*John Hawku*

# John Hawkwood

## An English Mercenary in Fourteenth-Century Italy

WILLIAM CAFERRO

The Johns Hopkins University Press

*Baltimore*

This book has been brought to publication with the generous
assistance of the Lila Acheson Wallace–Reader's Digest Publications
Subsidy at Villa I Tatti.

Johns Hopkins Paperback edition, 2015
2 4 6 8 9 7 5 3 1

Johns Hopkins University Press
2715 North Charles Street
Baltimore, Maryland 21218-4363
www.press.jhu.edu

*The Library of Congress has cataloged the hardcover edition of this book as follows:*

Caferro, William.
John Hawkwood : an English mercenary in fourteenth-century Italy / William Caferro.
p. cm.
Includes bibliographical references and index.
ISBN 0-8018-8323-7 (hardcover : alk. paper)
1. Hawkwood, John, Sir, d. 1394. 2. Mercenary troops—Italy—History—To 1500. 3. Soldiers
of fortune—Great Britain—Biography. 4. British—Italy—History—To 1500. 5. Italy—
History—1268-1492—Biography. I. Title.
DG536.H4C34 2006
355.3'43'092—dc22
2005016597

A catalog record for this book is available from the British Library.

ISBN-13: 978-1-4214-1841-4
ISBN-10: 1-4214-1841-X

*Special discounts are available for bulk purchases of this book. For more information,
please contact Special Sales at 410-516-6936 or specialsales@press.jhu.edu.*

Johns Hopkins University Press uses environmentally friendly book
materials, including recycled text paper that is composed of at least
30 percent post-consumer waste, whenever possible.

# CONTENTS

*List of Figures and Maps*     *vii*

*Preface*     *ix*

*Hawkwood Chronology*     *xiii*

Introduction     1

1  John Hawkwood in Perspective: *The Man and the Myth*     8

PART I     MAKING OF A WARRIOR

2  Essex Lad, King's Soldier, and Member of the White Company,
1323–1363     31

3  Italy and the Profession of Arms     62

PART II     RISE OF A MERCENARY CAPTAIN

4  The Fox and the Lion: *The Pisan-Florentine War, 1363–1364*     97

5  John Hawkwood of Pisa and Milan, 1365–1372     116

6  In the Service of God and Mammon, 1372–1375     144

PART III     THE MOST SOUGHT-AFTER CAPTAIN IN ITALY

7  John Hawkwood and the War of Eight Saints, 1375–1377     175

8  Love and Diplomacy, 1377–1379     191

9  At Home in the Romagna, 1379–1381     209

10  Neapolitan Soldier and Tuscan Lord, 1381–1384     226

PART IV     VETERAN CAPTAIN AND FLORENTINE HERO

11  The Deal with the Devil, the Birth of a Son, and a Victory at Castagnaro,
1385–1387     253

12  At the Center of the Storm:
*Florence and the Military Buildup, 1387–1389*     271

13  The War against Milan, 1390–1392     289

14  Two Weddings, a Funeral, and a Disputed Legacy, 1392–1394–1412     310

Conclusion     332

*Appendixes     347*
*Notes     353*
*References     417*
*Index     449*

FIGURES

1. John Hawkwood, detail from Paolo Uccello                                    10
2. Hawkwood's autograph and seal                                              11
3. Coggeshale coat of arms and Hawkwood coat of arms                          40
4. Hawkwood's raid in 1375                                                   163
5. John Hawkwood                                                             319
6. Inquest 1403, involving John Sampson                                      326
7. St. Peter's Church in Sible Hedingham                                     328
8. Hawkwood memorial at St. Peter's Church, Sible Hedingham                  329
9. Detail of a hawk, St. Peter's Church, Sible Hedingham                     330

MAPS

1. John Hawkwood's Military Campaign in Northern Italy                        xvi
2. John Hawkwood's Italian Holdings                                         xviii
3. Gilbert Hawkwood's Interests and John Hawkwood's Interests                 32
4. Italy in Middle of Fourteenth Century and Visconti Domain                 52
5. Initial Route of White Company                                            53
6. The Kingdom of Naples                                                    233
7. Battle of Castagnaro                                                     264

This project began more than fifteen years ago as part of a larger inquiry into the role of war in the economic, political, and social transformation of Italian society in the fourteenth century. Those researches first brought me into contact with that "nefarious" species of human being known as the medieval mercenary, of which John Hawkwood was the most egregious example. My primary objective in this book is to bring those soldiers and the wars they fought from the periphery of the historiographical discourse, where they currently dwell, to the center, where I believe they belong. In this regard, Hawkwood represents a particularly important subject of study. He was the most notorious soldier of his day, and his career was the most singular. Consequently, he is most easily removed from his milieu, treated as an exception, a medieval anomaly, a figure who, as my graduate adviser suggested, would best be dealt with as fiction. But such romantic approaches have already been undertaken, and by writers far more skilled than I. The purpose of this study is to replace the romantic Hawkwood with a more realistic one, to situate him in the context of the society in which he operated, to examine how he affected that society and how that society in turn affected him. Hawkwood was an exceptional character, but he was not an external one. The true value of his career is indeed as a unique entrée into the study of fourteenth-century society, one that sheds new light on old issues and raises entirely new questions.

War is always a distasteful subject, especially in recent times in which conflict has become ubiquitous and the threat of violence constant. It is not without reluctance that I, an economic historian in the first instance, have undertaken such a study. But reclaiming the historical John Hawkwood involves reclaiming the Italian military history of the second half of the fourteenth century, a history that has been poorly treated, dismissed since the days of Machiavelli as backward and hardly worth study in its own right. The lacuna has only grown worse in recent years, particularly in the American academy, where military history has languished on the fringe and the term *military historian* has become a sort of scholarly pejorative. The problem lay both with traditional humanist historians, who, uncomfortable with the very topic, have too often dismissed it out of hand, and with military historians themselves, who have not always adequately situated their work in its broader societal context. But no aspect of fourteenth-century society was left untouched and unaffected by war, and any depiction of that society without reference to war is apt to be skewed and artificial.

The book is divided into four parts, corresponding to the rhythms of Hawkwood's career. Unfortunately, the career does not come into sharp focus until Hawkwood was at least forty years old. Thus the presentation must lack a neat symmetry. It is with this in mind that I have begun the book with an essay (chapter 1) that serves to introduce Hawkwood as both a man and a warrior and to distinguish him from the prevailing myths and legends about him.

The first part deals with the shadowy early phases of Hawkwood's life, from his young days in Sible Hedingham to his exploits as a member of the celebrated (but often misrepresented) White Company and his entry into Italy. Part I ends with a description of the military milieu in which Hawkwood operated in Italy and an assessment of Italian warfare at the time.

The second and third parts detail Hawkwood's rise to prominence as an independent captain and the establishment of his reputation both militarily and financially in the service of several employers, including his king, Richard II. It was an eventful period in which he contemplated several times returning home.

The final part presents Hawkwood as a veteran captain, settled primarily, if uneasily, in the pay of the Florentines. The period witnessed Hawkwood's most notorious military victories and with them the attainment of the last bit of his martial fame.

During the many years of research involved in this project, I have relied on the help and advice of numerous friends, colleagues, archivists, and librarians from throughout Europe and the United States. The manuscript, completed in 2001 and accepted by the Johns Hopkins University Press in 2002, has endured a protracted publication process, and I thank Henry Tom for his steadfast support and help in seeing it through to publication. As the book went to press, there appeared two popular works on Hawkwood, by Duccio Balestracci and Frances Stonor Saunders. Kenneth Fowler has previously announced a comprehensive study of Hawkwood in the context of the larger English mercenary community in Italy, based on his excellent article. It is my hope that the confluence of studies—after more than a hundred years of scholarly neglect—will broaden our knowledge of the man and his era.

I wish first and foremost to acknowledge two institutions, the Institute for

Advanced Study in Princeton, New Jersey, and Villa I Tatti in Florence, which provided the financial and intellectual support for this and other projects. Without them there would be no book. At the Institute I benefited greatly from the scholarly and professional guidance of Giles Constable and Peter Paret and from the collegiality and support of the other fellows, notably Sharon Farmer, Beni Kedar, Bernard Bacharach, Barbara Diefendorf, Amy Remensnyder, Gary Dickson, Wolfgang Mueller, Jane Sharp, and Patricia Labalme. I owe them all a profound debt.

At Villa I Tatti I wish to thank Michael Rocke and Allan Grieco for arranging a seminar at which I presented some of my ideas on war and Italian society, and Humphrey Butters and Michael Mallett for an invitation to talk about Hawkwood at the University of Warwick symposium (1998) in Venice. I thank also my fellow Tatiani: Alessandro Arcangeli, Cecilia Asso, Jane Fair Bestor, Michele Bordin, Philippe Costamagna, Nicholas Eckstein, Carlo Falciani, Geraldine Johnson, Luca Molà, Marina Montesano, Michele Mulchahy, and Mary Vaccaro. I value the close bond we formed. I acknowledge in particular the help of Marcello Fantoni, who shared his substantial knowledge of war and court culture, and John Najemy, whom I relied on heavily in all matters involving medieval Italian society. I am grateful to Eve Borsook and Peggy Haines for discussing the project with me and for their assistance with sources, both secondary and primary. I thank Niccolò Capponi for helping me understand the technical aspects of war. Likewise, I thank Suzy Butters and Sabine Eiche for their friendship and advice with regard to sources in Mantua and England, respectively.

I wish also to express my gratitude to John Law for numerous references, particularly regarding John Ruskin. I thank Andrea Barlucchi for his help in the Florentine archives; Edward English for pointing out sources I missed in the Sienese state archives; Lorenzo Fabbri for his assistance at the Opera del Duomo; Paula Clarke for furnishing me with references in both Bologna and Florence; and, above all, Sarah Blanshei for navigating me through several Bolognese archives and spending much too much time answering my inquiries.

I am greatly indebted to Andrew Ayton and Maryanne Kowaleski for their enormously helpful reading of the chapters relating to England and for their advice on English sources. Similarly, I thank Clifford Rogers, Lt. Col. Kenneth J. Thompson, and Bernard Bachrach for their comments on chapter 3. I thank David Peterson for his advice on chapter 8 and Anthony Molho for his reading of chapter 13. Most of all, I wish to thank Benjamin Kohl for his comments on the overall text and for his efforts in helping me shape this into something resembling a book.

At Vanderbilt University I would like to thank my colleagues Peter Brush, James Epstein, and Helmut Smith for looking at early drafts of chapters. I also thank my undergraduate students Richard Bray, David Park, and Andrea Neeley, to whom I gave the task of reading over the initial chapters and who gleefully tore into my prose. I am grateful to Dean Ettore Infante for allowing me a year's leave to take up the fellowship at I Tatti. Most important, I acknowledge the help of my late colleague and friend Simon Collier, who, like Hawkwood, was an Essex man who played out his life in foreign lands. His enthusiasm for the project rivaled my own, and I miss him.

I dedicate this book to my wife and best friend, Megan Weiler, who has helped me at every stage and with every detail. Ours is a collaboration that now goes back twenty years to our days as undergraduates. I also dedicate the book to my wonderful family: my mother, Rose, and my sisters, Donna and Patricia.

| | |
|---|---|
| 1323 | Hawkwood's birth in Essex County, England |
| 1340 | Death of his father, Gilbert Hawkwood |
| 1342/43 | Probable first campaign in France with William Bohun |
| 1346 | Battle of Crécy |
| 1348 | Black Death |
| 1356 | Battle of Poitiers |
| 1360–61, December–March | Raid of the Great Company against Pope Innocent VI at Avignon |
| 1361, May | Arrival in Italy (Lombardy, Piedmont) with the Great Company |
| 1361, November | First extant contract bearing Hawkwood's name |
| 1363, April | Victory at Canturino |
| 1363/64, Winter | Appointment as captain of Pisan forces against Florence |
| 1364, February | First offensive for Pisa in extremely cold weather |
| 1364, August | Defeat at Cascina |
| 1365–66, November–October | With Ambrogio Visconti and the Company of Saint George |
| 1367 | Victory over Sienese forces at Montalcinello |
| 1368, June | Wedding of Lionel, Duke of Clarence, and Violante Visconti |
| 1368, October | Death of Lionel |
| 1369, June | Defeat and capture of Hawkwood outside Arezzo |
| 1369, December | Victory on behalf of Milan at Cascina |
| 1372, June | Victory on behalf of Milan at Rubiera |

| | |
|---|---|
| 1372, October | Abandonment of Milanese service in favor of the church; children and mistress taken hostage by Milanese ruler, Bernabò Visconti |
| 1373, June | Grant from Pope Gregory of church office for his illegitimate son and grant of property near Bologna |
| 1375, June–August | Lucrative raid on Tuscany |
| 1375–78 | War of Eight Saints |
| 1377, February | Participation in the massacre at Cesena |
| 1377, April | Abandonment of papal service in favor of Florence, Milan, and their allies |
| 1377, June | Marriage to Donnina Visconti; receipt of dowry, including lands near Milan |
| 1378, July–August | On diplomatic mission to Milan with Geoffrey Chaucer on behalf of King Richard II |
| 1379 | Dispute with Bernabò Visconti and dismissal from Milanese service |
| 1379–81 | Residence in the Romagna; feud with Astorre Manfredi of Faenza |
| 1381, August | Sale of Romagnol lands to Niccolò d'Este of Ferrara |
| 1381 | Older brother John Hawkwood the elder listed in poll tax as a franklin |
| 1381 | Peasants' Revolt in England |
| 1381–84 | Acquisition of estates and castles in Tuscany and Umbria |
| 1382 | Appointment by Richard II as ambassador to Pope Urban VI and Charles of Durazzo |
| 1383 | Service in the Kingdom of Naples |
| 1385, July | Alliance with Giangaleazzo Visconti of Milan, restitution of dowry lands |
| 1386, February | Birth of son and heir, John junior |
| 1387, May | Victory for Padua at Castagnaro |
| 1387–88 | Employment by Florence |
| 1388–89, November–May | Service in the Kingdom of Naples |
| 1390–92 | Service for Florence and allies against Giangaleazzo Visconti of Milan |
| 1391, April | Grant of citizenship by Florence |
| 1394, 17 March | Death of Hawkwood |

| | |
|---|---|
| 1394, 20 March | Funeral |
| 1397, 1403 | Dispute over English inheritance |
| 1403 | Restitution to Donnina by Giangaleazzo Visconti of her Milanese properties |
| 1406 | Return of Hawkwood's son and heir to England |
| 1436, June | Completion by Paolo Uccello of mural honoring Hawkwood in the Florentine cathedral |

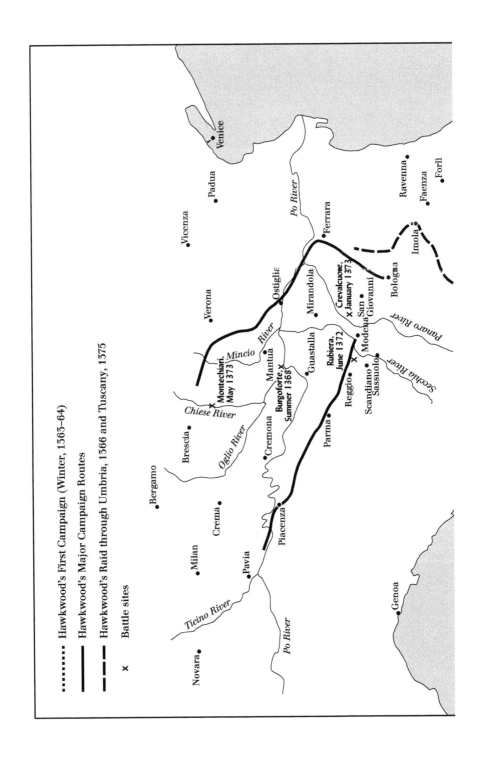

......... Hawkwood's First Campaign (Winter, 1363–64)

———— Hawkwood's Major Campaign Routes

– – – Hawkwood's Raid through Umbria, 1366 and Tuscany, 1375

x    Battle sites

Venice

Padua

Vicenza

Verona

Ravenna

Faenza

Forli

Po River

Ferrara

Imola

Bologna

Ostiglia

Mirandola

Crevalcuore,
x January 1373

San
Giovanni

Modena

Panaro River

Montechiari,
May 1373

Mincio River

Mantua

Rubiera,
June 1372

x

Reggio

Scandiano

Sassuolo

Secchia River

Guastalla

Chiese River

Burgoforte,
x Summer 1368

Brescia

Oglio River

Cremona

Parma

Bergamo

Piacenza

Crema

Milan

Pavia

Ticino River

Po River

Novara

Genoa

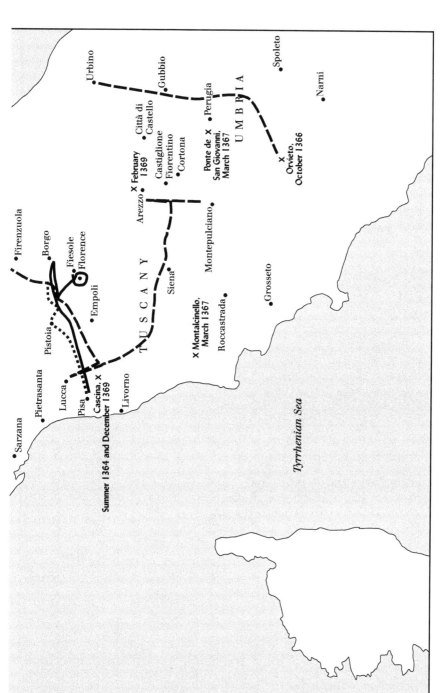

Map 1. John Hawkwood's Military Campaign in Northern Italy

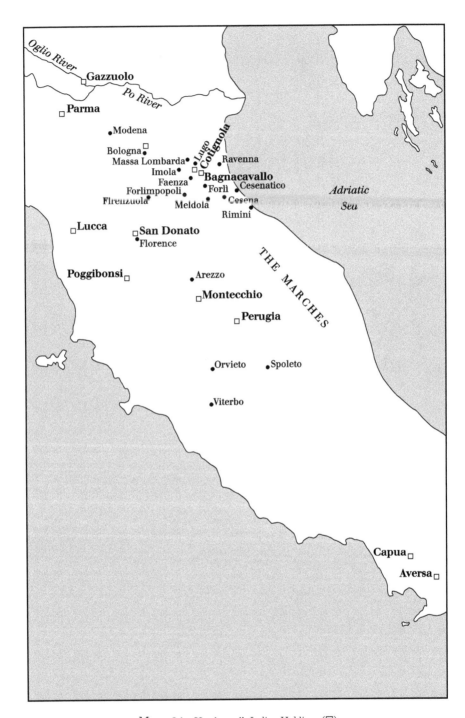

*Map 2.* John Hawkwood's Italian Holdings (□)

*John Hawkwood*

# *Introduction*

In novella 181 of his *Trecentonovelle,* the fourteenth-century storyteller Franco Sacchetti has John Hawkwood encounter two Franciscan monks near his fortress at Montecchio. The monks greet the Englishman.

"Monsignore, God grant you peace," said the monks.

"And may God take away your alms," Hawkwood responded immediately.

"Lord, why do you speak to us this way?" asked the frightened monks.

"Indeed, because you spoke thus to me," replied John.

"We thought we spoke well," said the monks.

"How can you think you spoke well," said Hawkwood, "when you approach me and say that God should let me die of hunger? Don't you know that I live from war and peace would destroy me? And as I live by war, you live by alms. So that the answer I gave you is the same as your greeting."[1]

John Hawkwood indeed lived by war, and no one was more successful at it. From modest roots in England, he rose to become the premier mercenary captain of his day, achieving fame on the battlefields of Italy, where he served for more than thirty years of his career. "He managed his affairs so well," Sacchetti wrote in a postscript to the above novella, "that there was little peace in Italy in his times." The nineteenth-century English writer James Granger ranked Hawkwood alongside the great Scottish patriot William Wallace ("Brave Heart") as a model of medieval military prowess.[2]

Hawkwood learned his craft as a minor player in the battles of the Hundred Years' War in France, crossed into Italy with the famed White Company in 1361, and became a full-fledged captain in 1363. From that time until his death in 1394, he rode with local armies in legitimate service and at the head of marauding companies when unemployed. Italian states alternately sought to hire him and to protect themselves from him. When he died, the Florentines, his last employer, buried him with great ceremony in their cathedral. His likeness, painted by Paolo Uccello, remains there on the west wall. The historian Ferdinand Gregorovius could not help but point out the irony that Florence had denied its greatest citizen, Dante, a final resting spot in the city but afforded a place of honor to that "robber of a Hawkwood."[3]

Hawkwood achieved an international fame during his lifetime. He served as ambassador alongside Geoffrey Chaucer, received angry letters from Saint Catherine of Siena, and sat in the company of the Flemish chronicler Jean Froissart and the Italian humanist Francis Petrarch at a lavish wedding feast for King Edward III's son Clarence. Contemporaries both admired and reviled him. Tommaso, the Marquis of Saluzzo in Piedmont, described him as "the most brave and wise captain Italy has seen in the last hundred years."[4] The anonymous English author of the *Westminster Chronicle* said his deeds in Italy were "so marvelous that his like had never been found there."[5] But the Tuscan poet Antonio Pucci called him an "English serpent."[6] And the popular Italian proverb "un inglese italianato è un diavolo incarnato" (an "italianized" Englishman is a devil incarnate) is said to have derived directly from Hawkwood's activities.

Hawkwood's notoriety has extended well beyond his lifetime. His name appears in the works of the Renaissance humanists Niccolò Machiavelli, Poggio Bracciolini, Leonardo Bruni, and Paolo Giovio, as well as those of the great modern historians Jacob Burkhardt and Edward Gibbon. On the eve of the English Civil War (1640), Lord John Maurice, grandson of King James I, assembled the materials to write Hawkwood's biography (including, curiously, a copy of Nostradamus's prophecies) but never completed the work.[7] Thirty-seven years later, Lord William Winstanley published a short romance (*The Honour of the Taylors or the Famous and Renowned History of Sir John Hawkwood*) placing Hawkwood in a tailor's shop and at various military and amorous adventures.[8] In 1776, the Society of Antiquaries in England commissioned from Richard Gough an account of Hawkwood's life, *The Memoirs of Sir John Hawkwood*, which was then read, "for want of something better," before the assembled members.[9] The nineteenth-century art historian and social critic John Ruskin frequently referred to Hawkwood in his lectures and letters.

For all his fame, however, Hawkwood has long presented an enigma for historians. His modest background and itinerant lifestyle do not lend themselves easily to biography. Lords and merchants leave obvious traces; mercenaries do not. A recent scholar spoke of the "immensity of the research" involved in reconstructing the lives and careers of such men.[10] Hawkwood's case is, ironically, made more difficult by its spectacular nature. His feats of arms over the years have drawn the attention of legions of amateur historians and fiction writers, who, rather than undertake new research, have chosen to trumpet more loudly and creatively the existing information—hoping to render the Englishman's deeds all the greater by

means of purple prose. It is instructive that there have been more fictional accounts of Hawkwood than nonfictional ones. The greatest of the genre is Arthur
Conan Doyle's classic *The White Company*, a sweeping adventure in which Hawkwood appears as a minor character. This was followed by William Beck's *Hawkwood the Brave* (1911) and Hubert Cole's trilogy: *Hawkwood* (1967), *Hawkwood in
Paris* (1969), and *Hawkwood and the Towers of Pisa* (1973).[11] In 1989, Andrew P.
O'Rourke published *Hawkwood*, the story of a Vietnam veteran who was nearly
killed in a plane crash, developed amnesia, changed his name to Hawkwood—
whom he had heard about in a Renaissance history class—and then traveled to
Argentina to fight as a soldier of fortune in the Falkland Islands War.[12]

The nonfiction works are few. The standard full-length biography is John
Temple-Leader and Giuseppe Marcotti's *Sir John Hawkwood*, published originally
in Italian in 1888 and then translated into English in 1889.[13] Temple-Leader
planned and wrote it; Giuseppe Marcotti did the fact gathering in local archives.
Temple-Leader was not a professional historian but an Englishman of the lordly
class, who, like the subject of his book, passed many years of his life in Italy. He
made excellent use of Tuscan archival sources and relied on a short Italian biography written a century earlier by Domenico Maria Manni (*Commentario della vita
del famoso capitano Giovanni Aguto Inglese, General condottiere d'armi fiorentini*)
and the above-mentioned *Memoirs* by Gough, written at about the same time.
Temple-Leader's work has served as the starting point for subsequent studies,
most of which follow closely the lines of his research.[14] Kenneth Fowler's recent
article is an exception. It extends, amplifies, and refines some of earlier writer's
conclusions, using an impressive array of archival sources.[15]

In the absence of adequate scholarship, John Hawkwood has emerged as more
of a cartoon figure than a human one. Fiction writers have idealized him into a
romantic, swashbuckling knight-errant. Doyle's John Hawkwood is a jolly mis-
creant who laughs into his long beard. Hubert Cole's Hawkwood moves coolly
from battlefield to amorous affair and back again. More scholarly-minded writers
have portrayed Hawkwood as a virtuous, "honest" man, an exception in an otherwise dishonorable profession. John Ruskin's Hawkwood is a "decorous" thief comparable to Robin Hood and Sir Francis Drake.[16] Temple-Leader fashioned Hawkwood in his own image, as an adoptive Florentine, whose public funeral capped a
lifelong love affair with that city. Others have seen Hawkwood as a precursor of
fifteenth-century developments. The nineteenth-century Italian historians Ercole
Ricotti and Giuseppe Canestrini argued that Hawkwood represented a precocious
instance of the trend whereby individual captains emerged from their bands and
ultimately took over the states they served. Hawkwood's attainment of landed
estates and his long-term service to Florence are interpreted as a precursor to the

careers of later Italian captains such as Braccio da Montone, who assumed control of Perugia, or the Sforza, who ruled Milan.[17]

This book takes a fresh look at John Hawkwood's life, relying almost wholly on documentary sources. It draws on material from archives in Italy and England, including diplomatic dispatches, personal letters, budgets, contracts, wills, and chronicles. The archival apparatus mirrors Hawkwood's own movements, which, despite Temple-Leader's assertions, were not restricted to Tuscany but covered a wide geographical area. The research has proved both logistically and method-ologically challenging. Ambassadorial dispatches, a major source of information, often focused on larger issues rather than on Hawkwood himself; they were sometimes confused, on account of faulty reconnaissance, and sometimes inten-tionally misleading, to gain diplomatic advantage.[18] The dating of the letters presented difficulties. The authors frequently did not give the year, and the events covered and people involved (especially the Visconti wars with the papacy) were often strikingly similar. Chronicle sources possess their own slants. Writers tended to embellish battle descriptions and, often, to relate feats of arms in terms of ancient paradigms, the Romans and Greeks, comparing contemporary captains to legendary heroes such as Hannibal, Caesar, or even Alexander. Interestingly, the victorious side often overstressed the strength of the vanquished. All sources had to be read carefully with regard to the circumstances in which they were written and the potential bias of the authors.

Given the broad arc of Hawkwood's activities and the enormous amount of ground he covered, no claim is made here for completeness. But the documents make it possible to get a new reading of the soldier and person. The portrait of John Hawkwood is of a man who was an extraordinary military leader, if not always an admirable human being. More than any other, he developed the skills of a great military strategist and inspired in his fellow soldiers an unrivaled loyalty. He was a savvy and uncompromising negotiator who played his cards close to the vest and managed to gain a reputation for "honesty" even while beating his opponents at their own game of duplicity and manipulation. He could be cruel and savage but also conciliatory. He retained a close connection with his home in England and a keen sense of his English identity. He served King Richard II as an ambassador and slowly built a patrimony in his native Essex on which he hoped to retire. Throughout Hawkwood kept his true intentions to himself, and in the end few contemporaries knew him well.

The predatory nature of Hawkwood's behavior possesses a certain timeless quality. The historian Charles Tilly has recently drawn intriguing parallels be-tween Hawkwood's "opportunism" and that of modern-day soldiers in Chechnia and Rwanda.[19] Analogies can also be found in the activities of the so-called German military enterprisers of the later sixteenth century studied by Fritz Redlich, the "corsaires" of seventeenth-century Malta described by Michel Fontenay, or the eighteenth-century Hessian mercenaries discussed by Charles Ingrao.[20]

But like all historical figures, Hawkwood is best understood in the context in which he operated. Hawkwood's story is that of the fourteenth-century mercenary. His experience, as a foreigner fighting in Italian lands, was shared by many soldiers—Germans, Hungarians, Frenchmen, Bretons, Catalans. These men were some of the most colorful figures of the day and included characters such as the German Oswald von Wolkenstein, who purportedly knew ten languages and wrote vernacular poetry, and Werner of Urslingen, whose armor bore the forbidding motto "I am the enemy of pity, God and charity." Hawkwood was one of numerous Englishmen—a group that included people of middling background, bastard sons of nobility, and even the occasional lord, like Edward le Despenser—who came for Duke Lionel's wedding and had a turn as a marauder in northern Italy. One obscure man-at-arms, John Carrington, wrote a brief diary of his experience.[21] What was unique about Hawkwood was the degree of his military success.

Most important, Hawkwood's story is the story of fourteenth-century Italy. It has long been customary in archival studies to tell the history of medieval and Renaissance Italy in discrete units, focusing on individual states, most often the great powers such as Florence, Milan, and Venice. But John Hawkwood worked all over Italy and never fully integrated into any single place. His perspective is pan-peninsular; his vantage entails, willy-nilly, a more careful accounting of the greater whole. Thus, tracing Hawkwood's life affords a useful methodology for understanding and interpreting the machinations of states in which he took part.

Indeed, Hawkwood's career provides a prism through which to view more broadly the historical events and developments of his time. The period was one of profound economic, social, and political changes on the peninsula. It saw recurrent famine and plague (most notably the Black Death of 1348), demographic crisis, intensification of regional and interregional rivalries, popular uprisings, and dissension in the church culminating in the papal schism in 1378. The transformative era, known to Italianists as the "crisi del Trecento," has been the subject of intense study and debate. Scholars have identified such trends as political and economic consolidation, the emergence of territorial states, the stirrings of republicanism, and the birth of a so-called Renaissance mentality pointing toward modernity. Hawkwood's activities were perforce bound up with these events and trends. He participated in the wars between the rival popes arising from the schism, in the territorial expansion of Milan, and in the establishment of Florentine hegemony in Tuscany. He was also involved in popular uprisings: he was in Pisa when Giovanni dell'Agnello took power, in Florence when the populist

Ciompi regime fell, and he participated in the events that led to Giangaleazzo Visconti's usurpation of power in Milan.

Although scholars have long acknowledged the importance of war, and indeed some, like Hans Baron, have afforded it a critical role in political events, there has been remarkably little research on the subject itself. A generation ago, the great Annalist historian Fernand Braudel complained in his study of the Mediterranean civilization that scholars were "as ignorant about war as the physicist is about the true nature of matter."[22] This remains true, particularly with regard to Italy, for which there exist only a handful of studies on war for the first part of the fourteenth-century and none for the second half.[23] As a result, many of the conflicts in which Hawkwood fought have not been studied at all. Thus it is part of the task of this book to reconstruct them.

A similar lacuna exists for the related field of diplomacy. Little has been written since the publication of Garrett Mattingly's pathbreaking *Renaissance Diplomacy* in 1955. Mattingly focused on the fifteenth century and later. Yet he explicitly credited the fourteenth-century mercenary with sharpening the skills of the Italian diplomat and thus helping to pave the way for the refined, permanent embassies of the fifteenth century.[24]

But neither war nor diplomacy can be understood in the abstract. It is the fundamental objective of this book to follow Peter Paret's injunction, stated most conspicuously in his *Understanding War*, that war be treated as an intrinsic part of "all other areas of society and culture."[25] The point deserves special emphasis here, since fourteenth-century Italian wars involved foreigners and thus it is especially easy to view them as external to other societal phenomena. This has in fact been the particular malady of Italian scholarship, which has dealt with mercenaries, both foreign and native, as "outsiders," separate from the mainstream of Italian life, or at best as symptomatic of the decay of that society. The pioneering works of Michael Mallett, John Hale, and Piero Pieri have helped correct this notion as it was applied to Italian mercenaries of the fifteenth and sixteenth centuries.[26] But any attempt at revision has been hampered by lack of attention to fourteenth-century soldiers and by the general belief that warfare conducted by these men was little more than a "negative intermezzo," hardly worth study in itself. The meager scholarship consists mostly of studies by Italian and German scholars, dating from the nineteenth century, and is suffused with nationalistic biases and limited by a preference to study foreign soldiers less for their own sake than as a stage in the broad evolution of Italian warfare.[27]

Hawkwood's career emphasizes the inherent impossibility of separating mercenaries from Italian society. Though an Englishman—and proud of it—Hawkwood was a fundamental part of the society he served. Contemporary diplomats, politicians, and chroniclers never mentioned Hawkwood apart from the events he participated in; nor, more generally, did they separate the wars he fought in from the course of their own daily lives and the destinies of their cities and states. Scholars who remove Hawkwood from his Italian milieu perpetrate an unfortunate alchemy.

Hawkwood was, as we shall see, involved in diplomacy as much as in war. Mercenary-related diplomacy played an important part of the overall diplomatic strategies employed by states, and Italian politicians often used mercenary issues to manipulate the larger political context. Hawkwood's actions always had a political dimension to them, particularly in the later stages of his career, when he accumulated a large patrimony of Italian territories. The deterioration of relations between the cities of Siena and Florence in the late 1380s, for example, can be properly understood only with recognition of Hawkwood's role as a landed lord in southern Tuscany. Hawkwood's funeral, beyond its function in commemorating the captain, formed part of a larger discourse among Italian states and became a means by which the Florentines propagandized and projected images of power to their neighbors.

After 1375, Hawkwood often served as ambassador for King Richard II of England, a role through which he became an instrument of English foreign policy in Italy and vice versa. More broadly, Hawkwood's career, and that of the foreign mercenaries in general, can be viewed apart from a strictly military context as a species of cultural exchange, which brought men of different national backgrounds together and helped on all sides to engender a sense of ethnic, even national, identity. The twentieth-century German historian Friedrich Gaupp goes so far as to make Hawkwood the embodiment of the spirit of the Renaissance, an example of Burckhardtian "illegitimacy" rising to leadership by dint of native skill and industry.[28]

Finally, Hawkwood's career sheds light on that most elusive aspect of fourteenth-century Italian society, the "very special sort of social organization" (as John Hale called it) known as the medieval army.[29] The following pages will elucidate the military environment in which the foreign mercenary operated, giving snapshots of the day-to-day vicissitudes of camp life, the relations among the soldiery, tensions between troops and civilians, negotiations between troops and their employers and between armies and their victims. It will be evident that beneath the glamour of battles won and lost the life of the soldier was often one of marches through obscure fields and of a struggle simply to manage in the face of limited resources and inadequate pay. It will also, I hope, become evident that war was a pervasive phenomenon on the peninsula, which should be viewed, to quote G. N. Clark, not as a "succession of occurrences" but as its own institution, with a "regular and settled mode of action."[30]

# CHAPTER ONE

# John Hawkwood in Perspective

## The Man and the Myth

Hawkwood, Anglioorum decus et decus addite genti Italicae.

*Julius Feroldus*

The physical John Hawkwood is a hazy figure, and the task of separating fact from fiction begins with a description of his appearance. According to Joseph Jay Deiss's popular account, Hawkwood was a "heavy set sort, a young ox in the shoulders, powerful of arm and hand. . . . His brown eyes were large, calculating and set wide apart under heavy brows. His nose was long and irregular and came to a point . . . his straight chestnut hair hung carelessly."[1] The Italian writer Indro Montanelli, on the other hand, depicts Hawkwood as a man with "thin and nervous lips" and "a head of frizzy chestnut hair."[2] The sixteenth-century humanist Paolo Giovio in his *Elogia veris clarorum virorum bellica virtute illustrium* and the eighteenth-century antiquarian Richard Gough in his so-called *Memoirs of Sir John Hawkwood* also offer idealized portraits that have no basis in fact.

The truth is that for all the extant documents relating to Hawkwood, a contemporary physical description of the man has yet to turn up. This is surprising because numerous depictions of other captains exist. Hawkwood's younger Italian contemporary Muzio Attendoli, for example, was known for his large hairy hands and hooked nose. The Englishman Andrew Belmont, who rode with Hawkwood in the White Company, was distinguished by his good looks, the German captain Rudolf von Hapsburg for his clean-shaven face ("Count Beardless," contemporaries called him). The fifteenth-century mercenary Braccio da Montone is rarely mentioned without reference to his distinctive limp.[3]

The only real source of Hawkwood's personal appearance is Paolo Uccello's great fresco in the Florentine cathedral. The portrait does not derive from firsthand observation but is a copy of an earlier original. A relatively small John

Hawkwood sits dressed in armor atop a large horse (fig. 1). It is difficult to adduce physical characteristics such as body type and size. Indeed, recent scholarship has pointed out that Hawkwood's very pose is suspect and that the composition was probably a piece of Florentine propaganda, intended to convey the image of the obedient captain conducting an inspection of troops.[4]

Uccello nevertheless gives a clear view of the captain's face, or at least the part that extends from beneath his captain's hat. It is a face of regular features, neither excessively pleasant nor excessively stern—devoid of any single distinguishing characteristic. Perhaps it is this lack of anomaly or peculiarity that caused contemporaries to remain silent about Hawkwood's physical qualities.

Biographers proudly affix to Hawkwood the title "Sir." The name rarely occurs without its modifier—most often Hawkwood is referred to simply as "Sir John Hawkwood." The appellation is fair enough. Hawkwood was knighted, though it is unclear when, where, and under what circumstances. But the term should not be used to infer anything about the character of the man. Knighthood conferred distinction on a soldier, but it was not so exclusive an honor as some modern writers have portrayed it. All major mercenaries of the day, however base and unsavory, were knights. Hawkwood was no more or less a "sir" than was Ambrogio Visconti, the bastard son of the Milanese tyrant Bernabò Visconti, who joined Hawkwood in marauding bands in the 1360s and 1370s, or Francesco Carmagnola, son of a local cowherd, who was ultimately executed by the Venetians for treason. Despite the rhetoric attached to it, knighthood did not preclude abuse of the lower orders and raids on peasants' fields. Success on the battlefield was the basic prerequisite for the title.[5] The ambiguity has led the historian Maurice Keen to wonder whether the distinction, and the cult of chivalry that went with it, were not just "a tinsel-covering disguising the ugliness of war and political strife."[6]

Hawkwood's surname presented a challenge for his non-English contemporaries. The British antiquarian Philip Morant complained that it was "strangely disfigured by foreign writers."[7] There were indeed quite a few variations, particularly in the Italian language, which does not lend itself well to rendering the name, since its alphabet has no *h* or *w*. Local documents give some interesting variants: "de hakeude" in the captain's first Italian contract with the Marquis of Montferrat, "Aucgunctur" in a Perugian document, "haughd" in a Lucchese document, "Hauvod" in a Florentine document, and "Hankelvode" in a papal document.[8] Most Italian contemporaries tried to piece the name together phonetically. The Paduan leader Francesco Novello addressed his letters to "Giovanni Augudh."[9] Hawkwood's Italian wife, Donnina Visconti, added an extra syllable, "Auchevud."[10] Hawkwood referred to himself in his own letters as "Haukevvod," "Haukwode," or "Haucod" (fig. 2.)

*Figure 1.* John Hawkwood, detail from Paolo Uccello. Scala/Art Resource, New York

The most common name applied to Hawkwood during his career was "Giovanni Acuto." This was not another Italian mispronunciation but a nickname, the type reserved for prominent men: renowned painters, warriors, and, nowadays, Brazilian soccer stars. The fifteenth-century Italian mercenary Erasmo da Narni was known by the name "Gattamelata," or "Honeyed Cat," while his contemporary Muzio Attendoli called himself "Sforza," or "Force." The German captain Philip von Sulz was dubbed "Dominus Malaspiritus," or "Lord Evil Spirit."[11]

In his fictional account of Hawkwood's first days in Italy, the novelist Hubert Cole has Hawkwood himself explain that the name "Acuto" was "the closest these blubber chops [i.e., the Italians] came to my real name."[12] But "acuto" was in fact a conscious pun. It simulated the pronunciation of his name while at the same time pointing to Hawkwood's most prominent characteristic in the eyes of his Italian contemporaries—his cleverness and cunning (the meaning of *acuto*). Hawkwood was literally "John the Astute" or "John Sharp"—his martial qualities blended into his name. The Florentine chronicler Filippo Villani, the first to give a detailed description of the English captain, understood the distinction well. "His surname in the English language was Hawkwood," Villani wrote, "which in the Latin tongue means Hawk of the Forest or in the Forest." Noting Hawkwood's "fox-like and crafty nature," Villani self-consciously chose to call him "acuto."[13] That "acuto" was indeed a nickname is confirmed in a Florentine document from 1382, which explicitly refers to "Hawkwood" ("Hauvod") as the captain's given name and "acuto" as the sobriquet, "by which he is known locally."[14] In general, the Florentines, who had long had commercial dealings in England, understood names of that country well. Villani himself was a shareholder in the Peruzzi bank, which had a branch in London and conducted business with the English crown.[15]

There is some question as to Hawkwood's overall learning and education. He clearly was not a refined soldier-scholar in the mold of a Federigo da Montefeltro or Castiglione's ideal courtier. Some claim that he could neither read nor write, an assumption based on the fact that his contract with Florence in 1385 was read aloud to him. This is, however, unfair, since reading contracts to captains was a common practice throughout Italy. The Flemish chronicler Jean Froissart, who met Hawkwood in person, gave conflicting testimony. In describing Hawkwood's correspondence with the Count of Armagnac prior to an invasion of Milan in 1390, Froissart said that the Englishman either "read or had read to him" the count's letters.[16] Hawkwood himself authored numerous letters, but these were dictated to scribes and notaries. He conducted most of his financial business either through agents or, after 1377, through his wife, Donnina, who was clearly a very literate woman. Whether this was because Hawkwood was unequal to the task or simply occupied with other affairs is unknown. It seems reasonable to assume that if Hawkwood was educated, it was at a most rudimentary level. The humanist Pier Paolo Vergerio, who witnessed Hawkwood's speech to his troops near Verona in 1391, described the Englishman as "more able with hand and industry than with tongue."[17]

*Figure 2.* Hawkwood's autograph (by a notary) and his seal (a hawk) on a letter from 1378. Richard Gough, *The Memoirs of Sir John Hawkwood* (London, 1776)

During his stay in Italy Hawkwood became fluent in the Italian language. His more than thirty years of residence there, his close relationship with locals, and his eventual marriage to an Italian woman afforded him much practice. Interestingly, the first time Hawkwood is directly quoted by a local chronicler—by the anonymous author of the *Annales Mediolanenses* in 1372—he utters not an Italian word but a French one, deriding Milanese notaries as little more than "escrivains," or scribblers, who exercised too much authority in wartime decisions.[18] The recourse to French is not surprising for a man who passed much of his early career on French battlefields and who came from an English society in which Norman French was still in widespread use. There are, in fact, several extant letters in Italian archives written by English soldiers in a French-like Italian dialect— including one by Hawkwood's lieutenant John Thornbury.[19] We may therefore imagine Hawkwood and his fellow Englishmen speaking a French-style Italian, which their hosts did their best to understand.

Hawkwood enjoyed, however, speaking his native language wherever he could: with his countrymen and with those Italians who knew it. The Florentine businessman and ambassador Simone di Ranieri Peruzzi boasted that his facility with English helped him develop a good relationship with Hawkwood and gave him an advantage in negotiations. There remains to this day among the peasants in the countryside near Florence the story that the Italian word *bistecca* derived directly from Hawkwood's requests in English for a hearty "beefsteak" whenever he was in that region.

Two of Hawkwood's surviving letters are in English and are among the earliest examples of private correspondence in that language. They were written toward the end of Hawkwood's life, to an associate back home in Essex, and involve his wishes regarding his legacy. The text of the epistle dated 8 November 1392 is cited below in the original.

> Dere S' I grete you wel and do to wytyn that at the making of this lettre I was in god poynt I thank god. I sende Johan Sampson bryngere of this lettre to you enformed of certeyn things quiche he schal tellyn you be mouthe. Qwerfore I preye you ñat ye levyn hym as my persone. Wrytyn at Florence, viii day of Novembre.
>
> John Haukwode, chevalier[20]

Hawkwood's letters in Italian archives are all in Latin. Hawkwood himself did not know the language, which was used in diplomatic correspondence among Italian states. His Latin epistles were written for him by chancellors and notaries in his employ. Some German mercenaries from the noble class apparently were skilled enough at Latin that they could converse in it and give orders on the battlefield. The same was true of Hungarians of similar background.[21]

Hawkwood's Latin letters focus mostly on issues related to military and political affairs. They convey well day-to-day activities in camp, reconnaissance, battlefield conditions, and the diplomatic machinations of states. They are, however, less revealing of his personal life. Of Hawkwood's amorous adventures we have only the lyrical vaporings of fiction writers. William Winstanley penned a curious tale in the seventeenth century, depicting Hawkwood as a tailor's apprentice (a "right dexterous lad"). Winstanley's Hawkwood falls hopelessly in love with the master's daughter, "the faire" Dorinda, "a virgin compleat in beauty," who was already betrothed to another man. "Tush, Tush," Winstanley has Hawkwood say at one point, "love is that which baffles Reason . . . a thing that takes the Diadem from Queens, and makes a Conquest over prince and peasant."[22] The story continues from there: Hawkwood is beaten by highwaymen and left for dead; a naked, overweight, red-haired woman appears in the guise of his ghost; Hawkwood fights a tournament against two giant brothers, leaves England for adventures abroad, and finally reunites with Dorinda, who had disguised herself as a man to escape her betrothal. Hubert Cole's fictional Hawkwood is a more bawdy character who links up with a series of willing women and eventually marries a French woman, Chantal. Chantal returns to her husband's childhood home at Sible Hedingham, where she is mistreated by his elder brother and dies an unhappy death.[23]

It is, however, possible to reconstruct the broad outlines of Hawkwood's personal life. Hawkwood's memorial in St. Peter's Church in Sible Hedingham, now lost, once contained the likenesses of two wives.[24] The identity of the first woman, almost certainly English, is unknown, as is the date of her marriage to Hawkwood. She bore John at least one child, a daughter named Antiochia, who married William Coggeshale, scion of a prominent Essex family with close ties to the Hawkwood family.[25]

Hawkwood's second marriage is well documented. In 1377, he wed Donnina Visconti, the illegitimate daughter of the Milanese ruler Bernabò Visconti, in a splendid public ceremony, described in a letter by an anonymous guest. Hawkwood himself told of the event in an epistle (in Latin) to the city of Lucca.[26] The marriage was not a love match but part of a deal that brought Hawkwood into the service of Milan and its then ally Florence during their war against the pope. Bernabò married several of his daughters to mercenary captains in an attempt to gain long-term loyalty from them, a ploy that did not work. But Donnina proved a good companion for Hawkwood. She was forceful character, in the mold of her father and the Visconti women in general. A contemporary Florentine letter spoke of her as "a consort worthy of such a man."[27] She entered the marriage with a substantial dowry in cash and land and diligently managed both her own and her husband's affairs. After Hawkwood died, Donnina moved forcefully to recoup his legacy in England, which had been co-opted by the heirs of his first wife. The couple had three daughters, Janet, Catherine, and Anna, and a son also named John.

Like many in his profession, Hawkwood had mistresses and illegitimate children. These are first mentioned in 1370, when they were settled in the city of Parma, and again three years later, when they were residing in Ferrara. Hawkwood's bastard children included two sons, John and Thomas. In 1372, Hawkwood used his connections with the pope, who owed him a great deal of money, to secure for John junior a sinecure back in England, in the church of St. Paul in London. Thomas Hawkwood, taken hostage in 1376 by Bologna, also returned to England and had a career as a mercenary captain.[28]

Whatever Hawkwood lacked in formal educational training and eloquence, he made up for by force of character. By all accounts he was an imperious man who did not suffer fools gladly. Hawkwood frequently displayed contempt for the machinations of politicians. "You go weave your cloth, and leave me to guide your soldiers," Hawkwood told the Florentine politician Andrea Vettori after a contentious consultation on military matters.[29]

He was similarly ill disposed to challenges to his military authority from fellow soldiers. In 1389, Hawkwood refused to link his brigade with that of the German mercenary Konrad Aichelberg because Konrad insisted on having equal status. "The dispute is this," wrote an ambassador who witnessed the dispute, "Konrad wants to call himself the captain . . . but John does not want him to do so."[30] Hawkwood also dealt severely with insubordination. When in 1379 a brigade under the command of the Englishman William Gold, a close comrade, repeatedly disobeyed orders, Hawkwood threatened them all with execution.[31]

The most important personal characteristic ascribed to Hawkwood by modern writers is his steadfastness in performing his obligations to his employers. The Englishman is portrayed, in both fiction and nonfiction, as the one "honest" man in a profession known for the opposite. "Fidelity," wrote Geoffrey Trease "was the keynote of Hawkwood's character." Trease compared him in this regard to "a modern lawyer" who "fights for his criminal clients with cool professional integrity."[32]

But the term *fidelity* must be understood here as a relative one. Hawkwood gained his reputation primarily from a single incident at the beginning of his career, when he refused Florentine bribe money while in the employ of Pisa. As we shall see, the incident is not without nuance, and Hawkwood's behavior in other instances was hardly honorable. Not only did he not uphold his contracts, but he routinely disobeyed and misled his employers. Hawkwood abandoned Milanese service twice under suspicious circumstances: the first time prompting his employer, Bernabò Visconti, to kidnap his family; the second time raising such anger in Bernabò that the Milanese tyrant, now his father-in-law, offered a monetary reward to anyone who "seized or killed" Hawkwood or any member of his troop.[33] The Florentines, for their part, repeatedly scolded Hawkwood when he was under contract with them—for not engaging the enemy, for trying to augment his band, for unilaterally negotiating with the enemy. When local officials conducted an inspection of Hawkwood's troops shortly before the war with Milan in 1389, they kept an official with him at all times to make sure that he did not parade his army, like Mussolini before Hitler in the modern age, more than once. Hawkwood even managed to get the better of Giangaleazzo Visconti, generally considered the craftiest ruler of the era. In the uncertain days after seizing power from his uncle Bernabò in 1385, Giangaleazzo signed Hawkwood to a lucrative contract, granting him a high salary and large tracts of land. But Hawkwood never lived up to its terms and spent much of the subsequent years fighting against Giangaleazzo's armies on the battlefield.

Contrary to his modern reputation, Hawkwood was in fact a master of deceit and manipulation. The very language of his letters is indicative of this trait. In the same epistle to Lucca in which he announced his wedding to Lady Donnina, Hawkwood crassly pressed the government to absolve a friend of his crimes against the city. He informed officials that his army was "not far away" and reminded them that "one hand washes the other" (his exact phrase).[34] In letters to the ruler of Mantua, whose lands Hawkwood frequently molested, the captain frequently alluded to "favors" he would bestow in return for concessions and help. Hawkwood received concessions, but the favors were never returned.

Hawkwood was most calculating when bargaining for bribe money. The negotiations he conducted during a raid in Lucchese territory in 1383 were a paradigm of deception. Hawkwood toyed with the Lucchese ambassador Andrea da Volterra sent to him. He assured Andrea of his affection for Lucca and his intention not to harm the city. He then sent him to his co-captain Richard Romsey, who cursed, complained, and expressed the desire to ride on Lucchese lands. "I am sent," lamented Andrea, "from Pilate to Herod."[35]

The Florentine chronicler Stefani also complained bitterly about the way the captain did business. Although Hawkwood had signed an agreement the previous year not to "molest" Florence, he arrived in 1379 in Tuscany with a large band of unemployed soldiers and "requested" that Florence and its neighbors "hire" his men. "They broke faith with the commune," wrote Stefani, "not openly, but in effect, more than openly. They said, 'I will not make you pay me, but you will hire me . . . whether you want to or not.' "[36]

In Hawkwood's own lifetime contemporaries rarely spoke of his honesty. The

TABLE 1
*John Hawkwood and Florentine wages, 1380–1381*

| Name | Position | Salary (yearly) |
| --- | --- | --- |
| Coluccio Salutati | Chancellor of Florence | 100 florins per year[a] |
| Heinrich Paer | German mercenary captain with 50 lances | 600 florins |
| Richard Romsey | English mercenary captain with 112 lances and 54 archers | 1,614 florins |
| Eberhard von Landau | German mercenary captain with 100 lances | 2,760 florins |
| John Hawkwood | English mercenary captain with 23 lances and 18 archers | 4,000 florins |

[a]Salutati's salary figure is before taxes. The salaries of the mercenaries were exempt from taxation.

reputation emerged only after Hawkwood was safely in his grave. It originated in Florence, where local officials were intensely grateful to the captain for keeping his army from capture during the darkest days of the Milanese war in 1391. Hawkwood's death shortly thereafter, and the continued military threat from Milan over the next forty years, fixed the "hero" image in the Florentine imagination and allowed locals to forget the prior years of trouble and conflict with the captain. But those Florentines who dealt with Hawkwood in his lifetime were under no illusions about the moral character of the man.

If, as Trease asserts, Hawkwood resembled "a modern lawyer," it was in the sense that he derived motivation from large paychecks. No one sought money more eagerly, and no one was more effective at acquiring it. This should not be surprising for a medieval mercenary, whose existence depended on the accumulation of coin. But Hawkwood was unusually adept at wrangling high salaries from his employers, augmented by interest-free loans, under-the-table gifts, and other preferments. When he worked for Florence in 1381, Hawkwood was the city's highest-paid official, with a yearly salary of 4,000 florins (333–1/3 florins per month), granted tax free. By contrast, Coluccio Salutati, the famous chancellor and the city's chief executive, earned a mere 100 florins a year, a salary that was subject to taxation. Hawkwood received higher pay than any other soldier on the Florentine payroll, though his brigade was one of the smallest (tables 1, 2).

When the payments stopped, however, Hawkwood also stopped work. If slowing the pace and intensity of service improved his bargaining position and profits, then Hawkwood slowed the pace. His employers suffered such behavior because their incessant wars created a constant need for mercenaries and because the Englishman was the best at fighting them.

Hawkwood's salary constituted only a part of his earnings. During the summer of 1375, Hawkwood extorted more than 200,000 florins in bribes, a sum that exceeded the annual revenue of whole cities, like Siena, Perugia, and Pisa. He also amassed jewels, silver plate, and expensive baubles, which he deposited in Bologna, Milan, Venice, and other places.[37] He diversified his financial portfolio. He had shares in the public debt in Florence and at one point purportedly had more than 100,000 ducats in investments in Venice.[38] After 1375, Florence paid Hawkwood, in addition to his salary, a pension of 1,200 florins yearly for the rest of his life, whether or not he served the city.[39] He also received long-term annuities from Lucca, Naples, and Milan.

Hawkwood coveted land most of all and worked to accumulate castles and estates both in Italy and back home in England. His Italian properties were often given to him in lieu of salary. In this regard, the pope, perpetually strapped for cash, was a leader in ceding land. Hawkwood prized the properties for both their monetary and military value—they could be sold or pawned in times of need and used while on campaign to recruit and garrison soldiers. Some lands produced modest revenues. At various points in his career, Hawkwood had castles through-out Italy: in Lombardy, the Romagna, Umbria, the Marches, the Kingdom of Naples, and Tuscany. He held for a time the great abbey of Sant' Alberto, located high above the Val di Nizza not far from Pavia. The abbey played host to the emperor Frederick Barbarossa in the twelfth century and, according to legend, was the final resting place of Edward II, the deposed English king, who purport-edly escaped his English captivity and hid in the abbey. There is notice of the existence once of a tomb honoring Edward, and it is perhaps this English connec-

TABLE 2

*Hawkwood's monthly salaries and employers, 1366–1394*

*(in gold florins)*

| Year | Brigade Size (Cavalry) | Monthly Pay | Employer |
|---|---|---|---|
| 1366 | | 600 | Pisa |
| 1370–1372 | 300 lances | | Milan |
| 1372 | 500 lances | 40,000 (whole company) | Pope |
| 1375 | 800 lances | 3,200 | Florence and allies |
| 1380 | 200 lances | 1,000 | Florence |
| 1381 | 18–23 lances | 333⅓ | Florence |
| 1382 | 17 lances | 1,000 | Florence |
| 1387 | 500 lances | | Padua |
| 1387 (Apr.) | 82 lances | 500 | Florence |
| 1388 (Jan.) | 100 lances | 500 | Florence |
| 1389 (June) | 400 lances | 500 | Florence |
| 1390 | 200 lances | 500 | Florence |
| 1391 | 220 lances | 500 | Florence |
| 1392 | 220 lances | 500 | Florence |
| 1393 | 25 lances | 500 | Florence |

*Note:* The salaries were often augmented by bonuses and thus were in reality higher.

tion that accounts for Hawkwood's interest in the abbey. But the connection is unlikely and has not been substantiated by scholars.

Among Hawkwood's other notable possessions were his estate just north of Florence, at San Donato a Torre in Polverosa, on the current site of the Villa Demidoff (where he married two of his daughters); and the small fishing town of Gazzuolo on the Oglio River, between Cremona and Mantua (where he installed his Italian wife just after he was married). We know by far the most about affairs at Gazzuolo, owing to Hawkwood's correspondence with the lord of Mantua, who owned half of the town. The letters are preserved in the rich Archivio Gonzaga.

Many of Hawkwood's properties stood in key strategic locations. In the 1380s Hawkwood controlled much of the southern access to Tuscany, including portions of the Via Francigena, the great medieval highway that ran from France to Rome.

It is a tribute to Hawkwood's cunning that for all the money Italian officials paid him, they never knew how much he actually had. The vagaries of war and campaigning surely produced an ebb and flow in Hawkwood's fortunes, but to judge from contemporary statements, particularly those of the captain himself, he was always poor. When Hawkwood bought land in Florentine territory in 1383 and thus appeared on the city tax rolls, he continually evaded his obligations, seeking special breaks and routinely claiming poverty and indebtedness.

Hawkwood had good reason to keep his earnings vague. Italian society resented watching its wealth flow to mercenaries, particularly foreign ones. Hawkwood knew well the story of his famous predecessor, the Provençal knight Montreal d'Albarno, who had amassed a huge fortune and was seized by the citizens of Rome in 1354 and beheaded. His last words were: "Romans I am dying unjustly. I am dying because of your poverty and my riches."[40]

Hawkwood's success at the bargaining table was an extension of the qualities that made him successful on the battlefield. Hawkwood was the craftiest soldier of his day. His tactics included feigned retreats, ambushes, and the dissemination of false information. Before escaping from Milanese territory in 1391, Hawkwood solemnly accepted his opponent's challenge to battle and agreed to meet him the next morning on the field. That night, at dusk, Hawkwood picked up camp and quietly escaped through back routes, placing his battle standards and banners high on the trees so that the enemy would assume he was still there. He then detached a contingent of his men and placed them in the woods to entrap the enemy as it pursued.

Contemporaries emphasized such attributes in their praise of Hawkwood. The anonymous author of the Este family chronicle lauded him for his "ingenuity and cleverness" in battle and characterized him as "the most skilled strategist" (doctissimus machinator) of the day.[41] The Venetian chronicler Daniele di Chinazzo, whose city often tried unsuccessfully to hire Hawkwood, described him as "a great master of war."[42] The Florentine chronicler Filippo Villani referred to him as "a fox," an image that was incorporated into Hawkwood's memorial in Sible Hedingham—a sign that the captain himself took it as a compliment.

Niccolò Machiavelli, for all his disdain for mercenaries, foreign ones in particular, strongly approved of the tactics of deception. Though he described men of Hawkwood's profession as "dangerous" and "ruinous" to the well-being of Italy, Machiavelli gave his ideal military captain in book 3 of *The Discourses* the very skills displayed so deftly by the Englishman. Machiavelli specifically commended the captain who used "fraud" on the battlefield, calling it a "praiseworthy and glorious" trait.[43] It is a tribute to Hawkwood's expertise in the praiseworthy art that he deceived the old master himself, who never noticed the Englishman's duplicitous qualities. In *The Prince* Machiavelli implicitly accepted the view that Hawkwood was an honest man, but he protested that the Englishman's faith was never really tested.[44]

The art of deception was advocated in manuals on warfare, which were available at the time in vernacular translations in both France and Italy.[45] The most famous of these, the *Epitoma de re militari*, written by the fourth/fifth-century Roman author Vegetius, spoke of the utility of scams and tricks on the battlefield, of maintaining secrecy and carefully controlling the dissemination of information ("the safest policy on expeditions is deemed to be keeping people ignorant of what one is doing").[46] An earlier work, Frontinus's *Strategemata* (first century AD), gives explicit examples of how Roman and Greek generals employed ruses to fool opponents. The chapters deal with such subjects as "concealing one's plans," "laying and meeting ambushes while on the march," "concealing reverses," "deceiving the besieged," and "surprise attacks."[47] The ideas contained in these works were current in Hawkwood's day. A fourteenth-century military treatise by Teodoro Paleologus, originally in Greek but available in French translation as *Les enseignements*, advocated such ploys as attacking enemies at night—a tactic employed by Hawkwood and his companions of the White Company when they first arrived in Italy.[48]

Hawkwood learned much on the battlefields of France, where he passed the early part of his career. He became schooled in English methods of war, most notably the practice of dismounting from horses and taking the defensive position at the start of battle. He used these tactics to great effect in Italy at Castagnaro in 1387, a battle reminiscent of the famous English victory at Poitiers. But Hawkwood did not arrive in Italy wholly formed; nor should his career be taken as an instance of superior English military skill applied to an Italian context. The famed

English longbow, one of most important military innovations of the Hundred Years' War and a significant factor in the success of the English against the French armies, did not figure prominently in Hawkwood's success in Italy. Extant contracts show clearly that he and his fellow Englishmen used longbowmen in their brigades, but the number of such soldiers remained small, too small for them to play more than a subsidiary role in battle, alongside other missile weaponry such as crossbows.[49] The crucial phase of Hawkwood's development as a military leader and strategist occurred in Italy, where he was exposed to a variety of military skills, including those of German, Hungarian, Breton, Catalan, and other soldiers. Italian warfare is traditionally depicted as backward with respect to the rest of Europe, owing to the use of mercenaries. But the use of mercenaries, in fact, made Italy a unique crucible in which to learn the skills of war. Mercenary captains frequently changed sides, so that those who opposed each other one day fought together the next. Familiarity furthered the need for cunning and honed Hawkwood's ability in that regard.

In any case, Hawkwood's talent did not manifest itself in Italy at once. His first campaign as a full-fledged captain in Pisan service in 1363 was a failure. He drove his men relentlessly through the snow and extreme cold, only to find the enemy territory stripped of provisions and the passes well guarded. But Hawkwood learned his lessons, and quickly. In subsequent years, knowledge of terrain and use of the physical conditions on the battlefield would be a hallmark of his success. He would prove most effective in Lombardy, where the open, flat plains, intersected by rivers and canals, were conducive to war of maneuver.[50] His frequent battles and years of residence in the region gave Hawkwood intimate knowledge of the physical structures and lay of the land.

In general, however, Hawkwood fought few decisive battles. He spent the bulk of his time moving his army from place to place, managing limited resources, and conducting limited raids. He preferred to avoid risks, a preference shared by his employers. In the eyes of the Florentines, Hawkwood's greatest military feat was his long retreat from Milanese territory, through a barren countryside and across three rivers. Locals praised Hawkwood for his "prudence" in not exposing his forces and with it the Florentine state. Hawkwood's epitaph in the Uccello fresco is taken from a eulogy of Fabius Maximus, the ancient Roman general who, through consistent retreat and avoidance of pitched battle, managed to wear out Hannibal. The text praises Hawkwood as a "cautissimus" (most prudent) warrior.

Hawkwood's ability to outmaneuver his foes depended greatly on his ability to gather information. Hawkwood established the best network of spies and informers in Italy. He derived much of his information from petty nobles and exiles who, owing to the fractious nature of local politics, existed in copious numbers in the Italian countryside. They were often willing, indeed anxious, to share information with Hawkwood, particularly if it could harm those who had mistreated them. Vegetius specifically advised generals to seek reconnaissance from "intelligent men, from men of rank, and those who know the localities."[51] Hawkwood showed a particular predilection for men whose lands lay in areas of strategic importance. He maintained an ongoing relationship, for example, with the noted Florentine exile Giovanni d'Azzo degli Ubaldini, whose clan controlled the Apennine passes near Faenza, which formed the important entryway into northern Tuscany.[52] Similarly, Hawkwood forged ties with the Sienese exile Raimondo Tolomei, whose properties lay near an access point to southern Tuscany. Hawkwood selected Tolomei as the godfather of one of his children and would buy properties from him around the town of Poggibonsi.

Hawkwood also gathered information from men who took up long-term employment in his bands. These included local notaries and merchants, who, in search of profits, offered their skills as chancellors and treasurers. Hawkwood employed men from various parts of Italy: Martino di Giacomo de Robbis of Città di Castello, Jacopo da Terrinca da Pietrasanta of Lucca, Andrea del Pace of Arezzo, and Dionisio della Strada of Milan. Jacopo da Pietrasanta, a Lucchese exile, became one of Hawkwood's most trusted advisers, working for the Englishman for more than twenty years. Through his ties back home, Jacopo kept Hawkwood well informed of events in Lucca. Hawkwood's Milanese chancellor Dionisio della Strada, from a prominent local family, was similarly useful.[53]

It is important to stress the range of information that Hawkwood had at his disposal. He gathered news not only from throughout Italy but from France, England, and elsewhere in Europe. He was informed of events on the French battlefields; he sent messengers directly to England and to his home county of Essex. In Italy, he knew details of negotiations among states, of the movements of ambassadors, of the plots of political exiles. During his negotiations with Hawkwood in 1383 the Lucchese ambassador Andrea da Volterra learned of the political machination in the Kingdom of Naples and of the movements of ships off the coast of Genoa.[54]

For all the reconnaissance he gathered, Hawkwood kept tight control of what left his camp. He made his men swear not to divulge information and often kept them in the dark about his broader schemes. In his own letters, Hawkwood passed on information selectively. It was his habit to give freely generic news—the election of a new pope, the status of this or that soldier—while not revealing anything of his own intentions. His epistles thus often have the appearance of being forthright when in reality they were not.

Hawkwood's ability to control the flow of information formed part of his larger skill at managing his men. He retained the same employees over many years and kept about him a core of trustworthy, courageous warriors, who joined him in numerous campaigns. Many of these were Englishmen, who had fought with Hawkwood from his first days in Italy.[55] Among Hawkwood's closest companions was William Gold. Gold became known locally by the nickname "Cocco," perhaps an indication that he began his military career as a cook, or *cuoco* (in Italian). He proved his skill as an independent captain in the employ of Venice in 1379 and was rewarded by the city with a lifetime pension and citizenship.

Hawkwood inspired loyalty in his men by working tirelessly on their behalf. The Italian archives contain many letters he wrote lobbying for his comrades: seeking favors, demanding restitution for stolen goods, prodding employers for extra pay for his soldiers. Hawkwood's insistence on the last caused Florentine officials to scold him during the Milanese war in 1390. "Tell him," they wrote to their ambassador stationed with the captain's army, "to spend less time advocating for his men and more time preparing to fight the enemy."

Hawkwood's ability as a captain of "free" companies also contributed greatly to his military reputation. As in traditional war, he accounted for such factors as terrain, weather, and enemy activities. He took care to avoid narrow mountain passes, where his men could be ambushed, and chose as his initial targets easy prey in lightly defended regions such as the Maremma lands near Siena. Apart from the ever present risk of malaria, the region was given to grazing and animal rearing and was, in short, a good place to feed armies. Hawkwood's companies often advanced in smaller units, behind individual corporals, to enhance maneuverability, facilitate provisioning, and maximize damage. Like all "free" captains, Hawkwood took in local exiles, which gave his bands a political and social dimension, which further frightened cities and towns and made them more willing to settle quickly to avoid potential internal uprising. The raids invariably ended with the extortion of bribe money. Here Hawkwood's skills as a negotiator allowed him to co-opt some of the largest sums of the era. It is instructive, however, that when called on by an Italian employer to oppose a mercenary company Hawkwood often took a hard line and advocated violence rather than negotiation.

It is important to stress that a key component of Hawkwood's success as a captain was his brutality. In their attempt to soften Hawkwood's image, modern scholars have often minimized this aspect of his personality. But Hawkwood was a ruthless man, and his troops committed some of the era's most violent crimes. His soldiers dismembered their enemies, raped women, and savagely murdered peasants. His raids on the cities of Faenza and Cesena in 1376 were widely considered two of the cruelest and most violent acts of the entire fourteenth century. Hawkwood himself murdered a young nun while plundering a local monastery. Two of his corporals had gotten into a tug-of-war over who would rape the attractive young girl first. Hawkwood swiftly settled the dispute by plunging a dagger into the girl's heart.[56]

Such episodes cast a shadow over Hawkwood's moral character and raise basic questions about his religiosity. Throughout this book we will see Hawkwood routinely sacking monasteries and holy places. He harassed the pope at Avignon, and later at Viterbo and Montefiascone, and responded rudely to Franciscan monks in Sacchetti's famous tale. Hawkwood ignored several papal summons to go on crusade, as well as the famous appeal by Catherine of Siena for him to leave the "devil's service and pay" and abandon his attack on Tuscany during a time of famine.[57] Hawkwood never went on pilgrimage and in this respect fell short of many other mercenary captains of the day. The list of his contemporaries who undertook crusades is a long one and includes many of the men he worked with or fought against: Walter Leslie, John Bourchier, Humphrey Bohun, John Coggeshale, Galeotto Malatesta, Amadeus of Savoy, Otto von Brunswick, Amieneu Pommiers, Enguerrand Coucy, Jacopo dal Verme, and many others. Even his fearsome countrymen Robin Knowles and Hugh Calveley traveled to Jerusalem late in their careers.

It would nevertheless be incorrect to portray Hawkwood as a wholly godless man. Documents in the Archivio Segreto Vaticano reveal that early in his career in Italy Hawkwood asked for and received permission from the pope to have a portable altar to conduct mass while on campaign.[58] Such requests were common among pious bankers and other itinerant men, whose frequent travel made regular attendance in church difficult. In Sible Hedingham, Hawkwood gave liberally to the church of St. Peter's, whose facade contains numerous hawks, the emblem of its benefactor. He gave also to the local parish church in the adjacent town of Castle Hedingham. In Italy, Hawkwood almost surely helped endow a hospice for English pilgrims dedicated to Saint Thomas in Rome in 1380.[59]

Hawkwood's ambivalent behavior reflects the inherent difficulty of reconciling the Christian ethic with acts of war.[60] German mercenaries would bless their weapons and banners in church before battle and then move forward and loot monasteries and religious sites as well as attack the enemy. Robin Knowles led a mercenary company against the pope at Avignon but later in his career endowed a church in his village in England, as did Hugh Calveley. The great Gascon mercenary Arnaud de Cervole was a minor cleric; the Provençal Montreal d'Albarno was once a monk. This ambiguity was basic to the profession of arms. Even Hawkwood's murder of the young nun in Faenza was not without redemptive Christian value. The Sienese chronicler who reported the deed in fact commended Hawk-

wood for Solomon-like wisdom. He praised Hawkwood for preventing dishar-
mony among his troops and for preventing the violation of the young girl. The
latter was a Christian act in that it allowed the girl to maintain her vow to God and
die with honor.

The church itself added to the confusion by condemning the acts of the mercenaries one day and lauding them the next. When Hawkwood fought for Milan
against papal armies in 1371, the pope denounced him as "a son of Belial." When
Hawkwood joined the pope the next year and won several battles, he was hailed as
"an athlete of God and a faithful Christian knight."[61] The devastations wrought by
Hawkwood at Faenza and Cesena had in fact been directed by the church, specifically by Cardinal Robert of Geneva, who later became the antipope Innocent VII.
When mercenaries died, religious authorities buried them with great pageantry in
local churches. Many of the men discussed in subsequent pages—Konrad and Lutz
von Landau, Konrad Aichelberg, and Tiberto Brandolino, to name a few—found
their final resting places in Italian cathedrals. Hawkwood was interred with the
highest of honors in the Florentine cathedral.

One of the most enduring myths about Hawkwood is that he was transformed
during his years of service on the peninsula into an Italian, specifically a Florentine. "From all that is indicated in his actions and customs," wrote Pier Paolo
Vergerio about Hawkwood in 1391, "he no longer has any foreign blood . . . and has
become regenerated more strongly and more healthful in fiber and body under
the moderating sky of Italy."[62] This image was carried into the modern era by
nineteenth-century Italian historian Ercole Ricotti, who described Hawkwood in
his two-volume work *Storia delle compagnie di ventura in Italia* as either "the last
of the foreign condottieri or the first of the Italian ones."[63] For the nationalistic
Ricotti, the praise was singular.

Much of the contemporary work of "italianizing" Hawkwood was done by the
Florentines, who came to view the captain as a full-fledged hero after his successful service against Milan (1390–1392). His death shortly thereafter engendered a
species of idol worship. A song recounting his life and deeds made the rounds of
the city. The famed merchant of Prato Francesco Datini made regular reference to
the Englishman in his correspondence with his friend Lapo Mazzei. "Is it not
true," Lapo wrote to Datini soon after Hawkwood's death, "that Solomon was not
better than all of the Italians and that John Hawkwood was not worth 500
lances?"[64] Paolo Uccello's famous portrait in the cathedral, painted in 1436, represents the culmination of Florence's admiration of Hawkwood.

The fresco has strongly influenced modern writers, who have tended to inter-
pret Hawkwood's career almost wholly in terms of Florence. The title of D. M.

Manni's eighteenth-century biography of Hawkwood, the first scholarly treatment of the man, is translated as "Commentary on the life of the famous English captain, John Hawkwood, *general captain of Florentine armies*" (italics added). Manni emphasized Hawkwood's feats of arms on behalf of Florence and largely ignored his service to other states. Manni's English contemporary Richard Gough, though ostensibly claiming Hawkwood for his native country, in fact portrayed the captain as very much a Florentine.[65] A century later, John Temple-Leader followed in this tradition, presenting Hawkwood as a "Florentinized" Englishman, whose career revolved around his relationship with that city. Temple-Leader stressed Hawkwood's receipt of a lifetime annuity from Florence in 1375, the purchase of Florentine property in 1383, and, just before his death, the taking of local citizenship. The twentieth-century German historian Friedrich Gaupp pushed the connection still further. He portrayed even the negative interactions between Hawkwood and Florence in a positive light: Hawkwood's attack on the city in 1375 was "a brutal wooing" and "species of marriage proposal."[66]

But though the Florentines came to revere Hawkwood, there is no evidence to suggest that Hawkwood ever felt the same toward them. He did not work for Florence until he had been in Italy for sixteen years. For much of that period, he fought against and harassed the city, which plotted ways to remove him altogether from Italy. Hawkwood's famed "pension" in 1375 was the product of bribery; he had already received a similar deal from Naples. The shift to Florentine employ in 1377 was in reality a shift to Milanese employ. Indeed, a better case can be made for Hawkwood's attachment to the city of Lucca, from which he accepted citizenship years in advance of Florence. He also held property in the city, received a lifetime pension, and, along with several of his fellow Englishmen, did much of his banking there with the city's largest firm, the Guinigi.[67]

The proper understanding of the captain and his career is one that does not equate him with any particular Italian state. Hawkwood's primary allegiance was and always remained to his native England. He identified with his home and always intended to return to his native Essex, to live the life of a landed lord off his Italian profits. The years Hawkwood spent in Italy, under the "moderating sky" of the peninsula, only strengthened his sense of national identity. Like his fellow countrymen, Hawkwood usually had inserted into his Italian contracts an explicit clause barring service against opponents who were allied to the king of England. Later contracts even contained a provision allowing him the right to "cross the sea" and return home before the termination of his service.

Hawkwood's allegiance to England is most apparent in his service to King Richard II, which began shortly after the monarch assumed power in 1377. Richard appointed Hawkwood to diplomatic missions on his behalf—to the Visconti of

Milan, to the Holy Roman Emperor Wenceslaus, to the Hungarian prince Charles of Durazzo, to Pope Urban V, and others. He entrusted Hawkwood with negotiating treaties, marriage alliances, and business ventures. The king valued Hawkwood and men of his type for their ability to offer personal loyalty apart from feudal ties.[68] Hawkwood became an important intermediary through which English foreign policy was conducted in Italy.

Hawkwood's duty to England was such that it influenced his choice of whom to serve militarily in Italy. The notion that he was an entirely "free" captain is erroneous. Already in 1367, we see the guiding hand of King Edward III, who, at odds with Pope Urban V, instructed Hawkwood and the English soldiers in Italy to support the pontiff's archrival Bernabò Visconti. Fifteen years later, however, King Richard's efforts at forging a closer alliance with Pope Urban V were instrumental in Hawkwood's decision to serve the papal cause. Hawkwood's service in that war, conducted during a time of famine and plague, brought him little profit and can only be understood in terms of his obligation to the crown. The chronicler Froissart even claimed that Hawkwood left Milanese employ in 1372 because he did not wish to fight against the French lord Enguerrand Coucy, since he was married to the daughter of King Edward III.[69]

Within Italy, Hawkwood became a leader of the English expatriate community of soldiers. Englishmen were often reluctant to oppose him in the field. A Perugian ambassador reported how in 1383 a brigade of Englishmen sent by the city against Hawkwood had dissolved before him. "They do not wish in any manner to be opposed to John Hawkwood, whom they see as their champion and protector."[70] Hawkwood's brigades became a favorite among Englishmen seeking employment, including many from Hawkwood's home base in Essex. William Coggeshale joined Hawkwood's brigades as a teenager, riding with him for years and eventually marrying his daughter.[71] John Coe undertook long-term service, with John Ball and Richard Stisted, for Florence from 1386 to 1394; the three men always fought together with a brigade of about fifteen to twenty men.[72] It was not only soldiers who joined Hawkwood. John Hedingham, a prominent London merchant, made several trips to him to conduct business; John Northwood served as Hawkwood's envoy to King Richard in 1382; and John Sampson repeatedly shuttled back and forth, from Hawkwood's camps to Essex, handling the captain's personal affairs and his correspondence with his representatives and family at home. The author of the *Westminster Chronicle* tells of an unnamed associate of Hawkwood's who returned to England from Italy in January 1386 and issued dire prophecies about future events in the island.[73]

Throughout his career in Italy, Hawkwood openly expressed the desire to return to England, particularly when his financial fortunes were at an apex. He prepared for a comfortable retirement by investing in estates in Essex, near his childhood home in Sible Hedingham, and in adjacent counties.[74] Donnina Visconti makes explicit mention of the purchases in a petition she sent to the king after Hawkwood's death, hoping to gain possession of them. She noted how her husband had sent "sums of gold at various times to 'feofees' to buy land and tenements" on his behalf.[75] The feofees, or representatives, included several close associates back in Essex, whom Hawkwood in his own letter of 20 February 1393 called "myn frendes." They managed his lands and held the rights to them until he returned.[76] The most important of the feofees was Thomas Coggeshale of Boreham (Essex), with whom Hawkwood first went to war in France and who was the uncle and former guardian of Hawkwood's son-in-law William. Hawkwood left it to Thomas to effect his last wishes before his death in 1394. At that point, Hawkwood's holdings included the famous Leadenhall in London, a meat, fish, and poultry market and nowadays a thriving retail space.

Despite his preparations, Hawkwood never returned home to live on his English estates. In the last months of his life, aware that death was close at hand, he summoned all his strength to arrange his passage to England. He died before he was able to make the journey. In this respect, Hawkwood fell short of contemporaries like Robin Knowles, who, after the glories won on the battlefields of France, lived a comfortable retirement on his estates in Cheshire, or John Thornbury, who returned from Italy to settle down on estates at Little Maldon in his native county of Hertfordshire.[77]

Yet Hawkwood's fame and military reputation ensured him a lasting fame in England. Hawkwood emerged in his native land as a hero of epic proportion. The fifteenth-century English writer and book publisher William Caxton afforded him a singular honor. In his translation of Christine de Pisan's book he placed him alongside Lancelot, Galahad, and the Knights of the Round Table as men "whoos names shyne gloriously by their vertuous noblesse and actes that thy did in thonour of thordre of chyualry."[78]

# PART I

# MAKING OF A WARRIOR

# CHAPTER TWO

# Essex Lad, King's Soldier, and Member of the White Company, 1323–1363

I would serve, since serve I must, in a foreign land, somewhere where a brave deed, were it my hap to do one, might work to make me a name.

*Quentin Durward to his uncle in*
*Sir Walter Scott's* Quentin Durward

Where a good man can always earn a wage, and where he need look upon no man as his paymaster but just take what he wants: To the White Company!!

*Arthur Conan Doyle,* The White Company

The story of John Hawkwood begins just north of London in the rolling hills of Essex, England. "A fair county," wrote the seventeenth-century antiquarian Thomas Fuller, "bearing the full proportion of five and thirty miles square, plentifully affording all things necessary to man's subsistence, save that the eastern part is not very healthful in the air thereof."[1] Hawkwood came not from the east but from the parish of Hinckford in north-central Essex. The region was given primarily to farming and sheep grazing, with an active export business in raw wool. In Hawkwood's day, a prosperous cloth-making industry grew, producing distinctive items such as Coggeshale whites and Colchester russets, which were marketed throughout Europe.[2] Along with its woolens, Essex had a reputation as a center of what one scholar has called "deeply rooted anti-authoritarianism."[3] In 1381, Essex participated in the greatest social uprising in medieval English history, the Peasants' Revolt, in which commoners rebelled against the crown.

It was in the town of Sible Hedingham, an old Roman outpost, a short pass up the Colne Valley from Colchester and not far from the Norman castle of the powerful de Vere family, that John Hawkwood was born. He was the second son of

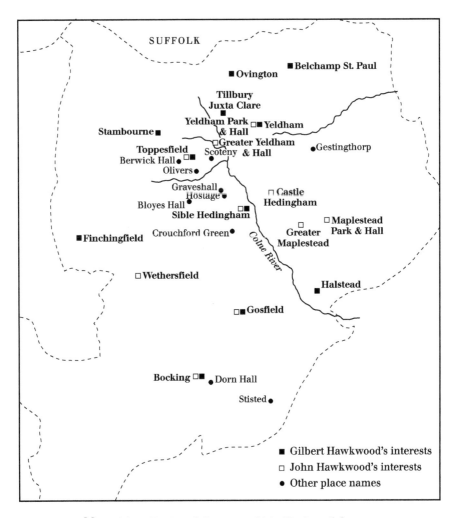

*Map 3.* Gilbert Hawkwood's Interests and John Hawkwood's Interests

Gilbert de Hawkwood ("de Haukewode," "de Hauekwode," or "de Haukwode," according to extant documents).[4] To the frustration of modern historians, Gilbert gave the boy the same name as his older brother, making our protagonist not only a second son but also a second John. The redundancy, common enough at the time, underscores the rather unremarkable circumstances of Hawkwood's birth.

Biographers have long claimed that the Hawkwood family was of low rank and station. This has allowed for a dramatic portrayal of John as "the poorest soldier in the army," who then rose to fame and glory against all odds.[5] The facts, however, tell a different tale. They indicate that the young Hawkwood grew up in reasonable comfort, on ample estates, attended by at least one maidservant. Gilbert Hawkwood, supposedly a tanner, was a landowner of considerable wealth.[6] He had property in two of Hinckford's largest and most prosperous villages: Sible Hedingham, the main family home, and Finchingfield, an adjacent town to the east.[7] According to the Lay Subsidy of 1327, a tax assessment based on movable wealth, Gilbert ranked seventh out of forty-five families listed for Sible Hedingham and eighth out of fifty-two in Finchingfield.[8] His business interests extended to the nearby villages of Gosfield, Bocking, Halstead, Toppesfield, and Great Yeldham; north into Stambourne, Langham, Tillbury Juxta Clare, Ovington, and Belchamp St. Paul; and into the adjacent county of Suffolk (map 3).[9]

Gilbert's circle included an array of men both above and below him on the socioeconomic scale. Most were local landholding families, such as the Baynards, Hodings, Ostags, and Listons from nearby villages (table 3).[10] It was through the Baynard family that Gilbert gained access to the Coggeshales, one of the most important clans in Essex. John Coggeshale, husband of Isabel Baynard, served for many years (1334–1339, 1340–1341, 1343-1348, 1352–1354) in the distinguished post of sheriff of Essex. The Coggeshales in turn formed marriage alliances with the Bourchiers, another notable family. Robert Bourchier represented Essex in Parliament (1329, 1330, 1332, 1339) and became chancellor of King Edward III in 1340.[11]

The above characters formed the social background of John Hawkwood's young life. He maintained contact with them throughout his career. He fought in France alongside members of the Liston, Coggeshale, and Bourchier families, and when his earnings from abroad allowed, he bought lands near these families, hoping to retire among them. Thomas, son of John Coggeshale, served as one of Hawkwood's chief representatives through whom he made investments in England while in Italy. Hawkwood later married his daughter Antiochia to Thomas's nephew William. Among Hawkwood's last wishes, as he lay dying in Florence in 1394, was that his wife return to England to live on the estates he had purchased from the Ostag and Liston families.

TABLE 3

*Business transactions involving Gilbert Hawkwood*

| Year | Transaction | Source |
| --- | --- | --- |
| 1314/15 | Litigation with John Graveshale over 300 acres of land, 18 acres of meadow, 10 acres of pasture, 75 acres of wood, 48 soldi of rent, and 1 messuage (i.e., a site for a home and associated building— bakehouse, barn, etc.) | *Feet of Fines for Essex,* 2:158 |
| 1329 | Collection along with Walter Roughley of Sible Hedingham and John de Nunthey of Halstead of £408 in outstanding debts owed by Robert Darre, Nycholas de Twynsted, John de Chilton, John Knyvet, and John le Cupere of Docking and Sudbury | *Calendar of Close Rolls, Edward III, 1327–1330,* 574 |
| 1336 | Witness to grant from Richard de la Lee, rector of Bradwell, to Sir Thomas Chaddeworth, clerk, and Robert Chaddeworth of all lands "had by fine" from Sir Thomas de la Lee, his brother, in Till-bury, Ovington, Great Yeldham, and Belchamp St. Paul and "reversion" of 70 acres of land, 2 acres of meadow, and 4 marks' rent on Stambourne and Toppesfield, which Elizabeth de Croxton held for life | ERO, D/DCW/T 46/3 |
| 1336 | Witness, along with John Summoner, to land deal involving a bequest by John Longwood "of Gosefield" to Henry Hughes of Wethersfield | PRO, DL 15/1999 |

*Note:* ERO = Essex Record Office Chelmsford, England; PRO = Public Record Office, London.

The sources make no mention of John's mother, who apparently died well before her husband did. It is possible that Mrs. Hawkwood came from the Munne family, which figures most prominently in Gilbert's will and later contested his legacy, perhaps an indication that the Munne family believed it deserved more on familial grounds. Gilbert's wife may also have been related to the Longwood family, a clan with interests both in Gosfield and in Sussex County. When John Longwood died in 1336, Gilbert stood heir to his estates. A web of relations, often difficult to discern, tied many of the local families together.

Gilbert Hawkwood and his wife had seven children. In addition to the two Johns, there were Nicholas and four girls: Agnes, Johanna, Alice, and Margaret. Nicholas, the youngest son, took up a career in the church and is mentioned in a document as a "poor priest of the diocese of London." In 1363 he received a small benefice at a monastery in Normandy, where presumably he lived out the rest of his life.[12] Johanna, the eldest daughter, married into the neighboring Graveshale family, once among Sible Hedingham's wealthiest, more recently reduced to a status roughly equal to that of the Hawkwoods. Gilbert Hawkwood and John

Graveshale senior, Johanna's father-in-law, had been involved in litigation in 1314–1315 over conflicting claims to large tracts of land, perhaps related to Johanna's dowry.[13] Agnes Hawkwood married Thomas Roughy, a modest local landholder. The youngest girls, Alice and Margaret, remained unmarried at the time of their father's death in 1340.

The most fortunate of the children was John Hawkwood the elder, who, by custom, inherited Gilbert's estates. He managed the family patrimony well, extending it especially in the direction of Gosfield, where he bought the village's largest manors: Parke Hall, Listons Hall, and Gosfield or Bellowes Hall. The last manor became known thereafter as "Hawkwood's Gosfield" or Hawkwood Hall and served as the main family base. John drew on Gilbert's personal network and solidified the family contacts, particularly with the most powerful of all the local families, the de Veres, the earls of Oxford, whose Norman castle dominated the local skyline. In 1371, John Hawkwood senior served as one of the executors of Thomas de Vere's estate. By 1381, he was the second largest landholder in Gosfield, listed in the poll tax of that year as a franklin, a title that signified status just below that of the gentry. His household included a wife, Margery, whom he married sometime before 1343, a maidservant named Alice, and, to further confound historians, a son whom he named John.[14] This John Hawkwood, first mentioned in documents in 1344, lived his life in Essex, appears briefly as a witness to a land transaction in 21 September 1368, and then is heard of no more.[15]

Scholars have often confused the several John Hawkwoods, particularly John the franklin with his younger brother John the mercenary. One clear distinction between them was their personal seals. John Hawkwood the mercenary affixed to documents the symbol of a hawk; his elder brother used a rampant lion over a bend with a tendril above and on each side. The latter seal appears in red-brown wax at the bottom of a document, dated 1341, in the Public Record Office in England. Unlike his younger brother, the elder John Hawkwood preferred to live in the shadows and eschewed public life and service. In 1348 he had himself exempted from serving on "any assizes, juries or recognitions" and "from being made mayor, sheriff, coroner, escheator or other bailiff or minister of the king."[16] Apart from a brief stint as a tax collector in 1377, he successfully managed to avoid office.[17]

## Boyhood and Birth

The sketch of the Hawkwoods thus far is of a rather stereotypical medieval landholding family—daughters given in marriage, the oldest son inheriting the patrimony, and the younger landless sons taking up careers in war and the church. The fiction writer Hubert Cole portrayed the two older Hawkwood brothers as at odds with each other, the elder scolding the younger and treating him with condescension.[18] The modern historian Barbara Hanawalt has affirmed that such fraternal rivalries were common in England at the time.[19] But whatever difficulties may have existed between the boys, they worked closely with each other when they became adults. John Hawkwood the mercenary sent money back home to John Hawkwood the franklin to buy land and make investments. The connection may help explain the elder John Hawkwood's own fiscal rise, which coincided with plague years when local landholders were generally hard pressed. John the franklin served along with Thomas Coggeshale and several other men as his brother's "foofee," purchasing estates and holding them until John the mercenary returned from Italy. But the younger John Hawkwood never came home, and after his death a bitter legal battle ensued between his wife and his feofees.

The lack of concrete information regarding the boyhood of our protagonist has given rise to some curious tales. The sixteenth-century bishop and humanist Paolo Giovio claimed that Hawkwood passed his early days among "the Frisian race of Germans."[20] The Florentine chronicler Filippo Villani, on the other hand, placed Hawkwood's birth in a forest. "His mother, about to give birth, had herself carried into a forest, and here the boy was born." Thus the name "Hawkwood," Villani concludes, is descriptive of the event: John was literally the "hawk of the wood."[21]

Giovio's depiction was, of course, the purest of fantasy. The Italian bishop even supposed that Hawkwood was a descendant of a German king named Memprecius. But Villani's tale has a strangely familiar ring. The story of a young woman giving birth in the woods was the subject of two ballads current in Hawkwood's day, "The Cruel Mother" and "Fair Janet." In the former, the expectant mother gives birth in the woods as she leans with her back against a tree; in the latter, she produces her child under a greenwood tree.[22] Since Villani probably met John Hawkwood in person, it is possible that he learned the story from the Englishman himself, who may have given in to the temptation to make sport of the Florentine by relaying to him as fact a story he heard as a boy.

The year of Hawkwood's birth has been the subject of much discussion. Dates of birth were not formally recorded in medieval England but come to light only from indirect evidence, such as coroner's inquests, when prospective heirs needed to prove they had reached the requisite twenty-one years of age to inherit estates.[23] Citizens themselves often did not know their ages, and military men had a tendency to exaggerate in order to enhance their feats of arms. John de Sully, who fought in the battle of Najera in 1367, claimed to be 105 years old at the time.[24]

As a consequence, there have been diverse opinions regarding the year of Hawkwood's birth. A typeset of an anonymous article in the Essex Record Office puts it at 1323; a manuscript among the papers of the Majendie family makes a claim for "the beginning of the reign of Edward III" in 1327.[25] The eighteenth-century antiquarian Richard Gough preferred 1320, as did the nineteenth-century writer John Temple-Leader. The influence of Temple-Leader brought wide acceptance of this last date, which has found its way into modern accounts.

A better case, however, can be made for 1323. Temple-Leader based his conclusion primarily on the fact that Hawkwood served as one of the executors of his father's will in 1340, which he supposed could have occurred only when Hawkwood was twenty-one years old. But the role of executor was open to seventeen-year-olds, and the commissions of array that enrolled men for war in Hawkwood's day accepted youths as young as sixteen.[26] Placing Hawkwood's birth at 1323 allows him to have been old enough to be executor of his father's will and yet younger when he began his advancement in the military profession in the wars in France and more youthful when, toward the end of his career in 1390, he effected a daring and physically demanding retreat from Milanese territory. The chronology still allows for Hawkwood to have been sufficiently aged—forty years old—when he arrived in Italy to warrant Villani's description of him as an "old fox." The average life expectancy in Hawkwood's native Essex was between thirty-six and forty years, and English ecclesiastical sources defined fifty or more as "old age." Men in Italy described themselves as "old" at fifty or younger.[27] The battlefields of the fourteenth century were generally the province of young men; some of the commanding officers in the English armies were still in their early twenties.[28] Just prior to calling Hawkwood an "old fox," Villani complained about the youth and poor quality of Florence's political leaders, who, on account of the recent plague, came to office having "not yet passed adolescence."[29]

## London Tailor and King's Soldier

In 1340 Gilbert died, and the elder John took over management of the household.[30] Gilbert was buried in the nearby parish church of St. Peter's in Sible Hedingham; in his will he had set aside 10 marks for the burial along with an additional 19 shillings for memorial candles.[31] Altogether Gilbert left 156 marks' (£97 ¼) worth of cash and movables—including livestock, furniture, and grain—to family, friends, clergy, and pious institutions. He gave more than 20 marks to chaplains at St. Peter's and to the vicar at Gosfield, 10 marks to the poor, and a small sum to the family maidservant, Basilea. The younger John Hawkwood received 37 ½ marks (£25), an allotment of grain and oats, a bed, and a full year's maintenance (appendix 1).

John did not, however, remain at home. His name is conspicuously absent from the deed drawn up at Sible Hedingham in 1341, which lists the entire male Hawkwood household, including John the elder; Johanna's husband, John Graves-hale; Agnes's husband, Thomas Roughy; and close family associates John Liston, Thomas Hoding, John Ostag, and John Oliver.[32]

Where was the younger John Hawkwood? It appears he went to London to work for a time as a tailor. The author of the contemporary *Westminster Chronicle* specif-ically identified Hawkwood as "an apprentice of a London hosier." The anonymous continuator of Ranulf Higdon's *Polychronicon* likewise spoke of Hawkwood par-ticipating in the "artem sartoriam" in London.[33] Hawkwood's home in Hinckford was a center of the Essex woolen industry, and there was a steady flow of appren-tices and masters to and from London. The historian Sylvia Thrupp has shown that fourteenth-century London was filled with apprentices of "every English dialect," representing "every social group in the kingdom, paupers and nobility excepted."[34]

The image of Hawkwood, future commander of large armies, wielding a nee-dle and scissors is certainly an incongruous one, and scholars have, not surpris-ingly, rejected it outright.[35] The great Roman authority on war Vegetius claimed that "all who shall seem to have dealt in anything pertaining to textile-mills should . . . be banned far from camp."[36] But it was fact that "meek" tailors were often transformed into effective warriors in the Middle Ages. In the twelfth century, the Earl of Leicester had numerous weavers in his army; textile workers in fourteenth-century Flanders defeated French armies.

Hawkwood did not remain a tailor for long. To use Fuller's felicitous phrase, he soon "turned his needle into a sword and thimble into a shield" and left England to fight in the wars in France.[37] The opportunities for soldiering abroad were good. In 1337, England began a long war with France. King Edward III claimed the right to the French throne through his mother, sister of the deceased French king Charles IV. The French bypassed Edward and chose instead Charles's first cousin Philip. The dispute culminated in a conflict that would continue in episodic fashion for the next hundred years and more.

The war offered landless younger sons like Hawkwood a chance for adventure as well as financial and social gain. According to tradition, Hawkwood joined King Edward's army as a longbowman. The assertion lacks direct evidence but accords reasonably well with Hawkwood's background. Bowmen were drawn from a broad sector of society, including men of some wealth and standing. Those recruited from the county of Cheshire, studied in detail by Philip Morgan, often held status equal to that of regular men-at-arms. Moreover, the demand for archers was at this time high, as English armies came to rely increasingly on "mixed" retinues consisting of men-at-arms and longbowmen—a development that some scholars have called "the Edwardian military revolution." The numbers of archers and men-at-arms began to reach parity in English armies by the middle decades of the fourteenth century.[38]

The archers used the famed longbow, a six-foot piece of sturdy Spanish yew, painted white. The weapon required considerable skill and strength to operate. The longbow had the advantage over the more traditional crossbow in that it could be fired more quickly yet still had enough striking power under the right conditions to penetrate armor. Archery and shooting contests were then popular in England and encouraged by the state as the wars in France progressed.[39] Long-bowmen earned 6 denari a day, a decent salary. But what lured men to the profession was the potential for profits from booty. In this sense it was a natural precursor to a life as a mercenary soldier, though advancement within the army through the ranks to the status of captain was admittedly not common.[40]

The standard account, taken from Temple-Leader, is that Hawkwood fought in France in the retinue of John de Vere, the seventh Earl of Oxford, with whom he passed his entire career. De Vere lived in the neighboring village of Castle Heding-ham.[41] He was a distinguished soldier from a long line of warriors, the "fighting de Veres," and had participated in royal campaigns in Scotland (1336) and in France (1339).[42] Hawkwood purportedly first joined de Vere for the offensive in Brittany in 1342/43. De Vere's retinue for that campaign consisted of a banneret (a senior knight with the right to command the other troops and to display the contingent's banner), seven knights, twenty-six esquires, and twenty-four mounted archers. But the documents do not give the identities of these men, and Hawkwood's name has not yet turned up among the letters of protection, a common means of distinguishing soldiers.[43] The connection between Hawkwood and de Vere is based primarily on the grant by the latter to the former of a "knight's fee," an estate given in return for military service.

But Hawkwood undoubtedly served more directly under a subcontractor, a lesser knight or esquire who recruited him, an arrangement that was common in English armies. Numerous neighbors and family associates went to war in France. Hawkwood may, for instance, have initiated his career under John Longwood, the associate of his father, who was in the retinue of the knight Hugh Neville, or with John and William Wauton, whose names appear in documents relating to the Hawkwood family. The most likely scenario, however, is that Hawkwood began alongside members of the Liston, Coggeshale, and Bourchier families.[44] John and Thomas Liston, John Coggeshale and his son Thomas, and Robert Bourchier and his son John all went to France at the same time Hawkwood did. The families, as we have seen, had close ties with Hawkwood and with one another. John Liston was part of Gilbert's inner circle, perhaps even a relative, and may well have been the "uncle and great master" who Filippo Villani claimed schooled Hawkwood in

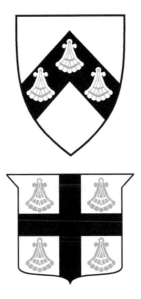

*Figure 3.* Coggeshale coat of arms (top) and Hawkwood coat of arms (bottom)

the ways of war.[45] The documents refer to John Liston at this time as a knight.[46] The Hawkwoods and Bourchiers had done business together since 1343, and after John Hawkwood's death, the chantry in his honor was made in conjunction with one for John Bourchier. The most obvious connection is between Hawkwood and the Coggeshales. John Hawkwood's eventual coat of arms, argent on a chevron sable with three scallop shells, closely resembles that of Thomas Coggeshale, whose emblem was argent on a sable cross between four scallops (fig. 3).[47] Thomas later served as one of Hawkwood's feofees in England.

The association between Hawkwood and the above-mentioned men indicates that if indeed he began his career in Brittany in 1342/43, it was most probably not in the retinue of de Vere but with William Bohun, Earl of Northampton. John Coggeshale and Robert Bourchier both fought under Bohun in 1342/43, as did John and Thomas Liston.[48] Bohun was a distinguished military man in his own right. He did not live near Hawkwood, as did de Vere, but he was nevertheless highly active in recruiting men from Essex and from Hawkwood's region in particular. The interpretation does not contradict the evidence of a knight's fee, which was granted only in 1361, well after Brittany and, significantly, a year after Bohun's death.[49]

In any case, Hawkwood's service to Bohun did not preclude service to de Vere.

It was common practice for soldiers to shift retinues during their careers, and we should allow that Hawkwood did the same.[50] One of Hawkwood's neighbors in Sible Hedingham, Thomas Shardelowe, held a knight's fee from de Vere but also fought with the Earl of Warwick (1346/47).[51] Another neighbor, Nicholas Picard, held a knight's fee from de Vere but also fought with William Bohun.

It has long been supposed that Hawkwood participated in two of the great battles of the war, at Crécy in 1346 and at Poitiers in 1356. Here again the direct evidence is meager. But Hawkwood's subsequent military career in Italy bears the imprint of the battles, such that the presumption should be judged valid. Traces of the methods of Crécy are evident in Hawkwood's service for Pisa; elements of Poitiers are apparent in Hawkwood's service for Padua and his conduct of the battle of Castagnaro.

At Crécy, both John de Vere and William Bohun were commanders of the English army. John Liston served as banneret for Bohun, along with Robert Bourchier; thus it is most likely that Hawkwood was also with the Earl of Northampton.[52] Bohun occupied the vanguard of the army, along with the king's sixteen-year-old son, Edward, Prince of Wales. John de Vere took up position behind the vanguard with King Edward III. The overall army consisted of between 10,000 and 15,000 men, two-thirds of whom were archers and foot soldiers.[53] Essex County sent contingents of 200 men-at-arms and 38 longbowmen,

The vicissitudes of the Crécy campaign are well known but are briefly stated here from Hawkwood's proposed vantage. The English army arrived on the continent at St. Vaast-La-Hougue in July 1346, traveled some three hundred miles, and then, short of food and pursued by the French, set up camp just north of the village of Crécy, on a hill above what is now called Vallée des Clercs. On 26 August, the French army, overzealous and not well organized, moved against the English.[54] The vanguard bore the brunt of the attack. The archers, most likely arrayed on the flank, let fly a hail of arrows, which dropped so many French horses that, according to the French chronicler Jean le Bel, they "piled up like piglets."[55] A rout ensued; the English shattered the French army, inflicting a large number of casualties, compared recently to those suffered by the Allied army during the D-Day invasion of Normandy on 6 June 1944.[56]

The English army followed up the victory with the siege of Calais, a strategically important and well-fortified city known as the "bolt and key" to entry into France.[57] The campaign was difficult for both sides, and several Essex men died, including John Coggeshale junior and William and John Wauton.[58] The town eventually capitulated in August 1347.

It was at the battle of Poitiers in 1356 that Hawkwood is said to have come of age as a soldier. John Stow claimed that John won the direct praise of Edward, Prince of Wales, who knighted him.[59] An anonymous nineteenth-century manuscript in the Essex Record Office claimed that Edward valued Hawkwood so much that he placed him at the head of his own contingent of 250 archers and even consulted him "in weighty affairs."[60]

Many of the participants at Poitiers were the same as those at Crécy. The Prince of Wales stood at the overall commander of the army. William Bohun was now dead, but John de Vere occupied the vanguard, along with the Earl of Warwick and the Gascon nobleman Captal de Buch. We may suppose that Hawkwood was with this group.

The royal army contained 6,000–8,000 men, with slightly fewer archers than men-at-arms. It advanced first on Gascony, where England and Prince Edward had claims. It rode through nearby Provence, robbing and looting rich towns, and then retired with its profits. The army set out again, pursued by King John and the French army. The two sides eventually met on the morning of 19 September 1356, facing each other across hedges and vines. Oxford, Warwick, and the vanguard retreated with the baggage train over a narrow bridge to a secure area behind a wood. This much discussed maneuver (a retreat or a feint?) drew the attention of the French, who sent a contingent of cavalry after the vanguard. According to the chronicler Geoffrey le Baker's account, John de Vere and his archers then played a critical role. They shot at the "hind parts" of the oncoming French, who, remembering Crécy, had placed armor on the front parts of their horses but, unfortunately, neglected the back parts. The result, wrote le Baker, was "horses being galled and wounded . . . tumbling with them that sat on their backs . . . making greater slaughter upon their own masters."[61] The French then threw the full weight of their army against the English; but they were overwhelmed, and King John himself was captured. The tactical highlight of the fighting came again from the vanguard. At the height of battle, Captal de Buch led a contingent of sixty knights and one hundred archers on an enveloping move that cut off escape.

The similarity between the decisive maneuver at Poitiers and Hawkwood's tactics at Castagnaro suggests that Hawkwood may well have been among the one hundred archers who accompanied Captal de Buch in his march. But if King Edward knighted Hawkwood after the battle, there is no evidence of it. Edward's famous "Register" lists honors bestowed on a wide array of men, including the knighting of a tailor, William Stratton.[62] But the erstwhile tailor John Hawkwood is nowhere mentioned. The author of the *Polychronicon* claims that Hawkwood received his knighthood in Italy.[63]

## Marauding Mercenary

The English army dispersed after Poitiers. The Black Prince returned home, as did John de Vere and other leading soldiers. Captal de Buch went on crusade in Prussia. The novelist Hubert Cole romances that Hawkwood too returned home, with a lusty French bride, Chantal. More likely, however, Hawkwood stayed in France, as did other soldiers of his status, roaming about the countryside.

The Florentine chronicler Matteo Villani appeared to have pinpointed the Englishman in the summer of 1359. He spoke of the marauding activities in southwestern France of a "Gianni dell' aguglia," or "John of the needle," whom he described as an "English tailor," who had "a great heart for feats of arms" and "took delight in doing evil." He said that Gianni's brigade was composed of "plunderers and Englishmen" who "devoted themselves to living by prey."[64] The reference is admittedly vague; there is no evidence that Hawkwood ever took the name "John of the Needle." And Villani, though generally well informed about events in southern France, placed his Gianni dell' aguglia in the unlikely setting of Pau, a city in the relatively barren province of Béarn, known more for producing mercenaries than for enticing them to plunder. The coordinates of Gianni do not readily correspond to those of a known band. The closest was the "Great Company" of Robin Knowles and Hugh Calveley, which rode through nearby Provence and harassed the town of le Puy. Did Villani mistake Gianni for Robin Knowles, who was once described by the French chronicler Jean le Bel as a tailor? Did he confuse Pau with le Puy?

Or did Villani actually see Hawkwood? Interestingly, Filippo Villani, Matteo's son and successor as chronicler, used the term "aguglia" not to mean needle but as a variant of "aquila," or eagle. Filippo spoke of the "aguglia" used by the Pisans as a symbol of the city, emblazoned on military banners during their war with Florence (1362–1364). If we understand "aguglia" as eagle, then "John of the Needle" becomes "John of the Eagle," an appellation much closer to "John of the Hawk," or Hawkwood. In the language of heraldry, there was little distinction between the eagle and the hawk. And, as we have already seen, Hawkwood used the hawk as his seal and most likely placed it also on his military banners.

The problem of marauding bands only grew worse when France and England signed the treaty of Brétigny on 8 May 1360. The treaty brought a temporary end to the war, but it encouraged the formation of the so-called free companies, which now spread throughout France. The largest and most formidable of the bands was the "Great Company" ("Magna Societas"), which came together in eastern France.[65]

John Hawkwood joined this band alongside an assortment of colorful characters, including the Périgord captain and self-proclaimed "king of adventurers" Seguin Badefol, the Gascon Bernard de La Salle, the German Albert Sterz, the English former convict John Verney, and the Italian adventurer Giovanni Guccio, who claimed to be King John I of France.[66] The French monk and chronicler Jean de Venette described them as "sons of Belial and men of iniquity, warriors from various lands who assailed other men with no right and no reason other than their own passions, iniquity, malice and hope of gain."[67] The English chronicler Knighton, not displeased to watch the French suffer, saw them as "brave and battle-hardened men, experienced and vigorous, who lived by what they could win in war."[68]

The band moved about initially in Champagne and Burgundy and then descended the Rhone Valley to harass the pope at Avignon.[69] On the night of 28/29 December 1360 it seized Pont-Saint-Esprit, a fortress about twenty-five miles north of the papal city, which was then serving as the collection point of taxes for Languedoc to pay the ransom of King John, who had been captured at Poitiers in 1356. The company remained in the environs of Avignon for the next three months, where it effectively blockaded Avignon from the north.[70] Veterans from throughout France joined it, as did soldiers from as far away as Lombardy, Genoa, Savoy, and even Spain.[71]

Hawkwood played a leading role in the Great Company, but given its amorphous nature, it is difficult to know his exact coordinates. Hawkwood has been identified as one of the men to whom Pope Innocent VI wrote on 15 February 1361 seeking peace. Innocent addressed his letter to three of the band's leaders: " 'Waltero,' knight and captain of the Great Company; 'Johanni Scakaik,' marshall; and 'Riccardo Mussato,' the black squire."[72] The first was likely Walter Leslie, a Scottish knight (the Earl of Ross), who had participated in the Baltic crusade in 1356 and had come to France in 1359; the last was probably Richard Musard, an Englishman, who later took up service with the Count of Savoy.[73] "Scakaik" is supposed to have been Hawkwood, based on the assumption that "Scakaik" was a misspelling of John's last name. If so, Hawkwood held the rank of "marescallo," or marshal of the company, a post just below that of the overall captain, Walter Leslie.[74] But although popes had a notoriously hard time rendering Hawkwood's name into Latin, the word "Scakaik" in truth bears little resemblance to "Hawkwood" and could just as easily have been a reference to someone else.

The company committed atrocities at Pont-Saint-Esprit.[75] Pope Innocent VI condemned and excommunicated the band in January 1361 and called out a crusade against it.[76] The enterprise failed, in part because many of the hired men, themselves mercenaries, went over the company. But the reappearance of plague in southern France did much to restrain the band and make its stay progressively uncomfortable. In March 1361 the pope and the company made peace.[77] The agreement was in the form of separate accords with the various contingents that made up the company. The pontiff engaged them for service across the Pyrenees in Spain and across the Alps in Italy.[78]

Hawkwood took up with those who went to Italy, where Pope Innocent was engaged in a war with his long-time adversary Bernabò Visconti, lord of Milan. Bernabò had recently launched an attack on the city of Bologna, the seat of the pope's vicar. Together with his brother Galeazzo, Visconti threatened much of northern Italy. Innocent allied with the city of Genoa and marquisate of Montferrat, states also endangered by Visconti expansionist policies.[79] The pope arranged to have the band work for John Palealogus II, the Marquis of Montferrat, a man of noble bearing, "handsome, virtuous, wise and valiant," who was roughly the same age as Hawkwood. Palealogus came in person to lead the band over the Alps.[80] The pope and the Genoese shouldered the costs.

The passage to Italy did not proceed smoothly. Members of the company broke off and ravaged the countryside near Rodez, forcing Montferrat to return to Pont-Saint-Esprit to seek more soldiers.[81] The band proceeded in a more orderly fashion the second time, through the Maritime Alps via Provence and Nice and the Valle Vermenagna. The band ravaged the suburbs of Marseille, however, when locals refused to sell them food. It arrived in Piedmont in May 1361.

An extant contract in the state archives of Turin provides a partial roll call of the men who crossed into Italy with Hawkwood (appendix 2). His brigade was captained by the German mercenary Albert Sterz, accompanied by seventeen corporals, fifteen of whom appear to have English names.[82] The men were veterans from the French wars, some familiar, others obscure, several undoubtedly using assumed names, a custom common among soldiers, particularly those wanted for crimes.[83] Notable among the corporals were Robin du Pin, sometimes taken for the Englishman Robin Knowles but more likely a relative of French mercenary (from Poitou) Guiyot du Pin, and Andrew Belmont, probably an illegitimate son of Henry Beaumont, Earl of Buchan (d. 1369), who had distinguished himself in the Scottish wars at Dupplin Moor and Halidon Hill and had once come to Italy in 1322 on behalf of Pope John XXII.[84]

The chronicler of Savoy, Jehan Servion, paid especially close attention to du Pin, whom he took as the overall captain of the band. Andrew Belmont was widely admired by local writers for his good looks. Another of the men, William Boson, would forge close links with Hawkwood and fight alongside him for the much of the next twenty years. Hawkwood's name appears among those of the corporals. He is identified as "Iohannes de Hakeude," a form surprisingly close to that used in documents back in Essex. He is among the first mentioned in document, along with Beaumont and du Pin, an indication, according to the established convention, that his rank was high.

The precise list of those who crossed the Alps with Hawkwood will, however, never be known for certain. The extant contract is dated 22 November 1361, a full seven months after the band arrived in Italy. It was preceded by three earlier contracts, none of which have survived.[85] In the meantime, the membership of the band fluctuated. The English chronicler Knighton spoke of a general ebb and flow of soldiers between Lombardy and France. The Italian writer Matteo Villani told how some of members turned back shortly after arriving, including a "bold woman," the "countess of Harcourt" ("la donna di siri ricorti," perhaps the wife of Jean V, Count of Harcourt), who had joined Montferrat at Avignon.[86] Papal registers show that Pope Innocent recruited additional soldiers directly from England in July and August 1361.[87] Some of the men who crossed into Italy broke off from the company and worked elsewhere on the peninsula. Walter Leslie, erstwhile captain at Avignon, does not appear in the contract of 22 November; he went to Venice with other English mercenaries.[88]

The official name of Hawkwood's band was the "Great Company of English and Germans," essentially the same as back in Avignon. The reference to Germans was probably a nod to Sterz. Local writers, however, explicitly identified the company as an English one. The French-speaking Servion called the band the "compagnez des angloys." Latin documents in the archives in Turin described it as "societas angliciis," as did the Milanese chronicler Azario.[89]

The contract makes no mention of the company's size. The accepted figure is that given by the chronicler Matteo Villani, who estimated that the band consisted of 3,500 horses and 2,000 infantry.[90] But Villani's calculation is not trustworthy. It was made two years after the company entered Italy, when it reached Tuscany in 1363. In any case, it bears uncomfortable resemblance to the estimate he gave for the German Great Company just pages earlier. Azario, who saw the band before Villani did, put the number of horsemen at only 2,000.[91] A better—though hardly imperfect—means of approximation is to compare the extant contract of 22 November 1361 with a later one from 1365, which contains the overall number of horseman (5,000) as well as the number of corporals (30). If the company in November 1361 was configured in the roughly the same way as its counterpart in 1365, that is, in brigades of roughly 167 men per corporal, then it had 2,839 horsemen—a figure midway between that of Villani and that of Azario.[92] This would make the company large in comparison with its counterparts in Italy: the famous German Great Company of 1350 had 2,375 horsemen, and its counterpart in 1358 had 1,500–2,000 horsemen.[93]

## The White Company

It was in Italy that the Great Company came to be known more surely by its famous nickname, the White Company, popularized in modern times by John Ruskin, Arthur Conan Doyle, and others. Ruskin claimed that the name derived from the band's habit of wearing highly polished plate armor,[94] which appeared "white" in the sun. He based this supposition on Filippo Villani's famous description of the band.[95] The explanation has become standard.

But Villani never linked the practice of polishing armor to the name; nor did any other contemporary.[96] Villani noted only that the armor appeared like "mirrors." The Milanese writer Azario, in fact, described the band as modestly armored: some soldiers had iron breastplates, others wore hardened leather doublets; some men had bacinets without visors, others had no helmets at all.[97] The discrepancy again derives from the different vantages of the authors: Azario saw the band just after it crossed the Alps, when it was likely impoverished from the trip, while Villani witnessed the band two years later, after it had become rich from large advances on pay from the city of Pisa. But documentary evidence suggests that the band was never heavily armored, at least not with respect to other soldiers in Italy. Florentine legislation from 1369 governing the outfitting of that city's armies indicates that the English generally wore less armor than their contemporaries, particularly native Italian soldiers.[98] Indeed, the very notion that the English awed Italian contemporaries with their armor is prima facie unlikely given that it was the Italians, notably the Milanese, who were the primary manufacturers of plate armor at this time and exported their wares to England, where there was little local industry.[99]

The name White Company thus more likely came from the custom of wearing surcoats over armor.[100] The Knights Templars, a distant model for mercenary companies, traditionally wore red surcoats over their armor. In a later description of the English corporal Andrew Belmont, Villani noted that he "dressed all in white." The Englishman included by the artist Andrea di Bonauti in the Spanish chapel (1366–1368) at the Santa Maria Novella in Florence is shown wearing white.[101]

It was nevertheless in Tuscany, and with Tuscan writers, that the name White Company gained wide currency. Locals may have been more inclined to use the appellation in order to distinguish the band from at least two other "Great Companies" then operating in the region. The chronicler of the city of Perugia, Del

Graziani, claimed that when the band arrived in Tuscany there was also a band called the Black Company.[102]

Whatever its genesis, the name White Company is a highly evocative one and has, in the hands of modern authors, become a synonym for a rough-hewn manly virtue.[103] Arthur Conan Doyle's Lady Maud in *The White Company* places her hand on her heart and is moved to tears by the mere sight of the men going off to battle.[104] The reality, however, was that the men behaved with little honor. The band's first moves on Italian soil were intensely brutal. It entered the Piedmont region setting fires, looting, raping women, maiming noncombatants, and mistreating prisoners.[105] Azario called them "better thieves than any others who have preyed on Lombardy." Villani said they were "young, hot and eager" and "accustomed to homicides and robbery, current in the use of iron, having little personal cares." Azario vividly described how the band shut captives in boxes and threatened to drown them to hasten payment of ransoms, how the band systematically dismembered victims, beginning with the hands, then the nose, the ears; the trunks of the corpses were left in ditches outside castles to be eaten by dogs. The crimes are noteworthy, even if we acknowledge the tendency for hyperbole in local chronicles.[106]

But apart from lurid tales of misdeeds, Azario and Villani had a great deal to say about the manner in which the company made war. They spoke at length about tactics, organization, and discipline, issues that bear directly on Hawkwood's eventual military career and are thus useful to dwell on in some detail.

Both writers applauded the band's fighting technique. Azario described how "in open battle" the soldiers dismounted from their horses and fought on foot. "They had very large lances with very long iron tips. Mostly two, sometimes three of them, handled a single lance so heavy and big that there was nothing it could not penetrate. Behind them, toward the posterior of the formation, were the archers, with great bows, which they held from their head to the ground and from which they shot great and long arrows." Villani confirmed that the band "almost always fought on foot" and added the detail that the soldiers left their horses with pages during battle. He described the typical English battle formation as "almost round," with two soldiers wielding a single lance. He compared their method of fighting to "the manner in which spearmen hunt a wild boar." The lance was held low, and the men moved slowly in small steps toward the enemy. They were supported by "ready and obedient" longbowmen, who made "buona prova" (i.e., were skillful). Villani did not say how the bowmen were deployed.[107]

The habit of descending from their horses and fighting on foot set the English apart from other mercenaries. The Germans favored cavalry charges; Hungarians shot arrows at opponents from their mounts. Filippo Villani claimed that the band introduced into Italy the cavalry unit known as the "lance," named after the weapon.[108] It consisted of a man-at-arms supported by a squire and a page, each with his own horse; the page, usually a boy, rode a pony. The formation was well adapted to fighting on foot; during battle the page took care of the dismounted horses, and the squire provided reserve and support for the man-at-arms. Michael Mallett has shown that the lance unit predated the advent of the company in Italy; indeed, precursors can be found as far back as a century earlier in Rule of the Templars, which allowed knights to have three and sometimes four horses. But Mallett rightly credits the English with exploiting the unit's potential in the context of fighting on foot.[109]

The precise manner in which the English fought on foot is not at all clear. The formations described by Azario and Villani do not have obvious parallels in English technique in France. The circular array of closely packed soldiers with long spears vaguely recalls the Scottish shiltrom, which performed well against English armies prior to the wars in France. The movement of soldiers toward the enemy in small steps with their lances pointed downward is reminiscent of the habit of the Swiss pikemen of the later fourteenth and fifteenth centuries.[110] What seems indisputable is that the formations were difficult to break and had strong counteroffensive potential.

But even more than technique, what impressed Italian contemporaries was the band's martial spirit and practical experience of battle. The men possessed a ferocity uncommon among foreign mercenaries. Petrarch spoke directly of this in a letter written about the same time that the company entered Italy: "In my youth the Britons . . . were taken to be the meekest of the barbarians. Today they are a fiercely bellicose nation. They have overturned the ancient military glories of the French by victories so numerous that they, who were once inferior to the wretched Scots, have reduced the entire kingdom to fire and sword."[111] Filippo Villani singled out the physical conditioning of the men and their ability to endure the elements, "to march at night as well as during the day, in winter and summer," traits he compared favorably with those of both the ancient Romans and Carthaginians.[112] Villani stressed the band's ability to intimidate its opponents—indeed, his description of its highly burnished armor was intended in the first instance as a statement on the means by which the company instilled fear. The English also frightened the enemy with loud shouts, which they made as they moved forward to attack. The practice contrasted with the silent Hungarians, who did not even use the customary fife and drums at the start of battle but merely slapped their saddlebags to signal assent to their commander.

The band also distinguished itself by its adaptability to its new environment and its ability to negotiate the Italian terrain. The band was highly mobile, able to move across large distances very quickly, skilled at what Matteo Villani called smisurato "viaggio," or "boundless travel."[113] The company enhanced its elusiveness by breaking into small units under individual corporals when on the march. The practice had the practical effect of giving corporals like John Hawkwood experience leading men, and this likely contributed to his later success. Azario lauded the leadership provided by the band's captain general Albert Sterz, whose "virtue at war made all the others virtuous."[114] Azario credited Sterz's effectiveness in no small measure to his ability to speak the English language and thus communicate directly with his soldiers.[115]

The skill most praised by Azario and Villani was, however, the band's talent for surprising enemies, in particular by launching attacks on towns in the middle of the night.[116] Azario said that the men slept "for the most part" during the day, so that they could better cause trouble at night. Villani thought the ruse an extension of the more general trait of "craftiness," which he saw as basic to the nature of the English race. But the band may have received instruction in the tactic from its employer, the Marquis of Montferrat. The marquis's father, Theodore Paleologus, wrote a military treatise (*Les enseignements*) in the first half of the fourteenth century, which advocated nocturnal attacks and gave details on how to effect them.[117] Italian states had themselves used the stratagem, but success was exceedingly rare, and the company deserves credit for exhibiting singular skill. The band's ability to storm towns was facilitated by the use of special scaling ladders, which could be put together and taken apart in small sections and could be made large enough to surmount even very high walls.[118]

What does not appear to have played a major role in the band's success was the longbow. The numbers of longbowmen were always small, and their feats of arms do not appear prominently in the battle descriptions. There is evidence, as we shall discuss later, of the English augmenting the bowmen with Hungarian archers.

The key to the company's achievement in Italy therefore lay in a combination of readiness for battle, cohesion, brutality, and deceptiveness—all traits that John Hawkwood would exhibit in his own career. The one contemporary criticism of the band's military ways was its penchant for "excessive boldness." According to Filippo Villani, this made the company restless and inclined to set up camp in "poor order."[119] This same tendency would be characteristic of John Hawkwood's own early days as an independent captain.

## War in Piedmont and Savoy

Unfortunately for the pope, the initial acts of violence perpetrated by the White Company occurred not in the lands of the enemy, the Visconti, but in those of Amadeus VI, the ruler of Savoy, who was in fact neutral in the war. Amadeus governed a rugged little Alpine state, which extended on both sides of the mountains, from the Saône River in France to the plains of the Po River in Italy. He and Montferrat had overlapping territorial interests, and several years earlier Amadeus had used his own war against the Visconti as a pretext to attack Montferrat's lands. Montferrat now extracted revenge on Amadeus, who, despite his neutrality, leaned uncomfortably toward Galeazzo Visconti, for whom he was acting as intermediary in marriage negotiations with the French royal house. Amadeus had attempted to inhibit the company's passage into Italy by stationing his forces near the two main Alpine passes into his territory, at Mont Genevere and Mont Cenis.

Montferrat and the company advanced instead through the Maritime Alps (map 4). They attacked first at Savigliano, a prosperous town on the western edge of Amadeus domain (forty-five kilometers south of Turin). The target had symbolic value; Amadeus had taken it from Montferrat only a year earlier. The band attempted to breach the walls but was unable. It set fire instead to the surrounding countryside.[120] It then advanced north into the Canavese region, a stretch of land extending from Turin up into the Val d'Aosta which was a focal point of tensions between the two states. The region was traversed by one of medieval Italy's most important roads, the Via Francigena, which ran north through the city of Ivrea to the San Bernardino Pass into France and south all the way to Rome. The road brought a lucrative traffic in merchants and pilgrims and thus promised the company excellent profits.

The company launched a full-scale attack on the town of Rivarolo, in the heart of the Canavese, twenty-five kilometers north of Turin (at the foot of the Alps). It scaled the town walls in the middle of the night, robbed the surprised inhabitants, and then harassed surrounding fields and villages.[121] It then went to Ivrea, located directly on the Via Francigena, and seized the local bishop, Pierre de la Chambre, and ransomed him for a large sum of money.[122] The band then returned to Rivarolo, where it set up its base.

The company remained in Amadeus's lands for nearly a year. The depredations fell heavily on the Alpine state, whose largest towns numbered only about two thousand inhabitants and were thus no bigger than the company itself.[123] The chronicler Servion said that the band was simply "too large for the region."[124] The

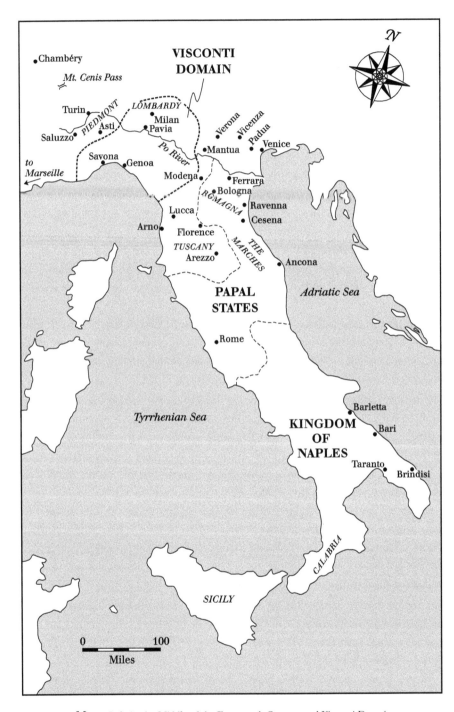

*Map 4.* Italy in the Middle of the Fourteenth Century and Visconti Domain

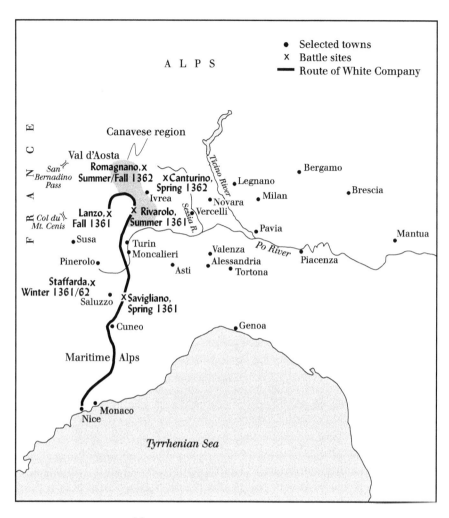

*Map 5.* Initial Route of the White Company

company's actions engendered in Amadeus a singularly personal animus, motivated in part by his inherent dislike of mercenaries as a subspecies of humankind. Amadeus considered himself a chivalrous knight and viewed warfare as an honorable pursuit to be practiced in an honorable manner. He saw mercenaries as little more than "ribaus" and "gens de riens."[125]

His attitude was, however, disingenuous. He had himself employed a "Great Company" of German mercenaries only a year earlier, and his inner circle included the English mercenary Richard Musard, who had been one the leaders of the Great Company at Avignon in winter of 1360/61.[126] Musard, known as the "black squire," became a sort of personal bodyguard and received numerous honors, including membership in Savoy's chivalric order of knights, the Order of the Collar, in 1364.[127] His career is an interesting parallel to Hawkwood's.

Amadeus made a stand against the company in the fall of 1362 at the town of Lanzo, eighteen kilometers southeast of Rivarolo, located on a high ridge overlooking the Stura Valley.[128] He went there with a contingent of men to reinforce the local fortress. But the company surprised Amadeus by launching an attack in the middle of the night, trapping him in the fortress.[129] The band easily gained entrance into the town, which lacked protective walls, and proceeded to rob with such diligence that, according to financial records, it took even pots and pans from homes.[130] The Savoyard chronicler Servion provides a colorful description of the episode. He claimed that Amadeus arrived in the town the day before the enemy and, "as befitting his youth," passed the early evening singing, dancing, and feasting with the local ladies. He then went to bed in the fortress, forgetting to post guards. One of the members of Savoy's entourage, an Englishman named William de Grandson, who was wounded and captured in the subsequent attack, made an impassioned plea to the band on Amadeus's behalf. "Sirs, I marvel that you who all your lives sought honor, should now without cause, without quarrel, without right, wage war on one of the most good, noble, valiant lords of the whole world. Had you asked anything of him, be it supplies or money, he would never have refused you."[131] The speech apparently moved the leaders, who then agreed to withdraw from the fortress and release the count in return for a bribe.[132] Servion asserted that Grandson succeeded because he already knew some of his captors, a statement that has been viewed skeptically by scholars. But it is in fact likely that Grandson was familiar with the men. Grandson had served as King Edward's ambassador to the mercenary bands in France back in the summer of 1360 and had negotiated with the Great Company, just before its descent to Avignon, when it was in the Champagne region.[133] Indeed, Grandson's role at Lanzo provides further proof of a connection between the Great Company that operated in the Champagne region in 1360 and the one now in Italy.

It was directly after the victory at Lanzo that the Marquis of Montferrat signed the company to the contract dated 22 November (appendix 2). The pact was drawn up at Rivarolo, where the company returned with its spoils. The document is atypical of its genre. It does not contain such usual stipulations as army size and rate of pay. Much space is devoted to issues of jurisdiction and the adjudication of improper behavior and fraud—a clear indication that Montferrat was uneasy about his employees. The most intriguing clause is the final one, in which the company refused "to oppose another society of Englishmen or other subjects of the Lord King of England."[134] The provision would appear in subsequent contracts, including those of John Hawkwood. It reveals that the band, despite the presence of soldiers of other nationalities, had a strong sense of its English identity and duty toward its king. German mercenaries often displayed regional sympathies, and Hungarians invariably had close ties to their monarch at home, but neither had equivalent clauses in their contracts. It must be stressed, however, that the English oath was *conditional.* The company would not fight its own countrymen so long as they were not directly employed by Montferrat's enemies. Should English soldiers take up with the enemy, the company was obliged to fight. English mercenaries did indeed end up fighting one another in Italy, and often.

The contract of 22 November 1361 also explicitly forbade the company to attack the Count of Savoy. But Savoy, humiliated at Lanzo (where locals wrote insulting words about him on the town gate), formally abandoned his neutrality and on 26 December allied with the Visconti. The treaty called "first and before everything else" for "the destruction of the society of Englishmen."[135] To facilitate this, Amadeus recruited a German band, which he dubbed "parva societas" (little society), a play on "prava societa" (evil company), his favorite name for the English.

Savoy staged a counterattack against the English in February 1362 at Staffarda, a small town some forty kilometers south of Turin, near the Po River. The chronicler Servion claimed that Amadeus scored a major victory, followed by a very unchivalric revenge, in which he hanged the prisoners he captured rather than ransom them.[136] But in fact the battle at Staffarda was a minor affair, involving a brigade of Englishmen whose connection to Sterz and Hawkwood's company was dubious. The main body of the company remained up north near Rivarolo, which was a significant distance from Staffarda.[137]

## War in Lombardy and the Victory at Canturino

As stipulated in its contract, the company now moved more directly against the Visconti. It undertook an offensive against Galeazzo Visconti in western Lombardy, advancing in March 1362 toward Tortona and Pavia, two of Galeazzo's most important and prosperous cities (map 5). As earlier, the targets had both strategic and economic value. Tortona was a commercial center on a key trade route leading to Genoa and the Champagne fairs up in France; Pavia was situated on the Via Emilia, which led, among other places, to Bologna, the epicenter of the war. Galeazzo Visconti attempted to slow the band by clearing the countryside of goods and securing citizens behind fortified structures.[138] Provisions were already scarce owing to the plague, which afflicted the region. Azario estimated that, because of the contagion, the band had declined to fifteen hundred horses. Galeazzo attempted to reduce the company still further through bribery but managed to corrupt only a few men.[139]

The company struck first just outside Tortona at the town of Castronuovo, ten kilometers up the Scrivia River. Predictably, the attack came at night. The band entered the city on 30 March with the help of traitors from within and, according to Azario, "committed atrocities too horrible to hear."[140] Galeazzo Visconti sent Konrad von Landau, the premier German mercenary of the day, to Castronuovo to oppose the band.[141] But Landau showed little inclination to fight and allowed the enemy to escape and advance to the gates of Tortona and then across the Po River to the environs of Pavia, where Galeazzo himself resided. It burned harvests and set off rebellions in several towns.[142]

The company remained in the environs of Tortona for three months. Despite the concerns about treachery expressed in the contract of 22 November, the band proved faithful to the Marquis of Montferrat's cause. Galeazzo Visconti continued in his attempts to buy off the band, but it held firm. "They responded," wrote Azario, "that they were prepared for war, that they had entered Lombardy to wage war as stipendiaries of the Marquis of Montferrat, whom they wished to serve loyally, just as they were currently doing."[143]

Azario's praise of the English must be understood, however, in terms of his frustration with Konrad von Landau and the German mercenaries. "The Germans didn't care about the wars in Lombardy, but, rather, they feared peace. Thus . . . Lombardy was destroyed; and the local people were plundered both from within and without, having no German as a friend. So it was, is, and will always be."[144]

It was at this point, when the band received high praise for its fidelity, that Hawkwood purportedly deserted the company, left Italy altogether, and returned to France to take part in the famous battle of Brignais near the city of Lyon on 6 April 1362. Hawkwood served as one of the commanders of a mercenary band that routed a French royal army—the high point in the history of the free companies. This interpretation appears in all modern accounts of Hawkwood's life.[145]

That such a journey was possible is undeniable. Passage through the Alps was not prohibitive. The Count of Savoy took six days to move from Lombardy to southern France using the Mont Cenis pass.[146] In fact, Savoy's bodyguard Richard Musard took that very route to Brignais and fought for the royal cause against the mercenaries.[147]

But beyond this fact, there is little evidence that Hawkwood went to Brignais. He was contractually bound to Montferrat and required to serve until July 1362, three months past when the battle occurred. To leave would have been to betray his troop, give up steady employment, and risk uncertain prospects up north. Moreover, if he traveled to Brignais, he apparently did so alone, since none of the other corporals listed in the contract of 22 November are mentioned as having participated there.

Indeed, the only source linking Hawkwood to Brignais is Jean Froissart's famous *Chroniques*.[148] But the Flemish writer was notorious for playing fast and loose with the facts, and nowhere is this more evident than in his description of Brignais. One recent historian has called it "as unreliable as anything Froissart wrote."[149] Froissart dealt with Brignais three times. The first passage, in temporal sequence, includes a long list of the captains who participated in the battle, but it does not mention Hawkwood.[150] The second, part of the reminiscences of the old mercenary Bascot of Mauleon, a figure somewhere between reality and fiction, does mention Hawkwood, not explicitly in terms of Brignais but as one of members of the Great Company at Avignon in the winter of 1360/61. Unfortunately, Froissart, through Bascot, commits an error in chronology and places the events at Brignais *before* those at Avignon. Thus the association of Hawkwood with Brignais is purely inferential, based on a misstatement of the progression of events. We assume Hawkwood was at Brignais because he was at Avignon and could not have avoided being at the former.[151] Froissart's final treatment of Brignais is embedded in a larger discussion of Hawkwood's career and events in Italy for the year 1378. This time Froissart explicitly places Hawkwood at the battle. But by then Hawkwood was famous and accomplished, and Froissart, unaware of his earlier mistake, exaggerated an initial career to suit the man's later accomplishments.[152] It seemed only fitting that the greatest mercenary captain in Italy should have participated in the greatest mercenary triumph of the day.

The most reasonable deduction is that Hawkwood remained in northern Italy in the spring of 1362, along with the rest of the company, burning and pillaging near Tortona. The war had reached a critical stage. Pope Innocent now moved to press his cause more aggressively. He brought Visconti's neighbors, Ferrara, Verona, and Padua, into a military league and planned a major assault on Milan—to take the war directly to Bernabò Visconti, the more formidable of the brothers.[153]

Galeazzo Visconti tried to hem the company in at Tortona by sending against it his most effective captain, the Italian mercenary Luchino dal Verme. Dal Verme had captured Pavia two years earlier on Galeazzo's behalf and was one of the most respected soldiers in Italy. The arrival of the Italian captain in fact induced the company to retreat from Tortona. It moved north toward Novara, taking several small towns on its way, including Romagnano, a strategic outpost on the Sessia River (twenty-eight kilometers from Novara and seventy from Milan), where it set up its base. The itinerary was somewhat curious, since the plague ravaged the region with particular ferocity. The company lost numerous men on the march; Azario estimated the number of horsemen now at five hundred. At Romagnano, the company received reinforcements of men and arms from the pope's allies, Genoa and Hungary.[154]

Dal Verme himself fell sick from the contagion. This allowed the company to stage a raid to the east, devastating a broad arc of land from Alessandria to Voghera. But the impetus of the attack quickly dissipated; and the pope and the Visconti initiated peace talks at Valenza, a small town on the Po River, just north of Alessandria.

The negotiations are significant because Hawkwood took an active role in them, the first time he engaged in what would become a familiar activity during his career. Hawkwood took part in the papal delegation along with Albert Sterz and other leaders of the company. The talks failed, however, and Hawkwood and the others returned to the band's base at Romagnano.[155]

In January 1363, the company renewed the offensive, launching an aggressive raid on Milanese territory. The band crossed the Ticino River, broke into small units, and fanned out over a wide area, damaging the towns of Legnano, Nerviano, Castano, and others. The band reached the outskirts of Milan at night and caught local citizens off guard, while they were out socializing and playing their nightly games of checkers. According to Azario's evocative description, the band exhibited singular greed. Soldiers robbed women of their jewelry and tied up citizens with ropes and led them away to be ransomed later. A single Englishman dragged off as many as ten captives at once, constrained in this activity only by a shortage of rope. To the band's credit, however, it did not violate women, as it had in the past. Azario attributed this not to moral rectitude but to haste and the desire of soldiers to move quickly elsewhere to gain more loot.[156]

The attack on the suburbs of Milan produced what Azario called "fat spoils," estimated at 100,000 florins.[157] The Visconti sent out urgent pleas for additional mercenary soldiers and again opened up direct negotiations with Albert Sterz, trying to bribe him and members of his band. Azario described the talks as constituting a subtle game of manipulation at which the Visconti notoriously excelled. But Sterz proved himself equally crafty. "Albert, knowing better," wrote Azario, "deceived art with art."[158]

Sterz's acumen contrasted sharply with the lassitude and dullness of Visconti's commander, Konrad von Landau, who remained unwilling to actively engage the enemy. Azario now accused him of being a drunken German captain, who passed too much time drinking wine at the banquet table.

The company meanwhile continued to devastate lands near Novara, due east of Milan. Galeazzo Visconti sent Konrad von Landau, who was stationed nearby, to defend the region. He dispatched the envoy Giovanni Caimmi, a noted military man, who ultimately convinced Landau to ride out against the enemy.

Landau's decision set the stage for a pitched battle, the first involving the company, after nearly two years in Italy raiding fields and overwhelming enemies by surprise. Landau met the company on 22 April 1363 near a bridge at the town of Canturino not far from the company's base at Romagnano. Landau initially acquitted himself well and forced the English to retreat. But the band quickly rallied, with the help of reinforcements from a nearby castle. At the point of battle, the English horsemen descended from their mounts; Landau and his men did the same. The two armies engaged. Landau's Hungarian horsemen, however, deserted the field, refusing to fight their countrymen in the opposing army. Azario relates a sad tale of how the German captain vainly shouted in his native tongue, "Alt! Alt!" to his fleeing Hungarian troops. Almost simultaneously he was struck in the face by a rock, which broke the nose piece of his helmet, and then was wounded in the mouth by a lance and another under the right arm. Landau was captured by the English and died in captivity shortly thereafter. "He had terrorized the whole of Italy," wrote Azario, "and yet the clever Count died indiscreetly, snuffed out by robbers and unarmed infantrymen.... What benefit was nobility, power, good looks, industry, uprightness . . . when . . . with one motion, when not looking, he was cut down and made a corpse."[159]

Azario's sketchy description of Canturino makes it difficult to assess the particulars of the battle. There is little that can be said of tactics. The spectacle of Landau appealing to his Hungarian troops in a language they did not understand suggests that, for all Azario's complaints about cowardice and lack of military zeal, a more pressing problem within the German captain's army was poor coordination. Just before the battle, Landau had lost numerous men to desertions.[160] It may well have been the case that pay was lacking for the soldiers.

The decision of the horsemen to dismount and fight on foot may be taken as evidence of the influence of English tactics in France. But it would be unfair to depict Canturino in national terms, as a victory of Englishmen over Germans. With the reduction of forces from plague, both armies had taken in many reinforcements of different nations. The English had many Hungarians, as did the Germans. The longbow, so important at Crécy and Poitiers, does not appear to have played a meaningful role. The climactic event, the unhorsing and death of Landau, occurred as the result of flying rocks.

More immediately, the battle of Canturino brought an end to the company's career in Lombardy and Piedmont. A truce followed the victory. Two envoys from the city of Pisa, Francesco Zaccio and Pietro da Peccioli, came to Novara and began negotiations to bring the company to Tuscany. Pisa was at war with its rival and neighbor Florence and sought reinforcements.[161] Florence also attempted to hire the company and sent its representatives. The commander of the Florentine army, the Italian mercenary Piero Farnese, urged his employers: "Other than those of Cocoar, you will find no better men than the English—born and raised as they are in war, cunning in military ways, and without fear. He who has them and can bear them for not too long will, without fail, be the superior in the war."[162] Villani believed that Florence had the edge in negotiations because of its long-standing economic connections with England through the wool trade and banking; Florentine bankers, in fact, held a good portion of the accounts of King Edward III.

Florence's advantages notwithstanding, the Pisan envoys prevailed. The final deal has been variously estimated at between 7,000 and 11,500 florins a month, for either four or six months of service, a sum that probably constituted at least 50 percent of Pisa's normal revenue.[163] The Florentines balked at the price. Villani quotes one official as asking: "Who will pay?"[164]

The band left Lombardy at the beginning of July 1363. Galeazzo Visconti allowed the company free passage through his lands. It rode alongside the Po River past Piacenza and arrived in Tuscany in the middle of the month. Its departure gave Galeazzo a chance to repair the damage to his state. He slowly retook the local towns and strongholds that had either rebelled or had fallen to the company.

The memory of the band, however, remained active in local minds. It had distinguished itself as the most terrifying and effective fighting force in Italy. The Florentine poet Antono Pucci summed up the episode succinctly in verse:

> In Lombardia avea una compagna
>
> Ch'era chiamata La Compagna Bianca
>
> tanto crudele, e con ogni magagna
>
> che tutta Lombardia aveva stanca
>
> Firenze, che ancora se ne lagna
>
> La rifiuto; e la volpe l'abbranca.[165]

In Lombardy there was a band
that was called the White Company
so cruel and with every vice
that it had worn out all of Lombardy
Florence, now regretful,
refused it and the fox [Pisa] embraced it.

# CHAPTER THREE

# Italy and the Profession of Arms

It is our custom to rob, sack and pillage whoever resists. Our income
is derived from the funds of the provinces we invade; he who values
his life pays for peace and quiet from us at a steep price.

*The German mercenary Konrad von Landau to the*
*papal legate Albornoz prior to invading church lands*

The Italy that John Hawkwood and the White Company encountered in the
second half of the fourteenth century was a landscape of turmoil. The vibrant
beginning of the century had given way to an onslaught of plagues and famines,
rampant violence, and social unrest. Contemporary writers described life in pessimistic terms. "The world," wrote a Sienese chronicler, "is a great shadow."[1]

War was endemic to the peninsula, which consisted of a patchwork of competing states that jostled each one another for position within limited geographical
confines (map 3). The historian J. K. Hyde described Italy in the best of times as
little more than a "confused happening," "fragmented among tumultuous republics and unstable tyrannies."[2] The wars in Piedmont between the Marquis of
Montferrat and the Count of Savoy, and in Lombardy between the pope and the
Visconti, were two of many rivalries. The commercially sophisticated and competitive Tuscan cities often fought one another. The Visconti family exerted especial
pressure, moving out from their capital cities of Milan and Pavia, systematically
subjugating their neighbors to the north and west in Piedmont and Lombardy and
south to Emilia-Romagna and Tuscany. Visconti attempts to establish a bridge-
head at Bologna, a city that was part of the papal domain, led to four wars with the
pontiff between 1350 and 1375.

The pope experienced difficulties within his own domain. His departure to
Avignon in 1305 created a power vacuum that was filled by local strongmen who
often disobeyed papal authority and fought with one another. The Kingdom of
Naples, ruled since the thirteenth century as a papal fief by the French house of

Anjou, faced civil strife between rival factions of the family and by independent-minded local barons. When the Great Schism broke out in 1378, the kingdom became the main theater of the rancorous battle between the rival popes. The maritime republics, Venice and Genoa, though more focused on international trade than on events in the peninsula, also participated in local wars. The Genoese resisted Visconti attempts to take their city, while the Venetians battled the Paduans over mutual interests in the Friuli region. The two cities fought their most intense wars against each other. The War of Chioggia (1378–1381) exhausted both sides.

Foreign powers regularly intervened in Italian affairs. The Hungarian branch of the Angevin family maintained interests in Naples and challenged Venetian expansion in northeastern Italy, actively aiding Venice's rival Padua. The Aragonese opposed French interests in Sicily. German emperors, with vague but long-standing legal rights in Italy, regularly descended on the peninsula to collect money. Henry VII came in 1310, followed by his son Ludwig of Bavaria in 1327, who was then followed by Charles IV in 1355 and again in 1363. Each "visit" touched off violence, particularly factional disputes within cities. The French, for their part, maintained diplomatic contacts with local states, most notably Florence, which often sought military assistance from them.

The constant struggles made the mercenary soldier a common figure on Italian battlefields. States had employed mercenaries since the twelfth and thirteenth centuries. The structure of Italian society encouraged the practice: the large number of independent political entities provided job opportunities, while wealth from trade and industry, particularly in northern and central Italy, provided the wherewithal to spend. Internal rivalries, notably the rise of the middle class, or *popolo*, against the nobility, brought the widespread political exclusion of nobles, who hired themselves out as mercenary soldiers. The pope, absentee ruler of an amorphous papal state, had little choice but to recruit mercenaries to fight his wars. Frequent military interventions by foreign princes left behinds cadres of foreign soldiers: Germans, Catalans, Hungarians, French, who took up service locally.

Officials initially recruited individual soldiers and small groups and placed them alongside citizen contingents.[3] As the scope of the Italian wars increased, the practice evolved. By the end of the thirteenth century, mercenaries occurred, like Shakespeare's sorrows, "not in single spies but in battalions." They formed into autonomous units, the largest of which had their own hierarchies of command, with corporals and captains distinct from the rank and file. They hired themselves to the highest bidder, and when dismissed from service, they coalesced into brigades known generally as "free companies" and locally as "companies of adventure" (compagnie di ventura). They sustained themselves during truces by ravaging the countryside, ransoming men and women and extorting bribes from intimidated cities. The phenomenon reached its peak in the middle of the century, at just the time that Hawkwood and the White Company arrived in Italy. The English band was therefore a familiar sight to contemporaries.

## Companies of Adventure

The "companies of adventure" have received a great deal of attention from both professional and amateur historians. The interest, bordering in some cases on obsession, has led writers to overstate the pervasiveness of the phenomenon.[4] Large autonomous companies were never the predominant military form; nor did they ever completely "replace" smaller units. At any given time only a handful of such bands operated in Italy. States continued to hire modest contingents of mercenaries for their armies along with native troops. The companies constituted the most conspicuous and powerful entities, which weighed heavily on the minds and finances of contemporaries. Their impact was greater than their numbers, but their careers were short lived. By the turn of the century, the companies were gone, replaced by individual captains and the development of permanent armies.

The exact event that initiated the phenomenon of the companies is disputed. Contemporaries singled out the German captain Werner of Urslingen and his band in 1339 as the first of "this plague of societies."[5] But Werner himself drew on the more distant example of Roger de Flor, a renowned Catalan adventurer, who in 1302 formed the so-called Great Company. Roger made a profound impression on the age, and his exploits, described by one modern scholar as the "most fantastic of the later Middle Ages," deserve brief notice here.[6]

Roger's career began at the age of eight, when he snuck aboard a boat belonging to the Knights Templars that was moored in the harbor near his home in Brindisi. According to the account of the chronicler Muntaner, Roger distinguished himself immediately, first by his ability to jump about the rigging "as lightly as if he were a monkey" and then as "one of the best mariners in the world," running missions to and from the Holy Land and gaining a sizable fortune thereby. He was eventually dismissed by the Templars for malfeasance and hired himself out as a mercenary in the wars in southern Italy. When these ended, he formed a mercenary brigade, which he called the Great Company (1302), and took employment in Byzantium, where a civil war was in progress. The band proved a spectacular success, indeed so much so that it unnerved its employer, the Byzantine emperor Andronicus, who feared that it would grow too powerful. Andronicus treacherously murdered Roger at a sumptuous banquet, purportedly in his honor.

What followed was the "Catalan revenge." The remnants of Roger's company rode for four years inflicting a bitter and prolonged retribution on their Byzantine hosts.[7] The Great Company defeated whole armies sent in its path and ultimately avenged itself directly on the Byzantine emperor by capturing his son and slowly killing him with thirteen knife wounds, the last of which disfigured his face.[8] The company then left Byzantium and took up service with the Duke of Athens, Walter of Brienne. Once again it disagreed with its employer and turned against him. The band defeated the duke, captured Athens, and held it for the next sixty-three years.

The success of the Catalan company would never again be duplicated. But it remained a powerful image in the collective consciousness of mercenary soldiers. The company's organization and modus operandi provided a useful model. When Werner of Urslingen assembled his band from veterans of the war between Pisa and Florence, he consciously called it the Great Company, after Roger de Flor's group. Werner affixed to his armor a defiant Latin tag proclaiming him to be the "enemy of God, pity and mercy" and rode throughout Lombardy and the Romagna raiding and pillaging. A decade later another Great Company coalesced around the Provençal adventurer Montreal d'Albarno, who had served under Werner of Urslingen. Montreal took his band, veterans of the wars in Naples, through the Marches and along the east coast of Italy, seizing forty-four castles. This Great Company represented the culmination of the phenomenon. Contemporaries compared it to a "moving state," which was virtually unstoppable for the better part of the next two years. When d'Albarno died in 1354, the German Konrad von Landau took over command and guided the band for the next nine years. In subsequent years brigades of various sizes rode through Italy: the Company of the Star, the Company of the Hat, the Company of the Flower, the Company of the Rose, the Company of the Hook, and at least three with the name Company of Saint George.

The companies generally grouped themselves around specific nationalities. Werner of Urslingen built his bands from a core of German soldiers, the Hungarian John Horváti formed his company in 1380 around fellow Hungarians, the Italian Alberigo da Barbiano in 1379 relied on Italians; we have already seen the English preference for their own. Italian chroniclers and writers often identified the companies in terms of those nationalities, eschewing the actual names in favor of appellations such as "the German company" or "the English company." These were not always accurate, as Italians sometimes had difficulty distinguishing one foreigner from another, particularly Englishmen from Germans. The bands themselves took their national association seriously and drew strength from camaraderie with their compatriots. The rivalry that broke out between the German Company of the Star and the English White Company in 1365–1366 had, as we shall see, a strong national dimension.

The point should not, however, be taken too far. Few bands were homogeneous. For all its English identity, the White Company contained Italian, German, and Hungarian mercenaries. Werner of Urslingen's German band included Italian, Hungarian, and Catalan soldiers. In general, the bigger the company, the more heterogeneous it was.

Scholars typically stress the prominent role played by rabble and base men. Matteo Villani described Montreal d'Albarno's Great Company as consisting of "twenty thousand rascals," serviced by a horde of women, who were little more than whores.[9] But the depiction is unfair. Villani's oft quoted statements constitute exaggerations borne of anger and resentment. Free companies took care to recruit good employees. Chief among these were Italian political exiles, who often possessed considerable military skill and had access to vital reconnaissance and information. Their mere presence in the bands elicited fear in officials in their native cities, who worried about the effect on internal factions. Fear was a highly desirable quality; the effectiveness of bands depended a great deal on their ability to terrorize.

Despite Villani's depiction of them, the women who traveled with the companies were not merely whores. Many were wives and loved ones, and some even fought in the field. The women in the Catalan company donned armor and served as soldiers when the number of men grew short. At the battle of Gallipoli, they performed admirably, fending off the enemy by flinging rocks from the ramparts of castles.[10] Villani himself conceded that the women in the Great Company did more than satisfy the carnal desires of the men. "They washed the clothes, cooked the bread, and each, equipped with a hand mill made from little rocks, ground the grain."[11]

The bands were thus also social units, consisting of component parts that played their own important role. On the military side, the band possessed hierarchies of commanders who oversaw military matters, treasurers who managed financial matters, and chancellors and notaries who tended to legal and diplomatic matters. The captain general, as he was technically called, stood at the head of the band, followed in order of authority by the marshals and corporals. The captain general attained his position through election. This fact has led some to speak of a "democratic aspect" in the bands. But in truth we know little of the electoral process: who voted and how. The marshals and corporals retained a significant degree of power and autonomy. They headed their own contingents within the company, which answered directly to them. The marshal coordinated the activities of the corporals and adjudicated disputes arising among the rank and file. He also provided the logistics for the provisioning of the men and the horses.[12]

Major decisions involving mobilization were decided on collectively by the captain general and his officers. When serving a state, the band also conferred on matters of tactics and strategy with the local captain of war, who commanded the overall army, and with government officials. The involvement of so many opinions often led to considerable friction.

The legal and financial positions within the companies were usually filled by Italian citizens, who, like the mercenaries themselves, sought profit and adventure. The chancellors were notaries, judges, and, generally, men trained in law. Their job involved drawing up legal documents, serving as intermediary between the band and states, and prospecting for future opportunities. Hawkwood took in chancellors from all over Italy, mostly men of experience and skill who had been exiled by their native cities. The critical role of treasurer was often staffed by a merchant, practiced in handling money. Michelotto Attendoli's mercenary band in the early fifteenth century employed a cloth merchant from Arezzo, Francesco Viviano, whose account books have survived.[13] The White Company seems to have relied on an Englishman, William Thornton, whose identity is unknown.

Mercenary bands were corporate in structure. The captain stood at the head of his brigade in a manner similar to the way a modern CEO stands at the head of his firm. When the captain decided to leave, the company did not disband but retained its name and elected another man.[14] The White Company remained the White Company after Albert Sterz left in 1365; Hugh Mortimer de la Zouche was appointed in his stead. The Great Company existed in one form or another for nearly twenty years, with Urslingen, d'Albarno, and Landau as its successive leaders.

The bands emphasized their corporate nature by referring to themselves not as "armies," strictly speaking, but as "societies," the same term used by contemporary Italian businesses. Cloth firms, banks, and trading companies were all "societies." When marauding as free companies, the bands took the name "society of societies," a label that stressed that they were a collection of businesses—corresponding to individual military brigades—linked together for the enrichment of its members.

Such terminology and structure make clear the intensely entrepreneurial character of mercenary bands, as well as, in military terms, the autonomy of individual brigades and decentralized nature of authority. The captains, marshals, and corporals of the bands were analogous to owners and shop managers of industrial firms. The rank-and-file soldiers may be said to resemble artisans and craftsmen. Indeed, it is not pressing the comparison too far to see in the fourteenth-century battlefield a species of stock market, in which the intrepid could make substantial profits. But the earnings in the highly speculative business of war were even more fragile than those in the nonmilitary realm. The Bascot de Mauleon, a colorful captain from the pages of Froissart's chronicle, gave succinct expression to the financial vagaries of the soldier's life: "Sometimes I have been so thoroughly down that I hadn't even a horse to ride, and at other times fairly rich, as luck came and went."[15] The downside to the military market was that a soldier could lose not only his earnings but also his life.

The mercantile aspect of companies has led some historians to see in them the antithesis of the feudal system. If we define feudalism as an honor-based system by which members of the aristocratic class exchanged land for military service, then mercenaries, with their lower-class roots, opportunistic behavior, and prefer ence for gold coin, would appear much the opposite. One popular author went so far as to equate the advent of the companies with the decline and eventual disappearance of feudalism.[16]

The assertion, though persistent in the literature, is nevertheless erroneous. Apart from superficial appearances, the mercenary and the feudal knight were hardly antithetical. This fact is critical in understanding the career of John Hawkwood. Mercenaries had always sprung up in the interstices in the feudal system—a system that was not all-encompassing and is, in any case, difficult to apply to Italy. But even the army recruited by William the Conqueror from Normandy—a region synonymous with feudalism—to invade England in the eleventh century contained mercenaries. Subsequent English, German, and French royal armies in the twelfth and thirteenth centuries routinely relied on hired soldiers.[17] Indeed, it is difficult to find an instance when mercenaries were not widely used or, conversely, when the archetypical medieval host, with the king attended only by vassals on forty-day service, actually took the field.

Mercenaries, of course, were around long before the Middle Ages, and even the great companies of the fourteenth century had more distant roots. France had already suffered the ravages of bands of armed men known as *routiers* in the twelfth century. These behaved in much the same manner as their later counterparts.[18] Roger de Flor's Great Company bore a striking resemblance to Xenophon's famed Greek "Ten Thousand," which marched through Persia in the fourth century BC. The "Ten Thousand" was a mercenary band, which, like Roger de Flor's company, had been forced to fend for itself in enemy territory.[19] Its formation had nothing to do with the medieval feudal system, which had not yet been born.

In general, the distinction between the honorable knight and the marauding mercenary in the Middle Ages was more theoretical than real. The excesses committed by the marauder against peasants brought no inherent dishonor because the victims were, strictly speaking, of too low a station to be included by the chivalric code that bound aristocratic warriors to respect others. Many of the soldiers' misdeeds—looting, stealing, ransoming—were considered part of the normal course of war. The Prince of Wales showed himself particularly skilled at such methods in his great *chevauchée* in France in 1355. But no one would have mistaken the Black Prince for a mercenary. Even the lowly backgrounds of some mercenaries did not necessarily separate them from their more gentle-blooded counterparts. War, as Maurice Keen in particular has stressed, was itself an ennobling activity. Success on the battlefield could gain de facto access to the gentry class. There has not yet been a study of the socioeconomic origins of the mercenaries operating in Italy, but many clearly came from the aristocracy.[20] The Germans Urslingen and Landau were of noble families, as were their counterparts Konrad Aichelberg, Konrad Prassberg, and Johann and Rudolf von Hapsburg.[21] The historian Stephan Selzer has pointed out a particularly large concentration of Swabian German nobles in the service of Italian states throughout the fourteenth century. Hungarian mercenaries were all nobles. The most famous of them, John Horváti, was a rich, powerful landholder, with close ties to the Hungarian king.

But the profession of arms carried its own mystique and provided its own inherent justification for bad deeds. Thus mercenaries, whatever their backgrounds, could properly claim priority as honorable men and portray their service as laudable. The very names they gave to their companies reflected this attitude. These were not, as one scholar suggested, "chance names" but often appellations of chivalric distinction. The "Company of the Star" formed by the German captains Albert Sterz and Hannekin Baumgarten in 1364 took its name from the chivalric Order of the Star, inaugurated thirteen years earlier by King John of France. The several brigades called the "Company of Saint George" that rode through Italy in the later years of the fourteenth century chose their name from the patron saint of chivalry, George, who was likewise the patron of King Edward's Order of the Garter (England).

In any case, the surge in mercenary activity in fourteenth-century Italy depended little on issues related to feudalism. The most obvious factor was the pace of war both within and outside the peninsula. The Hundred Years' War in France created the White Company and a steady stream of soldiers who would seek service in Italy. Italian wars, generally small and infraregional in the twelfth century and early thirteenth, grew progressively in scale and size, involving cities in different regions and thus necessitating more and better trained troops. Plague and famine increased the demand for foreign soldiers by reducing the local population. At the same time these crises intensified the competition among states for limited resources, which in turn touched off tensions that led to war. Declines in the value of land and increases in the cost of labor—two classic features of demographic crisis—may well have worked to force aristocrats and petty holders off their lands and into the mercenary business to support themselves. Although economic historians have not yet sorted out the effects of the great mortality on warfare, it is possible that while the overall population declined in Italy, the percentage of men-at-arms increased.

For both the impoverished landholder and the base adventurer, Italy remained the best place to make money. Despite the difficulties of the second half of the fourteenth century, Italy was still more economically advanced than the rest of Europe. It remained home to Europe's banking industry and was a leader in manufacturing and commerce. Plague damaged overall production and decreased the volume of trade, but Italian merchants moved into lucrative luxury businesses such as the manufacture of silk, for which demand remained high. The contemporary German writer Konrad of Megenberg instructed poor young German noblemen to begin their careers in Italy and increase their fortunes through wages there.[22]

The modern historian Yves Renouard described the situation from the Italian side. "Was it not reasonable and economical," he asked rhetorically, "to avoid mobilizing the most efficient citizens and to pay mercenaries who could fight whilst merchants, active in their counting houses, earned money to pay them?"[23] The English scholar Maurice Keen took the point further, arguing that the financial strength of Italy created a "spurious demand" for soldiers, who flocked to local states. The states then became more inclined to wage wars.[24]

Both assertions are compelling but go too far. Keen's depiction of a "spurious demand" is contradicted by evidence showing Italian states actively recruiting foreign mercenaries. Officials routinely sent ambassadors to foreign courts seeking soldiers. Milan appealed directly to German princes; Padua lobbied the king of Hungary; Florence sent envoys to the royal and noble houses of France and the Holy Roman Empire. The flow of military men also went in the opposite direction. The city of Genoa sent its crossbowmen to fight for other European states; Milan sent cavalry units to German princes.[25]

Renouard's depiction of the canny, pacific Italian merchant motivated by purely financial considerations is contradicted by evidence showing that officials carefully weighed numerous factors in their decision to hire mercenaries, the most important and obvious—and overlooked—of which was military skill. English, German, and Hungarian soldiers were considered good soldiers. We have already seen the admiration and fear evoked by the English. Hungarians were praised for being "unconcerned with death and willing to place themselves in every danger," while Germans were lauded for their courage, discipline, and "mastery of martial skill."[26] Modern historians have traditionally slighted the fighting ability of foreign mercenaries. But their criticisms derive in large part from the negative statements of contemporary humanists such as Francis Petrarch and Niccolò Machiavelli, whose judgments were hardly even-handed. Machiavelli displayed a general bias against foreign troops; both he and Petrarch, steeped in classic literature, based their assessments more on their reading of Roman history than on reality. As foreign mercenaries had been a symptom of the decay of ancient Roman society and a factor its decline, so too were their later counterparts evidence of the decadence of fourteenth- and fifteenth-century Italian society.

Italian states, in fact, sought foreign mercenaries precisely because they were foreign—a point that needs to be stressed. Italian states were tenuous aggregates of powers in which rivalries—rich versus poor, merchant versus noble, urban dweller versus country rustic—often led to violence. The fractious nature of political and social life caused local officials to think carefully before hiring their own for military service. A successful native captain might seek political gain at home; an unsuccessful captain might provoke scandal and internal quarrels between his supporters and opponents. After the victory at Campaldino in 1289, Florentine nobles who participated in the battle rode through the streets assaulting and murdering ordinary citizens.[27]

Foreigners, on the other hand, had little at stake locally. They could be hired and fired without political repercussion and were uninterested in local politics. The extent to which Italian states adhered to this principle is clear from the way they chose their own internal security forces. These were headed by a podestà, a kind of mayor/chief of police, who was always from another city or part of Italy. The rationale for this was explicit: to avoid employing those who had vested interests in the city and might therefore be biased and troublesome.

## Contracts for Service

When mercenaries took employment with a state, the relationship began with the signing of a contract, or *condotta*.[28] These contracts came in many varieties, but all stipulated basic terms such as the length of service, the size of the brigade, and the rate of pay. The Italian *condotta* bore resemblance to the English indenture contract used to recruit soldiers for service in France and was therefore not unfamiliar to Hawkwood and his fellow English mercenaries. The tradition in Italy was, however, much older, the contracts more sophisticated, the mutual responsibilities more clearly delineated, and the terms far more lucrative.[29]

*Condotte* were effected by means of formal ceremony. Soldiers were required to swear on the Bible. They placed one hand on the Gospels and raised a finger on the other hand, while an Italian official read the contract aloud. This last was to facilitate understanding for the illiterate and minimize misinterpretation for the more educated. The contracts were written in Latin, the official language of legal documents, but translators often spoke the terms to foreign soldiers in their native language. The captain and his commanders then affixed their seals to the document; those who could write also gave their signatures. Albert Sterz and nineteen corporals (John Hawkwood included) of the White Company attached their seals to the *condotta* with the Marquis of Montferrat. Four years later the *condotta* between the White Company and Florence contained twenty-four seals.[30]

The contracts generally called for brief stints of employment, lasting between four and six months. Historians have explained this as resulting from the employer's desire to retain mercenaries only for the campaigning season and to rid themselves of the soldiers quickly should they prove unreliable.[31] The practice has been contrasted with that of the fifteenth century, when states, moving toward permanent armies, extended longer terms. The point has, however, been overstated. Although fourteenth-century employers preferred short-term contracts, they also offered ones of longer duration. The *condotta* binding the White Company to the Marquis of Montferrat was, as we have seen, for eight months of service. Florence, reputedly the most steadfast in adhering to short-term contracts, routinely issued contracts for one year, two years, or longer. The city hired the German Konrad von Weitingen in 1376, the Italian Giovanni Pepoli in 1386, and the Englishman John Beltoft in 1390 all for one full year's service.[32] Hawkwood often served Florence for a year at a time. The Tuscan captain Primerano Torelli and his brother Francesco received ten-year contracts in 1365,[33] while Orlando, Jacopo, and Naddo Malavolti and Bertoccio Tolomei, all from the nearby town of Siena, were extended contracts in 1394 that allowed them "to serve as long as they wished."[34]

Indeed, the evidence indicates what should perhaps be obvious. Florence offered different *condotte* depending on the circumstances of employment. Beltoft was hired just prior to a war with Milan that threatened to be a long one. The Malavoltis and Bertoccio Tolomei were Sienese exiles who had helped the Florentines against Siena. Their long-term employment was both a reward for services rendered and enticement to others to do the same.

But even short-term contracts did not necessarily imply short-term service. If a state was pleased with a soldier, it rehired him again and again. Milan retained the services of the German captain Michael Colm for ten consecutive years, from 1347 to 1356. Florence kept Heinrich Paer on the payroll for sixteen years (1364–1379);

TABLE 4
*Mercenaries and long-term service*

| Name | Length of Service | Employer |
| --- | --- | --- |
| Hanneken Hul | 12 yrs (1347–1358) | Milan |
| Michael Colm | 10 yrs (1347–1356) | Milan |
| Heinrich Paer | 16 yrs (1364–1379) | Florence |
| Tilmann von Alzen | 5 yrs (1379–1384) | Florence |
| Heinrich von Lupfen | 13 yrs (1350–1372) | Papacy |
| Heinrich von Troisdorf | 17 yrs (1334–1350) | Papacy |
| Fritz von Shiltach | 14 yrs (1355–1368) | Papacy |
| Sobb von Issendorf | 17 yrs (1334–1350) | Papacy |
| Heinrich Suler | 14 yrs (1355–1368) | Papacy |

*Sources:* Archivio della Fabbrica del Duomo di Milano, cartelle 81; Archivio di Stato di Firenze, Camera del comune, Provveditori, poi massai, specchi, 1, fol. 24r; Provvisioni, registri, 68, fol. 93r; Provvisioni, registri, 72 fol. 115r; Provvisioni, registri, 73, fol. 141v; Schäfer, *Deutsche Ritter*, 1:118.

the pope employed Huglin von Schöneck continuously for twenty-three years (1354–1376) (table 4). The practice had precedent back in the thirteenth century. The Catalan William de la Torre worked for the city of Siena for nine years from 1277 to 1286. Diego de Rat worked for Florence consecutively from 1305 to 1313.[35]

In addition to the length of service, contracts also stipulated the number and type of soldiers. Cavalry was expressed in terms of individual horsemen or standard military units such as the *barbuta*, consisting of two men, a knight, and a page; the lance, consisting of three men, a knight, a squire, and a page; or the banner, consisting of twenty to twenty-five knights. The *barbuta* was popular among German mercenary bands and took its name from the type of helmet used by soldiers of that nationality. The lance, as we have seen, was used by the English and eventually became standard in Italian armies.[36] The banner, a popular formation in the early trecento, fell largely into disuse in the second half of the century.

It is commonly held that *condotte* involved exclusively the hire of cavalry. But in fact contracts usually included archers, crossbowmen, and various infantrymen. The German captain Hannekin Baumgarten's *condotta* in 1371 called for the hire of 300 infantrymen, half of whom were crossbowmen and the other half shield bearers. *Condotte* with English bands usually provided for contingents of longbowmen. John Clifford's contract with the city of Bologna in 1377 contained provision for 107 lances of cavalry and 32 longbowmen.[37] John Berwick's contract with Florence in 1379 included 20 longbowmen.[38] All of Hawkwood's contingents had longbowmen in them.

Salaries were generally figured according to a monthly rate. The wages of the captains usually depended on the size of their bands—the more troops, the greater the pay. This gave incentive for captains to increase the size of their bands. Sometimes employers used a precise formula, such as 1 florin per *barbuta* or lance;

TABLE 5

*Some monthly salaries paid by Florence to foreign mercenary captains*

| Year | Captain | Salary | Number of Soldiers in Contingent |
|---|---|---|---|
| 1343 | Gottfried Roher | 30 florins | 20 horses |
| 1350 | Janni Dornich | 30 florins | 25 horses |
| 1358 | Janne de Bolicha | 27.4 florins | 20 horses |
| 1372 | Heinrich Paer | 70 florins | 70 lances |
| 1385 | John Threlkeld | 100 florins | 100 lances |
| 1390 | John Beltoft | 300 florins | 77 lances |
| 1394 | Konrad Aichelberg | 150 florins | 200 lances |

*Sources:* Archivio di Stato di Firenze, Camera del comune, Camarlinghi, uscita 2, fol. 4v; Camera del comune, Camarlinghi, uscita 68, fol. 1v; Camera del comune, Camarlinghi, uscita 127, fol. 1r; Comune, Camarlinghi, uscita 205, fol. 6r; Dieci di balia, Deliberazioni, condotte e stanziamenti, 2, fol. 2r; Dieci di balia, Deliberazioni, condotte e stanziamente, 4, fol. 186v; Dieci di balia, Deliberazioni, condotte e stanziamenti, 6, fol. 7v.

other times the method of calculation was less obvious (table 5).[39] Famous mercenaries like Konrad von Landau and John Hawkwood always received high salaries, no matter what the conditions. The pay of captains of lesser reputation depended more on the vagaries of the marketplace. When wars were widespread throughout the peninsula and thus demand at a high, they earned well.

The salaries of rank-and-file soldiers were likewise affected by market conditions. The pay for lance units in Florentine service reached a peak—22 florins a month—in the mid- to later 1370s when the War of Eight Saints and War of Chioggia engaged much of Italy and rendered the market in soldiers tight. By the 1390s, the salaries of lance units started to decline, a trend attributed to the consolidation of Italian states and the lessening thereby of the number of potential employers. In 1394 Florence paid 16 florins per month for a lance; by 1401, 15 florins.[40]

There was surprisingly little connection between the wages of cavalrymen and those of the captains for whom they worked. Service for a renowned mercenary did not result in higher pay. The famous Italian mercenary Giovanni d'Azzo degli Ubaldini earned an impressive salary of 500 florins a month in Sienese service in 1381. But his cavalrymen earned only 6 florins a month, the same as those in the employ of the obscure mercenary Riccardo Dovadola, whose own monthly stipend was 24 florins.[41] The appeal of working for a well-known captain lay in his ability, through victories, to bring earnings beyond salaries in the form of spoils of war and, perhaps, through his reputation, to increase the likelihood that an employer would pay wages he promised.

Officers received additional compensation above their basic salaries as cavalrymen. The position of marshal was generally well paid. The two in the mercenary band of Hugo von Melchingen and Hermann von Winden in 1364 each received 32.5 florins a month in addition to their regular pay. The corporals of the band earned 14 additional florins a month. This fell far short, however, of the salary of Hugo and Hermann themselves, who received 150 florins a month each. The pay structure provided obvious financial incentive for cavalrymen and officers to seek advancement to the leadership of companies.[42]

Scholars have yet to determine the standard of living in Italy in the second half of the fourteenth century; thus it is difficult to assess the true meaning of mercenary wages in terms of the overall economy. It does appear, however, that captains and officers were well paid in comparison with people in the nonmilitary sector. In 1390 in the city of Florence a typical construction worker earned an average daily wage of 9.4 soldi, a farm laborer was paid roughly the same, a spinner of wool cloth earned 12.7 soldi a day, and a master builder received 17.1 soldi a day.[43] John Hawkwood's salary that year was 500 florins (37,500 soldi) a month, a sum 72 times greater than the wage of a master builder and more than 140 times greater than that of a construction worker. Meanwhile, a lance unit in Hawkwood's brigade earned 18 florins a month (a daily rate of 44 soldi). This was two and a half times the wage of a master builder, nearly three and a half times that of a spinner, and almost five times that of an unskilled construction worker or farm laborer.[44] But it should be noted that the 18 florins sustained three men with three horses, making it less impressive than it superficially appears.

The wages of infantrymen were less notable. Crossbowmen in Florentine service in 1390 earned 4 florins a month, or 9.7 soldi a day, roughly the same as construction workers and farms laborers. Less specialized infantrymen were paid only 3.8 soldi a day.[45]

One historian of fourteenth-century Tuscany, Giuliano Pinto, has estimated subsistence level at 3 soldi a day. According to this, Hawkwood, his officers, and his cavalrymen lived very well, but his infantrymen were barely able to manage.[46] A kilo of grain in Florence in 1390 cost on average 2.1 soldi and a liter of wine 2.3 soldi. Thus Hawkwood's 500-florin monthly salary was worth 17,857 kilos of grain (approximately 992 bushels) and 16,304 liters of wine (approximately 401 barrels of wine).

It needs to be stressed, however, that salaries were not exclusively paid in coin. Specie was often in limited supply in the second half of the fourteenth century, and employers sometimes gave a part of their soldiers' salary in commodities. The city of Lucca in 1383 paid part of the stipend of the German mercenary Johann von Eberhardsweiler in gold-embroidered silk and purple velvet. Thirty-five years later, the same city paid 10,000 florins of the 35,000 florins it owed the Italian captain Braccio da Montone in silk cloth. Payment in cloth appears to have become part of some formal contract with soldiers by the fifteenth century.[47]

Regular salaries of captains were frequently augmented by bonuses. These were sometimes woven into contracts in the form of payments for so-called dead lances or dead *barbute*, contingents that did not exist but whose salaries the employer agreed to pay. A captain could claim up to 10 percent of his brigade as "dead" and thus collect wages for soldiers he did not have. There are numerous examples of this practice. According to his contract with Bologna in 1391, Giovanni da Barbiano's brigade numbered 210 lances, but officials paid him for 231 lances, 10 percent more than he had.[48]

Bonuses also came in the form of sub-rosa cash payments, sometimes disguised as loans or as gifts, the latter bestowed on captains during holidays such as Easter and Christmas. Gifts usually consisted of expensive vanity items of little military use: silver helmets, golden utensils, jeweled cups. They were easily transportable and fit into satchel bags. Exceptional service could result in grants of houses, estates, and citizenships. The Venetians allowed their favorite captains palaces along the Grand Canal.[49] The Pisans agreed in one instance to pay off the debts of a company of German soldiers. The pope offered a less tangible but no less valuable gift to his mercenaries in 1365 when he granted them immunity from future excommunication.[50]

The extent of gift giving will never be known for sure because employers often concealed the practice. They did not want their citizens, whose taxes ultimately paid the bills, to know the extent of expenditure. Nor did they wish to set off jealousies among mercenaries, vain men who took careful note of what their counterparts received.

Distinct from bonuses and gifts were cash advances given to captains by employers when they signed their contracts. These were intended to help assemble the band.[51] But captains had to repay the advances, which were deducted from their pay. Captains were almost always expressly forbidden to increase the size of their bands on their own account. The right was retained by the employer.

One cannot overemphasize the degree of distrust that existed between the two sides. Employers worried especially about being defrauded by their soldiers and with this in mind spelled out explicitly rights and responsibilities. States included in contracts clauses requiring the bands to be in good fighting condition ("suitable for war") and captains to refrain from using horses that might be "blind, asthmatic, lame," or "sick from incurable illness."[52] Sometimes a minimum monetary value was set on horses; other times there were specific stipulations regarding the quality of soldiers, disallowing, for example, service by any man who was a thief or in debt.[53] All contracts insisted that soldiers swear a solemn oath "not to molest" their employer or his allies or associated territories during their term of service and to desist from turning against the employer, "as marauder or stipendiary of other state," for a set period of time after dismissal.[54] In return, employers promised not to defraud soldiers from their side, to make sure, for example, that their merchants sold goods to them at fair market value.

In order to enforce the terms of the *condotta* and to maintain the quality of the army, employers retained the right to inspect the band periodically. The inspections were called *mostre* and were usually held once a month.[55] If armies proved lacking, inspectors had the right to assess fines, which were deducted from the soldiers' pay. Florentine legislation from 1388 lists a variable set of fines: 5 lire (about 1½ florins) for a man-at-arms without his bacinet; 6 lire for both longbowmen and crossbowman without their weapons; and 1 lire for a shield bearer without his shield.[56]

Those who conducted the *mostre* took particular care examining horses. Healthy mounts were critical to the prosecution of war. Many contracts contained special *mendum* clauses, by which employers agreed to compensate soldiers for horses injured and killed in action.[57] This was, however, easily abused, as soldiers, interested in maximizing their revenue, claimed the loss of horses that were not their own. In England men-at-arms were obliged to prove the death of their horses by presenting officials with the ears and tail of the deceased. Some Italian states insisted on the same. But progressively employers refused to grant the clause at all and gave in only when desperate for troops. By the last decades of the fourteenth century the *mendum* passed largely out of existence. Even John Hawkwood, at the height of his prestige, was explicitly denied the privilege.[58]

One of the most problematic issues between the mercenaries and their employers involved the mechanism of settling disputes. Bands usually retained the right to deal with their own internal squabbles. But since quarrels could damage the overall effectiveness of the brigade as a fighting force, employers often sought more direct control. In a contract from 1364, Florence reserved to itself the right to punish crimes within a band if they involved murder. Its rationale was that the death of a soldier affected the size of the force, which reduced its capacity to fight. Altercations between mercenaries and civilians were usually handled by a joint commission made up of members of both sides.[59]

Two additional issues that caused significant dispute were the distribution of wartime booty and the payment of bonuses for victories on the battlefield. The tradition regarding the former was that bands retained the right to "movables" such as equipment, cash, and livestock, while the state had the right to "immovables" such as castles, towns, and lands. Some employers, however, placed limits on the right to movables, allowing the mercenaries the spoils only if they took the town or fortress by force. The state held them in the case of surrender.[60] In reality, there was little an employer could do to prevent the soldiers from seizing what they wanted when they entered cities. The Count of Savoy added an interesting twist in a contract of 1371. He granted the soldiers the right to all valuables, whether they took a town by force or not, but he made them swear to refrain from raping or harming local women.[61]

The mercenaries were permitted to ransom prisoners, but they had to turn over political enemies, that is, exiles and rebels, to the state on demand. It was this last issue that proved particularly contentious. Ransoms constituted a major source of revenue for soldiers, and to give prisoners to the state was to forgo substantial profits. The distinction between political exile and enemy combatant was in reality difficult to draw. For their part, employers disliked the way mercenaries treated captives, ransoming for themselves wealthy locals who brought good returns and allowing others, notably men of their own nationality, to go free. The Italian jurist Giovanni da Legnano complained about how German soldiers invariably dismissed their countrymen captured in battle. "They lift their finger, raise their visor, surrender and are instantly set free."[62]

The payment of bonuses for battle victories was a long-standing issue. The disagreement centered not on the validity of such payments, which was readily recognized, but on definition of the term *victory*. What constituted a victory worthy of a bonus? According to a Florentine contract of 1362, such a victory was gained by defeating an enemy force of at least two hundred horsemen.[63] This earned soldiers a full month's extra pay at double the usual rate (*paggia doppia*). The definition was put to the test a year later when the mercenary band defeated a garrison of more than two hundred horsemen outside Pisa. The band demanded its bonus. But Florentine officials rejected the demand, maintaining that the garrison, though large enough, was not taken by force but surrendered of its own accord. The band became enraged, formed into a free company, and vowed vengeance on Florence. Meanwhile, the Florentines officials changed the rules, defining a bonus-worthy victory as one on the battlefield over five hundred or more enemy horsemen.[64]

Perhaps the most problematic issue of all was the mechanism for renewing or ending contracts. Employers required their captains to give them advance notice, usually months ahead of the expiration of the contract, should they wish to serve another employer.[65] This was to protect the employer from having its army precipitously change sides, a potentially devastating act. Contracts usually explicitly forbade the bands from fighting against their former employer for a set period of time. Conversely, employers had to give the band notice months in advance if they intended not to renew the contract. This protected the mercenaries from capricious dismissal and gave them time to find a new employer. The reality, however, was that neither employer nor employee followed the rules, leaving both sides embittered.

## A Troubled Relationship: Mercenaries and Employers

The extent to which mercenaries did not live up to their contract and disappointed their employers is well documented. Contemporary Italian writers complained bitterly about indifferent performance in the field, maltreatment of civilians, and secret dealings with the enemy. Petrarch condemned the mercenaries as poor fighters and compared them to women and "buffoons," who "snore and perspire not manfully, but feverishly" in battle.[66]

But abuses existed on both sides. Employers also did not live up to their obligations. Most important, they frequently failed to pay salaries on time. This was the inevitable consequence of the high costs of war, which placed a great burden on local finances, which were barely able to meet expenses in the best of circumstances. The city of Milan paid 288,720 florins for the services of 1,203 lances for its war with Florence in 1390, a sum that was four times the annual budget of a mid-sized city like Lucca.[67] An anonymous Milanese diarist wrote that the expenditure created a tax burden on citizens that was so "heavy and continuous" that "subjects . . . were forced to emigrate because they could not bear the load."[68] Cumbersome and inefficient fiscal machineries rendered the conversion of tax revenue into soldiers' salaries exceedingly slow. The Sienese government in 1371, needing funds to pay its armies and frustrated by difficulties involved in the collection of taxes, sent armed soldiers to the home of citizens to force the issue. The men, in the words of the chronicler, "rode away, with God and the money they had collected."[69] Even when states were able to raise the necessary funds, they often found it difficult to physically transport the money to their armies. Bandits infested roads and often robbed official convoys. The pope sent a shipment of gold coin guarded by 150 cavalry from Avignon to his armies in Lombardy in 1328. The convoy was attacked and more than half of the money lost.[70]

In the absence of pay, soldiers were often left to fend for themselves economically, which increased the recourse to looting and robbing. The complaints of employers about such behavior are well known, but the mercenaries also complained, in numerous letters buried in Italian archives. Their laments are not in the elegant, polished prose of their more educated Italian contemporaries but in awkward, straightforward language. The English captain John Thornbury's letter to Siena in 1380 is typical of the genre: "I am greatly amazed that you do not wish to maintain your promises. . . . If you do not make the aforementioned payments as you are obliged by your pacts, you will have to excuse us that we also do not obey the pacts between ourselves and your commune."[71]

The relationship between the mercenaries and their employers also suffered from the manner in which the latter assembled armies. States rarely relied on a single band during wars but usually hired several mercenary contingents as well as native troops and auxiliaries from other cities. Although officials did their best to try to coordinate them, these multinational forces often did not get along among themselves. German and English soldiers were notoriously hostile to each other, a problem we shall discuss more fully in the next chapter. But rivalries existed among all the nationalities. Italian and German soldiers fought while in the mutual service of the pope in 1323; Hungarian and German contingents feuded while working for Milan in 1368; English, German, and Italian soldiers engaged in a three-way feud during their service to Venice in 1372.[72] In fairness to military planners, their actions were to a large degree conditioned by the vagaries of the mercenary market. With numerous soldiers available to the highest bidder, states often took on additional soldiers not so much because it was the best decision militarily but to prevent the men from seeking employment with the enemy. In this regard Italian states implicitly followed Vegetius's dictum that "what made the enemy weaker, helped you."[73] But the policy frequently made for ill-fitting armies.

Difficulties arising from logistics and provisioning raised tensions further. Italian states cleared the countryside of goods when facing invasion, locking away livestock, fodder, hay, and all means of sustenance in castles. This often left soldiers hard pressed to sustain themselves. Impoverished troops pawned their arms and armor, often to innkeepers and local lenders, many of whom charged exorbitant interest rates. Soldiers and their employers quarreled about billets. Armies sought comfortable accommodations, where they could be protected from the elements, such as in local monasteries, churches, or private houses. Employers preferred for the men to remain in their tents, if possible at a distance from local towns.[74] In 1381, the Florentines expressly forbade John Hawkwood from billeting his army in religious houses and "buildings connected to them."[75]

In general, military camps were unsavory places, rife with drunken brawls, thefts, and disputes over money and women. The Venetians took care to place billets in subject areas and rural areas, always at a safe distance from Venice, fearing the fate of the food supply.[76]

The task of smoothing relations between armies and their employers rested primarily with civilian officials known as commissaries. They were usually prominent citizens, often with experience as ambassadors. The Milanese tyrant Bernabò

Visconti recruited his commissaries, which he called *collaterali*, from noble families with close connection to his court. They rode with armies and kept the flow of information going between the politicians at home and the captains in the field. Milanese *collaterali* were sometimes called on to extend loans to impecunious soldiers so that they would not desert the field.

The activities of the commissaries have elicited mixed reviews from scholars.[77] Some assert that they performed well; others, like the nineteenth-century Italian historian Ercole Ricotti, denounced the profession in general as "more fitted to spying and punishing failures, than to facilitating victories."[78] The Florentine commissary assigned to the army in 1364 rallied a poorly disciplined force and roused a lethargic captain, who had actually fallen asleep just before battle.[79] On the other hand, a Venetian commissary in the fifteenth century stood accused of seducing the mistress of the captain of the army, which led to an acrimonious feud and disarray in the ranks.[80]

## Italian Warfare

Strained relations between soldiers and states and difficulties coordinating armies were in many ways the inevitable result of the basic nature of fourteenth-century Italian warfare. Contests were usually long, drawn-out affairs, involving much maneuvering and relatively little direct engagement of the enemy.[81] As in contemporary France, offensives usually began with raids against enemy territory, the primary objective of which was to destroy harvests, steal livestock, and damage fields and physical structures. These resembled the *chevauchées* of the Hundred Years' War. With the conjunction of plague and famine, armies struggled to maintain themselves in the field and to manage meager resources.

It was fundamental to Italian warfare that states did not seek pitched battles unless they possessed a clear and overwhelming advantage.[82] Claude Gaier's statement for France is applicable to the Italian situation: "A campaign brought to a conclusion constituted an exception."[83] In this, Italian military planners followed Vegetius's injunction that "attacks be made on favorable terms" and that "good generals do not attack when the risk is on mutual terms."[84] The anonymous author of the Milanese *Annales* explicitly warned against pitched battles and preached caution with respect to military affairs on the grounds that "the outcome of war is doubtful."[85] States preferred circumspect captains who could keep their armies intact and avoid major losses. In the fifteenth century the careful, if unimaginative, Federigo da Montefeltro was more sought after as a commander than his more daring contemporary and rival Sigismondo Malatesta.

Italian wars were thus often ones of attrition, in which economic factors played a paramount role. Offensives were designed first and foremost to inflict financial pain. Barns and livestock were a farmer's most expensive possessions; loss of them exacted a heavy economic toll. A Perugian force came to Tuscany at harvest time in 1396 armed with scythes not to kill the enemy but to reap grain before locals could.[86] The Florentines attacked Pisan shipping, aware of the importance of seabound commerce to that city. The Venetians and Genoese did the same to each other. The Hungarians attempted to stop the flow of exports of precious metals to Venice in 1374 and 1378.[87]

A critical effect of economic pressure was to destabilize opponents socially and politically. Cutting off trade routes and the food supply raised tensions within states and with it the hope of rebellion and thus victory without undertaking a risky military strike. Military planners often routed armies through or near towns in enemy territory where political dissent ran high, hoping to set off a spark. The city of Piacenza in Lombardy had a reputation for contrariness within the Visconti state, and for that reason Milan's opponents, most notably the pope, began their offensives there, reinforcing armies with local exiles. Since few cities or states in Italy were without significant internal discord, the strategy was employed frequently. The pope often used his position as the head of the church to incite disobedience among the clergy. He also sowed discord through excommunications and interdicts, effectively loosing the populace from its obligation to the state.

Such methods of war made reconnaissance and information gathering particularly important. Assessing the internal dispositions of states and maneuvering armies for long periods in the field required a sophisticated network of spies, informants, and advance scouts. Armies gained information from exiles, who, as we have seen, existed in large numbers throughout the Italian countryside and were often eager to plot against those who had humiliated them. States also hired spies, an indistinct class of people whose very work rendered their identities obscure. The fourteenth-century French soldier and writer Philippe de Mézières (1327–1405) thought spies so valuable that he recommended that governments devote one-third of their budgets to them. Military treatise author Teodoro Paleologus, strongly advocated the use of "good and loyal spies" on the battlefield.[88]

It is not clear how much was spent on spies, but Italian states often maintained large networks of them. In 1373, fearing rebellion and external threat, the city of Siena sent spies throughout Italy, in Venice, Perugia, Rome, Padua, Mantua, Todi, Gubbio, Forlì, Naples, Ferrara, Sarzana, Treviso, Verona, Milan, Arezzo, and various parts of the Romagna. The Sienese coordinated the activities of its spies through a separate governmental bureau, which also oversaw the town's supply of weapons.[89] Florentine budgets contain somewhat more vague references to "explorers" who "went out and got information and secrets."[90] It is likely, however, that many of the informants were not professionals but ordinary merchants and ambassadors who moved around quite a bit, met many people, and kept up on events. Contemporary letters citing secret information usually refer to sources in vague terms: "I heard from a friend that" or "A person worthy of faith told me" or "I have it from a friend, who heard it from another."

The sources show that informants often went to extraordinary lengths both to procure information and to conceal it from others. They rendered important revelations into cipher, hid letters in loaves of bread, and allowed intentionally erroneous information to fall into the hands of enemies in order to confuse them. Those caught spying were subject to the death penalty, often preceded by imaginative tortures. Conversely, those who succeeded were often highly rewarded by their clients. An otherwise obscure man known only as Luparello received a lifetime pension from the Florentine government for revealing important information that helped lead to the capture of the town of San Miniato.[91]

One of the activities undertaken by spies was poisoning enemies. The tactic was so popular that it can properly be counted as basic to fourteenth-century Italian warfare. Given the tenuous ties that held armies together, military planners knew well that the removal of an important captain could make the key difference. Thus poisoning, if successful, constituted a cheap and effective means of blunting enemy offensives.[92] The Florentines could not stop Giovanni d'Azzo degli Ubaldini and his Sienese armies on the battlefield in 1390. But they managed to taint a bowl of cherries, Ubaldini's favorite dish. When Ubaldini died, the impetus of his army ended. The Sienese war effort never recovered. In 1353, the Sienese tried to poison the entire army of Montreal d'Albarno by offering it grain laced with arsenic. The trick was discovered. More typically, enemies poisoned wells and drinking water in local towns to stop the momentum of their enemies.

Also critical to the prosecution of war was the use of field fortifications, a subject that has received surprisingly little attention from scholars. These structures, known as *bastite* or *bastie*, were erected throughout Italy to facilitate the movement and provisioning of armies. They were usually made of wood and earth, surrounded by a protective ditch; a variant from the first half of the fourteenth century is depicted in the top left-hand corner of Simone Martini's famous portrait of Guidoriccio da Fogliano. The papal legate Albornoz erected two *bastite* outside Orvieto to help recapture that town in 1354. Rinaldo Orsini built four *bastite* near Spoleto in 1383 to help him defend the city; The Venetians built a *bastita* not far from Padua to help carry the war to that city.[93]

Some *bastite* were fairly elaborate, such as the one constructed by Bernabò

Visconti outside Modena, which purportedly cost 60,000 florins and held thirty-six wagonloads of provisions. Others were simpler. The *bastita* outside the town of Carpi was built in Milan and then transported whole in 1370.[94] The structures, big or small, housed troops and weapons and were placed in strategically important locations, often near rivers and roads to control key crossing points and the flow of goods or near cities to help facilitate or protect against sieges. They were serviced by carpenters and craftsmen, who rode along with armies.[95]

The recourse to *bastite* underscores the essentially static nature of Italian warfare and the importance states placed on maintaining their armies in the field for the long run. The siege remained popular in fourteenth-century Italy. It was generally initiated against modest-sized towns; there was relatively little hope of success against major cities. When armies penetrated to the walls of large towns, they often eschewed outright attack and undertook instead ostentatious jest and discourtesies. This peculiarity of Italian war is best understood as a species of "psychological" warfare.[96] Armies held lavish banquets below the town walls, ran horse races, and sounded trumpets throughout the night. The merriment was perverse; the races involved not only horses but also prostitutes. Mock trials were held, which condemned enemy leaders in absentia; animals, representing those leaders, were condemned and hanged in plain view. The army meanwhile changed its positions or feigned attack in order to keep the enemy confused and off guard.

When armies did attack town walls, they invariably used artillery. There existed several rock-throwing machines described loosely by contemporaries as trebuchets and mangonels. The difference between the two is not always clear, owing to the imprecise manner in which the terms were used. The trebuchet appears to have launched larger rocks than the mangonel.[97] A recent scholar has estimated the average size of the stones at 100–150 kilos (220–375 pounds) and the distance traveled as 150–240 meters.[98] The Perugian chronicler Del Graziano claimed that his city had manufactured a device that threw balls as heavy as 1,500 pounds, but reconstructions using modern, more durable materials have succeeded only in launching stones of 1,400 pounds.[99] A Sienese chronicler maintained that his city used as many as three hundred trebuchets against Florentine positions in the Tuscan hills in 1390.[100] The figure is impossible to confirm.

In general, trebuchets and mangonels proved effective weapons, often doing extensive damage to town and castle walls. Italian officials gave the machines nicknames, like the heavy guns used in World Word I. A trebuchet aimed at clergy hiding in the Perugian citadel during the War of Eight Saints was, for example, called the *cacciaprete* (priest chaser.) The devices required stonemasons to operate them, as well as carpenters to help build, service, and maintain them. Such men rode with armies, accompanied by a separate official, the *maestro di traboccho* (master of the trebuchet), whose job was to look after the apparatus in the field. The *maestro* earned a good wage. The Florentines in 1363 paid 10 florins a month, 4 florins a month more than they paid their cavalrymen.[101] The salary is indicative of the skill of the *maestro* and the importance contemporaries placed on the siege.

*Maestri* often shot their stones over the walls directly into towns and fortresses, a tactic strongly advocated by Teodoro Paleologus in his *Enseignements* and intended to cause injury and confusion within. Castles maintained their own rock-throwing devices and hurled stones back in the other direction, sometimes aimed at enemy trebuchets. There are instances in which carefully aimed shots actually hit their mark.[102]

In addition to trebuchets, indeed sometimes alongside them, Italian armies used cannons. These were known generically as *bombarde*, a term applied to all weapons requiring gunpowder, including handguns. There are references to *bombarde* in Italian sources as early as the thirteenth century. By the second half of the fourteenth century they were commonly employed on Italian battlefields.[103] Local craftsmen, usually stonemasons, manufactured the weapon, which came in various sizes and shot both stone and iron balls. Like the trebuchet, the cannon required a full-time attendant, a *maestro della bombarda*, who was paid well for his services. A *maestro* employed by Florence in 1391 received 8 florins a month, similar to the wage of those who operated trebuchets.[104]

The cannon was an inconsistent weapon. It was just as likely to injure those who fired as it was the enemy—provided, of course, it worked, which was not always the case. But there are instances when the cannon proved effective, particularly when placed atop a town wall to inhibit enemy attempts to scale or surmount the edifice.[105] The mere noise and tremor jarred men from their positions. We shall see in subsequent pages how John Hawkwood's own attempts to scale walls were blunted in this manner.

It is myth, however, that mercenaries were hostile to gunpowder weapons, seeing in them the eventual obsolescence of their own profession.[106] Jacob Burckhardt's depiction of the fifteenth-century mercenary Paolo Vitelli threatening to put out the eyes and cut off the hands of those soldiers who used firearms remains curiously influential among modern works, particularly those of a popular nature. But mercenaries embraced the weapons and used them often. Hawkwood carried cannons, trebuchets, and whatever other items that might help him in battle. Indeed, the most intriguing reference to the use of handguns involves mercenaries. According to Del Graziani, German soldiers used guns "as long as hands" in

1365 against the White Company. The chronicler claimed that the guns were the crucial factor in the battle and that the bullets penetrated the armor of the English. The story, however, cannot be confirmed.

For all the diffuse and sporadic nature of wars in Italy, military planners did concoct grand strategies, involving the coordination of armies over long distances. In 1390, the Florentines planned to link up armies advancing from France with those from Bologna for a major strike at Milan. Twenty years earlier the pope contrived a similar plan by which the Count of Savoy would advance on Milan from western Lombardy and John Hawkwood and the rest of the papal army would move on the city from the south.

Such strategies were hammered out by committees and war councils. Republican regimes like Florence, Siena, and Lucca elected special committees called *balie*, with extraconstitutional powers to manage wars, including authority to impose taxes and raise money for the effort. The members of the *balie* discussed strategy with commissaries and military commanders.

Rational calculation was often augmented by recourse to the stars. Astrology was serious business in the Middle Ages, especially with regard to war. The pervasive attitude seems to have been that war was too important a matter to be left solely to worldly or even Christian considerations. Officials relied on pagan portents to decide such issues as when to mobilize armies and when to engage in battle. The inauguration of the captain of war, the head of all forces, was usually planned to coincide with favorable astrological signs.

The Florentine chronicler Matteo Villani strongly condemned the practice, calling it a "hereditary vice" from Roman times and "the near and almost partner of the stupidity of the auguries."[107] But it remained popular. Before his campaign against Padua in 1386 the ruler of Verona, Antonio della Scala, sought the advice of an astrologer, who informed him that his men "would enter Padua." Pleased by the prediction, Antonio sent his men forward. They entered Padua, but, unfortunately for Antonio, as prisoners of war after a humiliating defeat.[108] Such setbacks did not eliminate the practice. John Hawkwood himself resorted to diviners, soliciting opinions from as far way as France. Captains did not always follow the omens, but they were careful to consider them.

Most grand strategies failed. This was not due to bad portents but most often to unforeseen mishaps, poor communication, or tensions over lack of pay. Neither the Florentines' scheme nor that of the pope to link their armies in Milan succeeded: the former owing to the rashness of a poorly disciplined French force, the latter because the pope had fallen seriously behind in paying his army.

Although the intention was to avoid them, armies did occasionally engage in pitched battles. These usually occurred when one side perceived that it had a clear and overwhelming advantage or saw that the enemy was exhausted, distracted, or both. Many took place near streams or rivers, often while armies were preparing to cross them. One scholar has called the waterways of the flat Lombard plain "facilitators of battles."[109] The most important river in the region, the Po, ran through or near some of the largest cities, including Piacenza, Cremona, and Pavia. It was a major means of moving men and material, and the Milanese, who dominated the region, patrolled it with a fleet of boats, as did Mantua, Ferrara, Venice, and others. Offensives undertaken on the rivers were often done in conjunction with maneuvers on land.[110] Sometimes the waterways themselves were used as weapons of war. The Po, Adda, and Adige rivers tended to rise significantly during spring rains. Armies hired engineers to rupture their banks and send water on the enemy.

Pitched battles were typically intense, brutal affairs. They involved hand-to-hand combat and fierce individual contests between armored knights. Missile weaponry played an important role. Crossbowmen and archers shot their bolts and arrows, while trebuchets shot boulders and nearby civilians defended their homes with rocks. Trumpeters and drummers played their instruments at the start of battle, and the soldiers followed with screams, intended as much to intimidate the foe as to embolden the faithful. The English soldiers were reputedly the loudest.[111]

But it is necessary to distinguish between brutality and mortality. Pitched battles were violent affairs, but the actual number of deaths was often not high. The modern historian Daniel Waley claimed with admitted hyperbole that more horses may have been injured than men.[112] He stressed that the aim of knights in combat was to knock their opponent off their mounts and that missiles were often shot at the horses. The surviving books of Micheletto degli Attendoli's army show that only 15 of the 512 men in his charge died during the period the band was active, from 1425 to 1449.[113]

But the point must not be overstated. Machiavelli, denying the martial spirit of mercenaries, called their battles "bloodless" affairs. This is not true. Losses sometimes ran as high as a thousand or more men. Fourteenth-century mercenaries did not lack martial spirit; they lacked the incentive to kill large numbers of men. Both the soldiers and their employers understood that the enemy was more valuable alive than dead and that capture and ransom helped pay the high costs of war. Italian writers frequently described battles in purely fiscal terms. The Bolognese chronicler boasted of a local victory in 1384 as "a great earnings."[114]

## Composition of Armies

One must take care when speaking of the "typical" Italian army of the second half of the fourteenth century. The size and composition of forces varied from one campaign to the other.[115] The Milanese army that performed defensive duties outside Burgoforte in 1368 consisted of a couple of thousand men; the Veronese army sent to the great battle at Castagnaro in 1387 contained fifteenth thousand men, and the Bolognese/Florentine army that opposed Milan in 1390 had that many or more. All figures must be given with care. As Michael Mallett has rightly pointed out, the total number of men recruited differed from the number of men actually put in the field, which differed from the number who participated in battle. We have already seen how armies consisted not only of military personnel but also cadres of engineers, who operated trebuchets and diverted rivers; carpenters, who built *bastite;* and various other noncombatants. Armies also included auxiliaries sent by allies. These often did not fight but inflated overall numbers.

The most conspicuous component of armies was the cavalry. By the late fourteenth century it was almost always arrayed in lances, consisting of three men and three horses. Florentine legislation of 1387 gives a detailed physical description of the unit. The leader, the man-at-arms or "corporal," was heavily armored, with a bacinet, a mail shirt, a breastplate, arm pieces, leg pieces, and iron gloves. He carried a sword, a smaller dagger, and a long lance or pole, which he used to knock opponents off their mounts. The squire or "rider" wore only a breastplate, a simple helmet, and iron gloves and carried a sword and dagger; the lance was optional.[116] The page wore no armor and rode a pony called a *ronzino.*

The corporal bore the brunt of combat in pitched battles and took financial responsibility for the other men. The squire transported baggage and booty and procured food. He also acted as what the Italians called a *saccomano*, an important role that involved setting fire to fields and farms. The page was responsible for the care for the horses of the other men.[117]

The overall size of lance brigades varied widely from army to army and within individual armies. The Bolognese/Florentine army of 1391 contained brigades consisting of 300, 212, 210, and 151 lances commanded by renowned captains, as well as more moderate-sized contingents of 92 and 70 lances led by the lesser-known captains and small brigades of 10 and 3 lances under obscure captains.[118] Military planners generally preferred to use smaller brigades to lessen the potential impact of desertion. But the mercenary market and the reputations of the prominent captains often made this impossible. Well-known mercenaries successfully lobbied for more men and with them more pay.

Scholars have traditionally minimized the role of infantry. F. L. Taylor, for one, depicted foot soldiers as irrelevant to Italian armies into the fifteenth century.[119] The argument is well known. The thirteenth century was a "golden age" for Italian infantry, while the fourteenth century saw the triumph of mercenary cavalry, the "loss of native martial spirit," and the virtual elimination of the native foot soldier. According to one recent estimate, cavalry outnumbered infantry by the second half of the fourteenth century ten to one. Another put the ratio at a more modest three to one.[120]

The truth, however, is that the Italian infantry did not disappear but remained an important component of armies.[121] It was not at the focal point of strategic plans, but foot soldiers performed well in their limited roles and sometimes better than that. The full weight of their contribution is in part obscured by the tendency among contemporary writers to speak of them only in the most general terms—a tendency that derived as much from sociopolitical reasons as military ones. Where writers often gave exact (if erroneous) figures for cavalry—including the names of commanders—they resorted to the vaguest of estimates for foot soldiers, describing them generically as "many men" or a "mass of men." The higher social status of cavalries, as well perhaps as their foreignness, rendered them more visible.[122]

The imprecision of contemporary accounts notwithstanding, it is clear that the numbers of infantrymen were far greater than has been believed. Where figures are available, they indicate that infantry size was often comparable to or greater than that of the cavalry. A Milanese army in 1351 consisted of 7,000 horses and 6,000 infantry; the force that opposed it had 1,500 horses and 3,500 infantry. A Paduan army in 1390 consisted of 500 lances and 2,000 infantry. The Milanese army that defeated the Count of Armagnac in 1391 had 2,000 lances and 4,000 infantry.[123]

As with overall army size, the number of infantrymen depended on the nature of the campaign. More were needed during sieges, when the range of cavalry activities was limited. In such instances, *guastatori,* or sappers, played an especially important role. Their job involved setting fires, digging ditches, and mining below fortifications. They were often country rustics with little training who served in amorphous contingents. But their contribution to war efforts cannot be minimized.[124]

Other infantrymen were more highly skilled. Crossbowmen, themselves a species of mercenary, had a long distinguished history as warriors dating from the Crusades. They existed in large numbers in Italian armies in the thirteenth century and played a decisive role in such battles as Campaldino in 1289. Their numbers declined in the fourteenth century, as Stefano Salvemini's dated but still useful study of Florence suggests.[125] But they remained a significant presence in local armies and played a valuable role in war. The pope's army of 3,000 lances in 1366, for example, contained 1,500 crossbowmen. Milanese and Florentine armies at the end of the fourteenth century had at least that many crossbowmen, sometimes more.[126]

The importance of crossbowmen to Italian armies was proportional to the importance of missile weaponry to Italian war. As we have noted above, and as we shall see throughout this book, this was particularly so in pitched battles, which involved heavy use of projectiles, including bolts from crossbowmen, arrows from English longbowmen and Hungarian archers, and rocks from trebuchets and mangonels. Even local citizens were known to hide in buildings and toss stones at the enemy. The battle of Canturino was won largely by a well-aimed rock that felled Konrad von Landau. The fact is that Italian armies rarely went forward without considerable missile capability, though the occasion for using it did not always arise. The scholarly emphasis on mercenary cavalry has unfortunately obscured this fact.

To aid the deployment of crossbowmen, states often hired them in conjunction with shield bearers. When Florence recruited five hundred infantrymen in 1395, it required that they be divided equally between crossbowmen and shield bearers.[127] The shield bearer was intended to provide protection for the crossbowman when he fired his weapon—a tactic used widely in the thirteenth century and still common in the fourteenth.[128]

The integration of the two soldiers provides further evidence that the fourteenth century was not merely a "negative intermezzo" in the history of Italian warfare, as it is currently conceived, but a period of at least modest continuity and experimentation.[129] English brigades, as we have seen, brought in Hungarian archers to make up for the absence of sufficient numbers of native longbowmen.[130] Archers were in turn integrated with cavalry units, serving in lances. The Florentine army in 1387 specifically allowed the substitution in its lance brigades of a Hungarian archer, "armed with a *stambecchino* [a small flexible bow]" for a mounted squire.[131] The innovation was not restricted to Florence. The joint army contracted by the cities of Bologna, Siena, Lucca, Florence, Perugia, and Pisa in 1381 allowed for the inclusion of up to 200 Hungarian archers in the total of 1,600 lances.

Even the venerable longbow of the Hundred Years' War underwent alteration in the Italian context. The English and their Italian employers experimented, creating two types of longbowman: the "single" or "simple" archer, with longbow and horse; and the "double" archer, with longbow and horse attended by a page on a pony, in a manner similar to that of the squire of the lance.[132] The innovation likely derived from the desire to better integrate the longbow with the lance, as well as, on the part of the English, to increase wages. The double archer received a monthly pay of 11 florins, 7 soldi a month in 1387; the single archer was paid a monthly salary of 6 florins, and 13 soldi.

Such experimentation is not surprising given that Italy was the meeting place of soldiers from different countries and different military traditions. The evidence strongly contradicts the current notion that Italian warfare grew up in "isolation" and was shocked into "reality" only by the great French invasion in 1494.

## Perpetual Warfare

The most distinctive feature of warfare in Italy, however, was its perpetual nature. Violence did not end with formal declarations of peace. Seeking to maintain their earnings or to make up for wages unpaid or in arrears, demobilized mercenaries coalesced into free companies around notable commanders and corporals, who allied together by means of a formal oath. Soldiers from throughout Italy gravitated toward them.

The modus operandi of the bands resembled that of traditional armies. They conducted raids in the countryside, torched local houses, stole livestock, and ransomed citizens. Churches and monasteries, rich and poorly defended, were popular targets. The French canonist Honore Bouvet wrote sarcastically that "the man who does not know how to set places on fire, to rob churches and . . . to imprison priests, is not fit to carry on war."[133] The companies kidnapped both human beings and animals. Prominent citizens and important military men returned large ransoms; humble laborers brought more modest profits. Companies redeemed farm animals when the need for money outweighed the need for food. The farmers were willing to buy back the animals because it was cheaper than buying new ones.

Modern scholars often depict the itineraries of marauding companies as random. But this was not so. Companies selected their targets and routes with some care. They preferred areas where the pickings were good and the resistance was light. The Tuscan Maremma, a sparsely populated region where farmers sent their herds to fatten, and the Romagna, where grain was abundant, were favorites with bands. Small companies usually preferred to avoid large towns and cities to stay out of the path of local militias that might oppose them. Larger companies were more self-assured. The mightiest took the urban route and focused on areas in which there was a cluster of prosperous cities in close proximity to one another. The companies tended to be vengeful and often singled out former employers who owed them money or towns that had sent armies against them earlier. Until they reached town walls, however, the large companies usually moved about in smaller contingents under the command of individual corporals. This enhanced the arc over which they could steal and plunder and reduced the risk of being ambushed in narrow passes. The latter was especially important: companies greatly feared negotiating constricted spaces, where they could be ambushed. When they approached town walls, the companies reconstituted themselves to maximize their ability to intimidate and improve their chances of extorting bribe money.

Companies traversed, where possible, established roads. A favorite was the Via Francigena, a major highway that ran the length of north-central Italy, from France to Rome. It was much used by pilgrims and merchants, who served as ready targets for the bands. The Italian road network determined to some degree which cities were victimized. The city of Siena, for example, lay on the Via Francigena and was easily accessible from both the north and south. It became a chief target of mercenary companies, as did Lucca, also on the road, and Arezzo, accessible by the old Roman highway the Via Cassia. Florence, though the richest of the four, was more difficult to approach. It stood at the nexus of several roads but was protected from the north, most notably the Romagna region, by the Apennines. There were several passes through the mountains, but each was narrow, difficult, and insecure.

The most spectacular aspect of the raids was the bribes they extorted from cities. The Great Company in 1357 purportedly extorted 100,000 florins from Naples. The Company of the Star in 1364 took 38,650 florins from the city of Siena, a sum that was more than half the city's expenses that year. The figures are, however, maximums. Smaller companies extorted more modest sums, sometimes as little as a few thousand florins or less.[154] The size of bribes generally varied with respect to the capacity of the victim to pay. Bands were greedy, but they were also practical.

The bribes usually took shape through negotiations. Both sides hoped to settle the issue quickly: the state wished to avoid further damage; the companies wanted to move on for a payday someplace else. Cities sent ambassadors to the camps of the companies, who then communicated with the captains and the corporals. Given the heterogeneous quality of the companies and the significant autonomy of the subcommanders, ambassadors usually had to deal with many people. This was not easy, and ambassadors often complained about being bandied about. Corporals and commanders often had different agendas; one might hold a personal grudge against a city, but another might not. Yet the situation also provided the opportunity for a clever ambassador to exploit the differences and pit some members of a band against others, perhaps even break up the band.

The bands, for their part, played sport with the ambassadors by giving false information. A favorite ruse was to offer conflicting reports about their itinerary.

The mercenaries were also not reluctant to use violence, or the threat of it, as a bargaining tool. They occasionally threatened ambassadors with physical harm.

The end game was, however, surprisingly legalistic. When the two sides finally agreed on terms, they signed a contract, which resembled the *condotta* for legitimate military service. The document set the size of the bribe and the method of payment and outlined mutual responsibilities. States usually pledged free passage through their territories and food at market price or, sometimes, free of charge. Companies promised to leave local territory quickly, usually within several days and by routes that could easily be observed. The mercenaries almost always received additional emoluments such as payment for injured horses (the *mendum* clause) and personal gifts: horses, silk cloths, wine, ceremonial armor, wax, cakes, and candied fruits. The chancellors of the company, who drew up the document, received "tips" for their services. Cecholo da Imola, the chancellor of the Company of the Star in 1364, gained a bonus of 150 florins.[135]

As distasteful as the whole process was, there was little that cities and towns could do to protect themselves from the marauding companies. Modern historians, following Machiavelli and nationalist Italian scholars of the nineteenth century, have largely condemned states for cowardice and failing to meet force with force. The twentieth-century scholar Ferdinand Schevill ridiculed the city of Siena for "cringing behind its town walls" as a succession of bands looted its countryside.[136] But such charges are unfair. Italian states did defend themselves militarily, or at least made efforts to do so.

The most common means of defense was a military league, or what contemporaries called a *taglia*. These were collective armies contracted jointly by several states—often from the same general region—that felt threatened by the bands. The term *taglia* refers to the "cut" or share of troops each city was expected to provide, usually in proportion to its economic capacity.[137] The tradition dated from the thirteenth century and the famous Guelf league of 1260, which brought together militarily those communes that supported the claims of the pope and Charles of Anjou in southern Italy.

The antimercenary leagues of the fourteenth century were enacted frequently, such that there was hardly a single year from the middle of the century when one was not in force. But as we shall see throughout this book, the leagues proved ineffective. The participants quarreled, often over issues that had nothing to do with the mercenaries. Clever politicians used them as a means of diplomacy, to feel out opinion on broader issues, and to isolate enemies and exploit rivalries. As military entities, the league armies were, ironically, staffed by the same mercenaries Italian states were trying to eliminate and thus in some measure only perpetuated the system.[138]

But when pushed too far, individual states put together armies on their own and made war directly on the companies. The city of Siena—Schevill notwithstanding—defeated a band, the so-called Company of the Hat, in 1363. The triumph gave the Sienese an enormous emotional lift, but the effect was fleeting. Within a year they were again paying bribes; on several other occasions their armies were defeated by the bands.

Confronted with the same challenges regarding mercenary bands as Italian states, the French king Charles V came up with perhaps the most novel solution to the problem. He set the task before his physician and astrologer, Thomas de Pizan. Thomas, the father of Christine de Pizan, one of the foremost female writers of the Middle Ages, consulted his astrological charts. He then hammered out five metal figures of naked men and placed astrological signs on the jaw and breast of each. He filled in their hollowed-out backs with dirt taken from different parts of France and buried the figures in the regions where the dirt came from. He recited incantations as he dug.[139] He assured Charles that the companies would disappear. They did not.

# PART II

# RISE OF A MERCENARY CAPTAIN

# *The Fox and the Lion*

## The Pisan-Florentine War, 1363–1364

> We entered through the Golden Gate . . . to such a clamour of
> shouting and trumpeting. . . . The main streets, darkened by great
> towers even in the bright daylight were crammed with citizens
> cheering themselves hoarse.
>
> *John Hawkwood in Hubert Cole's*
> Hawkwood and the Towers of Pisa

"Better death in the house than a Pisan at your door"—so goes an old Tuscan proverb, still used today by Florentines to poke fun at their neighbor to the west. In the year 1363, however, Florence literally faced both death in the house and a Pisan at the door. Death came in the form of a renewed outbreak of the plague, which swept through the city. The Pisan came in battle regalia in the guise of John Hawkwood and the White Company, which rode to the town walls.

The Pisan-Florentine war marked the beginning of Hawkwood's career as a full-fledged captain. At nearly forty years of age, he assumed command of the Pisan army in the winter of 1363/64, six months after the White Company arrived, when its initial contract for service ended.

As captain of Pisan forces, Hawkwood elicited for the first time the full attention of local chroniclers. Both Filippo Villani and Sozomen of Pistoia described him as "a great master of war" (gran maestro di guerra), a generic epithet applied to many contemporary commanders. But the writers also gave additional details, notably that Hawkwood had long experience in war and was not an especially young man. They offered a strikingly accurate account of his social background: "he was not from the noble class; his father was a gentleman merchant and 'antico borghese,' as were his ancestors."[1] But the writers furnished no physical description—unusual particularly for Villani, who fancied such asides and just earlier in his chronicle had described a German mercenary in Florentine employ, Rudolf von Hapsburg, as being "handsome and of noble aspect."[2] Villani called Hawkwood an "old fox" and portrayed his vulpine qualities as being native to the English race. Pisan writers, on the other hand, had curiously little to say. Where Villani self-consciously called Hawkwood "acuto" to stress his foxlike cleverness, the anonymous Pisan chronicler rendered Hawkwood's surname as "auti," a word evocative of the Italian for "help" but which was probably little more than a clumsy attempt to piece together his name phonetically.

The fox image served as part of a larger metaphor for the Pisan-Florentine war itself. In their accounts of the conflict, Florentine writers repeatedly cast Pisa in the role of the fox and Florence in the role of the lion—the crafty, smaller commune versus the larger, more potent one. In his famous poem, Antonio Pucci described Pisa's hiring of the White Company as an instance in which "the fox knew more than the lion" (seppe la volpe piu qui del lione). He said that the war would decide whether "the lion is more able than the fox" (che puote pie il lion, che non la volpe).[3] The Florentine chronicler Marchionne di Coppo Stefani often referred to the Pisans as foxes in his account of the conflict.[4]

The fox-lion metaphor is most familiar from Machiavelli's use of it in the sixteenth century. Machiavelli applied it to his ideal prince, who should be a combination of lion and fox. Hawkwood, at the height of his military career, would combine the traits of both. At this point, however, he still had much to learn and was inclined, despite Villani's judgment, to favor too much force over subtlety, to act the lion rather than the fox.

The Florentine-Pisan war was the result of long-standing commercial rivalry and conflicting territorial claims between the two cities. In 1356, Pisa had angered Florence by placing a tariff on that city's goods entering its port, Porto Pisano. Florence responded by routing its merchandise through the Sienese port of Talamone. The tensions simmered and erupted into open violence in May 1362, when Florence seized Pietrabuona, a disputed town in the Valdinievole near Pisa.[5] The Florentines held the early advantage in the fighting, both on land and at sea. The Italian mercenary Piero Farnese, captain of the land forces, acquitted himself particularly well, conducting two successful offensives: the first resulting in the capture of the opposing captain, the second bringing the Florentine army to the gates of Pisa.[6] It was after the latter campaign that the Pisans aggressively recruited the White Company. The hire constituted a major coup for the city, not the least because it was achieved by outbidding the financially more potent Florentines.[7] Pisa's prospects improved further when Farnese suddenly died from the plague in June 1363, a month before the company arrived in Tuscany. Matteo

Villani noted a "sudden breeze" accompanying Farnese's passing, followed by a "remarkable passage" of crickets (*grilli*) so dense that they blocked out the sky.[8] Both were augurs of bad tidings for Florence.

The advent of the White Company changed the course of the war. The band in fact scored its first victory before it even reached the region. While it was still north near Piacenza, Pisan officials pretended that the company had arrived, sending out Pisa's own army under the cover of darkness in the middle of the night and having it return the next morning, raising as much noise and dust as possible, welcoming it with feasts and celebrations. The intention was to deceive the Florentines, whose army was nearby besieging the town of Montecalvoli. The Pisans here took explicit advantage of the White Company's reputation for marching at night, a tactic, as we have seen, that was used to great effect in Piedmont and Lombardy. The ruse worked. The Florentines, mistaking the Pisan army for the White Company, quickly lifted their siege and retreated. Rather than condemn the maneuver, Villani praised Pisa for its "cunning."[9]

The real White Company arrived with little fanfare shortly thereafter (July 1363).[10] Pisan officials joined it to the rest of the army, which was commanded by the Florentine exile Ghisello degli Ubaldini. The overall force numbered approximately 3,200 horses and 6,000 infantry. Albert Sterz captained the English; Hawkwood was as yet still a corporal. In August the army rode against Florence, advancing north and east via the plain of Pistoia and then south to Brozzi, to the western gate of the city.[11] The White Company displayed the same ferocity, maneuverability, and talent for nighttime attack that had distinguished it in Lombardy and Piedmont.[12] Within a week, the army reached the gates of Florence, stopping at Rifredi. The Englishmen, still unaccustomed to the ways of Italian cities, mistook the sound of church bells from the town for the battle alarm and briefly retreated.[13]

The army then initiated series of carefully choreographed insults below the city walls, mocking the Florentines with loud feasts and celebrations, running races, playing music through the night, minting gold florins with disparaging insignia on them, and hanging animals, on whose collars they affixed the names of members of the major families of Florence: Strozzi, Ricci, Albizzi, and Medici.[14] The spectacle was revenge for similar actions undertaken by Piero Farnese before the Pisan city walls months earlier. "Behold," wrote Filippo Villani, "how the wise communes of Florence and Pisa spent millions of florins renewing such villanies."[15]

The army returned to Pisa and renewed the offensive in late September. This time it took a more southerly path, through the Val d'Elsa to Castelfiorentino, touching on Sienese lands, into the Val di Pesa to the town of Figline, southeast of Florence.[16] The itinerary angered Siena, which was technically neutral in the war. The army seized Figline and stayed there for several weeks. During that time Andrew Belmont, the "handsome" English corporal, began an affair with Mona Tancia, "a woman of beauty and noble manners,"[17] who was the wife of a prominent citizen, Guido della Foresta. Villani described it as an instance of "good knightly love" and said that Tancia's husband received Andrew honorably and courteously. Andrew made sure that the army refrained from looting della Foresta's lands.

The army advanced north from Figline toward Florence and defeated a poorly coordinated army at Incisa, capturing much of the Florentine high command. One of the prisoners, Luca di Totto da Panzano, wrote an account of his experience in his diary. His words provide a succinct statement of the fundamentally economic nature of Italian war. "I was wounded in the face," wrote Panzano, "and lead away. I lost that day horses, arms, supplies, a silver belt and gold rings."[18] The company then returned to Pisa, loaded with prey and prisoners, so much so that, according to the Lucchese chronicler Giovanni Sercambi, "the English . . . became rich."[19]

## First Campaign

It was after the White Company returned to Pisa from Incisa that Hawkwood took over command of the army. Pisan officials elected him to the post of captain of war, a position that placed him in charge of the overall army but which did not de facto make him captain of the company, which, like all bands, chose its leader by internal election. But when Pisa chose Hawkwood as captain, it dismissed all other troops that were not part of the company, effectively making Hawkwood commander of both. It is unclear whether Hawkwood's elevation was later confirmed within the company itself and what effect this development had on the band's longtime captain, Albert Sterz. The circumstances may well have sowed the seeds of tensions that later followed.

Hawkwood's contract with Pisa has not survived. The chroniclers Villani and Sozomen report that the band received 150,000 florins in salary for six months, but they do not indicate how much Hawkwood himself earned. They estimated the size of Hawkwood's force as approximately 3,500 horsemen and 2,000 infantry— thus slightly smaller than the army that had preceded it. Documents in the Pisan archives indicate that the band retained as the official name "Great Society," the same one it had when it entered Italy. "White Company" was thus still a nickname bestowed on the band from the outside. We should not, however, stress too much the continuity between Hawkwood's army and the band that crossed into Italy in 1361. The original Great Company incurred substantial losses in Lombardy and had taken in soldiers of various nationalities, most notably Hungarians, Germans, and Italians. The Perugian chronicler Del Graziani claimed that the band now had four hundred Hungarians, but the figure is impossible to confirm. One notable Hungarian soldier whose presence can be confirmed is Nicholas Thod, who had defected from Konrad von Landau's army at the battle of Canturino in 1361 and now served Hawkwood as a corporal.[20] Pisan archival sources indicate, however, that the largest numbers of additional soldiers were Germans and Italians—though here again we possess no certain numbers. We do know, however, the names of the musicians who accompanied the army. They were Italians: Antonio, Marco, and Marcuccio—a drummer and two trumpeters, respectively.

The English maintained a significant presence, particularly among the officers. Andrew Belmont, William Boson, and William Thornton—all original members of the company—remained with the army as corporals. Two other men, Richard Romsey and William Gold, both likely members of the rank and file of the original company, emerged at this time as soldiers of notable skill and achieved the status of corporal. They forged especially close ties to Hawkwood himself. Pisan documents give additional names of English soldiers, including such men as Robert Astor, Robin Castel, Thomas Berton, William William, and two others known only as "Jack of London" and "the Bastard."[21] At some point the band was joined by the English nobleman Hugh de la Zouche, son of the lord of Ashby castle in Leicestershire and a distant relation of the famous Roger Mortimer, who had overthrown King Edward II in 1327 and romanced his queen, Isabella. Hugh would eventually become the captain of the White Company.

Hawkwood's first order of business as captain was to retain the services of his English soldiers. Their success had produced a substantial demand for them. The Venetians attempted to hire three hundred English soldiers in December 1363 to help put down a revolt on their colony of Candia.[22] In addition to high pay, they offered free passage to the Holy Land (via Cyprus and Rhodes) on their ships at the termination of the contract should the soldiers ultimately wish to go on crusade. The documents indicate that a "John of England" acted as a middleman in the negotiations with the Venetian envoy Peglio de Vonico. A modern Venetian archivist has identified this "John" as John Hawkwood himself, but this is unlikely, since John was a common name among both English mercenaries and Englishmen in general. There is no reason to believe that Hawkwood, recently promoted to captain, would deal in such petty details. The Venetian efforts continued into February. The city did not obtain its desired quota but did manage to hire 110 Englishmen.[23]

John Hawkwood and the main body of the army meanwhile remained quartered in the environs of Pisa. Their reputation and profits from war engendered in them an arrogance and taste for good living. Villani complained that members of the band took up residence in the best palaces in the city, touching off resentments among the local citizenry. A group of soldiers quartered near the Florentine town of Pistoia, harassed the local population, stealing goods and raping women. Pistoiese officials sent much of the female population to Genoa, where "they were able to sleep honestly."[24]

Hawkwood chose not to remain demobilized for the winter. In February, he undertook his first offensive as an independent commander. He did this even though the winter was one of the coldest on record in Tuscany, a winter in which, according to Villani, the "snows never stopped, and the ice from the cold winds was great." Villani was impressed that Hawkwood would even consider such an enterprise, and he compared the Englishman's resolve to that of the ancient Romans, who "rode at unusual and uncomfortable times, bringing to mind the old saying: 'Roman it is to do and suffer great things.' " The Florentine chronicler also drew parallels between Hawkwood and the great Carthaginian general Hannibal, whose success derived from *astuzia*, or cleverness, the same trait Villani applied to Hawkwood.[25]

Hawkwood departed from Pisa at the end of February 1364 (map 4). His plan was ostensibly a good one. He intended to advance east toward Vinci, a town belonging to Florence but where anti-Florentine sentiment was high. He would receive help from the local citizens and then ride to the Mugello, a fertile valley northeast of Florence, known for its stores of corn and oil and its abundance of animals. There he could sustain his army at local expense and then move south toward Florence. Hawkwood's offensive was augured in Florence by a lightning bolt that suddenly fell from an otherwise clear sky and struck the campanile of Santa Maria Novella.[26]

Florence opposed Hawkwood by assembling a substantial mercenary army of its own. The decision constituted a shift in policy. Officials had initially employed a combination of small mercenary brigades and rural levies against the White Company. But the Florentines now sought larger contingents of foreign soldiers and sent envoys outside the peninsula, to royal and ducal houses in France and Germany, to recruit them. Their efforts succeeded best in southern Germany, where they hired the prominent and powerful Swabian nobles Wolfard von Veringen, Heinrich von Montfort-Tettnang, and Johann and Rudolf von Hapsburg, each with substantial bands.[27] The men were connected by family ties: Johann and Rudolf von Hapsburg were brothers; their sister was married to Heinrich von Montfort-Tettnang. Florentine military planners appear to have intended to match the cohesion and esprit de corps of the English by creating a German band with both regional and familial bonds. Villani was clearly proud of this. He described the men as physically imposing, "big and handsome of body," though he thought Rudolf von Hapsburg pretentious and "puffed up with pride."[28] Officials added two more Swabian captains, Hugo von Melichingen and Hermann von Winden, with one thousand German *barbute*.[29] But these men and their soldiers were less impressive than the others. Hugo had recently suffered defeat at the hands of a Sienese army, and his band arrived in Florence poorly equipped. Florentine officials needed to distribute lances and other arms to the soldiers.

Hawkwood advanced to Vinci with little resistance and then proceeded northeast toward Prato, past the towns of Carmignano and Montemurlo, through the Valdimarina, to the entry point to the Mugello. He found the passes, however, well guarded and few provisions available. Local citizens had locked themselves and their goods in forts and behind town walls, leaving little on which Hawkwood could sustain his army. Rather than risk the passes, which were narrow and difficult to cross even in the best of conditions, Hawkwood turned back. But snow and intense cold made even that option difficult. On the way back he lost many horses from lack of fodder and the intense cold; several Englishmen died as well. The remnants of the army returned to Pisa with meager spoils: some fifteen prisoners from Vinci and nothing more.[30] Hawkwood first offensive ended in failure. Both sides demobilized their armies for the remainder of the winter.

With the approach of spring and the return of the campaigning season, the Pisans moved to augment their army still further. This time (March 1364) they recruited the renowned German captain Hannekin Baumgarten and his band of three thousand *barbute*. The hire rivaled that of the White Company in terms of magnitude and public relations, no less so because it was effected, as earlier, by outbidding the Florentines, who had long appealed to Baumgarten but failed to win his services.[31] The reputation of the White Company probably helped Pisa recruit Baumgarten, who was enticed by the prospects of lucrative booty that could be earned working alongside the English. But rather than undertake battle immediately, Pisa used Baumgarten's hire to gain an edge in negotiations. With the clear advantage in mercenary power, the Pisans hoped to gain favorable terms. As the Florentines negotiated, they cast about to find new recruits, particularly in France. An important figure in this was the Florentine treasurer Spinello Alberti, who, "fully informed of the income and expenditure of the commune, and its debts," advised Florentine leaders about the feasibility of military actions and involved himself directly in hiring troops. Spinello would later play an important role in Florence's relations with Hawkwood.[32]

The peace initiatives failed. In April, Pisa undertook a new offensive. Hawkwood and Baumgarten's army, consisting of approximately sixty-five hundred cavalrymen, brought along numerous contingents of sappers (*guastatori*) to assist in burning fields and tunneling below fortifications—an indication that Pisa intended this time an aggressive siege against Florence. The Pisan army was not integrated into a coherent whole; nor did it even travel as a single unit. The English brigades answered directly to Hawkwood, the Germans to Baumgarten.

Baumgarten and Hawkwood left Pisa together on 13 April 1364 and rode along the familiar path, northeast toward Pistoia and then to Prato. At Prato, a contingent of English soldiers caused panic by seizing a drawbridge and preventing it from being lifted up. The brigade withdrew but returned at night (15 April) and attacked the city, riding up to the town walls, seizing cattle, and taking prisoners. A small band of soldiers approached the town gate, rapped on it loudly, and then ran away. The curious maneuver seems to have been a psychological ploy intended only to discomfit the enemy.

At this point, Baumgarten and Hawkwood went in different directions. Baumgarten moved southeast, directly toward Florence, stopping at Peretola, not far from the western gate of the city. Hawkwood traveled north to the Mugello. Unlike the previous winter, he found the passes unguarded. There were plentiful provisions, including wine and fodder. According to Villani, this owed to a decision by the Florentine government to double the tax on these items, which induced some unhappy *contadini* to leave their harvest in the field.[33] Hawkwood made camp near the town of Barberino, some fifty kilometers north of Florence.

Florence sent its captain of war, Pandolfo Malatesta, to cut off Hawkwood's march. Pandolfo was a noted Italian mercenary who had gained considerable fame several years earlier by defeating Konrad von Landau's Great Company in the passes of the Val di Lamone, not far from the where Hawkwood's army currently stood. Pandolfo established camp several miles west of Hawkwood, outside the towns of Scarperia and Borgo San Lorenzo. Hawkwood dispatched small contingents of men, who conducted raids on local fields. A contingent of a hundred or so Englishmen encountered thirty of Pandolfo's German mercenaries. As the sides prepared for battle, a German corporal known only as Heinrich descended from his horse, took up his lance, and rushed headlong at the English. He knocked ten soldiers off their horses, killing two. The crazed maneuver rallied the Germans, who rode on the English and forced them to retreat. "We have with pleasure recorded this deed," wrote Villani," because in our days such prowess is rare."[34]

Heinrich's bold action, coupled with concerns that the passes into Florence had become too dangerous to attempt, induced Hawkwood to change his itinerary. He retreated farther into the hills and with difficulty doubled back to Prato. He renewed the advance toward Florence by a more southerly route through Sesto and Colonnata, following Baumgarten's path. He systematically burned and looted those villages not already damaged by Baumgarten. The Florentine government was angry at Pandolfo Malatesta for allowing Hawkwood to escape the Mugello and ultimately dismissed him for this and other transgressions.

Hawkwood and Baumgarten linked up just north of Florence in the hills of Montughi and Fiesole. They rode south and east to Rovezzano, just below the town walls.[35] The Florentine forces assembled behind three barricades outside the city, joined by a multitude of citizens who incautiously rushed forward to help man the defenses. Florentine officials tried in vain to get them to withdraw and get out of the way of the army.[36]

On May Day, the Pisan army attacked just outside the gate of San Gallo in the northeast corner of the city. The English corporal William Gold and his contingent led the first charge against the barricades.[37] Villani credits him with displaying great personal bravery and prowess. He was accompanied by a German named Eberhard—most likely Eberhard von Landau, the half brother of Konrad von Landau. Together they succeeded in opening a breach in the Florentine defenses.[38] English archers shot arrows on the enemy, which seemed to Villani "like hail stones." Florentine crossbowmen, stationed on the town walls and other high points in the city responded with volleys of iron bolts. The battle was noisy, both sides let out ferocious shouts. Amid the confusion, Baumgarten knighted Gold, a ceremony that occurred "within a crossbow bolt's throw" (una gittata di balestro) of the city gates and was punctuated by "thunderous" celebratory shouts.[39]

The fight was carried right up to the town wall. Hawkwood and his men moved about torching everything in sight. Eberhard von Landau penetrated so deeply behind the barricades that he found himself face to face with Heinrich von Montfort-Tettnang, whom Villani now called "a mass of iron, enemies were never wont to test."[40] The results of the encounter of these two men are nowhere recorded. Both lived to fight again.

With the approach of nightfall, the Pisan army retreated to Montughi and Fiesole. Within full view of Florence, the men held feasts and celebrations. They ran horse races and undertook an intricate dance, in which members of the different brigades threw torches back and forth to one another. In the middle of the night, Hawkwood sent trumpeters and drummers to the gate of Porta della Croce with instructions to play their instruments as loudly as possible to discomfit those within. Convinced that the enemy army had returned, frightened citizens "ran here and there"; women, fearing violation, placed lights in their windows and armed themselves with rocks.[41]

Hawkwood and his men also lay waste to much of Fiesole itself. Their targets included the castle at Vincigliata, just above the current site of Villa I Tatti,

Bernard Berenson's old villa and now the home of the Harvard Center for Renaissance Studies. Hawkwood set fire to the castle, which was later purchased and rebuilt by John Temple-Leader, a nineteenth-century gentleman who wrote his biography.[42]

The Pisan army returned to Florence the next day. It descended from Fiesole and moved counterclockwise around the city, passing over the Arno at "la Sardigna," ravaging the suburbs at Legnaia, Verzaia, and Arcetri. Velluti gives an evocative description of the army trampling the harvest, stealing goods and provisions, and, at Verzaia, letting go a torrent of arrows into the city. The army took the battle up to the gate of San Friano (now Frediano), the western entry point of the city.

## Defection of the Pisan Army

With the overwhelming advantage on their side, the Pisan army suddenly gave up the offensive. Its impetus was stilled not by Florentine forces but by bribe money. The anonymous Pisan chronicler wrote that the Pisan captains were corrupted by gold coins fitted into flasks of wine. He singled out the perfidy of Albert Sterz.[43] The Florentine writer Donato Velluti claimed that Hannekin Baumgarten and Andrew Belmont took the lead among the traitors, while Filippo Villani included mention also of Hugh de la Zouche.[44] John Hawkwood was the lone commander to remain faithful, with a contingent of approximately twelve hundred men.

The circumstances of the desertions are confused and unclear. Contemporary writers gave few details, and these are contradictory.[45] Villani estimated that the bribes paid before the Florentine walls totaled 114,000 florins: 9,000 florins to Baumgarten, 35,000 florins to his band, and 70,000 to the English.[46] Velluti, on the other hand, offered smaller numbers: 30,000 florins to the Germans and 50,000 florins to the English.[47] Florentine archival sources confirm Villani's figures for the English, who were paid in three installments: 20,000 florins up front, followed by 40,000 florins weeks later, and the rest in a series of smaller disbursements, including a personal subsidy to Andrew Belmont of 2,000 florins.[48] But the Florentine registers are incomplete with respect to the German brigade.

The Florentine documentary evidence does make clear, however, that only Hugh de la Zouche directly joined the Florentine army with a small brigade of twenty-five lances. His name alone appears in Florentine budgets.[49] Baumgarten, Belmont, and Sterz behaved more ambiguously. After abandoning the fight at the Florentine walls, they rode south toward Arezzo.[50] They now claimed to be a "free" company, whose contract with Pisa had expired. They attacked Sienese lands, under the name the Company of the Star, and openly demanded a bribe in the usual manner of a marauding band. Florentine officials claimed no prior conspiracy. But the actions of the brigade corresponded well with Florentine intentions, if not open policy. Relations with Siena had grown tense during the war. Florentine officials had accused their neighbor of surreptitiously supporting Pisa and, most recently, of defeating a band of mercenaries (the Company of the Hat) that Florence had hoped to use against Hawkwood. The raid by Baumgarten, Belmont, and Sterz was therefore a measure of revenge, a covert activity on the part of the Florentines, which doubtless corresponded also with the wishes of the band, which stood to increase its profits. The company in fact extorted nearly 40,000 florins from Siena.[51] The Sienese angrily and openly blamed the Florentines for the attack.[52]

After their raid on Sienese territory, Baumgarten, Sterz, Belmont, and their band rode back toward Pisa, stopping not far from the city at San Piero in Campo. Hawkwood wrote to officials to warn them not to open the gates to the army, whose loyalties were now suspect. The treachery now apparent, Florence dispensed with secrecy and openly sent an ambassador, Lapo dei Fornaino de' Rossi, to sign the band to a formal contract. De' Rossi concluded two separate pacts: one with Baumgarten and the Germans, another with Sterz and Belmont and the English. The deal with Baumgarten, dated 1 July 1364, called not for active service but for the band to "remain at peace with Florence for five years." In return, it received 27,000 florins in three installments.[53] The pact with the English, completed several weeks later (28 July), called for overt military duty, for six months, "against all the enemies of the commune of Florence," in return for a lump sum payment of 100,000 florins.[54] The different terms most likely owed to the fact that Florence already had in its employ significant numbers of German mercenaries, including Johann and Rudolf von Hapsburg. Officials wanted to oppose Hawkwood with an English force of its own. Interestingly, it was Baumgarten and his German brigade that retained the name "Great Company," while the English brigade now called itself "the society of Englishmen." The latter is a bit of a misnomer, since, as the contract makes plain, the English company contained numerous Hungarian soldiers.[55] In one of the many ironies of Hawkwood's career, Lapo dei Fornaino de' Rossi became Hawkwood's neighbor when the Englishman purchased land in Florentine territory twenty years later.

A critical figure in the negotiations with the English—indeed, the man most responsible for convincing the soldiers to desert the Pisan cause—was the Scottish knight Walter Lesley, the erstwhile captain of the Great Company at Avignon, to whom the pope addressed a letter in the winter of 1359/60.[56] Lesley was in Italy in connection with the pope's call for a crusade, which he eventually undertook.

His willingness to participate may have derived from his involvement in that enterprise. Lesley negotiated with English along with his brother, Norman, and the Florentine Luca di Totto da Panzano, who had been captured by English at Incisa several months earlier. Florentine documents cite Walter as the man who "reduced the White Company to benevolence and friendship with the city of Florence." He was paid the considerable sum of 3,000 florins for his services.[57] He remained Florence's envoy to the English throughout the rest of the war.[58] Lesley's service was a precursor of Florentine policy toward Hawkwood, which initially focused on using English-speakers to negotiate with him.

The full amount of the money paid to the German and English brigades will never be known with certainty. Florentine records show that officials purposely did not record all the expenditures in communal account books for fear of upsetting local citizens.[59] The sixteenth-century Florentine historian Scipione Ammirato told of widespread concerns about the costs of the war and how officials justified bribing the enemy on the grounds that the money spent would otherwise have gone to mercenary companies from southern France, whose services city officials had throughout the war tried to obtain.[60]

The defections left John Hawkwood as the one faithful commander in the Pisan army. The famous episode has been cast by modern historians in decidedly moral terms, as a defining moment in Hawkwood's career, in which he emerged from his squalid profession as the lone "honest" mercenary.[61] But the point has been overstated or, more specifically, removed from its context. There is, for example, evidence to suggest that the salaries of the deserting contingents were in arrears. The English contract of 28 July 1364 with Florence contains reference to an outstanding debt of 60,000 florins "still owed by Pisa" to the band. This is confirmed in a letter written a month later by Andrew Belmont, who, citing money owed him by Pisa, expressed the desire to ride on the city to obtain the sum.[62] This was perhaps inevitable given the gap between Pisa's revenue, which was modest in the best of times, and the expense of its troops, which were the most costly in all of Italy. The discrepancy was so apparent to contemporaries that it had raised suspicions from the start that the Pisan war effort was receiving financial help from elsewhere, notably from Bernabò Visconti.

Dissensions also likely existed within the Pisan army itself. As noted above, Hawkwood's elevation to command through Pisan election may have engendered ill feeling among his English comrades. In April, just before the army mobilized for its attack on Florence, members of the English brigade were negotiating with Pope Urban V, who wished to send them on crusade in the East. Albert Sterz apparently showed interest in the pope's proposal and at one point sent a messenger to Urban in Avignon indicating his readiness to serve. He ultimately chose not to go, but the impulse clearly remained with him, for in the contract of 28 July there is an explicit escape clause, allowing Sterz to leave Florentine service should he wish.[63] Such divided loyalties could hardly have engendered unity in the band and may well have made it more receptive to Florentine bribe money.[64]

In any case, the Pisans were less shocked by the behavior of their troops than modern scholars have been. The anonymous Pisan chronicler assumed an almost wistful tone, lamenting more the breakup of the powerful fighting force than its perfidy: "It is certain that they would have ruled all of Italy if they had not broken apart, so powerful and valiant were they!"[65]

As for John Hawkwood, he may not have followed the rest of his companions, but it is not at all clear that the conditions that impelled his mates to desert also existed for him. As titular commander of all forces, he likely had higher priority with respect to pay than the others. The pope's plea, as well as crusading activity in general (as we shall see later), held little interest for Hawkwood. Nor did the "treachery" of his comrades offend his sense of morality. Hawkwood later took these very men back into his services, and whatever tensions existed were eventually smoothed over. He would himself desert his employer before the town walls of the enemy eight years later.

## The Battle of Cascina

In practical military terms, the defection of the English and German contingents shifted the balance of mercenary power in favor of Florence. Hawkwood's army, a shell of its former self, retreated to Pisa, giving space to the Florentines to launch a counterattack against Livorno, a city that was not protected by walls. Frightened citizens were forced to hide on boats moored in the harbor, and many drowned.[66]

The Pisans built up their depleted force with German mercenaries, Genoese crossbowmen, and communal levies. The Sienese chronicler claimed that the Pisans recruited so many local citizens that "few people remained" in the city.[67] The Pisan chronicler Ranieri Sardo, who had been in charge of furnishing the army with grain in the early phases of the war, estimated the size of the army at 5,000 cavalrymen and 500 Genoese crossbowmen with "many infantrymen" and auxiliaries from Lucca.[68] Hawkwood remained the captain of war.

In Florence, Galeotto Malatesta took command of the army, replacing his unpopular nephew Pandolfo. Galeotto was a venerable old captain who had recently distinguished himself in papal service.[69] Villani called him "the most famous man then in Italy."[70] Malatesta's army contained about 4,000 horses and

11,000 infantry. On 29 July 1364 it mobilized for an offensive against Pisa. The departure date was chosen to coincide with the anniversary of the humiliation suffered at the hands of the Pisan army at Rifredi a year earlier. The army rode unimpeded to Cascina, a strategically important town on the left bank of the Arno, six miles from Pisa, flanked on one side by a steep mountain, the Verruca, and on other by the Pisan plain. Galeotto set up camp there.

Filippo Villani described the atmosphere at Cascina as resembling more that of a summer camp than a military one. Galeotto Malatesta, old and frail, had trouble keeping discipline among his much younger troops. The weather was very hot, and the soldiers wandered out of the town on their own, foraging for food and bathing in the Arno.[71] Meanwhile, Galeotto, secure behind barricades, took long naps and paid little attention to reconnaissance and the movements of the enemy.[72]

John Hawkwood and the Pisan army advanced to meet Malatesta at Cascina. They stopped six and a half kilometers away at the town of San Savino, separated from the enemy by a dusty plain. Hawkwood made several feints at the Florentine camp. The battle-crier repeatedly gave warning; the army was roused, only to find that the Pisans were not there. This annoyed Galeotto, who, according to Villani, did not like being taken from his midday naps. He threatened to cut off the crier's foot if he sounded the warning bell again without explicit permission.[73]

Hawkwood's tactics presage many of those that would distinguish him as a commander in his later career. He took precise account of the terrain and physical conditions of the battlefield. He positioned his army so that the wind would be at its back and thus blow dust into the eyes of the enemy. He also had the sun behind him, so that it would affect the vision of the enemy.[74] The strategy recalls the battle of Crécy and lends further support to assertions that Hawkwood was present there. He instructed his cavalrymen to dismount their horses at San Savino and advance on foot across the plain to Cascina—a ploy intended to enhance the element of surprise. According to Villani, Hawkwood spurred on his men by telling them of the riches they would gain from captives and booty.[75] Villani also claimed that Hawkwood dismissed the Florentines as "ignorant in the use of arms," but this was likely the chronicler's own frustration spoken through Hawkwood.

It is not clear whether Hawkwood's intention was to take advantage of the disarray in the Florentine camp and make an all-out attack or whether he hoped only to draw the Florentines from their camp and, perhaps, squeeze them into a strategically disadvantageous position near the Arno and the forbidding Verruca mountain. He nevertheless forced the issue, a strategy that differed strongly from that used at Crécy, where the English army relied on a defensive position. Also contrary to Crécy, Hawkwood made little or no use of longbowmen, whose numbers were probably quite small owing to the recent desertions.

Hawkwood's army reached the enemy in the late afternoon, when the sun was low on the horizon and at its most distracting.[76] Malatesta and the Florentine army drew up behind barricades. An advance guard of Hawkwood's men attacked the barricades with great fury. The Florentines acquitted themselves well, meeting the impetus with bolts from Genoese crossbowmen, who were hiding in houses and public buildings. The German mercenaries Heinrich von Montfort-Tettnang and Rudolf von Hapsburg led a counterassault. The Florentine diarist Giovanni Morelli gives a picturesque account of how Rudolf von Hapsburg (whom he called "Count Beardless") pushed the barricades aside, shouting "open the barricades to Count Beardless!" He then rushed at the enemy with his sword raised high.[77]

The battle lasted several hours. According to Villani, the turning point came when Manno Donati, a Florentine civilian commissary, effected an enveloping move with a contingent of auxiliaries and local infantry which cut off Hawkwood's advance guard from the rest of his army. Hawkwood, who had positioned himself at the back of the formation, ordered a full retreat. He left those who had been trapped to their own devices and rode off toward San Savino, hoping to minimize the damage. The Florentines pursued. Hawkwood's retreat devolved into a mad rush, with fleeing soldiers "dispersed here and there, tired and frightened."[78] Hawkwood himself lost his battle standard, a banner of black satin, seized by a German corporal from Johann von Hapsburg's brigade, who received double pay from Florentine officials as a reward.[79]

The Florentines took many of Hawkwood's men, as well as wagons of wine and provisions. The Pisan chronicler Ranieri Sardo claimed that the enemy captured an "infinite number of prisoners, more than is possible to record."[80] Florentine documents show, however, that the actual number was 356 men, a figure similar to that given by the diarist Monaldi.[81] The prisoners included prominent Pisan citizens and soldiers of various nationalities—such as Rubino de Sassi of France, Berlinghieri Cantini of Barcelona, Andrea Adano of Palermo, and Anselm Brinetti of Corsica—as well as a Franciscan friar known only as Raniero.[82] Florence took no English prisoners but let them go on their own recognizance. Officials wished to maintain good relations with these special fighters, perhaps with the thought that they might still entice them into service at a later date.

The captives were brought back to Florence in forty-two carriages, paraded throughout the city as trophies, and placed in prison. The Florentine historian Scipione Ammirato claims that they were subjected to forced labor, made to work on the roof of the Palazzo dei Priori. Ammirato could not resist saying that the roof was, architecturally speaking, ugly.[83] The fifteenth-century diarist Giovanni Morelli claimed that each prisoner suffered the additional indignity of being required to kiss the rear end of a small lion cub as he passed into the city via the San Friano gate.[84] In the metaphorical language of the war, the lion had humiliated the fox.

## Cascina Reevaluated

The "great defeat at Cascina," as the chronicler of Bologna called it, was a devastating blow to Pisa.[85] "Our city," wrote Sardo, "endures great pain and sadness."[86] Florentine writers, on the other hand, expressed disappointment that their army had not gone far enough. Velluti had hoped for complete annihilation of the enemy. "It is certain that if our army had followed them, there would have been a great carnage."[87]

Cascina was Hawkwood's second defeat as captain of the Pisan army. Contemporaries nevertheless spoke well of his conduct of the campaign. Villani described Hawkwood's actions in positive terms. He credited Hawkwood with exhibiting "fox-like craft" and contrasted this trait with the lack of the same exhibited by the Florentine commander Galeotto Malatesta. The Pisan Ranieri Sardo blamed the loss not on Hawkwood but on lack of discipline in the Pisan ranks, for which the civilian commissaries were responsible. Sardo criticized native troops, who, driven by "rage and craziness," rushed out of Pisa toward the battle front while Hawkwood and his corporals were still arranging the details of their contracts of service. "Our citizens," he wrote, "are to blame for everything."[88] The anonymous Pisan chronicler faulted German mercenaries, who he claimed did not follow up the first wave of battle. The Lucchese chronicler Giovanni Sercambi and the Sienese chronicler Donato di Neri concurred.[89] Neri claimed that the Germans were so poorly integrated into the army that they were "much dispersed and without the guidance of a captain."[90] Roncioni, author of a later, staunchly pro-Pisan history, described Hawkwood as a "valorous man" despite the defeat.[91]

In modern times, as the legendary John Hawkwood has come to replace the real John Hawkwood, historians have transformed the battle of Cascina into a heroic stand against insurmountable odds.[92] Both Temple-Leader and Joseph Day Deiss claimed that Hawkwood was greatly outnumbered.[93] Deiss said that Hawkwood had a "puny" force of no more than eight hundred Englishmen. "The odds," he wrote, "were impossible, the risk tremendous."[94] Neither author, however, drew on Pisan sources, which make clear that the armies were both about the same size.

Their attitude reflects an earlier refashioning of Cascina that occurred almost immediately after Hawkwood's death, in Florence, the Englishman's last and most grateful employer, where a cult of worship developed. The humanists Leonardo Bruni (d. 1444) and Poggio Bracciolini (d. 1459) enthusiastically applauded Hawkwood's deeds. Bruni praised Hawkwood's "great cleverness" at Cascina and described his march across the plain on foot as proceeding with "wonderful silence" thereby "surprising the enemy."[95] Bracciolini depicted Hawkwood's generalship as that of "a most clever man," who was "prudent in the military arts and long practiced in war."[96]

A more careful reading of the contemporary accounts of Cascina indicates, however, that Hawkwood's actions were not entirely blameless. If, as all writers agree, the army was poorly disciplined and poorly coordinated in battle, the responsibility for this rests at least in part with Hawkwood, whose job as captain included handling such issues. Filippo Villani, for all his praise for Hawkwood, indicates that the captain made a tactical error. He points out—without emphasis or negative aside—that Hawkwood misjudged the distance between his camp at San Savino and the enemy at Cascina, thinking the dusty plain much shorter than it actually was. The mistake was a significant one. The heat on the day of the battle was intense, "burning the earth," in Villani's evocative phrase.[97] Hawkwood's men arrived at Cascina already tired and worn. It is telling that in the immediate aftermath of the battle, many of the soldiers rushed to the Arno to quench their thirst. Loaded with armor, a great number of them fell in and drowned.[98] Hawkwood had in essence committed at Cascina the same error he made in his first campaign, when he pushed his troops too far in the winter snows. Villani put it kindly when he said that Hawkwood had at Cascina put "too much faith in the youth and bravery of his Englishmen."[99]

## The Rise of Agnello and the End of the War

In practical terms, Hawkwood's defeat at Cascina left open the road to Pisa. The Florentine army advanced to the town walls and undertook the now familiar insults and taunts. The soldiers ran celebratory horse races; smiths minted mock Pisan coins showing John the Baptist (the patron saint of Florence) holding the chains of the gates of Pisa. Responding directly to the earlier Pisan display, the Florentines hanged animals before the city gates. The Lucchese chronicler Sercambi said that they hanged two donkeys, two sheep, and a dog and placed a placard below them, which read "You come like sheep and dogs to assault our camp, and like sheep and dogs we treat you."[100] The Sienese chronicler Neri gave a different account of the placard, claiming that it contained the message "We come with donkeys, sheep and with dogs to gnaw at the bone!!"[101] He did not explain what the message meant.

After this, the Florentine offensive stalled. Galeotto Malatesta fell into a bitter dispute with Florentine officials over whether his troops deserved "double pay" for their victory. Florentine leaders denied his request, and Galeotto halted his army. Meanwhile, the German and English mercenaries in his band quarreled—the Germans were purportedly jealous of the elevated status and wealth of the English. The dispute culminated in a riot, which left several high-ranking soldiers dead, including Rudolf von Hapsburg.[102] The incident set off a feud between the two nationalities that continued beyond the Pisan war and would ultimately involve John Hawkwood. For the time being, the Florentines were forced to physically segregate the two brigades, damaging the efficacy of their army.

The calls for peace, which had persisted throughout the "tedious" war (as Villani called it), grew stronger. In Pisa, tensions erupted into rebellion. On 13 August 1364, Giovanni dell' Agnello, a prominent merchant, staged a coup, installing himself as ruler.[103] Hawkwood played a key role, the first but not the last time he would become involved in domestic upheaval in Tuscany. Hawkwood went where the money was. Just prior to seizing power, Agnello paid the Englishman and his brigade a sum of 30,000 florins to secure their loyalty. Hawkwood then entered the city and took up strategic places, in the piazza and the communal palace. He and his men watched as Agnello, with ostentatious ceremony, assumed the title of "doge for life." Hawkwood accompanied Agnello to the cathedral, where the transfer of power was formally made. The Englishman and his troops swore personal allegiance to the new ruler.[104]

Agnello promised to reduce taxes and uphold "reason and justice" and immediately removed Pisa from the war.[105] He signed a peace accord with Florence on 28 August 1364.[106] The agreement called for a return to the prewar territorial status quo, with the exception that the contested town of Pietrabuona, where the war began, was ceded to Florence. Pisa would allow Florentine merchandise to again move through its port and agreed to pay an indemnity of 100,000 florins over ten years, as well as 50,000 florins for the release of its hostages still held in Florence.[107] The deal was criticized in both cities. Many Florentines believed that the spoils were too meager. Carlo Strozzi, a chief proponent of the accord, had to be confined to his home until the furor in the city died down.[108]

Giovanni Morelli provided a succinct postscript to the conflict: "the war was bitter and very damaging, for us and for them."[109] The gravest damage was not to human life but to the finances of both cities. A contemporary Florentine source claimed that the city had spent more than 1.7 million florins, a staggering sum. A more modest modern estimate put the figure at 1 million florins.[110]

The chief beneficiaries of the great outflow of money were the mercenary soldiers. And despite their perfidy before the Florentine walls, the reputation of the men as fighters grew greatly, especially that of the English, which was already considerable before the war. Local writers openly credited the English with being the critical difference. When they fought for Pisa, Pisa held the upper hand; when they fought for Florence, Florence had the upper hand. Donato Velluti said straightforwardly that the hiring of the English meant victory in the war.[111] Like their counterparts in Lombardy, Tuscan writers marveled at the band's ferocity and appetite for war. Villani said that opponents had to remind themselves that the English were "merely men and not beasts."[112]

Conversely, the reputation of native fighting men suffered. Apart from the efforts of the local contingent that helped effect the enveloping maneuver at Cascina, the Florentines were generally dissatisfied with their own troops. They were particularly unhappy with the performance of Italian mercenary captains, who hardly seemed to measure up to their foreign counterparts. In their two years of fighting against Pisa, the Florentines employed six Italians as Captains of War. Other than Piero Farnese and Bonafazio di Lupo (Florence's first captain), they did not distinguish themselves to the locals. Rudolfo da Camerino and Galeotto Malatesta were described as "lazy," Ranuccio Farnese as "inexperienced," and Pandolfo Malatesta as "duplicitous."[113] At the end of the war, the Florentine government appointed Coppo de' Medici to head a commission to look into ways to reform the existing military system.[114]

Hawkwood's own performance as an independent commander showed that he still had much to learn, particularly about managing and coordinating his men. But Hawkwood already exhibited some of the traits of an outstanding military leader, including careful calculation, knowledge of local terrain, and courage in the face of adversity. For the time being, he remained with Pisa, in the service of the new doge. The Florentines meanwhile worked to protect themselves from their new neighbor and find ways to remove Hawkwood from Italy.

# CHAPTER FIVE

# *John Hawkwood of Pisa and Milan,*
# *1365–1372*

In these times, Charles, king of Bohemia, was emperor and Innocent
VI was pontiff. The latter sent into Italy, Egidio, cardinal of Spanish
birth ... who ... crushed and captured the Englishman John
Hawkwood ...        *Niccolò Machiavelli in Florentine Histories*

In this time flourished the renowned English knight, John
Hawkwood, who now against the church ... waged war and
performed many great wonders with his men.

Polychronicon Ranulphi Higden

The period following the Pisan-Florentine conflict was one of the most confused and complicated in the history of the mercenary companies. The peace
between the two cities coincided with the end of the prolonged war between the
papacy and Milan, leaving men-at-arms throughout Italy free to roam the countryside. English soldiers in Lombardy and Piedmont committed such excesses that
even the Black Prince back home denounced their deeds as "evil."[1] Pope Urban V
issued a general condemnation of the mercenaries as "pagans, and people not
redeemed by Christ's blood."[2] Italian states, however, exploited the turmoil and
used the mercenaries to jockey for position under the cover of peace.

John Hawkwood was one of the few foreign soldiers in Italy to remain in local
service. He stayed in Pisa after the war, helping the new doge, Giovanni dell'
Agnello, consolidate his hold on the city. Hawkwood's employment with Agnello
involved allegiance also to Bernabò Visconti of Milan, who supported the doge and
shouldered a portion of his military expenses.[3] Bernabò's assistance was, however,
covert, and its exact nature still eludes historians.

Hawkwood's employers were two of the most conspicuous despots of the age.
Agnello, grandiose in manner and style, dressed in gold cloth and held a golden

staff in his hand. At home in his palace, he sat by the window on golden cushions, so that, according to Filippo Villani, passersby could look on him "as if he were a sacred relic."[4] Bernabò, on the other hand, was known for his bellicose and cruel character. He supposedly favored his hunting dogs over his citizens and had a legendary sexual appetite, which produced thirty-six children by eighteen women.[5] Jacob Burckhardt described Bernabò—and the Visconti in general—as "the incarnation of the worst of the Roman emperors."[6]

Scholars have spoken of a "secret pact" by which Hawkwood acted as a kind of bodyguard to Agnello.[7] Agnello added a personal element to their association by making Hawkwood the godfather of his son Francesco, whom he gave the incongruous middle name "Aguto."[8] The pact has not survived, but its terms were almost surely those of a *condotta in aspetto*, a device that bound Hawkwood directly to his employer for a set fee but allowed him to pursue other possibilities when he was not immediately needed. This explains why Hawkwood appears at times to have followed his own agenda, acting more as independent marauder than as communal employee. It is, however, difficult to separate Hawkwood's motives from the broader political machinations of his employers. Bernabò in particular was a master of diplomatic manipulation and was widely accused of using Hawkwood and the "free" companies to continue his war against the pope by proxy. In truth all states were guilty; and when they were not, they still suspected one another. Thus even when he was acting in own interests, Hawkwood remained closely linked to his employers in the popular imagination. The Emperor Charles IV referred to him as "Aguto of Pisa," apparently unaware that the captain was in fact an Englishman.[9] But as we shall see, the English crown also played a direct role in Hawkwood's actions, as well as those of the English soldiers in Italy in general.

Hawkwood's own agenda involved seeking profits, supporting his fellow Englishmen, and wreaking vengeance on those who opposed him. He gained valuable military experience, fighting throughout northern and central Italy, though not always achieving success. With the fall from power of his mentor Agnello and the outbreak of open war between Milan and the pope in 1368, Hawkwood moved definitively into the employ of Bernabò Visconti, for whom he would win several important victories.

## The English versus the Germans

Outside Pisa and Milan, the first order of business was to try to remove John Hawkwood altogether from Italy. Pope Urban V continued his efforts, begun back in the spring of 1364, to recruit mercenaries for crusades in Asia Minor and

Spain. He envisioned sending them against the Turks, who had recently taken Adrianople and menaced the Byzantine capital at Constantinople.[10] The pontiff arranged for shipping through Venice and Genoa and offered the men plenary indulgence for their sins and absolution from debts owed to Jewish pawnbrokers.[11] He convinced the Holy Roman Emperor Charles IV to pledge financial support and appointed his legates Androin de La Roche and Gil Albornoz to take charge of the Italian operations.[12] Thomas Ufford, the son of the Earl of Suffolk, and William de la Pole, lord of Ashby, agreed to lead the Englishmen and traveled to Avignon to confer with the pope.[13]

The Florentines were lukewarm to the pope's plan but exceedingly eager to see Hawkwood leave Italy. They sent the ambassadors Doffo dei Bardi and Simone Simonctti (16 July 1365) to offer to pay his way to the Middle East. The embassy provides the first glimpse of the manner of diplomacy used by the Florentines in dealing with Hawkwood. The envoys were instructed to flatter the captain to his face and to fashion their proposal as a "courtesy" extended to him on account of his being "a rare friend and son" of the city of Florence. At the same time, however, they were to get Hawkwood to accept the "lowest sum possible" for the journey, by "reminding" him of the financial difficulties currently experienced by the city and the "great sacrifice" the offer entailed. "Tell him . . . how on account of recent wars and great expenses, we are very needy and much less potent than he might think."[14]

The choice of Doffo dei Bardi as one of the envoys is significant. Doffo was the son of Giovanni Bardi, founder of the great Bardi bank in England, the largest firm in that country. Doffo himself spent years in England working for the bank, where he came to know personally King Edward III, the firm's chief customer. This connection added a layer of prestige to Doffo's embassy, as well as the practical advantage that he likely communicated Florence's plans in English.[15]

Hawkwood appears to have entertained the notion of the crusade or at least made pretense that he did. But he ultimately declined. His former comrade Walter Leslie, captain of the Great Company back in the Avignon days, did take up the cross. He sailed with his brother Norman to Alexandria, where Norman most likely met his death.[16] Thomas Ufford went on crusade to Prussia; William de la Pole went only as far as Thebes and turned back.[17]

John Hawkwood remained in Italy and became involved in the bitter feud between English and German mercenaries that had erupted in the last days of the Pisan-Florentine war. A violent brawl broke out in the Florentine camp between the two nationalities in September resulting in the death of Rudolf von Hapsburg, which left bitter enmity. After Florence dismissed the army, the brigades went their separate ways: the English reconstituted the White Company, with Hugh de la Zouche in command and Andrew Belmont, Richard Romsey, Hugh Heton, Thomas Marshall, John Brice, and others serving as corporals.[18] The Germans created the Company of the Star, with Albert Sterz, recently departed from the English, and Hannekin Baumgarten as co-captains and Johann von Rietheim, Andreas Rod, Johann von Hapsburg, and most of the major German mercenaries in Italy as corporals.[19] Both companies took in reinforcements of Hungarian and Italian mercenaries and headed south from Florence, looting and pillaging along the way.[20] They faced each other in November 1364; the German band defeated the White Company.[21] By the summer of 1365 the two were in Umbria, near Perugia, poised to battle each other again.[22]

John Hawkwood rode with one hundred soldiers from Pisa toward the trouble spot. According to the standard account, he went to take over the leadership of the White Company at the request of Bernabò Visconti. Bernabò wished, in the guise of the English, to discomfit his longtime rival, the pope, who now employed the Germans. The interpretation is doubtful, however, since neither Bernabò nor any Italian ruler had the authority to insert his own man at the head of a mercenary company. The White Company would not in any case have accepted such intervention. Hawkwood's mission was one of relief on behalf of his English comrades, which coincidentally followed Bernabò's general antipapal policy.[23]

The White Company needed Hawkwood's help. It had fallen into dire straits. In January 1365 it had taken up service briefly with Pope Urban and Queen Johanna of Naples. But the sides quarreled, over pay and authority, and Urban dismissed the company and hired the Germans instead.[24] The pontiff succeeded in denying the band food and forage. The chronicler of Orvieto reported how by the summer of 1365 the formerly "very rich" company suffered from hunger and disease.[25]

Urban tried to forestall Hawkwood's march by offering him a bribe of 3,000 florins.[26] Hawkwood took the money but continued forward. The Florentines, keeping a close watch on Hawkwood, sent Doffo dei Bardi and Simone Simonetti with instructions "to draw out of Hawkwood his purpose, the condition of his company, how many men he has with him, and what they intend to do, whether they expect to get larger, and if so, with what men—in short, get from him everything that you think necessary and expedient for us to know."[27] Bardi and Simonetti were told to focus particular attention on Hawkwood's corporals. They were to take "careful note" of the language each spoke, the "general aspect and attitude" of each and, most important, whether any "might be induced to leave"

Hawkwood's band. This was, as we shall see, a favorite means by which to break up companies. The Florentines also sought information about Hawkwood from the German Company of the Star. They sent a separate embassy to Baumgarten and Sterz to ask about the "condition" of Hawkwood's band, whether they knew the Englishman's "intentions," and whether the brigade "was getting larger or staying the same."[28]

Hawkwood never reached his comrades. He made it as far as the eastern limit of Sienese territory. But before he could cross into Umbria, the Company of the Star attacked the White Company (22 July 1365) just outside Perugia, at San Mariano. The English fled to a local castle near Lake Trasimene, where, short of water and supplies, they surrendered, by means of a letter signed "your impoverished, imprisoned servants, the English."[29] The Germans took much of the English high command prisoner, including Andrew Belmont and John Brice, and placed them in jail in Perugia.[30] The captain of the company, Hugh de la Zouche, did not, as some assert, die from the wounds he suffered on the battlefield. He was captured, made full recovery, and emerged to fight again.[31] The Perugian chronicler Del Graziani claimed that there were 1,600 English captives; the Sienese and Orvietan chroniclers give more modest figures of 500 and 200 captives, respectively. Most of the prisoners were freed within a week, but the members of the English high command remained locked away for much longer. Hugh de la Zouche languished in jail for nearly four years, until 1369. The Perugians ignored all pleas for his release, including one from the pope in September 1368.[32] Perugian fiscal records indicate that at least he was treated well. He was served wine and meat during his stay.[33]

In his *Florentine Histories*, Niccolò Machiavelli claimed that Hawkwood himself was "crushed and captured" in the encounter—an assertion that has found its way into numerous modern works.[34] But Machiavelli, who despised mercenaries, foreign ones above all, is guilty of wishful thinking. The documents make clear that Hawkwood was not at the battle. The Perugian chronicler Del Graziani explicitly identified the captives of San Mariano as the same men whom Baumgarten and Sterz had defeated back in November 1364. Hawkwood, then in Pisa, was not part of that group.[35]

The defeat at San Mariano was, however, a crushing blow to the White Company, which now ceased to exist as a distinct fighting force. Many of the defeated Englishmen streamed to Hawkwood's banner. Hawkwood emerged more surely as a leader of the English expatriate community in Italy, a mantle he willingly assumed. He played champion to the commanders held in Perugia and, as we shall see, worked to secure their release.

## All Sides against Hawkwood

The defeat of the White Company left Hawkwood isolated in Sienese territory, alone to face the Company of the Star. He had little choice but to run. The Perugians and the Sienese actively aided the Germans with men and supplies while working to deny Hawkwood the same. The two cities formed a joint army and sent it after him.[36]

The turn of events encouraged the Florentines to plot more aggressive ways of eliminating Hawkwood from the Italian scene. They now wrote to Gomes Albornoz, the head of papal forces, urging mutual action to effect Hawkwood's "confusion and destruction."[37] They suggested that the pope, the queen of Naples, the Sienese, and the Perugians actively support the Germans with money and troops. This was to be done "covertly, so that we will not be discovered." Once the Germans "destroyed" Hawkwood, the allies would then absorb the victors into their own armies, with the pope and the queen taking two-thirds and Florence, Perugia, and Siena taking the remaining third. Florence offered the plan as a means not only of defeating Hawkwood but also of taming the Germans and thereby solving the vexing problem of the marauding bands.[38]

The pope did not embrace the idea but instead continued to promote a crusade or, failing that, a pan-Italian league against the companies. The Florentines sent embassies to Avignon to discuss the matter, including one headed by Giovanni Boccaccio, who was instructed to offer five ships and five hundred *barbute* for the crusade.[39] But there was in fact little enthusiasm in Florence for the pope's plan. Officials doubted its efficacy and had concerns that a pan-Italian league might ultimately be used against Bernabò Visconti, the pope's traditional enemy, with whom Florence had no quarrel.[40] In a meeting of ambassadors on 17 October 1365, the Florentines expressed reservations about the usefulness of leagues in general. "It does not seem to us that the way to remove the companies from Italy is by hiring more of the same people who are currently molesting us, to add, as it were, a barbarian force to that which we already have. The course of action that seems most effective to us is to send them away with money."[41] The statement, articulated by the envoys Piero di Filippo degli Albizzi and Michele di Vanni di Ser Lotto, constitutes not only a rebuttal of the papal scheme but a rationale for the long-standing policy of paying off marauding companies. That the statement came from Florence, one of the few states wealthy enough to consistently make such payments to mercenaries, is perhaps not surprising.

In the meantime, Hawkwood, with all of Tuscany except Pisa arrayed against him, worked to extricate himself from Sienese territory. The joint Sienese-Perugian army chased him through the Val d'Orcia in the southeastern part of the Sienese state, past San Quirico along the famous medieval highway the Via Fran-cigena. Hawkwood evaded the enemy by moving west into the difficult but lightly defended passes of the Maremma, a region of marshy land and malarial insects.[42] It was Hawkwood's first journey through a zone that he would traverse many times in his career. Hawkwood then headed north toward Pisa. Reports indicate that he received reinforcements of men, including Englishmen, from as far away as France.

The Company of the Star picked up the pursuit, following Hawkwood north beyond Sienese territory.[43] The chase proceeded past the outskirts of Florentine territory. Florence sent envoys to Baumgarten and Sterz offering them 300–500 florins to avoid local roads. The messengers also pressed the Germans for informa-tion regarding Hawkwood.[44] The two companies rode west and north to Lucca and then toward Sarzana, where Tuscany gives way to Liguria.

At this point, Ambrogio Visconti, the twenty-one-year-old bastard son of Ber-nabò Visconti, joined Hawkwood's brigade. Ambrogio had fought against Hawk-wood as a corporal in Konrad von Landau's army in Lombardy back in 1362. He now brought reinforcements of men and provisions, including contingents of crossbowmen and infantrymen. The band took the name the Company of Saint George, in honor of the patron saint of warriors and Ambrogio's recently de-ceased great-uncle Lodrisio, who had led a band with the same name twenty-five years earlier.[45]

## The Company of Saint George

The alliance with Ambrogio Visconti gave Hawkwood's actions a more dis-tinctly political coloring. The Company of Saint George now appeared an overt instrument of Milanese policy. This has, at least, been the view taken by most modern scholars.[46] Even the author of the *Storia di Milano*, more sensitive than most to the Milanese point of view, called the Company of Saint George "an intelligent attempt" by Bernabò to manipulate the situation and damage his enemies.[47] But a case can also be made that Bernabò acted in self-defense. By advancing to Sarzana, the German Company of the Star threatened to transgress a long-established boundary at which Bernabò had, according to a treaty of 1353, agreed to limit his hegemonic policies. Given the German band's association with the pope and the help it received from the Tuscan cities, Bernabò had reason to feel threatened. The situation was exceedingly complicated and exemplifies the politically charged nature of the so-called free companies. Florentine policy reflects an intricate tangle of considerations and motives at play. The city had little love for the German mercenaries it was now supporting. But the Florentines knew that to eliminate Hawkwood was to weaken their main rival, Pisa. This had to be done, however, without alienating Bernabò Visconti, who was not an enemy, and without seeming to favor the pope, who was a traditional ally.

The combined force of Hawkwood and Visconti slowed the impetus of the German Company of the Star. The two sides opened negotiations near Sarzana. Hawkwood took the lead for the English; Albert Sterz, his former comrade, fluent in the English language, served as chief spokesman for the Germans. Hawkwood began by demanding the release of all English prisoners still held in Perugia. Sterz and the Germans flatly refused. Several tense days passed. Dissension arose in the German camp. Sterz wished to continue negotiating, but Hannekin Baumgarten did not. The two men quarreled; Baumgarten accused Sterz of being too close to the enemy and of not having pursued his former mates energetically enough when they were in Sienese territory.[48]

While Sterz and Baumgarten argued, the Company of Saint George enhanced its bargaining power by taking in more troops. Italian soldiers from the old Company of the Hat joined the band, as did contingents of English and Hungarian soldiers. Italian political exiles also entered the company, most notably the powerful Florentine expatriate Giovanni d'Azzo degli Ubaldini, an excellent soldier, who would forge a close relationship with John Hawkwood.[49] Ubaldini's lands near Faenza lay at the entryway into Tuscany from the Romagna, and thus he was a valuable ally.

The new recruits transformed the band into what one scholar has called the "most colossal that had ever formed in the garden of the empire."[50] It now consisted of 43 corporals and approximately 7,000 horses, more than twice the size of the White Company when it first came to Italy. Interestingly, the band's basic structure, 163 horses per corporal, closely approximated that of the original White Company (167 horses per corporal).

The Company of the Star meanwhile disintegrated. Albert Sterz, his credibility lost, left the band and took up employment with Bernabò's brother, Galeazzo Visconti, lord of Pavia. The rest of the company scattered in various directions. Many, including Baumgarten, went south to plunder Sienese territory.[51]

The Company of Saint George also turned toward Tuscany. Whatever larger political motives it may have had, it is clear that Hawkwood now intended to gain revenge on those who had previously opposed him. He and Ambrogio arrived in the region in late September 1365 and remained for six months.

The Florentines, fearing Ubaldini as much as Hawkwood, immediately sent ambassadors to the company. Their embassy was again led by Doffo dei Bardi, who employed the same obsequious manner he had used earlier. He met Hawkwood and the band in Pisan territory. He spoke first with Hawkwood and told him of the "high esteem" Florence had for him and reminded him of the "many favors" the city had done on his behalf. Doffo claimed credit for helping to enlarge Hawkwood's band by releasing from Florentine service Hungarian soldiers, who took service with him. Bardi told Hawkwood that Florence did this "despite the fact that we knew how dangerous the growth of a company can be for us." Doffo spoke next with Ambrogio Visconti. He stressed "the singular friendship and peace that existed between his father and our commune" and urged him to maintain that relationship.[52] At the same time, the Florentines also sent ambassadors to Hannekin Baumgarten for information that might be used to break up the band. They asked about its size and composition, the languages the corporals spoke, and any other useful information that Baumgarten, "if he was so inclined," could give them.[53]

Hawkwood and Ambrogio paid little attention to Bardi's entreaties and pressured Florence by moving closer to its territory. The Florentines dispatched Bardi again, but this time to discuss money: specifically how much of it Hawkwood and Visconti wanted to avoid Florentine lands. Doffo was instructed to begin by claiming penury. "Tell Hawkwood how much fatigued we are by war and how through war we have extended ourselves beyond our means so much so that now even a small sum is impossible to pay." Doffo was then to offer the band a "gift" of 5,000 florins, "betokening the honor and benevolence that we bear the English."[54] He was authorized to increase the amount by 2,000 florins if Hawkwood remained dissatisfied, but he was not to speak openly of this. Doffo was permitted, however, to promise freely the use of guides through Florentine territory and provisions from local merchants at a fair price. In return he was to extract from the company a pledge that the band would not oppose or damage for five years "local towns, forts, walled territories and all Florentine territories" including those of the allied cities Pistoia, San Miniato, Volterra and Arezzo. Doffo insisted that Hawkwood, Visconti and all their corporals swear "with oaths and seals" to uphold the terms of the contract, even if the company should later change its captain or name—a ruse often used by bands to evade their obligations.

Negotiations lasted for several days. It is significant that although the talks took place in Pisan territory, Hawkwood, who claimed to be a "free"captain, did not make any monetary demands on that city. Disagreement arose not over money but over the length of the pact. The company would agree to respect Florentine territory for four years, not five, and insisted that Florence agree not to send troops to assist neighboring cities. The latter is proof that the band intended to do further harm to Tuscany and did not wish to be impeded. But Florence had already promised its neighbors, notably the Sienese, reinforcements in the case of mercenary attack.

The two sides concluded a pact on 4 October 1365. The band received 6,000 florins in bribe money—1,000 more than the initial offer but 1,000 less than Bardi's maximum. It was also allowed guides to lead it through local territory and provisions at a fair price. In return, company agreed not to return to Florentine territory for four years.[55] Unable to renege on its outstanding obligations to send soldiers to its neighbors, Florence promised to send only small contingents with the explicit understanding that they could not be used directly to fight the company.

The Company of Saint George now advanced toward Siena. Not only did Hawkwood have his own score to settle with the city, but so too did those soldiers who had joined the band from the Company of the Hat, which had been defeated by the Sienese back in 1363. The band entered local territory northeast of the city, by way of the Via Francigena, and, eschewing negotiations, proceeded on a circular tour of destruction, burning and looting along a broad arc, from the monastery of San Galgano up north, south to Roccastrada, then west to Buonconvento, then northeast to Berardenga and finally to Badia a Isola.[56] Sienese officials compared the company to "a snake which hides in the grass and belches poisonous liquid." Unable to make an accord with the company, officials attempted to raise an army. They contacted Hannekin Baumgarten, but he was not interested. They wrote to Doge Agnello, who disingenuously expressed "shock and regret" but did nothing.[57] They appealed to the Florentines, who sent a brigade of men, but, because of its agreement with the company, with instructions that the soldiers could be used only for defensive purposes. They urged the Sienese to work for a negotiated settlement.[58]

Hawkwood and Visconti plundered Sienese territory for two and a half months before retreating through the Valdelsa toward Pisa in early December.[59] The Sienese chronicler proudly claimed that Hawkwood was forced out by a "well-ordered and spirited" army composed mostly of citizen recruits. It is more likely, however, that the company left of its own accord, with the approach of winter. On the way north, it damaged Florentine territory, drawing bitter complaints of betrayal from officials there.[60] As it approached Pisan territory, Doge Agnello wrote to Siena requesting military help, a sham intended to distance himself from the band's actions.[61]

At this point it is worth pointing out the difference between the Sienese and Florentine strategies in dealing with Hawkwood. Florence consistently used the same ambassador, Doffo dei Bardi, to handle negotiations. Doffo, as we have seen, spent much of his career in England, in the highest circles, and was familiar with the English language and customs. The Sienese, on the other hand, had no coherent strategy. The city sent a variety of ambassadors, none of especial skill or prestige and none who knew English. Whereas the Florentines were keenly aware of Hawkwood's background, the Sienese, despite their many encounters with him, had little understanding of him. The local chronicler Donato di Neri believed that Hawkwood was in fact a German and referred to him now as "Giovanni Agud, tedesco."[62]

From Pisa, the company continued north, through Lucchese territory to La Spezia (16 December) and then Genoa, ravaging the Riviera de Levante. The passage to Liguria constituted an overtly political act—a pro-Milanese, antipapal act.[63] Genoa had long been a focal point of contention between the pope and Milan. The city served as a nexus through which the pontiff maintained the lines of communication between Avignon and the papal states, and it had recently fought for the papacy in its recent war against the Visconti. The Visconti coveted Genoa for its strategic value and had briefly held it in 1353. In 1363, there was an uprising in city, which both sides had tried to manipulate.[64] The arrival of the Company of Saint George in the winter of 1365/66 touched off new revolts. Ambrogio Visconti actively aided the rebels. He penetrated as far as the town walls twice, in late January and late February 1366, but was repelled each time by a Genoese force.

The raid on Genoa exacerbated the already deteriorating relations between the pope and Milan.[65] Interestingly, the Genoese chronicler Giorgio Stella notes only the presence of Ambrogio—"the natural son of Bernabò," as he called him[66]— before the town walls, not that of Hawkwood. It may be that the Genoese writer, convinced that the band was an instrument of Bernabò's policy, thought of Ambrogio as the only relevant party. But it may also have been the case that Hawkwood detached himself from the band. Stella estimated the company at 5,000 horses, substantially smaller than the 7,000 horses it purportedly had in Tuscany. While Hawkwood clearly advanced with the company as it initially rode toward Genoa, letters in the Sienese and Vatican archives suggest that Hawkwood returned south as early as January to resume harassing anew the city of Siena. Ambrogio did not quit Genoa until March, after which he also descended on Siena. In this instance, the company appears to have been a double-headed monster.

Hawkwood's attack on Siena was his third in less than nine months. He brought only a portion of the English brigade he had originally led north.[67] William Boson and a band of men broke off at Genoa, formed their own company (the Company of Genoa), and went to fight in Piedmont. Hawkwood replaced them with the Germans Albert Sterz and Johann von Hapsburg, who had been in Umbria but had outstanding claims against Siena.[68] Ambrogio Visconti and the rest of the Company of Saint George arrived later.[69]

"The band did great damage," wrote the Sienese chronicler, "burning, destroy-ing and robbing around Siena for twenty miles."[70] On 21 April 1366 the sides reached an accord whereby Siena agreed to pay a bribe of 10,500 florins in return for a promise by the company to leave Sienese territory. Officials also granted additional payments or "gifts" to "honor" the company, including 1,000 florins' worth of wax and sweetmeats and a new suit of armor for Johann von Hapsburg.[71] Sienese authorities unwisely allowed some of Hawkwood's men into the city to collect their pay. The result was a wild brawl. According to the Sienese account, Hawkwood's soldiers misbehaved, taking hostages, including the ambassadors who arranged the accord. Bolognese ambassadors (stationed in the city), on the other hand, claimed that the Sienese themselves provoked the melee by pay-ing less than they had promised and by trying to poison the men with tainted food.[72] Whatever the truth, the episode strengthened Hawkwood's grudge against the city.

Pope Urban, exasperated by the activities of the Company of Saint George and the mercenary companies in general, issued his strongest condemnation to date.[73] On 13 April 1366 he promulgated the bull *Clamat ad nos*, which excommunicated all the mercenary bands operating in Europe as well as those who employed or assisted them.[74] "The miserable multitude of orphans and others robbed and despoiled call out," wrote the pope, "as do the violated and burnt churches and ruined monasteries, as well as the noble and the plebs, the rich and the poor."[75] The pope gave the bands a month to disband and called on all employers to cancel their contracts with them.

The pope also increased his efforts to create a pan-Italian league against the mercenaries. His vigorous diplomacy succeeded on 19 September 1366 in convinc-ing Siena, Perugia, Pisa, Florence, Arezzo, Cortona, and the queen of Naples to join. Urban invited Bernabò Visconti to participate, but the Milanese ruler knew that the pope's efforts were really meant to isolate him. He sent pleasant words through his diplomats but did not join.[76] The league called for a common army of 3,000 horses and 3,000 infantry, with 1,500 crossbowmen. The pope provided the largest share, 850 horses and infantrymen, and the little city of Cortona provided the smallest share, 15 horses and infantrymen.[77] Unfortunately, the contracting parties would agree only to oppose future bands: the major bands operating in Italy; Hawkwood, Ambrogio Visconti, Baumgarten, and Johann Hapsburg's bands were specifically excluded. The league expired quietly less than a year after it was inaugurated. It accomplished nothing.

John Hawkwood and Ambrogio Visconti meanwhile rode on. At the same time that the pope worked to arrange his antimercenary league, they ravaged his lands.[78] In June and July, they traveled through Umbria and the Marches, harassing Urbino, Gubbio, Orvieto, and numerous other towns in the papal states. To help with reconnaissance, Hawkwood added to his brigade the Umbrian captain Niccolò da Montefeltro, bastard son of the Count of Urbino. Niccolò was not the most successful of soldiers, but he knew Umbria well and helped Hawkwood traverse the region. He also served as Hawkwood's chancellor, conducting business for him with local towns. In late June, he went to Perugia to negotiate on Hawkwood's behalf for the release of the English hostages who remained in the city. The Perugians refused but, according to city budgets, paid Hawkwood 1,053 florins for unspecified reasons.[79] The band advanced as far south as the outskirts of Rome. The anonymous chronicler of Orvieto claimed that it contained twenty-five thousand horseman and infantry, but this is certainly an exaggeration.[80]

The impetus of the Company of Saint George was stopped not by force of arms, however, but by negotiation. Urban and Bernabò, who repeatedly exchanged embassies in the hope of reducing tensions, reached an accord in October 1366. Bernabò agreed to withdraw his son, who left the company at Orvieto and returned home to Milan.[81] The Company of Saint George, after nearly a year of activity, quietly passed out of existence.

John Hawkwood remained, however, in the field at Orvieto, with a now small company, consisting of only four corporals, two Englishmen, and two Hungarians. The English corporals were Hugh Heton and Thomas Marshal, both veterans of the White Company.

The band was attacked outside Orvieto by a larger papal army commanded by Ugolino de Montemartre. Montemartre defeated Hawkwood and took several Englishmen hostage, including Hugh Heton. The two sides signed an accord on 29 October 1366 by which Hawkwood and his company agreed not to oppose the church "in the manner of society or stipendiary" for one year and to move amicably away through church lands "at a pace of at least ten miles [sixteen kilometers] a day." Hawkwood ("Johannes Hauchowode anglicus") affixed his seal to the document, as did his four corporals, including Hugh Heton, who, contrary to the report of the local chronicler, appears to have been immediately released from prison.[82]

The precise nature of the deal with the church is unclear. Shortly after the accord, there were rumors that the pope, through his papal legate Gil Albornoz, then active in Umbria, had made a secret agreement with Hawkwood to attack Perugia and claim the independent city on behalf of the church.[83] Allegedly, Albornoz and three mysterious Englishmen from Hawkwood's brigade, known only as "Rubino, Rubelutio and Tubaro," intended to move first against nearby Assisi with five hundred horses and then raise a revolt in Perugia. They would be joined there by Albert Sterz, who had been hired the previous summer as captain of Perugian forces.

Modern scholars have yet to confirm or deny the conspiracy. Hawkwood had motive to attack Perugia, which continued to hold his English comrades hostage. The pro-Perugian historian Maria Pecugi Fop claimed that there was a plot; Francesco Filippini, biographer of Albornoz, says nothing of one. A Florentine diplomatic dispatch dated 10 November reveals that Albornoz intended to hire members of Hawkwood's brigade, but this was to be done in conjunction with Florence for the apparent purpose of breaking the band up and thus removing it as a threat.[84]

In any case, the suspicions set off a chain of events that brought about the demise of Hawkwood's longtime comrade Albert Sterz. The Perugians accused Sterz of complicity, seized him, and executed him on the chopping block in November 1366.[85] Curiously, they then let Andrew Belmont out of prison to re-place Sterz. The decision was a colossal mistake. Rather than perform his charge, Belmont did just what officials feared Sterz would do; he deserted and joined Hawkwood's band.[86] Belmont used the advances on salary given to him by the Perugians to buy arms and weapons, which he then brought to Hawkwood's camp in Pisa.[87] The two now prepared a violent offensive.

## The Revenge of the English

Hawkwood's actions over the next months proved his capacity for vengeance. Together with Belmont, he embarked on vindictive raids against the Perugians and Sienese. The men had no political agenda but intended only to punish those who had offended them: the Perugians for the long imprisonment of the English and the murder of Sterz, the Sienese for general treachery and monies still owed. Those mercenaries who had recently served under Albert Sterz joined in the enterprise. Niccolò da Montefeltro was again present for reconnaissance in the region.

Hawkwood and Belmont attacked Siena first. On 6 March 1367, they shattered a Sienese army at Montalcinello, in the southwest part of the Sienese state—a battle that purportedly left "many dead and wounded and many taken prisoner."[88] The prisoners included the Sienese captain of war Ugolino da Savignano and virtually all of the high command. Rather than make a truce, Hawkwood and Belmont followed up the victory by ravaging the countryside, inflicting damage so severe that officials were constrained to postpone normal state functions, includ-ing criminal proceedings and court cases.[89]

Hawkwood and Belmont advanced next on Perugia, which they attacked with similar fury. On 31 March 1367 they defeated the Perugian army at Ponte di San Giovanni, just outside the city. The battle lasted for three hours and has been described as "one of the bloodiest of fourteenth-century Italy"—with between 1,500 and 1,800 of the enemy killed.[90] The captives were so numerous that the Perugians had to borrow money from Venice and Florence to redeem them.[91] In addition, Hawkwood extracted a bribe of 4,000 florins, as well as 3,300 florins in *mendum* to pay for injured horses.[92] The Perugian chronicler claimed that so many public mills were burned that all local grain had to be ground in private houses.[93]

Hawkwood and Belmont then returned to Sienese territory, to collect the final installment of bribe money and to redeem prisoners, including Ugolino da Savignano. Hawkwood humiliated the city by requiring it to compensate him for those horses injured during his battle with Siena as well as those injured while fighting Perugia.[94] The latter was a penalty assessed on Siena for having sent troops to the Perugians to help them defend themselves. The papal legate Albornoz, pleased with the defeat of Perugia, agreed to return to Hawkwood and Belmont the rest of the English prisoners taken by Montemartre at Orvieto—who had apparently languished in jail. The deal may perhaps be evidence that Hawkwood and Albornoz did indeed have some sort of understanding.

The band moved back north toward Pisa. The Florentine envoy Doffo dei Bardi, who had made several embassies to Hawkwood while he was in Sienese and Perugian territory, gave the band a "gift" of 500 florins to avoid passing through Florentine territory.[95]

## The Return of the Pope and the Outbreak of War

Hawkwood arrived in Pisa in late April 1367. He came home to the news that Pope Urban V, after years of urging by Italian states, intended at last to return the papacy from Avignon to Rome. The news was greeted enthusiastically throughout the peninsula. The Florentine chancellor Coluccio Salutati wrote: "I will always be happy that this happened while I was alive."[96] Urban arrived in Genoa on 24 May 1367.[97] Doge Agnello hoped to greet the pope at his next stop, Livorno, and instructed Hawkwood to ride with him with a band of approximately a thousand horses. Agnello's intentions were unclear. Why bring John Hawkwood, who had been so closely associated with Ambrogio Visconti, the son of the pope's sworn enemy? Did Agnello intend to welcome Urban or intimidate him? The Pisan chronicler Ranieri Sardo claimed that Agnello sincerely wished to greet the pontiff. Modern scholars have, however, judged Agnello at the very least guilty of egregious naïveté.[98]

Pope Urban remained on his ship at Livorno and refused go ashore and meet with Agnello and Hawkwood.[99] He eventually granted Agnello a personal audience, but only with the stipulation that John Hawkwood and his military entourage remain behind on the shore.[100] Urban then sailed on, stopping briefly at the Sienese port of Talamone and then going on to his temporary court at Viterbo.

The pope's motives soon became more clear. Shortly after reaching Viterbo, Urban concluded a new league against the mercenary bands (21 July 1367). It was a thinly disguised anti-Visconti alliance.[101] He appealed first to Milan's neighbors—Mantua, Ferrara, and Padua, which were directly threatened by Visconti expansionist policies, and then to those who had suffered at the hands of the Company of Saint George—Perugia, Siena, Cortona, and Queen Johanna of Naples.[102] The Holy Roman Emperor Charles IV, who had signaled his willingness to come to Italy to take on the mercenaries back in August 1366, now assumed the title of "protector of the church" and agreed to journey to Italy in support of Urban.[103]

The cold war fought by mercenary proxies had turned very warm. Bernabò Visconti responded by unleashing his son Ambrogio on the pope. Ambrogio rode south from Milan toward the papal states. He sacked the city of Urbino and then descended into the Kingdom of Naples. His impetus was, however, stopped by a papal army commanded by Gomes Albornoz, which defeated Ambrogio outside the city of Otranto in late September/early October 1367. A Sienese ambassador stationed in Rome claimed that Ambrogio had been killed along with all his men.[104] But Ambrogio in fact survived and was imprisoned in a local castle for the next four years. Three hundred of his men were put to death on the scaffold.[105]

## War along the Po River

Hawkwood took no part in Ambrogio's actions. He most likely remained in Pisa, though his exact whereabouts are unclear. He reemerges in the spring of 1368, when the war between the pope and Milan broke out in earnest.[106] On 5 April, Bernabò Visconti, along with his allies Agnello of Pisa and Cansignore della Scala of Verona, launched a preemptive strike against Mantua. Hawkwood rode to Lombardy at the head of a Pisan contingent of forty lances (map 3).[107]

For the first time, Hawkwood's service to Milan was open and unambiguous. His employment must, however, be understood in terms of English foreign policy. The Milanese cause now had a distinctly English dimension to it. King Edward III's relations with Urban V had become strained in recent years. Dissension arose initially over the Flemish succession and competing efforts by the French and English royal houses to gain the hand of the rich heiress of Burgundy, Margaret de Male. This was followed by attempts on Edward's part to arrange a marriage alliance directly with Bernabò Visconti, the pontiff's enemy. Edward pressured Urban by instructing Hawkwood and English mercenaries in Italy to support Bernabò. We know of this from a letter written by Bernabò to Edward in February 1367, thanking the English king for his assistance. It may well have been this English connection that contributed to the pope's decision to stay aboard his ship in late May 1367, while Hawkwood waited ashore. That same month Edward concluded a marriage agreement with Visconti, matching his son Lionel, Duke of Clarence, with Bernabò's niece, Violante. Humphrey Bohun, son of William Bohun, under whom Hawkwood probably began his military career, played a critical role as intermediary. Bohun came to Italy to help arrange the union.[108]

The now overt Anglo-Milanese alliance undoubtedly made service to the Visconti attractive to Hawkwood. Pope Urban tried to forestall Hawkwood's participation, as well as that of other English soldiers, by appealing directly to Edward. He wrote a series of letters, imploring the king to prohibit his men from serving Milan. The pontiff meanwhile excommunicated the Visconti, a now familiar sentence, and granted plenary indulgence to those who fought against him.[109]

By April 1368 the war was in full swing. The pope's ally, Niccolò d'Este, the lord of Ferrara, countered Bernabò's attack on Mantua with a strike against Visconti's interest at Parma. Hawkwood took up position not far from Mantua, at the town of Luzzaria, near the Po River. Unable to seize Mantua, Bernabò focused on pressuring the city by controlling access to it along the Po and Mincio rivers. He set up camp just north of Hawkwood, along the Po at Guastalla, from where he dispensed supplies. He erected two bastions: at Burgoforte, an entryway to Mantua four miles due south of the city on the Po River; and at Governolo, a town at the confluence of the Po and Mincio rivers. The bastion at Burgoforte was particularly formidable, staffed by 200 knights and 1,200 foot soldiers and equipped with a rock-throwing trebuchet that Bernabò nicknamed "Troy."[110] Bernabò conducted raids along the Po, burning farms and mills on the banks of the river (map 4).[111]

Hawkwood met substantial resistance at Luzzaria from the local citizenry, who attacked his band. He moved north, across the Po, toward Bernabo's bastion at Burgoforte. He made his camp about a mile or so away.[112] The Mantuan army meanwhile tried to lure him into a trap. A group of a hundred or so knights and infantrymen hid in the underbrush, while a small brigade of Hungarian mercenaries revealed themselves, hoping to induce Hawkwood and his men to chase them. Hawkwood did just that, pursuing them all the way to the gates of Mantua, to the *porta cerese* on the south side of the city, where the rest of the Mantuan army lay hidden. The ruse might have worked, except that overeager infantrymen left their hiding place too early and engaged Hawkwood's troop. Hawkwood and his men dismounted from their horses and battled the enemy back to the *porta cerese*. Hawkwood's brigade lost six knights, one of whom, according to an ambassadorial dispatch, was purportedly a "relative" of his. The letter does not say who the relative was.[113] Hawkwood retreated from the gates of Mantua, taking a circuitous route—south to the town of Serraglio, then southeast toward Burgoforte, then east to San Niccolò on the Po, then due west to Scorzarolo (just two miles from the enemy positions at Frasenelli)—to evade the enemy. He rode to Bernabò's camp at Guastalla, where he received an infusion of supplies.[114]

At this point (1 May 1368), a violent brawl broke out among German and Italian mercenaries garrisoning the bastion at Burgoforte. The feud was apparently long standing, dating from an earlier dispute at Parma.[115] Bernabò sent Hawkwood to calm the situation and reinforce the bastion. The Englishman appears to have restored order, but we know none of the details of how he did this.[116]

In the meantime, Pope Urban prepared a major assault. He amassed his forces at Ficarolo, a small town on the Po west of Mantua, near the allied city of Ferrara. Emperor Charles IV arrived at the town on 23 May 1368. The conjunction of his army with that of the pope produced a large multinational force, described by the Milanese diarist Corio as consisting of "more than 20,000 troops" from "almost every Christian nation."[117] The anonymous author of the *Annales Mediolanenses* claimed that there were 50,000 horses, including some Muslim Turks.[118] The actual numbers are not known, though sources agree that the army was very large.

Francis Petrarch provides a compelling account of the realities of the military buildup along the Po River. Petrarch had met with Charles near Pavia when the emperor first arrived in Italy. In order to return to his home in Padua, Petrarch needed to travel on the Po River through the war zone. He recounted his experience in one of his *epistolae seniles*. "We could not find at any price a boat that would venture the perilous journey . . . [and] after more than a full month of hunting I finally found a captain less timorous than the rest. We met everywhere with armed fleets on the water and embattled soldiers on the banks. Our sailors and servants trembled and turned pale." But the soldiers recognized Petrarch as he passed, and rather than oppose him, they sent gifts of wine and food. "I was delayed not by the ferocity of the soldiers, but by their generosity."[119]

## An English Wedding, a Feast, and a Fall

On the last day of May, the papal-imperial army launched an attack from Ficarolo against Visconti positions west of Mantua at the town of Ostiglia. The

Milanese successfully resisted. Charles then advanced on Bernabò's bastions at Governolo and Burgoforte

What happened next was, in the words of a modern scholar, "a very strange thing."[120] With the enemy moving toward his bastions, Bernabò Visconti summarily left the battlefield and returned home to Milan to attend the wedding of his niece Violante. Bernabò brought with him a brigade of English troops to escort the groom, Lionel, through Milanese territory. Although the scanty sources do not give the names of the soldiers in the brigade, John Hawkwood, by now Bernabò's most distinguished English captain, was surely one of them.

Bernabò's decision was not so "strange" as it seemed. He brought only a small contingent of men with him and left the bastions at Burgoforte and Governolo well protected and garrisoned. They could be taken only by a lengthy siege. Moreover, Charles IV's army, though large, was composed overwhelmingly of cavalry and was thus ill suited to siege warfare. Bernabò's absence at the head of his army was not unusual. Though the Milanese ruler often participated in his own wars, he typically did not lead his army into battle.

Bernabò and his brigade of Englishmen met up with the Duke of Clarence at Pavia, the home of the bride's father, Galeazzo Visconti. They then rode together toward Milan, where the wedding was to take place. The procession was a colorful one; brightly dressed maidens and knights moved forward atop caparisoned horses. Lionel's entourage included Amadeus of Savoy and his favorite English mercenary, Richard Musard, who had served as the duke's guides through the Alps; the Flemish chronicler Jean Froissart, who provided songs along the way; the English knight (and friend of Froissart's) Edward Despenser; his son, Hugh; and possibly Geoffrey Chaucer, of whom the duke was an early patron.[121]

The wedding took place at the Basilica of Santa Maria Maggiore in Milan on 5 June 1368. It was followed by a magnificent reception, "one of the great moments in medieval culinary history," with a menu that consisted of thirty courses, purportedly enough "to feed 10,000 people."[122] The first course included gilded suckling pig and crabs, followed by roasted hare and pike; then gilded calf and trout; then duck, heron, carp, and capons (in garlic and vinegar sauce). Francis Petrarch attended the affair as a guest of Galeazzo Visconti.

Unfortunately, Lionel died five months after the wedding, on 17 October 1368.[123] The English suspected treachery and refused to give back Violante's dowry. Edward Despenser and a group of English knights who had come to Italy with Lionel declared war on Galeazzo Visconti.[124] They linked up with William Boson and the English soldiers of the Society of Genoa, who been in northern Italy since leaving the Company of Saint George back in 1366.

John Hawkwood did not involve himself in the controversy but returned to

Burgoforte to reinforce Bernabò's army there. Charles IV had been unable to dislodge the Milanese garrison and now instructed his engineers to rupture an embankment of the Po River, swelled by spring rains, to send the water on Bernabò's men. Hawkwood purportedly saved the day by anticipating the enemy maneuver and rupturing the embankment farther upstream, thus sending the waters back on the enemy, a ruse judged "brilliant" by modern historians.[125] The reality, however, is that Charles's men miscalculated and ruptured the embankment in the wrong place, inadvertently forcing the water back on themselves.[126]

The war devolved into a stalemate, and the two sides agreed in August 1368 to a truce.[127] Charles IV left behind the burned farms and flooded fields of Lombardy and advanced south for an eventual rendezvous with the pope in Rome. His path lay through Tuscany, where local cities feared that his presence would destabilize the region. As Holy Roman Emperor, Charles possessed legal rights to bestow titles and confirm offices. His last trip to Tuscany, in 1355, set off revolts, including one that toppled a Sienese government that had been in power for nearly eighty years. A similar reaction occurred this time. Charles's arrival in Lucca in September 1368 touched off a popular reaction both in that city and in Pisa. The Lucchese sought imperial approval for their claims to independence from Pisa; Doge Agnello wanted official recognition for his regime. According to the Lucchese chronicler Giovanni Sercambi, Agnello conducted the talks at the same time that he secretly plotted to murder Charles. Unfortunately for Agnello, it was he who emerged the loser. As he plotted strategy at the church of San Michele in Pisa, Agnello strayed out on to the portico of the cloister to read a letter given him by Charles's representative Antonio da Ghivizzano. The structure suddenly collapsed, sending Agnello and several of his close advisers hurtling to the ground. Agnello broke his leg, not a serious injury but enough to incapacitate him at a critical moment and give impetus to his political opponents in the city. Charles sided with Agnello's foes and formally deposed the doge, a sentence that, as emperor, he had a legal right to impose.[128] Agnello was forced into exile. Piero Gambacorta took over Pisa.

Agnello's demise occurred too rapidly for any effective resistance. Hawkwood could do little for his former mentor. He remained up north, garrisoning Visconti forts in Lombardy, where an uneasy truce had taken effect.[129] It is likely that Bernabò dissuaded Hawkwood from any action—if the captain was indeed so inclined—to maintain the truce.

## War in Umbria

Bernabò bided his time and waited for an opportunity. It came in Umbria, where a dispute between Perugia and neighboring Città di Castello developed into a larger conflict between Perugia and the church. Bernabò at first surreptitiously sent money to Perugia and then sent John Hawkwood. Visconti took care, however, to dispatch Hawkwood only after signing a league against mercenaries, thus deflecting responsibility from himself.[130] As Hawkwood advanced south, Bernabò tried to pass off his march as that of a free company. He even went so far as to write to Pope Urban to warn him of Hawkwood, as well as the "menaces" of other marauding companies. The sham was nevertheless readily apparent. A Sienese ambassador spotted Bernabò's representatives with Hawkwood as he rode toward Umbria and reported that they made a deal for service with him on behalf of Perugia.[131]

Hawkwood arrived in Perugia in February 1369 and took charge of the army alongside the local captain, Dinolus Bindi Monaldi.[132] Their force consisted of two thousand horsemen and included William Boson and members of the erstwhile Company of Genoa and numerous Perugian exiles.[133] They encountered the papal army on 12 June 1369 near Ponte di San Giovanni, the scene of Hawkwood's decisive victory over the Perugians two years earlier. This time, however, the opposition forces, led by the German captains Johann Flach von Rieschach and Johann von Rietheim, got the upper hand, forcing Hawkwood and his army to flee.

Three days later the two sides met again, a mile from the western gate of the city of Arezzo. Hawkwood had the larger army, but as he advanced to meet the enemy, the citizens of Arezzo rapidly assembled a force and sent it against him. For the first and perhaps only time in his career, Hawkwood was completely surprised and unprepared. He had miscalculated the intentions of the Aretines, who had only days earlier helped him escape. He soon found himself surrounded; he gave battle but was quickly forced to surrender. He was taken prisoner along with his co-captain, Monaldi.[134] "They made a terrible fight," wrote the Aretine chronicler Bartolomeo Gorello, "in which . . . many were killed, and almost all of the remaining men were taken captive, including the captain, John Hawkwood [Johannes Haud]."[135]

Ristoro di Simonciono, the chancellor of Arezzo, reported the victory in separate letters to Charles IV and Pope Urban. "The Holy Mother Church exalts and all its devoted followers celebrate such a great victory."[136] Gorello attributed the victory to the intervention of Saint Vito, on whose day it occurred.[137] The emperor Charles himself wrote back home that "the enemy had been destroyed." His chronicler, Benesch Krabice, exaggerated the event into a slaughter of epic proportions.[138] The captain Rietheim was knighted after the battle.[139]

Hawkwood remained in captivity for two months.[140] We know none of the particulars of his detention. The incident should not be viewed as unduly noteworthy. Captains in Italy were routinely captured in battle. The Italian Galeotto Malatesta, who defeated Hawkwood at the first battle of Cascina in 1364, was taken three times. Luchino dal Verme—probably the most esteemed soldier of the day—was made prisoner several times.

Hawkwood returned to the field in August 1369. He traveled north to Lombardy to confer with Bernabò Visconti. A Sienese ambassador reported that he had heard "from a reliable witness" that Hawkwood was preparing "to ride to Rome through the Romagna" to enact revenge on the pope.[141] This is indeed what happened. Hawkwood unleashed a frightening assault, described in detail by the Florentine diarist Donato Velluti.[142] Hawkwood rode to the doors of the papal palaces at Montefiascone and Viterbo. His archers sent volleys of arrows directly into the pope's residence in Montefiascone, and his infantry soldiers burned the fields and vineyards at Viterbo. Pope Urban bitterly condemned the raids and censured the Perugians for having been the original cause of them. Emperor Charles wrote to Galeazzo Visconti pleading with him to convince Bernabò to call back "the abominable Satanic society of English" and their "captain who is called John Hawkwood [Iohannes de Acuto]." Urban even tried to revive the idea of a crusade and offered to absolve Hawkwood and his men from their contracts if they took up the cross. Hawkwood refused.

Hawkwood's bold initiative did not, however, turn the tide of the war. With the approach of winter, Hawkwood withdrew from the papal states and went back up north. Charles IV, weary of his sojourn in Italy, began his journey back home to Prague.

## War against Florence and Vindication at Cascina

Bernabò shifted his attention from Umbria to Tuscany. This time he exploited growing tensions between Florence and San Miniato al Tedesco, an allied town located on a strategically important road midway between Pisa and Florence. San Miniato had used the confusion of Charles IV's entry into the region in the summer of 1368 to cast out Florentine officials and offer itself to Pisa and Doge Giovanni dell' Agnello.[143] The sudden collapse of Agnello's government prevented this from happening. But Bernabò kept the cause alive; Florentine officials accused him of secretly aiding the rebels. Suspicions grew over the summer of 1369.[144] Donato Velluti accused Bernabò of hatching a vast scheme whereby he would first relieve San Miniato, then seize Lucca and Pisa, reinstall Agnello in power, and finally subdue Florence by destroying the roads to the city through the Mugello and to Pisa, in effect cutting off Florence's trade and food supply and causing starvation of the populace.[145] "He acted," Velluti wrote, "like a faithless man and traitor, and like a person who believed that he would soon be lord of Florence and all of Tuscany."[146]

The situation reached a climax in the late fall of 1369, when Florentines began a siege of San Miniato. Bernabò sent Hawkwood to defend the town. Florence joined the pope's league against the Visconti (9 November), something it had heretofore avoided.[147]

Hawkwood arrived at San Miniato in late November.[148] His army now contained Johann Flach von Rieschach and Johann von Rietheim, the same German captains who had defeated and imprisoned him at Arezzo months earlier.[149] Bernabò hired them after they initiated a violent brawl in the streets of Lucca, which induced the pope to dismiss them.[150] Hawkwood's army also included the Lucchese exile Alderigo degli Antelminelli, whom, according to a Sienese ambassador stationed in Pisa, Bernabò wished to install as the ruler of Lucca.[151] Hawkwood and Antelminelli would forge a long-term and often problematic relationship. The Florentines countered Hawkwood by recruiting for their army "as many English as possible." They also tried to recruit Hawkwood himself and sent embassies induce him to leave Milanese service.[152] Hawkwood held firm.

Hawkwood advanced to San Miniato through Pisan territory, where his former allies did their best to make him uncomfortable, clearing the countryside of hay and animals and refusing him food and provisions. Pisan officials also hid all the boats along the Arno to prevent him from using the river to move on Lucca.[153] The Florentine army, commanded by the Italian captain Giovanni Malatacca, pursued Hawkwood. The two armies met in early December near Cascina, the scene of the Englishman's first defeat in 1364 as an independent captain.

Hawkwood triumphed this time at Cascina. The Florentine army initiated the encounter near the so-called Fosso Arnonico, a canal that served in those days to prevent the flooding of the plain between Pisa and Florence. As the enemy approached, Hawkwood retreated with the main body of troops, dismounted his cavalry, and placed some of his soldiers in hiding, preparing an ambush. The Florentines pursued, but as they maneuvered along the banks of the Arno, their horses sank in mud, made soft by recent rains. Hawkwood then executed a flanking maneuver and surrounded them. He captured much of the Florentine army, including the captain, Giovanni Malatacca; his subcommander, Giovanni Mangiadori; and the rest of the high command. The booty—including horses, mules, provisions, arms, and armor—was enormous and sold for great profit in Pisa. Hawkwood sent the banners of the Florentine army back to Bernabò Visconti as trophies of the victory.[154]

The second battle of Cascina was very different from the first. This time

Hawkwood took the defensive posture, whereas previously he had been the aggressor. His army was well coordinated, unlike the disjointed force of five years earlier; and he displayed a more nuanced knowledge of local terrain. Pisan and Florentine sources, however, differ widely in assessing credit and blame. The Pisan chronicler Sardo acknowledged Hawkwood's skill. He claimed that the Florentine army was "well ordered and well prepared" for the attack and that it initially took Hawkwood by surprise.[155] The Florentine writer Velluti, on the other hand, maintained that Florence's army was poorly organized and "very tired" from a long march. He blamed the Florentine captain, Malatacca, whom he characterized as a man so cowardly that he got drunk before the battle in order to summon his courage.[156] All sources agree, however, that the Florentine army was the larger of the two.

Hawkwood followed up his victory by riding to the Florentine town walls and mocking his opponent with the usual races and games. One of the merrymakers, Giovanni Pusterla, from a prominent Milanese family, was seized, however, by locals when he strayed too far from the rest of the army.[157]

Although Hawkwood had personally redeemed himself, the victory at Cascina produced little for the victors. The Florentines rebuilt their army, hiring the prominent German captains Konrad von Weitingen and Lutz von Landau, the Italian captain Rodolfo da Camerino, and several Englishmen including Hugh Despenser (Edward Despenser's son) and Richard Romsey.[158] The pope also sent reinforcements.[159]

Bernabò Visconti sent additional troops to Hawkwood. But the offensive lost its momentum, and Hawkwood and the Milanese army retreated. Soon after Hawkwood departed, the Florentines retook San Miniato, a victory won by bribing the local castellan to open the gates.

Hawkwood went back to Lombardy. Along the way, he rode through Pisan territory, looting the countryside, including a farm owned by the chronicler Ranieri Sardo. "They set fire to the woodwork," wrote Sardo, "and burned a great deal of my stores, including beams, benches and cupboards, bedsteads, stools and wardrobes."[160] Hawkwood settled for the winter not far from Mantua, where his men sustained themselves at local expense. To cast suspicion from himself, Bernabò wrote Mantua, with whom he now maintained an uneasy truce, to warn them of Hawkwood's arrival.[161]

Back in Florence, a confused Donato Velluti wondered why Hawkwood had retreated so abruptly. He speculated that they were hindered by the coming of winter and lack of pay. Mino di Carlo Montanini, a Sienese ambassador stationed in Pisa, also spoke of lack of pay and lack of supplies.[162] The Bolognese chronicler gave a similar account, as did Bernabò Visconti in his own letter on the matter.[163] It was also certain that Bernabò's objectives in Tuscany were more limited than Velluti believed. The Milanese ruler could hardly have wished to seize Florence, a dubious enterprise that would have been inconsistent with his previous policy toward that city. More probably he wished only to maintain a presence in the region, as a prelude to assisting Agnello.

This indeed became clear in the spring of 1370, when Bernabò moved to reinstall his old ally Giovanni dell' Agnello. The two men signed an agreement on 11 May 1370 by which Visconti agreed to lend the erstwhile Pisan ruler 1,000 lances and 1,200 banners of infantrymen. The contingents, according to the text of Bernabò's cession, were added to the 150 horsemen already ceded to Agnello, "which at present include John Hawkwood." The contract was for four months, beginning when the soldiers arrived in Pisan territory from Parma, and lists various contingencies should Agnello succeed in seizing either Pisa or Lucca. Agnello himself joined Hawkwood's brigade, along with numerous exiles and the German captain Johann von Rietheim.[164] The arrangement was the inverse of the former relationship between the men.

Hawkwood and Agnello advanced to the gates of Pisa on 16 May 1370. Piero Gambacorta closed shops and halted all internal activities in the city in order to squelch possible uprisings on behalf of Agnello.[165] The Milanese battle plan was an unusually audacious one; the army planned an all-out assault on the town walls. Anticipating such an attack, Gambacorta stationed crossbowmen and small cannons there. On 17 May, Hawkwood's men attempted to scale the walls. The defenders fired the cannons. "As they heard the bombards," wrote the anonymous Pisan chronicler, "the men of Messer John Hawkwood moved back; and from the great fear, they left the field."[166]

Hawkwood regrouped for another attack several days later. His men climbed the portion of the wall above the gate of San Zeno, using ropes and ladders. But once again they were beaten back. The Pisans captured and tossed four of Hawkwood's soldiers from the wall and took two others prisoner. One of the latter, a slave belonging to an English soldier, was tortured and hanged in plain view.[167]

Hawkwood and Agnello rode on Livorno and scored a measure of redemption by burning the city on 22 May. They made several additional raids on the countryside and then retreated north to Parma at the end of June.

In the wake of the unsuccessful coup, Bernabò abandoned his former ally. Giovanni dell' Agnello emerged from the affair, in the words of the anonymous Pisan chronicler, "a completely defeated man." He settled eventually in Genoa, where he died quietly in 1387.[168] "He came in misery, grew old in poverty and died poor."[169]

## War in Emilia Romagna and Victory at Rubiera

Hawkwood's reaction to the humiliation of his former mentor is nowhere recorded. He passed the summer of 1370 in the environs of Parma.[170] Bernabò disavowed any direct connection to the Englishman, maintaining that he had advanced into the region of his own accord at the head of a free company. But Hawkwood's itinerary corresponded too closely with Visconti military objectives. Having failed to take Pisa, Bernabò brought his war against the pope back up north, to the southern Lombard plain. He focused on the city of Reggio (thirty-eight kilometers from Parma), a dependent of the church, which had a restless noble class, some of whom were sympathetic to the Visconti cause. From there he intended to pressure Bologna, the center of papal power in the region and a longtime target of Visconti hegemony. Bernabò's designs were directly opposed by the nearby lord of Ferrara, Niccolò d'Este, who likewise coveted Reggio.

The coincidence between Visconti policy and Hawkwood's actions left Bernabò with little choice but to admit that Hawkwood was indeed on the payroll. But in a letter to Mantua, Visconti claimed that he was "forced" to hire him as protection from "the pretenses of the church." He nevertheless boasted that while Hawkwood was in his employ he intended to use him to wage "good fat war."[171]

Hawkwood initiated the "good fat war" in August 1370, together with his erstwhile comrade Ambrogio Visconti, recently freed from his Neapolitan jail. The two rode with two thousand horsemen against Bologna, "burning and looting" up to the town walls.[172] Papal forces launched a counterattack against Reggio, torching a bastion Bernabò had erected outside the city. In November, amid the snows of an early season storm, Hawkwood surprised the enemy outside the town of Mirandola as it returned from a raid on Visconti lands.[173]

In the spring of 1371 Bernabò captured Reggio. He sent Hawkwood and Ambrogio Visconti to take possession of the city.[174] Hawkwood's soldiers, however, misbehaved. They robbed and looted nearby lands, including those belonging to Mantua—a focal point of the war in 1368 but now neutral, a status that Bernabò, more interested in Bologna, wished to maintain. The depredations were themselves unexceptional, but they occasioned an intriguing series of letters, which include one of the earliest surviving ones written by Hawkwood himself. The epistles provide a direct glimpse not only into the captain's personality but also into his relationship with his employer and the intricacies involved in settling disputes over the violation of neutral lands.

The worst excesses of Hawkwood's troops took place in October 1371 in the town of Guastalla, a dependent of Mantua. Ludovico Gonzaga wrote to both Bernabò and

Hawkwood to demand compensation.[175] Bernabò wrote back promising restitution. Hawkwood himself responded directly to Gonzaga in a letter dated 22 October 1371.

> Magnificent and Exalted Lord. I hear that certain of the English brigade . . . inflicted damage on your territory. I am greatly grieved by the news. But since these Englishmen were soldiers of the magnificent lord of Milan [Bernabò] there is nothing I can do. Please excuse me. You know well that yesterday when I traveled through your territory with my own men no damage was inflicted. . . . Thus let it please your lordship to send word throughout your territories that my associates be allowed to pass freely through your land and that they be allowed food and provisions in return for their money.[176]

The letter is polite, but it contained no apology, no admission of guilt, and, most important, no offer to pay for damages. Hawkwood carefully distinguished between the actions of his "own men" and those of Bernabò, in effect blaming his employer rather than himself for the crimes. His main concern was that Gonzaga not retaliate by denying his men food and forage.

The reply did not please Bernabò, who sent Ambrogio Visconti to speak with Hawkwood. The substance of the conversations between the two mercenary captains is recorded in a letter by Giovanni Pico, soldier and ambassador from the town of Mirandola, who was present at them. Pico reported that the crux of the problem was that Hawkwood's contract with Visconti had expired and thus Hawkwood considered himself technically a free captain. Hawkwood now sought a new contract, and Bernabò obliged. They concluded a pact in the city of Parma on 26 October 1371.[177]

Reconciled with Bernabò, Hawkwood still needed to be reconciled with the lord of Mantua, who had not yet been compensated. Both Bernabò and Ambrogio wrote to Gonzaga assuring him of Hawkwood's good intentions. Bernabò even sent to Mantua copies of his correspondence with Hawkwood, which indicated that the Englishman's attitude had changed.[178] Hawkwood himself wrote (31 October) to Gonzaga and indeed took responsibility.

> My Dearest Friend. I have received your letters telling of the damages inflicted by the men. I am sorry as I can be, and so that further incidents do not occur, let me proclaim here that none of the remaining soldiers can go on Mantuan territory to do any sacking. And also, if it pleases you, I will send one of my men there to protect everything, from hay to any thing else. They will make sure that nothing is touched.[179]

But as conciliatory as the letter appears at first glance, what Hawkwood did not mention was financial compensation. Gonzaga complained, and Bernabò now sent two high-ranking officials, Guidone da Vicecamerato and Filippo da Desio (the latter a civilian military adviser [*collaterale*] of the Milanese army), to do "whatever they could" to sway Hawkwood. Ambrogio Visconti continued to play a leading role, conducting a kind of shuttle diplomacy between Hawkwood, Bernabò, and the injured parties.[180] After several days of talks, Desio wrote optimistically to Gonzaga that a solution seemed near: "John Hawkwood [Achuvud] wishes to see to it that what is owed is made up to your subjects in Guastalla. John promises to accomplish this expeditiously, so that your subjects can be deservedly satisfied."[181] Hawkwood then sent the soldiers that he had promised to protect Mantuan lands as well as two financial advisers from his brigade to settle the issue of compensation.

But there was no happy resolution. The sides could not agree. A frustrated Filippo da Desio wrote that, owing to the conflicting opinions, it was "impossible" to assess the losses.[182] Hawkwood gave assurances but offered no money.[183] At a final rendering of accounts held at Parma on 15 November 1371, the Bolognese ambassador, Bonaventura de' Pizolpilizari, spoke of contentious debate. Negotiations were abruptly ended by news that Bernabò and the pope had arranged a truce. Hawkwood and his men rode off; they never paid for the damage they caused.

The incident is the first example of what would become a hallmark of Hawkwood's career: the ability to get the better of his Italian interlocutors at the bargaining table. But soon after the event, Hawkwood proved his worth on the battlefield. The truce was little more than a cover for both sides to amass more troops, and in the spring hostilities recommenced.[184] On 2 June 1372, Hawkwood and Visconti defeated papal forces outside the small town of Rubiera. Hawkwood and Visconti commanded an army of 1,000 lances, with the anomalous feature that it possessed no infantry.[185] The papal force was the larger one, consisting of 1,200 lances and infantry brigades of unspecified size. The pro-papal Bolognese chronicler claimed that Hawkwood and Ambrogio's force was not especially well ordered and that at the point of conflict it sued for peace. This was likely one of Hawkwood's ruses, for when the armies engaged, Hawkwood overwhelmed his foe.[186] He outflanked and surrounded the enemy and took captive most of its high-ranking officers. The Bolognese chronicler predictably blamed his own side. He claimed that the lance units in papal army were overly large and that the corporals had too much autonomy. "Each corporal thought himself a 'lord' in camp," he wrote.[187] The judgment, whether exaggerated or not, suggests that Hawkwood's army was the better coordinated of the two.

The battle of Rubiera was Hawkwood's most impressive win since Cascina. Bernabò proudly announced the victory the next day (3 June 1372) in a letter to Mantua.[188] But the triumph brought no decisive results and was followed again by a truce. Hawkwood remained encamped with his army near Modena.

# CHAPTER SIX

# In the Service of God and Mammon, 1372–1375

> But certainly now I do not know what I shall say about these men of arms . . . they do not say, it seems to me, "I will fight for the Right"; rather they are consumed with greed.
>
> *John Gower, "Mirour de l'Omme"*

By 1372 John Hawkwood was established as an effective captain and frightening marauder. The breakup of the White Company gave him de facto leadership of the expatriate community of English soldiers in Italy, a position reinforced by the resumption of hostilities in France in 1369, which sent Hugh de la Zouche, Andrew Belmont, and other leading soldiers back across the Alps. Edward Despenser remained until 1372 and then returned to England to join King Edward's campaign in France the following year.[1] Italy nevertheless continued to attract Englishmen, and a flow of men persisted between the two places.

As his reputation rose in Italy, Hawkwood gained his first notice at home in England. The anonymous author of the chronicle of St. Mary's Abbey at York spoke of the activities of a "Sire Johan Haukeswode" in Lombardy in 1369 at the head of "plusours autres Engleis de la ioly compaigny."[2] Thomas Walsingham gave a more detailed and laudatory account of Hawkwood ("Johannes Haukwod") as "an outstanding and famous knight" who was "always victorious" in battle.[3]

Walsingham's hyperbole notwithstanding, Hawkwood was just emerging from a cadre of capable foreign captains. Many of these were Germans, such as Johann von Rietheim, Johann Flach von Reischach, Konrad von Weitingen, Johann von Eberhardsweiler, and Lutz and Eberhard von Landau. Their names are obscure today, but they were well known and much in demand in the middle decades of the fourteenth century. Rietheim and Reischach had defeated and captured Hawkwood near Arezzo in 1369; Eberhardsweiler had scored victories in Milanese service in Tuscany, as had Lutz and Eberhard von Landau.[4] The most renowned of the German captain was Hannekin Baumgarten, now twenty years on the peninsula, dating from the days of the Great Company of Montreal d'Albarno.

But John Hawkwood was clearly a star on the rise. His ascent was aided by shifts in the mercenary market. The ranks of the senior mercenary leadership were in fact thinning. Konrad von Landau, the most successful of the German captains of the decade of the fifties, died on the battlefield in Lombardy in 1363. Hawkwood's comrade-in-arms Albert Sterz was murdered by the Perugians in 1366. Hannekin Baumgarten still lived but, despite his fame, was a spent force, performing mostly defensive duties on behalf of the church until his death in 1374.

There was more generally a decline in the participation of German soldiers in Italy. They had dominated the mercenary market for three decades prior to Hawkwood's arrival, their numbers purportedly reaching as high as ten thousand or more men. The Italian jurist Giovanni da Legnano equated the very term *mercenary* with German in his famous treatise on war and dueling published in 1360.[5] But German involvement declined sharply after that, according to one scholar as the result of improved economic conditions at home, which created more opportunities for employment there. The Germans' place was taken in part by Italian mercenaries, some of whom—like Giacomo da Cavallo of Verona, Rodolfo da Varano from Camerino, and various members of the Malatesta family of Rimini—had achieved notable status. But the truly great Italian captains, whose careers would rival that of Hawkwood—Jacopo dal Verme (b. 1350), Facino Cane (b. 1360), and Alberigo da Barbiano (b. 1349)—were still young and unproven.

The decades of the sixties and early seventies belonged to the English, who became the most highly prized of the foreign mercenaries in Italy. Their desirability was enhanced by their relatively small number, which set off a lively competition for their services and kept their wages high.[6] Even relatively obscure men, untested in the Italian context, received important commands and lucrative contracts. This was the case of John Thornbury (a.k.a. John Wenlock), who had fought in France in the retinue of John of Gaunt and came to Italy in 1371 to work for the pope.[7] Without prior experience, the pope made him a captain of his army, granted him a generous salary, and set him against John Hawkwood.[8] The pontiff acted according to an increasingly popular notion that the best way to stop a brigade of Englishmen was to oppose it with another brigade of Englishmen. In Florence, English soldiers had reached such prominence that one of them, perhaps Humphrey, son of William Bohun, with whom Hawkwood had probably begun his military career in France, was included in Andrea Bonauiti's great Church Militant fresco in the Spanish chapel at Santa Maria Novella.[9]

The English also had a lasting impact on the organization of Italian armies. States admired their fighting technique to the point that they adopted the lance unit used in English brigades. The shift occurred in Perugia in 1367, the papal states in 1368, in Florence in 1369, Milan in 1370, and Siena in 1372.[10] Locals did not wholly abandon previous formations, notably the *barbuta*, but the lance formation clearly emerged dominant. With it came widespread adoption of the technique of dismounting from horses at the outset of battle.

John Hawkwood's own reputation remained closely tied to that of the English in general, and indeed some contemporaries viewed him less as an individual than as an exemplar of the martial qualities of his nation. Documents from the late sixties affirm that he arranged his personal brigades in the English manner of lances. It is uncertain, however, whether he drew up his men in battle in the circular formation described by Villani and Azario with respect to the White Company. But Hawkwood clearly maintained a preference for his fellow English soldiers, a fact made explicit in a Florentine letter in 1369, which quoted him as saying he had "more faith in his English soldiers than in others."[11] We may now discern in his brigades a cadre of close associates who regularly fought with him. The men included William Boson, John Brice, William Gold, and Richard Romsey—all veterans of the White Company—and eventually John Thornbury. They worked beside Hawkwood throughout the decade of the seventies; William Gold, Hawkwood's most valued protégé, continued to serve him well beyond that. We also find in Hawkwood's brigades men from his home in Essex, most conspicuously the teenager William Coggeshale, the nephew of Hawkwood's comrade-in-arms in France Thomas Coggeshale. Sources make tantalizing mention of a relative, purportedly a brother, who was with Hawkwood in 1369 and killed in battle against Florence. The statement is unlikely, unless we suppose that Hawkwood's younger brother Nicholas left his monastery in Normandy to join his brigades.

But for all his dedication to his fellow Englishmen, Hawkwood was also becoming more firmly attached to Italy, accumulating modest wealth and the beginnings of a landed patrimony. Pisan accounts indicate that in 1366 Hawkwood received the yearly salary from that city of 600 florins, a decent sum but, as we shall see, a fraction of his later earnings.[12] Through extortion, he gained the first of his lifetime pensions from Queen Johanna of Naples. Hawkwood possessed lands near Bologna and Pisa and up north at Milan.[13] By 1368, the principal locus of his activities was the city of Parma, where Bernabò Visconti granted him estates formerly belonging to the German mercenary Konrad Craxer. In Parma, Hawkwood settled his family, which now included a mistress and two illegitimate sons, named Thomas and John. With Hawkwood was also his daughter by his wife (apparently no longer living), Antiochia, who was still a young girl.

Hawkwood also became more familiar with the milieu of the Italian battlefield. Now independent of the White Company, which had effectively ceased to
exist by 1365, he gained valuable military experience fighting alongside mercenaries of various nations, learning from their techniques of war. It was the peculiarity of Italian warfare that the captains Hawkwood fought against one day
fought with him the next. Several months after they defeated him, the Germans
Johann Flach von Reischach and Johann von Rietheim joined Hawkwood's army
and helped him win his great victory at Cascina. The Hungarian captain Nicholas
Thod fought against Hawkwood at Canturino but joined his brigades shortly
thereafter and stayed until 1367. Hawkwood learned from these men. He relied
most of all on Italians, who brought not only military experience but critical
reconnaissance and knowledge of the local terrain and local mores. Hawkwood
took in a tutor for each region in which he fought. When he rode through
Lombardy, he did so with the Milanese captain Ambrogio Visconti, his companion
in the Company of Saint George, who helped him negotiate local territory. When
he raided Umbria in 1366, Hawkwood hired the Umbrian mercenary Niccolò da
Montefeltro as his chancellor. Prior to his offensive against Lucca and Pisa, Hawkwood joined with the exiles Alderigo degli Antelminelli and Jacopo da Pietrasanta. The latter would serve Hawkwood for much of the rest of his career.

Hawkwood's conduct of war showed marked improvement. His earlier tendency to overtax his men gave way to more reasonable expectations. His campaigns during these four years (1372–1375) were characterized by greater subtlety,
better planning and coordination, and increased knowledge of local terrain. The
lion was, to use the metaphorical language of the Pisan-Florentine war, becoming
more of a fox.

Hawkwood's foxlike reputation was further enhanced by his emerging talent
with respect to financial matters. It is during this period that his *astuzia* in
bargaining and in enhancing his personal income manifested itself most clearly.
His search for profits would lead him to defect from Milanese service in favor of
the pope. His greed gained him the condemnation of the holiest person of the day,
Saint Catherine of Siena, and would eventually lead to a raid on Tuscany that left
him rich and the whole region at war.

## A Test of Champions at Modena

Hawkwood demonstrated his flair for manipulation in the summer of 1372
after his dramatic victory over papal forces at Rubiera. Hawkwood was then in the
environs of Modena, where he had remained after the battle, at the command of
the Milanese army. The enemy, captained by Niccolò d'Este, stood in close prox-

imity. In July Este challenged Hawkwood to battle, hoping to reverse the results at Rubiera. But the challenge devolved into an agreement to put the matter to a trial by combat of champions.[14] Each side picked six men. Hawkwood led the Milanese contingent, and an Italian mercenary, Bartolomeo de Cancellieri, headed the papal side. What followed was a give-and-take of negotiations, in which each subtly sought the advantage over the other. Hawkwood showed himself a master of the genre.

The parties agreed to meet on 4 July at Hawkwood's camp, near the banks of the Secchia River, to arrange the details of the contest. Hawkwood greeted the men warmly when they arrived and led them to a feast in their honor. Bartolomeo de Cancellieri spoke first and suggested that the battle take place in a meadow near the town of Marzaglia, just outside Modena. Hawkwood complimented the proposal and called it "a good one." But he pointed out that the location was six miles from his camp and only one mile from Cancellieri's camp; thus his men would be placed at a disadvantage. Cancellieri disagreed politely and told Hawkwood that he was "mistaken," that the meadow was less than three miles from the Milanese camp, the same as from his own; thus neither side had an advantage. Hawkwood made a counterproposal. He suggested that the champions meet in a different location, near a meadow outside the nearby town of Arcieto, and asked Cancellieri and his men to go with him to see it. The soldiers rode to Arcieto. But now Cancellieri demurred. He called the site "a good one" but claimed that it was more than three miles from his camp and only one mile from the Milanese camp; thus Hawkwood and his men had the advantage.

The dialogue continued. The men discussed other possibilities, including creating a made-to-order battlefield by sending out sappers to clear a meadow. But as the talks continued, it became progressively clear that nothing would be done, and the papal champions departed from Hawkwood's camp feeling manipulated. On returning to his own camp Cancellieri wrote to a letter to Niccolò d'Este, the overall commander of the papal forces, in which he expressed the suspicion that Hawkwood had conjured the whole exchange as a ruse to gain time so that his army could amass reinforcements and thus grow larger for battle.[15]

But Hawkwood did not intend to engage in battle near Modena. Soon after the episode, his employer Bernabò Visconti sent him to Piedmont to reinforce the armies of his brother and ally, Galeazzo.[16] Galeazzo was engaged in a separate war against Hawkwood's first Italian employer, the Marquis of Montferrat, which became enmeshed in the larger Milanese-papal struggle. The conflict between Galeazzo and Montferrat grew from the failed marriage between Galeazzo's daughter to Lionel, Duke of Clarence. As noted in the previous chapter, the English soldiers in Lionel's entourage made war on Galeazzo after Lionel died in 1368 and were assisted by Montferrat, who was anxious to take advantage of the situation. When Montferrat died in 1372, leaving only two small sons, Galeazzo attacked the marquis's most important city, Asti, taken from Galeazzo fifteen years earlier. Otto Brunswick, who served as the marquis's regent, led the defense of the city, along with Amadeus of Savoy, who, though related by marriage to Galeazzo, chose territorial considerations over familial ones. Pope Gregory encouraged Amadeus to join his anti-Visconti league and made him commander of papal forces in western Lombardy, responsible for operations in the area near the Adda and Ticino rivers.[17]

Hawkwood joined the attack on Asti with a brigade of three hundred lances. He rode to the town walls, where he undertook a siege, along with the rest of the Visconti army. With Hawkwood was his old comrade Ambrogio Visconti, the Italian mercenaries Cavallino de' Cavalli and Stefano Porro, and two others, Jacopo dal Verme and Ruggiero Cane, who would figure prominently in Hawkwood's later career. The commander of the army was Giangaleazzo Visconti, Galeazzo's inexperienced twenty-year-old son.

The army erected a bastion to intercept traffic and impede the flow of goods. But the siege did not proceed well. There were complaints among the mercenaries about lack of pay, and several brigades deserted outright. The operation devolved into a series of feints and gestures. Among the latter was Giangaleazzo Visconti's challenge to his uncle, Amadeus, the Count of Savoy, to a duel. Savoy, the older and more experienced soldier, eagerly accepted. But the contest never came off. Meanwhile Galeazzo was forced to abandon the project. He directed Hawkwood and his men back to Bernabò, who sent them back toward Parma and Reggio to prepare for a new strike against Bologna.

## Break from Bernabò

The unsuccessful siege of Asti was not a turning point in the war, which continued. But it proved a turning point in John Hawkwood's career. For the first time since he had arrived in Italy, Hawkwood abandoned his employer and deserted to the enemy.[18] The famous incident is reported by the anonymous author of the *Annales Mediolanenses,* who explained the decision as the result of anger at a battle plan that did not engage the enemy forcefully, a plan that seemed intended more to protect young Giangaleazzo from harm than to pressure the Count of Savoy. Hawkwood specifically laid the blame on "scribbling notaries" who oversaw the war. "He never believed that he should be ruled in the feats of arms by a council of notaries."[19] The *Annales Mediolanenses* account, repeated in the chronicle of Piacenza (*Chronicon Placentinum*), has become the standard version in modern works.[20]

It is easy to imagine Hawkwood's frustration with the prosecution of the war. Little was accomplished at Asti. Giangaleazzo's call for a duel was unpleasantly familiar—it was the fourth time in little more than six months that Hawkwood had been involved in such fruitless posturing. But the *Annales* version is only part of the story. A series of letters from the Archivio Gonzaga in Mantua indicate that the main source of Hawkwood's discontent was money. A letter by Giovanni Pico dated 12 September 1372 outlined the basic issues. Hawkwood was approaching the end of his contract and wanted more men and higher wages. In particular, he wished to augment his brigade with 200 more lances and 200 more archers. Bernabò, on the other hand, hoped to rehire Hawkwood at the same terms as those in the previous contract. Pico cited as the source of his information Ambrogio Visconti, who was with Hawkwood at Asti.

> Magnificent and exalted lord, Ambrogio Visconti came from the camp against Asti and said to me that John Hawkwood [Haucud] is in the territory of Galeazzo and that in 12 days he will ride 25 miles and eat and drink here with his comrades. Bernabò wanted to sign him again according to the previous agreement, by which the English were to have 100 lances in Brescia, 100 lances in Cremona and 100 lances elsewhere. The English did not want that, but wanted to augment their band by 200 lances and 200 archers. According to the general opinion, they are coming toward Saint Benedict and will stop there and sign an accord either with my lord Bernabò or with whoever will give them the best terms.[21]

Pico's last sentence makes clear that Hawkwood's contract was at an end and he now made himself available to the highest bidder. He enhanced his bargaining position by withdrawing from the front. In a letter dated 18 September, Giovanni Pico reported that Hawkwood retreated toward Parma, his longtime base of operations, and sent up his camp five miles outside the city in the town of Collegi. "There they will stay until they have a response from Bernabò."[22]

Bernabò sent his son Ambrogio to Collegi to speak with Hawkwood. Giovanni Pico, citing the friendship between the men, thought that this was a good move and augured a successful resolution. "Ambrogio Visconti will find out from John what these English want to do."[23]

But the negotiations did not go well. On 20 September Giovanni Pico reported continued "discord" between Hawkwood and Bernabò.[24] Hawkwood remained steadfast in his demand for more men, and Bernabò refused to give them to him. For his part, Bernabò had not been pleased with Hawkwood's recent performance or with that of his English mercenaries in general. By Bernabo's estimation, Hawkwood and the English had shown little interest in fighting at Asti and passed much of their time complaining about money. An English contingent had in fact deserted to the enemy, an act for which Bernabò may have held Hawkwood partially responsible.

After the failure of talks at Collegi, Hawkwood moved southeast in the direction of Modena to the town of Scandiano. The itinerary was noteworthy because it brought Hawkwood closer to the papal army, specifically the brigades of the French noble Enguerrand Coucy, who had recently joined the pope's cause alongside his cousin the Count of Savoy. Giovanni Pico wrote on 20 September that Hawkwood intended "to place camp a mile from Enguerrand Coucy."[25]

On 23 September Hawkwood himself wrote a letter detailing the state of affairs. The letter is brief and understated but makes clear that money was indeed the crucial issue. "I am with my brigade four miles from Corregio in the abbey of Campagnola," wrote Hawkwood. "Since my contract runs out at the end of the month I will stay here some days until I know if the lord of Milan wishes that I remain further in his service or not."[26]

Although Hawkwood indicated that he was waiting for Bernabò's reply, he was in fact already involved in negotiations with Pope Gregory, who eagerly sought his services. Gregory, described by a recent scholar as the most "active and purposeful" of the Avignon popes, took an aggressive stance toward the Visconti. A Sienese ambassador who attended the conclave that elected him in 1371 called him as "a good man, a friend of Italians," but noted that he was "completely disposed to the destruction of the lords of Milan."[27] Gregory focused especially on mercenary soldiers, recruiting the best available for his army, while denying the Visconti access to the same.[28] Gregory tried to cut off the Visconti from their basic source of German and Hungarian mercenaries by ordering bishops in those countries to issue edicts condemning those citizens who enrolled as soldiers in Milanese service. Gregory ordered the patriarch of Aquilea, whose lands formed a point of entry into Italy, to seize men-at-arms who passed through his territory. The pope gave the similar orders to bishops at Constance, Brixen, Aosta, and Trento, lands that were also gateways into Italy. Gregory demanded that secular authorities arrest Milanese ambassadors who tried to recruit soldiers in the Tyrol region.[29]

To gain Hawkwood's services, Gregory granted him the very terms that Bernabò had been unwilling to consider. He allowed the Englishman 200 additional lances and 200 additional archers and an advance on salary of 40,000 florins.[30] Gregory then wrote to his ally, Queen Johanna of Naples, and instructed her to restore the annual pension she had granted Hawkwood years earlier. Gregory stressed to her the advantages of having John Hawkwood on their side. The pope, so condemning of Hawkwood during his years with Visconti, now referred to him as "our beloved son."

> Most dear daughter in Christ . . . Recently it has reached our ears that you made or gave . . . to our beloved son, the noble John Hawkwood, knight now for many years, a certain annual provision. . . . Since, however, the same John, whom we take from the services of Bernabò Visconti, enemy and persecutor of the whole church, intends to come over to the church and not to offend, invade or damage its subjects, and lands . . . we strongly ask and urge your serenity that you make good to the said John Hawkwood his provision which you previously so liberally granted.[31]

Hawkwood accepted the pope's offer. In so doing, he behaved in the same manner as his comrades in the White Company had back in the summer of 1364. He abandoned his employer before the walls of the enemy for a better deal as the end of his contract approached. But Hawkwood's defection was somewhat less sensational because it coincided almost precisely with a truce in the war, brokered by the king of France on 21 September 1372.

In his brief account of the episode, the Flemish chronicler Jean Froissart stressed the role played by Enguerrand Coucy. He claimed that Hawkwood did not wish to oppose Coucy because he was related through marriage to the English king (Coucy was Edward's son-in-law, married to his daughter Isabella).[32] The interpretation emphasizes Hawkwood's English loyalties, which, as we have seen, were indeed quite strong. Hawkwood had in fact moved in Coucy's direction just before deserting Milanese service. But given the prominence of financial considerations, it is likely that Coucy's role was more of intermediary through whom the pope negotiated with Hawkwood. Meanwhile, the contention in the Milanese *Annales* that Hawkwood acted out of frustration with scribbling notaries and an unrequited urge to wage aggressive war reveals more about the author's own frustrations regarding the war with the pope than those of Hawkwood. "If Hawkwood had been permitted to fight it cannot be doubted that he would have won; and if he had won, the enemy would have come upon the lands of Galeazzo and Bernabò as they did." The tone is of someone who was himself annoyed with the notaries at home.[33]

Bernabò was bitterly disappointed by Hawkwood's desertion and vented his rage by capturing and imprisoning Hawkwood's mistress and children in Parma. The act was accompanied by an angry letter from Bernabò's wife and sons, enumerating Hawkwood's crimes. Giovanni Pico, who was shown the epistle by the Milanese operative Pietro Arimondo, summarized its contents. "They contended that the English had defaulted on their agreements and robbed the lands of Galeazzo, allegations that they could not honestly refute."[34] Bernabò wrote directly to Hawkwood offering to forget the offenses if he returned immediately to Milanese service. But Visconti made it clear that he would only grant Hawkwood the same salary and same terms as in the previous year, which, he added, were no better than those he was currently offering the German captain Berthold Mönch, Hawkwood's intended replacement.

Hawkwood remained with the pope. His brigade of five hundred lances was composed overwhelmingly of Englishmen. The corporals included John Brice, William Boson, Richard Romsey, and William Gold. The newcomer John Thornbury, who had opposed Hawkwood as a captain of papal forces at Modena in 1371, joined with seventy-six lances.[35]

The larger papal army was a multinational one. In addition to Hawkwood, the pope recruited the Frenchmen Enguerrand Coucy and Raymond, Viscount of Turenne; the Italians Niccolò d'Este of Ferrara, Galeatto Malatesta of Rimini, and the Count of Savoy; the German Otto of Brunswick; and the Gascon Amanieu de Pommiers.[36] Pommiers, now an old man, had served with Hawkwood under the Black Prince at Poitiers in 1356.

Bernabò countered by assembling an international force of his own. In retaliation for the hire of Hawkwood, Bernabò lured from papal service Hannekin Baumgarten, one of the pope's captains, with 300 lances. He also hired contingents of 600 German lances, 300 Hungarian soldiers, 200 Milanese lances, 200 Piedmontese lances, and 300 English lances.[37]

Bernabò made one further effort to rehire Hawkwood, sending his treasurer, Massolus della Strada, to negotiate with the Englishman.[38] Through Massolus, Bernabò promised to set free Hawkwood's children and mistress, who were apparently still held hostage.[39] It is unclear what Massolus communicated to Hawkwood by way of financial considerations, but the Englishman was not enticed by the offer.

## Athlete of God and Faithful Christian Knight

Hawkwood rode to Bologna, which served as the headquarters of the papal army. The local chronicler enthusiastically praised him as "the greatest and most worthy foreigner who ever crossed the mountains."[40] The pope joined Hawkwood's brigade with those of Niccolò d'Este, whom Hawkwood had defeated months earlier at Rubiera, and Ugolino da Savignano, a relative of Este, whom Hawkwood had captured outside Siena in 1367. The combined force numbered about two thousand lances.

Although the truce was still in effect, Hawkwood and Savignano rode on Parma in October/early November 1372—an attack that was likely revenge on Bernabò for holding Hawkwood's family. The Milanese ruler responded by sending Ambrogio against Bologna. Ambrogio's army purportedly inflicted 400,000 florins' worth of damage on the environs of the city.[41]

The mutual raids reignited the war. Pope Gregory renewed his aggressive stance, which now manifested itself in plans for ambitious offensives that would bring the war to the gates of Visconti's principal cities. Gregory zealously pursued his designs for the next two years, constrained, however, by increasing financial difficulties.

Gregory arranged his first offensive for the late spring of 1372. His plan called for an attack on Pavia, Galeazzo Visconti's capital. To facilitate this, the pontiff intended first to raise rebellion among the clergy in the Visconti dominion, particularly in Piacenza, a city with a strong dissident faction and a history of popular revolt. "The people of Piacenza," the local chronicler wrote, "were by nature always prone to discord."[42] Gregory added the noted Piacentine exile and captain Donadazio Malvicini Fontana to Hawkwood and Savignano's brigade, in the hope that his presence would help stir up passions in his native city.[43] The pope also reinforced the army with additional mercenary hires and made the venerable old captain Amanieu de Pommiers titular commander of the entire force.[44] Hawkwood commanded the English.

The army advanced northwest from Bologna toward Piacenza along the Via Emilia.[45] As the pope had hoped, the army received aid along the way from clerics and disaffected nobles. Fontana's presence indeed encouraged rebellion in Piacenza, where, according to the chronicler, "great treasons were committed by one against the other."[46] The papal army did not enter the town but took several strategically important local castles. It then crossed the Po River and took castles in the environs of Pavia.[47]

Hawkwood had performed well in his first action on behalf of the church. Pope Gregory was immensely pleased. He wrote to Hawkwood on 7 December 1372 to commend him for his "fidelity and readiness" and to urge him to continue with his current behavior, which "gives grace to God, whose business you are doing."[48] Gregory then excommunicated the Visconti brothers and ordered their goods and those of their allies sequestered. The pope also suspended the offices and benefits of those churchmen who remained faithful to the Visconti.[49] The measures encouraged further revolts throughout the Visconti domain.[50] Bernabò retaliated by passing laws restricting the liberties of the clergy, particularly those who had settled in Milan from the outside.

Visconti launched a counteroffensive against Reggio and Parma.[51] This forced Hawkwood and the papal army to double back, leaving garrisons to oversee the captured castles at Piacenza and Pavia. Ambrogio Visconti led the Milanese army to the walls of Bologna and remained there for two weeks, systematically stripping the land and amassing booty.[52] Hawkwood and Savignano caught up with the Milanese at Crevalcuore, near the Panaro River, where Bolognese territory gives way to that of Modena.[53] Loaded down with booty and captives, Ambrogio Visconti was outmaneuvered by his friend and former comrade, who trapped him as he tried to cross the river. After a brief and intense battle, Hawkwood carried the day (21 January 1373). "Our men," boasted the pope's vicar general in Bologna, Pierre di Bourges, "carried the fight in a most manly fashion."[54] Bourges estimated the number of dead at 500 and the number of captives at 1,500. The Bolognese chronicler claimed that 2,000 of Visconti's men died, mostly from drowning in the river. The Bolognese chronicler also credited the victory in part to the role played by native Bolognese troops, who rallied to Hawkwood's army in defense of their city.[55]

The victory at the Panaro opened the way for decisive offensive against Pavia. The pope now envisioned a two-pronged attack, whereby Hawkwood's army would advance from the south and link up with Amadeus of Savoy's army, which would descend from the north. Bernabò sent urgent requests to Avignon to open up negotiations for peace. The pope ignored the overtures.[56]

Hawkwood's army was again routed through Piacenza, where a local abbot, Berengarius, laid the groundwork by fomenting discord among the nobility.[57] In a letter dated 10 February 1373, the pope informed Hawkwood of Berengarius's efforts and urged him to proceed as quickly and as "secretly" as possible.[58] Visconti tried to impede Hawkwood's march by destroying mills and hiding fodder and provisions.[59]

Hawkwood indeed advanced quickly. But Amadeus of Savoy, unfortunately, did not. Although bound by contract to be inside Milanese territory by mid-October 1372, Amadeus lingered in Piedmont and arrived in the city of Vimercate, just northeast of Milan, only in March 1373. Bernabò tried to stop him there by poisoning his stores of bread and wine. Bernabò's spies were, however, spotted, and Amadeus was warned. The Savoyard chronicler Jehan Servion portrayed the incident in heroic terms, claiming that Amadeus miraculously cured those men who had already ingested the poison by means of a ring that bore the likeness of Saint Maurice.[60]

Savoy's presence at Vimercate nevertheless gave hope that the pope's plan would be successful. Hawkwood remained encamped in the environs of Piacenza. Gregory wrote letters to both armies to urge them forward. But to the pontiff's great disappointment, Amadeus began negotiating with the enemy. The modern historian Eugene Cox has hypothesized that the count did not wish for a decisive blow against his brother-in-law but wanted only to maintain the integrity of his own territory.[61] In any case, the momentum of the attack was lost. Hawkwood retreated with his men back to Bologna.

Pope Gregory remained, however, undeterred, and in April 1373 he prepared a new offensive. He joined Hawkwood and his English brigade with that of Enguerrand Coucy and routed them this time through Ferrara, from where they would proceed west and then north to Brescia—deemed by the pontiff to be a weak link in the Visconti dominion. The pope intended for Coucy and Hawkwood to link with Amadeus of Savoy and his army near the city of Milan. After the failure of his negotiations with the Visconti and much cajoling by the pope, Amadeus agreed to mobilize his army.

The plan initially worked well. Coucy and Hawkwood advanced north and crossed the Po River without incident. Their route passed close to Mantuan territory, where the army did its usual damage and elicited the obligatory letters of complaint. Amadeus moved swiftly from Vimercate to Brivio and advanced to the Adda River, near the city of Bergamo.[62]

The Visconti this time undertook an active defense and threw the full weight of their army against Coucy and Hawkwood just south of Brescia.[63] The two sides met on the afternoon of 7 May 1373 at Montichiari, on the banks of the Chiese River.[64] The battle was the most hotly contested one of the war. Coucy and Hawkwood won the day. According to the standard modern account, taken from the *Chroniques* of Jean Froissart, Coucy was the aggressor, leading a charge against the enemy reminiscent of the "French impetuosity" at Crècy and Poitiers. Coucy was repelled, but Hawkwood then rallied the army to victory.[65]

The details of the battle can, however, be verified in Italian chronicle accounts and also in several contemporaneous letters, including one by Hawkwood himself. Hawkwood's epistle was addressed to Ludovico Gonzaga of Mantua, whose lands he intended to pass through on his way to Bologna to redeem his captives. It was simple and straightforward, written the day after the event.

> Magnificent and exalted lord . . . the count of Virtu [Giangaleazzo Visconti], the son of Galeazzo, came yesterday from Brescia with 2,000 lances and a great number of infantry. He wished to put his men to the test against us on the battlefield, hoping I would not be able to withstand him. By the grace of God who dispenses his counsels otherwise, we came to battle in a long and broad field above Montechiari. Through violent blows we succeeded in bitter fighting. Some of the knights and squires of the enemy were killed, and good warriors were captured, among them Marquis Francesco [Francesco d'Este] your lord. The count of Virtu and Hannekin Baumgarten,

through wise counsel, took flight. Because some of my comrades were wounded and on account of our great number of prisoners, it is necessary to go back to Bologna. For this reason it would please us if your lordship would make available provisions in return for our money.                    John Hawkwood [Johannes Haukevod], captain[66]

The battle is recounted in two other letters: one by Raimondino Lupi, a nobleman from Parma, in the service of Mantua, stationed in Verona; and another by an unnamed Sienese ambassador in Bologna.[67] Neither writer witnessed the encounter firsthand but relied on reports from others. Lupi, like Hawkwood, wrote the day after the battle.

Be aware, lord, that . . . a letter was sent to Cansigniore from the captain of Peschera, which contained the news that yesterday Bernabò's men fought with those of the Church in the vicinity of Gavardo [northeast of Brescia, due north of Montechiari]. The battle was strong and bitter. A good 300 of Bernabò's men died and many drowned in the river. The Marquis Francesco [of Ferrara] and other lords fled to a castle of Messer Bernabò. The field remained to the men of the church.

                    Raimondino Lupi[68]

The unnamed Sienese wrote nearly a month after the event.

The news is this. Messer Bernabò, hearing that Messer John Hawkwood had passed the ditch and wanted to pass the river called the Adda, which is next to Brescia, immediately contacted Messer Galeazzo, and he sent on Hawkwood, the count of Virtu, his son, with many men and all of the army of Bernabò. They gathered at Brescia, 1500 lances in all, and more than 500 infantrymen. Bernabò's men left Brescia and rode close to Hawkwood. The captains were these: the Count of Virtu [Giangaleazzo Visconti], Misser Ambrogiano [Visconti], Misser Anchino [Hannekin Baumgarten] and the Marquis Francesco [Francesco d'Este]. And the second Sunday of the present month [May], they fought together. The battle lasted more than three hours. Finally, the camp remained Hawkwood's. More than 300 of the enemy were wounded and more put to flight. More than 160 drowned and many were made prisoners. However, the Count of Virtue, Misser Ambrogiano and Misser Anechino fled to a castle in Brescia.[69]

The Sienese writer gives the most detail, including the context of the battle, its length, and precise figures regarding army size and casualties. His estimate for the size of the Milanese army—1,500 lances and 500 infantry—is similar to the one given by Hawkwood. Lupi and the Sienese writer put the number of deaths in the vanquished army at 160 and 300, respectively, figures that are less than half of what some modern authors claim. John Hawkwood does not quantify the losses, but he admitted without reserve that some of his own men were injured. The author of the *Chronicon Regiense*, who supported the Visconti cause, claimed that 700 men and 400 horses from Hawkwood's armies were killed—but this is clearly an exaggeration in light of the figures given by Lupi and the unnamed Sienese.[70] Lupi inexplicably reported that Francesco d'Este escaped capture, when Hawkwood, who would have known for sure, says that he was taken. The Sienese writer claimed that Ambrogio Visconti participated in the battle, but this is not true. Ambrogio's own letters in the Archivio Gonzaga indicate that he was in Bergamo at the time.[71]

The Sienese writer does, however, confirm Hawkwood's contention that Giangaleazzo Visconti attacked first, trying to prevent the papal army from crossing the Adda River. Indeed, the accounts in the *Annales Mediolanenses*, *Chronicon Placentinum*, and *Chronicon Regiense* all say that Galeazzo attacked first and in fact won the initial encounter. It was when the army went to plunder the "horses and banners of the English" that Hawkwood drew up the remnants of the papal army—described as a ragtag group of volunteers, mercenaries, and rustics—and reversed the outcome.[72] The Bolognese chronicler, who supported the pope, recounts a similar story, though his version is more generic and does not credit Hawkwood by name.[73]

The *Annales Mediolanenses* and *Chronicon Placentinum* add the detail that Giangaleazzo was knocked off his horse in the fray; and the author of the *Chronicon Estense* claimed that in his haste to get to safety, Giangaleazzo left his helmet and lance on the field. The Bolognese chronicler, who called the battle "a miracle of God," focuses on the casualties ("great mortality") suffered by the Visconti army, the unfortunate loss on the papal side of good horses, and the prospect for the victors of a financial bonanza ("great earnings") from the ransoms of so many captives.[74] The *Chronicon Estense* lists the captives by name. They included members of the Milanese nobility, the Visconti household, German and Hungarian mercenaries, and Bolognese exiles.[75]

Hawkwood's victory opened the very real possibility of a conjunction between his army and Savoy's. Pope Gregory enthusiastically urged Hawkwood on. "With enormous joy, we hear . . . of your victory against the cruel army of the tyrant and persecutor of the Roman church," he wrote just after Montichiari. "We request eagerly and urge your nobility that you quickly join in Milanese territory with our beloved son, the noble man Amadeus, the Count of Savoy, captain general of forces up north, so that the enemy army cannot revive nor recover from its recent defeat."[76]

Gregory praised Hawkwood and his band. "How much honor and praise redounds on you and the other English knights who set forth in our part of Italy, obedient to the Roman church. How much profit and rejoicing is received by the Roman Church and Republic from the diligence and indefatigable labors of yourself and your warriors."[77] The pope now styled Hawkwood a "warrior of Christ, athlete of God and faithful Christian knight," the same praise bestowed most recently on the Count of Savoy after his crusade fought against the Turks several years earlier.[78]

But once again the conjunction of armies did not occur. This time Hawkwood held back, choosing to remain in Bologna, where he had gone to redeem his prisoners. John Temple-Leader explained Hawkwood's action as an instance of good military judgment. "He coolly considered the superior forces which the Visconti could yet dispose, the many dead and wounded which the battle had cost the conquerors, the difficulty finding provisions, and the hostility of the peasants, and feared he might be cut off from his base of operations if he advanced."[79] Eugene Cox claimed that Hawkwood shared the Count of Savoy's limited objectives and did not desire to deal the Visconti a death blow.[80]

But money was once again a crucial issue. For all his effusive praise for Hawkwood, Pope Gregroy was in arrears with respect to his salary. Letters in the Vatican archives indicate that the pope was having considerable financial difficulties finding funds. In January 1373, Hawkwood's corporal John Brice traveled all the way to Avignon to speak directly to the pope about the issue. He returned to Hawkwood with papal exhortations to "remain patient," to meditate on the "eternal rewards and perpetual glory" attendant on church service, but no money.[81] In the summer of 1373 the pope's fiscal woes appear to have reached a nadir. Ironically, Gregory found the clergy in Hawkwood's native England among the most recalcitrant in paying the subsidies he requested for the war.[82] The prestige of the victory at Montichiari placed Hawkwood in a good position to press his demands for pay. He discomfited the pope by disbanding his brigade, which then moved into Mantuan territory. Ludovico Gonzaga complained of "infinite damage."[83]

Hawkwood's approach produced results, at least for himself. On 4 June 1373 Gregory granted him possession of a *hospicium*, or hospice, outside in the city of Bologna—property that he had apparently held sometime earlier.[84] Hospices were dwellings used primarily by pilgrims. They were usually located on major roads, fortified against highwaymen and thus with strategic value. Four days later, Pope Gregory awarded a church office to Hawkwood's bastard son, John junior.[85] The grant allowed John, still a child, eligibility for "all offices and canonries in Cathedral and Metropolitan churches in London" except for "principal dignities." The intention was to allow Hawkwood's bastard son a church career but not to allow him to rise too high in it. The act contained the proviso, however, that John junior not "imitate his father's incontinence."[86]

Such gifts, however, hardly made up the balance due and did little to satisfy the rank and file. The pope wrote to Hawkwood on 7 June and 11 June 1373 to urge him to ride forward to link up with the Count of Savoy's army. Gregory appealed to Hawkwood's sense of duty on behalf of the faith. He portrayed Visconti as a schismatic, a "cruel and tyrannical" enemy of the church. At the same time, Gregory counseled Hawkwood to have "patience with regard to stipends."[87]

Hawkwood did not mobilize, and his inaction left Amadeus of Savoy isolated in Milanese territory. The count extricated himself by means of a difficult journey, crossing both the Adda and Oglio rivers and passing through narrow ravines to avoid the Milanese army, which followed behind him. Galeazzo Visconti ridiculed Savoy for taking "roads that even goats and wild animals would find difficult."[88]

The pope passed much of the next year and a half exhorting Hawkwood and his army onward for another offensive. Pope Gregory held out hope for a victory on the battlefield: if not to impose his will on the Visconti, at least to gain good terms at the bargaining table. But the money for this remained lacking. A contemporary church official spoke of "a cruel shortage of resources to conduct the war in Lombardy."[89] The modern historian Jean Glénisson described papal finance as "désespérée," a situation exacerbated by the reappearance of plague in Lombardy and throughout Italy.[90]

Gregory appears, however, to have succeeded in collecting enough money to keep Hawkwood on the payroll. And in July 1373 he even convinced the captain to undertake a more limited offensive on Milanese territory along the familiar route through Piacenza. But the Milanese army, well informed of his movements, cut off Hawkwood's march.[91] The only enduring result of the offensive was to stir anti-Visconti rebellions in the nearby city of Bergamo, which brought the demise of his friend and former comrade Ambrogio Visconti, who went forth to subdue them.[92] The author of the chronicle of Reggio lamented Ambrogio's death. He wondered how a man so young (thirty years old) and full of life and "feared by his enemies and warlike to his foes" could be struck down by mere country "rustics."[93] The statement recalls Azario's similar one at the death of Konrad von Landau at Canturino twelve years earlier.

Hawkwood remained in the employ of the pope but did no more significant fighting. The issue of back pay dominated the discourse between the two; the rank and file of Hawkwood's army began to mutiny from under him, indulging in the familiar sport of ravaging Mantuan lands.[94] Hawkwood could do little to stop them. He wrote to Gonzaga to express both regret and frustration—perhaps even sincere emotions in this instance. "We received your letter today," Hawkwood said in an epistle dated 2 September, "saying in effect that our troops have committed many robberies and that on account of this you wish to put some horsemen here as you have informed us. We answer that it is not our intention that damage be committed in your territories, but rather it grieves us greatly. And well we believe what you write us because we are not able to be with our light cavalry always."[95] This letter was followed by another two days later.[96]

The pope nevertheless persisted in his calls for a major strike against the Visconti; Hawkwood and his corporals persevered in their attempts to collect their due. In April 1375 Gregory wrote to John Brice outlining a last plan for a "deadly blow," whereby Brice, Hawkwood, and the English would "prevent the enemy from reaping the coming harvest."[97] The pope coupled his proposal with promises to give both Hawkwood and Thornbury lands in the Marches of Ancona. He offered Hawkwood the castle of Montefortini and Thornbury the castle of Montalto.[98]

The pope's promises made little headway with Hawkwood and did nothing to satisfy his men. The pope himself admitted in a letter to John Thornbury on 3 May 1375 that the band seemed to be withdrawing its services from him.[99] Meanwhile, peace negotiations, ongoing throughout the war, now intensified. Representatives of Gregory and the Visconti met for intensive discussions in Bologna.

## Congress in Florence

With an unhappy mass of men at his charge, Hawkwood awaited the outcome of the negotiations. His soldiers passed the early days of May pillaging lands in southern Lombardy, where, according to the Bolognese chronicler, "they did great damage and extorted money from the lord of Mantua."[100] The actions not only elicited local resentment but raised fears elsewhere. The cities of Tuscany were concerned that Hawkwood would attempt to make up his losses at their expense, as he had done so many times before. A Florentine official, Niccolò Soderini, suggested that they send a secret embassy to Hawkwood and his company to find out their intentions and to prepare, if necessary, to pay Hawkwood off.[101] "Let all be done," said Simone di Ser Grandi, "so that it is obtained and provided by all means that the 'society' will not come into Tuscany."[102]

The Florentines' anxieties were heightened by the fact that their relations with the pope had become strained during his long war against Milan. Gregory XI was unhappy with Florence for its lukewarm support. The city had only reluctantly joined his anti-Visconti league and then summarily left it. Florence had grown uneasy about the intensity of the pope's martial zeal and growing power, particularly after the decisive victory at Montichiari.[103] Florentine officials were also angered by Gregory's refusal during the recent famine to allow the transport of much-needed grain from Umbria and the Marches to Tuscany. Gregory countered that Florence was promoting discord in church lands with rhetoric extolling "popular liberty."[104]

The context gave political coloring to Hawkwood's activities. A strike on Tuscany would be perceived as an act of aggression on the part of the pope. To lessen tensions, papal officials meet with representatives of Tuscan cities in Florence at the beginning of June.[105] Gregory sent two ambassadors: Jacobo de Itro, archbishop of Otranto, and Berengar, abbot of Lézat. Florence, Siena, Pisa, Arezzo, and Lucca also sent two ambassadors each. The papal envoys requested subsidies to continue the war against the Visconti—25,000 florins upfront and an additional 50,000 over six months. With this, they promised, they could keep John Hawkwood on the payroll and station him in church lands.[106] They maintained, however, that Hawkwood was, at the moment, without stipend and thus a free captain.

Before anything was decided, however, the congress was interrupted by the news from Bologna that the pope had contracted peace with the Visconti (4 June 1375). The embarrassed papal ambassadors in Florence apologized for their now meaningless embassy and said they had been deceived. But the Tuscan cities were not convinced. The Florentines produced two "secret" letters, one from a local spy warning that Berengar was not to be trusted; the other from a church official in Bologna declaring that Hawkwood remained on the pope's payroll, at a salary of 10,000 florins a month.[107] A Sienese ambassador claimed that he was approached privately by Berengar, who tried to put a wedge between Siena and Florence. The meeting disbanded.

The failure of negotiations increased resentments and preoccupation with Hawkwood. Letters in the Archivio Gonzaga place Hawkwood somewhere between Modena and Ferrara at the time of the dissolution of the ill-fated congress at Florence.[108] Florence sent the ambassador Giovanni di Bondi del Caccia to meet with Hawkwood in Ferrara. He confirmed their worst fears: Hawkwood intended to ride on Tuscany within the week.[109]

## The Great Raid on Tuscany

Hawkwood's raid on Tuscany in the summer of 1375 was one of the most important of the fourteenth century and reveals most clearly the fundamental connection between the activities of mercenaries and political fortunes of Italian states. The raid led directly to war between the pope and Florence, a signal event in Florentine history that involved breaking precedent with prior policy. The raid was also a signal event in Hawkwood's career through which he attained great

*Figure 4.* Hawkwood's raid in 1375 as represented in the Lucchese chronicle of Sercambi. Giovanni Sercambi, *Le croniche Lucchesi,* ed. Salvatore Bonsi. Fonti per la Storia d'Italia, vol. 1 (Rome, 1963)

wealth and summit of his prestige. Hawkwood's motives have been variously estimated and discussed, but the raid itself has never been studied.

Hawkwood advanced on Tuscany at the head of a formidable brigade (fig. 4). A Florentine witness described it as "a vast army," equipped with siege engines, scaling ladders, and "bombards." A Sienese ambassador claimed that the brigade's camp was "a good ten miles long."[110] The precise number of men is unknown, but its leadership was largely English. Hawkwood's longtime comrades John Brice and Willam Gold served as co-captains, as did John Thornbury. Richard Romsey was a corporal, along with John Clifford, John Foy, John Dent, William Tilly, John Coleman, William Best, David Roche, Nicholas Tansild, Philip Puer, and Thomas Beston—the last a corporal in the original White Company. The band also had two non-English contingents, headed by the German Nicolaus of Frisia and the Italian Bartolomeo da Gaggio.

The demeanor of the army was as forbidding as its size. A Sienese envoy sent to speak with Hawkwood at Ferrara claimed that he "had never been so frightened" in his life.[111] "In their talk," wrote the envoy, "the company ridiculed all people." A Florentine embassy reported that the band showed especial contempt for Tuscany: "They say they can defeat the cities of Tuscany because of their discords, and they speak a great deal about our city, saying that you don't pull one rope, but call the one and the other ghibelline."[112] The reference was to the traditional Italian party rivalries and indicates that Hawkwood had gained during his stay in Italy a sense of the political landscape around him. Indeed, just before he moved against Tuscany, Hawkwood met with a prominent member of an old Ghibelline family, the Lucchese exile Alderigo degli Antelminelli of Lucca—a meeting that caused much consternation in Antelminelli's native city.[113] Hawkwood expressed particular contempt, however, for his old employer Pisa, which he claimed owed him money and had reneged on a deal to give him a castle.[114] A Sienese envoy reported that Hawkwood also bore a personal grudge against Florence for the death of his "brother." The report is almost certainly false, since we know that Hawkwood's two brothers were back in England. It may well have been that the envoy refers to that "relative" killed during battle with Florence back in 1369.[115]

Hawkwood's slights against them notwithstanding, the cities showed a sense of solidarity. Local ambassadors worked closely together, exchanging information and reconnaissance and, in the case of Siena and Florence, sending copies of internal dispatches to one another. The frankness and honesty of this discourse between longtime competitors are of course open to the debate. But there was a sincere feeling among locals that their fates were linked. "If Hawkwood takes Pisa," wrote a Florentine ambassador, "Florence and the other cities will be lost."[116] Given the size of Hawkwood's band, Florentine officials saw little point in armed defense. The ambassador Filippo di Cionetti Bastari put the case succinctly: "There are two ways to handle the situation, either by defense or by accord. The latter is the most secure."[117]

Hawkwood advanced toward Tuscany along the Via Emilia in late June (map 4). On 21 June he was at Castelfranco, eleven kilometers from Bologna, and from there traveled to Ponte d' Idice, near the city of Imola, a point of passage into Tuscany.[118] Tuscan ambassadors met up with Hawkwood there and tried to come to terms with him before he entered the region.[119] Florence sent two envoys, Simone di Ranieri Peruzzi and Spinello di Luca Alberti. Peruzzi, like Doffo dei Bardi before him, was a merchant/banker, who could speak English. Alberti was the treasurer of city.

Peruzzi and Alberti were "shocked" by Hawkwood's initial demands and instructed officials back home to secure the citizenry behind the town walls and allow the company to ravage the countryside. But Florentine leaders instructed the ambassadors to continue the talks and try to make a deal.[120] They concluded a pact two days later. The city agreed to pay the company the majestic sum of 130,000 florins—40,000 florins immediately and the rest in monthly installments (July, August, September). In return, Hawkwood promised not to engage in "hostile acts against the city, contado and district of Florence and its dependent towns" for five years and to give four days' advance notice if he wished to pass through Florentine lands, in which case he would use only "clearly marked roads."

The Florentines would provide basic provisions—wine, poultry, and straw (for horses)—free of charge.[121]

A Bolognese envoy, Alberto Galuzzi, relayed the terms to Ludovico Gonzaga in a tone of disbelief.[122] The Florentine chancellor Coluccio Salutati boasted that neither Florence's own counselors nor Hawkwood himself supposed that they could meet such demands.[123] At one point in the negotiations, Peruzzi and Alberti offered Hawkwood a house in Florence, a lifetime monthly stipend of 100 florins, and citizenship—the latter was extended also to William Gold and John Thornbury. The men were apparently uninterested. "Hawkwood made mock of the proposal," Alberti reported, "and wanted nothing of these things."[124] Hawkwood's attitude is perplexing, in light of his subsequent behavior. He would eventually accept all these privileges from Florence.

Ambassadors from the other cities were unable to match the terms Florence granted to Hawkwood, and consequently he and his men crossed into Tuscany. They marched from Imola through the narrow Apennine passes near Firenzuola, traversing lands belonging to the Ubaldini family, a clan perpetually at odds with the Florentine government, which was doubtless complicit in the itinerary. The company proceeded in three large brigades, with Hawkwood at the head of one, Thornbury at the head of another, and Gold in command of the third. They entered the fertile Mugello region north of Florence, where, despite their promises, they "robbed like enemies." The soldiers took food, straw, and provisions, which, technically, Florence was supposed to provide for free; but they refrained from burning houses and stealing horses.[125]

The band moved east toward Pisa, reaching to within several kilometers of Prato on Wednesday, 27 June. Rumors surfaced in Prato, a dependent of Florence, that a local monk, Piero da Canneto, plotted to hand the town over to Hawkwood in the name of the church.[126] Florentine officials seized the monk along with a local notary and led them to an exquisite torture. Sienese ambassadors stationed in the city described the event in gory detail: the men were suspended by a cord, systematically mutilated, and then buried in the earth head down.[127] It remains unclear whether there was in fact a plot. But the episode further hardened Florence's feelings toward the pope.

At Prato, Hawkwood was met by an embassy of three men dressed as penitents. They were sent by Tuscany's most renowned citizen, Catherine of Siena, who was greatly displeased by Hawkwood's behavior. They carried a letter, addressed to " 'Messer Giovanni Aut,' the head of a company that came at the time of famine." In it, Catherine condemned Hawkwood's actions and demanded he leave at once and go on crusade, as a good Christian soldier was supposed to do.

Dearest gentlest brother in Christ Jesus would it be such a great thing for you to withdraw into yourself and consider how much pain and anguish you have endured in the devil's service and pay? . . . You find so much satisfaction in fighting and waging war, so now I am begging you tenderly in Christ Jesus not to wage war any longer against Christians, for that offends God, but to go and fight the unbelievers. . . . How cruel it is that we who are Christians, members bound together in the holy Church, should be persecuting one another! This must not be.

Catherine ended by reminding Hawkwood to look after the care of his soul. "I beg you, dearest brother, to remember how short your life is."[128]

Hawkwood received the envoys graciously.[129] One of them was a Burgundian soldier reputedly a man of "bad character" but "very effective at negotiations." Catherine appears to have intended to negotiate with Hawkwood on his own terms.

But Hawkwood ignored Catherine's entreaties and prepared to ride on Pisa. Florentine ambassadors tried to intercede on Pisa's behalf, but Hawkwood rebuffed them, saying defiantly that he would make an accord with the city on his own. He advanced toward Pisa along the left bank of the Arno, ravaging San Savino and San Casciano. He then crossed to the other side, stopping at the small town of Montemagnio di Calci, just twelve kilometers from Pisa. The Pisan chronicler Ranieri Sardo, who served as ambassador to Hawkwood, claimed that he kidnapped 200 people—men, women, and children—and stole some 1,000 animals "large and small."[130] The company maximized the area over which it did damage by dividing into smaller units. The Sienese ambassador stationed in Florence reported that the Pisan army defeated a brigade of 500 of Hawkwood's men outside the gates of Livorno.[131] But this was only rumor.

On 3 July, after a week of harassment, Hawkwood and Pisa reached an accord. The pact was signed at Hawkwood's camp near the Franciscan monastery at Nicosia in foothills outside Calci. Pisa agreed to pay the band 30,500 florins, with 3,000 florins going to Hawkwood personally, and 2,500 florins each to his co-commanders, John Thornbury and William Gold. Hawkwood's money was to be disbursed in yearly installment of 600 florins over five years. The remaining 25,000 florins were paid in two installments: the first (12,500) ten days after the accord and the second (12,500) by the end of September. As in the Florentine deal, Hawkwood promised not to molest Pisa for five years and to give advance warning should he need to pass through Pisan lands.[132]

Florentine envoys arrived in Hawkwood's camp the same day he signed the accord with Pisa. They brought the first installment of 40,000 florins owed by the city. Hawkwood assigned four of his men, Richard Romsey, John Foy, Robert Seaver, and William Tilly, to distribute the money to his troops.[133]

Ten days later, on 13 July 1375, Hawkwood came to terms with the city of Lucca. Owing perhaps to the city's fiscal crisis, Hawkwood took from Lucca a relatively small bribe of 7,000 florins.[134] But he extracted instead a promise of citizenship for himself, John Thornbury, and their "legitimate male heirs." The city also absolved the men from paying local taxes should they choose to settle in the city. The Lucchese city council approved the deal several months later, on 8 October 1375.[135]

The accord with Lucca apparently caused Hawkwood to reconsider Florence's earlier offer. On 12 July the Florentine city council granted Hawkwood a lifetime stipend. The legislation called for payment of 100 florins per month for the rest of Hawkwood's life provided that he remain in Italy.[136] The stipend was tax exempt, to be paid every July, to either John or a certified agent. The language of the bequest contains no evidence of coercion. The Florentines offered the stipend as a reward for Hawkwood's "nobility" and "virtue." Florence's steadfastness in paying the money would bear fruit for the city down the line.

Hawkwood rode next on Siena. He traveled back over the Arno and advanced south through the Val d'Era to the city of Volterra, not far from the northern border of the Sienese state. Despite his promise, Hawkwood looted Pisan lands along the way.[137] Sienese envoys met him at Volterra, hoping to forestall his entry into their territory. Like Lucca, Siena claimed penury and offered Hawkwood a relatively small bribe of 12,000 florins. But Hawkwood found the offer insulting, and a Florentine witness to the negotiations wrote back home that "the Sienese do nothing to help their cause." Hawkwood and his band looted Sienese territory for several days and then resumed talks. After some give-and-take, the two sides settled on 30,500 florins—the same amount that Pisa was required to pay. In return Hawkwood promised not to ride on Sienese lands for the next five years.[138] The disbursements were to be in three installments: 10,000 florins immediately and the remaining 20,500 in August and September. But Hawkwood inflicted an additional degree of humiliation on the Sienese by requiring them to give bonuses of 120 florins to his chancellor for drawing up the peace accord and nineteen barrels of wines, twelve sacks of fresh baked bread, and sixty pounds of confetti for himself and his co-captains so that they could celebrate their triumph in style.[139]

Hawkwood now advanced toward the city of Arezzo, his final target. He rode east, skirting the northern limit of the Sienese state, and then south through the Valdichiana to the town of Lucignano, on the border between Sienese and Aretine lands. Along the way he set fire to houses belonging to Sienese citizens (including the castle of a prominent Sienese noble, Niccoluccio di Francesco Malavolti) in retaliation for the city's lateness in paying the first installment of its bribe.

Hawkwood set up camp at the town of Laterina, just outside Arezzo.[140] The

company divided into the now customary three units and moved about the countryside robbing and looting. One contingent attacked a castle owned by the prominent Florentine family the Ricasoli and captured the garrison of fifteen infantrymen as well as "the beautiful" wife and the daughter of the lord Ricasoli. The
Florentines wrote an angry letter to Hawkwood, demanding he release the hostage and give back the castle.[141]

Hawkwood retreated to Laterina and undertook negotiations with both Aretine and Florentine officials. On 24 July 1375 he reached an agreement. The Pisan
chronicler Ranieri Sardo claimed that the city paid 8,500 florins. The Bolognese
envoy Alberto Galuzzi put the total at 13,000 florins, a figure that also appears in
Florentine sources.[142] Galuzzi also reported that as part of the deal Hawkwood
agreed to release his hostages and the Ricasoli castle into Florentine custody.

As Hawkwood settled affairs with Arezzo, the additional installments owed to
him by Pisa and Florence came due. The Pisan envoys Oddo Macchaione and Ser
Piero da Civoli arrived at his camp at Laterina with 6,500 florins; the Florentine
Spinello Alberti came with 30,000 florins.[143] According to one report, Queen
Johanna of Naples also paid Hawkwood a large bribe at this time. But the source
does not indicate whether the subsidy was for a past debt or to prevent Hawkwood
from proceeding south into her lands.[144]

At this point Hawkwood contemplated his next move. Rumors circulated, but
no one really knew what he intended to do next. Hawkwood intentionally fostered
an atmosphere of uneasiness by spreading misinformation and by breaking his
band into smaller contingents and changing his location. Giovanni Pico, stationed
in the city of Parma, said that he had heard reports that Hawkwood now intended
to quit Tuscany and go on to Genoa "to receive money from the said commune and
to burn everything that he can."[145] Alberto Galuzzi, from Florence, believed that
Hawkwood wished to go to Pisa and then to Bologna. Niccolò Martinelli, stationed
in Bologna, claimed that Hawkwood and his band would stay near Arezzo. Five
days after his initial report, Giovanni Pico changed his mind and said that he
thought Hawkwood wished to travel to Rome. Two days later, Giovanni admitted
that he was utterly confused.[146]

Martinelli's estimate proved correct. Hawkwood remained near Arezzo, where
he focused on collecting the money owed him.[147] The total he extorted became the
subject of speculation among contemporaries. The Bolognese chronicler estimated
that Tuscany paid Hawkwood more than 250,000 florins.[148] Giovanni Pico guessed
that the sum was about 200,000 florins ("John and his society received 200,000
florins in tribute from the time they formed the company").[149] The documentary
sources indicate that the total was approximately 215,500 florins, not including
stolen livestock and grain, which would have made the total much higher. The

magnificent figure was more than five times greater than the operating capital of the businesses of the famous merchant of Prato, Francesco Datini, one of the wealthiest men of the age; it was three times greater than the operating capital of the great Medici bank of the next century; and more than the combined yearly revenue of the cities of Lucca and Siena.

While Hawkwood counted his riches at Arezzo, the sentiment against him in the region reached a fevered pitch. The Florentines praised him as "noble" and "virtuous" to his face, but behind his back they condemned him and his men as "a society of thieves."[150] Officials pushed for a military league against his company and its purported boss, the pope. Negotiations among the Tuscan states began the moment Hawkwood crossed the Apennines. Florence spearheaded the initiative, sending letters and ambassadors in all directions. "They told us," wrote Sienese envoys on 29 June, "that . . . they want to make a league and concord with every lord of whatsoever condition and whatsoever type and with every community that wants to maintain its liberty."[151] On the same day that Hawkwood settled with the Aretines, an agreement was reached between Florence and Milan for a "defensive" league against the pope.[152] The league army was to have 2,350 lances with accompanying units of archers, crossbowmen, and infantrymen.[153] The bylaws stressed its strictly defensive nature. The distinction was important; Milan, at peace with the church, was therefore technically not in violation of its treaty. Siena, Pisa, Lucca, Arezzo, and Queen Johanna of Naples joined the league in short order.[154]

The anger toward the church was reflected in attempts to make clergy pay for the bribes. Sensitive to ecclesiastical privilege, officials usually took care to request small sums, in the form of loans, with explicit assurance of repayment. In 1375, however, Florence imposed a large loan on the clergy for 90,000 florins and made clear that it would be collected "by love or by force." The Sienese followed suit, with a loan of 40,000 florins on its clergy to be paid "in the manner of the Florentines."[155] In Florence, taxation was accompanied by expropriation of ecclesiastical property. Soon after Hawkwood's raid, city officials initiated a commission known as the *ufficiali dei preti,* with the authority to levy forced loans and sequester property. One historian called it the "most comprehensive liquidation of ecclesiastical land holding anywhere in Europe prior to the Reformation."[156]

Florence's chancellor, Coluccio Salutati, condemned both Hawkwood and the pope in the strongest terms. In an epistle to the Hungarian prince Charles of Durazzo dated 2 September 1375, Salutati outlined a grand conspiracy, beginning with the pontiff's refusal to sell the Florentines grain during famine. "It was necessary that we seek grain for our sustenance from Flanders, Burgundy, Spain and—still more merciless—from the Turks and islands of the Saracens. We found more charity from foreigners and infidels than from the Church!" Coluccio point-edly accused the church of directing Hawkwood and his company against Tuscany. "While we were exhausted from famine, the church set their eyes on us and all of Tuscany . . . they held a colloquium and offered remedy by hiring the company of soldiers so that they would—or so they said—not vex us. In this way, they prepared for our destruction . . . [and] within one day [Hawkwood's band] was united into a pestilential 'society' and sent upon Tuscany."[157]

Simone di Ranieri Peruzzi, the ambassador who had helped make the accord with Hawkwood at Imola, corroborated Salutati's version. He wrote in his *Ricordi* that "the pope in Avignon had an agreement with Hawkwood and his Englishmen (though pretending to be forced) that they ride up to the gates of Florence on the day of Saint John the Baptist up to Rifredi."[158] Sozomen, the chronicler of Pistoia, portrayed Hawkwood as little more than a papal agent.[159] The Florentine chroni-cler Marchionne Stefani offered a still more blunt assessment: "the cardinal sent his men on us as if to say: ' I will burn their harvest and when they are starving, I will make myself *signore* of Florence.' "[160]

Florence's suspicions were shared in Tuscany and elsewhere. Giovanni Pico, ally of Bernabò Visconti, stated firmly in a letter from Parma that Hawkwood and his company "had a stipend from the church when the society began."[161] The anonymous chronicler of Rimini also blamed the church, as did the chronicler of Piacenza.[162] The Milanese lord Bernabò Visconti—an inveterate foe of the papacy—expressed openly in a letter to Ludovico Gonzaga that he suspected that Hawkwood was on the pope's payroll.[163] The case against the church seemed all the more conclusive when in August 1375, shortly after the extortions in Tuscany were finished, John Hawkwood and John Thornbury finally received the castles in the Marches promised them a year earlier.

The case against the church was, however, anything but conclusive. The pope's own correspondence on the matter gives little evidence of a conspiracy. He wrote to several cities during peace negotiations with the Visconti in May 1375, warning that peace in Lombardy might bring Hawkwood to Tuscany.[164] Admittedly such letters, as we have seen with Visconti, could be intended to deflect blame. But the pontiff also wrote a letter to Hawkwood's corporal, John Clifford, calling for restraint and expressing fears that his own lands might likewise be targeted.[165] The fifteenth-century Milanese diarist Corio, no friend of the pope, wrote that Hawkwood's company formed after the peace accord between the Visconti and the church and was made up of former soldiers of both the Visconti and the church. Corio said explicitly that they were "were without stipend" and thus on no one's payroll.[166]

The situation was, in short, a very complicated one. What has been overlooked is the state of Hawkwood's band itself. It was an angry and unruly horde, lacking in pay. Like their civilian counterparts, Hawkwood's soldiers suffered from disease and food scarcity resulting from the famine and plague of 1374. Reports indicate that conditions were particularly bad in the late spring of 1375, just before the raid on Tuscany.[167] It should be remembered that it was the pontiff's inability to pay his troops that induced him to negotiate with the Visconti in the first place. But lack of funds made it more difficult for the pope to distance himself from the army or to dismiss it. What may have appeared to Tuscans as a conspiracy between pope and *condottiere* was more likely a continuation of a contentious dialogue over back pay. The pontiff was in an untenable position. The historian Gene Brucker is probably right when he says that if the pope was guilty of anything it was of "ignorance" and "poor handling" of the situation.[168]

Regardless of who bore the ultimate responsibility for it, Hawkwood's raid proved the casus belli. The defensive league of July was followed by the election in Florence of a commission, or *balia*, of eight men—dubbed the "eight saints"—to direct the war effort.[169] The *balia* commissioned a flag with the word "Libertà" on it and sent it to allied cities.[170] A local citizen, Gherardino Giani, confidently predicted that Florence would have victory within a year.[171] The Lucchese chronicler Sercambi sounded a dissenting voice: "Oh unwise community to take such actions against the Church of Rome; for he who is against God and acts against God, will be punished by God."[172]

# PART III

# THE MOST SOUGHT-AFTER
# CAPTAIN IN ITALY

# John Hawkwood and the
# War of Eight Saints, 1375–1377

> I am not able to write for you all the great cruelty they did there,
> which not [even] Nero committed.
>
> *The Bolognese chronicler speaking of deeds done*
> *by Hawkwood's men at Cesena, 1376*

The raid on Tuscany made Hawkwood a rich man. In addition to his share of
bribe money, he had gained a salary of 600 florins a year for the next five years and
a lifetime annual pension of 1,200 florins. According to a dispatch from Parma,
Hawkwood now meditated on various options, including leaving Italy altogether.
"John Hawkwood [Aukd] does not want stipend or provision from anyone, but
wants to stay in Venice, as he says, with his money, which they say is 100,000
ducats, and stay there as long as it seems appropriate to him, while he sees how
events in Lombardy proceed. And then he will accept stipend if it seems appropriate to him or otherwise . . . he will do his business and . . . it is believed, return to
England."[1] How serious Hawkwood was about returning to England is unclear. A
master of disinformation, he understood well the importance of being ambiguous.
From the point of view of bargaining with Italian states, uncertainty was helpful
in driving up the price for his service. Hawkwood had just months earlier taken
citizenship in Lucca and given that city vague indications that he might eventually settle there.

Hawkwood's raid on Tuscany, however, left Florence and the region at war with
the pope.[2] Florence's decision to oppose the church was, as scholars have emphasized, a traumatic one for the city, which had long supported papal policy and
owed much of its financial prosperity to the favorable position held by its bankers
at the papal court.[3]

The conflict spread quickly. Orte and Narni, small papal towns on the Tuscan border, revolted in October 1375, followed by Montefiascone and Viterbo.[4] From Viterbo the insurrection moved to Umbria, reaching Città di Castello on 3 December and Perugia four days later.[5] The poet chronicler of Arezzo, Bartolomeo di Ser Gorello, expressed his wonderment in verse: "Tell me, son, if you would ever believe, / That the great power of the holy Church could fall with such speed?"[6] The war was called the War of Eight Saints after the eight-man Florentine *balia* that directed it.

Florence showed considerable optimism about its military prospects at the outset of the war, believing the contest would be a relatively short one.[7] But the city had great anxiety about Hawkwood and focused much of its diplomatic activity on trying to hire him. Hawkwood's prestige was at its highest since his entry into Italy. He was now clearly the most sought-after captain in Italy.

Florence sent a steady stream of ambassadors—"homines aptes" (skilled men) Filippo Bastari called them—to try to coax the Englishman to their side. "It is," the Florentines wrote to Bernabò Visconti on 8 September, "a matter of the greatest importance."[8] Although they denounced Hawkwood in their private counsels and letters to allies, city officials praised him in the highest terms in their direct correspondence with him. Their letters began with the salutation "dear John Hawkwood, magnificent knight and our dearest friend."[9]

Florence counted heavily on the efforts of its ally Milan, particularly on the embassies of Ruggiero Cane, one of Bernabò Visconti's most trusted envoys.[10] Cane knew Hawkwood from their joint service in Visconti armies against the pope back in 1369 and 1372. In 1372, Cane had stood along with Hawkwood as one of the captains at Asti, and they purportedly became good friends. Cane was said to "know Hawkwood's moods and desires, as well as his secrets."[11] This was hyperbole. But Cane had earned the Englishman's respect and had the additional advantage of knowing well the current political situation, having acted as one of Bernabò's representatives at the ill-fated convention in Bologna on 4 June 1375.

Cane arrived in Tuscany by way of the city of Lucca in July. He attached himself to Hawkwood while the Englishman was still conducting his raid on Tuscany. His approach was noteworthy. He ingratiated himself with Hawkwood by actively working on his behalf, including helping him collect bribe money from his victims. On 14 August, for instance, Cane wrote to officials in Lucca to demand outstanding sums due Hawkwood.[12]

The Florentines encouraged Cane's embassies. They sent their own envoy to join him, the treasurer Spinello di Luca Alberti, who had arranged the pact of 21 June 1375.[13] Like Cane, Alberti was also said to have developed a good personal relationship with Hawkwood, to have gained the captain's trust by dint of his forthrightness and virtue. The fifteenth-century Florentine writer Giovanni Cavalcanti claimed that Hawkwood was so impressed by Alberti that he gave him back a portion of the bribe he had extorted in June. This too was hyperbole. Hawkwood used the ongoing dialogue with the two men to extort more favors. He asked Florence to allow his yearly stipend to be paid to him also in England, a condition explicitly forbidden under the original terms of the agreement. The request provides further evidence that Hawkwood contemplated returning home, or at least wished to make it appear so. The Florentines, however, became annoyed and told the ambassadors that they were inclined not to pay Hawkwood at all if he continued in the service of the church. "Tell him we will not give him a single *grosso,*" officials wrote to Alberti. Cane diffused the tension and wrote to the Florentines reminding them to use "prudence and solicitude" in handling Hawkwood.[14]

The dialogue continued, and Hawkwood remained unconvinced. The Florentines grew frustrated. When a detailed report on the movements of church forces from the ambassador Giorgio de Scali in August 1375 omitted mention of Hawkwood, angry officials admonished their envoy: "We are greatly amazed that you made no mention to us of Sir John since you know that it is our intention to have him in the service of Bernabò and us, and no one else."[15]

Cane and Alberti did, however, succeed in luring away four hundred English horsemen from Hawkwood's brigade in September.[16] Florentine officials enthusiastically greeted the news and lauded their new soldiers as "the best of all fighters."[17]

Although the Florentines claimed that Hawkwood had always been on the payroll of the church, Pope Gregory was in fact competing with them for Hawkwood's services. The captain's attitude toward the pontiff was ostensibly no more benevolent than it was toward the others. In a letter written to the cardinal of Sant' Angelo in mid-September, Hawkwood's co-captain John Thornbury described him as "very inflexible toward the pope" and in particular angry with Gregory for failing to give him a castle (perhaps Montefortini) he had promised back in the summer. Thornbury, however, indicated his own willingness to take up the papal cause for the right price.[18]

Hawkwood meanwhile passed much of his time in the environs of Arezzo and Siena. At the end of September he set up camp at Abbadia a Isola, a town just north of Siena on the Via Francigena. From there he pressed Sienese officials for outstanding monies owed him, most probably relating to the recent raid. Ambassadors reported that he spoke "disparaging words" about Siena and made threats against them.[19] Some in that city believed that Hawkwod intended to seize the town of Montepulciano to satisfy the debt, but this did not happen. The behavior of the Sienese differed markedly from that of Florence. While Hawkwood was encamped at Abbadia a Isola, the Florentine delegation, led by Spinello di Luca

Alberti, arrived with timely payment of the third and final installment of the bribe the city owed him. Florence clearly hoped that ready payments would help entice Hawkwood to its side. But the Sienese, Florence's ally, did the cause no good. By November Hawkwood still did not have the money he was seeking from them. John Thornbury sent the city a threatening letter.

> Magnificent Lords. I am greatly amazed that you do not wish to maintain the pact between your commune and the society, because you promised us, Richard Romsey and myself, through your own scribes, a certain sum. And you also promised us that the "menda" of horses injured would, according to tradition, be made in your territory, but neither the "menda" nor our payment was made. Therefore, if you do not make these payments as you are obliged by promises and pacts, you will have to excuse us that we also do not obey the pacts between ourselves and your commune.[20]

By that time, however, Hawkwood had already chosen to serve the pope.[21] A Florentine ambassador reported that a deal was concluded in the middle of October by which Hawkwood and his band were to receive 30,000 florins a month for four months of service. No mention was made of the number of troops, but the ambassador stressed that the agreement was a "renewal" of Hawkwood's contract—Florence had never believed that he had previously been a "free" captain. Although disappointed, Florentine officials expressed hope on the grounds that the church could not sustain the expense of Hawkwood's brigade for long.[22]

Hawkwood divided his band into two parts. He sent one to the Romagna to keep a watch on events at Bologna and the other to Umbria to keep a watch on Perugia—the two most important cities in the pope's domain. Hawkwood himself went to Umbria at the head of eight hundred lances.

Hawkwood would serve the pope for the next two years. He did little to further his military reputation but instead engaged in the now familiar sport of exploiting the pope's lack of revenue to accumulate favors and estates, in this case gaining lands in the Romagna, where the war caused chaos. Hawkwood's modus operandi was tantamount to diversification of his financial portfolio and was likely at the root of his decision to take service with the pope in the first place. Despite his self-serving ways and indifference as a soldier, Hawkwood nevertheless became involved in two of the worst atrocities of the war, the killing of civilian populations in Faenza and Cesena.

## Revolt in Umbria

Hawkwood moved first in December to relieve the pope's garrison at Città di Castello. The rebellion there was particularly brutal. Citizens hunted down papal officials, threw them from the windows of the communal palace, and hanged them from the city's battlements.[23] Perugia revolted a few days later. An angry crowd of "small and great, noble and non-noble citizens" in that city gathered in the piazza, shouting "death to the abbot and the pastors of the church."[24] The abbot was the papal governor, the Frenchman Gérard du Puy, who was known locally as the "abate di Monmaggiore" (abbot of Marmoutier). The crowd forced du Puy to retreat to the city's formidable citadel (*cittadella*) along with his military entourage, which included the Englishman William Gold, whom Hawkwood had sent ahead to protect the governor, and the renowned Breton mercenary Bernard de La Salle, whom the pope had hired to oversee the defense of the citadel.[25] The insurgents laid siege to the *cittadella*, which purportedly had a ten years' supply of provisions. They plowed up roads, cut off escape routes, and undertook a bombardment of its walls.

Hawkwood attempted to storm the walls of Città di Castello but was driven away. He rode then to Perugia and camped just below the city at the Ponte di San Giovanni, the scene of his great victory against that city back in 1368. But rather than relieve du Puy and those trapped in the citadel, Hawkwood remained in camp, content to hold back and watch the action from a distance. The ongoing bombardment inhibited a direct attack, as did the recent memory of the unsuccessful attempt at Città di Castello. Perugian sources indicate that Hawkwood's band was approximately three hundred lances, hardly enough to undertake a bold offensive.[26]

Hoping to restrain Hawkwood from despoiling their lands, the Perugians received Hawkwood more as an honored guest than as an enemy. Ambassadors visited his camp at Ponte di San Giovanni bringing gifts and small bribes.[27] Hawkwood was given a new horse on 19 December in anticipation of Christmas.[28] But local citizens set upon members of his brigade, robbing, among others, his corporal John Brice. Hawkwood immediately retaliated with a raid, taking hostages in return for the lost sum.[29]

The bombardment of the citadel proceeded with ferocity. The insurgents aimed at its walls the enormous trebuchet known as the "priest chaser" (*cacciaprete*), which, according to the chronicler's claim, tossed stones weighing fifteen hundred pounds. It was fired "all day long"[30] along with a smaller device, a *mangonella*, which launched stones of fifty pounds. The machine also hurled excrement and live animals.

The rocks damaged the citadel and forced the abbot and his entourage to surrender on 22 December 1375.[31] The Perugians rewarded Domenico Bonintende, the craftsman who had built the "priest chaser," with an annual bonus of 25 florins, a home in the city, and citizenship (he was Florentine by birth).[32]

Hawkwood sent the Italian corporal Bartolomeo da Gaggio to negotiate the terms of the surrender.

The deal involved three parties: the victorious insurgents, the defeated contingent of the citadel, and Hawkwood and his brigade. The conditions were surprisingly favorable to Hawkwood. Du Puy and his men were allowed to depart the citadel freely, provided that they did not take any provisions and materials belonging to the fort with them. Hawkwood and his band were required to leave Perugian territory within two days of the liberation and had to promise not to return or "offend either persons or things, or the contado, fort or district of Perugia" for six months, beginning 1 January 1376. In return, Perugian officials promised not to do "any damage" to the company or the church and to refrain from hiring away any of Hawkwood's band without Hawkwood's direct consent. Perugia also agreed to compensate Hawkwood for damages already done to his band, in return for a promise that he return all hostages. For his role in helping arrange the accord, Bartolomeo da Gaggio received landed estates bearing an annual revenue of 200 florins.[33]

Of the eleven articles that made up the treaty, only three involved overt obligations on the part of the vanquished to the victor. The Perugians even allowed members of Hawkwood's band into city, where some received horses, provisions, and arms. The Florentines were outraged and accused the Perugians of allowing themselves to be tricked by Hawkwood. "Are you not aware of the cunning [astuzia] of the English?? What does it mean that you receive them within your wall as if they are friends, and give them arms . . . and all martial material with which they will attack and offend you and the other people of Tuscany?"[34] Officials reminded the Perugians that Hawkwood cared little for them. "It is impossible for foreigners to care about your liberty," they wrote.[35] The Florentines conceded, however, that Perugia did well to come to an agreement with Hawkwood, so that "at least he will not harm you."[36]

The evacuation of the citadel was completed the day after Christmas.[37] The captives and their belongings were released into Hawkwood's custody.[38] Bernard de La Salle emerged first, followed by William Gold and, lastly, du Puy.[39] Their personal effects, stuffed into fifteen trunks, were handed over to John Thornbury, who handled the redistribution. William Gold's possessions included three silver goblets and an enameled helmet emblazoned with his crest. Bernard de La Salle had pieces of precious cloth, a purple hood, and a woman's tunic(!).[40]

Hawkwood treated du Puy more as a prisoner than an ally. He placed a guard over the abbot and then demanded back pay from the church, which was apparently already in arrears.[41] Hawkwood and his men rode with du Puy to Cesena and "consigned" him to Galeotto Malatesta, the pope's ally and lord of Rimini, who then relegated him to the garden of his palace. Perugian officials outlined Hawkwood's deal with Malatesta in a letter to Siena dated 14 January 1376. "John Hawkwood [Aukuud], captain of the English society, released the abbot . . . into the possession of Galeotto . . . with the promise from Galeotto to pay his [Hawkwood's] stipend and that of his brigade."[42]

Du Puy was for Hawkwood little more than surety for back pay. The *Cronache malatestiane* estimated du Puy's value at 130,000 florins, which, if true, indicates that the pope had not paid Hawkwood any of his salary over the past four months. This could well have been the case, since the turmoil in the papal states separated Pope Gregory from critical sources of tax revenue, thus exacerbating the pontiff's traditional problem paying his men.[43]

After redeeming du Puy, Hawkwood and his band stayed in the Romagna.[44] In early February 1376, they skirmished with the combined forces of Sinibaldo Ordelaffi, lord of Forlì; Antonio da Montefeltro, Count of Urbino; and Guido da Polenta, lord of Ravenna, who had joined the uprising against the church.[45] Montefeltro, in a letter to Città di Castello, derided Hawkwood's band as little more than a "diabolic plague." In the meantime the town of Castrocaro, just south of Forlì, rebelled against the pope.[46] Hawkwood rode there. The citizens of Castrocaro, fearing his approach, abandoned the town and fled to nearby Forlì.[47] This allowed Hawkwood to seize Castrocaro.[48]

Pope Gregory did not approve of the town's capture. He had intended only for Hawkwood to put down the revolt. But Hawkwood wished to force the pontiff's hand with respect to pay, which remained lacking. He refused to relinquish the town, and Gregory had little choice but to formally invest him with it, in return for uncompensated services.

In this manner, Hawkwood involved himself in a major subplot of the war: the grab for lands in the Romagna and papal states. Throughout the war, military captains and local strongmen (often one and the same) took advantage of the confusion and the pope's financial difficulties to co-opt land for themselves. Gregory gave towns to allies and friends in return for loans or to satisfy debts. Galeotto Malatesta, one of the pope's staunchest allies in the region, had been an especial beneficiary of the policy. In return for his financial support, Galeotto secured numerous towns, such as Santarcangelo, Cesena, San Sepolcro, and others.[49] There was in short a market in towns for those to whom the church owed money; and Hawkwood was one of the pontiff's principal creditors.

Shortly after taking Castrocaro, the pope invested Hawkwood with two other towns, Bagnacavallo and Cotignola, both in the Romagna. The bequests have received considerable scholarly attention, although the exact circumstances of their transfer remain unclear.[50] The sources do not agree on the date or even what additional (if any) territories were included. Some claim that Hawkwood received also the town of Bertinoro. Others claim he gained Mirandola and Conselice; some omit Cotignola, while still others include Castrocaro.[51] The confusion derives from the fact that Hawkwood held all these towns at one time or another during his service to the pope in this war. Local chroniclers were understandably confused about where papal largesse began and military force ended, which lands were given to Hawkwood and which he took by force.

Much has been written about the grants of Cotignola and Bagnacavallo, how they constituted a turning point in Hawkwood's career and more generally a turning point in the history of mercenaries in Italy—the initiation of the process by which "free"captains became territorial lords, which reached its culmen in the fifteenth century. But as we have already seen, Hawkwood possessed estates throughout Italy, and this was not unique to him. The most immediate signifi-cance of the papal grants of Bagnacavallo and Cotignola was that they formed strategically important bridgeheads in an important theater of the war. Hawk-wood used Bagnacavallo, for example, to station troops, to guard local passes, and as a base for supplies.

Meanwhile, the pope also granted John Thornbury the town of Meldola.[52] Shortly thereafter, he gave a church benefice to Thornbury's bastard son Philip— essentially the same honor he had bestowed on Hawkwood's bastard son several years earlier. Ironically, the pope presented young Philip, still a small boy, with a benefice that he had previously promised to the great church reformer John Wycliff. Wycliff's reaction is recorded in the third book of his *De Civili Dominio.* "The lord pope gave me a prebend in the church of Lincoln, and having taken care to collect the 45 lire first fruits, he [then] conferred the same prebend on a youth overseas."[53] Wycliff did not know that the youth was also illegitimate.

## The Sack of Faenza

Hawkwood left Castrocaro on 12 February 1376 and rode to the town of Faenza. He set up his camp outside the city. Faenza belonged to the church, but the mood within was tense, and the papal governor, fearing revolt, requested Hawkwood's protection. A letter written from that city by the Bolognese ambassador Alberto Galuzzi on 12 February gives a sense of the overall military situation.

> Today the 12 of February John Hawkwood [Agud] left Castrocaro andfortif ied his
> brigade at Forlimpopoli. . . . And he sent 100 lances to Cesena. John Thornbury left
> there with a certain brigade and moved toward the Marches. . . . John Hawkwood is
> the papal overseer of Bagnacavallo. . . . The majority of his brigade is fortified and he

is a little outside of Faenza, where he makes his residence. Sinibaldo de Ordelaffi is at Forlì, where he is made captain of the people for the defense of the city.[54]

Hawkwood remained encamped near Faenza until March, when he began a siege of the nearby (eight kilometers) small town of Granarola. He was forced to withdraw and returned to Faenza.[55] This time the papal governor arranged to have the gates to city opened to Hawkwood, who entered with his men and ordered the local inhabitants to surrender their arms under pain of death.[56]

What followed was a sad affair. "They robbed the whole land," wrote the Bolognese chronicler, "and they chased out the citizens small and great . . . so that there remained no one except the women, whom they kept to violate."[57] According to the Florentine chronicler Stefani, the English soldiers left only those women "who were old or rustic." A cleric purportedly stood watch at the town gate and shouted at the fleeing women: "Turn back, this is good for the army."[58] The Sienese chronicler told the story of two of Hawkwood's corporals who fell into a bitter fight in a local monastery over who would rape an attractive young nun. Hawkwood intervened personally, plunging a dagger into the chest of the young woman.

Stefani called the sack "cursed and dishonest." The Bolognese chronicler said it was "the greatest cruelty ever." The sources emphasize the all-consuming greed on the part of Hawkwood's men. The chronicler of Forlì said that Hawkwood's men made no distinction between ecclesiastics and laity, systematically stripping both of their goods.[59] The Florentine merchant court records (*mercanzia*) relay the tale of two Florentine merchants, Bartolomeo Petriboni and Francesco Bernadetti, who had been residing in the city. Just before the attack, the papal governor consigned his deposits to the men. But Hawkwood's troops robbed the men, and the governor, unable to recover his money, held the merchants responsible and threw them in prison. Bernadetti's wife petitioned the governor to absolve her husband and to intercede on his behalf with Hawkwood. The governor agreed and met with Hawkwood. But the Englishman would hear nothing of the matter. The merchants remained in jail.[60]

The frenzied search for money and the lawless behavior of Hawkwood's men at Faenza are further evidence that the army lacked pay. The soldiers even set upon one another. A violent brawl broke out over the distribution of booty, in which several men were killed. Thomas Belmont, the son of the long-departed Andrew, was wounded, as was John Brice, apparently seriously.

Contemporary sources did not blame Hawkwood so much as the pope and papal governor for the excesses. Stefani called the governor a "traitor"; the Bolognese chronicler said he was "the worst man in the world."[61] It is difficult, however, to separate propaganda from fact. Both Bologna and Florence were at this point ready to blame all ills on the church.

In practical terms, Hawkwood's capture of Faenza gave him a base from which to move on Bologna. While he was laying siege to Granarola in March, the city had revolted from the church.[62] The pope's legate in Bologna, Guillaume Noellett, the cardinal of Sant' Angelo, had been exiled and fled to Ferrara.[63] Hawkwood first sent a small advance force of soldiers, led by John Thornbury, William Gold, and Philip Puer, to monitor the situation. But before he was able to reinforce the brigade, a hundred or so "horsemen and their servants" were captured, including Puer and Gold and the bastard sons of John Thornbury and John Birch, named Philip and Lawrence, respectively. More important for Hawkwood, his own bastard son, Thomas, whom he apparently entrusted to the others while he ravaged Faenza, was also seized.[64] They were placed in prison; their possessions were seized and divided among the citizenry.[65]

Hawkwood's response to the provocation was immediate and violent. He led a band of eight hundred lances from his outpost in Faenza against Bolognese territory.[66] He captured the small town of Massa Lombarda, which was then ceded to him by the exiled papal governor Noellet.[67] The Bolognese tried to open negotiations, sending an ambassador, Roberto da Saliceto, to Hawkwood. But Hawkwood mistreated Saliceto and, according to the ambassador, "demanded such tremendous terms they could not have wanted more, even if they were citizens of Faenza." Saliceto concluded that "there are no worse people in the world."[68]

The sides nevertheless continued to talk. Alberto Galuzzi reported on 8 May 1376 that Hawkwood sought above all the unconditional release of his men and their children. Bologna for its part wanted Hawkwood to cede to it the town of Faenza, which was still in his possession, and Massa Lombarda.[69]

The negotiations continued over the next several days. One of the Bolognese captives, an Englishman called Giovanni Favella (John Spark?), served as intermediary between the two sides. On 11 May, Galuzzi reported that Hawkwood demanded monetary compensation of 130,000 ducats in addition to the return of his captives and their goods. In return he was willing at least to discuss the cession of Faenza. Hawkwood must have left the impression that he was willing to compromise, since another Bolognese official, Bornio da Sala, who was familiar with the talks, wrote on 12 May that he believed "that there will be without fail a truce for fourteen or sixteen months."[70]

Bornio's optimism was misplaced. Instead of making peace, Hawkwood staged a brief but destructive raid (15 May 1376) through the Bolognese countryside. He took prisoner three hundred people and "innumerable animals."[71] "They rode . . .

up to the canal between Ferrara and Bologna," wrote Niccolò d'Este in a letter to the Venetians dated 16 May, "and they did much damage capturing people, animals and great prey."[72]

His bargaining position improved, Hawkwood now began negotiations anew. He announced that he would return his captives, human and nonhuman, only if the Bolognese satisfied "all the pacts" he had sought earlier. Hawkwood insisted, first and foremost, on the release of his son and the sons of John Thornbury and John Brice. He offered in return only vague assurances about Faenza, saying that "should he decide do anything with the city, he would make it available to the Bolognese for 10,000 ducats less than for anyone else."[73]

Despite Hawkwood's hard-line approach, the Bolognese were eager to settle. Not only did they wish to forestall further depredations, but officials also saw hope in the disunity within the Englishman's army. They had taken careful note of the fight over booty at Faenza. "On account of this discord," wrote Alberto Galuzzi, "we pushed for peace more quickly. The reason was because the English, seeing themselves opposed on all sides, are inclined to stay together.... With peace made, however, we will have a dialogue with them and then we can try to divide them."[74]

The sides reached an agreement on 25 May 1376. Beltramo degli Alidosi, the lord of nearby Imola, also signed the deal. The terms are somewhat hazy. Hawkwood agreed to give up his hostages in return for those taken by the Bolognese. Hawkwood's son thus came back to him, as did his good friend William Gold. It is not clear whether Hawkwood received the 130,000 florins he demanded earlier. He did get Bolognese officials to formally acknowledge his right to the Romagnol towns he had already seized, a list that now included Bagnacavallo, Cotignola, Castrocaro, Massa Lombarda, and Bertinoro.[75] It is not clear how Hawkwood came into possession of the last.

The Bolognese did not, however, receive Faenza as they had hoped. Hawkwood was in fact negotiating the sale of the town for a purported 55,000-60,000 florins to Niccolò d'Este at precisely the same time that he was concluding the deal with Bologna.[76] But Hawkwood ultimately retained Faenza and used it as his base of operations in the region.

Hawkwood agreed to withdraw his army from the environs of Bologna within two days and to give four days' notice, and use clearly marked roads, should he seek to reenter local territory.[77] Bologna agreed to restitute the goods stolen from the English captives. But this proved highly problematic. Bolognese officals called on citizens to bring all the stolen property, "arms, horses and goods," to the cortile of the Anziani by 1 June.[78] This did not happen. Five months later, William Gold was still trying to get his belongings back.[79] The Bolognese citizens were themselves frustrated. Saluccio Bentivoglio had held Philip Puer captive at his own expense. He sought 220 ducats' worth of compensation from the government but received nothing in return.[80]

## Entertaining Offers

The diplomatic activity in the English camp at Faenza did not end with the signing of the accord of 28 May.[81] As Hawkwood finished negotiations with Bologna, he began talks with Venice. The Venetians sought Hawkwood's services against Duke Leopold of Austria, who had invaded their territory in mid-March.[82] They sent the ambassadors Niccolò Morosini and Leonardo Dandolo with an offer to hire him along with 800–1,000 lances and 600–700 archers—in effect his entire current army and more—for four months at between 100,000 and 120,000 ducats. The envoys also promised to give Hawkwood and his corporals a bonus of 10,000 florins.[83] If this did not please him, they would take a smaller force of 400 lances and 300 archers, so long as Hawkwood himself agreed to command them. Each lance would receive 28 ducats a month, a figure that was well beyond the market rate.

The Venetians had laid the groundwork for their embassy weeks earlier by serving as intermediary for the release of Hawkwood's son from Bolognese captivity. They took Thomas Hawkwood and the sons of Brice and Thornbury to Venice while John Hawkwood negotiated with Bolognese officials. They treated young Thomas well, setting him up with "some good people in Venice" who saw to his comfort. The envoys noted that their city was well suited to such service, since there were many "foreign-born people" living there.[84]

The Venetians had instructed their envoys to keep their negotiations with Hawkwood "secret." But this was not possible. There were at Faenza numerous embassies to Hawkwood, from Bologna, Milan, Florence, the church, and various other cities. The Bolognese envoy Alberto Galuzzi was in fact well informed of the activities of the Venetians and reported on them in the letter of 25 May.[85] Galuzzi also indicated that Hawkwood was conducting talks with the king of Aragon. The reasons for this are not entirely clear. The English had recently negotiated with Aragon for mutual action against Castille, which supported France and had recently been conducting raids with its navy on the English coast. But at the moment there was truce between the two Spanish kingdoms.[86] The dialogue with Aragon gives notice, however, that for all his involvement in Italian affairs, Hawkwood maintained contact back home and monitored the situation there.

Hawkwood showed interest in the Venetian proposals, or at least he pretended to. In early June he sent four of his men to Venice to discuss the matter further.

Betrando di Alidosi, from nearby Imola, said that he believed that at least a portion of Hawkwood's brigade would work for the city.[87] Giovanni Pico, writing from Parma, said that he had heard from Ruggiero Cane that Hawkwood was leaning toward the Venetians. Giovanni Pico cited as the reason the large amount of money the Venetians were willing to pay.[88]

But the deal with Venice did not come off. Alberto Galuzzi said that Hawkwood turned the Venetian embassy down because he was awaiting word from the king of Aragon. "The English said that they could in no way respond to them [the Venetians] until the middle of June."[89] The Venetians grew impatient and hired the Veronese captain Jacopo de' Cavalli to command their armies at a salary of 700 ducats a month.

Competing alongside the Venetians for Hawkwood's services were the perennial contenders, the Florentines, who had sent embassies to Hawkwood throughout the war. Officials stepped up their efforts in the spring and early summer of 1376 as they became more pessimistic about the course of the war. Pope Gregory now prosecuted the war more aggressively. At the end of March 1376, he published an interdict against Florence. He excommunicated those officials responsible for the decision to go to war and encouraged states to expel Florentine merchants and seize their goods.[90] In May Gregory recruited for Italian service a band of Breton mercenaries, reputedly among the most ferocious of all fighters, led by the noted captains Silvestre Budes and Jean Malastroit.[91] Gregory himself undertook to return to Italy, to personally oversee the war effort. He left Avignon in June and ultimately installed himself in Rome in December 1376. The Florentines opened up peace negotiations, but Gregory showed no interest.

The need to separate Hawkwood from the church was therefore more urgent than it had ever been. The chronicler Stefani expressed especial fear of a conjunction between Hawkwood's band and the Bretons. Francis Petrarch described the Bretons as "a fiercely bellicose nation which had reduced the entire kingdom of France by fire and sword." "It would a dangerous thing," wrote Stefani, "to allow these two companies to become one."[92]

In their internal councils, the Florentines discussed several options, including even hiring *both* Hawkwood and Venice's nemesis, the Duke of Austria.[93] But more realistic voices advocated focusing on Hawkwood. "Let us provide in every way [possible]," said Marco Giotti, "that we have the brigade of Englishmen." In direct contrast to the Venetian approach, Giotti suggested that "the task be done loudly and openly."[94] At the end of May, the Florentine government sent Hawkwood a letter promising to absolve him of all "betrayals, injuries, damage and offenses" he had committed against Florence.[95] The letter was followed weeks later by another, granting Hawkwood the right to receive his annual pension "in whatever lands" he fought, even "beyond the mountains"—the very condition officials had angrily rejected months earlier.[96] In their correspondence with Milan, however, the Florentines expressed frustration. They complained that the Englishman asked for "impossible things."[97] Filippo Bastari suggested that the best approach was perhaps to appeal to the rank and file of Hawkwood's band, which he described as "paupers" and thus potentially able to be won over with bribes.[98]

The key figure in negotiations was again the Milanese envoy Ruggiero Cane. Florence and other cities often deferred to Cane or spoke through him.[99] Cane was present at Faenza thoughout the negotiations with various parties. On 31 May, Giovanni Pico wrote that he thought that Cane's entreaties were working and that Hawkwood might leave the pope's service for Milan. Alberto Galuzzi, writing from Bologna that same day, said "that Bernabò will soon have them [the English] in his pay."[100]

But Cane did not succeed. Hawkwood remained with the pope. Whatever problems the pontiff had meeting salary payments, he had given Hawkwood sizable and lucrative properties, which were uniquely his to give. In August 1376 papal budgets show he also paid a substantial sum of 13, 520 florins to Hawkwood in cash.[101] What the papal budgets do not show, however, are similar payments to the rank and file of Hawkwood's army, a discrepancy that would soon have consequences.

## The Massacre at Cesena

Unable to hire Hawkwood or forestall the Bretons, the allies braced for the concurrence of the two.[102] The Bretons were purportedly so confident of success that when Pope Gregory asked Malastroit whether he could defeat Florence, the Breton commander purportedly replied: "Does the sun enter there? If the sun can enter there, so can I."[103] The company arrived in southern Lombardy at the beginning of July and took immediately to ravaging the environs of Bologna and Imola, aided by local rebels and exiles. They set fires throughout the countryside but avoided battle and fortified positions. One of the exiles was Bornio da Sala, the Bolognese ambassador who had taken part in negotiations with Hawkwood back in May. He was eventually captured and beheaded.[104]

The Breton commanders met briefly with John Hawkwood at Faenza. They then rode to Cesena, where they were received by Galeotto Malatesta, who held the town for the pope.[105] They set up their camp just outside the city.

John Hawkwood remained at Faenza. The chronicler Stefani described him as "rich in money and [well] provided with food." But troubles persisted among his men. "He has," wrote Stefani, "a brigade that is not happy with him, and he is not happy with them." The dissensions gave the Florentines the opening to follow Filippo Bastari's advice and break up the band. They succeeded in hiring away 700 lances and 300 archers. The expense was, however, substantial. Florence paid each lance a salary of 22–24 florins a month and gave each corporal (among them Philip Puer) substantial loans and advances.[106] John Giffard, a corporal of still limited reputation, received a 1,500-florins advance.[107] "Never were we accustomed to such pay," wrote Stefani, who personally oversaw the enrollment of the troops.[108] Bernabò Visconti was so troubled by the price, he refused to pay, leaving the Bolognese and Florentines to shoulder the burden between them.

The advent of winter initiated a series of events that led to tragedy in Cesena. The Bretons had, since late fall, encamped outside the town. But provisions became scarce, and soldiers jostled with locals over limited food and forage. As the weather became colder and the price of goods rose, Robert, the cardinal of Geneva, who had come to Italy with the Bretons and taken charge in Cesena, decided to let the band into the city (24 November 1376). "They came inside the city," wrote the author of the *Cronache malatestiane,* from Rimini, "where they devoured, consumed and forced everything out of men and women."[109] A riot broke out on 2 February 1377. According to the Sienese chronicler, it was precipitated by the murder of four prominent citizens by the Bretons.[110] Local citizens then took to the streets shouting, "Long live the church and death to the Bretons." They hunted down Breton soldiers and killed some 300 to 400 of them.[111] What followed next was a scenario reminiscent of Faenza, only more violent. The Bolognese chronicler succinctly called it "the destruction of Cesena."[112]

Urged on by the cardinal of Geneva, the Bretons went on a rampage. "Everyone—women, old and young, and sick, and children and pregnant women," the Sienese chronicler wrote, "were cut to pieces at the point of a dagger."[113] People were purportedly thrown from the city wall and into shallow ditches in the streets; babies were "taken by the feet and dashed against the town wall."[114] Some died trying to escape, drowning in the moats surrounding the towns walls. By the end of the massacre, Cesena was in ruins. The estimates of the death toll have ranged from 2,500 to 8,000 people. A Florentine letter written at the time claimed 4,000 citizens were killed.[115] The *Cronache malatestiane* reported that "there remained neither man nor woman" in the city.[116] The Sienese chronicler likened the tragedy to the fall of Troy.[117] A local notary, Ludovico di Ser Romano da Fabriano, penned a short invective, *De Casu Cesenae,* condemning the massacre, one of the first literary protests in European history.[118]

Hawkwood participated in the massacre. The day after the riot began, Robert of Geneva issued a decree promising to grant the citizens of Cesena clemency if they relinquished their arms. He then called Hawkwood into the city to help enforce the decree. Once inside, however, Hawkwood's men joined in the attack on the now unarmed populace. Robert also brought into the city the Italian captain Alberigo da Barbiano, who was then also on the church's payroll.

Hawkwood's participation in the events at Cesena has done much to blacken his image. The nineteenth-century Italian historian Luigi Balduzzi blamed Hawkwood for behaving "contrary to justice," for being—at Faenza as well as at Cesena—the "agitator" rather than "moderator" of the events. Hawkwood's contemporaries were somewhat less condemning. The *Chronicon Estense* indicts Hawkwood for committing violence and extorting money in Cesena but claims that he also sent a thousand women to Rimini for safekeeping.[119] The Sienese chronicler asserts that Hawkwood was reluctant to take up the cardinal's charge. He gives a much quoted but probably apocryphal account of the conversation between the two.

> "I command you to descend on the land and do justice" said the cardinal.
>
> "Sir, when you want, I will go and prevail upon the inhabitants, so that they give up their arms ands and render them to you . . ." Hawkwood replied.
>
> "No," the cardinal said, "I want blood and justice."
>
> "Please think about it." Hawkwood protested.
>
> "I command you thus," said the cardinal.[120]

The Sienese chronicler's failure to condemn Hawkwood is particularly noteworthy given the animosity between his city and the English captain. Although we may dispute the particulars of the purported discourse with the cardinal of Geneva, it is indeed likely that Hawkwood played a lesser (though still violent) role at Cesena. The same cannot be said of the cardinal of Geneva himself, who is portrayed in all contemporary accounts as the villain in the affair. Several writers attribute his cruelty to his being a hunchback.

Whatever Hawkwood's role, the events at Cesena proved an important turning point in his career. After the sordid episode, he left papal service and took up with Milan, Florence, and the allied league. The transfer was accompanied by marriage into the Visconti family and, ironically, a belated general pardon in his native England for his misdeeds while in France.

# CHAPTER EIGHT

# Love and Diplomacy, 1377–1379

Man zemet liephart, löwen wild, den puffel, das er zeucht; der
ainem weib die haut abfildt, und si die tugent fleucht, noch künd
man si nicht machen zam, ir üble gifft ist aller werlde gram.
[Man tames leopards and wild lions, and trains the buffalo to pull;
but if a woman flees virtue, no man can tame her, even if he flays
her; for her evil poison is inimical to the whole world.]

*German vernacular poem by the mercenary /*
*poet Oswald von Wolkenstein*

We authorize . . . payment to our beloved and loyal knight Edward
de Berkeley and our faithful esquire Geoffrey Chaucer who
represent us to the Lord of Milan, Barnabò and our beloved and
loyal John Hawkwood [Johan Haukwode], who is in Lombardy.

*Royal Warrant, 13 May 1378, to make payments for the embassy of*
*Edward de Berkeley and Geoffrey Chaucer to Lombardy*

The massacre at Cesena in February 1377 was the moral low point of Hawkwood's career. He retreated after the tragedy to his base at Faenza. Less than a
month later, however, he received the ironic news from England that, "at the special asking of nobles, magnates and commonalty of the realm," he had been
granted a "general pardon." The decree absolved Hawkwood ("John de Haukewod, knight of the county of Essex") of the misdeeds he had committed as a
marauder in the early days of his military career, not for the crimes done at
Cesena. The pardon, which Hawkwood must have requested sometime earlier,
cited his "good service rendered in the king's wars in France and elsewhere." It
was brought before the English chancery by a group of prominent citizens, including his feofees John Sargeant and Robert Lindsey of Essex, who "mainperned"
(gave surety) on behalf of his "good behavior." On the same day John Clifford, who
participated with Hawkwood in the raid on Tuscany in 1375 and remained in his

brigade, was also granted a pardon, absolving him of the murder in France of a fellow soldier, John de Coupland.[1]

Hawkwood's pardon ostensibly cleared the way for an honorable return home. But there was in fact little incentive to make the voyage. Hawkwood had grown immensely wealthy in Italy and was at the peak of his demand as a captain. The market for English soldiers was generally at an apex, owing to the involvement of so many states in the War of Eight Saints and the concomitant outbreak of war between Genoa and Venice. Soldiers had become scarce. A Lucchese official entrusted with recruiting men-at-arms for that city complained that their salary demands had become "ridiculous."[2] Thus Hawkwood did not return to England; his pardon instead became a prelude to diplomatic service in Italy on behalf of the English king and accumulating estates to Essex.

At Faenza Hawkwood was again the subject of intense recruitment efforts by local ambassadors. On 10 April 1377 Milan, Florence, and their allies at last succeeded in convincing Hawkwood to leave papal employ and join them.[3] The reasons for his decision are unknown, but the pointless and—perhaps more important—profitless slaughter of innocents at Cesena may well have played a role.

Hawkwood's contract, effective 1 May 1377, called for him to command a brigade of 800 lances and 500 archers for one year. For the first two months, Hawkwood and his men received double pay, a right usually reserved for armies that had scored a major triumph on the battlefield. Hawkwood's personal share was 3,200 florins per month; each lance unit received 42 florins and the archers between 16 and 28 florins monthly.[4] The sums were extraordinary, even in a seller's market. After the second month, the salaries of the lance units and archers were halved for the duration of the contract, bringing them more in line with the market price. Hawkwood's pay remained the same. Bernabò Visconti shouldered a third of the expense, while Florence and the rest of the allies—Perugia, Bologna, Siena, Arezzo, Viterbo, Ascoli, Forlì, Urbino, Fermo, Città di Castello, Guido da Polenta of Ravenna, Bartolomeo da Sanseverino, Bertrando Alidosi of Imola, and Rodolfo Varano da Camerino—picked up the remaining two-thirds.[5]

As Hawkwood prepared to leave the service of the church, he sold the town of Faenza, his base of operations, to Niccolò d'Este of Ferrara. The details of the sale were reported on 4 April by the Mantuan ambassador at the Visconti court, Bartolino Codelupo. Niccolò paid 50,000 or 60,000 florins, a substantial portion immediately, the balance at a later date. In return, the English agreed to leave the town in fifteen days, giving hostages as surety. According to the Bolognese chronicle, Niccolò acted on behalf of the pope.[6] Codelupo was not so sure. "Some say Niccolò bought Faenza from the church for his own purposes, others say he serves the church by safeguarding this city."[7] On 9 April, Niccolò entered the city, and a week later Hawkwood evacuated his men.[8]

Hawkwood's decision to serve the allies was received joyfully in Florence. Franco Sacchetti described the hire as a feat worthy of the labors of Hercules, tantamount to the taming of "the English serpent with a hundred heads." The anonymous Florentine chronicler said succinctly that it was "good news."[9] The commander of Florentine forces, Rodolfo Varano, was, however, jealous of the generous terms granted Hawkwood, of which he himself was constrained to pay a part; and he was angry that city officials would not allow him, as the pope had Hawkwood, to keep several local castles he had taken into his custody He summarily quit and went over to the church.[10] The Florentines branded him a traitor and painted a *pittura infamante* of him in the city, depicting him on the gallows attached at the neck to the devil.[11]

Despite Florence's enthusiasm and subsequent propaganda on the matter, the recruitment of Hawkwood was in fact a triumph of Visconti diplomacy, for which Bernabò took explicit credit.[12] Ruggiero Cane played a key role, arranging a marriage between the Englishman and Bernabò's illegitimate daughter Donnina. The deal was the culmination of the personal approach undertaken fifteen years earlier by Bernabò's ally Doge Agnello, who had made Hawkwood godfather of his son. It was done in conjunction with the marriage of another of Bernabò's illegitimate daughters, Elisabetta, to the German captain Lutz von Landau, who then joined the allied cause with his large army. The twin marriages created familial bonds between the soldiers and Bernabò—bonds that, as we shall see, Bernabò took seriously. It also created familial bonds between Hawkwood and Landau, two of Italy's most successful mercenaries. It is likely that Hawkwood's daughter Antiochia was also married around this time, to Hawkwood's longtime military apprentice William Coggeshale.

## Marriage to Donnina

Hawkwood's wedding took place in June 1377 in Cremonese territory, probably at Gazzuolo, a small fishing village on the Oglio River, half owned by the lord of Mantua. Hawkwood arrived in late May to make preparations. On 26 May 1377, he wrote to Ludovico Gonzaga of Mantua seeking permission for free passage of his personal effects and several staff members from Ferrara through Mantuan territory.[13] Five days later, Hawkwood sent a letter to the city of Lucca announcing the event: "Dearest brothers, we joyfully announce to you that we have become son to the magnificent and exalted lord, and our father, Lord Bernabò through marriage to one of his daughters, whom we are preparing to wed immediately with a most beautiful celebration."[14]

Bernabò Visconti attended the ceremony with his wife, Regina, and his extended family, as well as members of Hawkwood's brigade. The nuptials were celebrated with feasting and jousts and the presentation of gifts. An account was given by an unidentified Mantuan ambassador, whose main concern was not the wedding itself but keeping close watch on Hawkwood's activities, since Mantua feared he might afterward ride on its lands.

> Last Sunday, John Hawkwood led his bride with much honor to his home, which, they say, once belonged to the late Gasparre del Conte, the former bishop of Parma. The wedding was honorably attended by the Duchess [Regina] and all the daughters of Bernabò. Yesterday, after dinner, Bernabò and his Porrina [mother of Donnina] went to Hawkwood's home, where a joust was going on all day long. I am told that yesterday after dinner Regina gave a wedding gift of 1,000 ducats in a cup. Marcus [Bernabò's son] gave to him a tin of pearls worth 300 ducats and Lodovico [another son of Bernabò] gave pearls of the same value, as did many nobles. The English were also given gifts of much silver, estimated at 1,000 ducats. There was no dancing on account of reverence for the late Taddea.[15]

In addition to the expensive gifts of pearls and silver, Hawkwood received a dowry in land and cash. It is likely that the town of Gazzuolo was part of this. Bernabò also gave Hawkwood a cluster of estates "with lands, possessions and vineyards therein" just northeast of the city of Milan (fifteen kilometers) in the towns of Pessano, Bornago, Carugate, Valera, and Santa Maria alle Molgora.[16] The English *Polychronicon* claimed that the cash payment amounted to 10,000 florins.[17]

Hawkwood's marriage to Donnina further established the captain's credentials as the wealthiest and most powerful soldier in Italy. He now possessed substantial patrimonies in both Milan and the Romagna, lands near Bologna and Cremona, and, most likely, others that we do not know about. He had a lifetime pension from the Florentines and the queen of Naples—in addition to his "regular" pay as captain of the allied forces. Such fortune and prestige rendered quitting the Italian scene still less appealing. The union with Donnina brought kinship with one of the most prestigious and affluent families in the Italian peninsula, into which the English king Edward III had married his own son.

Even as he prepared to take Donnina as his wife, Hawkwood engaged in his usual business of coercion and intimidation. In the letter in which he announced his "joyous" wedding to the city of Lucca, Hawkwood pressured officials there to readmit an exile, Masseo Padino, who was a friend of his chancellor, Jacopo da Pietrasanta. In return for the favor, Hawkwood promised his "love and affection." He also reminded officials that "one hand washes the other" and that his army was not far from their territory.

## Chasing the Bretons

After the wedding, the allies sent Hawkwood to the Romagna to fight the Bretons, who remained at Cesena. Lutz von Landau was dispatched to the Marches to oppose Rodolfo Varano. Bernabò allowed Hawkwood some time with his bride by taking charge of his brigade and leading it to Modena, where the allied army was collecting. Hawkwood remained at Gazzuolo for four days and then rode off to join his men.

At Modena, Hawkwood received food, fodder, and arms from Bolognese officials and then advanced southeast on the road to Faenza and Cesena. As he passed Bologna, however, his army looted local lands as if they were those of the enemy.[18] The Bolognese objected, insisting that they were his allies and that he was contractually bound to respect their territory, according to the agreement he had signed back on 25 May 1376.[19] The captain's raid coincided neatly with the arrival in Bologna of two letters from Florence demanding that the Bolognese pay their share of Hawkwood's salary, the first installment of which had already fallen due. The Bolognese accused the Florentines of setting Hawkwood on them. Florence denied the charge and sent letters to Hawkwood condemning his activities and begging him "to have some compassion for the poor Bolognese, who had been so abused during the previous year."[20] Florentine officials sent copies of these letters also to Bologna. Bolognese officials ultimately paid Hawkwood 30,000 florins, but this appears to have been more in the manner of a bribe than legitimate salary.[21]

From Bologna, Hawkwood advanced on Faenza and now attacked the town that he had sold only two months earlier. Hawkwood received assistance in this enterprise from the former ruler of the city, Astorre Manfredi, who been displaced by the church in 1368. The attack roused the Bretons from nearby Cesena, who moved forward to defend the town. But seeing that Hawkwood and Manfredi already held the upper hand, they turned back. Hawkwood and Manfredi took Faenza; Manfredi was allowed to retain possession of it.[22] Manfredi then formally joined the league against pope.

Hawkwood briefly retreated from the front and went to Gazzuolo to tend to his wife. His presence there is recorded in a letter to the lord of Mantua dated 29 June 1377. "Today I was in Gazzuolo in order to arrange a certain house so that we may live in it with our wife." He then excused himself for not stopping to see the Mantuan ruler in person, explaining that he had to return to his army.[23]

Hawkwood now took up pursuit of the Bretons, who had left Cesena and traveled through the Romagna into Umbria toward the city of Perugia.[24] The Florentine chancellor Coluccio Salutati instructed Hawkwood to keep watch on the band but to engage it only if it directly threatened Tuscany. Hawkwood followed closely, short of attacking, but his band despoiled Perugian territory; this act prompted anger from local officials, who refused to give him logistical support, denying him guides and provisions, indeed, even musicians for his camp.[25]

The Perugians dispersed the Bretons with their own army, aided by reinforcements from Florence, Milan, and other league members. The band fled southwest to the Sienese Maremma and attacked the town of Grosseto, mounting a furious attack on the town walls, knocking holes in six places.[26] Hawkwood now moved toward Sienese territory, advancing through the Valdichiana. He set up his camp near the town of Montepulciano.[27] The Sienese greeted him as an honored guest, bestowing on him gifts, including a caparisoned horse (worth 150 florins), baked breads, sweets, and provisions for his army. But rather than ride out against the Bretons, Hawkwood showed no inclination to mobilize. As the Perugians before them, the Sienese sent out their own and, as earlier, succeeded dispersing the enemy. The event was described in heroic terms by the Sienese chronicler, who noted, among other things, the use of poisoned arrows by the city's army.[28] The Breton band broke apart shortly after the battle: one part went to work for Queen Johanna of Naples, another went back home; a third remained loyal to the pope.

The breakup of the Bretons was a blow to the pope's war effort. It underscored the futility of the conflict, which after three years had produced little apart from spectacular campaigns directed against innocent civilians. Both the pope and the league were financially exhausted, and peace negotiations gathered momentum. "They say," wrote the anonymous Florentine chronicler in June 1377, "that there will soon be an accord. May God so will it."[29] But the talks bogged down. By the end of the summer of 1377 only the Bolognese had signed a peace agreement with the pope, a unilateral move that greatly dismayed Florence and the other allies.[30]

## Milanese and English Diplomat

John Hawkwood was himself withdrawing his services. From Montepulciano, he had passively watched the activities of the Bretons. Frustrated Florentine officials wrote letters throughout September 1377 urging him to strike a decisive blow at the enemy. But Hawkwood paid them little heed.

Instead, Hawkwood undertook the role of the diplomat. From his camp, he initiated discussions with papal representatives and league members. The Florentines were appalled and told Hawkwood that if he wished to help negotiations, he should make a strong showing in the field to force the pope's hand and aid in obtaining favorable terms.[31] In a letter dated 27 September, they begged him to leave negotiations to the experts. "We pray you to pursue the war in the manly way you began. This is, we believe, the only way that will lead to a desirable peace with honor."[32] Officials pointedly contrasted Hawkwood's behavior with that of his brother-in-law Lutz von Landau, who had scored a major victory over Rodolfo da Varano in the Marches.[33] The Florentines lauded Lutz for his "manliness" and "audacity" and credited him with gaining for himself and the allied cause an "unextinguishable glory."[34]

Florence chastised Hawkwood for acting of his own accord. "How can you possibly make treaties," officials wrote to him on 30 September, "without our knowledge or that of Bernabò?"[35] In reality, however, Hawkwood was not working independently but together with his father-in-law. Bernabò, tired of the inconclusive war, had already turned his interests toward Verona, where the death of Cansignorio della Scala opened up an opportunity for Visconti hegemony. Cansignorio had left two illegitimate sons; Bernabò pressed his claim to city on behalf of his wife, Regina, who was Cansignorio's sister. Regina gave signal of her intentions when, early in 1377, she gave birth to a son and named him Mastino after her grandfather, the venerable old ruler of Verona. Bernabò's designs were, however, not yet apparent in Florence.

Hawkwood's activities were also directed from outside Italy altogether. Young Richard II, who had assumed the throne in July 1377, sought a marriage alliance with Bernabò's daughter Catherine. He called on Hawkwood to conduct negotiations on his behalf. Hawkwood was an ideal choice given his own marital connection to the Visconti family—a connection that may in fact have been directed from England in the first place. In October Richard sent the Franciscan friar Walter Thorpe to Hawkwood to help with the talks.[36] It was the first of a string of embassies that would stretch over more than a year and would ultimately bring the poet Geoffrey Chaucer to Hawkwood's camp.

The Florentines meanwhile continued to be frustrated by Hawkwood's inaction on the battlefield, particularly when news reached them in November that he intended to demobilize for the winter and quarter his troops in Florentine territory. "Magnificent Knight and Dearest Friend," officials wrote to Hawkwood on 16 November, "we heard recently from Spinello, the treasurer of our commune, that your brigade has decided to stay this winter in certain of our lands and districts and that it now prepares itself to enter there." They demanded that he advance into enemy lands and feed his army at the expense of papal states or the Marches or, best of all, Camerino, in the lands of their erstwhile commander Rodolfo da Varano.[37] Florentine officials made a strong appeal to Hawkwood's English pride. "It greatly pains us that it will be said that the undefeated and glorious band of Englishmen fled from the enemy and had to dwell for some time in a quiet place."[58]

Hawkwood held firm in his intention to quarter his men in Florentine territory. Officials, fearing that Hawkwood's presence would cause "dissensions and rebellions," persisted in their efforts to dissuade him. They took great care, however, not to make Hawkwood angry. "With the English it is necessary to proceed cautiously," wrote a government official. "We must treat them . . . in such a way as to not anger them . . . for if we do not they will do things to the commune that we will not like."[59]

After much effort, the Florentines ultimately convinced Hawkwood to station the main body of his army in Sienese territory, near the town of San Quirico, not far from his original camp at Montepulciano. The decision greatly distressed Sienese officials, and the Florentines sent envoys to try to appease them. Hawkwood nevertheless placed some his men in Florentine territory, near Pistoia and Prato.[40]

With his army settled in for the winter, Hawkwood stepped up his diplomatic activities. He traveled back and forth from Milan to Florence to Rome to San Quirico, his base, with occasional trips to the Romagna to look after his possessions there. Hawkwood met with representatives of Richard, Bernabò, Pope Gregory, and Florence.[41] He corresponded with his old ally Alderigo degli Antelminelli, who was one of the pope's bankers, and held talks with the English theologian and former chaplain of Duke Lionel, Thomas Edwardston, who had come to Italy with the duke and was in Rome. The exact nature of Hawkwood's business with Edwardston is unknown.

Hawkwood went with Edwardston from Rome to Florence to meet with officials there in December 1377. The men were joined by Bernabò's ambassador, Ruggiero Cane. The anonymous Florentine chronicler describes the arrival of the embassy in Florence on 7 December: they were greeted with gifts of precious silks and linen and feted at a banquet in their honor at the Palazzo Signoria. But that there was antagonism toward Hawkwood for his unwanted diplomatic service is clear from the chronicler's statement when the English left the city on 10 December: "May he never return!!"[42] Hawkwood returned for a new round of talks twelve days later.

Hawkwood's preoccupation with diplomacy diverted his attention from his army, which behaved badly in his absence. William Gold rode with a group of men on the small town of Corliano, attacking peasants, ransacking houses, and stealing livestock. The Florentines complained to Hawkwood—"we know that this displeases you no less than it does us"—and asked that he return to take charge of his men: "without you, we can neither control them nor send them to the help of the allies."[43]

But Hawkwood showed no inclination to return to his army or to change his course. The peace initiatives were in fact gaining momentum, and the Florentines themselves, despite their admonitions to Hawkwood, were increasingly eager to see them succeed. On 28 February 1378, Hawkwood held a meeting at his camp at San Quirico, attended by Edwardston, Antelminelli, Cane, and numerous others.[44] The group discussed peace at a lunchtime banquet table. The details were described by Lando Ongharro, an official sent by the Sienese. Lando arrived at San Quirico to find Hawkwood and his guests already seated and discussions well under way. Ongharro explicitly identified among the participants Hawkwood's comrades John Thornbury and John Brice, the Breton captain Bernard de La Salle, and ambassadors from Milan and the papacy. Hawkwood invited Ongharro and his companion to join the feast. "They [Hawkwood and his group] told us that they had already composed a truce and that they would send the news to all the lands of the Church."[45] Hawkwood promised Ongharro that he would respect Sienese lands as he departed the region, and Bernard de La Salle agreed to do the same.

The talks at San Quirico helped set the stage for a general peace conference in the town of Sarzana.[46] Hawkwood himself traveled there, leaving San Quirico the day after the lunch meeting. True to his word, Hawkwood passed peaceably through Sienese territory. He stopped briefly in the city, where he was greeted with "highest honors," and then proceeded north to Pisa, Lucca, and, finally, Sarzana.[47]

Negotiations at Sarzana initially went well, as both sides showed a willingness to compromise. But on the eve of what appeared to be a settlement, Gregory XI suddenly died (27 March 1378). "When the thing was almost at a conclusion," wrote the Florentine Stefani, "the cardinals left on account of the news . . . and so things were left all confused and the ambassadors went home."[48]

Talks soon resumed, and a treaty was ultimately made on 28 July 1378.[49] The two main antagonists, Florence and the papacy, were now occupied with other issues. Florence faced domestic rebellion from among workers (the so-called *ciompi*) in the wool cloth trade, which brought down the government. Gregory's death precipitated a church crisis that resulted in schism. The cardinals under pressure from a Roman mob elected an Italian, the archbishop of Bari, as Pope Urban VI. But the archbishop's blunt manner and desire for reform alienated many, and a dissident faction of cardinals repudiated the election and chose the French cardinal of Geneva—the same person who directed the massacre at

Cesena—as Pope Clement VII. The split initiated a cycle of violence in southern Italy that would ultimately involve John Hawkwood.

The War of Eight Saints meanwhile ended inconclusively. According to the treaty, Florence and its allies were required to pay indemnities to the pope—money that, as we shall see, ended up in the hands of mercenary soldiers.

## To the Walls of Verona

For John Hawkwood, the war had already ended with the breakup of the conference at Sarzana. A week after it, he traveled to Lombardy to join his father-in-law in war against Verona. He stopped briefly in Florence (3 April 1378) to inform officials in person of his decision and to demand 10,000 florins in back pay he claimed was still owed his army.[50] The latter issue went unresolved, and Hawkwood continued to argue his case by letter into May and beyond.[51] As he rode north past Mantua, his soldiers ransacked local territory, eliciting the now familiar protest letters from the lord Gonzaga. Hawkwood wrote back that the incident "grieved us to death" and promised to make good the damage. But he did nothing.

Hawkwood took up below the walls of Verona. His brigade included his long-time associates John Thornbury and William Gold and a notable newcomer named Nicholas Sabraham. Sabraham, one of the most mobile English soldiers of the era, had fought at Crécy and in crusades in Prussia, Hungary, Alexandria, and Constantinople.[52] The historian Maurice Keen has singled him out as a possible model for Chaucer's "worthy knight" in the prologue to *Canterbury Tales*.[53] It was through Hawkwood that Sabraham came to meet Chaucer personally, when the poet visited Hawkwood's camp several months later.

Bernabò hoped for a quick victory at Verona. Several months earlier he had tried to seize the city by subterfuge, sending two German captains and a band of one hundred lances on Verona, ostensibly to seek peaceful free passage but in reality to kill the rulers once inside the city. On the point of entry, however, the captains were bought off and revealed the plan. Bernabò denied everything and accused the men of acting on their own initiative.[54] With Hawkwood on his side, Bernabò now intended to use blunt force. He joined Hawkwood's brigade with the brigades of Jacopo de' Cavalli, the Veronese exile recently in the employ of Venice, and his other new son-in-law, Lutz von Landau.[55] Bernabò himself accompanied the army with a cortege of noblemen and noblewomen, including his favorite mistress, Donnina de Porri (the mother of Hawkwood's wife), and his sons, Carlo and Ridolfo. The army held banquets outside the walls, with music and songs and horse races.[56]

But victory did not come so easily. The Veronese conflict became entangled in the increasingly bitter War of Chioggia between Venice and Genoa. Verona allied with Genoa, Padua, and Prince Charles of Durazzo of Hungary, who came to Italy to fight Venice. Bernabò sided with the Venetians. For his part, John Hawkwood continued the same distracted and self-serving behavior he demonstrated during the War of Eight Saints. He again concentrated more on diplomatic matters than military ones, leaving camp on several occasions for that purpose. In the meantime, his army devolved into chaos and disorder, worse than at any time in his career in Italy. The problem was exacerbated by a general shortage of supplies.[57] John Thornbury would leave Hawkwood and return to England. William Gold would become so distracted with his favorite mistress that he would be of little use as a soldier. By year's end, Hawkwood himself left Bernabò's service under suspicious circumstances, causing a breach between the men that would never heal.

## An Unruly Camp, Geoffrey Chaucer, and William Gold

The bad behavior began the moment Hawkwood's army arrived at Verona. William Gold immediately broke ranks, raided local lands, and launched an attack against a nearby castle. This was followed by numerous other incidents, involving both individual soldiers and bands of men. The city of Mantua bore the brunt of the excesses. The locations of Hawkwood's camps—in the towns of Villafranca, Piubega, Castelgrimaldo, Monzambano, and Castelgoffredo—were all within easy reach of Mantuan territory. Mantuan citizens avenged themselves by robbing and kidnapping unsuspecting soldiers, usually when they moved about singly. Nicholas Sabraham had his horse and possessions—including a collection of swords and a traveling bag—stolen as he rode outside Monzambano. The French soldier Allen Donfol was robbed of his horse outside Piubega; the Italian soldier Tiberto Brandolino was himself taken prisoner as he made his way from his home in Bagnacavallo to join Hawkwood's camp at Castelgoffredo. Tiberto's travails are relayed in a letter by John Hawkwood, who worked to gain his release: "In the night while our dear Tibertus de Brandolino of Bagnacavallo wished to come to our camp, he landed in your land, where he was received willingly by your vicar. In the middle of the night, the same vicar, in whose house Tibertus was received and stayed, called Tibertus and told him that he must arise without delay, since there was at the door a certain Michael of Pisa, our representative, with 12 lances, sent by us to escort Tibertus to our camp. Believing this to be true, Tibertus got up immediately and went to the door . . . and was taken."[58]

Hawkwood ransomed back Tiberto for 60 florins and managed to recover Sabraham's traveling bag, though it was returned emptied of its contents.[59] Hawkwood wrote to Mantuan officials condemning William Gold's misdeeds—"we will speak to him and his corporals and make it clear that no damage will be tolerated . . . and they shall refrain from committing crimes, and will treat your territory as if it were the territory of our magnificent and exalted lord of Milan."[60] Hawkwood then wrote directly to Gold instructing him to apologize to Mantua.[61]

The difficulties could be passed off as typical of armies and their neighbors. But the problems in Hawkwood's camp ran far deeper. A general shortage of supplies and lack of pay engendered strong dissensions among the rank and file of the army. When the soldiers were not stealing from Mantua, they were stealing from one another. Numerous letters record episodes of peculation and thievery. "Last night," went a typical epistle written in July 1378, "a certain Ulrich, the German servant of my brother and comrade Hannekin Botarch, fled camp and took with him the bay horse of the same Hannekin, a breastplate and a flask made of silver."[62]

William Gold complained that he did not have adequate fodder for his horses.[63] Hawkwood himself noted that his band was "in need" and "unhappy for many reasons."[64] When two representatives from Mantua came to camp seeking restitution for outstanding damages committed against their citizens, Hawkwood demurred, stating that his band was "ill disposed" to settle.[65] Although we may suspect that this was a ploy on Hawkwood's part to avoid his obligation, he was in fact negotiating at that moment with the city of Florence over wages due his band from the last days of the War of Eight Saints.[66]

The morale in camp received a further blow when John Thornbury summarily quit the army. The documents do not make clear whether he defected to Verona or simply removed himself from Hawkwood's service. But in May 1378, only a month after arriving, he was in custody against his will, a captive, in the English camp. He wrote to Mantua seeking asylum, for "a residence or quiet dwelling" where he could, "with greater ease," see to his ransom, "so that my freedom may be provided for quickly."[67] The Mantuans allowed Thornbury his request.[68]

The episode effectively ended Thornbury's career with Hawkwood. He remained in Italy, worked briefly as an ambassador for Florence and as a captain in an antimercenary league army, and then returned to England. In April 1380 he received, like Hawkwood, a pardon for his misdeeds committed during the war in France. He rejoined the retinue of John of Gaunt, with whom he had fought before coming to Italy, and participated in Gaunt's campaign in 1382 against Castille. He settled thereafter into a comfortable life as a landed lord in his native county of Hertfordshire and even served as a member of Parliament.[69]

The difficulties with his men clearly frustrated Hawkwood. When William Gold ignored his warning and continued to harass Mantuan lands, Hawkwood threatened him with the death penalty. "Egregious knight and dear brother we send our proclamation that no one dare to damage the territory of Mantua under the penalty of death."[70] But Hawkwood's coercive power and ability to control the situation in camp were greatly compromised by his involvement in diplomatic affairs, which diverted his attention. Just weeks after he arrived at Verona, Hawkwood was visited by King Richard's envoy, Walter Thorpe, pressing the issue of marriage between the English king and the Visconti.[71] Thorpe's embassy was followed by another, more famous one, involving Geoffrey Chaucer and Edward de Berkeley. It was Chaucer's third trip to Italy and perhaps the second time he met Hawkwood—the first at the wedding for Lionel in Milan in 1368.

Chaucer and Berkeley arrived in Italy in late June/early July and joined Hawkwood at his base at the town of Monzambano, on the right bank of the Mincio River. The men rode together to Milan (121 kilometers west) to speak in person with Bernabò Visconti.[72] Ruggiero Cane also participated in the talks, which continued through the first week of August.[73] They did not, however, succeed. Hawkwood returned to his men at Monzambano, and Berkeley and Chaucer departed for London.

Richard continued to pursue the matter forcefully, sending additional ambassadors throughout the winter of 1378/79 and into March 1379. Hawkwood sent envoys from his brigade back to England to report on the progress of negotiations—among them we are able to identify a John Northwood, who, like his captain, came from Essex. Bernabò Visconti dispatched Ruggiero Cane to England to speak directly with Richard.

The marriage plans nevertheless fell through. Richard shifted his interests to the German royal house of Luxemburg, to Anne of Bohemia, daughter of the Holy Roman Emperor Charles IV. The match involved establishing closer ties to Pope Urban VI, who championed the union in the hope that it would consolidate his alliance with both England and the empire, whose help he sought in his ongoing war against the French antipope Clement VII.[74] Richard would soon appoint Hawkwood his ambassador to Urban.

When Hawkwood went on diplomatic mission to Milan, the already difficult situation in camp devolved still further. He had left William Gold in charge of the army at Monzambano. On the night of 30 July, Gold's mistress, Janet, a prize won in the battles in France, abandoned him, taking with her more than 500 florins of his money. On the surface, the event was little more than another in a string of thefts that troubled the army. But it soon became clear that Janet was the love of William Gold's life, and her defection constituted an act of betrayal that shook Gold to his very foundation and threatened to undo the army.

Gold's emotions emerge from a series of extraordinary letters written to Ludovico Gonzaga, lord of Mantua, between 30 July and 25 August. They are revealing not only of the man but more generally of the complexity of the relationships that existed between mercenaries and their mistresses. The latter fulfilled far more important roles than the historiography has afforded them. Gold's first epistle betrays little sentiment, mentioning only Janet's theft and seeking from Ludovico Gonzaga help in capturing her should she appear in Mantuan territory. But the letter indicates that Janet abandoned Gold while traveling to Venice, where she conducted business on his behalf. The statement suggests that, like Hawkwood, Gold had investments in that city and that, like Donnina, Janet helped oversee her man's financial affairs.[75]

Gold's subsequent letters display a rising tide of resentment. On 2 August, he wrote to Gonzaga stridently urging him "to search all the hospices of the city" and to arrest Janet on sight and place her "secretly in a secure place."[76] When Janet was found in Mantua two days later, Gold implored Gonzaga to hold her ("I beg you that this Janet not be allowed to leave Mantua!"), even if she resisted, and offered the curious promise to do more for Gonzaga's "honor" than "any French lady."[77]

Janet complicated the issue by claiming that she had, since departing camp, married another person and was thus no longer bound to Gold. The development seems to have pushed Gold to the edge. He now spoke openly (in a letter dated 6 August) of his feelings, how "sweet love overwhelms even the proudest of hearts."[78] He insisted that Gonzaga sequester Janet in a local monastery, even if it was against the law, and offered to pay 1,000 florins for her upkeep. Gold also promised to serve Gonzaga with 500 soldiers, in effect proposing to break up Hawkwood's army to get his mistress back.

A more introspective letter followed three days later, in which Gold pondered, by way of metaphorical language, the vagaries of love and the pain of loss: "Love overcomes all things, it even prostrates the stout, making them impatient, taking all heart from them, even casting down into the depths the summits of tall towers, suggesting strife so that it drags them into deadly duel, as has happened to me because of this Janet. My heart yearns so much towards her that I cannot rest or do otherwise. . . . Therefore on bended knees I beg your lordship that you do not allow Janet to leave Mantua or your territory until I send for her."[79] Returning to the theme of his 2 August letter, Gold ended the epistle promising to do more for Gonzaga—should he produce Janet—"more than a thousand united French women."

The resolution of the matter is unknown. In his last letter, dated 25 August 1378, Gold had not yet gotten Janet back, complaining that military affairs kept him away.[80] We do not know whether Janet was reunited with William, whether she remained in Mantua or went elsewhere. William did, however, eventually regain his composure and continued on with his fine military career.

## The Final Break with Bernabò

Hawkwood's opinion of Gold's behavior is nowhere recorded. But the preoccupation of his leading corporal as well as his own absences from camp greatly hindered the Milanese war effort. Verona gained time to regroup its forces, taking in five thousand Hungarian horsemen commanded by John Horváti, the *vaivode* (viceroy) of Transylvania, a close kinsman of Prince Charles of Durazzo. Horváti was known to Italians as "Giovanni Bano," or John Ban—the surname represented a title, similar to "duke" or "count." His army, disciplined and well supplied, was the antithesis of Hawkwood's. It moved swiftly and efficiently to take up position near the Veronese town walls in September 1378.[81]

Bernabò bought time by arranging a brief truce, during which he augmented his forces. He recalled Hawkwood and Landau to Milan to plan a new offensive. The men rode out with fourteen hundred lances in November 1378 and launched a preemptive strike on Veronese lands near Lake Garda.[82] They then crossed the Adige River in January and prepared a siege of Verona. John Horváti and his Hungarian army made a counterattack on Visconti lands, staging a prodigious raid on Cremona, which purportedly netted 1,700 human prisoners and 20,000 *bestie grosse* (large animals).[83] But as Horváti rode back toward Verona, Hawkwood and Landau intercepted him as he attempted to cross the Adige, and they stole back some of his prey.[84]

The seemingly minor event proved a turning point in both Hawkwood's and Landau's relationship with Bernabò. Visconti himself relayed the details of what happened next in a letter to the Holy Roman Emperor.

> They camped with the army at the Adige river, in a position very secure and favorable, well-furnished with food and every other necessity . . . from which spot within a few days I would have obtained victory over the commune of Verona. But Lutz and [his brother] Eberhard without my knowledge or command, without any reason or necessity, crossed back over the Adige with my army, abandoned the siege of the city and gave up the war, which had been begun so valiantly. When I found out about it and realized that they did not have valid motives for their retreat, I was stunned and repeatedly sent orders to them, threatening criminal proceeding and denial of pay, to return to the siege of the said forsaken city. But indeed Lutz and Eberhard, filled with evil spirit, without any concern for my orders and without any fear of retribution, did not wish to return to the siege, although I offered my services and those of Count of Savoy to accompany the army. Instead, they attacked the men and subjects of the lands I govern under the pretext that they were commandeering

their pay, which they had no legal right to, given their disobedience, committing homicides, slaughters, pilfering animals and kidnapping people.[85]

Bernabò's letter deals only with the actions of Lutz, his brother Eberhard, and the German troops, since they were under the jurisdiction of the emperor. Visconti makes it clear that he had desired a decisive blow against Verona and saw the action at the Adige, as well as the general behavior of the army, as unacceptable. Bernabò's outrage was increased by the fact that Lutz was his son-in-law; the Milanese ruler had expected familial bonds to produce better service: "I had nominated Lutz as Captain General of the German troops, believing that he and his brother, on account of the benefits received from me and the tie of marriage, would be more faithful and more intent and solicitous in their task."

Bernabò urged the German emperor to denounce the men throughout their native land. To facilitate this, the Milanese ruler sent a copy of the letter to other German dukes and princes including Leopold of Austria, Stephen of Bavaria, Frederick of Nuremberg, and Robert of the Palatinate.[86]

If Bernabò wrote a parallel letter to King Richard in England, it has not survived. But Visconti's wrath clearly applied also to the Englishman, for immediately after the event Bernabò stripped Hawkwood of the Milanese lands he had granted him as part of Donnina's marriage dowry and gave them to a bastard son, Etorre. Hawkwood wrote to his son-in-law William Coggeshale, who resided there (though it is unclear whether on the dowry lands), and instructed him to leave the city and go to Bagnacavallo. Coggeshale departed with an escort of sixty men; Hawkwood wrote to Mantua to secure free passage.[87] Bernabò then published an edict offering a 30-florin reward for any mercenary—German, English, or Italian—captured or killed.[88]

Both Hawkwood and Landau expressed regret at the turn of events. In a letter to the lord of Mantua dated 19 February 1379, the men wrote: "We are in some discord with the magnificent and exalted lord, our lord, of Milan, but we strive, with the help of God, to regain his good graces."[89] They continued to hold captives from Horváti's army and were anxious to redeem them near Verona, where they had set up an exchange.[90] But Bernabò showed no willingness to compromise. He refused to allow Hawkwood and Landau passage through his territoryand blocked their movements and thus their attempts to profit from their hostages.

The split between Bernabò and his sons-in-law caused general concern. Officials throughout northern and central Italy feared that it would cause Hawkwood and Landau to form a "free" company to recoup their losses and that the band would eventually find its way into local territory. Florence immediately sent envoys to try to smooth over the dispute. Among them was the chronicler Stefani, who made it clear that his city worried as much about social and political pressures as financial ones. The Ciompi uprising of the previous summer had left the city tense and uneasy. "Because of the little concord in the city," Stefani wrote, "we feared a great deal."[91] In addition, Tuscany was under threat from another band, calling itself the Company of Saint George, which also grew out of the Veronese war and sought passage through the region to take up employment with Pope Urban VI.[92] Florentines officials focused in their internal councils on Hawkwood and contemplated several ways to prevent him from entering Tuscany, including arming the passes through the Apeninnes and setting up an ambush.[93]

Stefani's attempts to reconcile Hawkwood and Landau with Bernabò did not succeed.[94] The men, as expected, formed a free company and advanced south, reaching Tuscany at the beginning of March.[95] The Tuscan cities sent ambassadors to try to head off the band. They reminded both Hawkwood and Landau that they were contractually obliged to be at peace with the region, according to the agreement they had signed at the end of the War of the Eight Saints. The captains denied the obligation on the grounds that their company had come not to fight but only to seek employment. They also used a familiar species of legal trickery, arguing that Eberhard von Landau, Lutz's brother, now a co-captain, had not been part of the original accord two years earlier. Thus the band was technically different and no longer bound by its agreement.

Local officials were under no illusion and saw the band for what it was: an invading force. The Perugian chronicler Del Graziani put the issue bluntly: "Count Lutz and Misser Hawkwood said they came . . . as friends, but they comport themselves very badly and do not . . . observe what they had promised."[96] Stefani was still less charitable: "They broke faith with the commune, not openly but in effect more than openly—'I will not make you pay me,' they said, 'but you hire me . . . whether you want to or not.' "[97]

Florence took the lead in the new round of negotiations.[98] It sent Spinello Alberti. at the head of a delegation of envoys from various cities, including a representative of the church, Buonaventura Badoer, an Augustinian friar from Padua, recently made cardinal by Pope Urban VI. Spinello also brought along a young apprentice named Benedetto di Ser Landi Fortini, who would later replace him as the city's leading ambassador to Hawkwood and whose son would pen the captain's famous epitaph at the bottom of Uccello's portrait.[99]

The talks were prolonged and difficult and stretched out over nearly three months. Florentine sources give unique insight into the details. Alberti and his delegation met Hawkwood's band near Bologna, where they spent twelve days engaged in negotiations. They rode with the band throughout the Valdichiana, into Umbria and then Sienese territory.[100] The Florentine government continuously sent Alberti instructions and supplies. The company made demands both petty and large. Richard Romsey, one of the corporals, demanded, for example, restitution for monies he claimed were owed to him by the church from his service during the War of Eight Saints. Buonaventura Badoer in his role as bishop dealt directly with this.[101] The Florentines hired John Thornbury for several days to talk with members of the band with whom he remained on close personal terms.[102] Thornbury was paid well for the service (250 florins).

An agreement was reached on 10 June 1379 at the town of Torrita in Sienese territory. The signatories included the cities of Florence, Perugia, Siena, Arezzo, and Città di Castello.[103] They agreed to "hire" the company for eight months, in effect absorbing it into local armies. Hawkwood's personal brigade, consisting of 1,000 lances (600 Germans and 400 Englishmen), was divided between the Florentines and Sienese.[104] He and the Landau brothers received bonuses of 12,000 florins from Florence and 2,000 each from Siena.[105] The Sienese also granted Hawkwood and Eberhard additional "gifts" of 1,600 florins; Hawkwood's chancellor Jacopo da Pietrasanta and assistant Gasparino da Bergamo were paid 78 florins for drawing up the agreement.[106]

Florentine officials invited Hawkwood, the Landau brothers, and their corporals to a feast in their honor in the city on 18 June 1379 to celebrate the accord. The event—and the agreement itself—did not go over well with the local citizenry, who called on Alberti to explain his actions. He claimed utility, that the large number of troops now on the payroll could be used internally "in the piazza, and other places, to guard the pacific state of . . . Florence."[107]

With their army now gainfully employed, Hawkwood and Landau went their separate ways. Landau rode toward the Marches and then back home, where he undertook diplomatic service with the Holy Roman Emperor Wenceslaus.[108] John Hawkwood, however, remained in Italy. With a force of three hundred lances, he headed to Bagnacavallo and Cotignola, the lands bequeathed to him by the pope in 1377. "We come to Bagnacavallo," Hawkwood wrote, "to take up in our home."[109] Hawkwood was accompanied by William Gold.

# CHAPTER NINE

# At Home in the Romagna, 1379–1381

The men in these parts are passionatissimi . . . pay heed to every
doubt here, lest you find yourself deceived.

*Cardinal Anglic Grimoard, about the Romagna*

Hawkwood arrived in the Romagna at the beginning of July 1379. The shift from captain of armies to independent knight/local lord is indicated in his letters, which were now signed "John Hawkwood, *milex*," rather than "John Hawkwood, *capitanus*."[1] He brought with him William Gold and a contingent of thirteen lances under William Olney. It is a tribute to Hawkwood's reputation and negotiating skill that he was able to constrain the Florentines to pay the salaries of Olney and his troops.[2]

According to the fourteenth-century writer Benvenuto of Imola's description of it, the Romagna was a veritable paradise on earth (map 6). "In it are assembled all the things that are sparse in other places: sea, land, mountains, plains, numerous rivers, fountains, hills, woods, healthy air and wine."[3] But for all its natural beauty, the Romagna was also famous for its political instability and chaotic internal dynamics. Uncertain and inconsistent leadership from the church, the nominal overlord of the region, allowed for infighting, rivalry, and the rise of local strongmen. Such men jockeyed for power, seized cities, and, through treacherous means, frequently displaced one another. In Hawkwood's day the terms *Romagnol* and *tyrant* were often used interchangeably. "One should not be surprised that the tyrants of Romagna are faithless," wrote Matteo Villani, "for they are both tyrants and Romagnols."[4] A French legate with much experience in the region in the service of the pope described the Romagnols as "so treacherous and extravagant that in feasting and falsehood they are little different from Englishmen."[5]

It was perhaps inevitable, then, that John Hawkwood should take up in this land of the self-made man. It was perhaps equally inevitable that he should encounter difficulties, find his neighbors faithless, and, ultimately, become embroiled in local intrigues and conflicts. His was an unfortunate experience that, in Temple-Leader's evocative phrase, transformed him briefly "from the first of the condottiere to the last of local lords."[6] But Hawkwood used his time in the region to build up his landed patrimony back home in England and, deprived of his Milanese properties, to shift his Italian interests toward Tuscany and Umbria. He also established tighter relations with the Florentines, just across the Apeninnes, who throughout his travails showed a willingness to employ him and the fiscal capacity to meet payments to him.

## Domestic Affairs and Investments

Hawkwood went with his entourage directly to Bagnacavallo, the larger and better maintained of the territories. Hawkwood had already been using the town as a depot for the distribution of supplies to his armies in the field and for quartering soldiers. During the War of Eight Saints and the Veronese campaign, Hawkwood had moved battles axes, arrows, and various military items to and from Bagnacavallo, along with fodder and other provisions.[7] He had established a permanent garrison of English troops there commanded by Nicholas Clifton. Clifton left the town when Hawkwood arrived and took up employment with Florence.[8]

Donnina Hawkwood joined her husband at Bagnacavallo in August. She had been living since their marriage in Gazzuolo, Hawkwood's Cremonese possession, just south of Mantua. Donnina was now the mother of two girls, Janet and Catherine, the elder a year and a half old, the younger still an infant. Hawkwood himself was fifty-six years old. Several months earlier, Hawkwood's daughter from his first marriage, Antiochia, and her husband, William Coggeshale, had gone to Bagnacavallo, after the breach with Bernabò Visconti. But just before Hawkwood himself arrived, William, having reached his twenty-first birthday, returned home to Essex, to the town of Halstead, to claim his inheritance. The legacy was a significant one, consisting of ten manors.[9] He rejoined his father-in-law shortly thereafter, remained for a year, and then returned with Antiochia to England for good. He went on to a notable career in Essex, serving numerous times in the prominent posts of sheriff and member of Parliament.

Donnina's journey to Bagnacavallo is well documented. She arrived on the morning of 26 August 1379 with her children and a small group of attendants. She traveled along the Via Emilia through the towns of Parma and Reggio. Donnina announced her itinerary in a letter to the lord Gonzaga of Mantua, through whose lands she had sent ahead her personal effects. "I go to Bagnacavallo," she wrote, "to the distinguished and powerful knight, Lord John Hawkwood [Auchevud], my consort."[10] "I beg your magnificence," she continued, "on behalf of my father, Lord

Bernabò and my consort, Lord John . . . that the goods be permitted to pass through without impediment and without any toll or tax." The goods included "beds and various sundry items," which had been set on a boat on the Po River. Several weeks later, Donnina sent for the rest of her belongings, as well as her personal servant Jacobo della Credenza.[11]

Bagnacavallo was in reasonably good condition when the Hawkwoods arrived. The fortifications had recently been restored by the Manfredi family, which had ruled the city for more than thirty years before giving way to the papacy in 1368.[12] In that year the pope sent his legate Anglic Grimoard to the town to make a detailed inventory of it. Grimoard estimated the population at approximately 2,215 and its annual revenue at 5,000 florins—a sum comparable to Hawkwood's earnings in a lean year.[13] The landscape was dominated by the local castle, which was staffed by a castellan and twenty-five retainers. The town wall was not in good repair; it had only two functioning gates, each protected by a captain and eight soldiers. A single official acted as both civil and criminal judge, assisted by various functionaries. The captains at the gates earned a salary of 20 florins a month, while the castellan and his staff were paid 72½ florins a month, and the civil and criminal judge received 63 florins a month.[14]

A characteristic feature of the town was its large concentration of mercenary soldiers. Tiberto Brandolino, who had fought with Hawkwood and been captured at Verona, lived there along with his notable clan. The Brandolini traced their roots to a Brando of Brandenburg, who had supposedly served under the great Byzantine general Belisarius in the sixth century.[15] Tiberto had had a successful military career, collecting honors and estates for his distinguished service.[16] Tiberto's son Brandolino rose still higher to become one of the premier *condottieri* of the fifteenth century.

Just beyond Bagnacavallo lay the lands of the counts of Cunio, who also distinguished themselves by their military prowess. They often directed their bellicose urges at Bagnacavallo itself, which was described by one observer as "a snack that whetted the appetite of all the counts of Cunio."[17] The most outstanding of the counts was Alberigo da Barbiano, who in 1378 scored one of the era's most famous military victories over Breton mercenaries outside Rome, for which he was hailed by the Pope Urban (his employer) as "liberator of Italy" from the barbarians.[18] It is a measure of Alberigo's respect for Hawkwood that he never moved against Bagnacavallo while the Englishman was there.

Hawkwood's other Romagnol possession, Cotignola, was the home of the Attendoli family. Some fifteen members of this clan were active as mercenary soldiers in various armies.[19] The most well known was Muzio, who served as a corporal to Alberigo da Barbiano and by the early fifteenth century became one of the most renowned captains in Italy.[20] Muzio eventually gained lordship of Cotignola by papal decree in 1414 in recognition for his military accomplishments. By then he had changed his surname to "Sforza" (force), a name that would become associated with the city of Milan, which Muzio's relatives would rule.

The presence of so many notable soldiers in Hawkwood's lands has given rise to a belief that the Englishman oversaw a "school" of mercenaries in the Romagna. There can be little doubt that Hawkwood influenced locals, who could not have helped but take note of him. But if indeed it is proper to speak of a school, this had been established well before Hawkwood arrived. Hawkwood had little to do with the careers of Barbiano and Attendoli, which were begun in armies other than his own. Attendoli was seven years old when Hawkwood became lord of Cotignola, and he gained his first experience of war under the Italian captain Boldrino da Panicale, a man of moderate skill, who most often fought against Hawkwood. Apart from their joint (and unsuccessful) participation in war at Verona, Tiberto Brandolini rarely fought with Hawkwood. Both he and his son settled into quasi-permanent service for Milan in the late 1380s and early 1390s, just as Hawkwood was establishing permanent ties with Milan's archenemy Florence. There are similarities between Attendoli/Sforza and Hawkwood in terms of fighting technique but no evidence to suggest that the former was trained by the latter.

Hawkwood devoted much of his energy to maintaining his estates. Some scholars assert that he paid little attention to Bagnacavallo, a town "in which nothing was lacking."[21] But Hawkwood's own letters show that there was a constant flow of materials into and out of the town. Much of this came via the waterways from his Cremonese possession, Gazzuolo. The Oglio River passed through Gazzuolo and led into the Po River. The Po proceeded east and south toward Ferrara and the Romagna region, and, unlike today, its course extended below the line now followed by the Reno River, flowing into the Po di Primaro, to the north of Conselice, Lugo, and Fusignano. It emptied into the sea nineteen kilometers north of Ravenna. Hawkwood's goods from Gazzuolo traveled by ship on the Oglio River to the Po di Primaro, then to the Senio River, and thence to Bagnacavallo. The traffic flowed in both directions and consisted mostly of food and arms, presumably for the immediate use of Hawkwood and the local population. But on occasion Hawkwood also shipped freight intended for trade and profit. In July 1380 he sent a valuable cargo of twelve hundred bushels of salt—worth about 1,000 florins at current market price—from Bagnacavallo to Gazzuolo for sale in Lombardy, where salt was scarce.

Hawkwood employed a staff of functionaries to manage his domestic affairs. The most important of these was the Englishman Adam Sale, who oversaw activities at Gazzuolo. Sale signed his letters "business manager and factor," the same designation used by top-level employees of Italian business firms. We may assume that Sale's responsibilities were no less sophisticated. Sale was accompanied in Hawkwood's service by numerous others, such as Pierino della Latta, Astolfo da Pavia, Giovanni da Napoli, Andrew Cantel, and Giannino da Cremona. Their surnames indicate that they came from various regions throughout Italy and likely joined Hawkwood while he was on campaign. The specific activities of the men are not known. The documents make clear, however, that they did not always get along among themselves. Adam Sale, for example, got into a dispute with Astolfo da Pavia over matters of priority and authority. Not surprisingly, Hawkwood sided with his English worker over the Italian one.

The commerce between Gazzuolo and Bagnacavallo necessitated establishing good relations with Ludovico Gonzaga, lord of Mantua, and Niccolò d'Este, lord of Ferrara, through whose lands Hawkwood's goods traveled. Although he had opposed Este at the beginning of the decade, Hawkwood now actively courted him. He had on several occasions sent his bastard sons and mistress for safekeeping at Ferrara (where illegitimate children were famously in abundance). When daughter Catherine was born, Hawkwood and Donnina chose Niccolò's sister-in-law, Isabella, wife of co-ruler Alberto, as godmother to the child.

Hawkwood was similarly solicitous of Gonzaga, who held joint possession with him of the town of Gazzuolo. Gonzaga lay claim to the part just north of the Oglio River; Hawkwood owned the southern half. For Hawkwood to move his ships out of "my Gazzuolo," as he called it, he had to pass through Mantuan territory. Each journey required gaining explicit permission. For this reason he made especial efforts to stay on good terms with Gonzaga. He visited him when he could and excused himself when military business rendered such niceties impossible. He apologized to Gonzaga in June 1377, when, because of his obligations in the War of Eight Saints, he could not stop by and present in person his new bride Donnina before installing her at Gazzuolo. In other letters, Hawkwood offered Gonzaga his "special devotion" and proposed reciprocal services, such as freedom from tolls in return for help in finding fugitives. Hawkwood also occasionally shared information and reconnaissance—but only items that were generic in nature, such as the election of the new pope in 1378.[22] The relationship was cordial enough that when one of Hawkwood's soldiers was wounded on campaign during the War of Eight Saints, Hawkwood wrote directly to Gonzaga to request the services of a doctor: "Dear magnificent and excellent lord it happened these days that a certain comrade of mine was gravely wounded and here in Parma I am not able to find an adequate doctor to cure him. I hear that in Mantua there is a skilled doctor, Bernardo de Angelo; I beg you with all my heart to send him."[23]

Efforts and good words notwithstanding, disagreements frequently arose between the neighbors. The richness of the Archivio Gonzaga gives insight into the disputes with Mantua. On 16 March 1379, a crew of Hawkwood's men accompanied a cargo of bread and arms from Gazzuolo to Bagnacavallo. They were stopped just south of Mantua at Burgoforte by Gonzaga's men, who demanded that they produce a free pass. A standoff ensued. The captain of Hawkwood's crew, Pierino della Latta, wrote to Gonzaga: "I beg humbly for the sake of my lord [John Hawkwood] . . . that you send to me your letters with which I may have free pass with the arms, people and other things on board our ship."[24] He explained that Hawkwood, in his preoccupation with military affairs, had forgotten to obtain the free pass. At about the same time, Adam Sale wrote a lengthy letter to Gonzaga complaining that Mantuan citizens had been allowed to poach on Hawkwood's land, illegally fishing in his streams and taking wood from his forests.

> Dear Magnificent and Egregious Lord, I understand that men from your jurisdiction often cross the Oglio river and go into the forests and ponds of the noble and egregious knight John Hawkwood and in those ponds they ply they trade, they fish without my license to the great damage and detriment to the said lord John and they do similarly in the forests, cutting and taking away wood of many types. I beg that those of your Gazzuolo and any other persons of your dominion will not come in the said forests and ponds of the said John Hawkwood and do any damage.[25]

Ludovico Gonzaga had his own complaints. In a long letter dated 6 September 1384, he sought redress for an attack on a Mantuan ship that had passed along the Oglio River near Hawkwood's part of Gazzuolo. Hawkwood's men pulled a vessel ashore to have its cargo weighed—presumably for the purpose of taxing it. But as the boat approached land, it was struck by a missile from a trebuchet, which damaged the hull. It was dredged ashore and its goods confiscated. There is no record of how the case was resolved.[26]

There is little evidence of major building projects undertaken by Hawkwood in either Gazzuolo or Bagnacavallo. At Bagnacavallo there remains a street, named Strada Aguta, which Hawkwood purportedly built during his stay in the town. The road opens toward the east of the city and ends near what was then a fortress known as the bastion of Villanova. It is generally believed that Hawkwood built the road to facilitate communications with the fortress, which protected the city. It is likewise thought that Hawkwood himself built the fortress, but no evidence for this has survived.

Hawkwood's renovations at Cotignola were more extensive and have been chronicled by the nineteenth-century local historians Girolamo Bonoli and Luigi Balduzzi. Cotignola was in poor shape when Hawkwood received it. Neglect and frequent inundations of the Senio River had left its fortifications in disrepair.

Hawkwood began work immediately, enlarging the existing fortress to five times its previous size. He erected a palazzo, of which only the bell tower survives.[27] Documents relating to Cotignola in the Este family archives in Modena show that Hawkwood purchased land from the bishop of Faenza to effect the enlargement of the fortress, paying 300 florins and three *corbe* of grain on 25 August 1380.[28] The extant bell tower is made of brick with square holes in it. In Hawkwood's day, the tower had eight small arched windows. Its chief function was, as with all such edifices, to watch the movements of enemies from afar. As we shall soon see, Hawkwood had much occasion to use the tower for this purpose.

It is at this time that we also have our first explicit evidence that Hawkwood was investing in land back home in England—an activity he undoubtedly had begun much earlier. The documents show that on 26 February 1380 he purchased the manor called Bloyes in his native Sible Hedingham and the manor called Padbury in the adjacent county of Buckingham. Both had formerly belonged to a John Cavendish, listed in the documents as a London "drapier."[29] A few weeks later, Hawkwood bought the manors of Berwick, Cardeux, and Scoteneys in Toppesfield and Sible Hedingham, as well as additional properties in Yeldham, Wethersfield, Gosfield, and Hedingham.[30] The transactions were made on his behalf by his feofees back in Essex, including Robert Lindsey and John Sargeant, the same men who had "mainperned" on his behalf for his pardon back in 1377, as well as Robert Rykedon and Hawkwood's brother, John the elder. All the men were from Essex; they held the land for Hawkwood with the understanding that he would reclaim it when he returned home. Rykedon was a prominent Essex lawyer and landowner from the village of Witham. Hawkwood and his older brother worked so closely together that their wealth and status grew in synchrony.[31] By the late seventies, as the younger John Hawkwood stood at the top of the mercenary profession, his elder brother had become one of largest landholders in the town of Gosfield, his primary residence. The two probably collaborated at this time in endowing the church of St. Peter's in Sible Hedingham, where their father, Gilbert, was buried.[32] The facade of St Peter's, particularly the west tower, contains numerous hawks, the mercenary's personal emblem.[33] One of the Hawkwoods—it is not clear which—sent money to King Richard II in the fall of 1379 for a planned offensive against France.[34]

Hawkwood transferred his Italian earnings back to England by means of bills of exchange, an Italian fiscal innovation used extensively by international merchant bankers, which allowed the movement of money from one place to another without the physical transportation of specie. In 1382 we have the only documented transfer involving a bill of exchange made through the Guinigi bank of Lucca, the largest firm in that city, with interests in England dating from the thirteenth century.[35] The bill was sent first to Bruges, to a Guinigi factor, Francesco Vinciguerra. This was common; Bruges was a flourishing commercial center with close economic ties to England, and many transactions involving the island passed through that city.[36] The beneficiaries of the bill were Hawkwood's now familiar feofees: Robert Rykedon, John Sargeant and Robert Lindsey.[37]

## A Feud with Astorre Manfredi

While Hawkwood focused on his personal affairs, his presence in the Romagna was deeply resented by his neighbors. From the moment he received the properties from the pope, he was subject to attack. As early as in August 1378, when he was still waging war at Verona, a group of Italian mercenaries from Cesena staged a raid on Bagnacavallo, dragging away much of the town's livestock.[38] In May 1379, Astorre Manfredi assailed Bagnacavallo at the head of a free company called the Company of the Star. Manfredi, the former ruler of Bagnacavallo and current lord of Faenza (whom Hawkwood had helped install in that city two years earlier) proved a relentless adversary. He had no intention of allowing Hawkwood to remain at peace in the region. The Company of the Star did to Hawkwood what Hawkwood had done so often, and so effectively, to others.[39] Astorre received material support from Bernabò Visconti, who was eager to discomfit his estranged son-in-law.

Hawkwood responded to Astorre's raid by sending a contingent of three hundred lances directly against his home base at Faenza.[40] Bologna and Florence, fearing that the contest would spill into their lands, sent ambassadors to try to arrange peace. Florence's approach was similar to that used by Ruggiero Cane to gain Hawkwood's services in 1377. The city openly advocated on the Englishman's behalf and argued his case to Manfredi in a letter dated 28 May 1379: "Dear Magnificent Lord and Dearest Friend, we understand from the outstanding knight John Hawkwood [Johannes Haucud], who has worked so much on our behalf that we cannot write of it all but are forever in his debt, that in his territory of Bagnacavallo certain disturbances have occurred through you and the Company of the Star, which is at the borders of his land. . . . If you desire to conserve our friendship . . . if you wish to have our great gratitude . . . please refrain."[41] What services Hawkwood had done for Florence are not clear; the last encounter between the two had involved a raid whereby Hawkwood forced Florence to hire his men against their will, an act bitterly condemned by the chronicler Stefani. In any case, Florentine diplomacy did not succeed; nor did similar efforts by the Bolognese.

The feud between Hawkwood and Manfredi was not easily resolved. It was entangled in the broader rivalries that engulfed the Romagna. Pope Urban's decision during the War of Eight Saints to bestow lands and privileges on those who gave him financial and military assistance intensified traditional jealousies and left the region, in the words of the Bolognese chronicler, in "great tribulation."[42] The lord of Rimini, Galeotto Malatesta, was among those most favored by papal largesse and, consequently, among those most despised by his neighbors. Manfredi's attack on Hawkwood in May 1379 in fact occurred in conjunction with a strike on Malatesta. Manfredi received assistance from the lord of Ravenna, Guido da Polenta, and the lord of Urbino, Antonio da Montefeltro. After ravaging Bagnacavallo, Manfredi joined the others and laid waste to Malatesta's lands up to the gates of Rimini. Hawkwood in turn allied with Malatesta and his supporters, Francesco Ordelaffi, lord of Forlì, and the city of Bologna. Hawkwood sent William Gold and a contingent of 250 lances to Forlì to forestall an attack there and 100 lances to Bologna. He himself oversaw the defense of Bagnacavallo with 50–60 lances.[43] A local noble, Giovanni Alberghettino, an inveterate foe of Manfredi's, helped reinforce Hawkwood's army at Bagnacavallo.[44]

Hawkwood did his best to keep secret his support for other Romagnol lords. He gave only vague reference in his letters to his activities on behalf of "certain Romagnol" lords but few particulars. It is a tribute to Hawkwood's subterfuge that his role in the affair has to this day remained hidden.[45]

Manfredi and Hawkwood waged war throughout the summer and fall of 1379. The fighting ended only when Astorre left the Romagna, probably at the command of Milan or Venice or both, and conducted his Company of the Star against Genoa (then at war with Venice, which was allied with Milan). Manfredi was soundly defeated at Genoa and taken prisoner.[46] Hawkwood immediately took advantage of the situation. He secretly sent soldiers to Giovanni Alberghettino and encouraged him to stage a raid against Astorre's garrison at Marradi, a small town in Val di Lamone in the Apennines which stood at the entryway into Florentine territory. Astorre's brother Francesco intercepted Alberghettino and beat back the offensive. The details of the obscure event are known only through Hawkwood's letters. According to Hawkwood, the battle at Marradi was a bloody one in which a "good one thousand" men were killed and "many others" captured.[47]

## Secrets by Firelight and Employment by Florence

The fight with Manfredi was financially burdensome, as were maintaining the Romagnol territories and building a patrimony in England. Hawkwood endeavored to increase his income where he could and in December 1379 found an opportunity for profit by exploiting his reconnaissance and connections within the

Italian expatriate community. He wrote a letter to the Florentines informing them that he had information regarding plots by exiles against their city.[48] The epistle was timely; it arrived at a moment when there was great concern about conspiracies. The new government that had taken power at the end of the War of Eight Saints in 1378 had from its inception faced threats from both within and without; these reached a peak in December 1379.[49]

Hawkwood offered to expose the plot in return for a cash payment. He proposed a sliding scale. He wanted 50,000 florins for the whole story, including the names of the conspirators; 20,000 florins for the plot alone, without any names. "And he wanted," wrote the chronicler Stefani, "the money brought to him at Bagnacavallo."[50] In the event that Florence chose the first option—full disclosure—Hawkwood insisted that the conspirators be spared their lives and their goods and at worst face banishment from the city. Hawkwood intended to profit from the exile community, but, still reliant on information from that source, he did not wish to appear wholly infamous.

Florence sent the ambassador Guccio Gucci, a man of excellent repute, judged by Stefani to be "wise, rich and faithful," to speak with Hawkwood. He was instructed to take the less expensive option of 20,000 florins and to try to negotiate the price still lower. He arrived at Bagnacavallo to find Hawkwood sitting in a dark room, lit only by the burning logs in the fireplace. Beside Hawkwood sat the informer, who apparently did little to conceal his identity.[51] Guccio succeeded in getting Hawkwood to lower the price to 12,000 florins. The informer then slowly revealed the details of the plot.

Hawkwood's revelations helped forestall the conspiracy. Shortly after Guccio's embassy, Florence seized six conspirators and put them to death and sentenced another fifty men to death in absentia and confiscated their goods.[52] This was not, however, the outcome that Hawkwood wanted.

Shortly afterward, Hawkwood began to entertain offers to return to service in communal armies. His rival Manfredi had not fully recovered from his defeat in Genoa. The Genoese had released him from prison, but on returning home he became involved in battle with his brother Francesco, who had usurped his place at Faenza.[53] Both Venice and Florence sought to hire Hawkwood. The Venetians were embroiled in an increasingly bitter war with Genoa and wished to employ Hawkwood to command their land forces for an offensive at Chioggia. But for the third time in his career, Hawkwood turned down the Venetians. He recommended William Gold in his stead. The Venetians did as Hawkwood suggested and hired Gold in February 1380. His service began inauspiciously, with a brawl between English and Italian soldiers as the army assembled on Pellestrina, a sandbar not far from Chioggia.[54] But Gold helped quell the disorder and later distinguished himself in battle.[55] The local chronicler Daniele di Chinazzo lauded Gold (whom he called "Cocho Engelexe") for his "valorous" performance.[56] The Venetian senate rewarded him in April 1380 with a grant of honorary citizenship and in July 1380 with a lifetime pension of 500 gold ducats a year, a bequest that induced him to settle in the city, where his son Bertram would remain after his father's death.[57]

John Hawkwood meanwhile negotiated with Florence. The city sought his service against the approach of a mercenary company calling itself the Company of Saint George. The band, formed mostly from remnants of Alberigo da Barbiano's Italian company of the same name, had come together in anticipation of the arrival in Italy of the Hungarian prince Charles of Durazzo, who planned to take it to southern Italy to assert his claims to the throne of Naples. But as the company took shape, it attracted numerous Florentine exiles, so many that the chronicler Stefani referred to it as "a brigade of Florentine exiles," whose main purpose, he claimed, "was to ride close enough to the city to raise rebellion within."[58] The view was seconded by the Sienese chronicler Donato di Neri: "They went about saying 'we are the Guelfs of Florence and we wish to return to our home.'"[59] The band arrived in Tuscany in February 1380 and extorted money from the cities of Siena, Perugia, Pisa, Lucca, and Cortona.[60] As it approached Florence, panicked officials ordered all shops closed. They sent out the army. But the force, commanded by Eberhard von Landau, acquitted itself poorly. Landau was himself struck in the mouth and lost two teeth. His English corporal John Berwick was severely wounded; several others were taken prisoner.

The poor showing induced Florentine officials to pursue Hawkwood aggressively. For Hawkwood's part, Florentine employment had distinctive advantages over service to Venice. It allowed him to remain close to the Romagna, in case the volatile situation there changed. It also pitted him against a relatively weak opponent, a mercenary band, rather than the army of a major state like Genoa. The Florentines called for a police action; the Venetians desired all-out war. Venice was also allied to Bernabò Visconti, with whom Hawkwood remained at odds.

Florentine officials nevertheless had strong reservations. Some felt that Hawkwood came at too high a price; others were uncomfortable with his closeness to exiles and worried that he might become involved in internal affairs in the city. The crux of the debate was whether a cheaper, less renowned captain, a "man of lesser weight," would still be effective.[61] The fear of the Company of Saint George ultimately convinced officials to take the more expensive option. When the band advanced to the town of Empoli, a short ride from the gates of Florence, officials elected Hawkwood as their captain of war. They granted him lucrative terms: command of 200 lances at a salary of 1,000 florins a month for six months.[62] The Florentines surrounded him with a largely English force. They hired his longtime comrade Richard Romsey with 109 lances and John Beltoft, a rising star in the profession, with 50 lances. Also on the payroll was a young Italian captain, Facino Cane, with 10 lances. Cane would soon make his mark as an enemy of Florence in the armies of Milan and as one of the greatest of the *condottieri* of the fifteenth century.

Hawkwood formally assumed the post on 6 April 1380. The anonymous Florentine chronicler described the event in detail. Hawkwood entered the city to the ringing of bells and the sounding of trumpets. He stayed a week, arranging the details of the contract and conferring with city officials on strategy. "On the morning of April 14, John Hawkwood, the Englishman, took the baton in the name of God, in the palace of the Signoria, from our lords as captain general of war . . . to the undoing and death of our citizens who had come back, and were in the cursed Company [of Saint George]. At terce he rode out from Florence with all the men at arms. A beautiful and excellent band it was."[63]

Hawkwood's election as captain of war marked his first independent service to Florence. The give-and-take between the two sides would set the pattern for their relationship for the next decade and more. Hawkwood continually sought additional considerations from his employer in order to maximize his profits and, inasmuch as possible, to get Florence to bankroll his activities in the Romagna. Florence, on the other hand, perpetually expressed anxiety over the costs and activities and did its best to rein him in without alienating him.

Hawkwood's hire brought immediate results. Before a single blow was exchanged, the Company of Saint George sued for peace. In fact, the band settled for half the sum of money (20,000 florins) it had initially demanded and then took the road south from its camp at Empoli through the Maremma, passing into papal lands.

Hawkwood returned to Florence and tried to use his success to improve the terms of his contract. He asked permission to increase his brigade to 300 men, a number he had apparently originally asked for. The city, wishing to lighten its financial burden, wanted to reduce his force to 130 lances. The talks went back and forth, and eventually the sides agreed to keep the terms the same: 200 lances at a monthly salary of 1,000 florins.

The sagacity of Florence's decision to keep Hawkwood on the payroll soon became apparent. The departure of the Company of Saint George was followed by the arrival in July of Charles of Durazzo, who, after many delays, finally came to Italy. He moved south from Verona with five thousand horses, passing through the Romagna to Bologna and then into Tuscany. With the support of his ally pope Urban VI, Charles intended to unseat the current ruler of Naples, Queen Johanna, who had allied with the French house of Anjou and Urban's French rival to the

Holy See, Clement VII.[64] The arrival of so powerful a prince as Charles in Florentine territory raised new fears of conspiracies and plots.[65] Charles had a very
enthusiastic following in Florence and stirred strong passions in the city—passions
that one scholar has described as "disproportionate to his stature and role in Italian
politics and thus difficult to explain."[66] The city of Gubbio gave itself to Charles in
August 1380; shortly thereafter, he seized Arezzo.[67] By late September, he was
camped in the hills of the Chianti between Siena and Florence.

Florence sent Hawkwood with the full Florentine army, nearly a thousand
lances, to keep watch on Charles. He was instructed to avoid open engagement and
only to make sure, as far as possible, that the Angevin prince respected Florentine
lands. But Hawkwood took an openly bellicose stance and asked permission to
attack. "If you wish," he told officials, "I will destroy these troops."[68] The bravado
was misplaced, or more accurately, disingenuous. The Florentines had no desire to
undertake war against Charles, who, though a troublesome presence, was nevertheless a nominal ally. His principal motive for passing through local territory
was to aid another Florentine ally, Urban VI. Hawkwood knew this well. Indeed,
his own monarch back home, Richard II, supported both Charles and Urban
against the French cause.

Hawkwood's warlike stance was a ruse, intended to take advantage of the
passions within Florence and win additional concessions from his employer. His
contract was coming due at the end of September. He sought various financial
considerations, most notably the right to take a temporary leave of absence with
pay after this engagement in order to attend his own affairs. Hawkwood had in
mind his feud in the Romagna with Astorre Manfredi, who had returned to the
offensive and was now harassing his lands. Hawkwood in effect wanted Florence
to pay the cost of his defense. The city, preoccupied with the threat of Charles,
granted the request. It even promised to hire an additional brigade of one hundred
lances for his defense captained by his son-in-law, William Coggeshale, now back
from England.[69]

Hawkwood responded by giving effective service against Charles, keeping close
watch on him and helping escort him south, to Sienese territory (to Abbadia a
Isola and Montepulciano) and then Naples. The Florentines facilitated Charles's
departure by granting him large loan, which he promised to pay back in five years.
The money was deducted from what Florence owed the pope from the indemnity
from the War of Eight Saints.[70]

With the immediate threat gone, on 1 November 1380 Hawkwood formally
signed a new contract with Florence, a *condotta in aspetto* that allowed him to
manage his own affairs. Hawkwood took his leave of absence and returned to fight
Manfredi. The two men battled throughout the winter of 1380/81. A Mantuan

ambassador stationed in Ferrara described the military situation as of 10 January: "Concerning the men amassing in the Romagna, I can relate that there are about 600 horses, which Lord John Hawkwood has at his service, making war against Astorre Manfredi at Faenza, together with count Francesco di Dovadola and Giovanni Alberghettino."[71] Hawkwood built a bastion at the town of Sezada, some five miles outside Faenza, from which to pressure Manfredi.

The fighting continued into the spring. On 8 March 1381, at the urging of Florentine and Bolognese ambassadors, Manfredi and Hawkwood agreed to peace talks.[72] The two stopped first in Florence, to consult with officials there. "If I had anything to do with it," wrote the anonymous chronicler, "I would pay them both off and have done with it."[73] The men then went to Bologna, where negotiations continued for a week. The talks were linked to a broader initiative to bring peace among the other warring parties in the region. On 20 March 1381, Manfredi and Hawkwood agreed to a truce. The next day Galeotto Malatesta of Rimini agreed to end his war with Antonio da Montefeltro of Urbino.[74] Only Hawkwood's ally, Giovanni Alberghettino, refused to lay down his arms and continued to fight.[75]

Florence's preoccupation with conspiracies arising from political tensions and the arrival of Charles of Durazzo compelled the city to keep Hawkwood on the payroll. He was hired again when his contract came due on 1 April 1381, less than two weeks after the accord with Manfredi.[76] As earlier, Hawkwood received permission to do his own bidding. He was granted a relatively small force of ninety lances and archers, but he could use them any way he wished, provided he did not venture more than seventy miles from the territorial limits of Florence. Hawkwood's territories in the Romagna were within the limits. The generous terms of the contract were introduced by an equally generous preamble that lauded Hawkwood as a man of "virtue, sound judgment, long experience and circumspection in labors regarding war." Hawkwood also constrained the Florentines to hire his comrade William Gold, now back from his service to Venice, as well as Richard Romsey, John Berwick, and several other Englishmen.[77]

## A Farewell to the Romagna

Although Florence had helped bring about peace, its liberality in granting Hawkwood a private army for his own use helped facilitate war. Hostilities between Hawkwood and Manfredi recommenced just two weeks after the truce. The routine was now all too familiar. Florence and Bologna sent ambassadors to smooth over the difficulties; Hawkwood and Manfredi—and their allies—remained obstinate. If the report of a Sienese ambassador is accurate, the Florentines also behaved in a self-serving manner. While openly advocating peace, they sent out a con-

tingent of soldiers on 25 July to fight against Hawkwood's ally Francesco da
Dovadola—and, by association, against Hawkwood himself. The reason for the
Florentine decision is unclear.[78]

But Hawkwood was growing tired of the conflict and began to contemplate
leaving the region. To live in the Romagna was to be embroiled in constant war.
Worse, possession of estates there allowed enemies a chance for reprisals. As a
leader of free companies, Hawkwood could attack the lands of others with a
certain degree of impunity. As Leonardo Bruni once observed, the great strategic
advantage of mercenary bands was that they had "neither city nor countryside to
lose."[79] As a Romagnol lord, Hawkwood relinquished this advantage.

Hawkwood's attention was also now diverted elsewhere. On 5 May 1381 King
Richard II appointed him ambassador to Pope Urban VI and sent from England
the envoys Nicholas Dagworth and Walter Skirlaw. Richard had several days
earlier concluded a marriage alliance with the House of Luxemburg, to wed Anne
of Bohemia, the sister of the Holy Roman Emperor Wenceslaus. The alliance
included Urban V, who sought support for the league against "schismatics of the
church," that is, his French Clementinist opponents.[80] The sides envisioned a
broad union, whereby Richard would receive papal sanction for his ongoing activities against France, the pope would gain help for his war against the French
antipope Clement, and Wenceslaus would get badly needed financial relief in the
form of subsidies from Richard. Interestingly, Wenceslaus's business was handled
in part by Hawkwood's brother-in-law, Lutz von Landau, who was now at Wenceslaus's court in Prague, advising him on Italian affairs. The talks were complicated
and prolonged; Hawkwood himself sent one of his own men, John Northwood,
back to England to confer with the king.[81]

The service to Richard gave Hawkwood further incentive to unload his troublesome Romagnol lands. A Sienese ambassador, Giacomo di Buonaventura, reported
rumors on 31 July 1381 that Hawkwood had already begun negotiations about
Bagnacavallo and Cotignola with Niccolò d'Este of Ferrara.[82] The rumor proved
true. On 10 August 1381 Hawkwood sold the towns "with bastions, palaces, towers,
gates, fortresses and everything else" to Este for 60,000 florins.[83] The deal was concluded in the town of Lugo, just downstream from Bagnacavallo and Cotignola, at
the ford in the river Senio. Hawkwood did not himself attend the meeting but sent
power of attorney to two representatives: an Italian, Antonio Porcari, and an
Englishman, John Rayner. Este sent the Italian mercenary Filippo Guazzalotti,
who had fought against Hawkwood during the days of the papal-Milanese war in
1372, to take possession of the towns on his behalf.

The deed of transfer makes clear that Hawkwood abandoned the towns because
"he was not sufficiently powerful to defend the said territories . . . from the raids

and insidious plots of his enemies." The deed also indicates that Hawkwood had operated at a financial loss: "the expenses of maintaining the territories exceeded the income."[84] Hawkwood insisted, however, on retaining possession of the bastion he had built at Sezada, near Faenza, a precaution against Manfredi and an indication that, although Hawkwood was leaving the region, their feud was not over.[85]

Freed from Romagnol lordship, Hawkwood returned, as Balduzzi wrote, to "his own particular genius," leading marauding mercenary companies against innocent victims.[86] The sale of Bagnacavallo and Cotignola coincided with the end of Hawkwood's contract as war captain with the Florentines, leaving him free to speculate. In fact, Hawkwood skipped the final rendering of accounts at Lugo and joined forthwith a mercenary band then forming under the leadership of the German Eberhard von Landau and the Hungarian John Horváti.[87] He took personal command of 840 lances and went directly to Faenza to punish Astorre Manfredi one last time.[88] He raided Manfredi's lands and then rejoined rest of the company, crossing with it through the Apennine passes into Tuscany.

Unlike the recent Company of Saint George, Hawkwood's band had little in the way of a political agenda. The rank and file were motivated by the familiar combination of greed and revenge. For example, Ugo Calisten, a German corporal who had worked for Florence for many years, had recently fallen into debt to local moneylenders and lost his job. He sought financial redress and personal vindication. Hawkwood for his part appears to have been interested in acquiring Tuscan properties to replace the Romagnol lands he had just sold. Indeed, as the band approached Florentine territory, Hawkwood, despite two years of generous contracts, wrote to city officials to demand a house, which he alleged he was at one point promised but never given. Hawkwood also claimed damages against Florence, owing to the city's attack against his ally Giovanni Alberghettino.

Hawkwood's demands caused great concern in Florence, where much general consternation remained about the movements of armed men arising from the ongoing war in Naples. One official, Giorgio Scali, suggested that the city respond "sweetly and with good words, welcoming Hawkwood in friendship," and that it should hire him in conjunction with Bologna, which would pay part of his salary. Uguccione di Ricci advised, however, that the city "prepare as if for an enemy." He called it "the more honorable and safer action."[89] The city ultimately took the customary approach; it elected Spinello Alberti as ambassador and sent him to discuss terms.[90] "Spinello is the one," said Giovanni Amerigo, "who knows best Hawkwood's intentions."[91]

Alberti met the band near Assisi, where it had set up camp. He employed the now standard divide-and-conquer strategy, negotiating separately with Hawkwood and the other two captains of the band, hoping to exploit the differences between them. He told Hawkwood privately that the city would be willing to hire him for three months.[92] But he did not offer him property, only vague assurances that the issue would be dealt with in the future. Hawkwood apparently consented to this. On 30 October 1381 Spinello concluded a pact with the band near the city of Assisi. Florence was required to pay 5,000 florins; the band pledged in return to respect Florentine territory only "eighteen days in the form of a company (society) and three months as stipendiaries."[93]

Hawkwood was more successful in his quest for property with the Perugians, who negotiated with him alongside Spinello. They granted him possession of a *mansione* and cloister ("for the use of the magnificent knight John Hawkwood [Haugut] and his daughter") in the city.[94] Sienese ambassadors, however, flatly refused Hawkwood's request for land. The decision further damaged the relationship between the captain and that city.

The raid brought Hawkwood full circle. He ended his stay in the Romagna the way he had begun it, at the head of a marauding army. His career as local lord was a signal failure, and he began the process of finding a new patrimony elsewhere. The dispute with Astorre Manfredi, however, was not over. The two men would continue to fight over the next few years and were never fully reconciled.

Hawkwood was drawing closer to Florence. His relationship with the city was often contentious; but Florentine officials actively and consistently courted him, using when possible the city's wealth to win his good graces. And Hawkwood, in turn, continued to give little indications of good will. He was becoming increasingly comfortable taking their money and employment—a prospect made more appealing by his break with Bernabò Visconti. Within a month of his raid on Tuscany, Hawkwood resumed employment with the Florentines as their captain of war.

# CHAPTER TEN

# Neapolitan Soldier and Tuscan Lord, 1381–1384

The cause of this fighting is a fiend's cause, for no one on earth knows which of these popes is a fiend to be damned in hell.

*John Wycliff*

At approximately the same time that Hawkwood was divesting himself of his possessions in the Romagna, a rebellion broke out back home in Essex, England. Men from several southern villages assaulted government agents investigating tax evasion. The violence spread to Kent, Norfolk, Hertfortshire, Cambridgeshire, Surrey, Middlesex, and parts of Sussex. The insurgents, chanting egalitarian slogans ("when Adam delved and Eve span, who then was the gentleman"), made their way along the Thames River to petition the king in London. They destroyed the palace of the Duke of Lancaster and seized the royal treasurer Robert Hales, the chancellor of the archbishop of Canterbury, and the physician of the Duke of Lancaster and put them to death. King Richard II, a boy of fourteen years old, showed remarkable fortitude in handling the crisis, listening patiently to the peasants' demands, thus diffusing the impetus of the group. He then struck back with a fury, unleashing the army, which included the mercenary Robin Knowles. Knowles cut the rebels down. The famous Peasants' Revolt of 1381 was over.

The news reached Italy through numerous ambassadorial dispatches. The Lucchese envoy Giovanni Vergiolesi cast the event in distinctly Italian terms as an issue involving the people (*popoli*) and the nobles (*nobili*). "Some dissolute nobles along with the people in London complained how the chamberlain of the King of England with other barons and courtesans spent all of the income of the kingdom and the king, for which reason they rose up in great numbers and went armed to the house of the chamberlain and there they cut him to pieces. A bishop tried to mollify their fury, but they killed him too."[1]

There is no record of Hawkwood's opinion of the revolt, but he was certainly affected by it. His daughter Antiochia was now settled with her family in Essex, and his older brother, John, was a prominent landowner, the second wealthiest in the village of Gosfield.[2] Hawkwood's own holdings do not appear to have been touched, but the home of his feofee Robert Rykedon at Witham was ransacked, and John Cavendish, from whom he purchased land in 1380, was killed by the rebels at Bury St. Edmunds.[3]

There is little doubt that Hawkwood's sympathies lay with Knowles and the authorities. Not only was he a member of the landholding class that was under attack, but he had forged links to King Richard himself and was in fact serving as the monarch's ambassador to Pope Urban VI at the start of the revolt.[4] Hawkwood's older brother, John the elder, had also established ties to the crown through his connections to the de Vere family. Aubrey de Vere was Richard's personal favorite and stood at the king's side when he rode out to meet the rebels. William Coggeshale served on the royal commission in Essex enacted to repress the revolt, as did Robert Rykedon.[5] Hawkwood's old comrade-in-arms Hugh de la Zouche took part in the royal commission in Cambridge.[6]

And Hawkwood managed to profit financially from the situation. He purchased properties that had belonged to Richard Lyons, a wealthy financier to the crown and prominent landholder in Gosfield who had been beheaded by the rebels in London. The sale was completed in May 1382 between Lyons's heirs and Hawkwood's feofees, which included John Hawkwood the elder, Robert Rykedon, John Sargeant, and Robert Lindsey. The lands were mostly in Gosfield but stretched also into the adjacent counties of Hedingham and Wethersfield; a portion had formerly belonged to the Liston family, longtime friends of the Hawkwoods.[7]

Less than a year later, Hawkwood became involved militarily in a rebellion in Italy. In December 1381, he had signed on to serve Florence again as its captain of war. A month into his tenure, however, long-simmering political and social tensions in the city erupted into violence that quickly escalated into what historians have called a "conservative or counter-revolution," bringing down the popular Ciompi government that had ruled the city since 1378. The drama began when a leading politician, a cloth shearer named Iacopo di Bartolomeo Amati, known as "Scatizza," accused a prominent citizen of plotting to overthrow the government. Scatizza was in turn himself accused and seized by the captain of the people. Some members of government supported Scatizza and tried to save him; others, backed by well-to-do merchants and wealthier elements of the city, supported the captain of the people.[8]

Hawkwood stood beside the captain of the people and the wealthier, conservative forces. He entered the city in the middle of January 1382.[9] According to the anonymous Florentine chronicler, he performed his task dispassionately, in the manner of a captain "conducting an inspection of his troops" (a modo di fare la mostra). Hawkwood's mere presence helped the captain of the people perform his duty; his soldiers did not themselves engage in violent acts.[10] With Hawkwood's support, Scatizza and his allies were subdued. On 20 January, officials reformed the government and established a new, more patrician regime, which favored the greater guilds over the lesser ones. But tensions remained high in the city in the coming weeks and months.

Hawkwood's efforts in the piazza constituted an important moment in his relationship with Florence. It engendered in the new government a heightened sense of confidence in him. It was understood that Hawkwood's support depended on financial incentive, but the new rulers acknowledged that the Englishman was instrumental in the establishment of their regime, a fact that provided motivation to seek his services in the future, despite his often indifferent attitude toward them. And whatever opinion Hawkwood held about Florence, its persistent and energetic pursuit of his services tied him more closely to the region and gave further impetus to his own inclination to acquire lands and estates there.

In addition to his service inside the city, Hawkwood also protected Florence from external threats. Political crisis was accompanied by pressure from mercenary bands. There was great concern throughout Tuscany and Umbria about the movements of soldiers spinning out of the ongoing conflict down in the Kingdom of Naples. At the start of the winter of 1381, Charles of Durazzo demobilized his army. Remnants of it formed into two free companies, commanded by Durazzo's captains Alberigo da Barbiano and the more obscure Hungarian Villanozzo of Brumfort. They moved north, joined forces, took the now familiar name the Company of Saint George, and made their base near Arezzo, Durazzo's stronghold in the region.[11] The situation was very similar to that of a year and a half earlier when Durazzo had first led his army through Tuscany toward Naples. Alberigo and Villanozzo wished to sustain their men at the expense of the rich cities and fertile fields of Tuscany.

The Florentines feared not only violence and extortion but also the social and political pressure that the company brought with it. Many of those who had fled the city or been exiled during the recent upheavals flocked to the company. Florentine officials saw the band as a potential instrument of counterrevolution, a matter that elicited much discussion in the Signoria and in ambassadorial dispatches.[12] The reports of the Lucchese envoy Niccolò Dombellinghi, stationed in Florence from 6 December 1381 to 10 February 1382, intertwine news of the unfolding political disturbances with news of the maneuvers and negotiations with the companies.[13]

For the sake of civic harmony, Florence was eager to settle.[14] But the band made steep demands, including a bribe of 35,000 florins. Officials sent Hawkwood out to follow the company, with instructions to keep a watch on it short of engaging it in battle. The Florentines feared that a strike against it would be perceived as a strike at Charles of Durazzo, whom they had no desire to offend. They meanwhile sent ambassadors to seek an accord and also dispatched envoys directly to Charles of Durazzo to ask him to withdraw the men.[15] Durazzo gave assurances that he would recall the band but did nothing. The Florentine envoys complained that he offered "good words" but left them in "suspense."[16]

Hawkwood rode out of Florence on the very day that officials met to reform the government (20 January 1382). His personal brigade consisted of one hundred lances, but the city gave him an additional hundred German lances and hundred English lances—the latter including contigents of sixty-five and thirty-five lances under John Beltoft and John Berwick, respectively, men we shall hear more about presently. Richard Romsey joined a month later.[17] Florence also sent to Hawkwood recently readmitted exiles, who were constrained to join his army under penalty of being banished anew. The move was intended to prevent the men from joining the company rather than to enhance the quality of Hawkwood's force. The cities of Siena and Lucca sent reinforcements according to the terms of an antimercenary league signed back in 1381.[18]

On 29 January 1382 Hawkwood and the company briefly skirmished outside the town of Marcialla, not far from the band's base at Arezzo.[19] The encounter—along with a week's worth of observation of the company—convinced Hawkwood that Florence should take a different approach. On 31 January, he wrote to officials: "Why do you wish to throw away your money. . . . The enemy is so frightened . . . that they do not have the heart to come into Florentine land . . . in their base at Arezzo they have a great lack of provisions, both for men and for horses; it is said that some of the knights wish to go toward Cortona . . . and others to Perugia."[20] Hawkwood suggested that Florence resist the impulse to pay off the company and instead delay, in the hope that lack of supplies and internal division would eventually weaken the band.

Florentine officials followed Hawkwood's instructions. Their assent was, however, contingent on Hawkwood's ability to keep the band out of Florentine territory. A give-and-take between the city and the band followed, continuing through the spring. Florence neither rid itself of the company nor paid a bribe. The company gained the advantage when another band (commanded by the German captain Wilhelm Filibach) arrived in Tuscany in April.[21] Florence stepped up its efforts to reach an accord.[22]

Officials allowed Hawkwood an active role in the talks. He went on several trips to the enemy camp with Spinello Alberti, Florence's most experienced ambassador, and met directly with the captains Villanozzo and Alberigo.[23] A deal was made in late May, in conjunction with the city of Siena.[24] Hawkwood himself announced the terms: "The communes of Florence and Siena are in concord with the society of Italians and Germans. The pacts are these: that the said societies cannot be against the communes in the manner of stipends for nine months and for 18 months in the manner of a society. The societies will receive 30,000 florins. Presently nothing else is new."[25]

## A Tuscan Patrimony

At the same time that Hawkwood attended to his responsibilities as Florentine captain of war, he also looked after his personal interests. When his defensive duties against the Company of Saint George brought him near Lucca in February 1382, he used the occasion—and the substantial force he had with him—to request "favors" from that city. He asked for a lifetime pension like the one he was receiving from Florence. With his Lucchese chancellor, Jacopo da Pietrasanta, to advise him, Hawkwood played his victim well. He exploited local fears about the proliferation of armed bands and, as in Florence, the activities of exiles. Lucca was in poor shape militarily and economically and was eager to remain on good terms with the Englishman. Hawkwood told officials that he was contemplating settling down with his family in the city. It is doubtful that Hawkwood was serious; he had already given indications to the Perugians that he wished to settle in their city, to ambassadors elsewhere that he intended to return soon to England, and, as we shall see shortly, he was currently telling Florentines that he intended to settle in their city.

On 17 March 1382 Lucca granted Hawkwood his request for a pension. He was to receive 400 florins annually, "while he is alive and in Italy." The preamble to the act spelled out the rationale: "because it is greatly useful to keep John friendly to the commune and people of Lucca."[26] In return, Hawkwood promised not to oppose Lucca militarily. Together with his pension from Florence, Hawkwood now had an annual income of 1,600 florins, whether or not he did any fighting. He received his first installment from Lucca in April. Jacopo da Pietrasanta, though an exile, was allowed to enter his native city to pick up the money. The funds—or a portion thereof—were used to buy the lands of Richard Lyons. Hawkwood received his yearly pension from Lucca until 1391, when his service for Florence against Giangaleazzo Visconti, then a Lucchese ally, led officials to rescind the privilege.

Hawkwood's finances now prospered. He had sufficient capital to arrange personal loans to his fellow soldiers. He gave 400 florins to William Boson, his military companion from the days of the White Company, and 1,000 florins to Robin Corbrigg, a more recent arrival in Italy. Hawkwood's longtime corporal William Gold supplied a portion of the money advanced to Boson.[27]

Hawkwood's loan of money to fellow English soldiers was nothing new; indeed, we have evidence for it dating from 1374. But the contracts involving Boson and Corbrigg, drawn up in Florence by the notary Jacopo di Bartolomeo, are significant because they are among the few of this type that have survived. They contain several notable features. Both Boson and Corbrigg were, for example, required to pay Hawkwood back "in either Tuscany or England or any other location he may be"—a clause that emphasizes the tight connection of Hawkwood and the English soldiers in Italy with their home. Neither Boson nor Corbrigg was required to pay interest, provided that they returned the principal on time. The balance was due sixteen months after the issuance of the loan. If late, however, the men were to pay twice the sum owed.

The disbursement of funds was supervised by two local Florentine money-changers, identified only as Ghino di Giovanni and Maso di Iacopo, and an Englishman, John Hedingham. Hedingham was a prominent London merchant with close ties to the crown, who was instrumental in helping King Richard raise money for his wars in France.[28] He is again mentioned in connection with Hawkwood two years later as a witness to the captain's contract with Giangaleazzo Visconti in 1385. The precise relationship between the men is unclear.

Unfortunately for Hawkwood, Boson and Corbrigg did not repay their loans. A full four years later, Hawkwood was still complaining about his loss of money. He worked, however, to get the city of Florence to make good the sum and submitted a formal petition to that effect.

At about the same time, Hawkwood also renewed his attempts, initiated in 1380, to acquire property in the environs of Florence. As earlier, Hawkwood wanted it bestowed on him free of charge. Florence remained steadfast in its refusals and told Hawkwood that it would only agree to allow him to purchase estates with his own money, a concession that involved sidestepping a city statute that prevented foreigners from holding local land.[29]

Hawkwood ultimately agreed. He submitted a petition in his and wife Donnina's name seeking the right to own property. He did so in conjunction with Richard Romsey, who had recently been married in Florence (to an English woman named Isabel) and also wished to settle there. The Florentine city council approved both petitions. The terms of the cession allowed "anyone from the city, contado and district of Florence to legally and without punishment sell, exchange, give, alienate, obligate, concede or transfer property to John, his wife and any of their children or descendants in the male line."[30] The legislation cited as justification that Hawkwood had exhibited exemplary "devotion to the commune of Florence" and had stated his intention "to live in the city and have possessions and property and to leave behind children and descendants."[31] These statements should be regarded, however, as formula. It was victory enough to constrain Hawkwood to pay for the property.

Shortly thereafter Hawkwood bought a farm and castle at San Donato a Torre in Polverosa, just north of the city, beyond the Porta al Prato, not far from where he conducted his first campaign as an independent commander in the service of Pisa back in 1363. The property lay near the monastery of the Umiliati monks, known since the thirteenth century for their cloth making, and the current site of the Villa Demidoff. Hawkwood married two daughters at San Donato and kept the property until he died.

Hawkwood also purchased a cluster of lands south of city, near the town of Poggibonsi, at the border between Florentine and Sienese territory.[32] He bought these from a Sienese exile, Raimondo Tolomei, for 6,000 florins in October 1383, just after he left Florence to fight in Naples. The money likely came from ransoms of prisoners during his service there.[33] The properties consisted of three estates, a castle, and seven strips of land, with numerous subsidiary houses, ringed with vineyards and orchards.[34] All were located beside the Elsa River; the most formidable was the fortress called la Rocchetta, which overlooked the Via Francigena, the main conduit from Siena to northern Italy and to Rome. Hawkwood's neighbors included some of Florence's most prominent families, such as Alberti, Corbizzi, and Adimari. Rocchetta bordered the property of Lapo Fornaini de Rossi, among the first ambassadors to Hawkwood, who played an instrumental role in corrupting the White Company before the Florentine walls in 1363.

## War in the Kingdom of Naples

Meanwhile, important events were occurring elsewhere which would draw Hawkwood out of Tuscany (map 6). The internecine war in southern Italy between the French and Hungarian branches of the house of Anjou and the rival popes had resumed in earnest. Charles of Durazzo had seized the Neapolitan throne and imprisoned Queen Johanna. Just before Durazzo's coup, however, Queen Johanna named Louis of Anjou as her heir. Johanna's ally, the French pope Clement, gave Anjou the title of Duke of Calabria and ceded all revenues of the region to him. Louis now began his descent into Italy to support his allies and wrest Charles from the throne of Naples. The historian Peter Partner has stressed the importance of Anjou's expedition, calling it "a supreme effort by the Avignon papacy to regain southern and central Italy."[35]

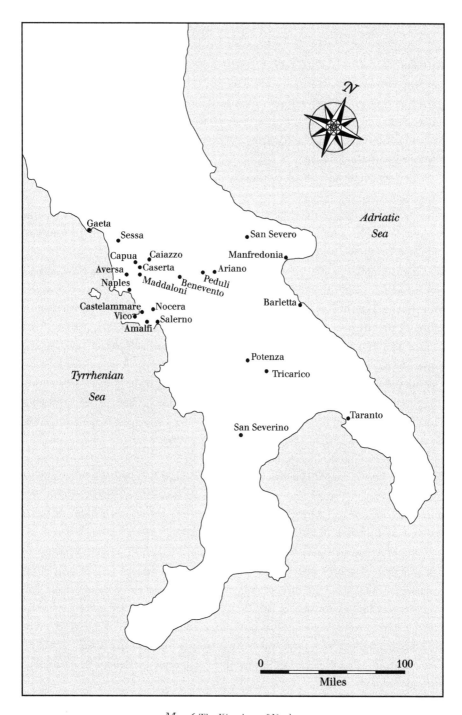

*Map 6.* The Kingdom of Naples

The conflict involved many of the same participants who had fought in the papal-Milanese war ten years earlier. Amadeus, the Green Count of Savoy, and Bernabò Visconti—who had earlier opposed each other—now were on the same side, supporting Louis of Anjou and Clement VII. Bernabò, always eager to oppose the Italian pope and ally himself with powerful royal houses, had married his daughter Lucia to Louis of Anjou—a match that brought the duke 200,000 florins in dowry and helped finance his army.[36] The German prince, Otto of Brunswick, also sided with the French.

Although Florence wished to remain neutral, John Hawkwood was himself already involved. King Richard of England supported Urban VI according to the alliance made between them back in 1381, for which Hawkwood had served as envoy.[37] When Richard's brother-in-law, the Holy Roman Emperor Wenceslaus, indicated in the winter of 1381/82 that he would enter Italy on Urban's behalf, the English monarch ordered all Englishmen there to gather under Hawkwood's command and assist the enterprise.[38] The directive was rescinded, however, when Wenceslaus chose to stay home, owing to lack of money. Nevertheless, the mobilization of the army of Louis of Anjou, and with it the direct participation of the French royal household in Italy, gave impetus to Richard's efforts on behalf of the pope. His support was linked to gathering momentum in England for crusade against Clementinist interests in Flanders, which was little more than a thinly disguised church-sanctioned offensive against France. Urban issued crusading bulls in England, and the bishop of Norwich, Henry Despenser, took up the cross. By the summer and fall of 1382, plans were well under way.[39]

Richard appointed Hawkwood as his envoy to both Urban VI and Charles of Durazzo.[40] The degree of Hawkwood's participation in Neapolitan affairs is made clear in a letter dated 26 June 1382 in which he was able to relay not only the maneuvers of Louis of Anjou's army—which had not yet entered Italy—but also the names of the nobles and barons who had taken up arms with him.[41]

Louis of Anjou arrived in Italy in July 1382. Pope Urban VI wrote to Florence to ask permission to hire Hawkwood as his captain of his army. "We pray most urgently . . . that you will without delay arrange that he enter our service." The problem was that Hawkwood was still on the Florentine payroll and his contract did not expire until October. The pope suggested a solution whereby the city would cede Hawkwood to him, and continue to pay him, but the money would be deducted from what Florence still owed of the indemnity payments from the War of Eight Saints.[42]

The proposition put Florentine officials in an awkward position. To allow Hawkwood to break his contract and fight for the pope would be perceived as support for Urban and aggression against the French cause. Florence wished to stay neutral. It decided on a more circumspect course, suggested in the Signoria by Ranieri di Simone Peruzzi, a man with experience in mercenary-related matters and with John Hawkwood in particular. Peruzzi suggested that the city hold Hawkwood until the conclusion of his contract in October and then allow him to do what he pleased. He added the telling postscript, however, that he was not sure whether Hawkwood would go along with the scheme, since "there is not much we can do to control Hawkwood once he has decided on his course."[43]

But Hawkwood behaved in this instance as Peruzzi and Florentine officials wanted. He waited until October, when his contract expired, and then transferred his services to the church. Even so, the shift did not appear neutral.[44] Despite the expiration of Hawkwood's contract, the city paid the first installment of his salary, which it deducted from the amount it owed the pope. The transaction did not go unnoticed by others.[45] In addition, Hawkwood's departure from Florence coincided with the arrival in the city of a letter from King Richard urging the government to support Urban and oppose the Duke of Anjou.[46] Louis of Anjou accused Florence of treachery and wrote home to France instructing officials to undertake reprisals against Florentine merchants there.[47] It was perhaps uneasiness over the issue that impelled the Florentine chronicler Stefani to minimize the size of the payment to Hawkwood, which he estimated as 12,000 florins. The pope's own letter indicates that the sum was 40,000 florins.[48]

Just before Hawkwood received the first installment of his salary, he was met by ambassadors of his estranged father-in-law, Bernabò Visconti, who wished to recruit him for the French Angevin side. They dangled the prospect of reuniting Hawkwood with his old comrade-in-arms Enguerrand Coucy, who was then contemplating entering war on behalf of Louis of Anjou. Bernabò was apparently willing to forgo his preceding enmity with Hawkwood on behalf of the cause. He apparently presented a convincing case, so much so that a Lucchese ambassador who sat in on the discussions thought that Hawkwood would in fact serve the French side.[49]

But Hawkwood rejected Bernabò's offer. Whatever regard Hawkwood may have had for Coucy, the Frenchman now directly opposed the interests of the English crown. Hawkwood served in Naples not only as a mercenary captain but as an agent of the king of England.

Hawkwood advanced toward the kingdom in late October at the head of a band of approximately twenty-two hundred horsemen. He moved very slowly, choosing to maximize his revenue in transit by extorting money from cities that lay in his path. He stopped in Sienese territory and demanded 1,000 florins, which he claimed he was owed in back pay. The Sienese refused, and Hawkwood sacked their lands and extorted a bribe of 14,000 florins.[50] Like Anjou, the Sienese blamed the Florentines for Hawkwood's behavior.[51] Hawkwood stopped next at Perugia. He again asked for 1,000 florins. The Perugians, having witnessed events in Siena, paid the sum immediately.[52]

By contrast, Louis of Anjou and the French army advanced toward the kingdom with regal pageantry. A Florentine merchant, Giovanni Corbizzi, who had seen the force assemble at Avignon, called it "the best band of men-at-arms in the world."[53] Another witness compared the army to that of Xerxes in ancient times. Louis linked up in southern France with Amadeus of Savoy, who arrived dressed from head to toe in green, the color of his household, including saddles, bridles, breastplate and crupper, and emerald surcoat.[54] The chronicler of Vicenza, Conforto da Costoza, estimated the size of the combined force at 40,000 horses, but a Lucchese ambassadorial dispatch put the figure at 16,000 horses when it crossed the Alps and 15,000 horses when it arrived in Milan. Bernabò Visconti received the army enthusiastically and dubbed it "patriots rather than mercenaries."[55]

The army moved out from Milan in late July, with the air of a crusading host.[56] Pope Clement VII excommunicated and anathematized his opponent. Amadeus of Savoy gave generously to churches and holy places he passed along the way; in one instance, he bestowed alms to a stray priest who asked for money for the burial of a poor man.[57] One of Anjou's soldiers was captured by locals sympathetic to Urban VI and chose to die of thirst because "he did not wish to drink with heretics."[58]

It was not long after the army traversed the limits of Lombardy that the glittering march bogged down. Anticipating resistance in Tuscany, Anjou and Savoy chose to travel to Naples via the Romagna and the Adriatic coast. The decision was an unfortunate one. It separated the army from its supply ships, which had traveled the other side of Italy via the Tyrrhenian Sea. As Anjou's men proceeded through the Romagna, they encountered resistance. Galeotto Malatesta of Rimini, a supportor of Urban VI, refused to allow Louis's army to purchase supplies.[59] An ambassador stationed nearby reported that "none of the lords of the Romagna were moved to do anything for the duke, except for he of Ravenna."[60] This was an overstatement, but the path was a difficult one for Anjou, and the problems were, unfortunately, augurs of still worse things to come.[61]

## A Great Misery among Men

The French army arrived in the kingdom in late August/early September 1382. The Count of Savoy advocated making a lightening strike against Pope Urban at Rome, to take advantage of the absence of Hawkwood, who was still under contract with Florence. But the Duke of Anjou vetoed the plan and chose instead to mass his forces for an attack against Charles of Durazzo in the city of

Naples. The French army set up its camp in the town of Aquila, at the northern edge of the kingdom. They were well received by local citizens and remained there for some time before moving slowly toward Naples, eventually taking up positions near the towns of Caserta and Maddaloni, just below Benevento (some seventeen miles from Naples). The prospects seemed favorable enough that the Lucchese ambassador, Niccolò di Carlino, stationed in Naples, reported back home that "things prosper for the duke of Anjou."[62]

But the conditions soon deteriorated. The years of conflict in the kingdom had left the region devastated. Ambassadorial dispatches paint a stark picture of a barren countryside lacking in food and supplies and of the effects of plague, which returned in full force in 1383. Soldiers in the French camp fell victim to hunger and disease; several prominent leaders, including the Count of Savoy, became sick as early as October.

John Hawkwood did not arrive until November. According to the Florentine chronicler Stefani, he went first to Rome to confer with the pope, where he was poorly received by local citizens, who were angry about his delay and threatened to harm him if he did not move out at once to engage the enemy.[63] The Neapolitan diarist Monteleone and the Sienese chronicler Montauri, however, claim that Hawkwood went straight to Naples to face Anjou's army.[64]

Hawkwood's service on behalf of Pope Urban constituted the first time he fought south of Rome. He joined his brigade with those of Alberigo da Barbiano and Villanozzo of Brumfort, the same men he opposed several months earlier in Tuscany. The Hungarian nobleman and mercenary John Horváti (Giovanni Bano), a close ally of Charles of Durazzo, commanded a separate Hungarian force consisting of 2,000 horses. Hawkwood, Barbiano, and Brumfort's army probably numbered between 2,000 and 3,000 horsemen. Interestingly, the sources make no mention of the use of lance units, the now prevalent formation in Italian armies. This may have been the result of the influence of Charles of Durazzo, who, as a Hungarian, eschewed the lance in favor of the more traditional "banner" of individual horsemen. The captains rarely moved about as one army but broke up into small units consisting of their personal brigades. The strategy was likely determined by the scarcity of resources.

Hawkwood's arrival at Naples forced the French army to abandon its offensive. Hawkwood pursued it and captured several high-ranking soldiers. He passed much of the month of December trying to collect the ransoms of his captive soldiers. The task proved difficult, and Charles of Durazzo eventually made good a part of the sum.

Amadeus of Savoy, who had escaped capture, nevertheless became convinced that there was little hope of victory and undertook negotiations. He wrote to

Hawkwood on 10 December 1382 to arrange a meeting. Representatives from both sides met on 4 January 1383. Savoy tried to broker a deal whereby Louis would abandon his claims to the Neapolitan throne in return for Durazzo's promise to relinquish rights to the county of Provence, to which he possessed the rights. But there was no agreement on the issue. At one point Savoy and Durazzo agreed to put the issue to a duel—a familiar device. But the contest never came about.

The difficult conditions induced both sides to continue discussions. Hawkwood outlined the sad state of affairs as of 27 January 1383 in a letter to the city of Lucca.

> Magnificent and potent lords, and most dear friends . . . We are here and we have our brigade in the val di San Severino opposed to the Count of Savoy. Villanuccius [of Brumfort] is also here, though his brigade is divided in the frontier regions. John Ban with his 2000 Hungarians has for a long while attacked up to the gates of Manfredonia; we expect him to dismiss his brigade and be here in three days. There is much talk of making peace with the Count of Savoy, but we have not to this point reached any agreement. On account of this, King Charles and the said Count have arranged to meet together in some place near here. . . . We truly hope there will be a good end to this, since both sides are exhausted by the war, especially considering the poverty of both parts.[65]

As the winter progressed, the "poverty" grew worse. Anjou's camp was in serious need of supplies. The Count of Savoy had to pawn his valuables and borrow heavily to meet payments to his brigade. The Duke of Anjou passed Christmas Day in Benevento morosely writing his last will and testament. Savoy's illness meanwhile grew steadily worse, and by 1 March 1383 he was dead. His army broke apart and slowly drifted home. The Duke of Anjou, now isolated, purportedly burst into tears when he found out the news.[66]

Hawkwood remained in camp at the Val di San Severino. He spent February conducting personal business with Florence and other cities. His wife, Donnina, submitted a petition in his name in Florence seeking exemption from taxation on the properties he recently purchased. Hawkwood asked for immunity on the grounds that he was not a citizen and therefore not liable. The Florentines allowed this but insisted that Hawkwood remain responsible for extraordinary taxes, such as forced loans imposed during wars.

After the Count of Savoy's death, Hawkwood rode through Calabria quieting opposition from local nobles hostile to Durazzo. In a letter dated 24 March 1383 Jacopo da Pietrasanta boasted that Hawkwood succeeded "by his prowess and the strenuous efforts of his brigade . . . to reduce the province of Calabria to the obedience to the king."[67]

In April, Hawkwood joined with Durazzo, Villanozzo, Barbiano, John Horváti, and an army of 16,000 for an assault on Anjou, whose brigade was now reportedly down to 8,000 men, only 2,000 of whom were cavalry. Durazzo issued a challenge to battle, which Anjou accepted. The armies arrayed for battle but engaged only in an inconclusive skirmish. Both armies withdrew.[68]

The difficult conditions continued to dictate the pace of the war. "Throughout the whole Kingdom," wrote the ambassadors Antonio Ristotili and Angelo di Lattinuccio at Naples, "there is war, famine and mortality, such that there is no remedy. For this reason the Kingdom is destroyed. . . . One can see that in this war money is king!"[69]

In May, Hawkwood conducted a siege against the enemy in the town of Paduli, six and a half kilometers northeast of Benevento. On the 28th of the month, Tommaso da San Severino, Count of Tricarico and ally of Anjou, led a counterattack with an army of 2,000 horses, 3,000 infantrymen, and 800 crossbowmen. He forced Hawkwood from the field, seized the bastion he had erected near the town, and took hostage twenty men. Jacopo da Pietrasanta was clearly shaken by the attack and described how he and Hawkwood's troop managed to return to Paduli only with the greatest difficulty.[70]

Hawkwood rode next with his men twelve miles east to Ariano, where Louis of Anjou had set up his camp and where the rest of Charles's army was amassing for a siege. According to Pietrasanta, Anjou's force was now between 5,000 and 6,000 men.[71] Alberigo da Barbiano, Villanozzo da Brumfort, and John Ban camped just outside the city and continually harassed Anjou. "Every day they ride up to the gates, four or five times!" wrote Jacopo da Pietrasanta on 23 June.

The activity further cut Anjou off from his supply lines. Money was sent from both Milan and France, but it did not get through. Pope Clement's ally, Rinaldo Orsini, lord of Orvieto, was supposed to relieve Anjou, but he took the pope's money and then installed himself in Spoleto, where he remained. Clement had hired Hawkwood's longtime comrade Richard Romsey and a contingent of English soldiers. But after receiving their pay, they too chose not to take up battle. "They do not wish," wrote Pietrasanta, "to be in any manner opposed to John Hawkwood, whom they see as their champion and protector."[72]

Pietrasanta now gave his most dire statement on the condition of the enemy: "They are all barefoot and nude and in the greatest poverty," wrote Pietrasanta; "you have never seen such great misery among men."[73] Hawkwood confirmed this account in his own letter: "the men endure such poverty that it is a wonder that they have the strength to continue living."[74]

If Pietrasanta's and Hawkwood's statements can be trusted, the allies were at the point of victory. But Hawkwood's contract was coming due, and, as he did so many times, he used the advantage to gain better terms. He demobilized his army and quartered it at Ariano and then went in person to Naples to speak directly with Charles of Durazzo. Pietrasanta said pessimistically that he thought the prospects were not good, given that Charles had no money. But Hawkwood left satisfied, gaining a contract for another three months. He rejoined his men at Ariano. Hawkwood himself reported the outlines of the agreement in a letter to Francesco Guinigi of Lucca dated 23 June: "We have agreed to place our band in the service of the king for three months, and we will go to that place [Ariano] to join our men to those others in the service of the king, believing that with such a force, all together, will prevail. We will pitch our tents against the duke and thus ultimately, with the help of divine virtue, we believe that the king will remain victorious."[75]

What Charles and Hawkwood decided—with the approval of Pope Urban—was to tap once again into the indemnity money owed the church from the War of Eight Saints, specifically that owed by Lucca. Hawkwood wrote to Guinigi, who was both a banker and prominent citizen, to look into the matter on his behalf. "Because we are owed here certain sums of money we would like you without delay to write to us . . . whether, if the pope is owed something, we may have this made out to us."[76] Hawkwood sought in essence the same financial arrangement he had made earlier with Florence. He also asked Guinigi to help collect a personal debt owed him "for a long time" from Alderigo degli Antelminelli, the Lucchese exile who first rode with Hawkwood's armies back in the sixties. During the War of Eight Saints, Antelminelli had served as one of the pope's bankers and had taken deposits of Hawkwood and of his wife, Donnina. Hawkwood's approach was noteworthy; he intended for the city of Lucca to bear responsibility for the debt of a citizen who was exiled over whom they had little control. Hawkwood did not care which of the parties made good the money.

In his 23 June letter, Jacopo da Pietrasanta had predicted that "who holds the field this summer, will be the winner" of the war. But the plague intensified with the warm weather, making all manner of movement by armies difficult. The coming weeks saw gestures and threats but no decisive encounters. Dissensions meanwhile flared between the Pope Urban and Charles of Durazzo. The two quarreled over Charles's refusal to cede the lands he had promised Urban's nephew when he was crowned king of Sicily by the pontiff back in 1381. Urban went to Naples to appeal personally to Charles, a move that only further complicated their relationship over the next months.[77]

The discord further strained the finances of both parties. Hawkwood did not receive the money he was promised and did no more fighting. Charles sent appeals to Pisan and Florentine merchants for funds, but with little success.[78]

When his contract expired in September, Hawkwood formed a free company. In a letter dated the 15th of the month, Jacopo da Pietrasanta announced Hawkwood's intention to leave the region. "John Hawkwood with his brigade has made a confederation with numerous others, including Giovanni d'Azzo degli Ubaldini. Together they will move at the end of this month toward Tuscany in the manner of a society."[79] Pietrasanta gave a succinct justification for the action: "because here they cannot live."[80]

The band grew to four thousand horses. The involvement of Ubaldini was an ill omen for Florence; the city had condemned him and his clan only a year earlier for their suspected participation in an uprising in Firenzuola.

Hawkwood went first to Pope Urban, who was temporarily settled at the city of Sessa, north of Naples. A member of the pope's entourage, Bartolomeo of Piacenza, claimed that Hawkwood demanded from the pontiff 25,000 florins in back pay and "would not leave until he got it." The Lucchese ambassadors Andrea da Volterra and Niccolò di Carlino reported that Hawkwood asked only for 13,000 florins.[81] They also said that Hawkwood went to Rome "at the petition of" Charles of Durazzo. But the envoys did not indicate the nature of Charles's petition and the business between the men. Bartolomeo of Piacenza, the source closer to the action, said that Hawkwood spoke ill of Charles and told the pope that he and his brigade intended to go next to Arezzo, Durazzo's stronghold, and make good the back pay owed by him.[82]

Hawkwood came to an agreement with the pope at Sessa. He received only a small amount of cash, no more than 2,000 florins, but Urban granted additional "pacts."[83] These were almost certainly grants of land, specifically a fortress at Carinaro near Aversa and other lands in Capua and Naples, which came into Hawkwood's possession at this time. The bequests were typical of the perpetually cash-strapped pope. We know none of the details, owing to the lack of Neapolitan documentary sources for the period. But Hawkwood clearly left Sessa satisfied, since he now agreed to further service on the pope's behalf. Urban instructed him to attack Rinaldo Orsini, an ally of the Duke of Anjou, who had seized city of Spoleto from the pontiff.[84]

Hawkwood and his company rode north from Sessa toward Spoleto, stopping in the environs of Orvieto on 18 November 1383.[85] But rather than continue on, Hawkwood took the road to Perugia. According to some reports, he was secretly paid off by Orsini; according to others, he failed to receive anticipated reinforcements from the pope and thus gave up the offensive.[86] Basic military considerations undoubtedly also played a role. Orsini had fortified Spoleto well, constructing four large bastions outside the city, manned by eight hundred horses.[87] Capturing the town was a dubious enterprise. Further, Hawkwood's band does not appear to have been in especially good fighting condition. During the passage to Orvieto, the company shrunk to about fifteen hundred poorly armed men.

Hawkwood's band nevertheless discomfited the Perugians. As it moved into Umbria, the company reinforced itself by taking in many Perugian exiles. Officials reacted fearfully, calling an emergency council (*balia*) and hiring troops to bolster defenses.[88] By the end of November, Hawkwood edged to within five miles of the city. The Perugians offered him a personal "loan" of 400 florins and gave 1,200 florins to his company.[89] A Lucchese ambassador claimed that the city spent overall 2,000 florins, a modest sum, which he explained was the result of the fact that the company "was not strong enough" to do any real damage.[90]

Accordingly, Hawkwood fortified his band. He took in as co-captain Richard Romsey, who had deserted Anjou and the French cause in the summer of 1383 and taken up briefly with Charles of Durazzo.[91] Romsey had advanced toward Spoleto at Durazzo's order, but he betrayed his employer and accepted bribe money from Rinaldo Orsini (200 florins for himself, 1,000 florins for his brigade). To show that he was not entirely infamous, Romsey refrained from joining Hawkwood until the latter extorted money from Perugia. Romsey had an extant pact with the Perugians, signed on 31 July 1383, by which he agreed not to "molest" them for two and a half years.[92]

Romsey formally entered Hawkwood's company on 29 November 1383 at Assisi. The three captains—Hawkwood, Ubaldini, and Romsey—swore an oath of allegiance in the church of Santa Maria degli Agnioli.[93] In a letter written on 6 December, Romsey gave an unusually frank statement of the band's motives: "We are associated with John Hawkwood [Johanne Haucutd] and Giovanni d'Azzo . . . to go to the territory of Siena and Pisa in order to get money from those parts."[94] Hawkwood corroborated this in a letter written three days later: "Since . . . we lack not a small amount of money, we decided to make recourse first to collecting our credits, and then demand subsidies from our friends."[95] Ubaldini, in his own letter on the matter, said that the company intended to enlarge itself further, and perhaps take in the Italian captain Boldrino da Panicale to better effect the extortions.[96]

Each of the captains had his own agenda. Romsey bore an especial grudge against the Sienese, who he claimed still owed him money from a raid back in September.[97] The city had further angered him by placing a bounty on his head, offering a cash prize to anyone who killed him or the other leaders of his band.[98] Ubaldini maintained a long-standing grudge against Florence, and Hawkwood focused his anger primarily at Lucca, though he had outstanding issues with Florence and never liked the Sienese.

The company moved first into Sienese territory, where officials settled quickly, paying the band a modest bribe of 8,000 florins—5,000 "openly," the rest under the table.[99] The company set up camp at Cortona, near the Sienese border with Perugia, and undertook negotiations with other cities. It is a measure of the fear that the band evoked that representatives from all over Italy—Milan, Ravenna, Rimini, Tuscany, Ancona, Fermo, and Ascoli—came to Cortona to discuss terms.[100] We are especially well informed of negotiations between Hawkwood and the city of Lucca from a series of letters written by the town's chief negotiator, Andrea da Volterra. They give perhaps the most complete portrait of intricacies involved in dealing with John Hawkwood and offer proof of his mastery of the art of manipulation. The episode is recounted in detail below.

## Negotiating with Barbarians

The first meeting between Hawkwood and Andrea da Volterra took place at Cortona a week before Christmas. The discussion focused on the outstanding debts owed Hawkwood by Alderigo degli Antelminelli. Hawkwood had pressed this issue for a long time in letters written to the city over a two-year period. He had even gotten Florence at one point to plead on his behalf.[101] Hawkwood continued to send letters as he departed the kingdom at the head of his mercenary company. The tone of the epistles, initially strident but polite, became progressively more threatening. In November 1383 Hawkwood wrote: "Alderigo de Antelminelli must give us a good sum of money of which, to this point, we have received nothing back. . . . We ask your lordship that since we will be in your vicinity with horses and infantry, you might want to make good the said money." In December, just prior to his meeting with Andrea da Volterra, Hawkwood wrote a more pointed missive, announcing that he would "visit" the city with his army if the money was not forthcoming.[102]

The Lucchese government took Hawkwood's claims seriously and tried to settle them back in June 1382. It appointed at that time a special committee of Lucchese citizens "neither allied nor contrary" to Antelminelli to compel him to pay. But the city had little coercive power over the powerful exile, and the attempt failed.

When Hawkwood sat down with Andrea da Volterra at Cortona, the parameters of their discussion were therefore already set. The obvious solution was for the city of Lucca itself to pay the sum. This is what Hawkwood wanted. But Andrea complained that the town was in difficult financial straits and that it could not raise the money. Hawkwood would hear nothing of it. "It isn't worth it for me to even mention that we have no money," Andrea wrote back home. "I can't seem to get it out of their heads that Lucca is filled with gold."[103]

Andrea da Volterra returned to Lucca to confer with town leaders. There was no alternative but to make good the debt themselves. The remaining question, however, was how much Hawkwood wanted and how quickly. Lucchese officials sent Andrea back with instructions to seek the smallest possible sum and the delay paying the balance.

The two men met the next day. Hawkwood said he wanted 7,300 florins, the total he claimed Antelminelli owed him. Andrea agreed but suggested that only 1,000 florins be paid immediately and the rest over six years. Hawkwood rejected the offer and demanded 2,300 florins immediately and the rest within a year. Andrea insisted that his city could not make the payments in less than four years. He debated the issue with Hawkwood until sundown. "God knows well," Andrea wrote, "it is difficult to deal with barbarians."[104]

The two sat down again two days before Christmas. This time the talks were held in Florence, which offered to act as arbiter. "Today I arrived in Florence at nones," wrote Andrea back home, "and right away went to Mister John [Messer G.] and after much reasoning and offers we came to a conclusion of the matter, in this form that now he will have 2,300 florins and the rest, that is 5,000 florins, in the next two years. I had wanted to fix a longer term, but there was no other way."[105] In essence, Andrea gave Hawkwood what he wanted but managed to gain an additional year in paying the balance.

Lucchese officials were not happy with the deal. They censured Andrea for exceeding his instruction and accused him of being intimidated by Hawkwood. Andrea defended himself: "I tried to deal with Hawkwood according to the commission you gave me, but I left without an accord—And it was not because I did not debate with Mister John from nones until vespers!!" Andrea insisted that Hawkwood had the upper hand in negotiations, backed as he was by his large army. "Everything depended on Hawkwood."[106]

Andrea made clear that Hawkwood exploited his advantage with skill. He said that Hawkwood always met him apart from his band and kept its whereabouts vague. Unable to gauge the nearness of the company to Lucchese territory, Andrea was never able to tell just how present the threat was. Hawkwood worked to gain Andrea's trust by generously supplying useless military reconnaissance, such as news of the capture of ships off the coast near Genoa and the fighting in Naples, while at the same keeping the more important information about his true intentions secret. He fueled Andrea's unease by passing reports that there was discord within the ranks of his company, that some of his corporals wished to ride on the city, and that there was little he could do to stop them.

Lucchese officials must have accepted Andrea's defense of himself because they continued to use him to negotiate with the band. After Hawkwood's personal business was settled, Andrea focused on appeasing the rest of the company.

Hawkwood served as the middleman, writing, at Andrea's request, letters to both Ubaldini and Romsey. He showed the letters to Andrea, who inspected them and approved them. Then Hawkwood went off to speak to the captains in person. Hawkwood's chancellor, Jacopo da Pietrasanta, assured Andrea that things would go well. "They will do," said Pietrasanta, "want John wants."

They did not, however, do what John wanted. Ubaldini fell into line, but Romsey remained intransigent. Andrea met with Romsey on Christmas Eve and described him as "severe and cruel" and "ill-disposed" toward Lucca. He also reported a rift within the band: " 'Messer' John wants to lead the brigade into the Marches and 'Messer' Richard does not want to listen to Messer John, unless he promises to lead the band to Lucca first."[107]

Whether this was a real disagreement or yet another sham orchestrated by Hawkwood is unclear. Richard did have outstanding claims against Lucca. Like Hawkwood, Romsey was owed money by Alderigo degli Antelminelli—a debt of 2,080 florins deriving from a disputed bill of exchange issued at Città di Castello years earlier. Romsey sought not only the principal but 1,000 florins in compensatory damages.[108]

What followed was a medieval species of good cop/bad cop, with Hawkwood cast in the former role and Romsey in the latter. While Hawkwood assured Andrea of his desire for peace and concord, Romsey made it known that he wished to ride on Lucca. "The whole camp shouts 'to Lucca, to Lucca.' " The conflicting signals exasperated Andrea. Hawkwood, for all his soothing words, showed no inclination to interfere with the wishes of Romsey or of the company at large. "And so," Andrea wrote, "I am sent from Herod to Pilate!!"[109]

After several weeks Andrea reached agreement with Romsey and the company. Romsey received what he wanted; the company sought 10,000 florins but appears to have settled for less. In his letter to officials back home, Andrea spoke only of an initial payment of 4,300 florins to the band, which also included money owed to Hawkwood.[110] There is, however, no record of the precise size of the bribe. An incomplete *capitolo* in the Lucchese archives enumerates only incidental sums totaling 1,100 florins "for the associates" (probably the commanders); 40 florins to Romsey and another corporal, John Thelkeld; 20 florins to a "Little Tom of Milan"; and 20 more to a man known only as "Giorgio."[111]

But for all the craft and drama involved in the negotiations, the resolution of payments was remarkably dull and legalistic. To complete the transaction, Andrea da Volterra requested from Hawkwood all documentation pertaining to the outstanding debt with Antelminelli. In return, he gave Hawkwood written pledges from the Lucchese government promising payment of the 5,000-florin balance within two years. Andrea then drew up a formal list of nine provisions, which, among other things, outlined the precise reasons for the payment, the time and place where the funds would be handed over, and an injunction that all matters involving the issue be effected in writing. The list reaffirmed that Antelminelli's debt was a "deposit" at the time of the War of Eight Saints which involved also Donnina.[112]

Andrea appears also the have done the legwork. A month after the agreement (February 1384), he rode in person to Hawkwood, then in Florence (probably San Donato in Polverosa), to arrange the transfer of the money, which was effected through local banks. Andrea arrived to find only Donnina at home; she told him that Hawkwood had left that day to join his soldiers. Andrea then rode out to meet Hawkwood in the field.[113]

Hawkwood's soldiers were now stationed near Borgo San Sepolcro and Città di Castello, north of Cortona and a relatively short ride from Florence. From there, Hawkwood negotiated with Pisan and Florentine envoys. The nature of the talks with Pisa is unknown; sources indicate only that the band extorted a "substantial" sum of money.[114] The discussions with Florence were complex. As he had done with Lucca, Hawkwood sought payment of debts owed to him by a third party. In this case the third part was Charles of Durazzo, or more precisely, his wife. Hawkwood asked that officials give him the savings belonging to her which were deposited in Florentine banks. The debt likely arose from Hawkwood's recent service in Naples and indicates that Charles still owed Hawkwood money and now wished to use his Florentines credits to settle the account. But Florence refused to give Hawkwood the money.[115] It offered instead to grant him funds belonging to Pope Urban in return for a promise that he would intercede on Florence's behalf with the pontiff to remove the remaining sanctions still in force against the city dating from the War of Eight Saints. Hawkwood went personally to Florence to negotiate, shuttling back and forth from his camp. In the end he received no deposits but constrained the Florentines to pay him a bribe of 700 florins.

Hawkwood quartered his company for the rest of the winter near Borgo San Sepolcro. He passed his time traveling to his properties in Florence, attending to personal business, and pressing, via letters, for favors from various cities. The band returned to its marauding ways in the spring. Hawkwood clearly wished to continue earning profits, or rather, reversing the losses he suffered from his service in Naples. To better accomplish this, he enlarged his company. In March 1384 he took in the German mercenary Eberhard von Landau, recently dismissed from Florentine service. There were reports from Milan that the band planned to move on Pisa and eventually rendezvous with a brigade of mercenaries, which was descending from Parma and Cremona.[116] But this did not happen. Instead, Hawkwood and his men set out for Arezzo, moving through the Valdichiana, along the border between Perugia and Siena, two of his favorite targets. Arezzo was Durazzo's stronghold, and the itinerary suggests that Hawkwood intended also to press his former employer for outstanding claims.[117]

The band plundered local lands. The Sienese decided on an active defense and sent out an army, led by the Italian mercenary Boldrino da Panicale. The decision was a mistake. Poorly coordinated and provisioned, the force never gathered momentum; it was reduced to eating its own horses and drinking urine. Hawkwood shattered the army and seized not only hostages but a valuable store of munitions and artillery.[118] He constrained the Sienese to pay 11,000 florins in bribes and then moved east to loot Perugian territory.[119]

The remaining details of the raid are obscure. But it proved personally lucrative for Hawkwood. As a result, he gained possession of the castle of Montecchio (now Montecchio Vesponi), located south of Arezzo, in the Valdichiana between the towns of Cortona and Castiglione Fiorentino. Montecchio was a formidable fortress town, which enclosed fifty-six homes, a parish church (San Biagio), a palace, and fields, vineyards, and woods. Its real value was strategic. It rose 364 meters from sea level and stood at the confluence of Sienese, Aretine, Perugian, and papal lands, guarding passage through the Valdichiana and overlooking a busy Roman road that brought merchants, pilgrims, and armies from Arezzo to Cortona and then Rome. The Carthaginian general Hannibal had driven his men along the road to his great victory at Lake Trasimene. Hawkwood himself had repeatedly traveled the road on his way to harass Perugia and Siena. It had served as a point of passage for other armies on the way south, notably Charles of Durazzo in 1380.[120]

We know none of the particulars of the grant to Hawkwood of Montecchio. A Lucchese ambassadorial dispatch dated 21 June 1384 claimed that Hawkwood obtained the castle from the Perugians in lieu of a bribe. The same letter also claims that Hawkwood made a similar demand from the Sienese for the town of Monte San Savino, not far from Montecchio, but was denied. For this reason, Hawkwood and the Sienese came to blows on the field.[121]

At this time Hawkwood also came into possession of two other towns, Migliari and Badia al Pino. Both were located near Arezzo and, like Montecchio, were well fortified and strategically important.[122] These may have been given to Hawkwood by the Perugians or perhaps by Charles of Durazzo; again, little is known of the transactions. What is clear, however, is that Hawkwood had now built for himself, in the aftermath of his service in Naples and divestment of properties in the Romagna, a significant patrimony in southern Tuscany.

## Enguerrand Coucy and Intrigue at Arezzo

The impetus of Hawkwood's free company was stopped not by a local army but by the arrival of his old French ally Enguerrand Coucy. Coucy came to Italy in July 1384 to aid his beleaguered countryman Louis of Anjou, who remained in Naples with a battered force.[123] He received support for this enterprise from Bernabò Visconti and descended south toward Tuscany in August, with Hawkwood's old friend Ruggiero Cane serving as one of his guides.[124] He continued on toward Arezzo, to oppose the garrison that Charles of Durazzo had established there. Coucy set up his camp nearby, outside the city of Cortona, in early September.

As Coucy passed into Tuscany, Hawkwood's co-captain Giovanni d'Azzo degli Ubaldini offered his services to the Frenchman.[125] Richard Romsey did the same, along with much of the rank and file of the band. The men now prepared to fight on behalf of the same French Angevin cause that Hawkwood had opposed just a year earlier.

Hawkwood did not join his co-captains. He kept in contact with Coucy through letters and envoys, but when the Frenchman approached Tuscany, Hawkwood traveled to the Romagna, where his old enemy Astorre Manfredi had attacked the bastion he had left there at Sezada.[126] Hawkwood passed much of July and August fighting Manfredi. At the beginning of September, however, Hawkwood left the region and traveled toward Coucy, his former captains, and the focal point of activities.[127]

Hawkwood's intentions are not at once clear. According to the one modern account of the event, he rode to oppose Coucy on behalf of the city of Florence.[128] Coucy had assured Florentine officials that he came in the tradition of the French-Florentine alliance as a "friend and brother" of the city, but he in fact harbored hostility, owing in large part to Florence's decision to "allow" Hawkwood to work for Charles of Durazzo.[129] Coucy's army looted Florentine lands as it passed through, and it demanded a "loan" of 25,000 florins, which was in reality little more than a bribe.[130] The Florentines treated Coucy courteously; they invited him to a banquet (11 September) in the city but refused to give him money.[131] When Coucy launched his attack on Arezzo on 28–29 September 1384, Florence sent eight hundred lances to help defend the city.[132]

But the assertion that Hawkwood helped the Florentines assumes that he and the city were allied. They were not. Neither the chronicler Stefani nor the merchant Guccio Benvenuti, both of whom wrote about the affair, mentions an alliance between Florence and Hawkwood.[133] The Sienese chronicle, on the contrary, states openly that Hawkwood supported Coucy and that in fact the Frenchman hired Hawkwood.[134] The statement is closer to the truth but nevertheless an overstatement. A extant letter from an ally of Charles's (Simone Caprese) who witnessed the action firsthand from the nearby castle at Castiglione Fiorentino (then called Castiglione d'Arezzo) said that Hawkwood lent support to Coucy but did so surreptitiously, through a third party.[135] The report is corroborated by the Lucchese ambassador Niccolò di Carlino, who claimed that Hawkwood was "obliged" to Coucy but made no mention of any overt military support.[136]

There was, in fact, little possibility that Hawkwood could have remained uninvolved. His recently acquired possessions at Montecchio, Migliari, and Badia al Pino lay close to the fighting. It made little sense for him to oppose Coucy; nor was it prudent to overtly support him and alienate Florence and its allies. Instead, Hawkwood appears to have played all sides. As he gave Coucy material support, he also maintained a cordial dialogue with Florence, exchanging letters and meeting regularly with ambassadors.[137] Both Coucy and Florence were anxious to stay on good terms with Hawkwood; neither wanted Hawkwood to take arms against them.

Hawkwood thus acted in the affair in the manner of a Tuscan territorial lord rather than a mercenary. His support for Coucy was, in fact, mostly logistical. He appears to have made his castle at Montecchio available to English soldiers and their families. Richard Romsey, for example, placed his wife, Isabel, there for safekeeping. Several times during the month of October Isabel tried to join her husband, but the Florentines refused to give her free pass. Several letters on the matter have survived, including two by Isabel, which give a sense of the toll that the struggle took on family members. The epistle of 25 October reads: "I wrote and spoke many times with the priors of Castiglione, whether it might please them to give a safe-conduct for me to stay with my attendant, servant and three horses in Castiglione. They did not, however, want to give it to me and I don't know the reason. From me they should not have any suspicion and for that I beg your dear friendship, if you might, to help me obtain the said safe-conduct. I am sure that from the grace and love you bear for Richard, you will do that which you can."[138]

Coucy succeeded in taking Arezzo and put Durazzo's garrison to flight.[139] But his march stalled thereafter. Just after capturing the city, Coucy received the news that Louis of Anjou was already dead—indeed, his life had ended more than a week earlier. The raison d'être of his campaign lost—and facing intense Florentine pressure as well as a shortage of supplies—Coucy decided to return to France.[140] He offered Arezzo to both Siena and Florence and cleverly exploited the rivalry between the two cities to drive up the price. Florence bought it for 40,000 florins in November 1384. The issue proved a point of departure in the relationship between Siena and Florence.

After the sale of Arezzo, Hawkwood returned to his marauding ways. He joined again with Richard Romsey and Giovanni d'Azzo degli Ubaldini, forming a new band, called the Company of the Rose.

# PART IV

# VETERAN CAPTAIN AND
# FLORENTINE HERO

# The Deal with the Devil, the Birth of a Son, and a Victory at Castagnaro, 1385–1387

Fortune allowed that after great and bitter battle . . . the Italians
and English under those wise leaders [Ubaldini and Hawkwood]
won, more by art and intelligence than force of arms.

*Gregorio Dati*, L'istoria di Firenze

By 1385 Hawkwood was over sixty years old, a veteran captain, with landed holdings in both Italy and England. His Italian patrimony had shifted southward in recent years, from Lombardy and the Romagna to Tuscany, Umbria, and the Kingdom of Naples. Although Hawkwood's wealth and prestige were lofty, it had been more than decade since he last won a major victory on the battlefield. His service as Florentine captain of war required mostly defensive duties; the war in the Kingdom of Naples was one of attrition, through which he acquired property but gained little military glory. Hawkwood passed much time in the role of diplomat and as captain of marauding bands, the latter adding further to his profits. Over the next two years, however, Hawkwood would reassert his military supremacy and score his greatest tactical triumph, at Castagnaro on behalf of the city of Padua. This was preceded by his proudest domestic victory, the birth to Donnina of a son and heir, John junior.

Hawkwood passed the spring of 1385 in a familiar position: at the head of a mercenary company in Tuscany. The band, calling itself the Company of the Rose, was a formidable one. It consisted of 3,000 horses and 1,000 infantry, led by five captains, each a renowned mercenary: Hawkwood, Taddeo Pepoli, Giovanni d'Azzo degli Ubaldini, Johann Eberhardsweiler, and Boldrino da Panicale.[1] Even the corporals included such respected military men as Giovanni degli Ordelaffi, who had recently led armies in Lombardy. The band extorted money from Perugia and Lucca in April and then moved north to Bologna.[2] These cities, led by Florence and Siena, assembled a joint league against it.[3]

On 6 May 1385, John Hawkwood received a letter from his brother-in-law Carlo Visconti. "We notify you today [5 May] in the late morning that in Milan the count of Virtu [Giangaleazzo Visconti] seized and detained the magnificent and exalted lord, Bernabò, our parent, along with our magnificent brother Lodovico Visconti. We are free at our fortress in Crema [twenty-five miles from Milan] and the castle of Porta Romana is held in our name."[4] Bernabò had ventured outside the walls of Milan to greet his nephew Giangaleazzo, who purportedly came to visit him on his way to make a pilgrimage to the shrine of the Madonna del Monte at Varese. Giangaleazzo arrived with an unusually large entourage, including the mercenary captain Jacopo dal Verme. At the appointed signal, dal Verme grabbed Bernabò, who had waited virtually unarmed. Giangaleazzo imprisoned him in a local castle.[5]

Although treachery within the Visconti family was nothing new, the sudden fall of Hawkwood's father-in-law was unexpected. "He whom almost all the universe held in fear and honor," wrote the Milanese diarist Bernardino Corio, "was by a timid youth made prisoner."[6] The usurper, Giangaleazzo, was a shy, retiring sort, who hardly seemed a match for his uncle. Giangaleazzo spent the rest of May consolidating his hold on Milan. He allowed citizens, frustrated by Bernabò's high taxes from perpetual wars, to set fire to local registers and initiated a formal *processus* against his uncle, charging him with a long list of crimes, ranging from homicides and rapes to torture and black magic.[7] The *processus* impugned all those associated with Bernabò, including the deposed ruler's favorite mistress, Donnina de Porri, mother of Hawkwood's wife. This brought the affair directly to Hawkwood, a circumstance that Carlo Visconti hoped to take advantage of.

Carlo was one of the few of Bernabò's sons to escape capture. His letter to Hawkwood on 6 May was an appeal for military assistance. He asked Hawkwood to come to Milan with as many soldiers as he could and promised to pay him well. "It is time," he wrote, "to show your manliness."[8]

Carlo's letter reached Hawkwood at his estates just outside Florence, where he had taken up briefly to look after his affairs, leaving his mercenary band in the environs of Bologna.[9] There is no record of a direct response by Hawkwood to Carlo. But the Englishman clearly did not rush forward to defend the honor of his brother-in-law and his wife, since he remained with the Company of the Rose. An extant letter by his chancellor, Jacopo da Pietrasanta, to the city of Lucca on 12 June indicates that Hawkwood intended to play both sides: "The band has reached an agreement with the city of Bologna for 15,000 openly, and 30,000 florins overall. And as was relayed to you . . . the brigade has reached an agreement with

Carlo Visconti, but, as you know, Bernabò has lost all and is no longer able to do those things that Carlo promised. Because of this the brigade has sent ambassadors to the Count of Virtu. Meanwhile, we await his response, and the money from Bologna. We will go next toward Modena."[10]

It is not clear what "things" Carlo had promised Hawkwood and was now unable to deliver—but most likely they were monetary. The company advanced to Modena and initiated negotiations with Giangaleazzo Visconti. Hawkwood himself reported on the talks in a letter dated 17 June 1385: "We are in accord with the Bolognese and we come now to Modena, where we believe that we will without fail have an accord with the Marquis of Ferrara. The Count of Virtu sends his ambassadors to us, seeking certain things, whence we send our representative to him. . . . If the society should make an accord with the Count, it will then go toward Tuscany."[11]

According to Pietrasanta, the discussions with Giangaleazzo went poorly. The sides continued to talk for ten days, at which point Pietrasanta pessimistically predicted that an accord seemed unlikely. "We are with the Count of Virtu, with whom we conclude nothing."

But later that same day (27 June 1385) Hawkwood did in fact make an agreement with Giangaleazzo Visconti. Visconti issued a decree from his capital at Pavia, restoring to Hawkwood those lands and properties originally given to him in 1377 by Bernabò as part of Donnina Visconti's dowry: "Considering the pure and sincere love which the distinguished and strenuous knight Hawkwood, our most beloved relative, has long borne and now bears us and our state, and from whom we expect in the future prompt and grateful service . . . we now restore freely . . . all possessions and goods with rights and appurtenances previously assigned by Bernabò Visconti, for the dowry or augmenting the dowry of Donnina, his wife and daughter of the said lord Bernabò."[12]

Hawkwood specifically regained those Milanese estates he had formerly owned just northeast of Milan (fifteen kilometers) in the towns of Pessano, Bornago, Carugate, Valera, and Santa Maria alle Molgora.[13] A month later, Visconti granted him return of his rights regarding the abbey of Sant' Alberto, near Pavia. It is a tribute to Hawkwood's dedication to the abbey—and its association with Edward II—that he accepted it with explicit agreement to pay all outstanding financial burdens.[14]

The "prompt and grateful service" Giangaleazzo expected in return was military. On 1 July 1385, Hawkwood signed a *condotta in aspetto,* promising to serve in Visconti's armies when called. In return, Visconti granted Hawkwood a monthly salary of 300 florins as well as a onetime bonus of 1,000 florins.[15] The contract was signed at camp near Modena and was witnessed by—among others—the

London financier John Hedingham, who had helped arrange loans from Hawkwood to two of his soldiers back in 1382.

To some scholars, Hawkwood's contract with Giangaleazzo was "shameful," an act tantamount to selling "his soul to the devil for mediocre gain."[16] But Giangaleazzo Visconti was not at this point in his career the devil incarnate that Florentine propaganda would later make him out to be. He was widely viewed as a potentially positive force. The Florentine chancellor, Coluccio Salutati, spoke enthusiastically of his ascension. "Now Italy can rejoice, Verona and Padua can be tranquil. Now Liguria and Emilia, Genoa, Bologna and Florence can enjoy peace. Now Venice can breathe. No other action was more salutary than this done by Giangaleazzo, whom his uncle had derided as an inexperienced boy until the time came for his well-merited punishment."[17]

Nor did Hawkwood's deal with Visconti constitute mediocre gain. The terms were exceedingly generous. The annual salary amounted to 3,600 florins, three times more than what Florence paid him and nine times what he received from the city of Lucca. The Milanese estates represented a valuable patrimony; Florence, by contrast, had never given Hawkwood land for free but made him pay for it.

The arrangement was one of mutual benefit. Giangaleazzo bought time to solidify his hold on Milan; Hawkwood acquired riches to sustain his career. If indeed Hawkwood held any personal resentment against Giangaleazzo on behalf of his brother-in-law and his wife, he understood that, practically speaking, there was at this point little he could do about it. The give-and-take between the Milanese ruler and the captain recalls the negotiations between Albert Sterz and Galeazzo Visconti in 1362, which the Milanese chronicler Azario described as an instance of "art deluding art." But Hawkwood received the better deal, so much so that we may suspect in Giangaleazzo's behavior an uncertainty, perhaps a fear that Hawkwood might yet attempt to move against him.

In the meantime, the Company of the Rose continued to hold the field. After signing the accord with Visconti, Hawkwood made good on his promise to move into Tuscany.[18] The company advanced on Lucca in early July, Siena in August, and Perugia in September, extorting bribes from each.[19] The raid on Sienese territory was particularly devastating. As he had in Milan, Hawkwood took advantage of political upheaval. The Sienese government, the so-called Riformatori, had recently fallen, leaving a chaotic interregnum. The company rode with little opposition and stole so many goods from local territory that the chronicler compared it to "a moving ant hill": "On Sunday the 13th of August there . . . came the many brigades of John Hawkwood, of which there were 2,500 horse, and immediately they were in the Val d'Arbia and the whole contado of Siena, up to the gates, and they plundered so many goods and took so many prisoners, as well as cattle, large and small, that one can neither write of it nor estimate. . . . They carried away more than six hundred pair of oxen, and more than eight thousand moggia of grain, and so many woolens and linens . . . and all departed . . . so that it seemed a moving ant hill."[20] The Company of the Rose appears to have broken up shortly thereafter; by September 1385 it is no longer mentioned in the sources.

The events in Milan reached a climax in the winter. On 19 December 1385, Bernabò Visconti died in his prison at the castle of Trezzo—purportedly from a tainted bowl of mushrooms. The very next day King Richard II of England appointed Hawkwood as his ambassador to Giangaleazzo. Richard was anxious to remain on good terms with the new ruler, whose grasp on power was now assured. He sent his familiar envoy Nicholas Dagworth to Hawkwood, and the two went to Milan to discuss the king's business.[21]

Hawkwood spent much of the winter and spring of 1385/86 engaged in diplomatic activity on behalf of the English crown. In addition to Milan, Hawkwood also represented Richard in the Kingdom of Naples, where the situation had not improved. The French prince Charles of Anjou was now dead, and Enguerrand Coucy had returned to France. But the relationship between the erstwhile allies Urban VI and Charles of Durazzo had become further strained. In January 1385 Urban excommunicated Charles, and Charles responded by besieging the pope at his palace at Nocera. Richard made Hawkwood ambassador to Charles a month later. Charles returned to Hungary in the fall of 1385 and was murdered in February 1386. The French antipope Clement took advantage of the situation to make gains in Naples.[22]

Hawkwood's diplomatic missions to Naples are mentioned in the letters of Andreina Acciaiuoli, the Contessa of Altavilla, whose lands the captain traversed along the way. Andreina, preoccupied with the business of marrying her daughter, does not relate the substance of the embassies, which took place between March and June 1386.[23] They may have been related to Urban's efforts to revive interests in England in a crusade against his Clementinist opponents. Bulls on the matter, originally issued in 1382, had been republished in England in February 1386, and John of Gaunt, the uncle of King Richard, was making preparations to use the papal charge for an invasion of Castile.[24]

The connection between Hawkwood and England was in any case quite close at this time. The anonymous author of the *Westminster Chronicle* reported the arrival at the king's court of a squire from Hawkwood's brigades in the winter of 1386: "He told about a man of religion living in those parts, who predicted that within the ensuing three years the English nation, because of its evil life, would be mercilessly punished, chiefly, so he said, by famine and pestilence, but that after this the country would be the happiest of all the kingdoms, since its people would be so trustworthy and reliable that every man would be able without hesitation or the risk of deceit to believe their bare word."[25]

Hawkwood used his service as diplomat also to enrich himself. In a letter to the city of Lucca, Pope Urban said that Hawkwood took up the topic of debts owed him from Alderigo degli Antelminelli. Despite the settlement with Lucca two years earlier, Hawkwood claimed that outstanding sums remained, and he requested that the pope pay him what was owed. Urban appears to have done as Hawkwood asked.[26]

Hawkwood also pressed claims against his favorite victim, Siena. He wrote to officials there demanding 1,000 florins in back pay, which he claimed was owed both him and his corporals from the Company of the Rose. The Sienese negotiated the figure down to 800 florins, a sum they then borrowed from a wealthy citizen, Niccolò Salimbeni. Hawkwood went in person to Siena with an escort of forty men to pick up the money.

In Florence, however, Hawkwood was cited for nonpayment of taxes. His properties near the city were, as we have seen, exempt from normal imposts, but he was, however, liable for extraordinary levies, particularly forced loans (*prestanze*), interest-bearing exactions made during fiscal emergencies.[27] Ironically, Hawkwood was assessed the loans as a result of the fiscal crisis brought on by his own mercenary band, the Company of the Rose.[28] Uncharacteristically, Hawkwood appears to have taken the debt seriously and paid the sum, 20 florins—which promised a 15 percent return. Thus Hawkwood paid for a small part of his own extortion. But the disbursement may be considered an investment.

The most welcome news came from the home front. In February 1386 Hawkwood's wife, Donnina, gave birth in Florence to a son, John junior. Donnina relayed the event in a jubilant letter to the wife of Alberto d'Este of Ferrara, the godmother of her daughter Catherine.

> To the most excellent and magnificent lady, most dear godmother.
>
> I notify you that to the joy of myself and my husband, a most beautiful male child has been born. That I trouble to inform you is because I know you share our joy with all your heart, you who raised Catherine from the sacred baptismal font. Be well.
>
> Donnina Visconti, consort of the magnificent knight John Hawkwood.[29]

The birth of an heir meant a great deal to Hawkwood. He would labor until his last days to ensure the boy's legacy.

## Paduan Service and the Battle of Castagnaro

While Hawkwood enjoyed blissful moments at home, important events were occurring in northern Italy which would soon bring him back to the battlefield. In the winter of 1385/86 long-standing tensions between the neighboring cities of Padua and Verona broke out into warfare. The causes were complex and involved also intrigues by the Venetians, who maintained a grudge against Padua and gave financial support to Verona.[30] Padua had supported Venice's rival Genoa in the War of Chioggia (1378–1381) and had in recent years encroached on Venetian interests in the Friuli. Milan, which had long coveted Verona, supported Padua. Bernabò had, as we have seen, attacked Verona in 1379; more recently, the city had antagonized Giangaleazzo by allowing the exiled Carlo Visconti to stay there. The new Milanese ruler preferred at this point to keep his role secret. He openly portrayed himself as the arbiter of peace, but at the same time he quietly funneled assistance to Padua in slow increments.[31]

The conflict had an ugly personal edge. Early in the war, the ruler of Verona, Antonio della Scala, challenged the Paduan ruler Francesco "il Vecchio" Carrara, to personal combat to decide the matter. Francesco's son volunteered to take up the charge on his father's behalf. But the elder Carrara stopped him and said: "Son, it is neither right nor honorable, that you and I, who are born of noble and legiti-mate matrimony, should fight with a most vile bastard, born from the stomach of a wretched baker woman."[32]

Hawkwood joined the conflict after it was already under way. The Paduans had gained the upper hand with a spectacular victory at Brentelles on 25 June 1386. Hawkwood's recent associate in the Company of the Rose, Giovanni d'Azzo degli Ubaldini, led the victorious army, which captured virtually the entire Veronese brigade, estimated at 6,000 horses, 38 bombards, 240 wagons of provisions, and 211 prostitutes.[33] With the help of Venetian money, Verona rebuilt its army. The Paduans then turned to Hawkwood, whom the Paduan chronicler Galeazzo Gatari called "the most famous and accomplished captain that there was in all of Italy and the most expert and circumspect in the feats of arms."[34] Hawkwood's hire was in large part a countermeasure against the Veronese decision to employ Hawk-wood's brother-in-law Lutz von Landau. Unfortunately for the Veronese, Landau deserted their cause before he took the field.

Giovanni d'Azzo degli Ubaldini went in person to recruit Hawkwood.[35] The two met in Ubaldini's lands in the Mugello not far from Faenza. Hawkwood agreed to serve at the head of five hundred horseman and archers. He rode toward Padua in January 1387, accompanied by Giovanni "tedesco" da Pietramala, a rising star in the mercenary profession, with a thousand horses. They advanced as far as the town of Montagnana, just southeast of Padua, left their army there, and then went personally to meet with Francesco il Vecchio. Carrara greeted the men with gifts and held banquets in their honor.[36]

The main body of the Paduan army was already in Veronese territory, just beyond the Adige River, at the town of Cerea. Francesco il Vecchio's son, Francesco Novello, escorted Hawkwood and Pietramala to camp. The band advanced through lands belonging to the Marquis d'Este, an ally of the Carrara, toward Castelbaldo, a fortified town on the Adige River, where Paduan territory gave way to Veronese territory. Recent rains had caused the river to swell and rendered crossing difficult. In addition, the enemy had stolen all available boats and taken up a local bastion nearby. According to the Paduan chronicle, Hawkwood did not wish to risk passage under these circumstances and prevailed on Francesco Novello to turn back to Padua. Novello, however, insisted that they move forward, and with his help the band succeeded in negotiating the river. The minor episode was, as we shall see, an augur of larger things to come.[37]

Hawkwood's arrival in camp presented an immediate problem. Francesco Novello had been the titular commander of forces, but Ubaldini, the hero at Brentelles, was the de facto head of the enterprise. The question was whether Hawkwood, a more renowned captain than Ubaldini, would be willing to play a secondary role.

The issue was settled in the initial war council held by the captains. Francesco Novello began the meeting with a speech advocating an immediate strike against the enemy. He then asked his colleagues for their opinion. There was a moment of silence as each looked at the other, and then Hawkwood said to Ubaldini, "Messer Captain, why don't you reply?" Ubaldini stood up and, facing Francesco, said: "Magnificent and generous knight, I have no response, nor am I disposed to give one, nor do I dare, on my honor, speak before my lord John Hawkwood does, even though I have held until now the honorable baton of the command of your Carrara army. Therefore here in your presence I refuse this honorable baton, because . . . I would not dare to carry it where there was also my lord John Hawkwood. So I give it to him, so that he can be leader and governor and captain of your army, and I intend to give him all my prompt obedience."[38] Ubaldini then handed the baton to Hawkwood, who accepted it "with many, many affectionate words" and with the promise that he would share it with Ubaldini. The council then prepared its offensive against Verona.

The Paduan army advanced swiftly: burning, robbing, and doing great damage as it went forward. It pushed to the walls of Verona but soon ran out of supplies. The Paduan chronicler Galeazzo Gatari spoke of great suffering, of soldiers going twenty days without bread and meat, "constrained to eat the vegetation and their horses."[39] The Florentine chronicle (*Cronica volgare*) attributed to Minerbetti gave a more conservative estimate of twelve days without bread.[40] Paduan officials sought to buy time by opening peace negotiations. They also appealed for more aid from Giangaleazzo Visconti, who showed interest but remained cautious.[41]

The Paduan army had little choice but to retreat and head back to its supply base at Castelbaldo. Castelbaldo, today a rustic town known for its apple and pear trees, was then furnished with a formidable castle, which the Paduans had provisioned with food and arms. Veronese forces tried to cut off the Paduan march.

Hawkwood's retreat took him through the old Paduan camp at Cerea, where he searched for food and fodder. The army found instead that the town wells and stores of wine were poisoned. The Paduan chronicler now credited Hawkwood with performing miracles, using "his ring" to undo the poison. The story is strikingly similar to one told by the chronicler Jehan Servion about Amadeus of Savoy in 1372, who placed his ring with the likeness of Saint Maurice in contaminated waters and purified them. Bartolomeo Gatari, who updated and corrected his father Galeazzo's chronicle, gave a curious clarification of Hawkwood's activity. "What is meant is that Messer John Hawkwood had with him a unicorn at Cerea, which I saw and I touched with my own hands, which was five feet long and which he cut into pieces and lowered in the wells."[42]

The Paduans renewed the march and advanced southeast to the town of Castagnaro, which lay just across from Castelbaldo, on the western side of the Adige River. With Ordelaffi and the Veronese army still at a distance behind them, the Paduans had an open to road to Castelbaldo. They chose, however, to stop just above Castagnaro and face the enemy.

The two armies opposed each other across "a large and wide plain," bisected by an irrigation ditch some six or seven feet wide. The Adige River lay on one side of the field, marshland on the other.[43] The position protected the Paduan army from cavalry assault both from the flanks and from the front. It was perhaps with this in mind that Hawkwood and his captains chose not to cross over to his supply base, which might easily have been surrounded by the enemy. Hawkwood could not, however, stop many of his hungry men from refreshing themselves at the base. "Men-at-arms abandoned their banners and went toward Castelbaldo," wrote the Paduan chronicler, "not having any respect for either their honor or what misfortune could occur."[44] Francesco Novello himself went to head off the deserters and organized men to ferry supplies back to the army.[45]

The stage was now set for the battle of Castagnaro, generally considered Hawkwood's finest victory and one of the greatest feats of military prowess of the era. Sir

Charles Oman in his classic *Art of War in the Middle Ages* called the battle "a triumph of old age" for Hawkwood and compared it to the epoch-making English victory over the French at Poitiers in 1356.[46]

According to Oman, Hawkwood and the Paduans were outmanned. He reckoned Veronese forces at 9,000 cavalry, 2,600 crossbowmen and pikemen, and several thousand native infantry; he put the Paduan forces at 7,000 cavalry and 1,600 infantry and archers. Oman took the figures from the Paduan chronicle and accepted them on the curious ground that they were reported "with great detail." His assessment has found its way into virtually all modern accounts of the battle, but there is in fact no independent verification of the Paduan chronicler's estimate. The Paduan writer may well have succumbed to the familiar temptation to exaggerate in order to make the subsequent victory seem more impressive.[47] What is certain, however, is that some of the most prominent mercenary captains of the day fought on both sides. Apart from Hawkwood and Ubaldini, the Paduan army contained the noted Italians Giovanni de Pietramala, Ugolotto Biancardi, Broglia da Chieri, and Biordo Michelotti—all of whom would play significant roles in Italian warfare in future years. Michelotti seized for a time the lordship of Perugia. The Veronese army had Giovanni degli Ordelaffi and Ostasio da Polenta, both from lordly families in the Romagna (Forlì and Ravenna), and the skilled Veronese mercenaries Ugolino and Taddeo dal Verme, cousins of Jacopo dal Verme, against whom Hawkwood would fight his last great battles in Italy.

The Veronese carried into battle a strange gunpowder apparatus, consisting of three large carts, each with 144 guns mounted on it. The guns fired balls the size of a hen's egg. It took four powerful horses to move the weapon, and each gun cart required three men to operate it. A modern scholar has compared it to the rocket launchers mounted on the backs of trucks employed by the Russians in World War II.[48] The Paduan chronicler was impressed enough by it that he gave a long, detailed description.[49] He said that the Veronese intended to use the weapon in the field "to break and divide the Carrarese battle formation and to take their flag."[50] The tactic, associated more with the so-called military revolution of the sixteenth century, was clearly ahead of its time. As we shall see, however, the contraption did not work; thus the tactic was never tested.

The two armies drew up for battle on 11 May 1387. The Paduan high command held a final council. Hawkwood advised the army take up the battle ("tuore la battaglia"), but he urged Francesco Novello to remove himself to safety at Castelbaldo. "Your person carries a lot of weight: so that if by chance it happens to our disgrace that we lose and you are captured, your state will be in great doubt. But God forbid such a disaster!!" Ubaldini seconded Hawkwood's opinion and added that should the army lose without Francesco with it, there would be "thousands of remedies." Francesco decided, however, to remain on the front line: "I am not a rogue . . . but disposed do battle."[51]

The Paduan chronicler gives a description of the battle formations—the most detailed we possess for an engagement involving Hawkwood. The Englishman arranged the Paduan army in three lines, consisting of eight contingents of men (map 7).[52] He placed himself at the head of the formation with 500 men-at-arms and 500 English archers, followed by Ubaldini and Giovanni da Pietramala with 1,000 horses and then Francesco Novello with 1,400 horses. A reserve of native infantry and crossbowmen was placed on the extreme right on an embankment near the Adige River. Ugolotto Biancardi expressed the opinion that the area near the Adige should be reinforced further, to prevent the enemy from making a naval attack. This appears to have been overruled. The *carroccio* (war carriage), the emblem of Italian cities, was protected by mounted troops and put, as was usual, at the rear of the formation.

Hawkwood filled in and smoothed out an area some twenty feet long where the irrigation ditch met the canal and the Adige River. This was done to create a pass over the river "if there were to be need of it."[53] This patch work proved crucial to the outcome of the battle.[54]

The Veronese army arrayed itself in six battalions, under Giovanni degli Orde-laffi, Ugolino del Verme, and Ostasio da Polenta. It is not clear where the multi-barreled bombard was placed.

The Paduan chronicler provides evocative details of the Paduan force. Hawk-wood coordinated the battle line atop a Thessalian destrier horse. Giovanni d'Azzo degli Ubaldini wore a pearl cap, while Francesco Novello placed over his armor a surcoat of white velvet with a red *carro* (cart), symbol of the Carrara family. He affixed to the top of his helmet two gold balls. Novello knighted five Paduan soldiers (mostly his relatives) to bolster morale; Hawkwood knighted several foreign soldiers.

The battle was engaged an hour before sunset—when, in the Paduan chronicler's poetic description, "the sun had already made its rapid journey toward the humid earth."[55] According to the Florentine Minerbetti, Hawkwood and the Paduans drew out the enemy by attacking with their light infantry and then retreating.[56] According to the Paduan account, Hawkwood began with blasts from his longbowmen, which fell on the foe "as if it were raining."[57] The Veronese then moved steadfastly toward the Paduan lines "in good order to subdue and destroy the hungry and weak Carrarese army."[58]

Both sides descended from their horses to fight on foot. The ditch between them was bridged by planks hastily thrown across it. An intense battle followed. Francesco Novello and Ugolotto Biancardi and their contingent fought with Ostasio da

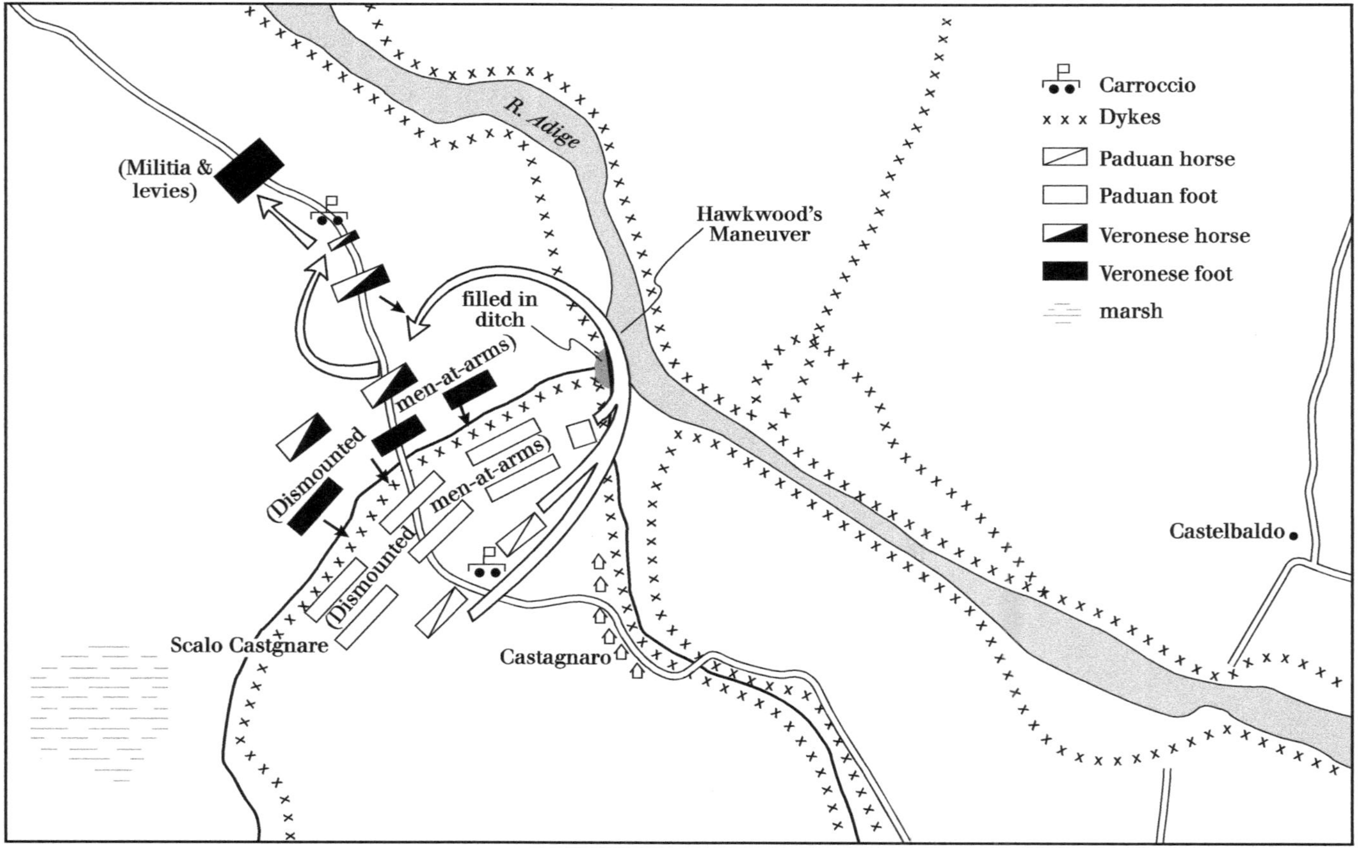

*Map 7.* Battle of Castagnaro

Polenta. In the melee, Novello's cousin, Francesco Buzzacarini, was knocked off his horse by a lance blow and fell wounded in a ditch. Francesco Novello then struck Ostasio with a strong lance blow to the chest, knocking him from his horse. Polenta was quickly removed to safety by his retainers.[59] The other contingents also engaged.

With the battle in full swing, Hawkwood made his decisive move. He gave over his contingent to Giovanni da Pietramala and rode out of the pack with a page to survey the scene. Seeing the left flank of the enemy exposed, Hawkwood ordered his men to advance to the extreme right of the battlefield, across the same patch he had filled in, where the drainage ditch and the canal met. Just before undertaking the maneuver he made one more attempt to convince Francesco Novello to remove himself to safety at Castelbaldo. Novello again refused, saying that he would prefer to die than to retreat. Hawkwood then tossed his commander's baton in the direction of the enemy, unsheathed his dagger, and shouted, "Carne, Carne [Flesh, Flesh]." The battle cry was a pun on the word *carro*, the Carrara symbol.[60] The shouts were accompanied by blasts from trumpets and the grunts of fighting men, such that "the whole sky resounded" with noise. Hawkwood crossed the ditch and the Adige and hit full force at the Veronese rear.

The effect of Hawkwood's stratagem was dramatic. The main body of the Veronese army scurried back to help, creating disorder and confusion. Hawkwood overwhelmed the enemy and seized not only the *carroccio* but the entire high command. A small infantry group refused to surrender. Poorly armed and badly equipped, the group was easily defeated and its commander taken prisoner.

The Paduan chronicle estimated that 4,620 fighting men were captured; the Este chronicler of Ferrara gave the more conservative figure of 2,000.[61] Among the spoils of war was the great Veronese multibarreled artillery piece, which either did not work or was too heavy and cumbersome to set up effectively on the battlefield. The Paduan chronicle put the number of dead at 716 men and the wounded at 846.

Hawkwood's generalship was admired and applauded throughout Italy. The most laudatory reviews came from Florence. Minerbetti titled the part of his work devoted to the battle as follows: "How the Lord of Verona Had Surrounded the Men of the Lord of Padua and Would Have Taken Them, If Not For the Wisdom and Advice of Misser John Hawkwood, Englishman, Who, Through his Sagacity Shattered the Enemy and Remained Free With All his Men."[62] Minerbetti credited Hawkwood not only with effecting the crucial maneuver but with doing so according to a carefully preconceived plan. The Florentine depicted the Veronese army as holding an overwhelming advantage and the Paduan army as having little chance of success. He put into the mouth of Hawkwood at the outset of the battle a speech not recorded by the Paduan chronicler. "Brave knights, if it were possible to fight the enemy in the open field, truly I know you would be victorious. . . . But seeing the manner in which they are fortified there it is impossible that they can be taken by force and defeated by us; but it is impossible to stay here, since we cannot survive but for a few days, and those in great necessity, we must beat the enemy with cleverness."[63] Minerbetti emphasizes Hawkwood's "cleverness" and "wisdom."

The Paduan account praised Hawkwood but stressed more the circumstantial nature of the battle. It explained Hawkwood's flanking maneuver as a response to momentary circumstance. The real hero of the battle was Francesco Novello, whose feats of arms are placed at the center of the chronicler's description. This is not surprising given that the chronicler, Galeazzo Gatari, was a partisan of the Carrara household, on behalf of which he often worked.[64] The chronicler told how Francesco fought like "a dragon throwing blazes of fire" and how his bravery "assured his eternal memory."[65] It was Novello who first showed Hawkwood how to cross the Adige when the English captain initially arrived in the Paduan camp. It was therefore Novello who deserved a portion of the credit for Hawkwood's later flanking move, which passed over the same ground for which Novello served as tutor. The traces of local pride were obvious. In reality, however, Hawkwood traversed the Adige many times and knew the vagaries of the local terrain well. It is unlikely that he need helped with the maneuver.

The other accounts of Castagnaro are brief and give few details of the fighting. The chronicle of Conforto da Costoza from Vicenza says only that Padua won a big victory. The Este chronicle lists the names of the leading prisoners taken by Padua but does not give much more.[66] The Sienese and Pistoiese chronicles are similarly terse. We unfortunately do not possess an account from the Veronese side to balance that from the Paduan point of view.

There are obvious parallels between the battle of Castagnaro and the battle of Poitiers. In both cases the opposing armies dismounted from their horses at the start of hostilities. They were separated from each other by a ditch, in the latter case dug by the English specifically to inhibit a French cavalry charge. The local terrains differed, but in both instances there were natural obstacles on the flanks. At Castagnaro, the field was hemmed in by the Adige River, at Poitiers by the Nouaillé wood (both times to the right of the victors). These would prove crucial to the results of the battle. Both the Paduan and English armies had the option of retreating to more fortified ground beyond the field but chose not to do so. If we accept the Florentine account of Castagnaro, the similarities are still greater. Hawkwood's initial feint drawing out the Veronese army was similar to the Earl of

Oxford's maneuver that began Poitiers. The enveloping move effected by Hawkwood at the height of battle reads like that of the Gascon captain Captal de Buch. Hawkwood crossed the Adige River; Captal de Buch advanced behind thickets of the edge of the forest and past a small hill. Both were lightning strikes that surprised the enemy and decided the outcome of the battle. The similarities are indeed so strong that it seems reasonable to conclude on this evidence alone that Hawkwood was at Poitiers.

But the point should not be overstated. There are also significant differences between the battles. Poitiers involved much greater use of the famed English longbow. The English army employed large contingents of these archers, who were instrumental in creating havoc in the French ranks. Hawkwood's army had few longbowmen. His own brigade of five hundred archers is the only one mentioned. They shot their arrows, but, the Paduan chronicler's mention of them notwithstanding, they do not appear to have made a difference to the outcome of the battle.

A wholly overlooked factor at Castagnaro was the effect of the great artillery piece brought to battle by Verona. It did not, of course, work. But it almost certainly had an impact on the way the armies prepared for and fought the battle. From the Paduan chronicler's description of it, it is clear that the weapon was much feared. One might speculate that the late start to the battle, which began as the sun was going down, may have been the result of frustrated attempts on the part of the Veronese to fire the weapon.

Most important of all, Castagnaro should not be understood solely in terms of what occurred at the much earlier battle of Poitiers, as Hawkwood now had nearly twenty-five years of experience as a captain on Italian battlefields. The tactics used at Castagnaro are in fact not at all surprising in light of his prior career. The knowledge of the terrain and the use of flanking movement are reminiscent of Hawkwood's great victory at the second battle of Cascina back in 1369 or even his victory against the papal army at Rubiera in 1372. In the former instance he outmaneuvered a larger Florentine army using the Arno River and the soft mud around it to his advantage. The tactic of dismounting from horses at the start of battle was by now routine in Italy; indeed, armies throughout the peninsula, whether English or not, employed the method.

## A Victory Turned Sour

After Castagnaro, the victorious army returned to feasts and celebrations in Padua. Francesco Novello's page, Giovanni Contarini, rode ahead of the army to inform Francesco "il Vecchio" Carrara of the victory. Contarini coyly offered il

Vecchio good news and bad news. The good news was that Paduan forces had won a great victory. The bad news was that Francesco Novello had offered the troops a month's double pay in the heat of battle. Contarini's second remark reflected the state of local finances, which were stretched to the limit by the war. Carrara smiled and went to the gates of the city to greet the army. He hugged John Hawkwood, Giovanni d'Azzo degli Ubaldini, and all the leaders of the army. He then turned to the captive enemy captain Giovanni degli Ordelaffi and said: "You are welcome here; I'm glad to meet you." Ordelaffi responded: "The feeling is not mutual; but as it pleases God, so be it!"[67] The army displayed its banners and war booty before a huge crowd of citizens shouting "carro, carro."[68] Feasting and drinking went on all through the night.

The war, however, was not over. Verona again regrouped and with Venetian aid rebuilt its forces. Giangaleazzo Visconti, wishing to back a winner and estimating that Padua was now in control, offered more open support. In April, he allied with Padua and, along with the city of Mantua, declared war on Verona. Visconti assumed the major share of the military expense, in return for a promise that he would receive possession of Verona in case of victory; Padua would get the city of Vicenza, which had allied with Verona.[69]

The battle was soon rejoined.[70] Ubaldini, now on the Milanese payroll, rode north and attacked Veronese territory near Lake Garda. John Hawkwood and Francesco Novello remained together and with the main body of the Paduan army prepared an attack on Verona proper. The two set out in April 1387. They found, however, that the Adige was well defended by the Veronese army and thus difficult to cross. There were also reports of little forage on the other side along their proposed route. Hawkwood advised the army to turn back. Novello disagreed. He was eager to strike a final blow at the enemy and did not want the army to lose its impetus.[71] In a scene reminiscent of their first interaction, Francesco Novello urged Hawkwood to cross the river. As the Paduan army mobilized, however, it was greeted by a storm of crossbow fire, which resulted in many casualties. Novello rallied his men by offering 100 ducats to the first soldier who crossed the river. The ploy worked. Several soldiers made a desperate dash, laying aside their arms and armor and swimming the fetid waters near a drainage ditch. The boldness of the few gave impetus to the whole, and the army managed by degrees to cross over. But once in Veronese territory, the army had limited success and, indeed, found it difficult to gather suitable forage for its horses. It was forced to turn back.[72]

At this point, Hawkwood quit Paduan service. The local chronicler says dryly that his contract had run out and thus he sought employment elsewhere. This was only part of the story. One would have expected Padua to make every effort to resign its best captain at so important a moment in the war. The chronicler of the city of Treviso makes the more pointed statement that "dissensions" arose between Hawkwood and his employer.[73] These were likely financial in nature, perhaps relating to the distribution of money from the ransoms of the prisoners taken at Castagnaro.[74] Francesco Carrara had, in fact, been heavy handed in that regard.[75] After Castagnaro, he published an edict asserting direct control over ransoms. This was contrary to the usual custom of allowing mercenaries a portion of the income. Carrara then dismissed many of the high-ranking captives, men who would have fetched a high price. This, combined with the overall economic constraints faced by Padua during the war, may well have put a financial squeeze on Hawkwood. It is, in fact, possible that his salary was also in arrears.

There is some proof that Hawkwood's service to Padua was not lucrative. Just before the battle, Hawkwood and his wife, Donnina, sent a petition to the Florentine city council (February 1387) complaining of large debts. This may be passed off as typical subterfuge on Hawkwood's part, but the complaint was coupled with an announcement that he intended to sell his lands in Florence, including the estates at Poggibonsi and at San Donato in Polverosa.[76] The petition sought only Florence's approval to do so.

Hawkwood's decision to quit Paduan service was also likely conditioned by issues of authority and command. Francesco Novello had frequently ignored Hawkwood's military advice. We have cited three instances in which Novello overtly countermanded Hawkwood's orders. The most recent instance, in which Novello insisted on crossing the Adige, must have been particularly annoying to Hawkwood, given his success at Castagnaro. The maneuver contradicted Hawkwood's basic instincts as a commander. It was rash, ill conceived, with much to lose and little to gain. Indeed, it was the very opposite of what Hawkwood had done at Castagnaro. As we have repeatedly seen, Hawkwood did not respond well to people—like the "scribbling notaries" at Milan in 1372—who told him how to conduct war.

Hawkwood's dissatisfaction with his employer may well have taken the form of insurrection. In his description of the Paduan army's crossing of the Adige, the chronicler Gatari makes no mention of Hawkwood's participation. It is possible that the angry captain refused to participate. This would help explain the curious assertion by the chronicler of Treviso that the lord of Padua wished to "behead" Hawkwood, a punishment appropriate to treasonous conduct. The nineteenth-century Italian historian Ercole Ricotti claimed that Hawkwood quit because he did not wish to serve Giangaleazzo Viconti, with whom he was angry over the capture and death of Bernabò.[77] But there is no evidence of this. Visconti had long been surreptitiously helping the Paduan cause. If Hawkwood hated Giangaleazzo as much as has been supposed, we might assume that he would have gone to work for Verona instead of Padua.

Hawkwood departed Padua at the end of May. He was replaced by the Italian captain Andrelino Trotto, a less expensive captain of modest reputation.[78] Andrelino's arrival at the Paduan camp was inauspicious. When he descended from his horse to greet Francesco Novello, the animal gave a sudden start, wounding Francesco severely in the leg. The Paduan commander had to be confined to bed for many days.[79] This was perhaps the most singular event in Andrelino's otherwise completely unremarkable career. The war continued through the summer and early fall of 1387. With the help of its powerful ally, Padua eventually emerged victorious (October 1387).[80] The city had little time to enjoy the victory.

Hawkwood meanwhile took up service again with the Florentines as their captain of war. He signed a six-month contract, placing him at the head of a personal contingent of eighty-two lances (each lance consisting of three horses and three men), forty archers, and two trumpeters for a handsome salary of 500 florins per month.[81]

The service for Padua constituted Hawkwood's last in northern Italy for an employer other than Florence. From this point until the end of his career, Hawkwood would remain in Tuscany in Florentine employ, with occasional service in the Kingdom of Naples. Florence proved itself the one employer that could consistently pay well and on time.

# CHAPTER TWELVE

# At the Center of the Storm

## Florence and the Military Buildup, 1387–1389

> Every day the Florentines make such injuries and so many and such
> bitter threats with companies . . . that it is impossible to recount
> them all.
>
> *Complaint by the Sienese chronicler Tommaso Montauri,*
> *summer of 1388*

When Hawkwood arrived in Florence in May 1387, he found the city pre-occupied with foreign affairs. The continuing wars in Lombardy and in the Kingdom of Naples and the recent intrigues of Pope Urban VI in Tuscany and Umbria caused considerable anxiety locally. Officials feared the movements of armed bands of soldiers spinning out of the contests. Internally, Florence faced a political crisis that led to the expulsion of several members of prominent families.[1] In his history of Florence, Leonardo Bruni spoke of a pervasive atmosphere of "suspicion."[2]

Florence's own hegemonic policies raised tensions further. Since the acquisition of Arezzo from Enguerrand Coucy in 1384, Florence had become more aggressive in its behavior toward its neighbors, particularly the Sienese, who had also coveted the town.[3] By the summer of 1387, relations reached a low point. Florence had taken from Siena possession of the town of Lucignano and now vied for control of Cortona and Montepulciano, two of Siena's most important satellites.[4] All the towns were located near Arezzo in the Valdichiana.

By agreeing to serve Florence as captain of war, Hawkwood placed himself at the center of a complex political and diplomatic contest. His presence was itself hardly neutral. Hawkwood had long been at odds with the Sienese, whom he found duplicitous and slow in the payment of outstanding debts. He took special pleasure in harassing them and had, in fact, staged a raid on the environs of

Lucignano just after Siena lost control of the town.[5] Hawkwood's lands in southern Tuscany, particularly the castle at Montecchio, posed a direct threat to Sienese interests. From its perch atop a hill 364 meters high, Montecchio overlooked the southern entry into the Valdichiana and the strategically important roads into the Sienese state. It lay close to both Cortona and Montepulciano, the focal point of the dispute with Florence. Thus Hawkwood had his own vested interests and functioned not only as Florence's leading soldier but also as a political entity in his own right (map 6).

The Sienese worried greatly about Hawkwood, and from the moment he assumed office, they sought assurances that he would not move against them. The Florentine officials immediately wrote to Siena, promising that "in as much as is possible and with all promptness" they would "work hard to see that John Hawkwood has the same regard for your land as he does for our land."[6] The Sienese nevertheless kept close watch on Hawkwood through spies and ambassadors. Diplomatic dispatches written in that city during the summer of 1387, no matter what their larger theme, invariably contained information about Hawkwood's movements.[7] And despite Florence's assurances, the Sienese were convinced that Hawkwood intended to harm them. The letter of the ambassador Mino di Simone dated 12 August 1387 was typical of the genre. After outlining the diplomatic state of affairs with Florence and much of Italy, Mino added the postscript that Hawkwood was spotted near Arezzo, plotting "some evil" against Siena.[8]

Despite Sienese fears, Hawkwood maintained a relatively low profile in the initial months after his hire. He passed much of his time prospecting for money to replenish his funds depleted from his service with Padua. He tended his lands and took care of his young family, which now included two girls, ten-year-old Janet and nine-year-old Catherine, and a son, John junior, barely a year old. He worked also on behalf of his English military comrades and induced the Florentines to hire Nicholas Payton and seventeen English lances for his personal brigade.[9] Hawkwood likewise persuaded Florence to employ three English corporals from his home in Essex: John Coe, Thomas Ball, and Richard Stisted, each with twenty lances.[10] These men would remain in Florentine employ until Hawkwood's death in 1394.

Florentine officials had their own concerns about Hawkwood. He was expensive and notoriously difficult to manage. Some in the Signoria spoke of the need for a less costly captain and advocated dismissing Hawkwood once his contract expired. Others maintained that the benefits of having competent military leadership in such uncertain times outweighed the expense and favored continuing Hawkwood's employment.[11] These ambivalent feelings remained throughout the captain's service. They reflect a general uncertainty in Florence about foreign affairs—what one scholar has called "a congenital inability" at this time "to define her needs and priorities."[12]

The diplomatic climate grew still more tense in October 1387. The protracted war between Padua and Verona finally ended, with Padua emerging as the victor. According to the terms of its military alliance with Milan, Padua was to receive Vicenza, while Milan would get Verona. But the Milanese ruler Giangaleazzo Visconti did not live up to his promises and seized Vicenza, a move he justified on specious grounds.[13] The Paduans were outraged and accused Visconti of treachery. The Florentines also became suspicious, particularly when news reached them that Giovanni d'Azzo degli Ubaldini, the head of Visconti's forces in the Paduan war and Florence's most notorious exile, intended to take his now unemployed band south to Tuscany. Ubaldini reached Bologna in November with a large force of fifteen hundred lances, raided local lands, and then moved on Modena, Forlì, and Cesena, stopping not far from his family's base at Faenza, at the point of entry into Tuscany.[14] The Sienese ambassador Niccolò Malavolti stationed in Florence reported a widespread feeling of distrust in the city. "In speaking with great citizens," he wrote (12 November 1387), "it is clear that they have great fear of this Lord of Milan and don't doubt that Giovanni d'Azzo is at his petition."[15] The Florentine chronicle attributed to Minerbetti pointedly accused Ubaldini of being "at the secret petition of the count of Virtu [Giangaleazzo], and had money and provisions from him."[16]

Hawkwood, as he often did in such circumstances, proposed an aggressive remedy. He offered to pursue Ubaldini beyond Tuscan territory and annihilate his band. He requested 500 lances, 2,000 crossbowmen, and 1,000 infantrymen for the task.[17] The Florentines were not inclined to such dramatic measure, which they feared would pit them too directly against Milan. Officials took the more moderate course of sending troops to help the Bolognese and ambassadors to Ubaldini to try to make an accord with him.[18] They instructed Hawkwood only to guard the passes.[19] Giangaleazzo Visconti—wishing to defuse the tensions and perhaps to shift suspicion from himself—helped broker a settlement. The pact was far reaching, intended to settle all outstanding issues between Florence and Ubaldini. Ubaldini agreed to maintain perpetual peace with Florence in return for an annual stipend of 1,800 florins over the next ten years and the repatriation of members of the male line of his family.[20] In theory the accord ended their longstanding dispute, but in truth it changed little.

The Ubaldini threat was followed shortly by the arrival in Tuscany of another mercenary band, led by Bernard de La Salle, Eberhard von Landau, and Guido d'Asciano. Suspicion again fell on Milan. Guido d'Asciano had recently worked for Visconti; Bernard had fought in the Kingdom of Naples, but he had intended to go north to serve in Lombardy.[21] Hawkwood's presence in Florence, however, dissuaded the company from moving on the city. It rode instead north against Lucca and Pisa and then south against Siena.[22] Florence had been spared, but its neighbors became more disaffected. Pisa, Lucca, and Siena held Florence responsible for the raid. The Sienese were especially aggrieved because Hawkwood, who had pursued the band as far as the Sienese border, demanded from the city a bribe of 4,000 florins to avoid crossing into its territory. Hawkwood claimed he was owed an outstanding debt. Siena sent embassies to Giangaleazzo Visconti requesting the service of Giovanni d'Azzo degli Ubaldini to defend itself.[23]

It was now December 1387, and Hawkwood's contract was coming to an end. There was renewed discussion among Florentine officials whether to retain or dismiss him. The debate focused on costs, risks versus rewards, and the overall effect of Hawkwood on the diplomatic situation. Insight into the negotiations from Hawkwood's perspective comes from a letter sent to him by his chancellor, Jacopo da Pietrasanta, who spoke with Florentine officials.

> I went to Florence and was with the Lord Priors and the Eight, and your other friends, who received me with gracious spirit from their love of you. It seemed to me that there was much hope regarding the business between us and the King, because they claim that they have no money and it seems that it will be difficult to have anything from any of your other friends. Whence the Florentines say that in the case that they pay anything to anybody, they would rather give to you than to anyone else in the world. But they wish now not to pay stipends, and on that account, I am not able to do more, so that you can provide for your activities. It does not seem to me that you should come here, because there is great lack. About your stipend [Hawkwood's lifetime annual payment], they say that they do not wish to provide it, except for the past year, and they will give that to Donnina. They do not lack soldiers, and those English soldiers are unhappy and wish to be with you, if you are able to give them 4,000 florins, and the same for those English soldiers in Bologna. All are in debt.[24]

The letter reveals that Florence now claimed penury and was reluctant to make additional advances of salary. Pietrasanta makes brief mention of "business" with "the King." The reference is to the king of Naples, Ladilaus, the young son of Charles of Durazzo, who inherited the throne when his father was murdered in 1386. Hawkwood was in communication with Neapolitan officials about serving on behalf of Ladilaus and his mother, Magherita, who served as his regent. Ladilaus and Margherita were at war with their traditional enemies, the French Angevins and their ally the French antipope, Clement VII. According to some reports, Hawkwood had been negotiating with Margherita since the beginning of his service in Florence, if not earlier.[25] A Sienese ambassador claimed that Hawkwood in fact traveled there personally to discuss prospects, but this cannot be confirmed. Hawkwood's interest in Ladilaus and the Hungarian cause followed the general lines of English policy, which steadfastly opposed the interests of the French Angevins and the antipope Clement VII. But there is no direct evidence that Richard II was behind Hawkwood's actions. Florence also supported the Hungarian Angevin cause, but officials were also anxious not to alienate its traditional French Angevin allies.[26]

Hawkwood ultimately remained in Florentine employ. The city, despite its claims of poverty, resigned him in January 1388, though the vote in the Signoria was very close.[27] Hawkwood's new contract was the same as the previous one. It called for him to command one hundred lances at a salary of 500 florins a month for nine months, with an option for an additional six.[28]

## The Trot of the Wolf, May–September 1388

The first months of Hawkwood's service were noneventful. But in the spring the diplomatic situation deteriorated significantly. In May 1388, Visconti turned against Padua. He formed an alliance with the city's longtime enemy Venice and mobilized his army.[29] This convinced Florentine officials that Giangaleazzo was, like his uncle Bernabò, after conquest.[30] The opinion in the Signoria became progressively anti-Visconti in tone. "The Count," said Donato Acciaiuoli, is not to be believed; he wishes without a doubt to deceive us."[31]

Relations with Siena also worsened. After almost a year of relative quiet, problems resurfaced in Montepulciano. Citizens there demonstrated in the streets and shouted "long live Florence." Florentine officials discouraged the revolt, but the Sienese accused them of secretly manipulating the situation. The crisis intensified over the summer.[32] And despite Florence's protest of innocence, its behavior seemed unsavory even to those who were not directly involved.[33] A Lucchese ambassador accused the city of playing the part of "a Judas, full of evil and simony," and discerned in its actions "the trot of the wolf."[34]

By the summer of 1388 there was a palpable sense of impending war with Siena. "Every day," wrote the Florentine chancellor Coluccio Salutati, "the fear increases, and we cannot be tranquil seeing that a war so terrible is imminent."[35] The Florentines worked on the diplomatic front to diffuse tensions. At the same time, however, they firmed up alliances and undertook a substantial military buildup. Budgets reveal that expenditure on troops increased 62 percent from 1387 to 1388 (from 154,740 florins to 250,457 florins).[36] But the Florentines insisted that the troops they were amassing were really free and independent.

John Hawkwood played a key role, protecting Florence from "random" mercenary incursions and using his influence with men in his profession to try to gain for the city the services of the best available captains. Siena did not have, nor could it afford, such a protector. It drifted instead closer to Giangaleazzo Visconti, in whom it saw a counterweight to Florentine arrogance.[37] The city actively sought his military support, but Visconti, who had nothing to gain by openly antagonizing Florence, did not wish to be involved.[38] Siena's efforts to forge closer ties with Milan brought the region closer to a broad, pan-Italian war. In the highly charged atmosphere every movement of armed men was regarded with suspicion, and each sided blamed the other.

John Beltoft's raid on Tuscany in May 1388 is indicative of the many volatile forces at play. Beltoft had been stationed in Perugia in the service of Pope Urban VI, for whom he fought in the civil war in Naples.[39] In late April he left the papal camp and gave notice that he intended to ride through Florentine lands toward Cortona, a focal point of the Sienese-Florentine dispute. Beltoft apparently had a grudge to settle with the lord of the city.[40] The Florentines immediately sent Hawkwood to intervene. Rather than directing him to attack, they instructed him to speak with Beltoft, Englishman to Englishman, to reconcile him with the lord of Cortona, and to constrain him to avoid Florentine territory.[41] Hawkwood's possession of the castle of Montecchio, only miles away from Cortona, added a personal sense of urgency to his embassy.

Hawkwood convinced Beltoft to spare Cortona and avoid Florence. But Beltoft then veered into Sienese territory, ravaged the Maremma, and then rode north into Pisan territory.[42] He was joined by two other captains, Bernard de La Salle and Eberhard von Landau, who ignored recent agreements they had signed with Tuscan cities. The combined force inflicted heavy damage, extorting bribes and seizing two castles near Pisa.

Hawkwood had helped protect Florence, but his efforts led directly to damage to Florence's neighbors, who were now angry. The Sienese claimed that Florence not only aided Beltoft but in fact created his band for the explicit purpose of harassing them.[43] They blamed Florence retroactively for all the attacks by mercenary companies on their land over the past several years. The Florentines send an embassy to refute the accusations point by point.[44] Shortly after, Sienese leaders sent an embassy to Milan offering to place their city under Visconti's "protection," with the explicit proviso that he protect them from supposedly "free" mercenary companies. Visconti, occupied with the initial phases of his war against Padua, declined. But the argument between Siena and Florence continued, played out in large part in Visconti's court in Milan, where one Florentine envoy referred to the Sienese as "idiots."[45]

The truth in this instance, however, was that the Florentines were, as they protested, innocent. Rather than encourage the band, Florence had warned its neighbors when Beltoft first arrived in Tuscany.[46] It also wrote to Urban VI, accusing him of employing the band and demanding he call it back.[47] The pope, who was not on good terms with Florence, was unresponsive and in fact insulted the Florentine ambassador sent to speak with him.[48] Beltoft himself was hostile to Florence. Even though Hawkwood had convinced him to avoid Florentine lands for the present, Beltoft would offer no assurance that he would continue to do so in the future. Officials sent Hawkwood on another embassy to extract from Beltoft a "written promise," containing his seal. Hawkwood ultimately persuaded Beltoft to write the letter, but resentments lingered between the two.[49]

However, any broad claim of innocence by the Florentines was impossible to sustain. The city's military buildup, Hawkwood's presence, and its attempts to defend itself from companies cast a suspicious light on it. The arrival in May of Carlo Visconti, the son of Bernabò, only made matters worse. Carlo was Giangaleazzo's most ardent opponent. He had escaped Milan after Bernabò's capture, journeyed to Germany to find support against his usurping uncle, and then quietly returned to Lombardy. Although he tried to keep his movements secret, his arrival in Florentine territory was well documented by ambassadors.[50] The Florentines did not want him and the overt anti-Visconti baggage he brought with him.[51]

But here, as elsewhere, Hawkwood proved a critical factor. Carlo was Hawkwood's brother-in-law and was drawn to Florence by his presence there. Carlo had already prevailed on Hawkwood to take action against Giangaleazzo when Bernabò was first deposed. On arriving in Florentine territory, Carlo went straight to Montecchio and eventually settled at Cortona. Florentine officials tried to stop him, but there was little they could do.[52] Carlo's attitude was clearly bellicose; he openly advocated war with Milan. This appears to have had an effect on Hawkwood, who now became more open in his disdain for the machinations of diplomats and is quoted at this time as saying, "The deeds in Lombardy require action not show."[53]

Carlo's negative impact was exacerbated by the almost simultaneous arrival in Florence of Antonio della Scala, the deposed ruler of Verona, recently defeated by Giangaleazzo. As with Carlo, Florentine officials worked hard to distance themselves from their visitor. They sent embassies to Giangaleazzo assuring him that they intended to "rush" Antonio's departure.[54] Gravely ill and in difficult financial straits, Scala did indeed leave quickly. But Carlo Visconti stayed. Officials kept close watch on him and did their best to downplay their connection with him. This proved especially important, as it became progressively clear that Carlo was a man of rather limited virtue. The Minerbetti chronicle called him "base and foolish."[55]

He and Hawkwood, however, developed a close rapport and remain close until the outbreak of the war with Milan in 1390.

The events, notably the presence of Carlo, exposed the dangers in keeping Hawkwood on the payroll. In May and June, Florentine officials again debated whether to dismiss Hawkwood. For his part Hawkwood indicated a willingness to leave the Florentine service and go south to join the war in Kingdom of Naples. Hawkwood had become increasingly frustrated by the many and conflicting opinions and divergent orders from his superiors.[56]

The debates in the Florentine Signoria of 16 June reveal a divergence of opinion. Lotto Castellani spoke in favor of Hawkwood's departure, citing both the money and anxiety it would spare, and advised that the city hire the less expensive, less controversial Bernard de La Salle in Hawkwood's stead.[57] Ludovico Banchi concurred but suggested that the city hire the German captain Johann von Eberhardsweiler. Bono di Taddeo advocated avoiding foreign mercenaries altogether and instead employing a cavalry of two hundred citizens, a move that had the added advantage that the city could pay the soldiers below the current market rate.[58] Giovanni Biliotti argued that the city should not allow Hawkwood to leave until it reached an agreement with Siena and the rest of Tuscany and made an alliance with Bologna.[59] Alessandro di Niccolo, on the other hand, favored retaining Hawkwood, whom he judged "greatly useful to the commune."[60] Alessio Baldovinetti and Aliotto Quarata agreed and counseled that Hawkwood be denied permission to leave.[61]

Florence ultimately decided to keep Hawkwood rather than let him go. Tension with Siena increased in July and August. Giangaleazzo's projected conquest of Padua was well under way, and by July his army had penetrated deep into Paduan territory. The situation had become too unsettled.

The city decided instead to build up its forces. It now augmented Hawkwood's band with the very companies against whom he had recently defended the city. Florence hired both Johann von Eberhardsweiler and Bernard de La Salle, who had remained in Tuscany after their raid on Siena.[62] The instructions given to the envoys who recruited the men betray the sense of impending war. The envoys were to tell the captains that they would "soon be needed for certain things that may soon happen." Efforts were made to hire Beltoft, but he proved difficult. Florence offered him at one point a monthly salary of 3,000 florins, but he turned down the offer and signed with Urban VI.[63] This was not before he rode off with some advance money the Florentines had given him. Officials charged Beltoft with fraud and disregarding his signed and sealed promises.[64] But the Florentines ultimately got the better of Beltoft. They managed, through bribery, to separate the majority of his English corporals from his brigade.[65]

The defectors went directly to Hawkwood, who was stationed along the Sienese border at Cortona with his brother-in-law Carlo. Hawkwood waited for the renegade corporals of Beltoft's band with bags of money. He received them "kindly and sweetly" on Florence's behalf and assured them of the "affection" that the city felt for the action they had taken.[66] The group was soon joined by Johann von Eberhardsweiler's band. The Sienese watched the developments closely. "Messer John Hawkwood and corporals in great quantity and from many parts," wrote an ambassador, "go to Cortona, where they will serve under his baton and banner."[67] A Lucchese envoy estimated the combined force at between 4,000 and 4,800 horses.[68]

Shortly after the union of their band, Eberhardsweiler returned to Germany. He left his fellow German Konrad Aichelberg, the nephew of Lutz von Landau, in command.[69] Aichelberg's brigade contained a brash young corporal, Konrad Prassberg, who would later figure prominently in Hawkwood's life.[70] Aichelberg and Hawkwood, however, did not get along. Hawkwood found Aichelberg arrogant and desirous of too much authority and autonomy. A Lucchese ambassador stationed at Perugia summed up the problem succinctly: "The dispute is this— Konrad wants to call himself the captain of the Germans and John does not want him to do so."[71] Hawkwood wanted to be commander of the entire army, which as titular captain of war was indeed his right. The Florentines sent envoys to help smooth over the difficulty.

Officially Florence disavowed any direct connection to their large army, now amassed along the Sienese border. They tried to pass it off as a free company. In a strict legal sense, this was true. All the captains, including Hawkwood, were hired by means of *condotte in aspetto*, which technically left the men and their bands "free" to take employment elsewhere, but with the stipulation that they "not in any way be against our commune and that they come to our service when we ask."[72] The Sienese dismissed the denials. "It is all well and good that they say no," said an ambassador stationed near Cortona, "but this much is certain, the soldiers are at the command of that commune!"[73]

At the same time that Florence built up its army, it angrily complained about Milan doing the same.[74] Officials accused Visconti of maintaining "secret agreements" with German and English troops, of amassing them near Bologna, and, more generally, of evoking "wonder and suspicion" throughout Italy.[75] Some even blamed Visconti for the failure to hire Beltoft, claiming that the English captain was in Milanese service.[76] As a counter to Visconti pretensions in Siena, Florence in late August 1388 made an alliance with Bologna, which, among other things, allowed the two cities to share military costs.[77] Bologna was, as we have seen, a frequent target of Visconti expansion, and, for Florence's purposes, key to trade routes north.

In September Giangaleazzo tried to eliminate Carlo Visconti by a favorite stratagem, poison. According to the Florentine Minerbetti chronicle, the Milanese ruler corrupted a local doctor in Cortona, promising to pay him 30,000 florins to kill both Carlo and the lord of Cortona. The doctor placed the poison in a "most beautiful" basket of figs and in several flasks of wine and offered them to Carlo. Before the intended victim took the fateful step, a letter arrived from John Hawkwood, warning of the plot. The doctor confessed under threat of torture and was drawn and quartered. The four pieces of his body were hung on the four gates of the city.[78]

## Into the Kingdom

Meanwhile the Florentines faced the problem of what to do with Hawkwood's large army. For all the rhetoric and subterfuge, the war had not yet materialized. Indeed, by the early fall, the worst of the crisis at Montepulciano had subsided, and negotiations had gained momentum. Hawkwood's brigade, ill fitted and bellicose, was as much a threat to peace as a protection from enemies. Florentine leaders again debated their options in the Signoria, some advocating a reduction of forces, others seeking more aggressive measures. There was a growing sense that the real enemy of Florence was Milan. One official even suggested that Hawkwood be sent north to oppose Visconti directly at Padua.[79]

Hawkwood himself was frustrated by the confusion, by the many and conflicting opinions and the divergent orders from his superiors.[80] Even in the best of circumstances it was difficult to hold together a stationary brigade, positioned at the border, cut off from the prospects of profits from booty. As a "free"company, the soldiers received only half pay. Rumors circulated that they wished to leave Florentine service. A Lucchese ambassador in Perugia reported several possibilities: that Hawkwood would go with a portion of his men either to the Abruzzi and the Marches to conduct raids; to Apulia and Rome to work for Margherita of Durazzo; or to Lombardy to fight on his own account against Milan.[81]

The report involving Queen Margherita turned out to be the most accurate. Hawkwood decided to take up the service in the Kingdom of Naples that he had long contemplated. In addition to profits for his soldiers, employment there held out the possibility for him of receiving lucrative estates, such as had been granted to him in the past by Margherita's husband, Charles.[82]

On 3 November 1388 Hawkwood's chancellor, Jacopo da Pietrasanta, met with Margherita's ambassadors in the town of Todi, just south of Perugia. The next day the two sides signed an accord. Pietrasanta reported the deal to officials in Lucca but gave only its barest outlines. He excused himself on the grounds that Hawk-wood had not permitted him to say anything else.

But as Hawkwood prepared to depart, Florentine officials apparently had mis-givings. On the same day that Hawkwood concluded the deal with Margherita, they spontaneously offered him a payment of 3,000 florins. They fashioned it a "loan" for his army, but it did not require restitution if Hawkwood stayed in Florence.[83] A week later, officials granted Hawkwood another subsidy, to recruit additional soldiers from Beltoft for Florentine service.[84]

The efforts to retain Hawkwood grew more strident in the days and weeks that followed. They gained impetus from reports of Visconti machinations in anti-governmental conspiracies in Bologna and of Milanese military gains against Padua.[85] On 26 November Giangaleazzo's armies entered the city of Padua. This gave him mastery over the Lombard plain. The news coincided with the discovery that Florence's chief ambassador to Milan, Buonacorso di Lapo di Giovanni, had been corrupted and had betrayed important secrets in return for bribes.[86]

Hawkwood ignored Florentine pleas to return and slowly made his way south. Florence continued to send ambassadors to try to dissuade him. The envoy Ghino di Roberto reached Hawkwood near Perugia in early December and assured the captain that the posturing was over and that a military strike against the Visconti was at hand. He suggested that Hawkwood return via the Romagna and quarter his troops for the winter at the expense of Antonio da Montefeltro, lord of Urbino, with whom Florence was currently at odds.[87] Giovanni Orlandini followed Ghino to warn Hawkwood of the bleak conditions in the kingdom: "It does not seem to us that it is good either for him or for us or for his brigade to go into the Kingdom during winter time, as it is now. The weather is bad and there is nothing there, because the land has been destroyed and consumed by the long wars."[88] Hawk-wood replied to Orlandini that the battles in the kingdom would only improve his brigade and that Florentine officials could, in any case, still call him when they needed him.[89]

The army Hawkwood took with him to the kingdom was composed of English, German, and Italian soldiers, estimated at thirteen hundred lances. The corporals were mostly English and mostly named John: John Wenlock, John Sale, Johnny Butler, John Colpepper, Johnny Svim (?), Johnny Liverpool, John Lye, and John Balzan.[90] Hawkwood's brother-in-law Carlo Visconti commanded his own small contingent. True to his reputation, Carlo comported himself poorly, stealing and plundering on the way out of Florentine territory.[91]

Hawkwood advanced via Tivoli past Rome to Capua, where (March 1389) he joined forces with Otto of Brunswick, both a former comrade and a former foe.[92]

Otto, who had recently undertaken Margherita's cause, commanded an army of three thousand lances. The two captains planned an assault on the city of Naples, the stronghold of the French Angevins, garrisoned by Lord Mountjoy. Margherita gave her personal support to the offensive by traveling to Naples with an armada of warships. She hoped that her presence would induce loyalists within the city to rise up on her behalf.[93]

This did not happen. Mountjoy and the French garrison held on admirably, repulsing successive waves of attack by Hawkwood and Brunswick over several weeks.[94] Hawkwood and Margherita's army was forced to retreat in mid-April 1389 to Aversa.[95]

The military situation was exacerbated by the dire conditions in the kingdom. As the Florentines had warned, there was a lack of material resources and little money with which to pay armies. Reports indicate that what scarce supplies existed were more successfully gathered by the French Angevin side. A Sienese ambassador claimed that they "took the best soldiers."[96] The French antipope helped facilitate the payment of his troops by issuing a decree permitting the stripping of local churches of their silver and gold.[97]

Hawkwood stayed in southern Italy for six months and gained little. The Florentines, for their part, kept in close contact with the captain and continued to press their cause. They sent Pera Baldovinetti on 6 February with instructions to appeal to Hawkwood's sense of honor—"beseech Hawkwood affectionately and remind him that we did things for him and provided services that we didn't have to."[98] Donato Strada was sent a month later with orders to appeal to Hawkwood's greed, to promise money "for himself and his brigade."[99]

Hawkwood showed little inclination to do as the Florentines asked. He responded to the embassies by suggesting that Florence hire someone else in his stead. He recommended several comrades, including a relatively obscure captain, Piero della Corona, and a company of Breton mercenaries, with whom he had recently fought in Naples. Frustrated Florentine officials dispatched Guido Cavalcanti on 2 April 1389 with instructions to take a more blunt tone.

> Go find John Hawkwood wherever he is; and after salutations, tell him how we asked him through our two ambassadors that he come to our services, according to which he is obligated by agreements he has with us. And remind him how he did not come, but instead sent here his envoys making excuses and begging us to take into our service Messer Piero della Corona and the Bretons, who are in Naples. Therefore, from the start, ask him to serve us . . . for four months beginning the day he arrives in the plain near Spoleto or in the plain of Viterbo and Montefiascone. . . . And tell him to have 1,000 lances and 500 infantry and crossbowmen. And all these things he is

required to do according to the agreements we have with him. . . . We ask that you put this in writing. . . . And tell John also that because we are sure that he does not have but 500 of the required 1,000 lances we are happy to take into our service Messer Piero della Corona and the Bretons that are in Naples, following his counsels and doing such courtesy for him that they will remain content.[100]

Hawkwood's recalcitrance toward Florentine ambassadors was probably little more than a ploy to gain the best possible terms. The prospects in the kingdom were bleak; both sides had by mid-April demobilized their armies. There is also evidence that Hawkwood was himself experiencing a financial crisis. He was cited at this time in the Mercanzia court in Florence for unpaid debts worth 2,000 florins. Through his representatives Hawkwood placed in pawn his Florentine properties, including his estates at La Rocchetta and San Donato in Polverosa.[101]

Indeed, Hawkwood's hard-line approach gained for him advance money, including a first month's salary, made payable in Rome, though Florentine officials had insisted that they would not give him anything until he arrived back in Florence. By late April/early May there were indications that Hawkwood intended to return to the city. The Lucchese ambassador Andrea da Volterra reported two contrary rumors: that Hawkwood would work again for Margherita for another six months, in return for lands and property; or that he would go to Florence. "This last news," wrote Andrea, "seems more certain."[102] The report was confirmed by Sienese spies who spotted Hawkwood advancing north in May from Tivoli toward Tuscany. Two Lucchese businessmen stationed in Florence, Bartolomeo Forteguerra and Michele Guinigi, indicated that Hawkwood intended to serve Florence with five hundred lances.[103]

While the Florentines worked to bring Hawkwood back to Florence, Giangaleazzo Visconti actively tried to prevent it. Hawkwood had been an important topic in the ongoing diplomatic discussions between the two sides conducted throughout the winter and spring.[104] In a meeting of ambassadors in Milan on 20 January 1389, Visconti specifically asked that as an act of good faith, to lessen overall tensions, Florence disband Hawkwood's forces, as well the others in Florentine employ. Since Hawkwood was then just beginning his service in the kingdom, Florence, with justification, claimed that it could do little with him. But Florentine envoys went much further; they spoke of the inherent impossibility of the task, how, "as Giangaleazzo himself knew well, we do not have the power to breakup the companies." They admitted to an existing relationship—"certain pacts"—with Hawkwood, but they pointed to the Englishman's strong will and independent ways and denied that they could control his actions.[105]

What Florence said was true, strictly speaking. But Hawkwood was by spring on his way to the city, and despite the peace negotiations, Florence was making every effort to build its army in opposition to similar efforts by Visconti. In addition to Hawkwood, Florence actively recruited for service the captains Konrad Aichelberg and Bernard de La Salle with contingents of 400 and 315 lances, respectively, as well as several lesser-known soldiers.[106]

## Return to Florence and the Drift toward War, June–September 1389

Hawkwood left the kingdom to take up Florentine employ in May. He advanced north from Tivoli to Borgo San Sepolcro with a force of 400 lance and 500 infantry.[107] The Florentines had wanted a larger brigade. They requested that Hawkwood bring 1,000 lances, including Otto of Brunswick. The Englishman was either unwilling or unable to do this.

The Florentine ambassadors Andrea Vettori and Giovanni di Giovanni Iacobi met Hawkwood at Borgo San Sepolcro and inspected his band. The review was conducted in in an open field, where the entire company could be easily viewed. There were concerns that the service in the kingdom, where supplies were few, may have resulted in a poorly equipped band. The ambassadors used the opportunity to admonish Hawkwood one more time for taking so long to return to Florence: "We are amazed that you put off for so long coming here, despite having had from us so many requests!!"[108] The ambassadors then diligently went about their task, writing the names of the soldiers and the quantity and quality of horses, armor, weapons, and all military material.

After the inspection, Hawkwood went in person to Florence to sign a contract for service. The pact was for six months at a salary of 500 florins. It carefully defined Hawkwood's band as a "free company," thus technically not part of the regular Florentine army or overall military buildup. Hawkwood had the important right, however, to hire and fire his own men.[109] The band was stationed between Perugia and Cortona, near Hawkwood's fort at Montecchio.

The mood in Florence had changed since Hawkwood's last tour of duty. The preparations for war were more apparent, as was a pervasive sense that diplomacy could no longer avert conflict but only delay it.[110] The peace talks with Visconti fell through in late May 1389, at about the same time Hawkwood arrived in the city. Florence complained that its envoys had been "led by the nose" by Giangaleazzo. Visconti himself expressed the sentiment that war was imminent, though he was neither inclined nor prepared to initiate it.[111] Even the language of Hawkwood's contract reflected the more bellicose attitude. His initial pact in 1387 called generically for "service to Florence," but the contract of May 1389 called "for the defense, preservation, protection and security of the liberty of the state, city and commune of Florence and for resistance and offense against the enemies of the said commune." That same clause appears in the contracts of all Florentine captains hired in 1389.[112]

Hawkwood's absence had brought some stability to the Sienese border. But just prior to Hawkwood's return, Konrad Aichelberg and Bernard de La Salle conducted a raid up to the gates of Siena.[113] This rekindled passions. Siena renewed its appeals to Giangaleazzo for a union against Florence and spoke openly of war.[114] Officials countered Hawkwood's presence by hiring the Italian mercenary Paolo Savelli with three hundred lances. Giangaleazzo Visconti assumed the cost of the band.[115] Visconti also sent Giovanni d'Azzo degli Ubaldini to environs of Bologna. The Minerbetti chronicle judged the hatred of the Sienese so strong that "they would give themselves to the devil if they thought that it would undo the arrogance of the Florentines."[116]

Florence built its army around Hawkwood. As they had done the previous summer, officials joined Hawkwood's brigade to that of Konrad Aichelberg. They sent Gino Cortegiano to oversee the conjunction, which last time had produced resentments. There were again concerns because Konrad's salary was less than Hawkwood's, although the size of his brigade was the same. Cortegiano met first with Konrad and flattered him. He told the captain that the city "loved him above all the others."[117] He then reminded him that he had already earned more from Florence in the past year than Hawkwood and hinted at future possibilities of income. Cortegiano met next with Hawkwood. He took an entirely different approach: no flattery, just business. Cortegiano stated his case briefly, that Hawkwood would soon have occasion to use the army, which would bestow on him "honor and profit."[118]

Hawkwood's and Aichelberg's brigades were joined to those of Bernard de La Salle and the Italian captains Broglia da Chieri and Brandolino da Bagnacavallo—the last Hawkwood's old comrade. The overall force consisted of 3,000 lances and 1,000 infantry and was stationed near Cortona.[119]

Although war seemed inevitable, neither side wanted to be the first to initiate it. Florence was particularly eager not to alienate Perugia, Lucca, and Pisa, which had not yet committed themselves to Giangaleazzo Visconti. Florentine officials had stressed this to Hawkwood when he first arrived at Borgo San Sepolcro. They told him to behave circumspectly and counseled him at that time in particular "not to offend" Perugia, whose lands were then close by. Perugia, like Siena, had ongoing discussions with Visconti and had recently received a contingent of troops from him. Officials continued through envoys to remind Hawkwood—and all other captains—to respect their neighbors.[120] Florence even urged caution with respect to Siena, whose goodwill was long lost. The Florentines sent Gino Cortegiano on 25 June 1389 to extract from Hawkwood "written and verbal promises" that he would leave Siena alone. Others ambassadors, including Simone Altoviti, Lorenzo Machiavelli, and Matteo Arrighi, were sent to Hawkwood within a small space of time to remind him to respect Sienese land.[121] The same opinion was voiced in the Signoria.[122]

But the army at Cortona possessed a momentum of its own. Carlo Visconti was again in the Florentine camp and eagerly urged war. Konrad Aichelberg had a personal feud with members of the Farnese clan, whose patrimony lay perilously close to the southern edge of Sienese territory. Both sides suffered the effects of plague and famine, which forced them to move about in search of food and safe haven, thus heightening suspicion. Reports indicate that Hawkwood and Aichelberg were low on supplies.[123] A young noblewoman, Franceschina, whose properties lay close to where the soldiers were stationed, complained that her estates were overrun by Hawkwood's men searching for food.[124] The situation did little for the relationship of the two captains, who continued to get on badly and whose mutual animosity engendered poor discipline in the rank and file.[125] Hawkwood, despite repeated warnings, displayed open hostility toward Siena, which he saw as little more than a proxy for Giangaleazzo of Milan. He was encouraged by the presence of Carlo Visconti and Francesco Novello, the son of the deposed leader of Padua, who was now in the Florentine camp and anxious to begin war.

A game of cat and mouse developed along the Sienese border. The sources give an almost daily account of feints, insults, and accusations, as the two opposing armies stationed themselves just miles away from each other. Separating fact from fiction is almost impossible. The situation reached its most intense phase in the first weeks of August, ironically just after a new round of peace negotiations were initiated by Pietro Gambacorta, the ruler of Pisa.

The two armies themselves became drawn into the war of words between the states. On 10 August, Hawkwood wrote to the Sienese complaining about their buildup of soldiers and about their general "lack of courtesy" shown to his brigade. He claimed that his army was merely a "free company" and not in Florentine pay.[126] The Sienese responded by dismissing Hawkwood's claims and in turn accusing him of making threatening moves on the border and trying to harm their land "without any cause." They mocked the notion that Hawkwood and Aichelberg were really free men, saying that "everyone knows you are in Florence's employ." Hawkwood's corporal Konrad Prassperg took up the argument from there. He wrote his own letter, expressing "amazement" at Sienese suspicions. "By my faith I swear to you that we are free men, and that they [the Florentines] beg us truly not to go into your territory." The Sienese dismissed Prassberg's denial as the "the counsel and advice of the old wolf"—that is, Florence.[127]

Florence clearly played the part of the old wolf. On August 10, the same day that Hawkwood wrote to Siena and Florentine envoys were meeting with their counterparts from Siena and Milan, Florence sent a secret embassy to Hawkwood to advise him of what to do when the inevitable conflict broke out. The Florentines told him that in the case of battle he should flee "to a fortified place near the border," where both sides could easily see him. He was to pretend to be frightened, so that the enemy would believe he was uninvolved. The Florentines would then funnel food and provisions to him, but in such a manner that it looked "as if they forced you to give it to them."[128]

Violence indeed broke out, four days later. Not surprisingly, it was Carlo Visconti who started it. Claimed to have been insulted by Visconti's troops on the Sienese side, he crossed into enemy territory. Hawkwood followed, raising the battle cry "Long live the commune of Florence and Carlo Visconti." He was met by Paolo Savelli and the Sienese army, which countered with the cry "Long live Siena and the count of Virtù."[129] The engagement lasted for seven hours. The Sienese chronicle claimed that Savelli ultimately held the field. The Florentine chronicle said that Hawkwood got the better of the battle.[130]

The Florentines disavowed any connection with the affair. They claimed that Hawkwood acted on his own and publicly rebuked him for it. An ambassador was sent directly to Siena to tell officials there that Hawkwood acted entirely alone, spurred on by his personal dislike of Visconti, not by a desire to make war on Siena.

Privately, however, Florentine officials acted very differently. They admonished Hawkwood not so much for his action but for foolishly allowing his men to shout "Long live the commune of Florence," a battle cry that made the Florentines seem directly responsible for the action. They instructed Hawkwood to be more discreet. They then instructed him to return to Sienese territory and stay for a month, "doing as much damage as possible."[131] They offered him 1,000 florins for the service. To help they gave him detailed reconnaissance on the state of Sienese forces as well conditions within the city. "Siena is in bad shape," Hawkwood was told; "they have very great famine and lack both flour and bread."[132] The time to strike was now. Officials sent similar instructions to the other captains.

The war between Florence and Siena had now de facto begun. In subsequent weeks, Florentine officials did little to conceal their intentions. On 18 August, officials openly sent an envoy to Hawkwood with instructions to offer him the service of a hydraulic engineer to cut off water to Siena. On 2 September, Jacopo Arrighi went to Hawkwood to urge him to spend another month in Sienese territory. On 6 September, Biliotto Biliotti and Guido di Messer Tommaso prevailed on Hawkwood to ravage the Sienese Maremma, where there would be plenty of food and where he could link forces with Betholdo Orsini, the Count of Savona, an ardent enemy of the Sienese. On 26 September Lorenzo Machiavelli assured Hawkwood that if he needed money while in Sienese lands, the Florentines would find a way to get it to him. The Sienese chronicler clearly discerned the trot of the old wolf. "The Florentines continually ride on our lands," wrote the Sienese chronicler; "they destroy the roads, plot mischief and rob in the countryside of Siena."[133]

The state of affairs brought the consummation of Siena's relationship with Milan. On 22 September 1389 Siena placed itself under the protection of Giangaleazzo.[134] Visconti sent his treasurer Giovanni della Porta to the city to help pay for and arrange the hire of more troops. The Sienese worked to keep the arrangement secret from the Florentines, without success. Florence sent envoys throughout the peninsula and to Stephen of Bavaria, who was married to one of Bernabò's daughters, seeking troops.[135]

The Sienese-Florentine conflict threatened to burgeon into a pan-Italian war. But ambassadors continued to discuss peace under the auspices of Piero Gambacorta of Pisa. The talks produced a settlement on 9 October 1389. Milan promised not to seek to extend its influence south of Modena, while Florence agreed not to interfere with affairs up north. The contracting parties resolved to submit all future disagreements to arbitration and to deal collectively with the problem of mercenary bands. Each was required to reduce its armies, and Florence was specifically required to divest itself of Hawkwood.[136]

No one was satisfied. Siena hoped not for peace but for Visconti's assistance in war. The Florentines waited for the next crisis. Its lack of faith in Milan was such that the day after the pact, it signed a separate accord for a league with Bologna, Pisa, Lucca, and Perugia, which was little more than a precautionary measure against Milan. Hawkwood, in the meantime, descended south for his last turn of service in the kingdom. He did little more than bide his time, waiting for the call to return for the war against Milan.

# CHAPTER THIRTEEN

# The War against Milan, 1390–1392

Italians! Finally, the viper has undertaken to vomit forth the poison
it had concealed.

*Florentine letter to Bologna, 3 May 1390.*

Hawkwood's tour of duty in the Kingdom of Naples was brief. In April 1390 the long-anticipated war between Milan and Florence began. The Florentines recalled Hawkwood, and this time he moved quickly to return.

Hawkwood was in Rome when the news reached him. To confuse enemies who might oppose his passage north, Hawkwood sent messengers to seek safe-conducts from towns along several routes, and he then advanced by obscure and difficult passes through the Sienese Maremma. Sienese operatives nevertheless caught sight of him. "Today, the 27th of April at nones," wrote the podestà of Grosseto to Sienese officials, "John Hawkwood passed by with 150 horses, 300 infantry and a good 50 archers, and keeps to the road along the 'mouth' of Castiglione." The Sienese hoped that the local inhabitants would resist the Englishman, but they did not.[1]

Hawkwood and his men arrived worn, but safely, in Florence. "The people rejoiced," wrote the Minerbetti chronicler, "because he was the best leader of men who was then in Italy, and all the men-at-arms . . . had fear of his wise counsels and measures."[2] Florentine officials formally signed Hawkwood to a contract on 30 April calling for him to command a brigade of two hundred lances with an unspecified number of longbowmen for one year.[3] That same day the Sienese officially declared war on Florence, sending the symbolic "bloody glove of challenge."[4]

The Milanese-Florentine war ranks as one of the great events of the early Renaissance. Scholars have viewed it as a turning point not only in the political history of the Italian peninsula but also in its intellectual and cultural history.[5] The war involved much of northern and central Italy: Milan allied itself with

Siena, Perugia, the Gonzaga of Mantua, the Estense of Ferrara, and the Malatesti of Rimini; Florence joined with Bologna, Francesco Novello da Carrara of Padua, and Astorre Manfredi of Faenza. The two great seaport trading centers Venice and Genoa remained nominally neutral, while Pisa was pushed in both directions. Florentine propagandists fashioned the struggle as one of liberty versus tyranny. For the diarist Gregorio Dati, the contest evoked images of Rome's great battle with Hannibal—Milan cast in the role of a latter-day Cathage.[6]

The most bitter and most overlooked theater of activity of the war was along the Sienese border. There the standard conventions of fourteenth-century warfare—capture rather than murder, maneuver rather than battle—were largely ignored. "For everyone of ours killed," wrote the Sienese ambassadors Augostino d'Ugolino and Neroccio di Mariano, "we killed one of theirs; and many villagers from those castles of Valdinievole who descend to the plain to do business, are killed, for no one wants prisoners."[7] Espionage and treachery also played large roles. Florentine officials complained to their commissary Donato Acciaiuoli that "spies come everyday from Siena." "We want you to give the order," they instructed Donato, "that . . . whoever comes from Siena be seized, and, if suspected of spying, be hanged."[8] Officials implored Donato to punish first and ask questions later.

Most of the major mercenaries of the era took part in the conflict. Ugolotto Biancardi, Taddeo and Jacopo dal Verme, Facino Cane, and Paolo Savelli fought for Giangaleazzo. It is often said that Hawkwood was the only major mercenary not in the Milanese camp, but this is not true. The Florentines and their allies also had the services of the Italian captain Giovanni da Barbiano, the German commanders Konrad Aichelberg and Konrad Prassberg, and the Englishman John Beltoft. Beltoft shared with Aichelberg command of Sienese operations, giving the Florentines a strong English presence on both fronts. At no time, as some assert, did Konrad von Landau work for Florence and its allies. The mistake is based on a confusion of Aichelberg for Landau, both of whom were known locally as "Conte Currado." Landau had left Italy for Germany several years earlier, after a bitter row with the Bolognese and some minor service to Verona. Bolognese officials had accused Konrad of treachery and painted a *pittura infamante* of him on the town wall. Landau responded by drawing his own *pittura infamante* on the saddle of his mount, depicting the local politicians hanged by their feet, held collectively in the hand of a gigantic whore.[9]

Hawkwood consulted with Florentine authorities and then went to Bologna to oversee the defense of that strategically vital city.[10] He sent the majority of his brigade in advance and arrived with forty lances in the middle of May.[11] He conferred briefly with Bolognese officials. Afterward, he rode northeast along the Via Emilia to the town of San Giovanni in Persiceto to join the main body of the Bolognese army, commanded by Giovanni da Barbiano. The enemy army, led by the Veronese captain Jacopo dal Verme, was encamped just ten miles away at Crevalcuore. As was customary, the Milanese army contained many prominent Bolognese exiles, including members of the Peppoli, da Panico, and Galluzzi clans.[12] The Florentine-Bolognese army had numerous Milanese exiles, most notably Lucchino, Francesco, and Carlo Visconti, the last Bernabò's son and Hawkwood's brother-in-law. Carlo had reached camp several days after Hawkwood, at the head of thirty horsemen.[13]

Hawkwood's reputation preceded him. When he arrived at the Bolognese camp, the Milanese army quickly withdrew from Crevalcuore, back beyond Modena, all the way to Parma. "They fled," wrote the Bolognese chronicler, "because . . . they saw the great multitude of men joining our camp, and because John Hawkwood came to our camp; so that . . . they left from fear."[14] The Milanese diarist Corio condemned the retreat as one of "little honor."[15] Hawkwood and Barbiano pursued the Milanese army and captured prisoners and booty.

For the next month or so, the war along the Bolognese front consisted mostly of raids and counterraids of limited scope. It was harvest time, and both sides did their best to impede the other. Hawkwood and Barbiano rode on Modenese lands, harassing farmers, stealing grain, and seizing cattle. A small brigade of men burned the fortress outside the town of Visdomini, near Ferrara.[16] The Milanese army did the same. A contingent of about hundred lances advanced almost to the gates of Bologna, where it harassed local communities, intercepted the harvest, and captured prisoners and cattle.[17] Dal Verme and the main body of the army meanwhile conducted raids on Barbiano's personal possessions near Bagnacavallo. The attacks forced Giovanni to ride out with his men to protect his lands.[18]

The strategy and rhythm of the war were determined in large part by continuing effects of plague and crop failure, which rendered goods scarce. "They change camp every two or three days," wrote the Lucchese ambassador Francesco Dombellinghi from Bologna, "because it is necessary in order to live."[19] At the same time, both sides sought the advantage by increasing the size of their forces. Florence recruited soldiers from inside Italy and from abroad, as did Milan. Florence added the Italian captain Rinaldo Orsini with 50 lances and 350 infantry and Hawkwood's old nemesis, Astorre Manfredi of Faenza, with 70 lances.[20] Milan firmed up alliances with the Count of Savoy and Hawkwood's first Italian employer, the Marquis of Montferrat, who sent substantial contingents.[21]

Neither side showed eagerness to engage the other directly. "They don't wish to put themselves to the test in combat," wrote Francesco Dombellinghi, "because in battles one runs risks, and well they realize that they can win through exhaustion and by lack of money."[22]

The first turning point of the war came in the middle of June. On the night of the 18th, Francesco Novello, the deposed lord of Padua, advanced with a relatively small band of 500 lances and 2,000 infantry and retook his native city.[23] Novello's success was unexpected. A Sienese ambassador stationed in Venice described his army as little more than "unwarlike peasants, not accustomed to the exercise of arms."[24] But Novello had judged well the discontent with Visconti rule in the city, and the Milanese, underestimating him, did not send adequate reinforcements.[25] Nevertheless, officials in Bologna were sufficiently skeptical of the news of Novello's victory that they held off celebration for several days until the initial reports could be confirmed. Novello's entry into Padua touched off a spontaneous revolt against the Visconti in Verona.[26]

John Hawkwood aided Novello's enterprise by challenging the main body of the Milanese army at Crevalcuore to battle. On the morning of 21 June he sent his trumpeter with the "bloody glove" to his rival Jacopo dal Verme. The challenge forced the Milanese captain to keep his army in place and thus prevented him from reinforcing the Visconti garrison at Padua, allowing Novello to consolidate his hold on the city.[27] Hawkwood may well have acted of his own accord in this instance, for officials in Florence had that same day sent the captain a strongly worded letter specifically advising him to avoid inciting conflict at all costs.[28] As usual, Hawkwood appears to have understood the situation better than his employer.

Hawkwood did not intend to fight dal Verme, only to a delay him. The Milanese captain left Crevalcuore several days later and advanced north to Padua and Verona. Hawkwood pursued and harassed dal Verme's rear guard, seizing 200 horses and 50 men-at-arms from the retreating army; among the latter was Facino Cane, now captured for the second time in three years by Hawkwood.[29]

The fall of Padua was followed by news from the Sienese front that Giovanni d'Azzo degli Ubaldini had died. Ubaldini had proved himself Milan's most effective commander, retaking several towns along the Florentine-Sienese border, including the much contested city of Lucignano. The Sienese claimed that Ubaldini had been poisoned, citing a tainted basket of cherries, a fruit "of which Giovanni was very fond."[30] The Florentines strongly denied the charge. The Minerbetti chronicler dismissed it out of hand: "Many Sienese say and believe that 'Messer Giovanni d'Azzo' was poisoned, but this was not true." He turned the accusation around and charged the Sienese with poisoning the Florentine commander, Filippo Guazalotti.[31] A well-informed Lucchese ambassador stationed in Florence confirmed, however, the Sienese version and even named the culprits (Mortello Ciardi and his son). He described them as exiles and erstwhile confidants of Ubaldini, who received 10,000 florins and readmittance to good graces of the city for their work.[32] The Bolognese had no doubts that their partners had done the deed. The Bolognese chronicler wrote that "the Florentines gave him [Ubaldini] a good 'hit' to make him die."[33] Privately, the Florentines rejoiced. In a confidential letter to the Dieci di balia in Florence, which directed the war effort, Donato Acciaiuoli called Ubaldini's death "good news."[34]

The momentum of the war now shifted in favor of Florence and Bologna. "Every day," began a letter from the Dieci di balia to Donato Acciaiuoli, "the news from Lombardy gets better."[35] Giangaleazzo Visconti scored a measure of redemption by putting down the revolt in Verona. His captain Ugolotto Biancardi entered the city and then brutalized it, purportedly killing fifteen hundred of the inhabitants.[36] But Milan was on the defensive and needed to reallocate men and resources back north.

The recent events had exposed Milan's weaknesses. Visconti's hold on his subject lands in Lombardy was clearly tenuous. There was widespread dissatisfaction with the heavy burden of taxes resulting from the war. There were also reports of dissension within the Milanese army itself. "We have heard of great divisions," the Dieci di balia wrote to Donato Acciaiuoli on 3 July 1390, "that some seek money and others want to depart and go elsewhere."[37] They instructed Donato to "treat with" the unhappy troops and try to get as many as possible to defect.

Hawkwood returned to Florence to confer with officials and discuss strategy. They made plans for a major offensive that would bring the war to the gates of Milan. For this enterprise, Florentine officials hoped to reinforce Hawkwood's army with that of the German duke Stephen of Bavaria, who had promised to take up arms against the Visconti months earlier.[38] Stephen had a personal stake in the conflict; he was, like John Hawkwood, married to one of Bernabò Visconti's daughters, Taddea, now deceased (and legitimate, unlike Hawkwood's Donnina).[39] Getting Stephen to come to Italy, however, proved difficult. He moved slowly. Florentine officials coaxed him with a large salary—of which 52,000 florins alone were paid out in June—and expectantly commissioned expensive silk banners with the duke's arms for him to carry into battle when he arrived.[40] Stephen ultimately entered Italy via the Friuli region at the end of June with six thousand horses. The Venetians officially denied him passage but tacitly allowed him to move through their territory. On 1 July Stephen made it to Padua, where his presence helped Francesco Novello consolidate his hold on the city and capture the local citadel, which had remained in enemy hands.[41]

Unfortunately, Stephen's momentum quickly dissipated. Rather than mobilize for an offensive against Milan, the duke began negotiating on his own accord: first with Queen Margherita of Durazzo, whom he hoped to marry and thus secure the throne of Naples, and then with Giangaleazzo Visconti in the self-appointed role of herald of peace. This was not what the Florentines wanted, and they complained bitterly throughout the summer.[42] Stephen, unable to obtain his ends, eventually left Padua for Venice and Rome and returned home in the fall. The Florentines claimed fraud, and that Stephen had been corrupted by Visconti bribery.

The behavior of the Duke of Bavaria eliminated the possibility of a large-scale strike against Milan. Hawkwood, Giovanni da Barbiano, and the main body of allied forces remained near Bologna. They conducted modest raids on enemy territory at Modena and farther north just below Parma. The army took care not to harass Parma itself, hoping to foment discord within that city, which was said to be unhappy with Visconti rule. This did not occur, however. Milanese troops staged counterraids on Bolognese lands, and Hawkwood and his men returned south to protect the local harvest. At the same time that he sheltered Bolognese farmers, Hawkwood sent contingents to the countryside of Modena to harass farmers there.[43]

It was, however, Francesco Novello who again forced the issue. With reinforcements sent by Florence and Bologna, Novello moved against the Marquis Alberto d'Este of Ferrara in late September.[44] He attacked the marquis's defenses at Badia Polesine and in a short while took the town, castle, and some surrounding territory. The marquis, whose commitment to the war was never strong, abandoned the Visconti cause and signed a pact of neutrality.[45]

Este's defection gave Hawkwood and his army more room to maneuver. Hawkwood now rode unimpeded on Reggio and then Mantua. He inflicted significant damage on Gonzaga lands, taking "very great prey of beasts and prisoners."[46] Hawkwood then doubled back to Parma, where this time he chose robbery and pillage rather than restraint. The army captured a large amount of booty. As it prepared to return to Bologna, a Milanese force of two hundred lances staged a furious counterattack. A brief but intense battle ensued. Hawkwood won and took the majority of them hostage.

The recent successes gave renewed impetus to plans for a large-scale offensive against Milan. Florence was particularly anxious to regain the initiative lost by Stephen's betrayal. It moved aggressively to augment the army, stepping up efforts to recruit a French force under the command of Jean III, the Count of Armagnac.[47] Like Stephen, Armagnac had a personal connection; his sister Beatrice was married to Carlo Visconti. The French count also knew John Hawkwood from the

English captain's early days and, if Froissart is to be believed, held a very high opinion of him. The Florentines first contacted Armagnac in May, and Carlo Visconti himself had gone personally to appeal to his brother-in-law. But the political situation in France was complicated, and negotiations with the count were confounded by the fact that representatives of Milan were also at the French court seeking French help, as well as trying to undermine Florentine efforts. Giangaleazzo's daughter, Valentina, was married to the Duke of Touraine, the brother of King Charles VI. The king himself contemplated entry into Italy to forcibly install the French claimant to the papacy, Clement VII, in Rome.[48]

Florence secured an agreement with Armagnac in mid-October, calling for six months of service.[49] Officials at home were pleased: "Much is expected from the arrival of the count."[50] At the same time, Florentine officials also tried to hire the renowned Italian captain Alberigo da Barbiano, then working in the Kingdom of Naples. Here too Florence competed directly with Milan, which made its own play for Alberigo. When Florentine officials heard that Alberigo intended to board ship at Ancona for Milan to speak with Giangaleazzo Visconti, they immediately sent their most trusted ambassador, Donato Acciaiuoli, to Alberigo to head him off. Acciaiuoli offered him a six-month contract ("or six more if he wants") at 500 florins a month, the same salary as Hawkwood's. "If he is not content with this and wants greater things," officials wrote to Donato, "don't break with him, but give him good hope, without obligating yourself."[51] Alberigo, whose brother Giovanni was already one of Florence's captains, showed some interest and stopped briefly in Bologna to discuss the matter. He decided, however, to stay out of the conflict altogether.

Florence and its allies went forward with their plans for a major offensive. They chose Padua as the launching point for the offensive against Milan. The city had both symbolic and strategic value. Pier Paolo Vergerio, who witnessed the preparations of the army firsthand, deemed the city a good choice: "Situated between the Alps, Liguria and the Apennines there seems no better place from which to attack the enemy."[52]

Hawkwood and his men reached the city in the middle of November. The allies steadily amassed troops and munitions. Astorre Manfredi arrived in late December with 100 lances, followed shortly thereafter by Giovanni da Barbiano with 400 lances.[53] Florentine budgets show that they sent shipments of arms, including 9,500 arrows for English longbows and 24,350 iron bolts for crossbows.[54] The Minerbetti chronicler counted altogether 2,000 lances and 4,000 infantry and crossbowmen. The number included 200 lances under Francesco Novello and 600 German lances left behind in Padua by Stephen of Bavaria.[55] The Bolognese chronicle gave a slightly more conservative estimate of 2,000 overall lances and 3,000 infantry; the anonymous *Chronicon Estense* put the figures at 3,000 lances, 500 archers, and 2,000 infantry.[56]

Florence dispatched two members of the Dieci di balia to deal with Hawkwood directly. The sides engaged in vigorous negotiations. Aware of his importance to the campaign, Hawkwood sought favors for himself and his men. He got the representatives to agree to remove from his account back in Florence unpaid taxes for which he was liable. Hawkwood was exempt from income or property taxes, but as a landholder in Florence he was, like all citizens, responsible for "extraordinary" exactions, such as forced loans, raised during the war. In this way he ironically helped pay for the very war he fought. Officials canceled his debt, which stood at 22 florins, 2 soldi, and 9 denari.[57] Hawkwood next asked that his personal brigade be increased with one hundred additional longbowmen and that the contract of his fellow Englishman John Balzan, who served as marshal of the army, be renewed for another five months at a salary of 30 florins a month. The Florentine representatives agreed to these demands. They refused, however, to grant Hawkwood's request for increased pay to his corporal John Wenlock and his request that his brother-in-law Carlo Visconti be allowed to accompany the army on its march to Milan. On both points the Florentines were adamant. About Wenlock they said curtly: "We don't want to give him anything!" As for Carlo, they told Hawkwood that they deemed him a liability to the offensive. The aim was not to take Milan, a dubious enterprise at best, but to pressure Giangaleazzo Visconti by sowing discord within the Milanese state. Officials told Hawkwood that they much preferred that Carlo's brother Lucchino ride with the army because he was more popular locally than Carlo and thus more likely to raise revolt. To appease Hawkwood, they offered to "pay Carlo well" to remain behind. The issue clearly left the Florentines frustrated. "Tell Meisser John," the government back home wrote to its negotiators, "not to give so much trouble on behalf of others, since his own [demands] are enough for us."[58]

At the same time, however, the Florentines understood well how crucial Hawkwood was to the operation and made his happiness a top priority. When Christmas came, they gratuitously sent the Englishman a "bonus" of 1,000 florins. Officials spoke openly about the rationale behind the bequest: "because our entire state is in his hands."[59] Florence's sense of urgency was heightened by awareness that its main adversary, Giangaleazzo Visconti, was particularly skilled at subverting captains with bribes. The example of Stephan of Bavaria was still present. Indeed, the Florentines angrily scolded their less well-to-do allies, the Bolognese, about delays in paying soldiers. "Urge by every means," Florentine officials wrote to their ambassador at Padua in the middle of December, "that the Bolognese send their installment to Padua, or otherwise they will destroy our affairs and theirs."[60]

By January the allied army was ready to mobilize. In addition to John Hawkwood, the commanders of the force included Francesco Novello, his half brother Conte da Carrara, Giovanni da Barbiano, and Astorre Manfredi.[61] At Francesco Novello's request, the Florentines transferred the German Konrad Aichelberg from the Sienese front to Padua.[62] This did not please Hawkwood, who did not like Aichelberg, but the Englishman ultimately assented. Aichelberg's band was joined to a smaller one led by another German captain, Konrad Prassberg, recently transferred from Bologna.

The allied plan called for the army to advance first on Vicenza and Verona, two cities in the Milanese dominion deemed ripe for rebellion. To aid its designs, the allied force brought numerous exiles, chief among them Pietro da Polenta, the brother of Samartina, wife and widow of the deposed and now defunct former ruler of Verona, Antonio della Scala.[63] After raising revolts in the two cities, the army would then move west to rendezvous at Milan with the Count of Armagnac's French force, which would descend from the north and east.

Hawkwood and the allied army set out from Padua two hours before sunrise on the morning of 11 January 1391; the exact timing was set by the astrologer Alessio Nicolai, who rode along with Hawkwood's brigade.[64] The Milanese army, estimated at fifteen hundred lances under the command of Jacopo dal Verme and Ugolotto Biancardi, was stationed between Verona and Vicenza.

The allied army proceeded in two parts. Francesco Novello took the main body toward Vicenza along the road at Arzignano. Hawkwood led a smaller force along the Adige River via familiar ground at Castelbaldo. Novello notified the Florentines on 13 January of his progress: "I have, with my men and the greater part of the league army, camped at villa Barbarani and other villas in the environs of the city of Vicenza. There we await the arrival of the distinguished knight John Hawkwood [Johannis Augudh], who reaches us here today."[65] Novello reported little resistance from Milanese forces and a generally good reception from locals. Hawkwood joined Novello and laid siege to a local castle not far from Vicenza. The siege was unsuccessful, and the army then moved on toward the Adige River and into Veronese territory proper. They encountered opposition from a contingent of Visconti troops that contested the passage of the Adige. After a brief skirmish, Hawkwood and Novello succeeded in crossing the river. They raided local territory at Valpantena and Valpolicella and advanced to the walls of Verona. This time the Veronese people did not rise up against their Visconti overlords. The army then moved south to Mantua, hoping to detach the lord Gonzaga from his ally.

The offensive stalled at Mantua. Florentine sources reported dissension in camp, in particular that Hawkwood's old nemesis Astorre Manfredi planned to murder both the English captain and Francesco Novello. The Florentines blamed Giangaleazzo Visconti for seducing Astorre with bribe money. "Everything was done," wrote the Minerbetti chronicler, "at the petition of the Count of Virtu."[66] Pier Paolo Vergerio, however, praised Manfredi and spoke instead of scarce resources, which made provisioning difficult and produced in the army an overall "listlessness" (ignaviam).[67] It was indeed winter, and problems supplying an army were in fact very real. The Milanese had increased the pressure by removing all manner of food and fodder to secure locations. Astorre Manfredi himself, in a letter dated 11 February, described the region around Verona as "desolate and bare."[68] The allies may have had unrealistic expectations about their chances of success in light of Novello's rapid and stunning strike at Padua and had overestimated reports of widespread dissension within the Milanese dominion.

Reports of delays and problems with the Count of Armagnac's army further hampered morale. Florentine officials had expected him to arrive in Italy by November and to be well on his way toward Milan by January. But Armagnac had difficulty collecting men and then difficulty coordinating them and finding adequate billets.[69] His efforts were actively impeded by the king of France and by powerful rivals such as Gaston Phoebus, the Count of Foix, and the mercenary captain Merigot Marches.[70] The Florentines complained in hyperbolic terms that "all of Italy wonders at so much delay."[71]

Florence sent a steady stream of ambassadors hoping to keep Armagnac moving forward. They paid the first installment of his pay, some 50,000 florins, in December. They dispatched two commissaries shortly thereafter to coordinate his passage to Italy.[72] Florence also sent envoys to Hawkwood and Novello urging them to keep their present positions in anticipation of the count. The Florentines particularly feared that the soldiers would be corrupted by Visconti bribes. Donato Acciaiuoli personally met with Francesco Novello on 24 February to urge him "to proceed in a manly fashion to Milan, and . . . in no way to keep counsels with the enemy."[73] A week later Donato returned to Novello with the message that he should do his "utmost" to see to it that "the army does not leave enemy lands, but stays ready and in battle order, to turn toward Milan."[74]

The entreaties did little good. By early March, Armagnac was still not in Italy. The army in Verona began to split apart. Astorre Manfredi went home to Faenza with his men; Hawkwood and Novello retreated to Padua.[75]

The Milanese used the confusion to stage a counterraid on Bologna. The Florentine emissary Leonardo Beccanugi, stationed in Ferrara, described the attack as "very damaging."[76] The larger strategic hope was to draw Hawkwood and the rest of the army out of Lombardy to defend Bologna. But Bolognese defenses, led by Konrad Prassberg, who had split off from Hawkwood's army, ultimately stiffened. Prassberg's actions allowed Hawkwood to launch a retaliatory raid on Vicenza, netting booty and prisoners.[77]

The Florentines meanwhile did not give up on their planned offensive against Milan. But the news from France was not encouraging. Giangaleazzo Visconti's ambassadors continued to work there against Florentine interests. In March a French delegation including Giangaleazzo's son-in-law the Duke of Touraine and the Duke of Burgundy, a steadfast opponent of Armagnac, traveled to Italy to discuss an alliance by which Charles VI would send a force against Bologna in return for Visconti's support for the French king's proposed *voie de fait* on behalf of the antipope. A tentative agreement was made at the end of March. But Armagnac's preparations were not blunted by the king's plans. Florentine ambassadors reported that the count continued to amass men and remained eager to take up their cause.

With so much uncertainty surrounding Armagnac, the Florentines moved aggressively to fix Hawkwood more closely to them. The captain's contract was coming due, but rather than wait until its conclusion, they simply extended it a month early in March. On 8 April, city officials took the grander step of giving Hawkwood a lifetime pension of 2,000 florins a year, as well as dowries of 2,000 florins for each of his three legitimate daughters, a pension of 1,000 florins for his wife, "the noble lady, Donnina," and Florentine citizenship to John himself and "his sons and descendants in the male line, born and yet to be born." The monetary gifts were all tax-free; the 2,000 florins would be paid every three months, on top of the 1,200 florins he was already receiving. The citizenships came with the stipulation that Hawkwood's descendants could never hold office in Florence and Donnina's pension would be paid in the event of the death of her husband and so long as she remained in Florence.[78]

The grant constituted a huge financial windfall for Hawkwood. It is indicative of how seriously the Florentines took the offensive against Milan and how determined—as well as uneasy—the Florentines were in trying to maintain in Hawkwood that "faith in military matters" that they lauded him for in the act. But Florence's actions with regard to Hawkwood were also conditioned by Giangaleazzo Visconti's actions toward his own captain, Jacopo dal Verme. Just prior to the gift to Hawkwood, Visconti granted dal Verme citizenship and landed estates in Milan, followed by citizenship in Verona, Jacopo's home.[79] The utility of such moves was apparent: the emoluments held the captains to their service and reduced the risk of their going over to the enemy. The captains were jealous and well aware of priorities bestowed on each other.

With Hawkwood secured more closely to them, Florence and its allies continued their preparations for a spring offensive. Troops collected again in Padua. The army had many English and German mercenaries in it. The German contingents included the captains Konrad Aichelberg with 150 lances and Konrad Prassperg with 100 lances, as well as lesser-known commanders such as Albert Coiser with 92 lances and Konrad Rodisten with 70 lances.[80] Hawkwood's personal brigade remained at 200 lances, with his countryman John Balzan as marshal.[81] He was joined by numerous smaller English brigades including David Falcan's contingent of 79 lances and 37 longbowmen (double and single archers), Roger Nottingham's band of 10 lances and 5 archers, and similarly sized contingents under William Cook and Richard Croft and several other obscure English corporals.[82] Several of the lances were mixed, with Germans, Italians, Frenchmen, and Hungarians grouped together.[83] The Englishman Johnny Pip's three lances were composed of Hungarian, Italian, and French soldiers.[84]

Bolognese muster rolls add color to the brigades. Konrad Prassberg rode a black horse with a star next to the left eye and a white patch near the left side of its nose; David Falcan, a brown bay horse with a small star in the front; and Roger Nottingham, a brown horse with white spots on its feet.[85] The soldiers assembled behind bright red banners with the insignias of the cities of Florence and Bologna.[86] The Florentines fortified the camp with munitions and supplies. Fiscal accounts include purchases of large quantities of gunpowder.[87] The astrologer Alessio Nicolai was again hired to give "advice about the riding of men at arms." His monthly pay was 15 florins a month, more than anyone in the allied camp except the captains and corporals.[88]

The allies continued to wait for Armagnac, whose arrival constituted, according to a Florentine dispatch, nothing less than the "salvation of the state."[89] On 27 April Florence sent the envoys Giovanni de Ricci and Rinaldo Gianfigliazzi to Armagnac to make sure he received all the money and help he needed.[90]

By early May the army in Padua was ready. The allied battle plan remained essentially the same as it was six months earlier. Hawkwood and his men would move westward through Verona toward Milan, where, as earlier, they hoped to get help from discontents within the Milanese state.[91] Verona had already rebelled, and Hawkwood brought with him numerous contingents of Veronese exiles to help stir things up anew.[92] Cremona was also thought to be ripe for the taking. A local ambassador described the citizens there as "in an ugly temper."[93] Hawkwood would then cross the Oglio and Adda rivers and link up with the Count of Armagnac along the Po, outside Milan. Although the Florentines preferred that Hawkwood take only Lucchino Visconti to help raise rebellion in the environs of Milan, the captain also took along his brother-in-law Carlo.

Francesco Novello's role this time was not to ride on Milan but remain close to Padua and make raids on Visconti positions at Vicenza. Novello's half brother Conte da Carrara captained a Paduan contingent, which traveled with Hawkwood. Along the Sienese frontier, the Florentines put out the call for all-out offensive.[94] The strategy and commitment of resources for this offensive were therefore more ambitious than those of the previous winter.

In consultation with his astrologer, Hawkwood set out from Padua on 10–11 May. His army consisted overall of 2,200 lances, 1,200 crossbowmen, and "many" other infantrymen.[95] They moved in the direction of Vicenza and then west to Verona. The Adige River was crossed with little difficulty. An advance guard of Visconti troops gave only minor resistance. The main body of the Milanese army, fearing the advance of Armagnac, remained closer to home base. To help raise rebellion, Hawkwood instructed his men to take only the food and fodder they needed but to refrain from robbing and looting.[96] When insurrection did not occur, the Englishman pressed on. According to Vergerio, Hawkwood gave a brief speech to his troops, urging them toward Milan, where he assured them that there would be victory and "great earnings."[97] He said that their supplies would hold out, so long as "each man brought to bear the full weight of his spirit against the enemy." But he warned that the path to victory would not be easy. "We must cross many rivers, which only victory will allow us to ford anew."[98] The statement would prove prophetic.

Hawkwood and his army advanced past the Mincio River and into the environs of the city of Brescia. He established personal contact with some discontented nobles he knew in the city of Cremona but was unable to incite an uprising. He moved on toward the Oglio River. Here Hawkwood encountered his first serious resistance. According to the Minerbetti chronicler's account, Taddeo dal Verme and three hundred lances pursued Hawkwood from behind. Hawkwood set a trap. He encouraged dal Verme to follow and placed Konrad Aichelberg and three hundred lances in a "place well hidden." When dal Verme had advanced too far, Hawkwood turned to offer battle. Dal Verme gave the order to retreat but found Aichelberg behind him. Taddeo and his men made a mad, disorganized dash, which resulted in the capture of a hundred men and the death of many others, who drowned in the Oglio River.[99] Vergerio, for his part, does not mention dal Verme or Aichelberg's trap but says only that Hawkwood encountered resistance from the main body of the Visconti army, estimated at 9,000 horse and 3,000 infantry, as he approached the Oglio River. Hawkwood successfully repelled the attack and was able to get across the Oglio. He lost, however, some of his own men, who drowned in the river.[100]

Whatever the particulars, Hawkwood crossed the Oglio River and moved into the territorial space of Bergamo. Here too he skirmished with Visconti troops. The encounter was "contended with much blood," and several high-ranking soldiers on Hawkwood's side were injured, including Conte da Carrara.[101] Hawkwood then proceeded through the valley of San Martino, where anti-Visconti feeling ran high and where local rustics had, a decade earlier, killed Bernabò's son. Hawkwood received help from a friendly Visconti exile, who saw to it that local castles made food available for the army. Hawkwood then advanced to the town of Pandino, due south of Bergamo, just seven kilometers east of the Adda River, twenty-five kilometers east of Milan, and thirteen kilometers northeast of the main body of the Visconti army, which was amassing on the other side of the Adda at Lodi.

It was now June, and Hawkwood's arrival at the banks of the Adda caused great concern throughout the Milanese domain.[102] Giangaleazzo worked to augment his army at Lodi, sending out calls for reinforcements from allies and from within the state.[103] Some reports claimed that the Milanese lord was at the point of despair, weeping "every day from fear and from shame" and holding candlelight vigils to encourage the local populace.[104] This was probably not true, for Visconti continued his calculating ways, trying to buy off members of Hawkwood's band—including Carlo and Mastino Visconti—and making an agreement with the doge of Genoa. But Visconti was hard pressed. Hawkwood's advance on his territory was coupled with an offensive by the Bolognese against Parma and Piacenza. There continued to be reports of disaffection in Cremona and rumors that the citizens were arming themselves for rebellion. On the Sienese front, the Florentines had just launched a major offensive. Most important, there was the anticipated arrival of the Count of Armagnac from the north—a threat made more sinister by its diffuse nature. Visconti operatives could not determine precisely when or where the count would arrive. The Florentines conversely displayed great confidence. "The Count of Virtu," wrote Gregorio Dati, "had the greatest fear he ever had of losing his state."[105]

Meanwhile, Hawkwood and his counterpart at Lodi, Jacopo dal Verme, discomfited each other with frequent maneuvers and raids. At one point, the two agreed to submit the issue to a test of champions. They selected four captains and sixty men. But the contest never came off. Hawkwood and his army then renewed an old psychological ploy. On the day of the feast of John the Baptist (24 June), the patron of Florence, Hawkwood ran a *palio* in full view of the Milanese, signaling to the enemy his confidence of approaching victory.

Posturing aside, Hawkwood was in fact waiting for Armagnac, without whose help he knew he could do little. Unfortunately, however, Armagnac was again delayed. With help from his allies in France and his ambassador Niccolò Spinelli, Giangaleazzzo had bribed five hundred Breton lances in Armagnac's army when the count was at Avignon, readying to enter Italy.[106] Armagnac was constrained to take arms against the traitors, who were defeated only after a series of battles. The count executed several of the leaders, including the renowned captain Bernard de La Salle, who was beheaded just outside Avignon.[107]

The difficulties delayed Armagnac's descent into Italy until June, when Hawkwood was already well advanced into Milanese territory. Once in Italy, Armagnac moved with some dispatch. "Let us cheerfully attack these Lombards," Froissart reported him as saying; "we have a just quarrel and a good captain . . . and we are going to the richest country in the world; . . . and as the Lombards are rich and cowards we shall gain great profits."[108] But the army did not advance in the manner in which the allies had hoped. Rather than taking the proposed route along the right bank of Po River toward Pavia, Armagnac moved through the territory of Asti, needlessly attacking minor fortifications.

Armagnac's delay left Hawkwood isolated and overextended. Supplies had grown perilously scarce. The Milanese, wrote the Carrarese chronicler, "had the wisdom to burn all the straw in the environs of Milan and to secure everyone to the forts."[109] Hawkwood's army lacked food and forage and was reduced to eating its own horses.[110]

The only option was retreat, a maneuver that would involve recrossing three rivers, now swollen from spring rains. Milanese engineers rendered the passage more difficult by rupturing the embankments of the Adige, flooding the nearby plain. According to the Minerbetti chronicler, the Milanese army was so confident that Jacopo dal Verme wrote to Giangaleazzo: "Tell me how you wish me to deal with these enemies of yours, for they are not able to camp, and I will deliver them in your hands in whatever manner you wish."[111] Modern accounts invariably include the story of how dal Verme, "by way of a practical joke," sent Hawkwood a fox in a cage, to say that he had the clever Englishman trapped.[112] But if indeed dal Verme possessed such confidence, it was tempered by the knowledge that, however delayed, Armagnac was on the way and ultimately had to be dealt with. Dal Verme's advantage was therefore not so great as has been portrayed; nor was Hawkwood's situation so desperate.

Hawkwood's retreat from the banks of the Adda was nevertheless a masterpiece, worthy of his nickname "acuto." He manipulated and deceived his opponent and skillfully negotiated the most difficult terrain. He began with a show of strength, challenging dal Verme to battle. Dal Verme accepted and prepared his men. But Hawkwood discomfited dal Verme by immediately moving to within a mile of dal Verme, whereupon he made ostentatious preparations, including knighting ten of his soldiers. Dal Verme, suspicious of Hawkwood's sudden movements, remained in camp. Hawkwood then sent ambassadors to dal Verme to admonish him for not appearing on the field and to reiterate Hawkwood's desire to do battle. Having convinced dal Verme of his intention, Hawkwood prepared his escape. That night he instructed his men to tie the battle banners high on the trees and to light the usual bonfires. He then led the army quietly out of camp, leaving trumpeters there to sound the battle cry as well as horses and provisions to tempt the enemy into pursuit of booty and thus provide his army with still more time to escape.[113] When morning came, dal Verme advanced on Hawkwood's camp only to find it empty.

Hawkwood's maneuver was a worthy one and not unfamiliar to readers of the great military expert Frontinus. In his *Stratagems* the Roman writer recounted a similar ruse effected by Mithridates, king of Pontus, in the 1st century BC whereby he arranged a meeting with the Roman general Pompey, who had him trapped; Mithridates kept the camp fires burning and then fled through back roads under the cover of night. Likewise, Vegetius in his manual instructed generals on the importance of leaving baggage exposed to help cover a retreat.

Dal Verme pursued Hawkwood as far as the Oglio River. With the prospect of Armagnac's arrival he could not go any farther, a fact Hawkwood knew well. To inhibit the pursuers, Hawkwood sent Konrad Aichelberg into the woods to create a trap. Konrad and his men succeeded in harassing some of dal Verme's troop, including the unfortunate Facino Cane. Hawkwood and his men cross the Oglio without incident.

Hawkwood's odyssey was, however, not over yet. He still had to cross the greatly swollen Mincio River and the Adige, whose rupture left the plain submerged. Hawkwood lost a good number of men along the way but managed by 10 July to arrive safely at Castelbaldo. "It seemed," wrote the Minerbetti chronicler, "they escaped from death and returned to life."[114] They received provisions at Castelbaldo and entered Padua two days later.

Dal Verme meanwhile hurried back west to intercept Armagnac, who was now making his way through Piedmont and eastern Lombardy toward Alessandria, a town known primarily as the spot where Italian armies had effectively opposed the great German emperor Frederick Barbarossa. Dal Verme met the French army on 24 July. The French moved forward in poor order and in intense heat and were cut down by dal Verme's more disciplined troop. The Milanese captured Armagnac, who died almost immediately, either from heat exhaustion or, as the Florentines believed, from Visconti poison.[115]

The defeat of the French brought Hawkwood's virtues into sharper relief. Florentine writers like the Minerbetti chronicler blamed Armagnac for displaying "too much boldness," caused by the fact the he was "very young and accustomed to always winning" and, at the same time, unaccustomed "to using his wits."[116]

Conversely, Hawkwood was described as a "wise old man" who "escaped danger through his wisdom."[117] D. M. Manni lauded Hawkwood for his "prudence and vigilance,"[118] while Leonardo Bruni claimed that "no other captain but John Hawkwood would have been able to save the army from such difficulty." "Hawkwood was at an extreme age, which makes captains more prudent and cautious; because the young are most often led by audacity and fervor."[119] Pier Paolo Vergerio thought that Hawkwood's retreat gave him "the last and greatest elevation of his fame" and status in military affairs comparable to that of the ancients.[120]

Despite the praise he received, it would be wrong to credit Hawkwood with outright victory. There can be little doubt that Hawkwood displayed sound judgment, cunning, and great endurance. But it must be stressed that Hawkwood never really had the full attention of dal Verme, who was distracted by the impending arrival of Armagnac. On his way home, Hawkwood incurred rather serious losses. Numerous witnesses attest to the fact that his army was significantly smaller when it arrived in Padua.[121]

Although Hawkwood warrants praise, his counterpart, dal Verme, is at least as deserving. Not only did dal Verme succeed in chasing Hawkwood from the borders of Milan, but he also wiped out an invading army of superior size. What seemed like an insurmountable threat to the Milanese state in June 1391 had evaporated by August. It is only because the Florentine propaganda machine was more effective than that of Milan that the deeds of dal Verme have not received their due. The judgment of later historians reflects the Florentine sources. But outside Florence, Hawkwood's retreat did not receive unrelenting praise. Gatari, the Carrarese chronicler, spoke of it in generic terms ("Seeing that the count of Armagnac did not come and all of March and June were passed, and no longer being able to hold out Messer John Hawkwood decided to leave . . . and so on 2 July he led his army from the Milanese and rode so much that by 10 July he arrived in the Padovano and set up camp at Castelbaldo and on 12 July Hawkwood came to Padua to confer with the Signore Francesco Novello").[122] The anonymous author of the *Chronicon Estense* praises Hawkwood for his "ingenuity and cleverness" but says nothing of a Florentine victory.[123] Even the chronicler of Bologna, Florence's closest ally, does little more than relate the deed without comment or judgment.

That uneasiness existed in the minds of Florentines is evident from later attempts to recast the details of Hawkwood's retreat. Leonardo Bruni has Hawkwood's maneuver occurring after the defeat of Armagnac. Whether conscious or unconscious, Bruni's error adds more luster to Hawkwood's deed.[124] Bruni depicts dal Verme and the Milanese as "emboldened from the victory recently acquired" and ready "to have in their hands a second victory." Poggio Bracciolini followed

Bruni's lead and also put the battle with Armagnac before Hawkwood.[125] "Having succeeded [against Armagnac] beyond their greatest hopes, they [the army] went right away and with great speed to destroy the army of Hawkwood."[126] Bracciolini has Hawkwood disoriented by the defeat of Armagnac and adds, for good measure, the story of the caged fox. The versions of the two great humanists have cast a long shadow and were accepted by, among others, Ercole Ricotti in his famous history of mercenaries in Italy.[127] From there, the error has continued to find its way into numerous modern works. The sixteenth-century Florentine writer Scipio Ammirato must be credited with helping to set things right. In his *Istorie fiorentine,* Scipio placed the events in their proper order.[128]

In this instance perhaps the most judicious estimate comes from a Milanese source. The fifteenth-century diarist Corio offers a straightforward and artless description in which Hawkwood found himself, on reaching the Adda River, without provisions and opposed by an army larger than his own. "Whence, without losing any time he rode day and night without ceasing until he arrived at Padua." The retreat was, Corio said, "not without danger and intolerable damage to his men."[129] Corio blamed dal Verme for allowing Hawkwood to escape but later lauded the commander for his role in the defeat of Armagnac.

Hawkwood's retreat and Armagnac's annihilation nevertheless gave the advantage to Visconti. The northern frontier of the war now shifted to Tuscany. In August, dal Verme advanced south to Sarzana, at the edge of Tuscany, with an army of 2,500 lances and 3,000 infantry and crossbowmen.[130] The Florentines fortified their garrisons at Bologna and Padua and recalled Hawkwood to Tuscany to spearhead local defenses. Hawkwood took the road from Bologna to Pistoia with 1,200 lances and 1,000 crossbowmen and then set up camp just north of Florence at San Miniato. He was soon joined by Giovanni da Barbiano with 600 lances and 300 crossbowmen and reinforcements of 1,000 lances and 2,000 infantry sent up from the Sienese front.[131]

Once again the allies tied Hawkwood closer to them by means of financial bonuses. On 31 August 1391, the Bolognese city council voted Hawkwood a "gift" of 1,000 florins, 500 of which would be paid on Christmas and the other half on Easter. The same legislation granted Giovanni da Barbiano 600 florins, also in two installments on Christmas and Easter, and Konrad Prassberg 400 florins.[132] The Florentines meanwhile took care of Konrad Aichelberg, now stationed at the Sienese front. On 22 August, they granted the German commander a 1,200-florin lifetime pension.[133] The gift was as much to satisfy the ego of the captain, who was competitive with Hawkwood, as it was for services done. The Florentines also gave Konrad and his corporals gifts of silver, including eight large goblets, twenty-two cups, and two decorative silver bacinets, all made by the Florentine goldsmith Jacobo di Ser Zelli, worth 472 florins.[134]

The Milanese offensive in Tuscany consisted primarily of a series of maneuvers as dal Verme looked for an opening. He moved first from Sarzana toward Pisa, crossing the Arno and setting up camp at Cascina, the scene of Hawkwood's first major battle as a commander in chief. According to the Florentines, his army received food and supplies from the Pisans. He then descended south to Casole along the Sienese border to pick up soldiers trying to join his band. The reinforcement brought his force to about 3,000 lances and 5,000 foot soldiers. Hawkwood, thinking that dal Verme intended to ride on Florence from Cascina, went out to Montopoli to stop him. When he found out that dal Verme had proceeded south, Hawkwood too went south toward Casole and stationed his brigade in secure places at Staggia, Colle, and his own castle at Poggibonsi.[135] Seeing that Hawkwood had momentarily split up his brigade, dal Verme then raced back up toward Florence, damaging Florentine lands along the way. Hawkwood pursued with about a thousand lances but, perceiving dal Verme's force the stronger, gave only light battle. Dal Verme advanced across the Elsa River and maneuvered his forces perilously close to Florence, setting up camp just north of the city at Poggio a Caiano. Hawkwood set up his camp two miles away at Tizzano.

The Florentines moved furiously to reinforce Hawkwood's brigade. Large-scale levies were made from the countryside and *contado*, bringing, according to the Minerbetti chronicler's probably inflated estimate, some ten thousand rustics to the front. On 17 September, the city passed legislation erasing bans and sentences placed on murderers and criminals if they joined Hawkwood's band. The amnesty was contingent on their "proving themselves valiant against the enemy." It specifically excluded, however, political exiles and those declared "rebels."[136] The Bolognese passed similar legislation.[137]

The measure increased the size of the allied army, and dal Verme retreated from Poggio a Caiano back toward Lucca. Hawkwood believed that dal Verme and his men would proceed through Pistoia and sought to cut them off there. He guessed wrong and then sent one thousand lances and large contingent of infantry to race after them. The Florentine force caught up with the rear guard of the Milanese army and attacked. The strike caused confusion in the otherwise well-ordered army. The Minerbetti chronicler claimed that many of the enemy infantry were killed, some by their own horses, and that some horsemen were also captured, including the unfortunate Taddeo dal Verme. Informed of the victory, Hawkwood rode out with the main body of the Florentine army. He moved, however, very slowly and cautiously and neared the enemy when it was already dark. The two armies pitched camp, though the region was barren of food. In middle of the night, dal Verme raised his army and quietly left the camp, leaving behind crippled horses, supplies, and munitions, including several trebuchets and bombards. The next morning Hawkwood found the camp empty. Dal Verme had taken a page out of Hawkwood's own book, repeating on a smaller scale the Englishman's maneuver two months earlier at the Adda River.

Dal Verme reached safety in the environs of Lucca, where he was able to feed and furnish his hungry army. Hawkwood advanced to Pescia, where he found food and supplies, and then proceeded to Lucca. He saw that dal Verme was well fortified and supplied and returned to his defensive position just outside Florence at San Miniato.

In subsequent weeks the armies continued to maneuver in Tuscany. No new glory was won. Indeed, neither side was especially anxious to fight. The expensive war had taken its toll on all parties, exhausting them financially. The intention now was more to gain a military advantage for the purpose of extracting favorable peace terms. To this end, dal Verme's army in Tuscany focused on inflicting economic damage on Florence, in particular on closing down Florence's trade. The Milanese received help in this from their ally Genoa. They appealed to the Pisans, who were (despite Florentine accusations) not interested. Florence meanwhile worked hard to protect its commerce, sending large military convoys with its goods. The English captain John Beltoft escorted a shipment of grain from Pisa to Florence in the middle of December. He encountered the Milanese army at Cascina and, to his great shame, fled the field without uttering a word to anyone. This left Beltoft's co-commander the German captain Hugh de Montfort, along with 100 lances, to fend for themselves. The opposition had 2,000 lances. Montfort was captured, and Beltoft never worked for Florence again.[138]

The capture of the Florentine grain shipment was a victory for Milan. But as winter approached, the two sides, tired of the inconclusive war, stepped up negotiations for peace. They eventually took up the offer of the Genoese doge Antoniotto Adorno and the grand master of the Hospitallers of Rhodes, Riccardo Caracciolo, to mediate the dispute. On 20 January, after some rancorous negotiation sessions, a peace accord was signed. It essentially reinstated the *status quo ante bellum* in Tuscany, with the exception that Siena regained Lucignano and Florence kept Montepulciano. The most contentious issue was the fate of Padua. Francesco Novello was allowed to keep Padua but had to give up Bassano, Feltre, and Belluno. The Padua lord was also required to pay a yearly 10,000-florin indemnity for the next fifty years.[139]

With the end of the war, Hawkwood did not immediately go home. Florentine officials requested his help against a mercenary company that had coalesced around Biordo Michelotti, Broglia da Chieri, and other unemployed soldiers. The band sought passage through Bolognese territory to link up with Azzo da Castello and other marauders.[140] Hawkwood and his men succeeded in denying the company passage and put them to flight in the direction of the Sienese Maremma.

This service done, Hawkwood at last retreated from the battlefield and made his way back to Florence. It was the end of his military career.

# CHAPTER FOURTEEN

# Two Weddings, a Funeral, and a Disputed Legacy, 1392–1394–1412

So Worthies live; although they lose their breath, Their Fame does
live, and even conquers death.

*Winstanley's postscript to his* The Honour of the Taylors or the
Famous and Renowned History of Sir John Hawkwood, Knight

E come morto quel capitano,
il comune ordino di fargli onore;
e perche visse fior d'ogni cristiano
onorollo ciascun collieto core.

*From the Florentine* cantare *honoring Hawkwood.*

Hawkwood returned home from the Visconti war to a hero's welcome in Florence. For locals, the Englishman's performance was the one clear positive in a contest of decidedly mixed results. But Hawkwood left the battlefield a spent warrior, tired and most likely infirm. He moved quickly to settle his Italian affairs and prepared at last for a comfortable retirement in his native England.

Hawkwood endeavored first to arrange marriages for his daughters. Florentine officials had promised him 2,000 florins in dowry for each of the girls. Janet, fifteen years old, and Catherine, fourteen, had reached the proper age; Anna, six, was still too young.[1] Hawkwood matched Janet with Brezaglia di Porciglia, scion of a distinguished clan from the Friuli, with close ties to the Este family of Ferrara. Brezaglia's father served as the podestà of Ferrara; Isabella d'Este was the godmother of Catherine Hawkwood. The wedding took place in September at Hawkwood's estate just outside Florence at San Donato in Polverosa and was attended by numerous notables, including Ser Benedetto di Lando Fortini de Orlandini, the Florentine notary and treasurer who had for so long dispersed sums of money to Hawkwood. The transfer of dowry occurred shortly after the ceremony, sealed by a notarial deed dated 19 November 1392.[2] The couple lived out their lives in the Friuli and do not appear to have had any children.

Catherine Hawkwood's wedding followed shortly after Janet's. Catherine was paired with one of the rising stars of her father's profession, the German mercenary Konrad Prassberg.[3] Prassberg was a dynamic soldier who had worked with John Hawkwood in the difficult days along the Sienese border in 1388 and 1389 and during the Milanese war. He was of noble extraction, from the southern German region of Allgäu.[4] He had begun his Italian career in the early 1380s as a protégé of Konrad Aichelberg; his first job, ironically, had been to oppose Hawkwood in 1381 in the service of the city of Genoa. During the war with Visconti, Prassberg proved himself brave and effective, fighting primarily in the environs of Bologna. He went with Hawkwood (and Aichelberg) on the great offensive in the spring of 1391 and took part in the arduous retreat across the Oglio River, during which he was purportedly knighted by John Hawkwood himself.[5] After the war, Prassberg cut a dashing figure at local tournaments. At a joust in Bologna, Konrad captained his team to victory, earning a cap of pearls.[6] Several months later in Florence, he did the same, winning a pearl brooch fitted into the shape of a little lion.[7]

The marriage contract between Catherine Hawkwood and Konrad Prassberg was drawn up on 5 November and the wedding scheduled for 24 January 1393.[8] A temporary hitch developed, however, ten days before the ceremony. Prassberg wrote to the prominent Florentine citizen Donato Acciaiuoli complaining that the Hawkwoods were unable to dress the bride in the manner that the prospective groom had wanted. He asked Acciaiuoli to intercede with the Florentine government for an advance of 1,000 florins on his stipend so that he could take care of the problem himself: "I beseech you for the love of myself and the good fame of John Hawkwood that you will use your influence with the honorable Signoria of Florence that I may have 1000 florins owed my pension . . . so that Lady Donnina may dress my wife for the wedding on the 24th of this month. Lady Donnina writes that nothing is wanting except money to dress her. I have ordered them to make great celebrations, but they have put off so long the purchase of gowns for the maiden."[9]

It is not at once clear whether what Prassberg refers to is a financial crisis in Hawkwood household, a sudden miserly streak, or yet another ploy on Hawkwood's part to maximize his revenue, this time at the expense of his future son-in-law. There is evidence of economic difficulty. In the fall of 1392, Hawkwood was cited in Florence for an outstanding debt of 1,834 florins. A year later, on 11 July 1393, Hawkwood complained in a petition to the city council of the drain on his finances resulting from numerous expenses, including high interest he was paying on silver and jewels that he had pawned in Bologna and Venice. The statement must, however, be measured against a yearly income of at least 3,200 florins, a patrimony that included large tracts of land near Arezzo and Siena and estates back in his native England.[10]

The impasse was ultimately overcome, though it is unclear how. The wedding took place as scheduled on 24 January. As in Janet's case, the ceremony was attended by local notables and members of Hawkwood's personal entourage, including a Bolognese merchant, Piero Lucchini de Savi; Hawkwood's chancellor, the Milanese Francesco di Lorenzo; and Hawkwood's personal servant, the German Hermann Mattei di Aquis.[11]

The union of Catherine and Konrad produced three children: Konrad junior, Clara, and Hartmann. Konrad senior unfortunately died shortly after the youngest was born, on the battlefield in 1399. Catherine then departed Italy and went with her children to Konrad's German estates in the Allgäu. Her youngest son, Hartmann, took up his father's profession and returned for a time to Italy.[12]

It is noteworthy that despite the adulation and favors Hawkwood received from the Florentine government, he did not marry his daughters to local citizens. Instead he joined them with men of his own profession, mercenary soldiers—a practice that was not uncommon in Italy. Hawkwood's rival Jacopo dal Verme, for example, married into the family of Giovanni d'Azzo degli Ubaldini. Hawkwood's preference for men of his own profession provides further evidence that although Florence was the locus of Hawkwood's activities in the latter part of his career, he never came to identify with the city.[13] Years later, when daughter Anna came of age, she was married to a Milanese soldier, Ambrogiolo di Piero della Torre, exiled from his native city.

While settling the marriages of his eldest daughters, Hawkwood made final preparations to return home to England. He sent his "welbelived squyer" and comrade from Essex, John Sampson, on several trips from Florence to England to communicate his intentions to his feofees, notably to Thomas Coggeshale, Hawkwood's longtime friend and chief representative. Sampson's journeys occasioned the only known letters in English by Hawkwood, dated 8 November 1392 and 20 February 1393. In the epistle of 20 February, Hawkwood instructed Sampson to obtain safe-conducts for his return.[14] Sampson arranged to have five men and horses accompany Hawkwood home via the port of Calais.

In the summer of 1393, Hawkwood liquidated his property in Florence. He divested himself, via petition to the government, of his entire patrimony, including "a farm with houses, tower . . . in the place called La Rocchetta" near Poggibonsi and his estate at San Donato in Polverosa.[15] The petition makes plain, however, that Hawkwood had in fact started the process earlier, placing some of his holdings in the name of his seven-year-old son, John junior. The sale price is not recorded; nor is the name of the buyer. The Catasto records of 1427 list a Baldinotto di Antonio Baldinotti as owner, but it is not certain whether Baldinotti purchased the property from Hawkwood or from someone else.[16]

Hawkwood also sent personal representatives throughout Italy to collect outstanding monies and debts owed him. His wife, Donnina, did the same, settling her own affairs back in Milan and elsewhere. In Florence, on 11 March 1394, John Hawkwood arranged a last rendering of accounts. He requested that city officials convert his yearly stipends and landed estates into a lump sum of cash. Hawkwood in turn agreed to cede to Florence the strategically important fortresses at Migliari, Abbey del Pino, and Montecchio in southern Tuscany. Along with past salaries due, the Florentines consented to pay 6,000 florins. As a sign of goodwill, officials added a bonus of 1,000 florins to help facilitate passage to England. The grant was to be final and binding; Hawkwood could not at any future time ask for more.[17] It is a measure of the importance of the fortresses to Hawkwood that he kept hold of them until the very end.

As Hawkwood prepared to leave, Florentine officials devised a more public means of honoring him. On 20 August 1393 the city council voted to erect a marble statue "adorned with figures" on Hawkwood's behalf in the cathedral. This was, according to the preamble of the legislation, "so that the magnificent and faithful achievements of John Hawkwood, his fidelity and honor . . . to the Florentine republic, should not only be rewarded . . . but perpetually shown to his glory . . . that brave men may know that the commune of Florence recompenses true service with her recognition and beneficent gratitude."[18] The Hawkwood statue would be placed beside the wooden monument to Piero Farnese, hero of the Pisan war, who had been honored thirty years earlier. The Farnese memorial, now lost, was located then in the south aisle of the cathedral, near the door leading to the campanile.

Hawkwood's health, however, was failing. The great retreat and the rigors of the last campaigns of the Visconti war had left him exhausted. The plans for the monument in 1393 were in fact for a tomb; the language of the bequest indicates that officials sensed that the end was near. Hawkwood's own letters in the winter of 1392/93 suggest that he himself understood that his final days were approaching. He pointedly instructed Sampson to communicate to his feofees in Essex various contingencies "touchying my will and purpose," including what should be done should he "deye before coming hom." The prologue to the settlement of his Florentine accounts on 11 March 1394 described the captain as "weary with age and burdened with infirmity."[19]

Hawkwood died on 17 March 1394, less than a week after the final rendering of his accounts. According to the Minerbetti chronicler, the end came from a "subito accidente," perhaps a heart attack.[20] The captain would not realize his dream of returning home to England and living off the fruits of his victories.

## Burial and Funeral

Hawkwood's funeral was held on 20 March, three days after his death. Extant accounts describe a spectacular event.[21] The Minerbetti chronicler said that the city honored Hawkwood with "no regard for expense.[22] The diarist Naddo da Montecatini said that neither citizen nor foreigner has ever received such a tribute, an opinion seconded by the anonymous author of a song (*cantare*) in *rima ottava* commemorating Hawkwood, which circulated throughout Florence just after his death.[23] The Florentine writer Benedetto Dei, born twenty-three years after Hawkwood's funeral, claimed to know the *cantare* by heart.

The elaborate burial ceremony began in the Piazza della Signoria, where Hawkwood's bier was placed, dressed in vermilion velvets and golden brocades. In death Hawkwood now appeared much like his first full-time employer, Giovanni dell' Agnello of Pisa, had appeared in life. Donnina, her children, their spouses, and numerous retainers were there, dressed in traditional mourning clothes, supplied by the state. The guilds of the city contributed torches and candles, and their members came out in large numbers. The town fathers furnished three banners with the arms of Florence and a helmet with a golden lion holding a lily in its claw as the crest. Hawkwood's personal brigade sent fourteen caparisoned warhorses, bearing the Englishman's personal banner, his sword, shield, and helmet.

The funeral bier was then brought to the baptistery of San Giovanni. Cadres of mourners, hooded and dressed in black, and priests and monks followed the body, singing psalms and carrying torches. Citizens lined the path, and local shops were, by communal decree, closed for the occasion. Hawkwood's body was then placed on the baptismal font, draped with golden cloths, and laid out for public viewing. The Englishman's sword was placed on his chest and the commander's baton in his hand. Professional mourners sobbed over the body.

Finally, the corpse was transferred to Santa Reparata, the cathedral, which was lit up brightly with a multitude of torches and candles. It was put on a catafalque in the central choir. A local prelate—the name has not survived—gave a eulogy extolling Hawkwood's deeds. The author of the *cantare* relates the scene in the Tuscan dialect of the late trecento:

> E'n Santa Liperata fu portato
> tutto coperto a ricchi drappi d'oro
> quivi s'udiva un canto rilevato;

esposaron la bara a mezzo coro:

non e possibile aver racontato

le rilevate cose del mortoro,

ch' a raccontar parebbon cose istrane;

eppo'sonaron tutte le campane.

In Santa Reparata he was brought

all covered with rich golden cloth

there a notable song was heard;

his bier exposed in the middle of the choir

it was impossible to recount

all the notable deeds of the dead man

which would seem strange things to relate;

then all the bells were rung.[24]

The total cost of the ceremony was approximately 410 florins, a figure that would have been still greater without the largesse of the local guilds. In comparison, the funeral of Hawkwood's contemporary Coluccio Salutati, the great humanist chancellor who guided Florence for more than thirty years, cost a mere 250 florins.[25]

According to the modern historian Sharon Strocchia, not only was Hawkwood's funeral the most elaborate of an already "flamboyant" late trecento Florentine style, but it also constituted a species of civic ritual, with didactic and symbolic functions. City officials used the ceremony to emphasize "major themes of ceremonial politics" to the populace at large.[26] The placing of Hawkwood body in the baptismal font of San Giovanni rather than directly in the cathedral, as was the custom, represented a novel feature, aimed at conveying a sense of both loss and cyclical renewal. The font was where the Florentine citizenry was baptized. The wide-scale participation of the guilds in the funeral made plain the "corporate ethic" of the city; the extravagant display provided "a striking picture both of the triumph of flamboyance and of the commune triumphant."[27]

But Hawkwood's funeral fit a still larger context. The burial of mercenary captains in churches was by the end of the fourteenth century standard practice in Italy. Tibertino Brandolino, Hawkwood's comrade-in-arms from the Bagnacavallo days, had been laid to rest in the church of San Francesco in Venice; Jacopo de' Cavalli, who had fought along with Hawkwood outside Verona in 1379, was interred in the same city at SS. Giovanni e Paolo; and Paolo Savelli, who had opposed Hawkwood on the Sienese border during the Milanese war, was buried at the church of the Frari. The German captain Konrad Aichelberg would be interred in a local church in Pisa.[28]

For the most part, the death rites of the other men were less spectacular than those for Hawkwood. Cavalli, for one, paid for his own funeral.[29] But states kept careful watch on such ceremonies and judged their own actions in terms of those of the others. Embedded in the funerals was a dialogue, a posturing, a penchant for propagandizing. On the one hand, states sent messages to mercenary captains that good and faithful service was appreciated. On the other hand, they gave notice to one another of their willingness to compete in displaying civic loyalty and local pride.

Hawkwood's funeral is best understood in terms of events in neighboring Siena, Florence's longtime rival and bitter opponent in the Visconti wars. The ceremony honoring Hawkwood was preceded and followed by ostentatious state funerals in that city for Giovanni d'Azzo degli Ubaldini, who died three years before the Englishman, and Giovanni "tedesco" da Pietramala, who died almost exactly a year later. The two men not only had been important captains in Sienese armies but were also Florentine exiles, hated and despised in their native city.

Ubaldini had, in fact, died by Florentine poison during the Milanese war. His funeral, held on 28 June 1391, was described by the Sienese chronicler Tommaso Montauri as an extravagant affair, befitting "a pope or an emperor."[30] The magnitude of the ceremony provided a rallying point for locals during a difficult war while sending a message of defiance and scorn to Florence. That Hawkwood's funeral was staged as an emphatic response becomes clear from the close parallels between the two events. Ubaldini's body, too, was brought to the cathedral via solemn procession, attended by ornately decked out horses bearing the crests, helmet, sword, and spurs of the captain. By communal decree, all shops were closed, and the whole city (fifteen thousand citizens, according to Montauri) came out to mourn: men, women, children, monks, and priests.[31] The corpse was laid out amid candles and torches in the cathedral, and an abbot from the nearby monastery of San Galgano eulogized Ubaldini.[32]

The cost of this event was 462 florins, a figure quite close to the one for Hawkwood's funeral.[33] The financial condition of Siena was dire at this time; the city could barely meet payments to its employees, and its armies were wholly paid for by Milan.[34] Such an act of fiscal folly made little sense apart from its function in a war of propaganda.

The importance of this dialogue becomes clearer still when we consider the funeral of Giovanni "tedesco" da Pietramala, which in turn came as a response to Hawkwood's. Unlike Ubaldini, Pietramala had not been an especially effective captain in Sienese service. Nevertheless he received a spectacular send-off. "There was no one at this time," wrote Montauri, "who remembers having seen or heard such magnificence and honor made to such a man."[35] But in a postscript to his description of funeral, the chronicler admitted that the citizens were not excessively fond of Pietramala and did not regard him as particularly faithful. "Note that Pietramala would have had greater honor if it weren't that on the first of January past, he went to aid the Bretons [then at war with Siena] and defeated the camp and took many prisoners. This the Sienese were never able to forget."[56] If the Sienese were unable to outdo the Florentines on the battlefield, they were intent on outdoing them in homage to their fallen captains.

A similar discourse can also be detected in the efforts to memorialize Hawkwood with a monument. Such honors were, along with public burials, becoming increasingly common in the late trecento and would be even more so in the next century.[37] Once again, however, events in neighboring Siena were most important. Both Giovanni d'Azzo degli Ubaldini and Giovanni "tedesco" da Pietramala were commemorated by means of equestrian statues (now both lost) in the Sienese cathedral—the latter purportedly effected with especial skill in wood by Jacopo della Quercia.[38] The Ubaldini monument, completed in 1391/92, likely hastened the original plans to honor Hawkwood in 1393; the subsequent statue of Pietramala encouraged Florentine officials to keep the project alive.

The original Florentine plan to make a marble tomb for Hawkwood, initiated in 1393, was revived on 2 December 1395, soon after the Pietramala funeral. Officials decided to rework the old wooden monument to Piero Farnese, a proposal that would involve sculpting the Hawkwood and Farnese memorials in marble and placing them in the north aisle, pointing toward the high altar—Farnese was to have precedence of place, closest to the altar.[39] The project gave way shortly thereafter to a still larger design, perhaps conceived by the Florentine chancellor Coluccio Salutati, to erect a series of monuments in the cathedral commemorating men of action and men of letters, including Dante, Boccaccio, Petrarch, and the humanist theologian Luigi de' Marsigli.[40] A committee of experts chose the painters Agnolo Gaddi (d. 1396) and Giuliano Arrighi (known as Pesello, d. 1446) to draft the Hawkwood and Farnese tombs. They were instructed to sketch their models directly on the wall, on the site where the tombs were to go.[41] Both men had excellent reputations. Gaddi had painted the frescoes in the Castellani chapel and choir at the Santa Croce in Florence and more recently had worked on the stained-glass windows in Santa Reparata. Pesello had undertaken several commissions in Florence and would later be consulted about the construction of the great dome on the cathedral.[42]

For reasons that are not clear, however, the tombs were never made. The grand plan was abandoned in favor of a simple wall painting; Farnese's memorial was left in wood. Gaddi drew the figure of Hawkwood, and Pesello made the sarcophagus at the bottom. Each man received 15 florins for his work. Little is known of appearance of the painting, for which the first documentary reference dates from 16 June 1396.[43] Scholars have suggested that lack of funds, owing to the financial stress of war and pestilence, constrained officials to leave the project as it was; Florentine superiority with respect to painting technique perhaps contented the government with the decision.[44]

This may have been the end of the story, but the plan for a marble tomb to honor Hawkwood was revived thirty-seven years later, in May 1433, by the Albizzi government. The collapse of the regime several months later temporarily ended the project, which was taken up again by the Medici regime in 1436. They chose to replace the Gaddi and Pesello fresco with another painted work and hired the renowned artist Paolo Uccello in May 1436 to do the job. Uccello completed the project by 28 June. The *capo maestro* of the cathedral was, however, dissatisfied and on 7 July ordered Uccello to redo it. Uccello finished the new design on 31 August, for which he was paid 15 florins, the same as Gaddi and Pesello.[45]

It is Uccello's Hawkwood that has come down to posterity (fig. 5). It remains in the cathedral, in excellent shape, in the third bay of the northern wall, now accompanied by the painting of the poet Dante and the mercenary Niccolò Tolentino done in 1465 and 1465, respectively. Hawkwood's memorial dwarfs that of Dante and is considerably larger than the wall tombs dedicated to Bishop Corsini and Luigi Marsigli on the opposite wall; only Tolentino's memorial is of similar dimensions.[46] It was transferred to canvas in the nineteenth century (when it was also restored, several pieces having fallen off) and moved from the north to the west wall; in 1947 it was moved back to its present position.[47]

Hawkwood is set on a gray-green horse, with commander's baton in hand, dressed partially in armor, atop a fictive cenotaph. Uccello used a technique called *terra verde* to simulate an equestrian bronze statue. But the fresco is not monochrome. The background is dark red; Hawkwood's horse and tomb contain accents in red, black, white, and orange. The composition is large, measuring some 3.5 meters from the horse's hooves to the top of Hawkwood's cap. Art historians have pointed out the anomalous feature that the painting has two viewpoints: the horse and the rider are seen as if on a level with the spectator, whereas the cenotaph is seen from below. The cenotaph contains the inscription "Ioannes Acutus eques brittanicus dux aetatis suae cautissimus et rei militaris pertissimus habitus est" (John Hawkwood, British knight, most prudent leader of his age and most expert in the art of war). The words were supplied by Bartolomeo Fortini de Orlandini, the son of Benedetto, the former treasurer of Florence and Hawkwood's old ally. The epitaph was apparently added to the fresco some months after Uccello finished it.[48]

Scholars have wondered at the decision to honor Hawkwood so long after his

*Figure 5.* John Hawkwood. Scala / Art Resource, New York

death. The decision has seemed all the more incongruous because it was under-taken by two different regimes, the Albizzi and the Medici, which otherwise had little in common. Some have asserted that the Hawkwood fresco was redone in conjunction with the general refurbishing of the cathedral, on the occasion of its rededication as Santa Maria del Fiore by Pope Eugene IV in March 1436.[49] The original Gaddi and Pesello fresco was probably in need of restoration; the window next to it had been repaired several times in the early fifteenth century, suggesting that the elements got to it.[50]

But like Hawkwood's funeral, the commission of the Uccello fresco was linked to broader political and diplomatic issues. The circumstances in 1433-1436 were similar to those in the 1390s, when the plan to commemorate Hawkwood was first proposed. Florence was at war with Milan, which, as earlier, had found allies within Tuscany. In 1436, Florence's most bitter opponent was the city of Lucca, the struggle reaching a climax in the spring of 1436, at about the time Uccello was hired. The art historian Wendy Wegener has emphasized the connection between Florence and Lucca, how Uccello's commission coincided with the commission in Lucca of a monument to honor its chief mercenary captain, Niccolò Piccinino. The tribute to Piccinino had special significance in Florence because he had recently commanded the city's armies but had left under suspicious circumstances. On Piccinino's departure from Florentine employ, officials ridiculed him by painting a *pittura infamante* of him. Thus Uccello's fresco, undertaken shortly thereafter, provided an image of what a mercenary captain was supposed to be. Piccinino, conversely, was the image of what a mercenary ought not be.[51]

The very pose Uccello gave Hawkwood is emblematic of the larger political agenda. Hawkwood rides a show horse and conducts an inspection of his troops. He is relaxed, with the baton of command at his side; the gait of the horse is that of an ambio (amble), consistent with a commander slowly moving about his brigade. The movement of the legs confused Giorgio Vasari, the sixteenth-century author of lives of the Renaissance artists, who thought it a technical mistake, which marred an otherwise "most perfect" work. The modern scholar Lionello Boccia blamed what he perceived as an incongruous pose on restoration efforts of the nineteenth century.[52] But the depiction was intentional and didactic. Uccello and his Florentine employers wanted an idealized Hawkwood, in a stance suggestive of a loyal communal servant.

The interpretation is reinforced by a recent study using ultraviolet rays on the extant design (*modello*), which Uccello submitted to the *operai* of the cathedral to gain the commission. It shows that the painter had originally depicted Hawkwood in a more threatening pose, in the manner of a captain at the head of his troops, dressed in armor from head to toe, with only a small portion of his face emerging from underneath the helmet, his baton slightly raised and his horse at the ready.[53] It was for this reason that the *capo maestro* rejected Uccello's first effort as "not painted as it should be" and demanded that he do it again.[54] Art historians have traditionally cited as reasons for the rejection issues of perspective and color. But the real problem was meaning.[55] This is made still clearer by Bartolomeo Fortini de Orlandini's epitaph at the bottom of the painting. The words were taken from Plutarch's eulogy of Fabius Maximus, recently translated from the Greek by the Florentine scholar Lapo da Castiglionchio.

The propaganda value of Hawkwood's image was therefore critical to the city's decision to honor him. As in the 1390s, the survival of Florence was in doubt— indeed, in many ways even more so. The continued threat of Milan, along with the uneven performance of recent mercenary captains, provided fertile ground for the propagation of Hawkwood's legend. As the faithful and steadfast Fabius had saved Rome from an implacable foe, so too had Hawkwood saved Florence. In this manner the image of the "loyal" and "faithful" Hawkwood—a skewed and artificial image—was bequeathed to the modern world.

## Donnina Visconti and the Settlement of Accounts

The political utility of Hawkwood's image did not, however, preclude sincere admiration for the man. Whatever the larger function of his funeral and subsequent memorials, the Florentines remembered Hawkwood reverently as a man who stuck by the city in its darkest hour. To be sure, the sentiment arose only after the captain was safely in his grave. But it was sincere enough. The fourteenth-century novelist Franco Sacchetti had ridiculed Hawkwood in his lifetime as a robber and a thief, but the fifteenth-century writer Giovanni Cavalcanti, an otherwise harsh critic of Florentine politics and society, lauded the Englishman as "an outstanding captain" and a paradigm of prudence.[56] The humanist Leonardo Bruni (d. 1444) despised mercenaries in general but still praised Hawkwood throughout his history of Florence as an effective soldier. Bruni's younger contemporary Poggio Bracciolini (d. 1459) referred to Hawkwood in his history as a "wise leader" and "most expert in arms and 'virtù.' "[57]

Proof of the goodwill that the Florentines held for their captain was their treatment of his widow, Donnina. A month after Hawkwood's funeral (16 April 1394), the Florentine city council voted to give Donnina and her children Hawkwood's full salary for March, though he had died before the end of month and thus technically was not entitled to the whole share. The council also granted Donnina permission to collect all sums due her husband, including his annual pension of 3,200 florins as well as the 2,000 florins promised for daughter Anna's dowry and the 1,000 florins intended to aid Hawkwood's journey back to England—payments effected in three installments over the course of a year, ending in March 1395.[58] In return, Donnina agreed, as her husband had before her, to transfer his Tuscan fortresses to Florence. She wrote to the castellans to instruct them to relinquish control.

The disbursement of Anna's dowry and the 1,000 florins for Hawkwood's journey home proved thorny legal issues and required separate acts of the city council to countermand a law prohibiting such transfers. Donnina received help in navigating the complex Florentine legal system from Giovanni Jacopo de Orlandini, a relative of the Florentine treasurer Benedetto di Fortini de Orlandini, whom Hawkwood had given power of attorney before he died. Orlandini served Donnina's interests well and was received kindly by Florentine officials.

The necessary legislation was passed on 15 December 1394 and the disbursements duly made. A week later, the city council voted to protect the inheritance from taxation. In January 1395, John junior, now nine years old, was appointed to an honorary post as commander of two lances in the Florentine army.[59]

The Florentine city council made a final ratification of Donnina's award on 10 January 1395. Donnina signed the document at her home "at Santa Maria a Quarto, in the parish of San Stefano in Pane," an indication that she was now divested of her husband's Florentine patrimony.[60] Florentine officials made it clear, however, that she and her young family were welcome to remain in the city and reiterated an earlier decision to allow her a yearly stipend of 1,000 florins should she decide to stay.[61]

Although the terms were generous, Donnina nevertheless chose to leave Florence. After receiving the last installment, she undertook plans to complete Hawkwood's intended voyage to England and Essex County. Florentine officials wrote a letter commending her to King Richard II. The epistle, to the "most serene and glorious prince Richard," was sent on 29 March 1395. It outlined the city's desire to accommodate Donnina as tribute to her husband: "We cannot in any way neglect the posterity of the noble and brave knight John Hawkwood, who for a long time faithfully and honestly fought in our service . . . nor may we omit to render honor and service to him in every possible manner." The letter then gave justification for Donnina's decision: "The progeny of that man . . . find themselves as strangers and pilgrims in our city. . . . Therefore their mother, a consort worthy of such a husband, has decided, as soon as the age of her children will allow it, to transfer herself with them to England."[62]

A Milanese by birth, Donnina was indeed a "stranger" in Florence. But her decision to go to England was nevertheless a curious one. It involved traveling to a country she had never seen, whose language she likely did not know well, while giving up a lucrative Italian stipend. But the decision was based on sound financial reasoning. Her husband had provided well for her in England, leaving a lucrative legacy of manors and estates grouped near his childhood home in Essex and in the neighboring county of Buckingham and including the well-known marketplace of Leadenhall in London.[63]

The patrimony escaped the attention of Florentine officials, who apparently believed that Hawkwood had left his young family destitute. The diarist Giovanni Morelli, for one, interpreted the state sponsorship of the captain's funeral as in part an act of kindness to an impoverished widow. The impression was perhaps as Hawkwood had wanted it to be. But his English patrimony was a substantial one. Anticipating that Donnina might outlive him, Hawkwood gave explicit instructions to his feofees to provide for her should she return. Hawkwood specifically asked that Donnina be granted possession of the manors of Ostags and Listons in Sible Hedingham, the ancestral homes of two eponymous families, which had been close friends with Hawkwood's father, Gilbert. Hawkwood wanted Donnina to live there until John junior reached the age of inheritance, twenty-one years, at which point he would receive the whole of his father's legacy.

If Donnina had any lingering doubts regarding the journey, they were assuaged by a warm welcome from the English king Richard II, who now requested that Hawkwood's corpse be sent back to England. The English monarch wished to pay tribute to the man who had served him for so many years as ambassador, by granting his final wish, if posthumously.[64] The Florentines assented to the request in a letter dated 3 June 1395.

> Our devotion can deny nothing to the eminence of your highness. We will leave nothing undone that is possible to do, so that we may fulfill your good pleasure. So, therefore, although we consider it reflected glory on us and on our people to keep the ashes and the bones of the late brave and most magnificent captain John Hawkwood, who, as commander of our army, fought most gloriously for us and who at public expense was interred in the principal church of Santa Reparata . . . nevertheless, according to the tenor of your request, we freely concede permission that his remains shall return to his native land.[65]

To receive Hawkwood's body, preparations were undertaken for a tomb in the church of St. Peter's in Sible Hedingham.

Richard's request has been viewed by scholars as part of a larger pattern of involvement in the burials of prominent allies and favorites. Just before Hawkwood's death, Richard had intervened in the funeral of the bishop of Waltham; a few months later, the king oversaw the interment of the Hawkwood family ally Robert de Vere. De Vere, like Hawkwood, had died outside England. Richard had him returned and buried in the de Vere family plot at Earl's Coln. Richard himself attended the ceremony and ordered the coffin opened just before burial so that he could touch his friend one more time. A recent historian has described Richard's behavior in such matters as evidence of "narcissism" and "macabre sense," which afforded him a "uniquely theatrical way of displaying his power over . . . destinies even in death."[66]

But despite the liquidation of Florentine accounts and the direct appeal of the English king, neither Donnina's living body nor Hawkwood's dead one appears to have gone to England. Instead, a dispute arose between Donnina and Hawkwood's feofees, who did not wish to make room for her. The crux of the disagreement was over the validity of Hawkwood's instructions, communicated in the final months of his life through John Sampson to Thomas Coggeshale. Did these have the force of a legal will and last testament?

The Florentine archives contain no record of a written will by Hawkwood, from which scholars have concluded that Hawkwood never made one. But Florence was, as we have seen, a temporary stop for him, and he had already settled his accounts there before he died. The real issue was whether Hawkwood formally filed a will in England, where his business had for many years been handled by intermediaries, where he had a family by his first wife, and where his financial affairs were anything but settled. Hawkwood's English letters of 8 November 1392 and 20 February 1393 show that he made every effort to clarify his intentions. On 22 April 1393 John Sampson and Thomas Coggeshale drew up an indenture at the latter's home in Boreham, Essex, which in effect laid out on paper Hawkwood's last wishes. In addition to granting Donnina the right to Ostags and Listons, Hawkwood wished for John junior to receive everything when he came of age. He also wanted his feofees to sell his interests in Leadenhall, including the avowed-sons of the churches (the legal authority to appoint the parish priest), in order to purchase chantries in the churches of Sible Hedingham and neighboring Castle Hedingham on behalf of his soul and those of his comrades who fought with him. The indenture is cited below, written in the words of John Sampson.

> Atte ferst, he wolde that the leadene hall with avowesones of the Churches be sold and ii prestes yfounded in the nonnerie of hythingham to singen there in my maistre chapel and i preste in the parisshe chrurche of Hethyngham Sibille. And also yif my lady Haukwode overlive my maister Sir John Haukwode and kepe here sole and come in to Engelond he preyeth you and alle the other feffetz ye wolde eneffe here in Lisstones and Ostages in Hythngham to term of here lyf the reversioun to John Haukwode, the sone of here in the tayle. And the remenaunt to be kept in handis of the feffez til John my maistressone be of ful age. And at his ful age

enfeffyn hym ther in that is to weten to him and to his heires of his body getyn and for defaute of issue of his body he wele that the forsaide londes ben sold.[67]

The indenture notwithstanding, Hawkwood had in the end communicated his intentions only verbally. There was nothing in England in his own hand. The absence of a written document is confirmed in the Guildhall records of testament, which cite Hawkwood by name but make no mention of a will. Instead there is notice of commission for January 1397/98 to look into the matter of his legacy ("for the administration of all the goods of John Haukevodd alias 'Achud,' the knight"), initiated some three years after the captain's death.[68] The commission was occasioned by Donnina herself, who sent a formal petition to English authorities to protest her treatment. Donnina's petition recounted how her husband had over the years "sent sums of gold" to England for the purchase of "lands and tenements" but that his feofees now withheld the rightful possession of them. Donnina further complained that the deeds and official papers relating to these purchases and transfers had been removed from St. Paul's Church in London, where they had originally been placed.[69]

Little is known of the case. The Guildhall records indicate that Donnina appointed as her representative a Milanese clergyman, Matteo Maffolo de Conluxianus, associated with the church of Santa Fidele in Milan. The commission acknowledged that Hawkwood's official papers had in fact been removed from St Paul's, but it could not account for their whereabouts.

The problem regarding Hawkwood's legacy was perhaps inevitable for a man whose life was played out so far from his place of birth and who had two families by two wives. The particulars of the opposition to Donnina are nowhere recorded, but it is quite likely that a key role was played by Thomas Coggeshale's nephew and former ward, William Coggeshale, who was Hawkwood's son-in-law, husband of daughter Antiochia. Like all Hawkwood's feofees, he had economic incentive to oppose Donnina, but more so than the rest he had the power to do so. Since returning from Hawkwood's brigades in Italy in the early 1380s, William had become one of the most powerful men in Essex, serving in numerous distinguished posts, including that of sheriff, on important royal commissions and in the Parliament (ten times). William displayed particular zeal in building a landed patrimony, skillfully using his political connections both to the crown and, when it became fashionable, to antiroyal factions to gain his way.[70] He also exhibited an equal zeal for litigation, as evidenced by a bitter suit he leveled against the wealthy London merchant Walter Sibille, which lasted for many years and which he ultimately won. His direct link to the Hawkwood family ended, however, when Antiochia died in 1388, perhaps adding to his estrangement.

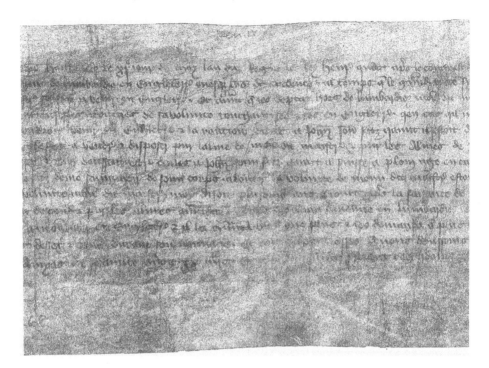

*Figure 6.* Inquest 1403, involving John Sampson. Public Record Office, London, C 270/29 #17

The dispute over Hawkwood's legacy continued beyond 1398. Another inquest was held in England five years later. A fragment of a testimony from this has survived; located in the Ecclesiastical Miscellany in the Public Record Office in London, it is written in first person by a "Sampson," most likely Hawkwood's "welbelived squyer," who had effected the indenture with Thomas Coggeshale back in 1393 (fig. 6).[71] Sampson's testimony indicates that the central issue was the rights of Hawkwood's son, John junior, now nearly of age, to his father's "lands in Essex and Bucks counties." In this instance, however, a settlement was reached, confirmed by the fact that John junior returned to England when he reached twenty-one and inherited his father's estates, a development that will be discussed presently. Donnina remained in Italy and eventually returned to Milan. In 1403, by special decree of Giangaleazzo Visconti, she was granted restitution of her marriage dowry, taken away when Hawkwood chose to serve Florence. The patrimony included the now familiar cluster of estates northeast of Milan, at Pessano, Bornago, Corugate Valera, and Santa Maria alle Molgora. She also received estates located between Bergamo and Cremona and at Terranova near Lodi. These two produced annual revenue in excess of 150 florins.[72]

Nevertheless, owing to the protracted dispute, the corpse of John Hawkwood senior does not appear to have been transferred to England, as King Richard had requested. The fate of Hawkwood's body has generated a surprising amount of speculation among professional and amateur historians alike and is one of the true mysteries regarding Hawkwood. In the spring of 1999, a local television station in England sought to settle the issue by digging up Hawkwood's tomb at St. Peter's in Sible Hedingham. The church, however, opposed this endeavor, wishing to protect its integrity. Ostensibly, there is little ambiguity. King Richard asked for Hawkwood's remains, and Florence agreed to send them. Most scholars have therefore concluded that Hawkwood was returned to England and placed in the tomb in his honor at St. Peter's, a deduction strengthened by the fact that his body has never been found in Florence.

The conclusion is, however, contradicted by documentary evidence in the archives of the Florentine cathedral. According to the books of the supervisors (*operai*), Hawkwood's body was still in Florence as of 1 January 1405.[73] The date is significant; it was just before John Hawkwood junior's twenty-first birthday, when he stood to gain his inheritance. It is likely that the subject was revisited in anticipation of the young man's return to England, perhaps with the thought that Hawkwood's corpse would accompany him. But the entry in the supervisors' book makes clear that Hawkwood's remains did not leave Florence but that his body was "moved from where it is and put beneath the ground, in the usual and customary place." As for the subsequent disappearance of Hawkwood's corpse, D. M. Manni gave the best answer when he said that it had most likely been buried in the old choir and was lost when a new choir was made and the floor was repaved with marble in the sixteenth century.

## Final Legacy in England

Hawkwood was nevertheless honored in England with a tomb in the church of St. Peter's in Sible Hedingham, located along the south wall, near a modern wooden altar.[74] It is not the work of artistic renown, such as the Uccello fresco, but is representative of a rather standard type of funerary monument then in vogue in Essex and in England more generally. Much of the paint has crumbled off, and the carvings have become worn with age (fig. 7).

The structure consists of a canopied arch with various figures. On the right side of the arch, one can still see a hawk, the symbol of John, and a boy sounding a conch shell (figs. 8, 9). On the left side of the arch there are emblems of hunting: a boar and a hare. On the two vertical pillars are a lion (left) and dragon (right). Under the arch is a low altar tomb with a slab of gray marble. Below that are five shields, once painted, now blank. At one time, the inside of the canopied arch, now

*Figure 7.* St. Peter's Church in Sible Hedingham. Photograph by author

whitewashed and walled over, contained the painted figure of John Hawkwood, standing in prayer, between his two wives. From Hawkwood's mouth emerged a prayer scroll in Latin which read, "Son of God, remember me." From his first wife's mouth came the words "Mother of mine, remember me," and from the second "Mother of Christ, remember me."[75] The gray marble slab may once have had traces of brass inlay, a common feature of funerary monuments of the time.[76]

As was the case in Florence and Italy, Hawkwood's legend grew in England after his death. The writer of the *Westminster Chronicle* made careful note of the captain's passing in 1394 and lauded him as a "marvelous" soldier.[77] Thomas Walsingham in his *Historia Anglicana* remembered Hawkwood as the "most distinguished knight in all the world."[78]

Hawkwood's son and heir John junior returned to Essex in 1406 when he reached twenty-one and claimed his inheritance. He was welcomed back by royal decree of King Henry IV, which formally extended to John junior full legal prerogatives and explicit right to the entirety of his father's legacy: "We concede to our beloved John, son of John Hawkwood, deceased knight, who was born in Italy, that he be treated as our liege and native in all things. including the right to have his inheritance and whatever other emoluments . . . maners [*sic*], lands, tenements, revenues, services, fiefs . . . liberties and whatever other possessions."[79]

John appears to have received his inheritance piecemeal. Robert Rykedon, the lone survivor of Hawkwood's feofees, handed over to him in July 1409 a substantial part of the legacy, including the manors of Bloyes, Listons, and Hodings in Gosfield and Sible Hedingham, as well as "appurtenences" in the surrounding villages of Halstead, Castle Hedingham, Great Maplestead, Bocking, and Wethersfield and "all lands and rents and services in Sible Hedingham called 'Potterstrete'

*Figure 8.* Hawkwood memorial at St. Peter's Church, Sible Hedingham. Photograph by author

*Figure 9.* Detail of a hawk, St. Peter's Church, Sible Hedingham. Photograph by author

and 'Ostags'" including the "manor known as Hawkwood's in Gosfield."[80] The last property, long the home of John Hawkwood the elder, indicates that John junior may have laid claim also to his uncle's legacy. In September 1410, William Coggeshale and others ceded to John junior the rights to the manors of Barwick and Scotneys in Toppesfield. The cession was contingent on John's marrying within five years—from which we learn that he came to England single and remained so to that point.[81] John junior in fact never married and appears to have died young, without issue. The only notice we have of his activities in England is through various deals, sales of land to other people.[82] In 1420, his inheritance reverted to a committee of executors.[83]

A Hawkwood legacy in England was, however, continued through his daughter from his first marriage, Antiochia. She had two daughters with William Coggeshale, named Blanche and Alice. Blanche married John Doreward of Bocking, son of John Doreward senior, both prominent members of Essex society.[84] Alice married John Terrell, another important Essex man, who was connected to the household of the Duke of Gloucester and served as speaker of the House of Commons and treasurer of the royal household. Alice died in 1427 and is remembered by a simple funerary slab in the parish church at East Horndon, which bears the inscription "Here lies Alice, daughter of William Coggeshale, knight, and Antiochia, his consort and once wife of John Terrell."[85]

A male Hawkwood legacy in England continued through Hawkwood's illegitimate son John, to whom the pope had given a sinecure at St. Paul's in London back in 1372 and who we may presume remained in that post, though there is no notice of his activities. The sources do, however, make intriguing mention of a Thomas Hawkwood, whose name corresponds to Hawkwood's bastard son taken in 1376 outside Bologna and ransomed in Venice. This Hawkwood appears to have been a dynamic character, more in the model of his father. Thomas took up the profession of arms and rose to prominence in Aquitaine in the service of John Tiptoft, seneschal of the region in the first part of the fifteenth century. If this Thomas was indeed Hawkwood's son, he provides a certain symmetry to our story. Thomas distinguished himself not only in the same profession but also in the same region in which his father had initiated his career.[86]

John Hawkwood, mercenary soldier and captain of Italian armies, received his final homage in his native England in 1412. On 20 October of that year chantries were founded for "the well-being of his soul" and those of his military companions in St. Peter's Church at Sible Hedingham and in the Priory Church at Castle Hedingham.[87] Chantries were then a popular means of honoring prominent men and endowing churches.[88] John Rykedon and his son supervised the task, along with John Coe from the nearby village of Gestingthorp, who had fought in Italy with Hawkwood from 1386 to 1394.[89] To help raise the money, Rykedon sold Hawkwood's interests in Leadenhall, thus belatedly enacting Hawkwood's verbal wishes and the terms of the indenture of 1393.[90] The chantries for Hawkwood were effected in conjunction with ones on behalf of members of the Bourchier family in Halstead, for which John Hawkwood junior provided some of the land.[91] The endowment for Hawkwood included nearly five hundred acres of land in Sible Hedingham, Castle Hedingham, Gosfield, Great and Little Yeldham, and Toppesfield and the appointment of a priest to say masses on behalf of the deceased.[92] The priest lived at Ostags, one of the manors that Hawkwood had intended for his wife, Donnina.[93]

The chantries no longer exist. The chapel commemorating Hawkwood in the church at Castle Hedingham was taken down in 1676. The scattered remnants were then set up in a farmhouse built on the lands of the dissolved nunnery.[94] The decayed monument remains in Sible Hedingham, along with a tile with the stamp of a hawk, now kept in a drawer.[95]

# Conclusion

The distinguished French knight Geoffroi de Charny (d. 1356), like Hawkwood, fought in the Hundred Years' War. Charny never met Hawkwood, but a passage from his *Book of Chivalry* reads like a summary of the Englishman's career:

> Now we must consider yet another category of man-at-arms who deserves much praise. That is the one who, for various compelling reasons . . . leaves his locality . . . before he has gained any reputation there, [although] he would have preferred to remain in his own region if he could well do so. But nevertheless they leave and go to Lombardy or Tuscany or Pulia or other lands where pay and other rewards can be earned. . . . Through this they can see, learn and gain knowledge of much that is good through participating in war, for they may be in such lands or territories where they can witness and themselves achieve great deeds of arms. And many times Our Lord has favored a number of those . . . both with renown for their physical strength and skill in the good armed combats . . . so that they drew profit as well as honor from them. And when God has, by his Grace, granted them honor for their great exploits in this military activity, such men deserve to be praised and honored everywhere, provided that they do not, because of the profits they have made, give up the exercise of arms too soon, for he who too quickly gives it up may easily diminish his reputation. And no one should give up performing great exploits, for when the body can do no more, the heart and determination should take over. . . . I therefore say: whoever does best is worth the most.

As we have seen, Hawkwood remained on the battlefield to the very end of his life; his great retreat from Milanese territory just prior to his death followed closely Charny's call for "heart and determination" to take over when "the body can do no more." Hawkwood's persistence indicates that, for all his manipulation of his employers and interest in profits, he was the quintessential soldier, who reveled in the practice of arms.

Charny's aim in the Book of Chivalry was to outline the qualities of the chivalrous knight. Whether Hawkwood met all these criteria is subject to debate. The concept of chivalry was, as we have frequently noted, an inherently ambiguous one, whose flip side involved harassment and abuse of innocents—activities at which Hawkwood particularly excelled.[1] Charney, an intensely pious man, stressed above all the knightly obligation to go on crusade.[2] But Hawkwood consistently refused to do this, and his behavior in this regard contrasted sharply with that of other men in his profession. The difference is perhaps most apparent in the events that occurred after the great Milanese-Florentine war in 1392. Hawkwood's rival in the conflict, Jacopo dal Verme, went on crusade to Jerusalem alongside the future English king Henry IV. Hawkwood, though the end of his life approached—and with it, presumably, the impulse to atone for his sins—eschewed the company of the English dauphin and remained in Florence putting his affairs in order.

But however problematic the term *chivalric knight* is as applied to Hawkwood, he undoubtedly influenced perceptions of his day. Terry Jones has made the provocative statement that Chaucer's "gentle" knight in the prologue to his *Canterbury Tales* was an ironic portrait, modeled on mercenaries like Hawkwood.[3] Chaucer, as we know, met Hawkwood in person, as well as many other men of his profession. But Hawkwood brought Chaucer together in Italy with Nicholas Sabraham, a knight and crusader who Maurice Keen, in his rebuttal of Jones's argument, has noted bears close resemblance to Chaucer's knight. Sabraham's peregrinations—to Scotland, France, Spain, Prussia, Hungary, Greece, Turkey, and Alexandria—mirror those of Chaucer's well-traveled crusader.[4]

One of the most important and distinctive features of Hawkwood's career was his role as a conduit between English and Italian society. Through him, most obviously, military knowledge flowed between the two places. Hawkwood brought with him to Italy English techniques of war developed in France and Scotland and used them to effect on the battlefield. But he also learned much from his Italian experience and sent information in the other direction. His exposure to the styles of war of soldiers of various nationalities, the switching of sides, fighting both with and against his fellow captains, enhanced Hawkwood's skills such that he developed into the most sophisticated strategist anywhere in Europe. Those who served in his brigades returned to England with improved skills, bringing what they learned back to the Hundred Years' War in France and Spain. Hawkwood's comrade John Thornbury, who had only mixed success in Italy, returned to England to the military retinue of John of Gaunt. Gaunt's retinue, one of the most studied by English scholars, contained at various times several men who fought in Italy, including John Kirkeby, Robert Clifton, and John Colepepper.[5] It is doubtless an overstatement to speak of "Italian methods" of war used by the English, but soldiers who served beyond the Alps were clearly valued by their contemporaries.

The exchange between Italy and England involved, however, much more than just military skill. Mercenary bands constituted a unique cultural exchange. The greatest failing of the current historiography on mercenaries is that it has entirely neglected the human element in the drama. Englishmen were exposed to different customs and political and economic systems. The interaction involved not only soldiers but men of various professions. Hawkwood's brigades played host to English merchants, churchmen, and ambassadors, as well as the captain's personal servants who traveled back and forth to conduct his business. Through Hawkwood these men gained experience of Italian society, and Italian society gained experience of them. The interchange occurred at the most basic domestic level. Hawkwood married an Italian, Donnina; his comrade John Thornbury married an Italian named Naverina, and Richard Romsey married another, named Isabella. German and Hungarian soldiers did the same.

Mercenary armies fostered what might be called a vertical social exchange.[6] The Italian mercenary system brought together a highly diverse group of men of varying social classes: petty thieves and highwaymen, to be sure, but also poets and artists, men of modest background as well as men of higher status. Italian battlefields were perhaps the most egalitarian spaces in all of fourteenth-century Europe. Service overseas blurred traditional societal markers and distinctions and forced soldiers into the unique position of re-creating themselves.[7]

This was, of course, the basic appeal of the mercenary profession and what brought Hawkwood and his comrades to Italy in the first place. The men established relationships across social barriers, both within their bands and with the outside world. Hawkwood's military skill placed him at the head of brigades beside men of higher social status. Many of these were German, Italian, and Hungarian captains, who were from the petty nobility. But on the battlefield Hawkwood shared equal rank and authority with them. This is not to say that there were not resentments; the Swabian lord Konrad Aichelberg did not like Hawkwood and did not wish to defer to him, even when he served in a subordinate role in armies. But the social boundaries were sufficiently fluid that Hawkwood was able to marry his daughter to Konrad Prassberg, who was also from the nobility. Such unions became common.

Class distinctions were more operative within the context of an individual national group. Hawkwood may have stood on equal footing with German and Hungarian captains of higher class, but Germans and Hungarians of lower rank, regardless of their martial skill, did not. The traditional hierarchies of those societies appear to have reasserted themselves in the new environment. The En-

glish case is somewhat unusual with respect to the others in that there seem to
have been relatively few soldiers from the nobility and many more from the
middle and lower levels of society. For that reason, there was de facto a greater
social mobility within English brigades. Nevertheless, those men-at-arms with
connections to noble houses, even tenuous ones, seem to have attained leadership
roles more easily. This was the case of Hugh de la Zouche, who led the White
Company in 1364, and Andrew Belmont (or Beaumont), who, though undistin-
guished as fighter, always stood as a corporal in brigades. Men like William
Gold and Richard Romsey, on the other hand, moved steadily through the ranks,
achieving first knighthood in Italy and eventually command of whole armies.
It was, however, unthinkable that Hawkwood would stand superior to a high-
ranking noble such as Edward Despenser, who fought in Italy in the late 1360s.
Nevertheless, Hawkwood took command of an army, in the Pisan war, in which
both Belmont and Hugh de la Zouche participated and were subordinate to him.
It may well have been partly for this reason that it so notoriously fell apart.

Hawkwood created within his personal brigades a system akin to the English
retinue. He attracted to his service men from his home county of Essex, for whom
he served as military mentor. We have spoken of some of them in the preceding
pages: William Coggeshale, John Coe, John Ball, Richard Stisted, John Northwood,
John Oliver, John Giffard.[8] There were certainly more, though we shall probably
never know the full role call. Hawkwood forged lasting associations with the men,
reinforced by economic, social, and even familial ties. Indeed, the social structure
within Hawkwood's brigades closely resembled the patron-client system—what
Christiane Klapisch-Zuber has called "parenti, amici, vicini [kin, friends, and
neighbors]," which constituted the underpinning of Florentine society.[9]

Scholars have traditionally viewed mercenaries as inherently rootless men.
Anthony Mockler called the fourteenth-century mercenary a "vagabond"; Guy
Arnold, speaking of the profession in general, claimed that such men inherently
lacked national feeling.[10] But it may be argued, in fact, that service abroad, fighting in a strange land among men of various nations, enhanced in soldiers a sense
of their own national identity.[11] Hawkwood always considered himself an Englishman above all else. Scholars of England have noted how the ongoing war with
France encouraged a general feeling of "Englishness" at the time—a point emphasized in the contemporary sermons of clergymen like Thomas Brinton, bishop of
Rochester, who advocated obligation to king and country and the willingness "pro
patria mori," to die for one's country.[12] We have seen how the sentiment was also
operative in Italy. It was expressed most obviously in the contracts of English
soldiers, which initially involved an oath of allegiance to the king and eventually contained the right for soldiers to return home when they wished. But it

also manifested itself—and perhaps most intensely—in feuds with soldiers of other nationalities. The English defined themselves most often against the Germans, with whom they frequently fought. The Florentine ambassador Simone di Ranieri Peruzzi made clear the pervasive nature of the rivalry when he commented that English and German were two languages that did not "go well together." The feud was at its most intense in 1365, after the two nationalities shared space in the Florentine army. They engaged in a homicidal struggle that culminated in the defeat of the English by a German band calling itself the Company of the Star. The English surrendered by means of a letter in which they specifically identified themselves by their nation—as "impoverished Englishmen." The sense of identity here can be understood less as political than as ethnic and cultural.

More noteworthy still, foreign mercenaries evoked patriotic sentiments on the other side, among their Italian employers. Scholars have long represented the use of mercenaries in Italy as the very antithesis of patriotic sentiment and native pride. But the foreign soldiers induced in their hosts not only local chauvinism but also broader regional and pan-peninsular sentiments. Pope Urban VI articulated this in his famous letter in 1378 lauding the Italian captain Alberigo da Barbiano's victory over Breton mercenaries as "the liberation of Italy from barbarians."[13] This has been taken as the exception to the rule, but the sentiment was pervasive and oft stated. In a far less renowned letter, the Florentine chancellor Salutati also praised Barbiano's victory in patriotic terms, as deriving from the "strength and virtue of Italians." He contrasted Italian virtue with the lack of the same among the English and Germans.[14] It was a pointed statement, since Hawkwood and his German brother-in-law Lutz von Landau were then on the Florentine payroll. The poet Petrarch derided the foreign soldiers in several places, most famously in the poem *Italia mia*, where he condemned the "German rage" and spoke of the "barbaric blood" of mercenaries as a blight on the "lovely body" of Italy.[15]

To be sure, there is rhetorical flourish in all these statements; Petrarch and Salutati were steeped in the classics and tended to see the present situation in terms of the fall of Rome, which had been caused in large part by the reliance on foreign mercenaries. But the sentiment was expressed elsewhere, with less flourish but equal intensity, in the little-studied military leagues, or *taglie*, by which states allied together to defend themselves against marauding bands. The *taglie* strongly advocated regional, sometimes pan-Italian, solidarity. Their preambles invariably contained antiforeign language and correspondingly strong patriotic feeling. The prologue to the military league of 1381 is one of numerous examples. It called on "all Italians and people of Latin blood" to link together against the "diabolical foreign scourge" of mercenary companies that acted as a "plague" on the peaceful states of the peninsula.[16] The image of the bands as a "diabolical foreign scourge" was an especially common one, as was the urge to solidarity.

As we have seen, the military leagues were rarely successful and indeed often brought out latent hostilities among states. It is premature to speak of nationalism in any modern sense; Italy would not achieve nationhood until the nineteenth century. But there were at least the stirrings of an Italian consciousness. This protonationalistic rhetoric was a principal reason that nineteenth-century Italian scholars took up the study of mercenaries at the very time that Italy was uniting as a country. The scholars implicitly saw in the fourteenth century a distant mirror of events in their day.

For all their sense of national identity, Hawkwood and his counterparts were not wholly "outsiders" in Italian society. It has been a fundamental aim of this book to show that fourteenth-century Italian war was inseparable from its social, political, and economic context. Rather than constituting evidence that war was distinct from the other functions of society, the use of mercenaries represented an implicit acknowledgment on the part of Italian contemporaries that a fundamental link existed. The hiring of foreign soldiers with no political or social agenda of their own was an unsuccessful attempt to separate the strands.

The very manner in which wars were fought emphasizes this point. The object was just as much political, social, and economic as it was military; and states fashioned their battle plans accordingly. We have repeatedly seen how Hawkwood's employers routed his armies through cities and areas deemed tense and volatile and timed his offensives to coincide with spring harvests in order to raise revolt even in more stable places. It was critical to Hawkwood's success, as both a captain and a free captain, to gain support from disaffected lords and exiles who inhabited the countryside. Hawkwood could not have maneuvered his armies as efficiently without such men, and his skill in establishing relations with them accounted in no small measure for his success.

Such technique of war underscores a basic lack of political cohesion in Italy. For all the discussion among scholars about the "taming of feudal outposts" and the "shipwreck of Italian feudalism" in the thirteenth century, the truth was that states were still relatively inchoate power aggregates (at least by modern standards) in which petty lords and local potentates continued to play important roles alongside urban governments.[17] The prosecution of war was proof of this. Cities had long excluded their feudal nobility from political participation, but the lords remained active and conditioned the manner in which wars were conducted. A critical point of entry into the Florentine state was, as we have seen, controlled by the Ubaldini family, and Florentine wars in second half of the fourteenth century cannot be wholly understood without reference to the clan. It is instructive of the divided contemporary mentality that many of rewards given to Hawkwood by his employers, notably rural estates, were of the nature of feudal grants, which perpetuated the system.

The scale and nature of Hawkwood's activities in Italy give impetus to see him less as an individual soldier than as a species of state. The classicist G. B. Nussbaum has equated the mercenary bands of the ancient world with "moving city-states."[18] The comparison is appropriate to Hawkwood, who employed his own spies, informers, legal advisers, treasurers, chancellors to draw up papers, business managers, and full-time employees to run his estates. His employees were paid well, indeed sometimes better than their equivalents in traditional states. Hawkwood's chancellor Jacopo da Pietrasanta was paid 150 florins in 1384 for drawing up a single contract; the Florentine chancellor Coluccio Salutati's yearly salary was, as we have seen, 100 florins. In no regard did Hawkwood more resemble his own state than with respect to diplomacy. He corresponded not only with states and rulers throughout Italy but also with their counterparts in France and England. He sent and received embassies and undertook long-term strategies in dealing with others, and they undertook long-term strategies in dealing with him. We have seen how the Florentines, especially in the early phases of Hawkwood's career, sent to him ambassadors who were English-speakers and treasurers; Milan preferred military men.

Hawkwood's earnings were, to be sure, more speculative than those of a traditional state. And it was the uncertainty of the profits, his own and those of his staff, which encouraged the recourse to war, in the form of the raids of free companies. The raids, to speak in business terms, offered a return that was usually worth the risk. This motivated Hawkwood to remain perpetually on campaign and helped make Italian warfare constant.

Hawkwood's state compares in this regard to those of Italian lords such as Galeotto Malatesta of Rimini, Astorre Manfredi of Faenza, or even Castruccio Castracane of Lucca from the earlier period. The men sustained themselves by hiring themselves out as mercenary captains. But Hawkwood's state was geographically diffuse. Its physical locus extended over a broad area, which shifted throughout his career.[19] Only in his later years did it become focused in Tuscany. But his holdings and activities were always international in scope, and the core of his state and its fundamental identity must be said to have been English. He never took employment that conflicted with his obligation to the crown and, after 1377, often conducted the business of King Richard. Hawkwood's activities repeatedly affected the political dynamic of the peninsula, and he was quick to exploit the weaknesses of others if it was to his advantage. And those states that failed to establish cordial relations with Hawkwood, were slow or duplicitous in meeting obligations to him, and did not extend him proper courtesy or dignity—states like Siena and Perugia—quite literally paid the price, in the form of raids.

Hawkwood compares especially well to a state with respect to his finances. His earnings for the year 1377 were 82,600 florins; for 1381 they were 67,533 florins. The sums are extraordinary and bear little semblance to typical personal salaries of the era, which were of a wholly different magnitude. The city of Lucca, with a population of about thirty thousand people, generated revenue of 65,571 florins in 1377 and 70,862 in 1381.[20] Siena, with approximately fifty thousand people, had an income of 93, 962 florins in 1377.[21] Hawkwood's profits in 1377 were more than twice the operating capital of the business empire of Francesco Datini, the famed merchant of Prato, whose interests stretched throughout Europe to Avignon, Valencia, Barcelona, and Palma de Mallorca. The Englishman's earnings that year even exceeded the operating capital of the famed Peruzzi bank, one of the largest businesses in the history of premodern Europe, a "pillar of Christendom" or "super-company," which had a "corpo" at its height in 1300 of 80,000 florins.[22] The historian Christopher Dyer has estimated baronial income in England at 200–500 lire yearly at the beginning of the fourteenth century, according to which Hawkwood did especially well, a fact that would have had particular significance to him. The yearly income of the wealthy Earl of Lancaster was 11,000 lire, a figure that is still only half as much as Hawkwood earned from Florence (21,000 lire) in 1380.

To be sure, Hawkwood did not always earn such high salaries. The sums for 1377 and 1381 represent maximums. But even in more modest years his income is comparable more to that of small towns and businesses than that of other individuals. His lowest yearly income, 600 florins from Pisa in 1366, was still as much as ten times the annual income of the typical baron in England.[23] And our estimates will always be conservative, since we will never have an accurate read on how much money Hawkwood was given under the table and how much he made in pensions, in ransoms of prisoners, and in seizure of arms, armor, and booty from the houses of innocent civilians. Table 6 provides an estimate of Hawkwood's earnings from 1364 to 1394.

Hawkwood's income made him a factor in the Italian economy. It is unfortunately difficult to place his profits in their precise economic context, since scholars have undertaken little research on the financial aspects of war. The great economic historian of Italy Frederic Lane chided economic theorists for defining their subject in precisely such a way as to purposely exclude the analysis of the use of violence.[24] Military historians, for their part, have been just as slow to take on economic issues.[25]

However, it is clear that Italian states labored under the weight of the fiscal

TABLE 6

*Hawkwood's income from salaries, pensions, sales of land, and mercenary raids, 1364–1394*
(in gold florins)

| Year | Salary, Pension, Land Sale | Marauding Company | Total |
|------|---------------------------|-------------------|-------|
| 1364 | (300,000—whole brigade) | | (300,000)[a] |
| 1365 | | 9,000 | 9,000 |
| 1366 | 600 | 12,000 | 12,600 |
| 1367 | | 7,800 | 7,800 |
| 1372 | (480,000) | | (480,000)[b] |
| 1375 | 1,800 | 215,000 | 216,800 |
| 1576 | 1,800 (480,000) | | (481,800)[b] |
| 1377 | 82,600 | | 82,600 |
| 1378 | 40,200 | | 40,200 |
| 1379 | 17,480 | 42,000 | 59,480 |
| 1380 | 13,200 | | 13,200 |
| 1381 | 67,533 | 15,000 | 82,533 |
| 1382 | 13,200 | | 13,200 |
| 1383 | 9,300 | 31,000 | 40,300 |
| 1384 | 1,600 | 11,000 | 12,600 |
| 1385 | 5,200 | 48,000 | 53,200 |
| 1387 | 7,600 | | 7,600 |
| 1388 | 7,600 | | 7,600 |
| 1389 | 7,600 | | 7,600 |
| 1390 | 8,600 | | 8,600 |
| 1391 | 16,200 | | (16,200)[c] |
| 1392 | 9,200 | | 9,200 |
| 1393 | 9,200 | | 9,200 |
| 1394 | 7,000 | | (7,000)[d] |

[a]Paid to the whole White Company at the rate of 150,000 florins for six months.
[b]Paid to the whole of Hawkwood's army at a rate of 40,000 florins per month.
[c]Includes gift of dowries for daughters and pension to Donnina Visconti.
[d]Final settlement with Hawkwood before his death.

pressure brought on them by Hawkwood. Even the relatively modest sum of 10,000 florins that Perugia paid Hawkwood in 1381 (about 12 percent of his income that year) left the city without sufficient funds to meet salary obligations to its employees. Officials raised revenue by doubling the tax on butchered meat,[26] a decision that angered the populace and exacerbated political and social tension within the city.[27] Hawkwood's extortions from Siena in 1385 intensified an ongoing crisis there that ended with legislation aimed at a whole-scale restructuring of the fisc.[28] The mere act of gathering coin to pay mercenaries was itself difficult. The supply of specie in premodern economies was always limited, particularly during war. The cumbersome fiscal apparatuses of states and their limited coercive powers to collect taxes were not conducive to the speedy turnover of funds needed to pay bribes. Desperate to remove Hawkwood from its lands in 1385, Siena allowed him to exchange debased coins for good ones, leaving the city exposed to the effects of Gresham's law.[29]

Given the sums that Hawkwood amassed, it is necessary to account for how he spent his money, which necessarily affected the Italian economy. We have seen that he scattered his profits in various directions, purchasing supplies while on campaign, loaning money to soldiers, and making improvements to his lands. Like others in his profession, he conducted business with moneylenders and pawn-brokers, from whom he borrowed money at high interest. We hear of debts to such men at various times in Florence and in Bologna. The papal decree in 1364 absolving Hawkwood and members of the White Company from obligations to Jewish lenders indicates that the captain also patronized that sector of the economy. Jewish money lending had increased markedly throughout Italy in the second half of the fourteenth century; and with it Jews had become more promi-nent in Italian cities. Officials issued contracts, similar to those made with merce-nary soldiers, allowing them to do business locally and in return taxed them to help pay for the wars and extortions in which Hawkwood played a prominent part. Jews specialized in pawns, which they accepted in return for high-rate loans. According to Paduan sources, a local soldier, Filippo Zerdo, pawned his goods to a Jewish moneylender just prior to setting off on campaign. Papal budgets fre-quently cite the involvement of Jews in matters pertaining to armies. In the 1370s two Jews, "Padono de Agate" and "Icharinde," are mentioned as selling goods to soldiers, including horses, saddle bags, and even missals.[30] As I have argued else-where, the connection between mercenary soldiers and Jewish lenders was an important one, deserving of more study. It likely constituted a significant means by which mercenary money was recycled into the larger Italian economy.[31]

Hawkwood's largest investments, however, were in Venice, where, as of 1375, he purportedly had 100,000 florins on deposit. Venice was one of the commercial capitals of Italy, a meeting place of merchants from throughout Europe. It is not clear in what form Hawkwood made his deposits there. The scholar Reinhold Mueller has outlined the appeal of such fiscal structures as the Venetian grain office, likening it to a Swiss bank, in which depositors, often very rich men—some of whom were mercenary captains—placed funds.[32] Later in his career, when working for Florence, Hawkwood held shares in that city's public debt (*monte*). According to Roberto Barducci, numerous soldiers invested in Florentine public debt in the fourteenth and fifteenth centuries.[33] Florentine officials allowed for the transfer of such credits, thus opening up a secondary market in which one could speculate. Anthony Molho has uncovered evidence that outside investment in government credits increased in times of war, raising the intriguing possibility that war itself served as stimulus to investment in that city.[34]

This pattern of investment in two of Italy's most financially potent cities is noteworthy. It points to a process whereby such states were winning the economic competition of the late fourteenth century. The investment brought money back into the economies of these states, which allowed them to better sustain themselves in the face of continuous war and made them more able to hire the most expensive mercenaries and gain their long-term services.[35] By the time Hawkwood reached the summit of his reputation, only the richest states could afford to employ him for the long term. And as we have seen, extended service induced captains to settle in the states they served, bringing their ample wealth with them and increasing the degree to which their money was recycled into the local economy.

The service also kept captains from raiding local territories or at least reduced the incidents of violence. This was true of Hawkwood's relationship with Florence and Milan. But his long-term arrangement with Florence had consequences for the neighboring cities. While Hawkwood's harassment of Florence declined greatly after 1380, when he settled into a more consistent employment with the city, his activities against Siena, a town he always had contempt for, increased. The basic difference in his relationship with the cities is made clear in the year 1385, when we find Hawkwood paying taxes in Florence while at the same time extorting a bribe from Siena. After 1387, when Florence and Siena were effectively at war, Hawkwood was almost constantly in Sienese territory. During this time he continued to collect a pension from the city of Lucca. In economic terms, Hawkwood provided a means by which Sienese and Lucchese money was recycled into the Florentine economy.[36]

The larger, fiscally more sophisticated states benefited from mercenary money, accentuating their advantage. Hawkwood and his contemporaries thus played an important role in the great economic competition among states and the attendant consolidation that ultimately reduced the political landscape to the five so-called Renaissance states.

Hawkwood's wealth, and mercenary money in general, also had an effect on the English economy. We have seen how some of Hawkwood's most notable investments—the purchase of manors and of Leadenhall (costing 2,000 marks)—were made back in England. In this respect, Hawkwood stood in a tradition noted by the historian K. B. McFarlane. McFarlane described how the fifteenth-century English soldier John Falstolf sent the considerable profits he earned fighting in France back to England, a fact that led McFarlane to make to the provocative statement that the Hundred Years' War may have been beneficial to the English economy of the time. The claim became the subject of a well-known debate with M. M. Postan, who denied the profitability of the French war and of war in general.[37]

The example of Hawkwood and his comrades shows that money was returning from the battlefields not only of France but also of Italy. John Beltoft, whose career flourished in the eighties, sent money home and even arranged for a lifetime annuity from the pope to be paid directly in England. Beltoft purchased military items, such as bows and arrows, in England for use in Italy.[38] Undoubtedly Beltoft also invested in land, but his premature death on the Italian battlefield in 1392 denied him the chance to return to England. Hugh de la Zouche, on the other hand, did return home in 1371 to a comfortable retirement on his estates in Cambridge, Leicester, and Sussex counties. His elevated status is reflected by his service on royal commissions and in important local posts until his death in 1399.[39] John Thornbury used his Italian profits to buy land in his native county in Hertfordshire and served as member of Parliament five times.[40] He continued to profit from his Italian connections while in England, gaining an annuity from the pope for his part in negotiations with a local abbey and, after much litigation, his share of William Gold's fortune promised him back in 1379, which helped sustain his son Philip's life as a landed lord.[41]

This is not to assert that investment from Italy brought overall profit to the English economy. The debate lies outside the scope of this study. Suffice it to say that many men-at-arms who served in Italy or France returned home poor. The reformer John Wycliff complained in his sermons about the problem of impecunious former soldiers,[42] and the Parliament in 1376 enacted legislation ordering such men to resume their original crafts.[43]

It needs to be stressed, however, that the practice of sending money home was not unique to English mercenaries in Italy. Hawkwood and his comrades followed a pattern already set by German men-at-arms. The famous captain Werner of Urslingen purchased estates in his native Swabia with the revenue he earned during his service at the head of the Great Company in the 1340s and 1350s and was able to retire in comfort on them. Hannekin Baumgarten bought lands in his native Cologne. There are many more examples.

Like Hawkwood, German soldiers used representatives (the equivalent of feoffees) at home, often relatives, to make the actual purchases. Johann von Rietheim bought property in Ulm with the help of his brother Wilhelm; Konrad von Weitingen worked with his brother Volz to purchase land near Radolfzell.[44] Huglin von Schöneck sent money home to Basel with the help of his brother Johann, a canon in St. Leonard's Church there. Schöneck subsidized the construction of a chapel in the church and, like Hawkwood, endowed a memorial in his own honor. In 1369 the pope allowed Huglin to send to the church a relic of Saint Theobald that he found in Italy.[45]

It was the uniqueness of the Italian economic system, the most sophisticated in Europe, which facilitated the movement of money. Both the Germans and the English returned their profits through bills of exchange, a medieval Italian innovation that was available to soldiers who worked in Italy. International merchant bankers, particularly those who serviced the pope, used the bills extensively to transfer sums over distances and to speculate in the money market. As we have seen, Hawkwood and his comrades drew bills on the Guinigi firm of Lucca. The German Johann von Riethelm used the Del Mayno bank of Milan, one of that city's most important firms. The German economic historian Wolfgang von Stromer has made the intriguing statement that German mercenaries took home not only profits but also knowledge of Italian business techniques. Bertold Mönch, who replaced Hawkwood in Milanese service when the Englishman defected in 1372, worked after his service was done as an agent for the Del Mayno bank and subsequently set up his own firm on the Milanese model in Cologne. Hannekin Baumgarten used his exposure to Italian business methods to help his heirs establish the Paumgartner company, a firm of German businessmen who conducted trade between Avignon, Barcelona, Milan, and Prague.[46] This is another instance in which mercenary soldiers functioned as a means of cultural exchange.

In terms of Italian history, the tendency of foreign mercenaries to export their profits constituted a drain on the economy. The shift from the use of foreign mercenaries in the fourteenth century to native ones in the fifteenth must therefore be viewed not only in military terms but also in economic terms. Native soldiers invested their money at home in Italy and thus enhanced the degree to which such funds were recycled into the economy. It may rightfully be said that fourteenth-century war constituted a greater economic drain than fifteenth century—a statement that has important implications for the overall economy history of the peninsula.

This book has stressed the importance of understanding Hawkwood's career in its context. It has been argued that Hawkwood was not an anomalous figure but one of continuity, who had much in common with his contemporaries.

Indeed, virtually all the distinctions and honors he attained have parallels in the careers of other men. The grants to him of land, citizenship, and pensions were standard practice in fourteenth-century Italy. The Venetians gave the obscure German captain Robotus von Engestorp land and citizenship in 1373.[47] The Perugians did the same for Albert Sterz and Hannekin Baumgarten in 1364.[48] The lord of Ferrara, Niccolò d'Este, gave the Tuscan captain Filippo Guazzalotti local estates and made him a citizen as well. Florence granted citizenship not only to Hawkwood but also to Konrad Aichelberg and, years earlier, Rodolfo da Varano, a decision officials came to regret. The precedent for Hawkwood's extended service to Florence was set a generation earlier by the Catalan captain Diego de Rat, who worked continuously for the city from 1305 to 1313 and took up residence in a local palace.[49]

Even Hawkwood's role as diplomat was common. Garrett Mattingly in *Renaissance Diplomacy* made a sharp distinction between the mercenary and the diplomat, claiming that "diplomacy was for rulers; war for hired men."[50] But there was in fact hardly a mercenary who was not also a diplomat. Jacopo dal Verme served the Visconti as an envoy to Pope Gregory XI during the War of Eight Saints and to his native city, Verona, in 1387. Lutz von Landau also acted as ambassador to his home, conducting negotiations in Italy on behalf of his monarch, the Holy Roman Emperor Wenceslaus.[51] He conferred with the emperor in person, sat at his court in Prague, and from 1379 to 1383 served as intermediary between the monarch and the city of Lucca in discussions about imperial recognition of the city's freedom.

In general, Hawkwood's career bears strong resemblance to that of his German brother-in-law Lutz. Like Hawkwood, Landau began his Italian career in the service of a legendary mercenary company of co-nationals, the German Great Company. He emerged as a respected independent captain in the late sixties and seventies, attained considerable wealth, and in 1377 married one of Bernabò Visconti's illegitimate daughters. Lutz was the subject, like Hawkwood, of a *novella* by Franco Sacchetti.

But it was in the end Hawkwood's success at war that most distinguished him from his contemporaries. He was ultimately a better soldier than Landau or any of the others. If his career was not an augur of a new phase in the history of mercenaries, it nevertheless represents an outstanding instance of the triumph of the individual. In this regard, it evokes Burkhardt's notion of the "Renaissance man." Burckhardt reserved the title for Italians, whom he called the "first born sons of modern Europe," and saw the native fifteenth-century *condottieri* as the apotheosis of the phenomenon.[52] Hawkwood possessed many of the characteristics outlined by Burckhardt, notably the ability to overcome circumstance and low birth by dint of talent and cunning, which manifested itself most clearly on the battlefield.

But John Hawkwood can perhaps even better be understood in terms of new historicist concepts of Renaissance identity.[53] He bears the stamp of what the literary critic Stephen Greenblatt has called a "self-fashioned" persona, characterized by the ability to assume a "calculated mask" within a specific cultural context. Greenblatt cites Shakespeare's Iago as one such example, as a "mobile personality" who dominates others by means of "empathy"—a term borrowed from sociologist Daniel Lerner and defined as a distinctly European trait that allowed early modern explorers to conquer new environments.[54] Hawkwood may be said to have manipulated Italy the way Greenblatt's Iago worked on Othello.

Greenblatt's self-fashioning occurred in the milieu of sixteenth-century court culture. Hawkwood molded his persona in the context of fourteenth-century Italy, on the battlefield and in diplomacy, both of which involved similar modes of dissimulation and coded behavior. His success as military strategist, diplomat, and blackmailer depended to no small extent on empathy, on his capacity to understand his opponents' mentality and anticipate their reactions. His deceitfulness and his elusive, changing identity lay at the source of his power.[55] The palimpsest of Uccello's obedient captain over the older, fiercer image represents a final retouching of the mask.

*1. Last Will and Testament of Gilbert Hawkwood (1340)*

In the name of God, Amen. This is the will of Gilbert of Hawkwood

First, I leave my soul to God and the Blessed Mary and to all of her saints and my body for burial at the church of St. Peter in Hengham Sibill.

Next, I leave to the church of St Paul in London two solidos.

Next, for expenses on the seventh day of my burial I leave 5 marks. And for expenses on the thirtieth day, two marks. And for the candles burned 10 solidos.

Next, for distributing to the poor and other expenses of my burial, 10 marks

Next, to my oldest son John, 10 libras

Next, to my younger son John, 20 libras

Next, to my son Nicholas, 10 marks.

Next, for Agnes, my daughter and Ruby, her husband, 100 solidos

Next, Johanna, my daughter and John of John Gravashale, her husband, 100 solidos, which I wish that are in the hands of my oldest son John, who will dispense as he sees fit.

Next, I leave my daughter Alice, 10 libras

Next, I leave Margaret, my daughter, 10 libras

Next, I leave John Calth, 40 solidos

Next, I leave the Vicar of Gosfield, 10 solidos

Next, I leave the chaplain of the parish, 2 solidos

Next, I leave William Ferour, chaplain, half a mark.

Next, I leave on behalf of the four chaplains celebrating [mass] in the church of Hengham, and elsewhere, 20 marks.

Next, Walter, son of Philip, a half a mark.

Next, William Cumbwell, half mark.

Next, Basilia, female slave, 12 denari.

Next, John Munne the elder, 40 denari.

Next, William, his brother, 40 denari.

Next, Gilbert, son of Stephen, 40 denari.

Next, Agnes Munne, 2 solidos.

Next, Matilda, her sister, 12 denari.

Next, Richard le Clerk, 6 denari.

Next, Walter Bernard, 5 solidos.

Next, Henry, my renter 40 denari.

Next, Agnes Ostag, 40 denari.

Next, Agnes, the Prioress of Hengham, half a mark.

Next, Sara, formerly "suprioressa," 3 solidos.

Next, to John my oldest son, six steer and 2 cows from my manor in Hengham Sibill.

Next, I leave to the same John, my son, 10 quarterias of grain and 10 "quarterias" of oats.

Next, I leave to John, my younger son, 5 quarterias of grain and 5 quarterias of oats.

Next, to Nicholas, my brother, five "quarterias" of grain and 5 "quarterias" of oats.

Next, I leave Walter Munne, 2 solidos.

Next, to John Munne, the younger, 2 solidos.

Next, I leave to my shepherds, 12 denari.

Next, to Thomas Munne, 2 solidos.

Next, I leave to my daughter Alice, beyond the previously mentioned 10 lira, 100 solidos and one bed.

Next, to my daughter Margaret, 100 solidos and one bed.

Next, to my son, John, the younger, 100 solidos and one bed.

Next, to my son Nicholas, one bed.

Next, I concede to the same Alice, Margaret, John and Nicholas support for one year.

Next, I leave all my other goods, that have not been specifically apportioned, to my executors, for the purposes of making and distributing, on behalf of my soul and the souls of my all my benefactors, in celebration of masses and to the poor, according to what is best for my soul and for the souls of all the faithful.

I constitute and make as executors of this testament, my son, John the elder; my son John, the younger; Lord John the vicar of the church of Gosfield. . . .

*2. The Agreement between the White Company and the Marquis of Montferrat*
*(22 November 1361)*

We John Marquis of Montferrat Imperial vicar, etcetera presently promise to the egregious and noble men: lord Albert Stertz captain of the great society of English and Germans, now in Rivarolo, Andree de Belmonte, Ioanni de Hakeude, Guillelmo Quatreton, Rubino de Pingo, Guillelmo d' Arras, Guillelmo Folifet, Ioanni Stocheland, Adam Scoto, Guillelmo Bosson, Iohanni Baxino, Roberto de Thorborough, Thome de Bomont constables of the said society and to Eyghino de Heton, Thome de Biston, Iohanni Borgelay, Thome Ludelay, Guillelmo Kerkebi and all others and each of the said society that up until next July we will not give aid, counsel or favor against the same society or state of the same. Rather, we will keep and treat all and each as our dear and faithful friends.

Item, that to them as our dear friends we will allow to be given food, merchandise, refreshment and other material that they need in any place or territory of ours in return for their money.

Item, that they are able to stay and depart from our lands as our dear friends provided that they come not in unwieldy numbers and provided that they have our letters conceding them license, that is, that in our lands and with our people and subjects they are able to associate and do business freely and securely.

Item, that to whomever of our enemies wishes to join the said company we will give transit and passage though our territories, if we are required, notwithstanding any obstructions, and on the condition that they obligate themselves to us by the same pacts as the others.

Also, that to Count of Landau and other Italian traitors or our exiles we do not wish to be held to give passage in any way. Indeed, we wish that these be handled carefully everywhere as traitors and exiles.

Item, that to the same [society] we will give in every case our authority, counsel, aid and favor, provided that they not oppose our subjects or those sworn to allegiance to us.

With the exception, however, that it is understood that they not oppose our nephew, the illustrious Count of Savoy, nor oppose his lands, his people or subjects, but rather, notwithstanding the above, it is permitted to ourselves to act toward our nephew the lord Count in whatever manner we wish.

And we promise to observe all and each of these things legally and in good faith without fraud, as they are expressed above until the aforementioned day.

We, also, Albert Stertz, knight and captain aforementioned, Andreas de Belmonte, Iohannes de Hakeude, Guillelmus Quatreton, Rubinus de Pingo, Guillelmus d'Arras, Guillelmus Folifet, Iohannes Stochland, Adam Scot, Guillelmus Boson, Iohannes Baxinus, Robertus Thoinborogh, Thomas de Bomont, constables, Eyghino de Heton, Thomas Biston, Iohannes Borgelay, Thomas Ludelay and Guillelmus Kerkebi for ourselves and all others and associates of our said society of English and Germans and others who are in the said society or will be in the future, promise to the previously mentioned illustrious and magnificent prince and Lord John, the Marquis of Montferrat, imperial vicar, etcetera, that until next July we will not oppose him or his honor and state or any of his lands, cities, localities, forts, people and subjects or the lord Doge and commune of Genoa and both subjects and those who are allied to, and we will do no injury either collectively or individually, publicly and secretly and we will not go over to the service of any of his enemies; but indeed, if we know anything or anyone to procure or treat of something that can go to the damage of the said Marquis and Doge and their subjects we will notify them and avoid those men as well as much as possible.

Item, that all and each lands, cities, forts and places of the Marquis and his subjects that we are or any of our men are in, we shall defend legally and faithfully, without fraud, against all persons the honor and state of the Marquis of Montferrat and the Doge of Genoa.

Item, to the same lord Marquis we will serve at his request well and faithfully against his enemies provided that [if only] he requires us to wage war or remove his enemies from camp if they are encamped in the territory and jurisdiction of any places or forts which the said lord Marquis holds or possesses or in the future will hold and that it is understood that the said places be left decently armed.

Item, that the person of the same lord Marquis and the illustrious lord Otto, duke of Brunswick, relative and brother of the said lord Marquis and lord of Captain of Genoa and each and all knights, noble, officials and subjects of the said Marquis and Doge while they are with us and in our company we will honor, defend and treat as the person of our own lords and just as our own dear and special brothers and friends, by custom of fraternity.

And that the said lord Marquis and said lords Otto and lord Captain and each and all other knights officials men and subjects of the said lords can with us, among us and in whatever place we are, come, stay, go, associate with, return by their own free will with each and all of their things, horses, merchandise freely and securely just as our dear friends and brothers by whatever way we can.

Item, that in all cases we will dispose of our charge wholly against whosoever of the enemies of the lord Marquis and the Doge and the nobles, people and subjects of their honor and state.

And to the same we forcefully give aid, counsel, and favor.

And that to any subject of the aforementioned Marquis and the said lord Doge we will do no violence

With the exception, however, that by the aforementioned we are not held to do anything against another English society or any subjects of the lord King of England if they should come to Lombardy, unless the same society is at the service of the enemies of the said Marquis.

And we promise, well and faithfully, to observe each and all of the aforementioned things in good faith without fraud as is stated above until the aforementioned date.

Given at Ripparolo [Rivarolo] on 22 November in the year of our lord Jesus Christ 1361. On the fourteenth indiction.

*3. Transactions involving John Hawkwood, the elder*

| Year | Transaction | Source |
|------|-------------|--------|
| 1341 | Renunciation of his right to the lands of John Longwood, recently died, in Langham and Stratford in Essex and Sussex counties. The deed was drawn up at Sible Hedingham; witnesses: John Lystones, "knight," Thomas Hodinge, John Ostag, John Graveshale, Thomas Ruby, and John Olyver. | PRO, DL 25/1736. |
| 1343 (Jan.) | Witness with Walter Rouhey and John Nunthey to grant of land of land involving Robert "Bourgchier" in Halstead. | *Calendar of Close Rolls, Edward III, 1343–1346;* *Feet Fines for Essex,* 2:256. |
| 1344 | Along with Margery, his wife, and John, "their son and heir," held "court" at manor of Bellowes in Gosfield. John Calth and John Galaunt also mentioned. | Morant, 378. |
| | Involved in litigation with the Munne family, John Calth, and John Galaunt, the vicar of Gosfield, over land in Gosfield, Sible Hedingham, and Bocking. | *Feet of Fines for Essex,* 3:72. |
| 1348 (June) | Received exemption for life from being put on "assizes, juries or recognitions, or from being made mayor, sheriff, coroner, escheator, or other bailiff or minster of the king, against his will." | *Calendar of the Patent Rolls, Edward III, 1348–1350,* 140. |
| 1350 (Mar.) | Witness to a grant involving John de Coggeshale and Isabel, wife of John Bernard. | *Calendar of Close Rolls, Edward III, 1349–1354,* 215. |
| 1353 | "Possessed of" manor of Bellowes, now called Hawkwood's Gosfield. | Morant, 378. |
| 1354 (Oct) | Received with wife, Margery, from John Bourchier (Bourgchier) pastureland in Gosfield formerly owned by John Lystones. | ERO, D/DCw/T 37/31 |
| 1360 | Involved with John Cavendish in land deals in Gosfield, Little Yeldham, Greater Yeldham, Sible Hedingham, and Castle Hedingham. | *Feet of Fines for Essex,* 3:128. |
| | Took possession of the manor of Parke Hall in Gosfield as of 1360. | Morant, 379. |
| 1361 | Mentioned in connection with "knight's fee" from John de Vere, the Earl of Oxford. | *Calendar of Inquisitions Post Mortem, Edward III,* 10:513–523. |
| 1368 | Involved in land deals in Gosfield, Sible Hedingham, and Bocking. | *Feet of Fines for Essex,* 3:15 4. |
| 1370 (Feb.) | Witness to lands acquired by John Bourchier in Halstead. | ERO, D/DCw/T 33/2, D/DCw/T 33/3. |

| | | |
|---|---|---|
| 1371 | Served as the executor of Thomas de Veer's will. | BL, Harleian MS 6148, fol. 143r. |
| 1373 (July) | Payment to John de Neuport of Essex for his lands. Mentioned as Hawkwood "of Gosfield." | *Calendar of Close Rolls, Edward III, 1369–1374,* 573. |
| 1375 | Suit regarding rights to lands in Finchingfield, Great Sampford, Great Berfeld. John Cavendish mentioned. | *Feet of Fines for Essex,* 3:176. |
| 1377 | Service as tax collector in Essex. | *Calendar of Fine Rolls, Richard II, 1377–1383,* 57. |
| 1380 | Tenancy of land in Gosfield (14 acres of land and pasture) and Sible Hedingham owned by the priory of Colne. | ERO, D/DPr/6 67. |
| 1381 | Listed in poll tax as "Franklin." Assessed at a rate of 5 soldi in Gosfield, the second highest next to that of Richard Lyons. | Fenwick, 210. |
| 1384 | Mentioned in "rental of the manor of Graveshall" as tenant of 2 acres of land yielding 6 denari a year. John Sargeant and John Oliver also mentioned as tenants. | ERO, D/DBm/m 164. |
| 1388 | Mentioned as "still alive" and married to Margery. | *Calendar of Inquisitions, Miscellaneous (Chancery), 1387–1393,* 92. |
| 1390/91 | Served with William Coggeshale as witness to a deal regarding land in Sampford. | ERO, D/DQ 61/194. |
| 1392 | Mentioned in connection with the litigation involving lands of Maud de Veer, mother of Thomas de Veer. | *Calendar of the Patent Rolls, Richard II, 1391–1396,* 98. |

*Note:* BL = British Library, London; ERO = Essex Record Office, Chelmsford, England; Morant = Morant, *History and Antiquities of Essex;* PRO = Public Record Office, London; Fenwick = Fenwick, *Poll Taxes.*

## *Abbreviations*

| | |
|---|---|
| ASBo | Archivio di Stato di Bologna, Bologna, Italy |
| ASF | Archivio di Stato di Firenze, Florence, Italy |
| ASL | Archivio di Stato di Lucca, Lucca, Italy |
| ASMa, AG | Archivio di Stato di Mantova, Archivio Gonzaga, Mantua, Italy |
| ASMi | Archivio di Stato di Milano, Milan, Italy |
| ASMo | Archivio di Stato di Modena, Archivio d'Este, Modena, Italy |
| ASPe | Archivio di Stato di Perugia, Perugia, Italy |
| ASPi | Archivio di Stato di Pisa, Pisa, Italy |
| ASS | Archivio di Stato di Siena, Siena, Italy |
| AST | Archivio di Stato di Torino, Turin, Italy |
| ASV | Archivio Segreto Vaticano, Vatican City, Italy |
| ASVe | Archivio di Stato di Venezia, Venice, Italy |
| ATL | Anziani al Tempo della Libertà, Archivio di Stato di Lucca, Lucca, Italy |
| BCA | Biblioteca Comunale dell'Archiginnasio, Bologna, Italy |
| BML | Biblioteca Medicea Laurenziana di Firenze, Florence, Italy |
| BRF | Biblioteca Riccardiana di Firenze, Florence, Italy |
| CG | Consiglio Generale, Archivio di Stato di Siena, Siena, Italy |
| CLRO, HR | Corporation of London Record Office, Hustings Roll, London, England |
| Conc. | Concistoro, Archivio di Stato di Siena, Siena, Italy |
| CP | Consulte e Pratiche, Archivio di Stato di Firenze, Florence, Italy |
| ERO | Essex Record Office, Chelmsford, England |
| PRO | Public Record Office, London, England |
| Reg Vat | Registri Vaticani, Archivio Segreto Vaticano, Vatican City, Italy |

## *Introduction*

1. Sacchetti, *Il trecentonovelle,* 448–449.
2. Ibid., 449. Granger, *Biographical History of England,* 59–60.
3. Gregorovius, *Geschichte der Stadt Rom,* 34.

4. "En Ytalie ne fu cent ans devant plus vaillant capitain ne plus sage de lui." Jorga, *Thomas III*, 127.

5. *Westminster Chronicle*, 521.

6. Pucci, *Poesie*, 253.

7. British Library, London, Additional MS 6395. This contains correspondence from 1640 to 1641 relating to Maurice's attempts to write Hawkwood's life. Brief early notices of Hawkwood's career are also in John Stow's *Annales* and del Migliore's *Firenze città nobilissima.*

8. Winstanley, *Honour of the Taylors*, 1.

9. Gough, *Memoirs of Sir John Hawkwood*, 2.

10. Andrew Ayton suggested that the task would "defy even the most determined researcher." Ayton, *Knights and Warhorses*, 139.

11. Beck, *Hawkwood the Brave;* Cole, *Hawkwood, Hawkwood and the Towers of Pisa*, and *Hawkwood in Paris.*

12. O'Rourke, *Hawkwood.*

13. Temple-Leader and Marcotti, *Sir John Hawkwood.*

14. See, among others, Stanley, "Sir John Hawkwood"; Sperling, "Sir John Hawkwood"; Trease, *Condottieri;* and Deiss, *Captains of Fortune.* In 1975, the Italian writer Marco Tabanelli wrote a biography based mostly on Temple-Leader and Marcotti (*Sir John Hawkwood*) entitled *Giovanni Acuto, Capitano di Ventura.* The work contains basic factual and chronological errors. The same is true of Hans Rosenberger's *John Hawkwood, ein englischer Soldführer in Italien*, which was originally a doctoral dissertation. Two recent additions to the popular genre are Duccio Balestracci's *Le armi, i cavalli e l'oro: Giovanni Acuto e i condottieri nell'Italia del Trecento* and Frances Stonor Saunders's *Hawkwood: Diabolical Englishman.* They appeared just as this book went to press.

15. Fowler, "Sir John Hawkwood and the English Condottieri in Trecento Italy."

16. Ruskin, "Letter 22 (October 1872)," in Ruskin, *Works*, 384–385.

17. Ricotti, *Storia delle compagnie*, 2:166–178; Canestrini, "Documenti."

18. Especially useful collections of ambassadorial dispatches exist in the state archives of Siena, Lucca, Florence, and Mantua and in the Archivio Segreto of the Vatican. There are also important collections at the Biblioteca Comunale dell'Archiginnasio in Bologna and the Biblioteca Medicea Laurenziana and Biblioteca Riccardiana in Florence. Several useful letters are in the Archivio d'Este in Modena, but the remainder of the documents appear to pertain to the fifteenth century. The Archivio Gonzaga in the state archives of Mantua is perhaps the best of all, although I found many of the letters misfiled and incorrectly dated by modern archivists.

19. Tilly, *Collective Violence*, 133–136.

20. Redlich, *German Military Enterpriser and His Work Force;* see also Redlich, *De Praeda Militari;* Fontenay, "Corsaires de la foi ou rentier du sol?"; and Ingrao, *Hessian Mercenary State.*

21. Copinger, *History and Records of the Smith-Carington Family*, 74.

22. Braudel, *Mediterranean and the Mediterranean World in the Age of Philip II*, 836.

23. A more extensive discussion of the literature on fourteenth-century mercenaries is in Caferro, *Mercenary Companies*, xiii–xx. Daniel Waley has treated some aspects of mercenary contracts in his "Condotte and Condottieri in the Thirteenth Century." The literature for the fifteenth century is far more extensive. In addition to the sources quoted in note 16 of this chapter, see Block, *Die Condottieri;* Waley, "I mercenari e la guerra"; Blastenbrei, *Die Sforza und*

*ihr Heer;* Lazzarini, *Fra un principe e altri stati;* and Covini, *L'esercito del duca.* For the still later period, see Hanlon, *Twilight of a Military Tradition,* 1–8.

24. Mattingly, *Renaissance Diplomacy,* 57–58. Apart from Mattingly, the literature on fifteenth-century diplomacy consists primarily of the studies of Vincent Ilardi. See his *Studies in Italian Renaissance Diplomatic History* and, with Paul Kendall, *Dispatches with Related Documents of Milanese Ambassadors in France and Burgundy.* For a more recent account, see Fubini, "Diplomacy and Government in the Italian City-States of the Fifteenth Century."

25. Paret, *Understanding War,* 14. Michael Howard has also stressed the connection between war and society; see his *War in European History.*

26. Mallett, *Mercenaries and Their Masters* and "Venice and Its Condottieri"; Hale, *Renaissance War Studies* and *War and Society in Renaissance Europe;* Pieri, *Il Rinascimento.*

27. The nineteenth-century nationalistic studies include Ricotti, *Storia delle compagnie;* Canestrini, "Documenti"; and Schäfer, *Deutsche Ritter.*

28. Gaupp, *Pioniere der Neuzeit in der Frührenaissance.*

29. Hale, *War and Society in Renaissance Europe,* 8.

30. Clark, *War and Society in the Seventeenth Century,* 9.

## One • The Man and the Myth

*Epigraph:* Gough, *Memoirs of Sir John Hawkwood,* 1.

1. Deiss, *Captains of Fortune,* 113.

2. Montanelli, *L'Italia dei secoli d'oro,* 375; Tabanelli, *Giovanni Acuto,* 18.

3. Trease, *Condottieri,* 187–188.

4. Borsook, "L'Hawkwood d'Uccello," 44–51; Wegener, "That the Practice of Arms"; Melli, "Nuove indagine sui disegni di Paolo Uccello." The Sercambi chronicle of Lucca contains a contemporary image of Hawkwood along with his band that raided Tuscany in the summer of 1375. Hawkwood is on the extreme right, below his banner, wearing the captain's cap atop his head rather than armor. The portrait is generic. His pose, however, bears similarity to that in the Uccello fresco. Compare figures. 4 and 5.

5. For a more complete discussion of this important subject, see chapter 3.

6. Keen, *Chivalry,* 37; see also Caferro, *Mercenary Companies,* 6, and now Kaeuper, *Chivalry and Violence.*

7. Morant, *History and Antiquities of Essex,* 288.

8. ASL, Consiglio Generale, 5, 116 (18 October 1375); ASV, Reg Vat, 271, fols. 136v–137r; Cognasso, "Note e documenti," 158.

9. BML, Ashburnham MS 1830, II-188.

10. ASMa, AG, busta 1606 (26 August 1379).

11. Selzer, *Deutsche Söldner,* 154.

12. Cole, *Hawkwood and the Towers of Pisa.*

13. F. Villani, *Cronica,* 5:256.

14. ASF, Notarile Antecosmiano, 11053.

15. Hunt, *Medieval Super-companies,* 269–271.

16. Froissart, *Chronicles,* 490.

17. "qui manu et industria potior esset quam lingua." Vergerio, *Epistolario,* 70.

18. *Annales Mediolanenses,* col. 750.

19. ASS, Conc., 1786, #12.

20. CLRO, HR, 124/6; *Calendar of Select Pleas,* 308.

21. Schäfer, *Deutsche Ritter,* 1:141–144; Canestrini, "Documenti," 73.

22. Winstanley, *Honour of the Taylors,* 2.

23. Cole, *Hawkwood.*

24. The memorial is described in a letter dated 23 February 1713/14. ERO, D/Y 1/1/70. See also Sperling, "Sir John Hawkwood," 72–74. The British Library in London contains an incomplete genealogy of the Hawkwood family. British Library, Additional MS 41 319. See also Weever, *Ancient Funeral Monuments.*

25. Roskell, Clarke, and Rawcliffe, *History of Parliament,* 2:616–618.

26. ASL, ATL, 439, #2012.

27. The document is reproduced in Temple-Leader and Marcotti, *Sir John Hawkwood,* 359–360 (document 69).

28. ASMa, AG, busta 1367 (20 September 1372).

29. ASF, Dieci di balia, Legazioni e commissarie, 1, fol. 79.

30. ASL, ATL, 571, #1403.

31. ASMa, AG, busta 2388, #253 (11 July 1378).

32. Trease, *Condottieri,* 73.

33. Pizzagalli, *Bernabò Visconti,* 126–127.

34. ASL, ATL, 439, #2012.

35. Ibid., 571, #1186.

36. Stefani, *Cronaca fiorentina,* 345.

37. In general, mercenaries showed great interest in jewels and expensive "vanity" items. When Hawkwood's comrade William Gold died, he left several chests containing silk cloth, gold, and precious stones, including diamonds, rubies, sapphires, and pearls. *Calendar of Select Pleas,* 308.

38. ASF, Monte Comune, 694, fol. 2r; ASMa, AG, busta 1367.

39. ASF, Capitoli, registri, 1, fol. 48r.

40. *Life of Cola di Rienzo,* 144.

41. *Chronicon Estense,* col. 499.

42. Chinazzo, *Cronica de la guerra,* 43.

43. Machiavelli, *Discourses,* 513.

44. Machiavelli, *Prince,* 40.

45. Contamine, *War in the Middle Ages,* 210–218. The Count of Savoy purchased a copy of Vegetius in 1347. See Cox, *Green Count,* 51.

46. Vegetius, *Epitome,* 74–77, 83–86.

47. Frontinus, *Stratagems and the Aqueducts of Rome,* 6–7, 88–89, 204–205.

48. Knowles, *Les enseignements de Théodore Paléologue.* See also Settia, "Gli 'Insegnamenti' di Teodoro di Montferrato," 11–28.

49. In English armies at the time the numbers of men-at-arms and longbowmen were reaching parity. But this was not the case in Italy. Hawkwood's personal brigade in 1386 consisted of 246 horsemen but had only 40 longbowmen; his brigade in 1387 had 300 horsemen and 55 archers. Ayton, *Knights and Warhorses,* 140. ASF, Camera del comune, Provveditori, poi massai, specchi, 4, fol. 81r; Camera del comune, Provveditori, poi massai, specchi, 5, fol. 85r. ASBo, Tesoreria e controllatore di tesoreria, 14, fol. 4r.

50. On Lombardy and war, see Mallett, *Mercenaries and Their Masters*, 155.

51. Vegetius, *Epitome*, 74.

52. Cavalcanti, *Trattato Politico-Morale*, 125.

53. Covini, *L'esercito del duca*, 154–155, 283; Lazzarini, *Fra un principe e altri stati*, 226–232.

54. ASL, ATL, 439, #1187.

55. Velluti, *Cronica Domestica*, 236; Cognasso, "Note e documenti," 158–159.

56. *Cronaca senese*, 637.

57. Catherine of Siena, *Letters*, 1:106 (letter 30).

58. Urban V, *Lettres communes*, 318.

59. Stow first mentions this in his *Annales* (335). He lists Hawkwood as a founder of the hospice along with numerous others, including the mercenaries Robin Knowles, Hugh Calveley, and the bishop of Rochester, Thomas Brinton. Temple-Leader dismisses Stow's statement as fiction. Temple-Leader and Marcotti, *Sir John Hawkwood*, 140, 178, 238. Recently, however, Margaret Harvey has proved the validity of several names on Stow's list, including Knowles. Although she found nothing either way for Hawkwood, her research indicates that Stow's claims were hardly groundless. Given Hawkwood's frequent sojourns to Rome (serving in the wars in the kingdom) and his oft demonstrated concern for his fellow Englishman, I think it very likely he supported the hospice. Harvey, *English in Rome*, 59–61.

60. Richard Kaeuper has asserted that the knightly attitude toward religion was to absorb ideas appropriate to the way of life and to downplay those that were not. Kaeuper, *Chivalry and Violence*, 45–48.

61. ASV, Reg Vat, 269, fol. 235v.

62. Vergerio, *Epistolario*, 68.

63. Ricotti, *Storia delle compagnie*, 2:166–178.

64. Guasti, *Lettere di un notaio*, 304, 424.

65. Manni, *Commentario;* Gough, *Memoirs of Sir John Hawkwood*, 32.

66. Gaupp, "Condottiere John Hawkwood," 311.

67. De Roover, *Money, Banking and Credit*, 39; Meek, *Lucca, 1369–1400*, 44, 200–202.

68. Jones, *Royal Policy of Richard II*, 130–133.

69. Palmer, "England, France and the Flemish Succession," 358–359; Froissart, *Chronicles*, 574.

70. ASL, ATL, 571, #1085.

71. In his study of medieval Cheshire Philip Morgan noted the tendency of men from that region to go directly to the bands of the renowned Cheshire soldier Hugh Calveley. Morgan also pointed out that local soldiers often bypassed service in France and went straight off to Italy to seek adventure and fortune. Morgan, *War and Society*, 163–178.

72. ASF, Dieci di balia, Deliberazioni, condotte e stanziamenti, 1, fol. 153r, Dieci di balia, Deliberazioni, condotte e stanziamenti, 3, fol. 26v; Dieci di balia, Deliberazioni, condotte e stanziamenti, 4, fols. 45v, 131r; Dieci di balia, Deliberazioni, condotte e stanziamenti, 5, fol. 185r; Camera del comune, Camarlinghi, uscita 300, fol. 15r.

73. *Westminster Chronicle*, 157.

74. *Calendar of Close Rolls, Richard II, 1377–1381*, 367–368; *Calendar of Close Rolls, Richard II, 1381–1385*, 137–138; Morant, *History and Antiquities of Essex*, 379–380.

75. PRO, C 66/348, m. 9, reverse side; *Calendar of the Patent Rolls, Richard II, 1396–1399*, 312.

76. CLRO, HR, 124/6.

77. Thornbury's return to England can be reconstructed from documents in the Public Record Office in London. See PRO, C 143/396/7; C 143/403/38; E 210/5550; E 211/310/B, C, E, F; E 326/2571; E 326/2576. See also *Calendar of the Patent Rolls, Richard II, 1377–1381*, 484; *Calendar of the Patent Rolls, Richard II, 1381–1385*, 55, 347, 465–466, 590, 592, 596, 598–599; *Calendar of the Patent Rolls, Richard II, 1388–1391*, 79–80.

78. Caxton, *Book of the Ordyre of Chivalry*, 123.

*Two • Essex Lad, King's Soldier, and Member of the White Company, 1323–1363*

*Epigraphs:* Scott, *Quentin Durward*, 91. Doyle, *White Company*, 49.

1. Fuller, *Worthies of England*, 163.

2. Reaney, *Essex*, 69–70; *Essex Sessions of the Peace*, 2; Page and Round, *Victoria History*, 2:313–319.

3. Poos, *Rural Society*, 229.

4. Scholars have erroneously referred to the "de" before Hawkwood's name as an "aristocratic particle." As Reaney points out, the particle indicates "no more than the place of origin or birth." Reaney, *Origin of English Surnames*, 36.

5. Gough, *Memoirs of Sir John Hawkwood*, 2; Sumption, *Hundred Years War*, 470.

6. According to R. L. Poos, a craftsman in Essex could also be an "agriculturalist" and vice versa. B. Hanawalt has noted that landowners often sought wages to supplement their income from agriculture. It nevertheless seems highly unlikely that a man of Gilbert's wealth was a tanner. Poos, *Rural Society*, 25–28; Hanawalt, *Ties That Bound*, 115, 134; Kowaleski, *Local Markets*, 293–303.

7. According to the Lay Subsidy of 1334, Finchingfield had the highest overall assessment, followed by Halstead and then Sible Hedingham. Glasscock, *Lay Subsidy of 1334*, 80. Poos (*Rural Society*) lists Essex towns according to size and occupational diversity, based on the 1381 poll tax. Bocking ranked second, Finchingfield third, and Sible Hedingham fifth.

8. Ward, *Medieval Essex Community*, 62–64.

9. PRO, DL 15/1999; ERO, D/DCw/T 46/3; *Calendar of Close Rolls, Edward III, 1327–1330*, 574; *Feet of Fines for Essex*, 2:158.

10. ERO, D/DCw/T 37; D/DBm/m 164; Morant, *History and Antiquities of Essex*, 329, 379; Ward, *Medieval Essex Community*, 64, 66–67.

11. Bourchier, though based in Halstead, was tied directly to Sible Hedingham through his marriage to Margaret Prayers, the daughter of Thomas Prayers, owner of a local manor. Jones, "Fortunes of War," 146; Ward, "Sir John Coggeshale," 61–66.

12. *Calendar of Papal Registers, Petitions to the Pope*; Morant, *History and Antiquities of Essex*, 379.

13. Ward, *Medieval Essex Community*, 63; *Feet of Fines for Essex*, 2:158.

14. *Feet of Fines for Essex*, 3:66, 72; Fenwick, *Poll Taxes*, 210–211.

15. ERO, D/DU 40/50.

16. *Calendar of the Patent Rolls, Edward III, 1348–1350*, 140.

17. *Calendar of Fine Rolls, Richard II, 1377–1383*, 57; Fenwick, *Poll Taxes*, 210–211; *Calendar of Inquisitions, Miscellaneous (Chancery), 1387–1393*, 92.

18. Cole, *Hawkwood*, 1–3.

19. Hanawalt, *Ties That Bound*, 213.

20. Giovio, *Elogia*, 316.

21. F. Villani, *Cronica*, 5:256.

22. Child, *English and Scottish Popular Ballads*, vols. 1 and 2, nos. 20, 64; Hanawalt, *Ties That Bound*, 216.

23. Even then the years were often rounded off. Bedell, "Memory and Proof of Age in England," 3–27; Hanawalt, *Ties That Bound*, 228.

24. Prestwich, " 'Miles in Armis Strenuus,' " 217–218.

25. ERO, T/Z 20/19; D/DMh/F35.

26. A boy could make a testament at fourteen, a girl at twelve, and a child was criminally liable at seven years of age. Fleming, *Family and Household*, 60.

27. Poos, *Rural Society*, 119; Hanawalt, *Ties That Bound*, 228; Gilbert, "When Did a Man Grow Old in the Renaissance?" 7–32.

28. Barber, *Edward, Prince of Wales and Aquitaine*, 90.

29. F. Villani, *Cronica*, 5:224, 256.

30. PRO, DL 25/1736. It is possible that John the elder took over management of Gilbert's estate before his father's death, probably through some form of retirement contract. On such contracts see Hanawalt, *Ties That Bound*, 229.

31. A mark was equal to 160 denari (silver pennies), and 240 denari was equal to 1 lira or pound. The pound was, however, a money of account and not a real coin. See Spufford, *Money and Its Use in Medieval Europe*, 223.

32. PRO, DL 25/1736.

33. The *Westminster Chronicle* was written in Hawkwood's lifetime. It is not clear when the continuation of the *Polychronicon* was written. *Westminster Chronicle*, 521; Higden, *Polychronicon*, 371.

34. Thrupp, *Merchant Class of Medieval London*, 210–211.

35. Here, as with his date of birth, there has been considerable disagreement. The seventeenth-century writer John Stow, author of the oft cited *Annales or General Chronicle of England*, claimed that Hawkwood went to London to become a tailor. Stow's contemporary William Winstanley expanded the statement into a sprawling romance, depicting Hawkwood as a "dexterous" tailor who "gained the applause of his customers." Cecil Clode carried the image into the nineteenth century. In his *Early History of the Guild of Mechant Taylors* he listed Hawkwood as a founding member.

But Temple-Leader dismissed the tailor story out of hand, as according ill with Hawkwood's background and as resulting from a later confusion among scholars of Hawkwood's nickname *acuto* (or in Tuscan form, *aguto*) with *ago*, the Italian word for "needle." "John the needle" became transformed into "John the tailor."

Moreover, the motives of the authors who identified Hawkwood as a tailor are suspect. Both John Stow and Cecil Clode were themselves members of the tailors' guild. William Winstanley stated in his introduction that his main purpose was to use Hawkwood's example to elevate the status of tailors, specifically "to obliterate" slights "touching their manhood." The loss of guild records prior to 1400 makes Clode's claim impossible to verify.

But the contemporary accounts placing Hawkwood in the tailor's shop support Clode and Winstanley and prove, contra Temple-Leader, that the story was not a later confusion of Hawkwood's nickname. Stow, *Annales*, 308, 309; Winstanley, *Honour of the Taylors*, 1; Clode,

*Early History of the Guild of Merchant Taylors;* Temple-Leader and Marcotti, *Sir John Hawk-wood,* 8.

36. Vegetius, *Epitome,* 7.

37. Fuller, *Worthies of England,* 163.

38. Ayton describes this as constituting as much a social revolution as a military one. Ayton, "English Armies in the Fourteenth Century," 29–33; Morgan, *War and Society,* 109.

39. Prestwich, *Armies and Warfare,* 126; Bradbury, *Medieval Archer,* 95–115, 160–170.

40. Prestwich, *Armies and Warfare,* 143.

41. Temple-Leader and Marcotti, *Sir John Hawkwood,* 8–9; Perroy, *Hundred Years War,* 115–116; Sumption, *Hundred Years War,* 370–410.

42. Anderson, *De Veres of Castle Hedingham;* Nicholson, *Edward III and the Scots,* 128, 177, 201, 246.

43. PRO, E 36/204, fols. 102v, 105v; C 76/17, mm. 19, 26. Ayton, *Knights and Warhorses,* 257 n. 7, 263. I thank Professor Ayton for the references.

44. Hawkwood's heirs donated land for the Bourchier chantry at Halstead in 1412. For the Bourchier chantry, see PRO, C 143/443/11. For the Hawkwood chantry, see ERO, D/DCw/T 37/37. The document relating to the bequest of land is PRO, C 143/443/24.

45. F. Villani, *Cronica,* 5:257.

46. PRO, C 143/239/6.

47. On the process of armorial dissemination, see Ayton, "Sir Thomas Ughtred and the Edwardian Military Revolution," 115–118.

48. PRO, E 36/204, fol. 86v; C 76/17, m. 39; C 81/1735, no. 21; C 81/1734, no. 24. I am again indebted to Professor Ayton for these references.

49. John Hawkwood is first mentioned as a recipient of a "knights fee" in 1361 and then again in 1371. *Calendar of Inquisitions Post Mortem, 1370–1373,* 102–103. ERO, D/DMh/F35.

50. Ward, *Essex Gentry,* 18; Morgan, *War and Society,* 49–56; Saul, *Knights and Esquires,* 83; Ayton, "English Army and the Normandy Campaign," 256.

51. Wrottesley, *Crécy and Calais,* 140.

52. A "prest" (advance of wages) exists for de Vere's retinue in 1346, but it makes no specific mention of personnel. PRO, E 403/336, m. 42. Bourchier's presence at Crécy is mentioned in Froissart, *Chronicles,* 163. See also *Knighton's Chronicle,* 62, and Murimuth, *Adae Murimuth Continuatio Chronicarum,* 264. Barber, *Edward, Prince of Wales and Aquitaine,* 50.

53. Scholarly estimates of the size of forces for the campaign have differed. Wrottesley, *Crécy and Calais,* 9–16; Sumption, *Hundred Years War,* 497. I have followed the estimates of Ayton and Rogers. Ayton, "English Army and the Normandy Campaign," 219–237; Rogers, *War, Cruel and Sharp,* 219–237.

54. Page and Round, *Victoria History,* 2:213; Wrottesley, *Crécy and Calais,* 60; Ayton, "English Army and the Normandy Campaign," 258–260.

55. *Chronique de Jean le Bel,* 103; Baker, *Chronicon,* 83–84. Matteo Villani claimed that even those who escaped were wounded by arrows. M. Villani, *Cronica,* 4:406. An excellent description of the campaign is in Rogers, *War, Cruel and Sharp,* 265–267.

56. Neillands, *Hundred Years War,* 104.

57. Sumption, *Hundred Years War,* 19.

58. Wrottesley, *Crécy and Calais,* 280; Ayton, "English Army and the Normandy Campaign," 257.

59. Stow, *Annales*, 308. See also Morant, *History and Antiquities of Essex*, 288.

60. ERO, D/DMh/F35.

61. Baker, *Chronicon*, 148, 303; *Chronique Normande du XIVe siècle*, 114; *Knighton's Chronicle*, 89; M. Villani, *Cronica*, 4:537–538.

62. This could have been because Edward's Register includes only those in his immediate circle; Hawkwood may have received his honors directly from de Vere, who is also not mentioned in the Register. *Register of Edward, the Black Prince.*

63. Higden, *Polychronicon*, 371.

64. M. Villani, *Cronica*, 4:213–214.

65. Froissart took the name Tard-Venus from Jean le Bel. Knighton and Venette preferred, however, to call the band the "Great Company," the name that appears in contemporary documents. The modern French historian, Henri Denifle, the foremost expert on the mercenary companies, favored "Great Company" and suggested that the appellation Tard-Venus "be left to Froissart." More recently, Kenneth Fowler has affirmed the correctness of the term "Great Company." Venette, *Chronicle*, 106; *Knighton's Chronicle*, 183; Denifle, *La désolation des églises*, 1:380; Fowler, *Medieval Mercenaries*, 2–5.

66. Froissart, *Chronicles*, 136; Sumption, *Hundred Years War*, 464.

67. Venette, *Chronicle*, 106.

68. *Knighton's Chronicle*, 183.

69. Denifle, *La désolation des églises*, 1:382–383; Froissart, *Chronicles*, 298; *Chronique de Jean le Bel*, 321; Hayez, "Travaux à l'Enceinte d'Avignon," 196–208.

70. Fowler, *Medieval Mercenaries*, 32.

71. Denifle, *La désolation des églises*, 1:389–90; M. Villani, *Cronica*, 5:50; *Thalamus parvus*, 357; Guigue, *Les Tard-Venus*, 9–55; Fowler, *Medieval Mercenaries.*

72. *Thesaurus Novus Anecdotorum*, cols. 882–883; Denifle, *La désolation des églises*, 1:391; Luttrell, "Juan Fernandez de Heredia at Avignon."

73. Macquarrie, *Scotland and the Crusades;* Sumption, *Hundred Years War*, 464; Cox, *Green Count*, 183.

74. Hawkwood was undoubtedly at Pont-Saint-Esprit, a fact attested to in later documents. He was probably with another contingent of the large and amorphous company. Walter Leslie and Richard Musard both passed into Italy, like Hawkwood, but never fought along with him once there. Fowler, "Sir John Hawkwood and the English Condottieri in Trecento Italy," 131–148.

75. *Thesaurus Novus Anecdotorum*, col. 858; *Chronique de Jean le Bel*, 323.

76. *Thesaurus Novus Anecdotorum*, cols. 849, 860; Denifle, *La désolation des églises*, 395; Guigue, *Les Tard-Venus*, 56; Labande, "L'occupation du Pont-Saint-Esprit," 146; Housley, "Mercenary Companies," 262; Cox, *Green Count*, 151–152; Henneman, *Royal Taxation*, 156.

77. *Thesaurus Novus Anecdotorum*, col. 909; M. Villani, *Cronica*, 5:59–60.

78. Fowler, *Medieval Mercenaries*, 35–36.

79. Cognasso, "L'unificazione," 408.

80. Azario, *Liber Gestorum*,110, 128, 174; Cognasso, "L'unificazione," 414; Gabotto, "L'età," 120.

81. M. Villani, *Cronica*, 5:60; Sumption, *Hundred Years War*, 468.

82. The full roster of corporals includes Hawkwood, Andrew Belmont, Robin du Pin, William Quartreton (Thornton), William of Arras, William Folifet (Folifait), John Stockland,

Adam Scot, William Bosson, John Bassin, Robert Thornborough, Thomas Bomont (Beaumont), Thomas Beston, Hugh Heton, John Borgelay, Thomas Ludley, and William Kirkeby. Cognasso, "Note e documenti," 158–159. There is no evidence to support Sumption's statement that "the minority" of the band were Englishmen. Sumption, *Hundred Years War*, 468.

83. John Kirkeby, for example, was probably the same who fought in the Breton campaign in 1342/43 in the retinue of Sir Walter de Mauny; William Folifet, perhaps a relation of Thomas Folifet, a mercenary who took part in the famed Battle of the Thirty; and Hugh Heton, likely a relative of David Heton, who rode with Robin Knowles's Great Company through Normandy and Loire in the summer of 1359. Determining the identity of the soldiers is, however, a most inexact science. The corporal Adam Scot, for example, may have been a relative of Walter "Scot" Leslie, but he may also have been related to William Scot, who fought with the Black Prince at Poitiers, or even to Robert Scot, a mercenary leader eventually executed in France for his activities. The subject is dealt with in Caferro, "Fox and the Lion." See also Hewitt, *Black Prince's Expedition*, 206, 211; John of Gaunt, *Register*, 215; Fowler, *Medieval Mercenaries*, 9, 19, 22, 104, 129, 149, 153, 175, 326; Ayton, *Knights and Warhorses*, 183, 240, 263, Walker, *Lancastrian Affinity*, 37, 204, 264, 272; Sumption, *Hundred Years War*, 354–355, 357.

84. Henry was married to Margaret, daughter of Hawkwood's patron John de Vere. Perhaps it was through this mutual connection that Andrew linked with Hawkwood. Mosely, *Burke's Peerage*, 227–228; Maddicott, "Sir Henry Beaumont," 52–53; Rogers, *War, Cruel and Sharp*, 30–39, 56–57.

85. The prior contracts were for two months (twice) and for four months. Romano, "Niccolò Spinelli da Giovenazzo," 378; Cognasso, "L'unificazione," 414; Cognasso, "Note e documenti," 23–169.

86. Fowler, *Medieval Mercenaries*, 4–5.

87. *Thesaurus Novus Anecdotorum*, cols. 882–883.

88. Ditchburn, *Scotland and Europe*, 27.

89. AST, Archivio camerale, conti della tesoria generale di Savoia, camerale Piemonte, castellania, Lanzo, mazzo 5–6, #28 (1360–1361).

90. M. Villani, *Cronica*, 5:203.

91. Azario, *Liber Gestorum*, 110.

92. The figure must nevertheless be considered a rough approximation. We cannot suppose that there was continuity or consistency in the size of corporals' contingents. Even regular English armies in these years lacked uniformity. A typical knight banneret in an English army consisted of sixty to seventy men. But retinues fluctuated significantly. Retinues in the army of 1359 ranged from nine to fifteen hundred men. Prestwich, " 'Miles in Armis Strenuus,' " 214–217; Ayton, "English Armies in the Fourteenth Century," 31–34; see also Caferro, "Fox and the Lion," 185–186.

93. *Codex Diplomaticus*, 419–426; Selzer, *Deutsche Söldner*, 64–65, 72–73.

94. The practice distinguished the English from German soldiers, who relied primarily on mail shirts and were conspicuous to locals for the way they fastened their sword, dagger, and headpiece to their armor with chains, and from Hungarians soldiers, who used little more than hardened leather for protection. Selzer, *Deutsche Söldner*, 39–40; M. Villani, *Cronica*, 3:176–179; Canestrini, "Documenti," xxxiii–xxxiv.

95. F. Villani, *Cronica*, 5:260. Plate armor was in fact known in Italy as "white" armor, at least by the fifteenth century. Prestwich, " 'Miles in Armis Strenuus,' " 207–209, and *Armies*

*and Warfare*, 23–24; Ayton, "Arms, Armour and Horses," 200–201; Edge and Paddock, *Arms and Armor*, 93, 99, 107.

96. Filippo's father, Matteo, and the contemporary English writer Thomas Walsingham both refer to the band as the White Company, but they do not say why. Matteo Villani used the term rather loosely, applying it first to the company that harassed Lyon just after the treaty of Bretigny in 1360. The Milanese Azario did not use the term at all; nor did Jehan Servion, the chronicler of Savoy. The French chronicler Cuvelier called the band that fought in Spain in 1366 the White Company. Walsingham, *Historia Anglicana*, 295–296; M. Villani, *Cronica*, 4:331–332, 5:49, 203. Cuvelier, *Chronique de Betrand de Guesclin*, 287, lines 7981–7984; Sumption, *Hundred Years War*, 533; Fowler, *Medieval Mercenaries*, 144, 196. A fuller discussion is in Caferro, "Fox and the Lion," 186–188.

97. Azario, *Liber Gestorum*, 128.

98. Ricotti, *Storia delle compagnie*, 2:104–105, 315–328.

99. Williams, *Knight and the Blast Furnace*, 53–59, 731–732.

100. On the use of the surcoat, see Edge and Paddock, *Arms and Armor*, 41, 45, 57–59, 73, 77. For a nonscholarly reference to white surcoats and the English, see Tuchman, *Distant Mirror*, 225.

101. Morelli, *Ricordi*, 307; Devlin, "English Knight of the Garter."

102. Del Graziani, "Cronaca," 193.

103. Ruskin, "Fors Clavigera, part I," in Ruskin, *Works*, 16.

104. Doyle, *White Company*, 127–128.

105. Servion, *Gestez et Croniques*, 118.

106. F. Villani, *Cronica*, 5:259–260; Azario, *Liber Gestorum*, 128. The nineteenth-century Italian historian Ercole Ricotti accused the English of "grotesquery." Ricotti, *Storia delle compagnie*, 2:141–142.

107. Azario, *Liber Gestorum*, 128. F. Villani, *Cronica*, 5:260.

108. F. Villani, *Cronica*, 5:258; Selzer, *Deutsche Söldner*, 56–58.

109. Mallett, *Mercenaries and Their Masters*, 36–37; Contamine, *War in the Middle Ages*, 67–68.

110. Oman, *Art of War in the Middle Ages*, 76–77.

111. Petrarch, "Familiares, XXII, 14 (27 February 1361)," in *Letters on Familiar Matters*, 184–185.

112. F. Villani, *Cronica*, 5:259–260.

113. M. Villani, *Cronica*, 5:120.

114. Azario, *Liber Gestorum*, 128.

115. Ibid.

116. M. Villani, *Cronica*, 5:120.

117. Knowles, *Les enseignements de Théodore Paléologue*, 73, 76, 97–98; Settia, "Gli 'Insegnamenti' di Teodoro di Monferrato," 19, 21–22.

118. F. Villani, *Cronica*, 5:259–260.

119. Ibid., 260.

120. Cox, *Green Count*, 156; Gabotto, "L'età," 122.

121. Cox, *Green Count*, 157–158; Gabotto, "L'età," 122, 275 (document 18).

122. Gabotto, "L'età," 117, 122, 275, document 16; Cox, *Green Count*, 140, 151, 158; Azario, *Liber Gestorum*, 160.

123. Cognasso, "Per un giudizio del Conte Verde," 1–2.

124. Servion, *Gestez et Croniques*, 118.

125. Cognasso, "Per un giudizio del Conte Verde," 1–2.

126. Azario, *Liber Gestorum*, 160; Gabotto, "L'età," 117.

127. Mugnier, "Lettres des Visconti de Milan," 388–391; Cox, *Green Count*, 181–183.

128. Cox, *Green Count*, 158; Cognasso, "L'unificazione," 415.

129. M. Villani, *Cronica*, 5:111.

130. AST, Archivio camerale, conti della tesoria generale di Savoia, camerale Piemonte, castellania, Lanzo, mazzo 5–6, #28 (1360–1361).

131. Servion, *Gestez et Croniques*, 120–121; Cox, *Green Count*, 159.

132. M. Villani, *Cronica*, 5:111; Ricotti, *Storia delle compagnie*, 2:140; Cox, *Green Count*, 160.

133. Denifle, *La désolation des églises*, 253, 385; Chérest, *L'Archiprêtre*, 125–128; Fowler, *Medieval Mercenaries*, 27–28.

134. Cognasso, "Note e documenti," 160.

135. AST, Ducato di Montferrato, mazzo 4, document 15.

136. Cox, *Green Count*, 16; Gabotto, "L'età," 125 n. 4. Servion, *Gestez et Croniques*, 120–121.

137. Gabotto, "L'età," 125; M. Villani, *Cronica*, 5:118.

138. M. Villani, *Cronica*, 5:84–85; Cox, *Green Count*, 150–151.

139. M. Villani, *Cronica*, 5:84; Azario, *Liber Gestorum*, 129.

140. Azario, *Liber Gestorum*, 110, 128; M. Villani, *Cronica*, 5:120.

141. Azario, *Liber Gestorum*, 128; Hóman, *Gli Angioni di Napoli*, 374–375.

142. Cognasso, "L'unificazione," 416.

143. Azario, *Liber Gestorum*, 129.

144. Ibid.

145. Temple-Leader claimed that Hawkwood simply turned around soon after arriving in Italy. He "did like the countess of Harcourt," wrote the authors, "and returned directly into France." Temple-Leader and Marcotti, *Sir John Hawkwood*, 12. Others, though differing in detail, have agreed that Hawkwood returned to France. Hennemen, *Royal Taxation in Fourteenth Century France*, 172; Sumption, *Hundred Years War*, 478; Fowler, "Sir John Hawkwood and the English Condottieri in Trecento Italy," 130. More recently, however, Fowler has expressed some doubts; Fowler, *Medieval Mercenaries*, 8–9.

146. Cox, *Green Count*, 155–156.

147. Denifle, *La désolation des églises*, 391; Guigue, *Les Tard-Venus*, 72.

148. Apart from Froissart, no other contemporary writer places Hawkwood at Brignais. Matteo Villani of Florence and the Petit Thalamus of Montpellier both describe the battle but say nothing of Hawkwood. Hawkwood is not mentioned in the scholarly accounts of Monicat, Denifle, Chérest, Delachenal, or Guigue.

149. Sumption, *Hundred Years War*, 478. Guigue also condemns Froissart. Guigue, *Les Tard-Venus*, 64.

150. Froissart, *Chronicles*, 294.

151. Ibid., 372–373. Ercole Ricotti, among others, repeats the mistake of Froissart about Brignais, putting it before Avignon. Ricotti, *Storia delle compagnie*, 2:136–137.

152. Froissart, *Chronicles*, 251.

153. Cognasso, "L'unificazione," 416, 418–419.

154. Azario, *Liber Gestorum*, 129; Cognasso, "L'unificazione," 416, 419.

155. Azario, *Liber Gestorum*, 160–161; Gabotto, "L'età," 126; Cox, *Green Count*, 170–171; Cognasso, "L'unificazione," 419.

156. Azario, *Liber Gestorum*, 160.

157. Ibid.

158. Ibid., 161.

159. Ibid., 164.

160. M. Villani, *Cronica*, 5:159.

161. Azario, *Liber Gestorum*, 164.

162. M. Villani, *Cronica*, 5:204.

163. Ibid., 205; *Cronaca senese*, 606; Velluti, *Cronica Domestica*, 231; Pucci, *Poesie;* Temple-Leader and Marcotti, *Sir John Hawkwood*, 18; Bayley, *War and Society*, 28. For Pisan revenue, see Meek, *Commune of Lucca under Pisan Rule*, 74.

164. M. Villani, *Cronica*, 5:204.

165. Pucci, *Poesie*, 235.

### Three • Italy and the Profession of Arms

*Epigraph:* Quoted in Caferro, *Mercenary Companies*, 55.

1. *Cronaca senese*, 652.

2. Hyde, *Society and Politics in Medieval Italy*, 1.

3. Waley, "Army of the Florentine Republic," 70–92, and "Condotte and Condottieri in the Thirteenth Century," 337–371; Caferro, *Mercenary Companies*, 3–4, and "Mercenaries and Military Expenditure," 219–247; Mallett, *Mercenaries and Their Masters*, 10; Varanini, "Mercenari tedeschi in Italia," 277–280.

4. Covini, "Political and Military Bands," 19.

5. The statement is from a league of mutual defense contracted between the cities of Bologna, Florence, Pisa, Siena, Lucca, and Perugia in 1385. Caferro, *Mercenary Companies*, 3–4, 196. See also Bianchi, "Gli eserciti delle signorie venete," 185.

6. Burns, "Catalan Company," 751; Contamine, *War in the Middle Ages*, 246–47; Sablonier, *Krieg und Kriegertum.*

7. Muntaner, *Chronicle*, 519.

8. Ibid., 527.

9. M. Villani, *Cronica*, 3:174.

10. Muntaner, *Chronicle*, 538, 540.

11. M. Villani, *Cronica*, 3:174.

12. Schäfer, *Deutsche Ritter*, 4:116, 169, 260; Selzer, *Deutsche Söldner*, 53.

13. Del Treppo, "Gli Aspetti organazzativi," 253–254.

14. Keen, *Laws of War*, 150.

15. Froissart, *Chronicles*, 288.

16. Mockler, *The Mercenaries*, 28.

17. Prestwich, *Armies and Warfare*, 145–153.

18. Housley, "Mercenary Companies," 257–258.

19. Xenophon, *Persian Expedition*, 225–229.

20. Schäfer, *Deutsche Ritter*, 1:108–117.

21. Shubring, *Die Herzoge von Urslingen.*

22. Kruger, "Das Rittertum," 312.

23. Renouard, *Les hommes d'affaires italiens du Moyen Age*, 237.

24. Keen, *Chivalry*, 230.

25. Cognasso, "L'unificazione," 529.

26. Varanini, "Mercenari tedeschi in Italia," 278–279.

27. Bayley, *War and Society*, 3–4.

28. Ibid., 9, 14, 46–47.

29. Goodman, "Military Subcontracts;" Walker, "Profit and Loss;" Mallett, *Mercenaries and Their Masters*, 80–82.

30. Cognasso, "Per un giudizio del Conte Verde," 12.

31. Mallett, *Mercenaries and Their Masters*, 82.

32. ASF, Camera del comune, Camarlinghi, uscita 295, fol. 4r; Camera del comune, Provveditori, poi massai, specchi, 3, fol. 65r.

33. ASF, Camera del comune, Camarlinghi, uscita 176, fol. 3r.

34. ASF, Dieci di balia, Deliberazioni, condotte e stanziamenti, 6, fol. 39r.

35. Waley, "Army of the Florentine Republic," 351–352; Mallett, *Mercenaries and Their Masters*, 25–26.

36. Caferro, *Mercenary Companies*, 52.

37. ASBo, Tesoreria e controllatore di tesoreria, 14, fol. 4r.

38. ASF, Provvisioni, registri, 68, fol. 122v.

39. Da Mosto, "Ordinamenti militari," 26.

40. ASF, Dieci di balia, Deliberazioni, condotte e stanziamenti, 3, fol. 10r; Dieci di balia, Deliberazioni, condotte e stanziamenti, 6, fol. 7r–7v; Camera del comune, Camarlinghi, uscita 331, fol. 4r; Dieci di balia, Deliberazioni, condotte e stanziamenti, 16, fol. 71v.

41. Caferro, *Mercenary Companies*, 53–54.

42. Canestrini, "Documenti," 50–51, 57–60.

43. The figures are taken from Goldthwaite, *Building of Renaissance Florence*, 436, 437; Pinto, *Toscana medievale*, 124–126, 147; Franceschi, *Oltre il "tumulto,"* 242–258. The exchange in that year was 1 florin = 75 soldi.

44. ASF, Camera del comune, Provveditori, poi massai, specchi, 7, fol. 50r.

45. Ibid., Camarlinghi, uscita 295, fol. 4v.

46. Pinto, *Toscana medievale*, 130–131.

47. ASL, ATL, 439, #1279; Waley, "I mercenari e la guerra," 116; Mallett and Hale, *Military Organization of a Renaissance State*, 127; Ryder, *Kingdom of Naples*, 278–279; Da Mosto, "Ordinamenti militari," 27–28; Blastenbrei, *Die Sforza und ihr Heer*, 200–201.

48. ASBo, Comune, Stipendiari, le bollette, 56, fol. 12r. There are numerous additional examples. ASBo, Tesoreria e controllatore di tesoreria, 15, fol. 63v.

49. Fop, "Il comune di Perugia," 63, 82.

50. *Codex Diplomaticus*, 423.

51. Mainoni, "Mutui," 11–12.

52. ASF, Dieci di balia, Deliberazioni, condotte e stanziamenti, 3, fol. 11r.

53. Canestrini, "Documenti," 52–54.

54. ASF, Dieci di balia, Deliberazioni, condotte e stanziamenti, 3, fol. 11v; Canestrini, "Documenti," 52.

55. Examples of *mostre* held once a month are in ASF, Provvisioni, registri, 50, fols. 99r–106r; Dieci di balìa, Deliberazioni, condotte e stanziamenti, 3, fol. 11v.

56. ASF, Dieci di balìa, Deliberazioni, condotte e stanziamenti, 3, fols. 82v–83r. The florin was worth 74 soldi at this time.

57. Prestwich, *Armies and Warfare*, 96.

58. ASF, Dieci di balìa, Deliberazioni, condotte e stanziamenti, 3, fol. 11v.

59. Cognasso, "Per un giudizio del Conte Verde," 17.

60. Bayley, *War and Society*, 13–14; Mallett, *Mercenaries and Their Masters*, 85–86.

61. Cognasso, "Per un giudizio del Conte Verde," 18.

62. Giovanni da Legnano, *Tractatus de bello*, 108. See also Bayley, *War and Society*, 48, and Schäfer, *Deutsche Ritter*, 1:141–144.

63. Canestrini, "Documenti," lx–lxiii; Bayley, *War and Society*, 9–10; ASF, Provvisioni, registri, 50, fol. 100r.

64. Canestrini, "Documenti," 51.

65. Ibid., 52–54.

66. Petrarch, *Letters on Familiar Matters*, 252.

67. Mainoni, "Mutui," 10. For Lucca, see Meek, *Lucca, 1369–1400*, 48, 153–155.

68. Quoted in Pullan, *History of Early Renaissance Italy*, 216.

69. Quoted in Caferro, *Mercenary Companies*, 139–140.

70. G. Villani, *Cronica di Giovanni Villani*, 5:122.

71. ASS, Conc., 1787, #72.

72. Franceschini, "Soldati inglesi," 144; Velluti, *Cronica Domestica*, 259.

73. Vegetius, *Epitome*, 116.

74. Canestrini, "Documenti," xxxii, 61–62.

75. ASF, Provvisioni, registri, 70, fol. 27r.

76. Mallett and Hale, *Military Organization of a Renaissance State*, 131–137, 185; Mallett, *Mercenaries and Their Masters*, 139–140, 142–143, 190.

77. A discussion of the origins of the commissary in Italy is in Connell, "Il Commissario e lo stato territoriale fiorentino," 591–617. The classic study of the office is Hinze, "Der Commisarius und seine Bedeutung," 242–274; Mallett, *Mercenaries and Their Masters*, 88.

78. Ricotti, *Storia delle compagnie*, 2:18.

79. F. Villani, *Cronica*, 5:287–288.

80. Mallett, *Mercenaries and Their Masters*, 89.

81. The literature for the fourteenth century is exceedingly small. Aspects of warfare in Italy prior to the fourteenth century are covered in Settia, *Comuni in guerra*. The later period is the subject of several studies. See, in particular, Pieri, *Il Rinascimento*; Hale, *War and Society in Renaissance Europe*; Blastenbrei, *Die Sforza und ihr Heer*; Covini, *L'esercito del duca*.

82. Avoidance of risks was common in medieval warfare. See Prestwich, *Armies and Warfare*, 11; Strickland, *War and Chivalry*, 43; Rogers, "Vegetian Science of Warfare."

83. Gaier, *Art et organisation militaire*, 204; Contamine, *War in the Middle Ages*, 219.

84. Vegetius, *Epitome*, 83.

85. *Annales Mediolanenses*, col. 750.

86. Waley, "I mercenari e la guerra," 114–115.

87. Venice banned all Florentine merchants when the city briefly supported its archenemy

Francesco Sforza of Milan in 1451. Bayley, *War and Society*, 72; Sambin, "La guerra del 1372–1373," 38–53; Lane, *Venice*, 192; Cozzi and Knapton, *La Repubblica di Venezia nell'età moderna*, 4–5; Mueller, *Venetian Money Market*, 151, 274.

88. Knowles, *Les enseignements de Théodore Paléologue*, 84.

89. Caferro, *Mercenary Companies*, 46–47.

90. ASF, Dieci di balia, Deliberazioni, condotte e stanziamenti, 6, fols. 75v, 129v.

91. ASF, Provvisioni, registri, 57, fol. 154r.

92. Mallett minimizes the importance of poison. Mallett, *Mercenaries and Their Masters*, 202–203.

93. ASL, ATL, 571, #25; *Corpus chronicorum Bononiensium*, 165, 281, 283.

94. M. Villani, *Cronica*, 5:198; *Corpus chronicorum Bononiensium*, 257.

95. Carpenters servicing Perugian *bastite* in 1384 are mentioned in ASPe, Consigli e riformanze, 32 fols. 108r, 153r; Partner, *Lands of St. Peter*, 341.

96. Trexler, "'Correre la Terra,'" 845 902.

97. Prestwich, *Armies and Warfare*, 282.

98. Hall, *Weapons and Warfare*, 20–21.

99. Del Graziani, "Cronaca," 223; Hall, *Weapons and Warfare*, 20–21.

100. *Cronaca Senese*, 733.

101. Canestrini, "Documenti," 51–52.

102. Contamine, *War in the Middle Ages*, 194; Prestwich, *Armies and Warfare*, 285.

103. Angelucci, *Documenti inediti*, 67–101; Pasquali-Lasagni and Stefanelli, "Note di storia dell'artigliera," 149–189; Contamine, *War in the Middle Ages*, 140; Prestwich, *Armies and Warfare*, 287. References to canons are frequent in the archival sources—ASBo, Governo, Signorie, Provvisioni in Capreto, 1376–1400, #299, fol. 37v; ASPi, Com A 136, fols. 16r, 17v, 21r.

104. ASF, Dieci di balia, Deliberazioni, condotte e stanziamenti, 5, fol. 78v.

105. DeVries, for one, has pointed out that the deficiencies of the cannon have been overstated. DeVries, "Impact of Gunpowder Weaponry," 227–255.

106. Burckhardt, *Civilization of the Renaissance in Italy*, 78; Deiss, *Captains of Fortune*, 25.

107. M. Villani, *Cronica*, 5:144–145.

108. Gatari, *Cronaca Carrarese*, 254–255.

109. Settia, "Il fiume in guerra," 34.

110. Mallett, *Mercenaries and Their Masters*, 172–176.

111. Canestrini, "Documenti," xxxiv.

112. Waley, "I mercenari e la guerra," 126–128.

113. Del Treppo, "Gli Aspetti organazzativi," 253–275.

114. *Corpus chronicorum Bononiensium*, 258, 286–287.

115. The figures never reach as high as the purported seventy thousand men put together by Florence and its Guelf allies at Montaperti in 1260. See Waley, "Army of the Florentine Republic," 78, and Davidson, *Forschungen zur Geschichte von Florenz*, 4:151.

116. ASF, Dieci di balia, Deliberazioni, condotte e stanziamenti, 3, fols. 82r–83r.

117. Blastenbrei, *Die Sforza und ihr Heer*, 100–113.

118. ASF, Dieci di balia, Deliberazioni, condotte e stanziamenti, 5, fols. 52r–54r; ASBo, Comune, Stipendiari, le bollette, 56, fols 63r, 147r, 316r; ASF, Camera del comune, Camarlinghi, uscita 295, fols. 4v–5v.

119. Taylor, *Art of War in Italy*, 5–6.

120. Barlozzetti and Giuliani, "La prassi guerresca," 55; Da Mosto, "Ordinamenti militari," 29.

121. Waley, "I mercenari e la guerra," 120; Blastenbrei, *Die Sforza und ihr Heer*, 113–114.

122. Blastenbrei, *Die Sforza und ihr Heer*, 113.

123. Bayley, *War and Society*, 20; Bueno De Mesquita, *Giangaleazzo Visconti*, 121; Cognasso, "L'unificazione," 561.

124. Bianchi, "Gli eserciti delle signorie venete," 176.

125. Salvemini, *I balestrieri*.

126. Caferro, *Mercenary Companies*, 57–58.

127. ASF, Camera del comune, Camarlinghi, uscita 110, fol. 3r.

128. Ibid., 68, fol. 4v.

129. Mallett and Hale, *Military Organization of a Renaissance State*, 65; Covini, "Political and Military Bands," 21.

130. ASF, Capitoli, registri, 12, fol. 248v.

131. ASF, Dieci di balia, Deliberazioni, condotte e stanziamenti, 3, fols. 82r–83r. The contract between Florence and the Englishman John Threlkeld in 1384 explicitly allowed him to include Hungarians in his lances. Ibid., 2, fol. 2r–2v.

132. Ibid., 3, fol. 10r–10v.

133. Quoted in Coopland, *Tree of Battles*, 189. See also Labarge, *Gascony*.

134. ASPe, Diplomatico, cassetta 36, 260.

135. ASS, Biccherna, 237, fol. 98r. The subject is covered extensively in Caferro, *Mercenary Companies*, 36–85.

136. Schevill, *Siena*, 246.

137. The recourse to *taglie* went back to the twelfth century. See Naldini, "La 'tallia militum,'" 75–113.

138. ASF, Capitoli, registri, 12, fols. 246r–254r.

139. Thorndyke, *History of Magic*, 801–802; Labarge, *Gascony*, 145.

### Four • The Fox and the Lion

*Epigraph:* Cole, *Hawkwood and the Towers of Pisa*, 34.

1. F. Villani, *Cronica*, 5:256–257; Sozomen of Pistoia, *Specimen Historiae*, col. 1076.

2. F. Villani, *Cronica*, 5:225.

3. Pucci, *Poesie*, 235.

4. Stefani, *Cronaca fiorentina*, 261.

5. M. and F. Villani, *Cronica*, 5:132–146; Ammirato, *Istorie fiorentine*, 95; Brucker, *Florentine Politics*, 187–188. A detailed description of the economic competition between the cities is in Caturegli, *La signoria di Giovanni dell'Agnello*, 17–41. See also Bayley, *War and Society*, 27.

6. M. Villani, *Cronica*, 5:200. For Farnese, see Zorzi, "Piero Farnese," 136–139.

7. *Chronica di Pisa*, col. 1041.

8. M. Villani, *Cronica*, 5:209.

9. Ibid., 213–214; Sozomen, *Specimen Historiae*, col. 1072.

10. Sozomen, *Specimen Historiae*, cols. 1071–1073.

11. Velluti, *Cronica Domestica*, 232.

12. *Chronica di Pisa*, cols. 1042–1043; Monaldi, *Istorie pistolesi*, 323.

13. F. Villani, *Cronica*, 5:222.

14. The sources disagree on detail. Donato Velluti said four donkeys were hanged; Filippo Villani and the Sienese chronicler Neri claimed that there were only three. F. Villani, *Cronica*, 5:221–222; Velluti, *Cronica Domestica*, 232–233; *Chronica di Pisa*, col. 1042; *Cronaca senese*, 601; Roncioni, *Istorie pisane*, 869.

15. F. Villani, *Cronica*, 5:221.

16. Ibid., 230–235. The Lucchese chronicler Sercambi erroneously puts the battle at Incisa before that at Figline. Sercambi, *Croniche Lucchesi*, 125.

17. F. Villani, *Cronica*, 239–240.

18. "Frammenti della Cronaca di Messer Luca di Totto Panzano," 71.

19. Sercambi, *Croniche Lucchesi*, 124.

20. ASPi, Com A 138, fols. 74v–76v; Hóman, *Gli Angioni di Napoli*, 374–375. Del Graziani, "Cronaca," 193.

21. ASPi, Com A 138, fol. 33r (9 October 1363).

22. ASVe, Collegio secreti e lettere secreti, registri, 1 fol. 114r. The folio numbers refer to those written in pencil on the document.

23. Ibid., fols. 132v, 137r.

24. F. Villani, *Cronica*, 5:257; Sozomen, *Specimen Historiae*, col. 1076.

25. F. Villani, *Cronica*, 5:258–259.

26. Ibid., 257.

27. ASF, Provvisioni, registri, 51, fol. 125r; Brunner, *Zur Geschichte der Grafen von Hapsburg-Laufenburg*, 94–118; Selzer, *Deutsche Söldner*, 81–82.

28. F. Villani, *Cronica*, 5:225.

29. Ibid., 266; Canestrini, "Documenti," 50–51, 57–60.

30. F. Villani, *Cronica*, 5:261.

31. Ibid., 262; Velluti, *Cronica Domestica*, 235.

32. F. Villani, *Cronica*, 5:262–263.

33. Ibid., 268.

34. Ibid., 269.

35. Ibid., 276.

36. Velluti, *Cronica Domestica*, 236.

37. F. Villani, *Cronica*, 5:275.

38. This is the first mention of Landau, who was thought by Stephan Selzer to have begun his Italian career in 1371. Selzer, *Deutsche Söldner*, 383.

39. *Chronica di Pisa*, col. 1045; F. Villani, *Cronica*, 5:275.

40. F. Villani, *Cronica*, 5:275.

41. Ibid., 274–276.

42. Temple-Leader and Marcotti, *Sir John Hawkwood*, 28.

43. *Chronica di Pisa*, col. 1045.

44. Velluti, *Cronica Domestica*, 236–237; F. Villani, *Cronica*, 5:284.

45. Modern scholars have relied on Leonardo Bruni's description, which is particularly vague with respect to the desertions. Bruni, *Istoria fiorentina*, 438.

46. F. Villani, *Cronica*, 5:284.

47. Velluti, *Cronica Domestica*, 238.

48. ASF, Provvisioni, registri, 52, fol. 3r.

49. ASF, Camera del comune, scrivano di camera uscita, 20, fol. 33r; scrivano di camera uscita, 21, fol. 26v.

50. *Chronica di Pisa*, col. 1045; *Cronaca senese*, 606–609; Sozomen, *Specimen Historiae*, col. 1078; F. Villani, *Cronica*, 5:284–285; Roncioni, *Istorie pisane*, 874; Professione, *Siena e le compagnie*, 35–37.

51. ASS, CG, 171, fol. 61v (9 June 1364).

52. Caferro, *Mercenary Companies*, 19, 44, 113; Professione, *Siena e le compagnie*, 35–39.

53. ASF, Capitoli, registri, 22, fols. 200r–203r.

54. Canestrini, "Documenti," 58 (document 10).

55. Ibid., 57–60; Bayley, *War and Society*, 32; Velluti, *Cronica Domestica*, 238.

56. Canestrini, "Documenti," 60; Macquarrie, *Scotland and the Crusades*, 81.

57. ASF, Camera del comune, scrivano di camera uscita, 22, fol. 13r.

58. ASF, Signori, responsive originali, 6, #14, 17.

59. ASF, Provvisioni, registri, 52, fol. 3r.

60. Ammirato, *Istorie fiorentine*, 148.

61. Trease, *Condottieri*, 73; Gaupp, "Condottiere John Hawkwood," 309.

62. Andrew Belmont's letter was addressed to the Florentine envoy Zenobio dell'Antella on 4 September. ASF, Signori, responsive originali, 6, #9. See also #17.

63. Velluti, *Cronica Domestica*, 237–238; *Chronica di Pisa*, col 1045; Canestrini, "Documenti," 59.

64. *Calendar of Entries in the Papal Registers Relating to Great Britain and Ireland*, 8–9.

65. *Chronica di Pisa*, col. 1045.

66. Ibid.

67. *Cronaca senese*, 609.

68. Sardo, *Cronaca di Pisa*, 157.

69. Jones, *Malatesta of Rimini*, 79–101.

70. F. Villani, *Cronica*, 5:292.

71. Ibid., 286–287; Bayley, *War and Society*, 32.

72. F. Villani, *Cronica*, 5:286.

73. Ibid., 288.

74. Ibid.; Manni, *Commentario*, 641.

75. F. Villani, *Cronica*, 5:289.

76. Monaldi, *Istorie pistolesi*, 324.

77. Morelli, *Ricordi*, 310.

78. F. Villani, *Cronica*, 5:290.

79. ASF, Camera del comune, scrivano di camera uscita, 22, fol. 33r.

80. Sardo, *Cronaca di Pisa*, 158. The nineteenth-century Pisan historian Raffaele Roncioni offered the more modest figure of five hundred captives. Roncioni, *Istorie pisane*, 876.

81. ASF, Provvisioni, registri, 52, fols. 30v–32r; Monaldi, *Istorie pistolesi*, 324.

82. ASF, Provvisioni, registri, 52, fols. 30v–32r.

83. Ammirato, *Istorie fiorentine*, 156; Bayley, *War and Society*, 33.

84. Morelli, *Ricordi*, 312.

85. *Corpus chronicorum Bononiensium*, 193.

86. Sardo, *Cronaca di Pisa,* 157.

87. Velluti, *Cronica Domestica,* 238–245; Pagolo Morelli also complained of the lack of desire "to follow up the victory." Morelli, *Ricordi,* 311.

88. Sardo, *Cronaca di Pisa,* 157; F. Villani, *Cronica,* 5:288–292.

89. *Chronica di Pisa,* cols. 1044–1045; Sercambi, *Croniche Lucchesi,* 125; *Cronaca senese,* 609.

90. *Cronaca senese,* 609.

91. Roncioni, *Istorie pisane,* 872.

92. Temple-Leader and Marcotti, *Sir John Hawkwood,* 32–33.

93. Ibid.; Deiss, *Captains of Fortune,* 120.

94. Deiss, *Captains of Fortune,* 120.

95. Bruni, *Istoria fiorentine,* 232.

96. Bracciolini, *Storia fiorentina,* 20, 22.

97. F. Villani, *Cronica,* 5:288.

98. Ibid., 291.

99. Ibid., 288.

100. Sercambi. *Croniche Lucchesi,* 126. Roncioni claimed that two sheep and a "grandissimo cane" were hanged. Roncioni, *Istorie pisane,* 877.

101. *Cronaca senese,* 609.

102. ASF, Signori-Carteggi, responsive originali, filza, 6, #2–19. These documents consist of letters written by Galeotto Malatesta, Andrew Belmont, and numerous participants in September 1364. F. Villani, *Cronica,* 5:295–296.

103. Caturegli, *La signoria di Giovanni dell'Agnello,* 69–71, 83. On the rise of Agnello, see also Silva, *Il governo di Pietro Gambacorta,* 29–30.

104. F. Villani, *Cronica,* 5:299–300.

105. The quote is from Sardo, *Cronaca di Pisa,* 161. See also Sercambi, *Croniche Lucchesi,* 127–128.

106. *Cronaca senese,* 610.

107. Bayley, *War and Society,* 34; Caturegli, *La signoria di Giovanni dell'Agnello,* 34–38; Silva, *Il governo di Pietro Gambacorta,* 30–31. Sardo and Sercambi give differing accounts of the indemnity and settlement. Sardo, *Cronaca di Pisa,* 162; Sercambi, *Croniche Lucchesi,* 128.

108. Monaldi, *Istorie pistolesi,* 325.

109. Morelli, *Ricordi,* 305–306.

110. Becker, *Florence in Transition,* 2:160. See also Brucker, *Florentine Politics,* 189.

111. Velluti, *Cronica Domestica,* 231.

112. F. Villani, *Cronica,* 5:277.

113. M. and F. Villani, *Cronica,* 5:142, 200, 228, 383; Velluti, *Cronica Domestica,* 232.

114. Bayley, *War and Society,* 34–36; Canestrini, "Documenti," 68–69.

*Five • John Hawkwood of Pisa and Milan, 1365–1372*

*Epigraphs:* Machiavelli, *Florentine Histories,* 44. Higden, *Polychronicon,* 419.

1. AST, Corti stranieri (esteri), Inghilterra, mazzo 1, documento 4 (4 November 1365).

2. *Codex Diplomaticus,* 430–437, no. 410; Urban V, *Lettres secrètes,* no. 1500. For the general

circumstance involving the bands, see Housley, "Mercenary Companies," 263–266; Henneman, *Royal Taxation*, 161–205.

3. Landogna, "Le relazioni tra Bernabo e Pisa," 142; Vittani, "Quattro lettere," 157–160; Pauler, *La Signoria dell'Imperatore*, 124.

4. M. and F. Villani, *Cronica*, 5:301.

5. Corio, *Storia di Milano*, 1:326–327.

6. Burckhardt, *Civilization of the Renaissance in Italy*, 11.

7. Caturegli, *La signoria di Giovanni dell'Agnello*, 97.

8. The Lucchese chronicler Giovanni Sercambi felt the need to explain the strange appellation, and the anonymous Pisan mistook it for the child's first name. Sercambi, *Croniche Lucchesi*, 132; *Chronica di Pisa*, col. 1047.

9. *Regest Imperii*, 388. The letter was to Mantua and was dated 14 May 1368.

10. *Calendar of Entries in the Papal Registers Relating to Great Britain and Ireland: Papal Letters*, 4:8; *Codex Diplomaticus*, nos. 403–4; Canestrini, "Documenti," 85–86.

11. ASV, Reg Vat, 246, fols. 153–168v.

12. Sautier, *Papst Urban V*, 62; Caturegli, *La signoria di Giovanni dell'Agnello*, 104; Urban V, *Lettres secrètes*, no. 1822; Housley, "Mercenary Companies," 273; Fowler, *Medieval Mercenaries*, 129–135.

13. The William de la Pole mentioned in the papal letters was not the famous merchant of the same name, who also lived at this time. Luttrell, "English Levantine Crusaders," 147–148; Bresc, *La correspondence de Pierre Ameihl*, 367–369.

14. ASF, Signori-Carteggi, Missive I Cancelleria, 13, fol. 50v.

15. Sapori, *La crisi delle compagnie mercantili*, 86; Hunt, *Medieval Super-companies*, 228, 241.

16. Macquarrie, *Scotland and the Crusades*, 81–85; Ditchburn, *Scotland and Europe*, 69, 200–201.

17. *Les chroniques de la ville de Metz*, 105; Housley, "Mercenary Companies," 265; Chérest, *L'Archiprêtre*, 302–324; Denifle, *La désolation des églises*, 480–484.

18. ASF, Provvisioni, registri, 52, fols. 29r–35v; Signori-Carteggi, Missive I Cancelleria, 13, fols. 8r, 9r, 32r.

19. ASS, Conc., 1774, #25; ASF, Signori-Carteggi, Missive I Cancelleria, 13, fol. 23r; Cognasso, "L'unificazione," 430.

20. ASF, Signori, responsive originali, 6, #63; Sautier, *Papst Urban V*, 58; Glénisson and Mollat, *Gil Albornoz*, 334–335; *Codex Diplomaticus*, 419–426.

21. Del Graziani, "Cronaca," 196–197; Fop, "Il comune di Perugia," 62.

22. *Cronaca d'Orvieto*, cols. 687–688; Sautier, *Papst Urban V*, 49, 56–58. ASS, Conc., 1774, #90 (dated 22 January 1365). The terms of the contract between the pope and the White Company are reproduced in *Codex Diplomaticus*, 419; Urban V, *Lettres secrètes*, 272. See also Glénisson and Mollat, *Gil Albornoz*, 333–334; Bresc, "Albornoz et le royaume de Naples," 701–702; Filippini, *Il Cardinale*, 364.

23. Sautier, *Papst Urban V*, 64.

24. ASS, Conc., 1774, #25; ASF, Signori-Carteggi, Missive I Cancelleria, 13, fol. 23r; Cognasso, "L'unificazione," 430.

25. *Cronaca d'Orvieto*, col. 688; *Codex Diplomaticus*, 428.

26. Glénisson and Mollat, *Gil Albornoz*, 339.

27. ASF, Signori-Carteggi, Missive I Cancelleria, 13, fol. 49v.

28. Ibis., fols. 48r–49r.

29. The letter is reproduced by the editor of Del Graziani, "Cronaca," 199–200; Fop, "Lineamenti," 619.

30. Del Graziani, "Cronaca," 200; *Cronaca senese*, 609; *Cronaca d'Orvieto*, col. 689. A letter from the Sienese archive dated 11 September specifically mentions the capture of John "Briz" or Brice. ASS, Conc., 1778, #15. The Perugians celebrated the victory with banquets and feasts throughout the city. They granted Albert Sterz and Hannekin Baumgarten honorary Perugian citizenships and houses in the city. ASPe, Conservatore della Moneta, 13, fol. 9v.

31. ASS, Conc., 1778, #15

32. ASV, Reg Vat, 249, fol. 160v.

33. ASPe, Conservatore della Moneta, 13, fols. 8v–9.

34. Machiavelli, *Florentine Histories*, 44; Ghirardacci, *Historia di Bologna*, 287.

35. Del Graziani, "Cronaca," 200.

36. Ibid., 201; *Cronaca senese*, 609.

37. ASF, Signori-Carteggi, Missive I Cancelleria, 13, fol. 54r.

38. Ibid., fols. 53v–54r. The Florentines also had an outstanding agreement with Sterz and the Germans. Bayley, *War and Society*, 36–37.

39. ASF, Signori-Carteggi, Missive I Cancelleria, 13, fol. 62 v; Werunsky, *Kaiser Karl IV*, 330–339; Cognasso, "L'unificazione," 432.

40. For papal efforts to convince the Florentines and others, see Urban V, *Lettres secrètes*, nos. 1249, 1298.

41. ASF, Signori-Carteggi, Missive I Cancelleria, 13, fol. 70r.

42. *Cronaca senese*, 609.

43. Sautier, *Papst Urban V*, 65.

44. ASF, Signori-Carteggi, Missive I Cancelleria, 13, fol. 55v

45. Ibid., fols. 63v–64r; Sautier, *Papst Urban V*, 67–68. For Lodrisio's earlier band, see Rendina, *I capitani di ventura*, 78–80.

46. C. C. Bayley claims unambiguously that Bernabò directed the company. Bayley, *War and Society*, 37.

47. Cognasso, "L'unificazione," 431.

48. ASF, Signori-Carteggi, Missive I Cancelleria, 13, fols. 63v–64r.

49. Franceschini, "Il cardinal legato Egidio d'Albornoz," 663; Filippini, *Il Cardinale*, 382.

50. Filippini, *Il Cardinale*, 383.

51. ASS, CG, 172, fol. 51r; Consiglio Generale, 173, fols. 12r, 32r.

52. ASF, Signori-Carteggi, Missive I Cancelleria, 13, fol. 66r.

53. Ibid., fol. 63v.

54. Ibid., fol. 67r.

55. Ibid., fol. 69r–69v.

56. *Cronaca senese*, 610–611. Professione, *Siena e le compagnie*, 42–43.

57. ASS, Conc., 1774, #104 (2 November 1365); Conc., 1775, #16 (6 December 1365).

58. ASF, Signori-Carteggi, Missive I Cancelleria, 13, fols. 71v, 77r.

59. Sautier, *Papst Urban V*, 75; ASF, Signori-Carteggi, Missive I Cancelleria, 13, fols. 78r, 84r.

60. ASF, Signori-Carteggi, Missive I Cancelleria, 13, fols. 78r, 84r.

61. ASS, Conc., 1775, #16 (6 December 1365).

62. *Cronaca senese*, 611.

63. ASS, Conc., 1775, #19; Stella, *Annales Genuenses*, 158.

64. Cognasso, "L'unificazione," 433; Werunsky, *Kaiser Karl IV*, 340–341.

65. The Florentines expressed concern about relations between the two in their internal discussions and ambassadorial dispatches. ASF, Signori-Carteggi, Missive I Cancelleria, 13, fols. 36r, 64v–65r; CP, fols. 41r, 80v–81v, 83v.

66. Stella, *Annales Genuenses*, 158.

67. Cognasso, "L'età," 151–152, 164, 282–284.

68. ASS, CG, 174, fol. 42r; Canestrini, "Documenti," lxix; *Cronaca senese*, 611; Sautier, *Papst Urban V*, 76–77. Johann's arrival in Sienese territory from the city of Todi is mentioned in a letter of Francesco da Casale of Cortona on 17 January 1366. ASS, Conc., 1775, #20.

69. ASS, CG, 174, fols. 18v, 31r; ASV, Reg Vat, 248, fol. 92r.

70. *Cronaca senese*, 611.

71. The chronicle claims that the deal was made on 23 April. But the documents have it as 21 April. *Cronaca Senese*, 611; ASS, CG, 174, fol. 42v.

72. ASMa, AG, busta 1215, #12; *Cronaca senese*, 611.

73. Sautier, *Papst Urban V*, 77; ASV, Reg Vat, 248, fol. 32 (21 January), Reg Vat, 248, fol. 193r.

74. *Codex diplomaticus*, 430–437; Sautier, *Papst Urban V*, 78–79.

75. *Codex diplomaticus*, 430.

76. Canestrini, "Documenti," 89–118; Bayley, *War and Society*, 38–39.

77. Bayley, *War and Society*, 38–42; Sautier, *Papst Urban V*, 83–85; Filippini, *Il Cardinale*, 388–389.

78. ASV, Reg Vat, 248, fol. 112r; ASF, Missive I Cancelleria, 14, fol. 8v; Cognasso, "L'unificazione," 431; Sautier, *Papst Urban V*, 86–87.

79. Payment was made on 20 June 1366. ASPe, Conservatore della Monete, 16, fol. 18r–18v.

80. ASMa, AG, busta 1066, #17. ASV, Reg Vat, 248, fols. 111r, 112r. Glénisson and Mollat, *Gil Albornoz*, 258–259, 358–360, 371–372, 376–377. The first attacks on Orvieto occurred from 8 to 16 July and are described in *Ephemerides Urbevetanae*, 89. See also Sautier, *Papst Urban V*, 86–87. A letter from Urbino verifies the presence of the company in the region in late September. ASMa, AG, busta 1066, #33.

81. ASF, Signori-Carteggi, Missive I Cancelleria, 14, fol. 8r–8v; ASV, Reg Vat, 248, fol. 160r; *Codex Diplomaticus*, 440; Cognasso, "L'unificazione," 436.

82. Bologna, Archivio Albornoziano, busta 361 (46); Franceschini, "Il cardinal legato Egidio d'Albornoz," 663–664, 678–679. Sautier, *Papst Urban V*, 88; Cognasso, "L'unificazione," 436; Filippini, *Il Cardinale*, 396–397.

83. Fop, "Il comune di Perugia," 65; Sautier, *Papst Urban V*, 87–89; Azzi-Vitelleschi, *Le relazioni*, 115.

84. ASF, Signori-Carteggi, Missive I Cancelleria, 14, fols. 22v–23r.

85. A papal letter from October notes the growing tensions regarding Perugia. ASV, Reg Vat, 228, fol. 167r. Partner, *Lands of St. Peter*, 355.

86. ASPe, Conservatore della Moneta, 19, fol. 10v.

87. ASF, Signori-Carteggi, Missive I Cancelleria, 14, fol. 35r; *Cronaca senese*, 613.

88. *Cronaca senese*, 613.

89. ASS, CG, 176, fol. 10r.

90. Sautier, *Papst Urban V,* 91; *Ephemerides Urbevetanae,* 90.

91. *Cronaca senese,* 613; Filippini, *Il Cardinale,* 398.

92. Sources also indicate that the victory may have owed in part to an uprising in nearby Assisi, an event blamed on the church, which diverted local attention. Albornoz was lurking in the hills with a contingent of five hundred cavalry. Azzi-Vitelleschi, *Le relazioni,* 117.

93. Fop, "Il comune di Perugia," 69.

94. *Cronaca senese,* 614.

95. ASF, Signori-Carteggi, Missive I Cancelleria, fol. 44r.

96. Quoted in Brucker, *Florentine Politics,* 231.

97. *Chronica di Pisa,* col. 1047; *Cronaca senese,* 614; Sardo, *Cronaca di Pisa,* 166–167; Pauler, *La Signoria dell'Imperatore,* 128; Werunsky, *Kaiser Karl IV,* 358.

98. Sardo, *Cronaca di Pisa,* 166–167; Pauler, *La Signoria dell'Imperatore,* 128.

99. *Cronaca senese,* 614.

100. Sardo, *Cronaca di Pisa,* 167

101. Werunsky, *Kaiser Karl IV,* 358.

102. Bayley, *War and Society,* 42.

103. The pope's accord with the emperor called for the latter to protect the church and its allies for seven years. Jensovsky, *Monumenta Vaticana,* 529–535.

104. ASS, Conc., 1776 (unnumbered, dated 2 October). A letter in the Archivio Gonzaga, dated the last day of September, has the defeat of Ambrogio occurring on 23 September. ASMa, AG, busta 805, #13. See also Sautier, *Papst Urban V,* 101.

105. Sautier, *Papst Urban V,* 102; Pirchan, *Italien,* 1:51; Cognasso, "L'unificazione," 440.

106. On preparations for war by both sides, see Cognasso, "L'unificazione," 440–441; Pirchan, *Italien,* 1:52, 55.

107. Pirchan, *Italien,* 1:148; 2:83; Cognasso, "L'unificazione," 445.

108. Negotiations regarding the union between Lionel and Violante were already under way in July 1366. Documents relating to this are in Lattes, *Repertorio Diplomatico,* 168. See also Trautz, *Die Könige,* 396–399; Rymer, *Foedera,* 3:782–783, 797; Luttrell, "English Levantine Crusaders," 151–153. For discussion regarding the Flemish succession, see Palmer, "England, France and the Flemish Succession," 342–358.

109. ASV, Reg Vat, 249, fols. 103r, 119v–120r, 142r–142v, 148v–249r.

110. Pirchan, *Italien,* 2:86.

111. Ibid., 84.

112. ASMa, AG, busta 2184 (13 May 1368); Pirchan, *Italien,* 2:83.

113. Ibid. (14 May 1368); Pirchan, *Italien,* 2:86.

114. Pirchan, *Italien,* 2:87.

115. Ibid., 33; Cognasso, "L'unificazione," 442.

116. *Annales Mediolanenses,* cols. 737–738.

117. Corio, *Storia di Milano,* 1:823.

118. *Annales Mediolanenses,* col. 738.

119. *Epistolae Seniles,* XI, 2 (from Padua, 21 July 1368), in Thompson, *Petrarch,* 46–48.

120. Cognasso, "L'unificazione," 446.

121. Cox, *Green Count,* 243–244, 249–250; Pirchan, *Italien,* 2:154; Walsingham, *Historia Anglicana,* 306. Chaucer was away from England from January 1368 to October 1368, and thus

he could have attended Lionel's wedding. The evidence is, however, only circumstantial. *Chaucer's Life Records*, 30.

122. Cox, *Green Count*, 251; Cook, "Last Months."

123. Cox, *Green Count*, 261.

124. Gabotto, "L'età," 163, 177–178, 180.

125. Both Temple-Leader and Gaupp give the above account. Their assertions likely derive from the fifteenth-century Milanese diarist Bernardino Corio, who credited the "militi de Bernabo," whom he described as "homini di grande animo e veterani in militare disciplina," with having ruptured the embankment of the Po in the "second hour of the night," forcing the water on the pope and emperor's men. But Corio, who had a decidedly pro-Milanese agenda, never mentioned Hawkwood or anyone else by name. See Temple-Leader and Marcotti, *Sir John Hawkwood*, 62; Gaupp, "Condottiere John Hawkwood," 309; Corio, *Storia di Milano*, 1:824.

126. Gustave Pirchan, working from both published and unpublished sources, gives the most authoritative and credible account of the event. He concluded that Charles's men miscalculated and ruptured the embankment in the wrong place, sending the water inadvertently back on themselves. Pirchan, *Italien*, 1:161; 2:99 n. 70; Cognasso, "L'unificazione," 446.

127. *Monumenta Vaticana*, 639–640.

128. Sercambi, *Croniche Lucchesi*, 146–147; Caturegli, *La signoria di Giovanni dell'Agnello*, 188–189.

129. Cognasso, "L'unificazione," 450–451.

130. Del Graziani, "Cronaca," 43.

131. ASS, Conc., 1777, #65.

132. Pirchan, *Italien*, 2:229.

133. Dupré Theseider, "La rivolta di Perugia," 85; Pirchan, *Italien*, 2:205, 230.

134. Pirchan, *Italien*, 1:424–427.

135. Bartolomeo di Ser Gorello, *Cronica dei fatti d'Arezzo*, 120.

136. The letter to the pope is reproduced by the editors of the Aretine chronicle of Bartolomeo di Ser Gorello and by Temple-Leader and Marcotti. Bartolomeo di Ser Gorello, *Cronica dei fatti d'Arezzo*, 295 (document 5); Temple-Leader and Marcotti, *Sir John Hawkwood*, 319 (document 7).

137. Bartolomeo di Ser Gorello, *Cronica dei fatti d'Arezzo*, 120. See also Urban V, *Lettres secrètes*, 512.

138. Quoted in Pirchan, *Italien*, 1:425; 2:229–231.

139. Selzer, *Deutsche Söldner*, 377–378.

140. According to Temple-Leader and Marcotti, Hawkwood remained a prisoner for a whole year. But they and other writers confuse Hawkwood's plight with that of the prisoners of the White Company several years earlier. Temple-Leader and Marcotti's error was then accepted by editors of chronicle of Bartolomeo di Ser Gorello, who date the battle at Arezzo at June 1368, a year earlier than it actually happened. The date is impossible, for, as we know, Hawkwood was at that very time defending the fortress at Borgoforte in Lombardy. The Bolognese chronicler makes clear, however, that the majority of the prisoners taken at Arezzo were let go soon after the battle.

141. ASS, Conc., 1778, #14.

142. Velluti, *Cronica Domestica*, 280; Cognasso, "L'unificazione," 459.

143. The Florentine preparations for war are in ASF, CP, 10, and Provvisioni, registri, 57. A letter relating to events in San Miniato is in the Mantuan archives, dated 22 October, from Giovanni Guazzoni stationed in Verona. ASMa, AG, busta 1595 (Verona). See also Salvestrini, "San Miniato al Tedesco."

144. ASF, CP, 10, fols. 115r, 118v, 119v. Brucker, *Florentine Politics,* 228–243.

145. Velluti, *Cronica Domestica,* 284.

146. Ibid., 281.

147. ASV, Reg Vat, 250, fol. 6v (letter dated 7 December 1369). ASS, Conc., 1778 (letter dated 27 November 1369).

148. *Chronica di Pisa,* col. 1055. Sardo, *Cronaca di Pisa,* 192–193. Lattes, *Repertorio Diplomatico,* 187.

149. Selzer, *Deutsche Söldner,* 377–378.

150. Sercambi, *Croniche Lucchesi,* 160.

151. ASPi, Com A 207, fols. 5r, 32v.

152. ASF, CP, 10, fols. 4v–5r.

153. ASS, Conc., 1778, #37.

154. Sardo, *Cronaca di Pisa,* 196; *Cronaca senese,* 633.

155. *Chronica di Pisa,* col. 1055; Sardo, *Cronaca di Pisa,* 192–193.

156. Velluti, *Cronica Domestica,* 286.

157. On Giovanni Pusterla, see Mainoni, "Capitali e imprese," 186–188.

158. ASF, Provvisioni, registri, 58, 113r–114r, 163r, 165r, 173r; Camera del comune, Camarlinghi, uscita 196, fol. 15v. M. Devlin claims that the pope's contingent included the Englishman Edward Despenser, who had remained in Italy to fight Galeazzo Visconti. Devlin, "English Knight of the Garter," 275. The pope's own letter (9 January) on the matter makes clear that Despenser remained at the time in Piedmont. ASV, Reg Vat, 250, fol. 19r. Devlin only uses the abbreviated version in *Calendar of Entries in the Papal Registers Relating to Great Britain and Ireland.*

159. ASV, Reg Vat, 250, fols. 6v, 19r; ASF, Provvisioni, registri, 57, fol. 119r. The Florentines also considered sending out to the king of Hungary for more troops. ASF, CP, 10, fol. 4v. See also Velluti, *Cronica Domestica,* 286.

160. Sardo, *Cronaca di Pisa,* 197.

161. Osio, *Documenti diplomatici,* 139.

162. ASS, Conc., 1778, #45.

163. *Corpus chronicorum Bononiensium,* 254; Lattes, *Repertorio Diplomatico,* 188 (document, 1629).

164. Caturegli, *La signoria di Giovanni dell'Agnello,* 203, 223; *Cronaca senese,* 638; *Annales Mediolanenses,* col. 744.

165. Sardo, *Cronaca di Pisa,* 199.

166. *Chronica di Pisa,* 201.

167. Sardo, *Cronaca di Pisa,* 201.

168. Ibid.; Caturegli, *La signoria di Giovanni dell'Agnello,* 207–208.

169. *Chronica di Pisa,* 201; Caturegli, *La signoria di Giovanni dell'Agnello,* 204.

170. ASMa, AG, busta 1329, #41; busta 1367; busta 1329, #134 (21 August).

171. Lattes, *Repertorio Diplomatico,* 191.

172. *Annales Mediolanenses,* col. 744; *Corpus chronicorum Bononiensium,* 256, 295.

173. ASMa, AG, busta 1313, busta 1329, #36.

174. Ibid., busta 1288. The busta contains numerous letters by Ambrogio Visconti from Reggio, nine of which are erroneously dated 1376. Additional letters describing events in Reggio are in busta 1306 (11 March–6 November 1371). A more general discussion of the vicissitudes of Reggio is in "Chronicon Estense," col. 496; Cognasso, "L'unificazione," 463, 466; Grimaldi, *La signoria di Bernabò Visconti*, 30, 34–37.

175. ASMa, AG, busta 2184 (minute), #65 (20 August 1371). On Gonzaga's neutrality, see Glénisson, "La politique de Louis de Gonzague," 248–249.

176. ASMa, AG, busta 1339, #19 (22 October).

177. Ibid., busta 1367, busta 1288.

178. Ambrogio Visconti wrote to Mantua on 27 October to tell them of the progress. "I notify you that my magnificent and exalted father and lord Bernabò wrote to John Hawkwood and his other English brigades that they must not offend your territory. I also wrote to them about this via letters which I have attached to this present letter." ASMa, AG, busta 1288. The quote is from busta 1321 (19 October 1371).

179. Ibid., busta 1339, #19 (31 October—no year given).

180. Ibid., busta 1339. There are two letters from Desio: #24 (3 November) and #25 (9 November).

181. Ibid., #24 (3 November).

182. Ibid., #25 (6 November).

183. Ambrogio Visconti seemed convinced that the English would pay. "I have information," he wrote to Gonzaga on 12 November, "that next Friday or Saturday . . . the English will make good their damage. And I, from the love I bear your dominion, will do everything I can to see that this happens." Ibid., busta 1288 (12 November).

184. Glénisson, "Quelques lettres de défi," 237–239, 246–248; Novati, "Un venturiero toscano," 88–90.

185. *Corpus chronicorum Bononiensium*, 274–275.

186. Novati, "Un venturiero toscano," 90–91; Glénisson, "La politique de Louis de Gonzague," 253; Grimaldi, *La signoria di Bernabò Visconti*, 48. Bernabò announced the victory to Mantua on 3 June 1372. Lattes, *Repertorio Diplomatico*, 210. See also Osio, *Documenti diplomatici*, 157.

187. *Corpus chronicorum Boniensium*, 274–275.

188. Lattes, *Repertorio Diplomatico*, 210. See also Osio, *Documenti diplomatici*, 157.

## Six • *In the Service of God and Mammon, 1372–1375*

*Epigraph:* Gower, "Mirour de l'Omme," in *French Works*, cols. 24049–24060.

1. Higden, *Polychronicon*, 378; Devlin, "English Knight of the Garter," 274–276; Luttrell, "English Levantine Crusaders," 152.

2. *Anonimalle Chronicle*, 56.

3. *Chronicon Angliae*, 64. Walsingham repeated the same description of Hawkwood in his *Historia Anglicana* (306). Hawkwood is also mentioned in relation to the events of 1369 in the appendix to the Ranulph Higden's *Polychronicon*, 371.

4. Selzer, *Deutsche Söldner*, 375–376, 379–381, 384–387.

5. Ibid., 28–29, 44–46.

6. M. Villani, *Cronica*, 5:204.

7. In his pardon for "good services" in 1380, the name Thornbury is cited as an alias for Wenlock. *Calendar of the Patent Rolls, Richard II, 1377–1381*, 484.

8. ASMa, AG, busta 2184, #72 (25 September 1372); *Codex Diplomaticus*, 522–523.

9. Luttrell, "English Levantine Crusaders," 150–151.

10. Selzer, *Deutsche Söldner*, 56.

11. ASF, Signori-Carteggi, Missive I Cancelleria, 14, fol. 38v.

12. It is in general difficult to trace earnings owing to lack of holdings in Milan and Pisa. ASPi, Com A 141, fols. 8r, 19v.

13. ASV, Reg Vat, 269, fol. 178r; Lattes, *Repertorio Diplomatico*, 166.

14. The details of the episode are revealed in a series of letters in the Este archive in Modena. Glénisson, "Quelques lettres de défi," 237–239, 246–248; Cognasso, "L'unificazione," 470; Grimaldi, *La signoria di Bernabò Visconti*, 49; Novati, "Un venturiero toscano," 88–90. On dueling in general, see Gordon, *Duel in European History*.

15. ASMo, Cancelleria Marchionale, leggi e decreti, fols. 81v–83r; Glénisson, "Quelques lettres de défi," 239–242, 248–254.

16. Pope Gregory wished to include Niccolò d'Este in the peace process; Bernabò did not. Cognasso, "L'unificazione," 470; Grimaldi, *La signoria di Bernabò Visconti*, 49.

17. AST, Trattati diversi, mazzo 1, 26; Cox, *Green Count*, 263; Glénisson, "La politique de Louis de Gonzague," 253–254; Cognasso, "L'unificazione," 461–462, 468; Gabotto, "L'età," 183.

18. Temple-Leader and Marcotti, *Sir John Hawkwood*, 72; Cox, *Green Count*, 274.

19. *Annales Mediolanenses*, col. 750.

20. The wording is exactly the same for the two accounts. Mussis, *Chronicon Placentinum*, col. 514.

21. ASMa, AG, busta 1367 (12 September). The year is erroneously given as 1373.

22. Ibid. (18 September). The year is erroneously given as 1376.

23. Ibid.

24. Ibid. (20 September)

25. Ibid. The arrival of Coucy is already mentioned in a letter from the pope to Johanna of Sicily of 11 October 1372. ASV, Reg Vat, 268, fol. 181r. The best source on Coucy in Italy is still Lacaille, "Enguerran de Coucy."

26. ASMa, AG, busta 1321 (23 September).

27. ASS, Conc., 1779, #69 (February 1372); Conc., 1782, #97.

28. Partner, *Lands of St. Peter*, 358.

29. An overview of papal policy is in Mollat, "Préliminaires," 237–244.

30. ASMa, AG, busta 1140, #49 (18 October).

31. ASV, Reg Vat, 269, fols. 179v–180r.

32. Froissart, *Chroniques*, 8:41m and *Chronicles*, 574.

33. *Annales Mediolanenses* col. 750; Mussis, *Chronicon Placentinum*, col. 514.

34. ASMa, AG, busta 1367 (20 September 1372). The letter is erroneously dated 1376.

35. Ibid., busta 2184, 72 (25 September).

36. ASV, Reg Vat, 264, fol. 44r; Reg Vat, 275, fols. 102v, 104, 106v, 140–141v; Partner, *Lands of St. Peter*, 360; Glénisson, "La politique de Louis de Gonzague," 255.

37. Cognasso, "L'unificazione," 473.

38. ASMa, AG, busta 1367 (25 September 1372). The letter is erroneously dated 1376.

39. Ibid. (23 September 1372). The letter is erroneously dated 1376.

40. *Corpus chronicorum Bononiensium,* 278.

41. The figure is given by the chronicler of Reggio. *Chronicon Regiense,* col. 78.

42. Mussis, *Chronicon Placentinum,* col. 517.

43. Ibid., cols. 515–516.

44. Ibid., col. 515; *Annales Mediolanenses,* col. 753.

45. Cognasso, "L'unificazione," 476.

46. Mussis, *Chronicon Placentinum,* col. 515.

47. Conradolus di Ponte of Reggio wrote to Lodovico Gonzaga about the advent of Hawkwood near Pavia. ASMa, AG, busta 1619, #383; ASV, Reg Vat, 264, fols. 81v–85r.

48. ASV, Reg Vat, 268, fol. 97r–97v. The pope wrote a similar letter to Fontana. Ibid., fol. 97r.

49. Cognasso, "L'unificazione," 477; Segre, "I dispacci," 41–43.

50. One such revolt, in Reggio, is described by Ambrogio Visconti himself in a letter he wrote 22 January to Ludovico Gonzaga. ASMa, AG, busta 1288 (22 January).

51. *Chronicon Regiense,* col. 79.

52. *Corpus chronicorum Bononiensium,* 281–282; Cognasso, "L'unificazione," 476; Grimaldi, *La signoria di Bernabò Visconti,* 64–65.

53. *Corpus chronicorum Bononiensium,* 283; Mussis, *Chronicon Placentinum,* col. 516.

54. ASL, ATL, 439, fol. 45r.

55. *Corpus chronicorum Bononiensium,* 283. The *Chronicon Regiense* gives no figures. *Chronicon Regiense,* col. 79.

56. ASV, Reg Vat, 269, fol. 120v (7 February 1373); Cognasso, "L'unificazione," 477–478.

57. ASV, Reg Vat, 269, fol. 100r.

58. *Chronicon Regiense,* col. 79.

59. ASMa, AG, busta 1619, #383.

60. Servion, *Gestez et Croniques,* 196.

61. Cox, *Green Count,* 276.

62. The letters of Ambrogio Visconti trace Savoy's movements. ASMa, AG, busta 1430, #131–135. See also Cognasso, "L'unificazione," 478.

63. Osio, *Documenti diplomatici,* 161 n. 95; Cox, *Green Count,* 277.

64. There are numerous papal letters relaying the details of the advance of the armies toward Montichiari. ASV, Reg Vat, 269, fol. 35v (10 April 1373); Reg Vat, 269, fol. 271 (13 May 1373). ASMa, AG, busta 1602 (11 April 1373); busta 1224 (8, 9 April; 6, 16, 23 May); busta 2092 (11 April 1373). See also Cox, *Green Count,* 277; Cibrario, *Storia della Monarchia di Savoia,* 229.

65. Froissart, *Chroniques,* 8:54.

66. ASMa, AG, busta 1599. "Magnificie et excelse domine noviter dominatione vostra quod Comes Virtutum filius domini Galeam veniens heri de Brixia cum duabus milibus lanceis et cum maximo numero peditum contra nos in campestri praelio experiri voluit vires suas sperans indubie nos prostrare. Ex divina vero favente clementia, que sua consilia aliter dispensavit, nos cum dictis gentibus venimus ad prelium in longhis et amplis pratis supra Montem Clarum quos duro peracto prelio ipsas gentes posuimus per pugne violentiam in conflictum in quo mortui fuerunt aliqui milites et scutiferi dictarum gentium et omnes boni armigeri capti inter quos captus fuit Marchio Franciscus, domino vostro, Comes Virtutum et Dominus Anichinus de Bongardo, sanius consilium capientes, fugam arripuerunt. Et quia in dicto prelio fuerunt aliqui

de meis sotiis vulnerata et etiam propter magnum numero praegioniorum nos oportet trans-
ferire versus Bonon quare placeat dominationi vostre providere quod in territoriis vostris habere
possimus de victualibus pro denariis nostris. date villa Calcinarie territorie Brixie, Johannes
Haukevod, capitanus."

67. Richards, *Altichiero,* 181–185.

68. ASMa, AG, busta 1595. "Sapia segnore che ancoy in li tredesore fu mandato una lettera a
Cansignore dal capetanio di Peschera in la quale se contegniva chel di da eri combate la zente di
messer Bernabo con la gente delagesia a prasso Gavardo e qui fu una forte meschia e dura per tal
modo che sono morti bene trecento di quelli di messer Bernabo e sono anegati molti ingeso e
che'l Marchese Francecho e i altri segnori sono fuziti a uno castello di Messer Bernavo e anno
optenute el campo la zente dela gesia e li praedicti consi a aviuto e dicto capetanio da oraeni di
quelli di Messer Bernabo fuziti de la ditta meschia. Raimondino Lupo."

69. ASS, Conc., 1783, #21. "la novelle e questa che Misser Bernabo sentendo che Messer
Giovanni Aguti era passato la fossa et volendo passare uno fiume che si chiama l'Adda il quale e
a lato di Brescia. Subito richiese Misser Galeasso e esso mando allui il conte di Virtu suo figlioulo
con molta gente e tutto lo sforzo di Messer Bernabo, si racolse a Brescia in tucto 1500 lancie per
impedire il detto passo e la detta giente di Messer Bernabo. Esci fuore di Brescia et con piu di
500 pedoni e acostavesi a presso Misser Giovanni Aguto, e erano questi cioe il conte di Virtu,
Misser Ambruogiano, Misser Anechino et il Marchese Franchesco e la seconda domenicha del
presente mese combattero insieme et la bactaglia durò piu di tre ore finalmente il campo rimase
a Misser Giovanni Aguti et fuorono morti de nemici piu di 300 lanci et piu mectendosi in fuga a
una a qua n'aforgarono piu di 160 comprese et prigioni assai. Ma il conte di Virtu, Misser
Ambrogiano et Messer Anechino si fugurono a uno castello de Brescia."

70. *Chronicon Regiense,* col. 80.

71. ASMa, AG, busta 1430, #131–135.

72. *Annales Mediolanenses,* col. 754; Mussis, *Chronicon Placentinum,* col. 518; *Chronicon
Regiense,* col. 80.

73. *Corpus chronicorum Bononiensium,* 286–287.

74. Ibid.

75. *Chronicon Estense,* cols. 497–498.

76. ASV, Reg Vat, 269, fol. 51r–51v.

77. Ibid., fol. 175r.

78. Ibid., fol. 235v.

79. Temple-Leader and Marcotti, *Sir John Hawkwood,* 76.

80. Cox, *Green Count,* 278.

81. ASV, Reg Vat, 269, fol. 100r.

82. Partner, *Lands of St. Peter,* 357–358, 360. For the pope's efforts to raise money, see
Glénisson, "Les origines," 145–168.

83. ASMa, AG, 2184, #78, minute (24 May 1373).

84. ASV, Reg Vat, 269, fol. 178r.

85. Ibid., 284, fol. 131r; Lunt, *Accounts Rendered,* 474.

86. ASV, Reg Vat, 284, fol. 131r. William Lunt's published accounts of the papal collectors in
England list the bequest to John junior as occurring on 20 November 1372, seven months before
the letter of the pope. If the date is correct, it may be that the pope offered the sinecure as part of
the package to lure Hawkwood into his service. Lunt, *Accounts Rendered,* 474.

87. ASV, Reg Vat, 269, fols. 175r, 51v.

88. Mugnier, "Lettres des Visconti de Milan," 403–405; Cognasso, "L'unificazione," 479; Cox, *Green Count*, 278–279; Osio, *Documenti diplomatici*, 161–164.

89. Segre, "I dispacci," 45; ASL, ATL, 530, fol. 12r. Quoted also in Brucker, *Florentine Politics*, 282.

90. Glénisson, "Les origines," 160–161.

91. Osio, *Documenti diplomatici*, 165.

92. *Annales Mediolanenses*, col. 755; *Chronicon Regiense*, col. 81.

93. *Chronicon Regiense*, col. 81.

94. Budgets show that Gregory made payments to Hawkwood in December 1373. Schäfer, *Die Ausgaben der apostolichen Kammer*, 471. The contract is mentioned in ASMa, AG, busta 1310 (28 July 1374); Glénisson, "La politique de Louis de Gonzague," 253. In January 1374 the pope once again urged Hawkwood to strike at Piacenza. ASV, Reg Vat, 270, fol. 3r (January 1374); Cognasso, "L'unificazione," 481. In the spring of 1374 the Count of Savoy made a separate peace with Galeazzo. Cognasso, "L'unificazione," 482–483.

95. ASMa, AG, busta 2388, #245.

96. Ibid., #246 (4 September 1374).

97. ASV, Reg Vat, 271, fol. 227v.

98. The offers were made in separate letters to Hawkwood and Thornbury. ASV, Reg Vat, 278, fols. 45r–45v, 79r. The pope also granted landed estates to a German mercenary. Ibid., 281, fol. 123v.

99. Ibid., 271, fol. 229r.

100. *Corpus chronicorum Bononiensium*, 295.

101. ASF, CP, 13, fol. 16r–16v (25 May).

102. Ibid., fol. 16r.

103. Glénisson, "La politique de Louis de Gonzague," 260.

104. Partner, *Lands of St. Peter*, 362.

105. ASS, Conc., 1786, #50; Brucker, *Florentine Politics*, 287.

106. ASS, Conc., 1786, #39.

107. Ibid., #51.

108. ASMa, AG, busta 1367 (5 June 1375); busta 1288 (4 June 1375). Osio, *Documenti diplomatici*, 175–176; Corio, *Storia di Milano*, 1:847.

109. "Lettere alla signoria," 172; Osio, *Documenti diplomatici*, 176 (document 115).

110. "Lettere alla signoria," 172–173; ASS, Conc., 1788, #74.

111. ASS, Conc., 1786, #74.

112. Ibid.

113. Fumi, *Regesti*, 75 (7, 8 June 1375).

114. "Lettere alla signoria," 173.

115. ASS, Conc., 1786, #50, 74.

116. ASF, CP, 13, fol 18r.

117. Ibid.

118. ASMa, AG, busta 1288, (21 June 1375).

119. Partner, *Lands of St. Peter*, 362.

120. ASF, CP, 13, fol. 20r–20v.

121. Gherardi, "La guerra dei fiorentini," 210–215 (document 6).

122. ASMa, AG, busta 1085, #13 (25 June).

123. ASF, Signori-Carteggi, Missive I Cancelleria, 15, fol. 5r; Gherardi, "La guerra dei fiorentini," 234–236 (#49).

124. Alberti's comments were recorded by Sienese ambassadors in Florence on 22 June. ASS, Conc., 1786, #74.

125. Ibid., #78.

126. Stefani, *Cronaca fiorentina*, 292–293.

127. ASS, Conc., 1786, #82.

128. Catherine of Siena, *Letters*, 1:106 (letter 30).

129. ASS, Conc., 1786, #83.

130. Sardo, *Cronaca di Pisa*, 210–211.

131. ASS, Conc., 1786, #82 ( 29 June 1375).

132. Sardo, *Cronaca di Pisa*, 211. Alberto Galuzzi reported the terms of the deal and claimed that the first installment was 15,000 florins. ASMa, AG, busta 1085, #15.

133. Gherardi, "La guerra dei fiorentini," 217.

134. The reason for the more favorable treatment is not clear. Lucca was on relatively good terms with the papacy; perhaps that was a factor. The city was also in difficult financial straits, and Hawkwood showed a tendency to extract money in rough proportion to a victim's wherewithal. ASL, Consiglio Generale, 5, 93 (13 July 1375).

135. ASL, Consiglio Generale, 5, 116–117 (18 October); Deliberazioni, 132, fols. 107v–108r; Consiglio Generale, 6, 621; Consiglio Generale, 7, 343, 347–348.

136. ASF, Capitoli, registri, 1, fol. 48r.

137. Sardo, *Cronaca di Pisa*, 211; Fumi, *Regesti*, 76.

138. ASS, Reg 3, fol. 305r; Caferro, *Mercenary Companies*, 37.

139. ASS, Conc., 77, fol. 25r; Caferro, *Mercenary Companies*, 41–42.

140. ASMa, AG, busta 1367 (24 July 1375).

141. Ibid., busta 1085, #16 (27 July 1375).

142. Ibid., #18 (14 September 1375); Gherardi, "La guerra dei fiorentini," 232 (#41).

143. Sardo, *Cronaca di Pisa*, 212.

144. ASMa, AG, busta 1367 (24 July).

145. Ibid.

146. Ibid., busta 1085, #18; busta 1140, #273; busta 1367 (29 July; 31 July).

147. Fumi, *Regesti*, 80.

148. *Corpus chronicorum Bononiensium*, 297.

149. ASMa, AG, busta 1367 (24 July 1375).

150. ASF, Signori-Carteggi, Missive I Cancelleria, 15, fol. 1r. It tells of the need for a mutual policy against the "scelestia" of the "anglice societatis."

151. ASS, Conc., 1786, #82. The letter proves, as Brucker suspected, that negotiations for the league had begun quite early. Brucker, *Florentine Politics*, 294 n. 154.

152. This accord was reached 24 July. Alberto Galuzzi reported the deal in his dispatch dated 28 July 1375. ASMa, AG, busta, 1085, #20.

153. Brucker, *Florentine Politics*, 297; Gherardi, "La guerra dei fiorentini," 219 (#14).

154. Gherardi, "La guerra dei fiorentini," 232 (#39).

155. On ecclesiastical taxation in the period, see Caferro, *Mercenary Companies*, 103–116, 145.

156. Peterson, "State-Building," 128–130.

157. ASF, Signori-Carteggi, Missive I Cancelleria, 15, fol. 5; Gherardi, "La guerra dei fiorentini," 234–236 (#49).

158. Sapori, *Il libro di commercio*, 522.

159. Sozomen, *Specimen Historiae*, col. 1094.

160. Stefani, *Cronaca fiorentina*, 292.

161. ASMa, AG, busta 1367 (21 August 1375).

162. *Cronaca Riminiese*, col. 915; Mussis, *Chronicon Placentinum*, cols. 520–521.

163. Osio, *Documenti diplomatici*, 175–176 (document 119).

164. ASF, CP, 12, fols. 6v–7r (3 May 1375).

165. ASV, Reg Vat, 271, fol. 229.

166. Corio, *Storia di Milano*, 1:848.

167. Partner, *Lands of St. Peter*, 361.

168. Brucker, *Florentine Politics*, 295–296.

169. Gherardi, "La guerra dei fiorentini," 222–231 (#24).

170. Stefani, *Cronaca fiorentina*, 293–294.

171. Brucker, *Florentine Politics*, 308.

172. Sercambi, *Croniche Lucchesi*, 214.

*Seven • John Hawkwood and the War of Eight Saints, 1375–1377*

*Epigraph: Corpus chronicorum Bononiensium*, 333.

1. ASMa, AG, busta 1367 (26 October 1375).

2. On the War of Eight Saints, see Trexler, *Economic, Political and Religious Effects of the Papal Interdict* and *Spiritual Power;* Brucker, *Florentine Politics*, 131–144, 265–335; Peterson, "State-Building," 128–130; Lewin, *Negotiating Survival*, 39–56.

3. Brucker, *Florentine Politics*, 294–296.

4. Partner, *Lands of St. Peter*, 363; Larner, *Lords of Romagna*, 89–91.

5. Franceschini, "Soldati inglesi," 181.

6. "Dimmi, figliol s'avessi mai creduto / che l'gran poter che avia la chiesa sancta / fussi in si breve tempo giu caduto." Bartolomeo di Ser Gorello, *Cronica dei fatti d'Arezzo*, 71.

7. Brucker, *Florentine Politics*, 308–309.

8. ASF, Signori-Carteggi, Missive I Cancelleria, 15, fol. 1v (8 September).

9. Ibid., fol. 8r; the salutation is the same in letters dated 2 September (fol. 16r), 6 September (fol. 19v), 10 September (fol. 2v), 12 September (fol. 3r), and 7 October (fol. 31r), all in 1375.

10. See Lattes, *Repertorio Diplomatico*, 170, 230, 248.

11. ASF, Signori-Carteggi, Missive I Cancelleria, 15, I, fol. 1v.

12. Lucchese sources have Cane in Lucca on 23 July 1375. ASL, ATL, 530, #102. Cane's letter to Lucca is dated 14 August 1375. Ibid., 439, #527. Cane's embassy was briefly slowed when he fell sick. Gherardi, "La guerra dei fiorentini," 232–233 (#40, 44).

13. ASL, ATL, 530, #102; ATL, 439, #527.

14. ASF, Signori-Carteggi, Missive I Cancelleria 15, I, fol. 1v.

15. Gherardi, "La guerra dei fiorentini," 236–237.

16. ASMa, AG, busta 1085 (18 September 1375); Gherardi, "La guerra dei fiorentini," 238–239.

17. ASF, Signori-Carteggi, Missive I Cancelleria, 15, fol. 13r.

18. Ibid., fol. 9r.

19. ASS, Conc., 1787, #49.

20. Ibid., #72

21. Glénisson, "Les origines,"167; Gherardi, "La guerra dei fiorentini," 236–237 (#52).

22. ASF, Signori-Carteggi, Missive I Cancelleria, 15, fol. 14v (16 October 1375 ).

23. This is described in a letter from the Città di Castello sent to the Sienese on 9 January 1375; ASS, Conc., 1790, #11; Franceschini, "Soldati inglesi," 182 n.1.

24. Del Graziani, "Cronaca," 220.

25. Ibid., 221; Dupré Theseider, "La rivolta di Perugia," 119–129.

26. ASPe, Conservatore della Moneta, 26, fol. 34r.

27. ASPe, Consigli e riformanze, 24, fol. 2r; Del Graziani, "Cronaca," 222.

28. ASPe, Conservatore della Moneta 26, fol 29r.

29. ASPe, Consigli e riformanze, 24, fol. 49v.

30. Del Graziani, "Cronaca," 223.

31. ASPe, Consigli e riformanze, 24, fols. 4v–5r, 103v–106v; Partner, *Lands of St. Peter,* 363; Franceschini, "Soldati inglesi," 182.

32. ASPe, Consigli e riformanze, 24, fol. 33r.

33. Dupré Theseider, "La rivolta di Perugia," 138–139, 159–161.

34. ASF, Signori-Carteggi, Missive I Cancelleria, 16, fol. 38v; Gherardi, "La guerra dei fiorentini," 222; Dupré Theseider, "La rivolta di Perugia," 135. But the Florentines ultimately accepted the accord and announced in a circular letter to various cities the "happy triumph of liberty in Perugia." Gherardi, "La guerra dei fiorentini," 222–223.

35. Gherardi, "La guerra dei fiorentini," 219–220; Dupré Theseider, "La rivolta di Perugia," 139–140.

36. Gherardi, "La guerra dei fiorentini," 220.

37. ASPe, Consigli e riformanze, 24, fols. 6v–7r; Dupré Theseider, "La rivolta di Perugia," 142–143.

38. ASPe, Conservatore della Moneta, 26, fol. 34r.

39. ASPe, Consigli e riformanze, 24, fols. 4v–5r.

40. On 7 January the Perugians elected officials to see to the restitution of the goods of the former prisoners. Ibid., fol. 12v. "Regestro e documenti," 547–553.

41. *Cronache malatestiane,* 40.

42. ASS, Conc., 1787, #89 (14 January 1376).

43. Jones, *Malatesta of Rimini,* 97.

44. ASS, Conc., 1787, #89. A Florentine letter of 4 February 1376 speaks of the English "infesting" the Romagna. Gherardi, "La guerra dei fiorentini," 226.

45. Franceschini, "Soldati inglesi," 183.

46. The rebellion in Forlì is noted in a Florentine letter dated 27 December 1375. ASF, Signori-Carteggi, Missive I Cancelleria, 16, fol. 37r.

47. Franceschini, "Soldati inglesi," 201 (document 2).

48. *Corpus chronicorum Bononiensium,* 307.

49. Jones, *Malatesta of Rimini,* 97–98; Larner, *Lords of Romagna,* 90–91.

50. Vancini, *La rivolta dei Bolognesi,* 16.

51. Balduzzi, "Bagnacavallo," 72–74. The Milanese diarist Corio has Hawkwood receiving

Mirandola and Bertinoro in addition to Bagnacavallo. This was in return for 100,000 florins owed the captain. Corio's chronology was, however, correct. Hawkwood received the towns just after the sack of Faenza in February 1377. Corio, *Storia di Milano*, 1:851.

52. ASMa, AG, busta 2388, #75.

53. Holmes, *Good Parliament*, 175–176. Holmes hypothesizes that the prebend was given to Thornbury sometime after 14 January 1376.

54. ASMa, AG, busta 2388, #75.

55. *Corpus chronicorum Bononiensium*, 309; *Cronache malatestiane*, 38–39.

56. *Corpus chronicorum Bononiensium*, 315.

57. Ibid.

58. Stefani, *Cronaca fiorentina*, 296.

59. *Annales Forolivienses*, 69.

60. ASF, Mercanzia, 1177, fols. 58r–75r. See also Brucker, *Renaissance Florence*, 78.

61. Stefani, *Cronaca fiorentina*, 296; *Corpus chronicorum Bononiensium*, 315.

62. Stefani, *Cronaca fiorentina*, 295.

63. *Cronache malatestiane*, 42; Vancini, *La rivolta dei Bolognese*, 24.

64. ASMa, AG, busta 1140, #300, 312. The Bolognese chronicle says incorrectly that two of Hawkwood's children were captured. Venetian sources show there was only one. *Corpus chronicorum Bononiensium*, 308, 318.

65. ASBo, Governo, Signorie, Provvisioni in Capreto, 1376 (9 October), fol. 7v.

66. *Corpus chronicorum Bononiensium*, 317–318.

67. ASMa, AG, busta 1140, #312.

68. *Corpus chronicorum Bononiensium*, 315.

69. ASMa, AG, busta 1140, #297 (5 May 1376), #298 (8 May).

70. Ibid., #299 (11–12 May 1376).

71. Ibid., #300 (20 May 1376). A modern account puts the theft at four thousand animals and four hundred human prisoners. Vancini, *La rivolta dei Bolognesi*, 30.

72. ASVe, Commemoriale, 8, fol. 11r (16 May 1376).

73. ASMa, AG, busta 1140, #300 (20 May 1376).

74. Ibid.

75. Ibid., busta 1227 (11 June 1376).

76. Ibid., busta 1140, #313; busta 1602, #632; *Annales Forolivienses*, 69.

77. ASMa, AG, busta 1140, #300.

78. ASBo, Commune, Capitano del popolo, Giudici del capitano, 805, fol. 15r.

79. ASBo, Governo, Signorie, Provvisioni in Capreto, 1376–1400, #299, fol. 40v.

80. Vancini, *La rivolta dei Bolognesi*, 24.

81. ASMa, AG, busta 1227 (11 June 1376), from Galeazzo Busoni records the negotiations—pope, Milan, and all sides courting Hawkwood. The letter also records the passage of the prisoners from Bologna.

82. Verci, *Storia della Marca*, 33–35; *Corpus chronicorum Bononiensium*, 320.

83. *Calendar of State Papers and Manuscripts, Existing in Archives and Collections of Venice*, 5:601–609 (hereafter cited as *Calendar of State Papers, Venice*).

84. Ibid. (document 986).

85. ASMa, AG, busta 1140, #301 (25 May).

86. Russell, *English Intervention*, 224–225, 249–256.

87. ASMa, AG, busta 77 (5 June 1376).

88. Ibid., busta 1367 (31 March).

89. Ibid., busta 1140, #301 (25 May).

90. Mirot, *La politique Française*, 98–178; Brucker, *Florentine Politics*, 309–311.

91. Schäfer, *Die Ausgaben der apostolischen Kammer*, 641.

92. Quotation from Caferro, *Mercenary Companies*, 11; Stefani, *Cronaca fiorentina*, 297.

93. ASF, Signori-Carteggi, Missive I Cancelleria, 15, fol. 66r.

94. One official, Jacobo Sacchetti, demurred, citing potentially "intolerable expenses." ASF, CP, 14, fol. 52r.

95. ASF, Signori-Carteggi, Missive I Cancelleria, 15, fol. 69r.

96. Ibid., 17, fol. 45r.

97. Ibid., 15, fol. 66r.

98. ASF, CP, 14, fol. 52r.

99. ASF, Signori-Carteggio, Missive I Cancelleria, 15, fol. 66r.

100. ASMa, AG, busta 1140, #302.

101. Schäfer, *Die Ausgaben der apostolischen Kammer*, 645.

102. ASF, CP, 14, fol. 53v; Balia 13, fol. 3r.

103. Stefani, *Cronaca fiorentina*, 300–301.

104. *Corpus chronicorum Bononiensium*, 320–332.

105. *Cronache malatestiane*, 42; *Corpus chronicorum Bononiensium*, 328.

106. Stefani, *Cronaca fiorentina*, 300–301. Stefani mentions only Philip Puer. Bolognese sources mention Dent and Giffart. ASBo, Governo, Signorie, Provvisioni in Capreto, 1376–1400, #299, fols. 37v–38v. Stefani does not say exactly when the deal was made with the English. The Bolognese records indicate that payments began in the second week of November. Both sources indicate that there were German mercenaries mixed among the English. Ibid., fol. 39v.

107. Ibid., #299.

108. Stefani, *Cronaca fiorentina*, 300.

109. *Cronache malatestiane*, 43.

110. *Cronaca senese*, 665.

111. *Ibid.; Corpus chronicorum Bononiensium*, 333.

112. *Corpus chronicorum Bononiensium*, 332.

113. *Cronaca senese*, 665. The indiscriminate slaughter of young and old and of both sexes was confirmed by the chronicler from Forlì. *Annales Forolivienses*, 69.

114. *Corpus chronicorum Bononiensium*, 333.

115. Robertson, "Cesena," 7; a Florentine letter to Bernabò also speaks of four thousand people killed. ASF, Signori-Carteggi, Missive I Cancelleria, 17, 90 (10 February 1376). The *Annales Forolivienses* puts the figure at three thousand people, 69. Gori, "L'eccidio di Cesena," 3–37.

116. *Cronache malatestiane*, 43.

117. *Corpus chronicorum Bononiensium*, 332–333; *Cronaca senese*, 665; *Annales Forolivienses*, 69; *Cronache malatestiane*, 43–44; *Chronicon Estense*, col. 500.

118. Robertson, "Cesena," 6; Partner, *Lands of St. Peter*, 365.

119. Balduzzi, "Bagnacavallo," 72–74; *Chronicon Estense*, 500.

120. *Cronaca senese*, 665.

## Eight • *Love and Diplomacy, 1377–1379*

*Epigraphs:* Jones, *Oswald von Wolkenstein*, 71. *Chaucer's Life Records*, 54.

1. *Calendar of the Patent Rolls, Edward III, 1374–1377*, 435.

2. ASL, ATL, 439, #2010.

3. ASMa, AG, busta 1140, #322.

4. ASF, Balìa, 13, fols. 178v–179r.

5. BRF, MS 786, fol. 36v. Cognasso, "L'unificazione," 491.

6. *Corpus chronicorum Bononiensium*, 340.

7. ASMa, busta 1602, #632.

8. BRF, MS 786, fol. 22r.

9. Sacchetti, *Il trecentonovelle*, 449. "Diario d'anonimo fiorentino," 330.

10. The Florentines had further angered Rodolfo by not allowing him to keep custody of the towns (Fabriano, Tolentino, and Sanginesio) that he had seized while on campaign. Gherardi, "La guerra dei fiorentini," 111.

11. "Diario d'anonimo fiorentino," 340; *Cronaca senese*, 669.

12. ASS, Conc., 1793, #5; ASMa, AG, busta 1602, #642. Franceschini, "Soldati inglesi," 183.

13. ASMa, AG, busta 1619.

14. ASL, ATL, 439, #2012 (31 May).

15. ASMa, AG, busta 1602, #641; Osio, *Documenti diplomatici*, 191–192. Osio places it in his collection after a document dated 20 June 1377. He reproduces only the second half of the letter. Temple-Leader and Marcotti offer a translation. Temple-Leader and Marcotti, *Sir John Hawkwood*, 128. The quotation above is my own translation of the same.

16. Santoro, *La politica finanziaria*, 2:2–3, document 5.

17. The figure cannot be confirmed, but it is similar to the amount estimated by the Milanese diarist Corio for Lutz von Landau's cash dowry (12,000 florins). Higden, *Polychronicon*, 394; Corio, *Storia di Milano*, 1:851.

18. *Corpus chronicorum Bononiensium*, 342, "Diario d'anonimo fiorentino," 333.

19. *Corpus chronicorum Bononiensium*, 342; Gherardi, "La guerra dei fiorentini," 286, #361, 362.

20. BRF, MS 786, fol. 43v.

21. "Diario d'anonimo fiorentino," 333.

22. *Corpus chronicorum Bononiensium*, 343; "Diario d'anonimo fiorentino," 334–335; Corio, *Storia di Milano*, 1:854–855.

23. ASMa, AG, busta 2388 (29 June 1377).

24. *Cronache malatestiane*, 44; *Corpus chronicorum Bononiensium*, 343.

25. ASS, Conc., 1792, #20 (9 September 1377); Franceschini, "Soldati inglesi," 201–202.

26. "Diario d'anonimo fiorentino," 338. *Cronaca senese*, 667; Del Graziani, "Cronaca," 225.

27. ASS, Conc., 1792, #94 (26 November 1377).

28. *Cronaca senese*, 667.

29. "Diario d'anonimo fiorentino," 332; Brucker, *Florentine Politics*, 324.

30. Brucker, *Florentine Politics*, 327; *Corpus chronicorum Bononiensium*, 339; Gherardi, "La guerra dei fiorentini," 281 (#341).

31. BRF, MS 786, fol. 55v (11 September 1377).

32. Ibid., fols. 60v–61r (27 September 1377); Temple-Leader and Marcotti, *Sir John Hawkwood*, 133.

33. ASS, Conc., 1792 (2 November); "Diario d'anonimo fiorentino," 342; Professione, *Siena e le compagnie*, 69.

34. BRF, MS 786, fol. 68v ( 9 November 1377).

35. Ibid., fol. 61r (30 September 1377).

36. PRO, Issue Roll 465 (October 1377); Perroy, *L'Angleterre*, 137; Jones, *Royal Policy of Richard II*, 83–84.

37. Temple-Leader and Marcotti, *Sir John Hawkwood*, 137.

38. BRF, MS 786, fol. 69v (16 November 1377).

39. Ibid., fol. 70r

40. Ibid., fol. 71r.

41. "Diario d'anonimo fiorentino," 346, 349.

42. Ibid., 344.

43. BRF, MS 786, fol. 80r (10 February 1378).

44. Ibid., fol. 82r.

45. ASS, Conc., 1793 (1 March 1377).

46. *Cronache malatestiane*, 44–45; Stefani, *Cronaca fiorentina*, 311; *Corpus chronicorum Bononiensium*, 348–349; *Cronaca senese*, 670; Gherardi, "La guerra dei fiorentini," 118; Cognasso, "L'unificazione," 491.

47. *Cronaca senese*, 670.

48. Stefani, *Cronaca fiorentina*, 311. For the larger context of the talks, see Lewin, *Negotiating Survival*, 52–54.

49. Gherardi, "La guerra dei fiorentini," 123–125, 292 (#392); *Cronaca senese*, 672.

50. "Diario d'anonimo fiorentino," 352.

51. BRF, MS 786, fol. 89v (6 April 1378), fol. 95v (17 May 1378).

52. Both Hawkwood and William Gold wrote letters relating to "Sabraam." ASMa, AG, busta 2388, #284 (30 July), and busta 1595 (6 August). Luttrell, "English Levantine Crusaders," 146, 149; Nicolas, *Controversy*, 125.

53. Keen, "Chaucer's Knight," 54.

54. Osio, *Documenti diplomatici*, 194–197 (document 131, 17 February 1378); Pizzagalli, *Bernabò Visconti*, 122.

55. Pizzagalli, *Bernabò Visconti*, 127.

56. Gatari, *Cronaca Carrarese*, 148; Corio, *Storia di Milano*, 1:863; Pizzagalli, *Bernabò Visconti*, 126.

57. BRF, MS 786, fols. 95v (letter to Hawkwood, dated 17 May 1378), 96v (to Bernabò, dated 20 May), 99r (to Bernabò, 8 June), 101r, 101v (to John Hawkwood, 6, 7 August).

58. Hawkwood wrote two letters on the subject. ASMa, AG, busta 2238, #254, 255. On Tiberto's career, see Esch, "Brandolino Brandolino," 13:29.

59. The letter relating to Sabraham is in ASMa, AG, busta 2388, #284; a letter on behalf of Donfol is in ibid., busta 2338, #268.

60. Ibid., #250.

61. Ibid., #283.

62. Ibid., busta 1595 (29 July 1378).

63. Ibid. (31 July 1378).

64. Ibid. (8 August 1378).

65. Ibid., busta 2388, #440 (8 August 1378).

66. BRF, MS 786, fol. 101v.

67. ASMa, AG, busta 1595 (30 May 1378).

68. Ibid., busta 2388, #270.

69. Walker, *Lancastrian Affinity*, 43, 109, 283; *Calendar of the Patent Rolls, Richard II, 1388–1391*, 79–80.

70. ASMa, AG, busta 2388, #253.

71. PRO, Issue Roll, 468, m. 5; Issue Roll 465, m. 16; Foreign Accounts, 2 Ric II m.F and 3 Ric II, m. D; Saul, *Richard II*, 84; Perroy, *L'Angleterre*, 137–138.

72. Pratt, "Geoffrey Chaucer," 188–193; Kuhl, "Why Was Chaucer Sent to Milan in 1378?" 15–18. See also *Chaucer's Life Records*, 53–61.

73. Pratt suggests that the talks were conducted between 15 July and 2 August. Pratt, "Geoffrey Chaucer," 190.

74. The details are discussed in Tuck, "Richard II," 218–219. Saul, *Richard II*, 85–86.

75. ASMa, AG, busta 1595 (30 July 1378).

76. Ibid. (2 August 1378).

77. Ibid. (4 August 1378).

78. Ibid. (6 August 1378).

79. Ibid. (9 August 1378).

80. Ibid. (25 August 1378).

81. Gatari, *Cronaca Carrarese*, 152, 155, 156.

82. Corio, *Storia di Milano*, 1:863. Corio has the hostilities recommencing in October.

83. Gatari, *Cronaca Carrarese*, 161.

84. Ibid., 162.

85. Osio, *Documenti diplomatici*, 214–216.

86. Ibid., 215–216.

87. ASMa, AG, busta 2388.

88. Pizzagalli, *Bernabò Visconti*, 126–127. The peace accord that ended the Veronese war is in Santoro, *La politica finanziaria*, 1:328–332 (document 455).

89. ASMa, AG, busta 2388, #258 (19 February 1379).

90. Ibid., busta 1430, #223 (18 February 1379).

91. Stefani, *Cronaca fiorentina*, 342.

92. ASMa, AG, busta 2338, contains nine letters written by the band, from 3 December 1378 to 30 April 1379. The band's activities are also dealt with in the chronicles: *Corpus chronicorum Bononienesium*, 356, and *Cronaca senese*, 674. See also Stefani, *Cronaca fiorentina*, 341–342, and Professione, *Siena e le compagnie*, 74–75.

93. ASF, CP, 17, fols. 12r–19v.

94. Stefani, *Cronaca fiorentina*, 342.

95. ASMa, AG, busta 2388, #259, 260. There is also a letter from Giovanni Cingola on the matter. Ibid., busta 2338, #282. *Corpus chronicorum Bononiensium*, 356–357; Professione, *Siena e le compagnie*, 76.

96. Del Graziani, "Cronaca," 227.

97. Stefani, *Cronaca fiorentina*, 345.

98. *Cronaca senese*, 675.

99. ASF, Provvisioni, registri, 68, fol. 93v; "Diario d'anonimo fiorentino," 388 (n. 6), 393.

100. "Cronaca del Laurenzi," 3:141, 143; Professione, *Siena e le compagnie*, 77; Del Graziani, "Cronaca," 227; *Cronaca senese*, 674–675.

101. ASF, Camera del comune, Camarlinghi, uscita 238, fol. 30r.

102. ASF, Provvisioni, registri, 68, fol. 93v.

103. Franceschini, "Soldati inglesi," 185.

104. ASMa, AG, 2388, #326; ASF, Camera del comune, uscita, 238, fol. 28r; Provvisioni, registri, 68, fol. 92v.

105. *Cronaca senese*, 675.

106. ASF, Camera del comune, Camarlinghi, uscita 238, fols. 29–30v.

107. "Diario d'anonimo fiorentino," 399.

108. ASMa, AG, busta 1388 (10 August 1379).

109. Ibid., busta 2338, #261.

## Nine • At Home in the Romagna, *1379–1381*

*Epigraph: Codex Diplomaticus*, 539.

1. ASMa, AG, busta 2388, #261 (3 July 1379), #262.

2. ASF, Signori-Carteggi, Missive I Cancelleria, 18, fol. 8r.

3. Benvenuto de' Rambaldi di Imola, *Commentum super Dantis Aldigheri Comoediam*, 301. See also Larner, *Lords of Romagna*, 5–6.

4. M. Villani, *Cronica*, 5:42; Larner, *Lords of Romagna*, 71–72.

5. Quoted in Larner, *Lords of Romagna*, 71. The humanist historian Francesco Guicciardini seconded the sentiment, adding that the region was one "where men are commonly dishonest, malignant and ignorant of honor." Guicciardini, *Opere inedite*, 393.

6. Temple-Leader and Marcotti, *Sir John Hawkwood*, 167.

7. ASMa, AG, busta 1619; busta 839 (17 July 1377); busta 2338, #256.

8. BRF, MS 786, fol. 100v (16 July 1378).

9. *Calendar of Inquisitions Post Mortem, 1–7 Richard II*, 118.

10. ASMa, AG, busta 1606 (26 August 1379).

11. Ibid. (7 September 1379).

12. Malpeli, *Dissertazioni*.

13. The population figures have been disputed. Malpeli based his assessment on 443 hearths (*fumantes*), supposing that each family had five people. Ibid., 147. John Larner, however, doubts whether each *fumante* corresponded to an individual family. Larner, *Lords of Romagna*, 209–219 (appendix 2). For the most up-to-date analysis, see Pini, *Città medievale e demografia storica*, particularly the essay " 'Focularia' e 'fumantaria' nel censimento del cardinale Anglico in Romagna nel 1371," 225–241.

14. Malpeli, *Dissertazioni*, lvii–lviii.

15. Ibid., 161.

16. ASMa, AG, busta 2388, #254, 255; Malpeli, *Dissertazioni*, 164.

17. Malpeli, *Dissertazioni*, 137.

18. ASMa, AG, busta 2338, #242.

19. Solieri, *L'antica casa*; Bignami, *Sotto l'insegna del Biscione*.

20. Mallett, *Mercenaries and Their Masters*, 67–69.

21. Bonoli, *Della storia di Cottignola;* Balduzzi, "Bagnacavallo," 74; Temple-Leader and Marcotti, *Sir John Hawkwood,* 108.

22. ASMa, AG, busta 2388, #249 (17 April 1378).

23. Ibid., busta 1367 (31 March 1376).

24. Ibid., busta 1388 #282.

25. Ibid., busta 2388, #89.

26. Ibid., busta 2184, #157.

27. Bonoli, *Della storia di Cottignola,* 74.

28. ASMo, Casa e Stato, cassette 20, #11.

29. *Calendar of Close Rolls, Richard II, 1377–1381,* 367; *Essex Sessions of the Peace,* 14, 17.

30. *Calendar of Close Rolls, Richard II, 1377–1381,* 367–368.

31. Hawkwood's purchases included the manor in Gosfield known as Bellows Hall, pasture-lands called "le hole and le hay" once belonging to the Liston family from John Bourchier, and other deals for land in Gosfield. ERO, D/DCw/T 37/31; D/DCw/T 33/2; D/DCw/T 33/3; *Feet of Fines for Essex,* 3:128, 154.

32. Davies, *Guide to the Church,* 2; Morant, *History and Antiquities of Essex.*

33. Davies, *Guide to the Church,* 2, 5.

34. Rymer, *Foedera,* 4:83–84.

35. *Calendar of Close Rolls, Richard II, 1381–1385,* 367; Holmes, "Florentine Merchants," 201–202.

36. In 1381, the Guinigi numbered sixteen persons, with three factors in Bruges, among them Vinciguerra. Kaeuper, *Bankers to the Crown,* 9, 81–82; Hunt, *Medieval Super-companies,* 58–59; De Roover, *Money, Banking and Credit,* 39; Meek, *Lucca, 1369–1400,* 44, 200–202.

37. *Calendar of Close Rolls, Richard II, 1381–1385,* 367; Meek, *Lucca, 1369–1400,* 213.

38. ASMa, AG, busta 2388, #256.

39. The poet Franco Sacchetti, who condemned Hawkwood, would come to know Manfredi as podestà in Faenza (1396) and compared him to the Trinity in a ballad (Larner, *Lords of Romagna,* 164).

40. ASMa, AG, busta 2388, #261.

41. ASF, Signori-Carteggi, Missive I Cancelleria, 18, fol. 16v.

42. *Corpus chronicorum Bononiensium,* 343.

43. ASMa, AG, busta 2388, #262.

44. Ibid., #264 (19 October 1379).

45. There is no literature on these events apart from Hawkwood's letters.

46. *Cronache malatestiane,* 50. There are various accounts of the demise of the company. *Cronaca senese,* 676; Gatari, *Cronaca Carrarese,* 183, 184; *Chronicon Estense.* The Sienese chronicle spoke of the capture and death of Antonio Visconti, the nephew of Bernabò. Gatari says that two of Hawkwood's children were captured at Genoa (184).

47. ASMa, AG, busta 2338, #264 ( 18 October 1379).

48. ASF, Signori-Carteggi, Missive I Cancelleria, 18, fol. 89r (8 December 1379). Manni, *Commentario,* 636–638. Temple-Leader and Marcotti, *Sir John Hawkwood,* 158–159.

49. Brucker, *Civic World,* 55–56.

50. Stefani, *Cronaca fiorentina,* 353.

51. Ibid.; Brucker, *Civic World,* 56.

52. "Diario d'anonimo fiorentino," 406.

53. *Annales Forolivienses,* 71.

54. Chinazzo, *Cronica de la guerra,* 105; Verci, *Storia della Marca,* 169; *Calendar of State Papers, Venice,* 1:28–29.

55. Chinazzo, *Cronica de la guerra,* 105, 107.

56. Verci, *Storia della Marca,* appendix document 1,724, 34–36.

57. ASVe, Commemoriale, 8, fol. 33r; *Calendar of State Papers, Venice,* 124.

58. Stefani, *Cronaca fiorentina,* 368–369. The anonymous Florentine put the number of exiles in the band at forty-eight. "Diario d'anonimo fiorentino," 410. On the political agenda of the band, see Caferro, *Mercenary Companies,* 8–9.

59. *Cronaca senese,* 678.

60. "Diario d'anonimo fiorentino," 409–411. The author enumerated the money they extorted: 4,000 florins from Cortona, 10,500 florins from Siena, 5,000 florins from Perugia, 10,500 from Pisa. According to the Sienese chronicle, the figure paid by that commune was 11,000 florins. *Cronaca senese,* 677. Stefani claims the Lucchese paid 5,000 florins. Stefani, *Cronaca fiorentina,* 369–370. Stefani wrote derisively: "The money they make the communes pay, they say they wish in loan . . . but actually, who doesn't want to lend is forced, robbed and burned." Stefani, *Cronaca fiorentina,* 370. On the presence of the company in Florentine lands, see Stefani, *Cronaca fiorentina,* 366, 368; "Diario d'anonimo fiorentino," 409; and *Corpus chronicorum Bononiensium,* 362, 364.

61. Stefani, *Cronaca fiorentina,* 371.

62. ASF, Camera del comune, Camarlinghi, uscita 241, fols. 9r–11r.

63. "Diario d'anonimo fiorentino," 410–412; Temple-Leader and Marcotti, *Sir John Hawkwood,* 161–162.

64. Valois, *La France,* 8–10; Cox, *Green Count,* 319–321.

65. Stefani, *Cronaca fiorentina,* 377; *Corpus chronicorum Bononiensium,* 369.

66. Brucker, *Civic World,* 75–76.

67. *Cronaca di ser Guerriero da Gubbio,* 21–22. Stefani, *Cronaca fiorentina,* 378–379.

68. ASF, Signori-Carteggi, Missive I Cancelleria, 18, fol. 22v.

69. ASF, Camera del comune, Camarlinghi, uscita 243, fol. 16v.

70. Stefani records negotiations. Stefani, *Cronaca fiorentina,* 380–381; according to the Florentine anonymous chronicler ("Diario d'anonimo fiorentino"), the figure was 45,000 florins, 418. This figure agrees with the Sienese chronicler, *Cronaca senese,* 681.

71. ASMa, AG, busta 1227, #104 (10 January 1381).

72. Ibid., #105 (8 March 1381).

73. Quoted in Temple-Leader and Marcotti, *Sir John Hawkwood,* 165.

74. Ansidei, "La tregua"; Jones, *Malatesta of Rimini,* 100.

75. ASMa, AG, busta 1140, #65. The truce was also mentioned in the letter of Alberto Galuzzi to Mantua dated 3 April.

76. ASF, Provvisioni, registri, 70, fol. 26v.

77. Ibid., fols. 15r–15v, 26v–27r, 47r.

78. ASS, Conc., 1802, #38; "Diario d'anonimo fiorentino," 427.

79. Bruni, *Istoria fiorentina,* 421–422; Caferro, *Mercenary Companies,* 102.

80. PRO, C 47, 28/6; Staçul, *Il cardinale,* 135–140; Perroy, *Diplomatic Correspondence,* 16, 191; Mirot and Déprez, "Les Ambassades Anglaises," no. cdxlvi, cdl; Rymer, *Foedera,* 4:114–116,

140; McKisack, *Fourteenth Century*, 427, 429–433; Saul, *Richard II*, 102–107; Tuck, "Richard II," 206, 218–219.

81. Selzer, *Deutsche Söldner*, 382.

82. ASS, Conc., 1802, #38.

83. ASMo, Casa e Stato, busta 486; Balduzzi, "Bagnacavallo," 80.

84. Balduzzi, "Bagnacavallo," 82.

85. The nineteenth-century Italian scholar Luigi Balduzzi claimed that Hawkwood handed over the towns in good repair. Niccolò d'Este, on the other hand, claimed the opposite. When he sold the towns thirteen years later to the da Polenta family, he said explicitly—in the extant deed of sale—that the towns were in "a bad state," particularly the physical structures. Balduzzi, "Bagnacavallo," 82. ASMo, Casa e Stato, busta 486.

86. Balduzzi, "Bagnacavallo," 78–79.

87. ASS, Conc., 1802, #38.

88. ASF, CP, 20, fol. 54r; ASMa, AG, busta 1140.

89. ASF, CP, 20, fol. 25r.

90. Ibid., fol. 27r.

91. Ibid., fol. 24r.

92. Ibid., fols. 26v–27.

93. Canestrini, "Documenti," 76–78 (document 14). The company next signed separate accords with the cities of Perugia and Siena. Professione, *Siena e le compagnie*, 92.

94. ASPe, Consigli e riformanze, 29, fol. 189r–189v.

## Ten • *Neapolitan Soldier and Tuscan Lord, 1381–1384*

*Epigraph:* Wycliff, *Select English Works*, 229–230.

1. ASL, ATL, 439, #844 (13 August 1381).

2. Fenwick, *Poll Taxes*, 210.

3. Rykedon's house was attacked on 18 June. *Essex Sessions of the Peace*, 24; Liddell and Wood, *Essex and the Great Revolt of 1381*, 98; Prescott, "Essex Rebel Bands in London," 58, 93, and "London in the Peasants' Revolt," 125–143; Holmes, *Good Parliament*, 56, 65–67, 72–74, 78–79, 89, 157.

4. Rymer, *Foedera;* Perroy, *Diplomatic Correspondence*, 16, 191.

5. Roskell, *Commons of the Parliament of 1422*, 169–170.

6. *Calendar of the Patent Rolls, Richard II, 1381–1385*, 75.

7. *Calendar of Close Rolls, Richard II, 1381–1385;* Morant, *History and Antiquities of Essex*, 379–380.

8. "Diario d'anonimo fiorentino," 434. Fumi, *Regesti*, 169; Stefani, *Cronaca fiorentina*, 392–393; *Cronaca Senese*, 691–692; Brucker, *Civic World*, 61–75.

9. Fumi, *Regesti*, 168; Stefani, *Cronaca fiorentina*, 398.

10. "Diario d'anonimo fiorentino," 435.

11. Eyewitnesses estimated the size of the band as four thousand horsemen. Fumi, *Regesti*, 177.

12. ASF, Provvisioni, registri, 71, fol. 16v. The discussion concerning what to do about the company is in CP, 20, fols. 115r–118r (26 January–4 February).

13. ASL, ATL, 571, #1038–1042; Fumi, *Regesti*, 168.

14. Fumi, *Regesti*, 168

15. ASS, Conc., 1808 (11 January 1382; 24 February 1382); ASMa, AG, busta 1099, #101.

16. Fumi, *Regesti*, 178.

17. ASF, Provvisioni, registri, 71, fol. 18r–18v.

18. "Diario d'anonimo fiorentino," 436.

19. ASF, Provvisioni, registri, 71, fols. 20r–21v.

20. ASL, ATL, 439 (31 January 1382). The lack of supplies is confirmed in other letters. Fumi, *Regesti*, 173, 176–177.

21. ASF, CP, 20, fol. 151v. Perugian sources speak of payments to Filibach at this time. ASPe, Consigli e riformanze, 50, fol. 15r

22. ASF, CP, 20, fol. 172r.

23. ASMa, AG, busta 1099, #101; "Diario d'anonimo fiorentino," 440.

24. Caferro, *Mercenary Companies*, 66.

25. ASMa, AG, busta 1099, #102 (30 May 1382).

26. ASL, Consiglio Generale, 8, 73 (17 March 1382).

27. ASF, Notarile Antecosmiano, 11053.

28. Holmes, *Good Parliament*, 72–74.

29. ASF, Provvisioni, registri, 71, fols. 126v–127r.

30. Ibid., fol. 126v.

31. Ibid.

32. Temple-Leader and Marcotti, *Sir John Hawkwood*.

33. Dini, "La Rocchetta," 20.

34. Ibid., 14–20.

35. On 1 June 1381 the pope invested Durazzo with the kingdom, and soon after Johanna appealed to Louis of Anjou. Documents relating to this and other events in the kingdom at the time are in BCA, B. 1145 (Lettere di Signori e del Comune di Firenze ed oltre missive responsive). See Frati, "Una raccolta," 129–144; Partner, *Lands of St. Peter*, 371; Bueno de Mesquita, *Giangaleazzo Visconti*, 19–20; Valois, *La France*, 1–16.

36. Cognasso, "L'unificazione," 512.

37. Rymer, *Foedera*, 4:140; Perroy, *L'Angleterre*, 159.

38. Rymer, *Foedera*, 4:114–116, 140; Staçul, *Il cardinale*, 146; Perroy, *Diplomatic Correspondence*, 16, 191, and *L'Angleterre*, 159; Saul, *Richard II*, 83–88, 94; Tuck, "Richard II," 206, 218–219.

39. *Westminster Chronicle*, 30–31; Tyerman, *England and the Crusades*, 333–338.

40. Perroy, *L'Angleterre*, 280, 287–88; Rymer, *Foedera*, 4:145.

41. ASL, CG, 8, 170, fol. 15r (26 June 1382).

42. Cutolo, *Re Ladislao*, 34–35, 37.

43. The deliberations are in ASF, CP, 21, fols. 61v–62v, 67v–68r, 71r–72r. See Lewin, *Negotiating Survival*, 74–75.

44. For French suspicions, see Durrieu, "La prise d'Arezzo," 167–168.

45. Stefani, *Cronaca fiorentina*, 421.

46. "Diario d'anonimo fiorentino," appendix, 535–536. The author of the *Chronicon Siculum* claimed that Florence pretended to dismiss Hawkwood. *Chronicon Siculum*, 48.

47. Durrieu, "La prise d'Arezzo,"168; Temple-Leader and Marcotti, *Sir John Hawkwood*, 181.

48. ASV, Reg Vat, 310 (8 September 1382).

49. ASL, Consiglio Generale, 8, 182; Fumi, *Regesti*, 161 (3 September 1382).

50. *Cronaca senese*, 696; Professione, *Siena e le compagnie*, 97.

51. Stefani, *Cronaca fiorentina*, 421; *Cronaca senese*, 696.

52. ASPe, Consigli e riformanze, 30, fol. 165r.

53. Giovanni Corbizzi's letter is filed among miscellaneous diplomatic dispatches in the Sienese archive. ASS, Particolari, Famiglie forestiere, #5. For Louis's initial moves in Italy, see Labande, *Rinaldo Orsini*, 137–138, 140. See also Staçul, *Il cardinale*, 163–164; Cutolo, *Re Ladislao*, 37.

54. Cox, *Green Count*, 332.

55. ASL, Consiglio Generale, 8, fol. 137r; Conforto da Costoza, *Frammenti di storia vicentina*, 28; Fumi, *Regesti*, 154.

56. Labande, *Rinaldo Orsini*, 141–142.

57. Cox, *Green Count*, 332.

58. The news was relayed by Niccolò di Carlino, a Lucchese ambassador stationed in Faenza. ASL, ATL, 439, #1065 (17 August 1382); Fumi, *Regesti*, 182.

59. ASL, ATL, 439, #1065 (17 August 1382); Fumi, *Regesti*, 182; Valeri, *L'Italia nell'età dei principati*, 231.

60. Fumi, *Regesti*, 182 (17 August 1383).

61. Feliciangeli, "Sul passagio di Luigi d'Angiò," 369–462.

62. Fumi, *Regesti*, 161.

63. Stefani, *Cronaca fiorentina*, 421.

64. Monteleone, *I Diurnali*, 33; *Cronaca senese*, 696.

65. ASL, Consiglio Generale, 8, fol. 31r. See also Fumi, *Regesti*, 183.

66. Cox, *Green Count*, 335–336.

67. ASL, ATL, 439, #1075 (24 March 1383).

68. *Chronicon Siculum*, 49; Cutolo, *Re Ladislao*, 38.

69. ASL, ATL, 439, #1086 (10 June 1383).

70. Ibid., 571, #1085 (23 June 1383).

71. Ibid., 439, #1086 (10 June 1383); ibid., 439, #1084 (23 June 1383).

72. Ibid., 571, #1085 (23 June 1383).

73. Ibid., 439, #1084.

74. Ibid., #1086.

75. Ibid.

76. Ibid.

77. But a group of cardinals refused to go, and dispute arose over that, with the deposition by the pope of Cardinal Mezzavacca in October. *Chronicon Siculum*, 50–52; Cutolo, *Re Ladislao*, 36; Staçul, *Il cardinale*, 166–168.

78. Valente, "Margherita di Durazzo," 462–463.

79. ASL, ATL, 439, #1098 (15 September 1383).

80. Ibid., #1098.

81. Fumi, *Regesti*, 207–208.

82. ASL, ATL, 571, #1174.

83. Fumi, *Regesti*, 198 (21 November 1383).

84. ASL, ATL, 571, #1174, 1137. The mission is also discussed in a letter by William, the "chancellor" of the lord of Cortona (18 November). Ibid., 439, #1133.

85. Ibid. (18 November 1383). Ibid., #1136. Fumi, *Regesti*, 197–198.

86. Fumi, *Regesti*, 211–212; Labande, *Rinaldo Orsini*, 167.

87. Fumi, *Regesti*, 208.

88. ASPe, Consigli e riformanze, 31, fol. 200v (22 November 1383), 204r. ASL, ATL, 439, #1096 (8 September 1383).

89. An additional 20 florins went to the chancellor Dionisio della Stada, who arranged the loan. ASPe, Consigli e riformanze, 31, fol. 204r; Conservatore della Moneta, 29, fol. 59v.

90. Fumi, *Regesti*, 210–211, #1176 (6 December 1383). Niccolò di Carlino reported that 1,500 florins were paid in cash and that with gifts the total reached 2,000 florins. ASPe, Conservatore della Moneta, 29, fol. 60 r.

91. For Romsey's employment with Durazzo, see Labande, *Rinaldo Orsini*, 164. The accord with the Perugians has survived and is in the Perugian archives. ASPe, Diplomatico, cassetta 36, #260 (31 July 1383). The mission against Orsini probably involved a plan to link up with Hawkwood. This is what Ninalberto da Todi believed. Fumi, *Regesti*, 198.

92. Labande, *Rinaldo Orsini*, 165.

93. Fumi, *Regesti*, 210–211, #1176.

94. ASL, ATL, 439 (6 December 1383).

95. ASL, Capitoli, 32, p. 307 (9 December 1383).

96. The letter appears to have been intercepted by the Lucchesi. ASL, ATL, 439 (9 December).

97. Ibid., #1096.

98. Professione, *Siena e le compagnie*, 100–101; Fumi, *Regesti*, 210.

99. ASL, ATL, 439, #1150. Internal Sienese records indicate, however, that the payment was a bit smaller: 7,000 florins in all. ASS, Biccherna, 267, fol. 187v.

100. Fumi, *Regesti*, 212.

101. ASL, Consiglio Generale, 8, 171 (17 June 1382); Consiglio Generale, 7, 638–639; ATL, 530, fol. 157r–157v.

102. ASL, ATL, 439, #1167; Capitoli 32, p. 307 (15 December 1383); ATL, 439, #2119 (19 December 1383).

103. ASL, ATL, 571, #1188.

104. Ibid., #1186.

105. Ibid., #1183 (23 December 1383).

106. Ibid., #1186.

107. Ibid., #1185 (24 December 1383), #1186 (26 December 1383).

108. Romsey had petitioned the Lucchese along with Hawkwood back in November 1381 and again in January 1383. Ibid., 530, 320 (22 December 1381).

109. ASL, ATL, 571, #1188.

110. Ibid., #1189.

111. ASL, Capitoli 32, 159 (13 January 1384).

112. Ibid., 161 (12 June 1383).

113. Fumi, *Regesti*, 217.

114. Ibid.

115. ASF, Camera del comune, Provveditori, poi massai, specchi, 1, fol. 25r.

116. Fumi, *Regesti*, 219 (2 March 1384); ASL, ATL, 471, #1203.

117. ASPe, Consigli e riformanze, 32, fol.103r.

118. *Cronaca senese*, 702.

119. ASS, Conc., 1813, #96 (23 July 1384).

120. On the importance of the Valdichiana and mercenary raids, see Caferro, *Mercenary Companies*, 71–72.

121. Fumi, *Regesti*, 221. Perugian sources indicate that the city still had possession of Montecchio as of 3 March 1384. ASPe, Consigli e riformanze, 32, fols. 28r–29v.

122. Bacci, *Strade romane*, 148–204.

123. Labande, *Rinaldo Orsini*, 177; Durrieu, "La prise d'Arezzo," 161–167.

124. Fumi, *Regesti*, 229.

125. Ibid., 226–227.

126. Ibid., 227.

127. ASPe, Consigli e riformanze, 32, fol. 190v.

128. There were reports that Charles of Durazzo's men attempted to poison Coucy along the way. Fumi, *Regesti*, 226; Durrieu, "La prise d'Arezzo," 168–169.

129. According to Lucchese ambassadorial dispatches, Coucy privately spoke ill of the city. Fumi, *Regesti*, 226–227.

130. Durrieu, "La prise d'Arezzo," 170–175; Professione, *Siena e le compagnie*, 104–112; Brucker, *Civic World*, 104–105.

131. Caferro, *Mercenary Companies*, 38, 115.

132. Fumi, *Regesti*, 231, 233.

133. *Ricordo della compra di Arezzo fatta dai Fiorentini.*

134. *Cronaca senese*, 704; Fumi, *Regesti*, 232.

135. *Il carteggio Acciaioli*, 131–148 (October); 149–158 (November).

136. Fumi, *Regesti*, 232.

137. Hawkwood had several meetings with Florentine ambassadors (among them Donato Acciaioli Bartolomeo di Niccolò Ridolfi, Jacopo di Bartolomeo de' Medici) from 17 October to 27 October. BML, Ashburnham MS 1830, II-243-246; *Il carteggio Acciaioli*, 140–141.

138. BML, Ashburnham MS 1830, II-548, II-549.

139. Fumi, *Regesti*, 231; Stefani, *Cronaca fiorentina*, 429–430.

140. The death of Anjou is mentioned in a letter by Antonio Sercelli to the bishop of Florence, dated 27 September. BML, Ashburnham MS 1830, II-56.

*Eleven • The Deal with the Devil, the Birth of a Son, and a Victory at Castagnaro,*
*1385–1387*

*Epigraph:* Dati, *L'istoria di Firenze*, 26.

1. ASL, ATL, 439, #1292 (12 June 1385).

2. ASPe, Consigli e riformanze, 33, fols. 79v, 107r; ASL, Min 3 (10 April 1385).

3. Professione, *Siena e le compagnie*, 117.

4. ASS, Conc., 1816, #5.

5. Bueno de Mesquita, *Giangaleazzo Visconti*, 31–36; Chamberlain, *Count of Virtue*, 75–83; Cognasso, "L'unificazione," 513–516.

6. Corio, *Storia di Milano*, 1:273.

7. The *processus* is published in *Annales Mediolanenses*, cols. 788–800.

8. The original letter is reproduced in Temple-Leader and Marcotti, *Sir John Hawkwood*, 350.

9. "Diario d'anonimo fiorentino," 461. Temple-Leader and Marcotti, *Sir John Hawkwood*, 188.

10. ASL, ATL, 439, #1292 (12 June 1385); Fumi, *Regesti*, 240; *Cronaca senese*, 713.

11. ASL, ATL, 439, #1293 (17 June 1385).

12. Santoro, *La politica finanziaria*, 2:2–3.

13. Ibid., 5–6 (document 10). The bequest was made on 26 July.

14. Santoro, *La politica finanziaria*, 2:5–6.

15. Osio, *Documenti diplomatici*, 249; see also Temple-Leader and Marcotti, *Sir John Hawkwood*, 189–190; Cognasso, "L'unificazione," 522; and *Calendar of State Papers and MSS., Milan*, 1:1.

16. Temple-Leader and Marcotti, *Sir John Hawkwood*, 190.

17. Salutati, *Epistolario*, vol. 15 ("Epistle V").

18. ASL, ATL, 439, #1292.

19. Ibid., #1297 (9 July 1385); ASPe, Consigli e riformanze, 33, fol. 175v.

20. *Cronaca senese*, 713; ASPe, Consigli e riformanze, 33, fol. 175v; ASS, Biccherna, 272, fol. 130r; Bueno de Mesquita, *Giangaleazzo Visconti*, 70, 85.

21. PRO, C 47/28/6.

22. BCA, B. 1145 (Lettere di Signori e del Comune di Firenze ed oltre missive responsive); Frati, "Una raccolta," 129–144; Partner, *Lands of St. Peter*, 373–374; Hòman, *Gli angioni di Napoli*, 461–466; Guldescu, *History of Medieval Croatia*, 227–232; De Regibus, "Il declino degli Angioni," 369–410; Mancarella, "Firenze," 95–106.

23. BML, Ashburnham MS 1830, II-50, II-52.

24. *Westminster Chronicle*, 140–143; Sherbourne, "Defence of the Realm," 98, 100–113; Palmer, *England, France and Christendom*, 67–85.

25. *Westminster Chronicle*, 156–159.

26. ASL, Dipl. #1315; Fumi, *Regesti*, 245–246.

27. ASPe, Consigli e riformanze, 33, fol. 193r.

28. ASF, Prestanze, 957, fol. 60r.

29. ASMo, Archivio per materie: capitani di ventura, busta 1.

30. Kohl, *Padua*, 229–242; Bueno de Mesquita, *Giangaleazzo Visconti*, 69–75; Collino, "La guerra Viscontea," 106.

31. Bueno de Mesquita, *Giangaleazzo Visconti*, 70. Salutati, *Epistolario*, 16:146–159.

32. Quoted from Kohl, *Padua*, 235.

33. Ibid., 235–236.

34. Gatari, *Cronaca Carrarese*, 258.

35. Pastorello, *Nuove ricerche*, 140–141 (document 6); Bueno de Mesquita, *Giangaleazzo Visconti*, 73–74.

36. ASF, Missive I Cancelleria, 21, fol. 4v.

37. Gatari, *Cronaca Carrarese*, 263–264.

38. Ibid., 265.

39. Ibid., 266.

40. *Cronica Volgare*, 26.

41. Cognasso, "L'unificazione," 530.

42. Gatari, *Cronaca Carrarese*, 267.

43. Ibid., 271.

44. Ibid., 268.

45. Ibid., 271.

46. Oman, *Art of War in the Middle Ages*, 2:296, 300. Brief accounts of the battle are in Mallett, *Mercenaries and Their Masters*, 160; Contamine, *War in the Middle Ages*, 160; and Ricotti, *Storia delle compagnie*, 2:185–186.

47. Oman, *Art of War in the Middle Ages*, 2:297.

48. Hall, *Weapons and Warfare*, 47.

49. Gatari, *Cronaca Carrarese*, 266–267.

50. Ibid., 267.

51. Ibid., 269.

52. Ibid., 270–271.

53. Ibid., 271.

54. Ibid., 270–271.

55. "Facieva gia il sole versso l'umida tera il suo velocie viagio." Gatari, *Cronaca Carrarese*, 272.

56. *Cronica Volgare*, 26; Temple-Leader and Marcotti, *Sir John Hawkwood*, 200.

57. Gatari, *Cronaca Carrarese*, 272.

58. Ibid., 270.

59. Ibid., 272.

60. Ibid., 273.

61. Ibid., 278; *Chronicon Estense*, col. 514. Sozomen of Pistoia put the number of captives at five thousand men. Sozomen, *Specimen Historiae*, col. 1129.

62. *Cronica Volgare*, 25.

63. Ibid., 26.

64. Kohl, *Padua*, xxi.

65. Gatari, *Cronaca Carrarese*, 272.

66. *Chronicon Estense*, cols. 514–515.

67. Gatari, *Cronaca Carrarese*, 276.

68. Ibid., 277.

69. Chamberlain, *Count of Virtue*, 100; Bueno de Mesquita, *Giangaleazzo Visconti*, 74.

70. Gatari, *Cronaca Carrarese*, 284; Pastorello, *Nuove ricerche*, 21, 144 n. viii.

71. Gatari, *Cronaca Carrarese*, 289; *Chronicon Estense*, col. 515.

72. Gatari, *Cronaca Carrarese*, 290; *Chronicon Estense*, col. 515.

73. *Chronicon Tarvisum*, col. 788.

74. Temple-Leader and Marcotti, *Sir John Hawkwood*, 204.

75. Cessi, "Prigionieri illustri," 153–170.

76. ASF, Provvisioni, registri, 75, fols. 209v–211r (5 February 1386).

77. Ricotti, *Storia delle compagnie*, 2:126.

78. Gatari, *Cronaca Carrarese*, 290.

79. Ibid.

80. Bueno de Mesquita, *Giangaleazzo Visconti*, 74–78.

81. ASF, Dieci di balia, Deliberazioni, condotte e stanziamenti, 3, fol. 10r; Camera del comune, Provveditori, poi massai, specchi, 4, fols. 80–81v.

## Twelve • *Florence and the Military Buildup, 1387–1389*

*Epigraph: Cronaca senese*, 721.

1. Brucker, *Civic World*, 77–86. See also Najemy, *Corporatism and Consensus*, 166–200.

2. Bruni, *Istoria fiorentina*, 307.

3. ASS, Conc., 1815, #37, 41, 67; Brucker, *Civic World*, 104–107; Caferro, *Mercenary Companies*, 19, 24, 34, 165–166.

4. The case was submitted to arbitration before the Bolognesi, who ceded the town to Florence in October 1386. Caferro, *Mercenary Companies*, 34; Brucker, *Civic World*, 107–109.

5. Caferro, *Mercenary Companies*, 34.

6. ASS, Conc., 1821, #10 (4 June 1387).

7. One of numerous examples is Niccolò Malavolti's letter of 18 July. Malavolti spoke at length about the general state of affairs but ended with a report that Hawkwood had stopped briefly in the environs of Arezzo. Ibid., #38 (18 July 1387).

8. Ibid., #60 (12 August 1387).

9. ASF, Dieci di balia, Deliberazioni, condotte e stanziamenti, 3, fol. 17r (14 June).

10. ASF, Camera del comune, Provveditori, poi massai, specchi, 4, fol. 66r–66v.

11. ASF, CP, 26, fols. 22v–27v.

12. Brucker, *Civic World*, 125, 129.

13. Cognasso, "L'unificazione," 534; Bueno de Mesquita, *Giangaleazzo Visconti*, 92–93; Kohl, *Padua*, 240; Law, "La caduta degli Scaligeri," 83–98.

14. *Cronica Volgare*, 49; Collino, "La preparazione della guerra," 213, 225–232.

15. ASS, Conc., 1822, #3a, 4, 5, 7, 8.

16. *Cronica Volgare*, 49. Peter Herde has argued that the first hints of Florentine anxiety about Visconti occurred in October 1387. Herde, "Politische Verhaltenweisen," 196 n. 217.

17. ASS, Conc., 1822, #3b (17 November 1387).

18. ASF, Signori-Carteggi, Missive I Cancelleria, fol. 280r (11 November 1387). Florentine officials wrote several letters to Ubaldini. ASF, Dieci di balia, Legazioni e commissarie, 1, fol. 50 (30 January 1388), fol. 55r (9 February).

19. ASF, CP, 26, fol. 211r.

20. Collino, "La guerra Viscontea," 147–148. The first payment to Ubaldini is recorded in ASF, Camera del comune, Provveditori, poi massai, specchi, 4, fol. 79v.

21. Novati, "Trattive," 574.

22. ASS, Conc., 140, fol. 20r. *Cronica Volgare*, 49; *Cronaca senese*, 720.

23. ASS, Conc., 124, #25, 26, 27; Conc., 134, #6.

24. Fumi, *Regesti*, 251–252 (28 November).

25. Ibid., 265.

26. ASF, CP, 26, fols. 38r–39v, 46v–48v, 63r–64r; Brucker, *Civic World*, 76–77, 114; Collino, "La politica fiorentino-bolognese," 137–139; Mancarella, "Firenze," 112–115.

27. ASF, Provvisioni, registri, 76, fols. 158r–159r.

28. ASF, Dieci di balia, Deliberazioni, condotte e stanziamenti, 4, fols. 85v–87v.

29. Salutati's letter of complaint to Venice on 12 May is in ASF, Signori-Carteggi, Missive I Cancelleria, 21, fol. 25. Cognasso, "L'unificazione," 537; Bueno de Mesquita, *Giangaleazzo Visconti*, 79; Kohl, *Padua*, 248–251.

30. Brucker, *Civic World*, 126.

31. ASF, CP, 27, fol. 10r.

32. ASS, Conc., 1821, #18, 24, 29; Collino, "La preparazione della guerra," 269–270.

33. Bueno de Mesquita, *Giangaleazzo Visconti*, 108–109, 341–342.

34. Fumi, *Regesti*, 260; Bueno de Mesquita, *Giangaleazzo Visconti*, 92; Brucker, *Civic World*, 122.

35. Quoted from Cognasso, "L'unificazione," 539.

36. ASF, Camera del comune, Provveditori, poi massai, specchi, 4, fol. 63r; Camera del comune, Provveditori, poi massai, specchi, 5, fol. 61r.

37. ASS, Conc., 143, fols. 26v–27r; Caferro, *Mercenary Companies*, 166.

38. Collino, "La preparazione della guerra," 286–289.

39. Caferro, *Mercenary Companies*, 169; Partner, *Lands of St. Peter*, 182; Professione, *Siena e le compagnie*, 133–135.

40. ASF, Dieci di balia, Legazioni e commissarie, 1, fol. 77.

41. Ibid., fols. 77–78.

42. Ibid., fols. 98r, 90.

43. *Cronaca senese*, 721; ASS, Reg. 4, fol. 182v.

44. ASF, Dieci di balia, Legazioni e commissarie, 1, fols. 107, 103.

45. ASS, Conc., 143, fols. 26v–27r; Caferro, *Mercenary Companies*, 165–166; Bueno de Mesquita, *Giangaleazzo Visconti*, 99–100, 341.

46. ASF, Dieci di balia, Legazioni e commissarie, 1, fol. 77.

47. Ibid., fol. 80.

48. *Cronica Volgare*, 59; ASF, Dieci di balia, Legazioni e commissarie, 1, fol. 83 (8 May 1388).

49. ASF, Dieci di balia, Legazioni e commissarie, 1, fols. 92, 93.

50. Giacomo Carapea, a Mantuan ambassador stationed at Arezzo, gave a careful account of Carlo's movements. The podestà of Ferrara wrote of Carlo's activities to the Sienese. ASMa, AG, busta 1099 (16 July 1388). The letter from the podestà of Ferrara is in the Sienese archive. ASS, Conc., 1823, #35 (1 May 1388). The anonymous Florentine chronicler mentioned Carlo's arrival as occurring on 4 May. "Diario d'anonimo fiorentino," 477. Romano, "Giangaleazzo Visconti," 26.

51. BML, Ashburnham MS 1830, III-43 (11 May 1388).

52. ASF, Dieci di balia, Legazioni e commissarie, 1, fols. 109r, 110.

53. Ibid., fol. 158.

54. Ibid., fol. 104.

55. *Cronica Volgare*, 60.

56. Temple-Leader and Marcotti, *Sir John Hawkwood*, 209.

57. ASF, CP, 27, fol. 23v.

58. Ibid., fols. 12v–13r.

59. This opinion was repeated by several other council members. Ibid., fols. 7v–9v.

60. Ibid., 26, fol. 215v.

61. Ibid., fol. 216r–216v.

62. Collino, "La guerra Viscontea," 7–8.

63. On 14 June 1388, Florence offered Beltoft a contract for three years with a personal salary of 1,000 florins annually. On 7 July the city increased its offer to 3,000 florins annually. According to William Horton, who negotiated on Beltoft's behalf, the Englishman found the promise of exclusive obligation to Florence too constraining. ASF, Dieci di balia, Legazioni e commissarie, 1, fol. 94.

64. Ibid., fols. 117–118, 119 (22 July 1388).

65. Ibid., fols. 115, 132.

66. Ibid., fol. 131 (19 August 1388). See also CP, 27, fol. 24v.

67. ASS, Conc., 1824, #4.

68. Fumi, *Regesti*, 277.

69. This is mentioned in the correspondence between two university professors from Siena and Perugia in May 1388. Zdekauer, "Tre lettere," 288–298.

70. ASS, Conc., 1824, #18.

71. ASL, ATL, 571, #1403. Fumi, *Regesti*, 276–277. Fumi erroneously dates this letter 30 October 1389. It belongs to 1388. It is part of M. Savini 's embassy to Perugia in October of that year. Fumi, *Regesti*, 268–269.

72. ASF, Dieci di balia, Legazioni e commissarie, 1, fol. 105r.

73. ASS, Conc., 1824, #4. The Florentine chronicler Minerbetti, for one, did not deny Florentine involvement with the English corporals. *Cronica Volgare*, 67.

74. A good summary of Florentine machinations is in Collino, "La guerra Viscontea," 19–24.

75. ASF, Dieci di balia, Legazioni e commissarie, 1, fol. 121 ( 22 July 1388).

76. This was voiced by Ludovico Banchi in the Signoria on 20 July 1388. ASF, CP, 27, fol. 20r.

77. ASF, Capitoli, registri, 12, fols. 153r–163r (20 August 1388).

78. *Cronica Volgare*, 67–68.

79. ASF, CP, 27, fols. 51v–53v; Brucker, *Civic World*, 130.

80. Temple-Leader and Marcotti, *Sir John Hawkwood*, 209.

81. *Cronica Volgare*, 67. There is an interesting letter by a Lucchese ambassador stationed in Perugia which describes the activities and composition of the band. ASL, ATL, 571, #1379 (15 October, 1388). See also Fumi, *Regesti*, 268–269. The ambassador was under the impression that Beltoft himself would soon join the band, but this was, of course, not true.

82. Cutolo, *Re Ladislao*, 85–87.

83. ASF, Dieci di balia, Deliberazioni, condotte e stanziamenti, 4, fol. 1r–1v.

84. Ibid., Legazioni e commissarie, 1, fol. 147.

85. Palmieri, "La congiura," 187.

86. There were also at this time renewed concerns about Montepulciano. ASF, CP, 27, fols. 43r–43v, 50r–52r. Cognasso, "L'unificazione," 541. Buonacorso eventually surfaced in Siena. *Cronica Volgare*, 70–71; Brucker, *Civic World*, 85–86.

87. Bueno de Mesquita, *Giangaleazzo Visconti*, 88; Collino, "La politica fiorentino-bolognese," 134–137; Brucker, *Civic World*, 112–113.

88. ASF, Dieci di balia, Legazioni e commissarie, 1, fol. 158.

89. Ibid.

90. The other English corporals included David Falcon, Richard Swinfort, Roger Baker, and Richard Norlant. Ibid., Deliberazioni, condotte e stanziamenti, 4, fol. 1v.

91. Ibid., Legazioni e commissarie, 1, fol. 114.

92. *Chronicon Siculum*, 80–81; Cutolo, *Re Ladislao*, 88.

93. *Chronicon Siculum*, 81–82; Partner, *Lands of St. Peter*, 374.

94. *Cronica Volgare*, 74; Monteleone, *I Diurnali*, 53.

95. Monteleone, *I Diurnali*, 53; Mancarella, "Firenze," 112–115.

96. ASS, Conc., 1823, #14 (9 April 1388).

97. *Cronica Volgare*, 54–55.

98. ASF, Dieci di balia, Legazioni e commissarie, 1, fol. 169.

99. Ibid., fol. 178.

100. Ibid., fol. 179.

101. The court gives the impression that Hawkwood in fact sold off La Rocchetta. ASF, Mercanzia, 1201, fol. 149r–149v; Notarile Antecosmiano, 10656, fols. 35r–37v. I thank Paula Clarke for alerting me to this document.

102. ASL, ATL, 439, #1398; Fumi, *Regesti*, 275.

103. ASL, ATL, 471, #1395.

104. The negotiations, initiated back in December 1388, focused on getting Giangaleazzo to agree to acknowledge the Serchio Valley as the extent of his sphere of influence in Tuscany. In return Florence promised to refrain from involvement in Lombardy. ASF, CP, 27, fols. 101r–104r, 127v–128v; Bueno de Mesquita, *Giangaleazzo Visconti*, 100–102; Brucker, *Civic World*, 131–132.

105. ASF, Dieci di balia, Legazioni e commissarie, 1, fols. 164–165, 167.

106. Ibid., Deliberazioni, condotte e stanziamenti, 4, fols. 4v–7r; Camera del comune, Provveditori, poi massai, specchi, 5, fol. 92v.

107. The most Florentine sources place Hawkwood near Città di Castello as of late May or early June. Hawkwood's name reappears in the discussions of the Signoria in June. ASF, CP, 27, fol. 127r. A letter by a Lucchese ambassador has Hawkwood still at Città di Castello as of 2 July. Fumi, *Regesti*, 279. The anonymous Florentine chronicler recorded Hawkwood's arrival in the city on 3 May 1389. "Diario d'anonimo fiorentino," 91–92.

108. ASF, Dieci di balia, Legazioni e commissarie, 1, fol. 199.

109. Ibid., Deliberazioni, condotte e stanziamenti, 4, fols. 37r, 39r.

110. There remained ostensible efforts at peace. Florence continued to negotiate, but with a decided air of cynicism. ASF, CP, 27, fols. 127v–128v.

111. Bueno de Mesquita, *Giangaleazzo Visconti*, 105–106.

112. ASF, CP, 27, fols 143v–144v (23 July 1389).

113. *Cronica Volgare*, 76, *Cronaca senese*, 725.

114. ASS, Conc., 1825, #50 (16 June 1389); Bueno de Mesquita, *Giangaleazzo Visconti*, 108; Favale, "Siena," 323; Caferro, *Mercenary Companies*, 166.

115. Caferro, *Mercenary Companies*, 166; *Cronica Volgare*, 76; Silva, "Il Governo," 248–249; Fumi, *Regesti*, 279; Bueno de Mesquita, *Giangaleazzo Visconti*, 106.

116. *Cronica Volgare*, 79.

117. ASF, Dieci di balia, Legazioni e commissarie, 1, fol. 201.

118. Ibid.

119. Ibid., fol. 209.

120. Ibid., fol. 199.

121. Ibid., fols. 205–206.

122. ASF, CP, 27, fols. 148r–151r.

123. ASL, ATL, 572, #1413; Fumi, *Regesti*, 279.

124. BML, Ashburnham MS 1830 (13 July 1389).

125. ASS, Conc., 1826, #17 (31 August 1389).

126. Ibid., #10 (8 August 1389).

127. ASL, ATL, 572, #1413. Fumi, *Regesti*, 279–280.

128. ASF, Dieci di balia, Legazioni e commissarie, 1, fol. 210.

129. Ibid.

130. *Cronaca senese*, 725.

131. ASF, Dieci di balia, Legazioni e commissarie, 1, fols. 210–211.

132. Ibid.

133. *Cronaca senese*, 727.

134. Bueno de Mesquita, *Giangaleazzo Visconti*, 109.

135. ASF, Dieci di balia, Legazioni e commissarie, 1, fol. 202; Bueno de Mesquita, *Giangaleazzo Visconti*, 107–108.

136. Bueno de Mesquita, *Giangaleazzo Visconti*, 110–111; Favale, "Siena," 351–370; Silva, "Il Governo," 263.

## Thirteen • *The War against Milan. 1390–1393*

*Epigraph:* ASF, Dieci di balia, Legazioni e commissarie, 1, fol. 181.

1. ASS, Conc., 1827, #11, 12, 13.

2. *Cronica Volgare*, 97.

3. ASF, Dieci di balia, Deliberazioni, condotte e stanziamenti, 4, fols. 159r–160v.

4. *Cronaca senese*, 732.

5. Baron, *Crisis of the Early Italian Renaissance.*

6. Dati, *L'istoria di Firenze*, 37.

7. ASS, Conc., 1829, #57.

8. BML, Ashburnham MS 1830, #57 (1 June 1390).

9. *Cronica Volgare*, 24.

10. Discussions in the Signoria about sending Hawkwood to Bologna are in ASF, CP, 28, fols. 63r–66r.

11. Hawkwood's arrival in Bologna is recounted in the dispatches (14–16 May) of the Lucchese ambassador Francesco Dombellinghi. Fumi, *Regesti*, 295. The event is also described briefly by the Bolognese chronicler on 14 May. *Corpus chronicorum Bononiensium*, 410.

12. Ibid., 408; Corio, *Storia di Milano*, 1:909.

13. ASL, ATL, 572, #1469; ATL, 572, 1470, 1471; Fumi, *Regesti*, 296. Vergerio, *Epistolario*, 69.

14. *Corpus chronicorum Bononiensium*, 410–411.

15. Corio, *Storia di Milano*, 1:909.

16. ASL, ATL 572, #1478, 1482 (letters dated 8–9 June); *Cronica Volgare*, 100; *Corpus chronicorum Bononiensium*, 412; Fumi, *Regesti*, 298.

17. ASL, ATL, 572, #1477, 1490; Fumi, *Regesti*, 297, 301.

18. ASL, ATL, 572, #1478; Fumi, *Regesti*, 298 (8 June).

19. ASL, ATL, 572, #1467; Fumi, *Regesti*, 295.

20. ASL, ATL, 572, #1483; *Corpus chronicorum Bononiensium*, 414; Fumi, *Regesti*, 299.

21. ASL, ATL, 572, #1488; Fumi, *Regesti*, 310.

22. ASL, ATL, 572, #17 (letter dated 13 June); Fumi, *Regesti*, 298.

23. Gatari, *Cronaca Carrarese*, 407–413; *Corpus chronicorum Bononiensium*, 416–417; Bueno de Mesquita, *Giangaleazzo Visconti*, 122; Cognasso, "L'unificazione," 555; Kohl, *Padua*, 265–269.

24. ASS, Conc., 1821, #19; Bueno de Mesquita, *Giangaleazzo Visconti*, 121–123.

25. Kohl, *Padua*, 266–267; Bueno de Mesquita, *Giangaleazzo Visconti*, 122–123.

26. BML, Ashburnham MS 1830, III-70; Bueno de Mesquita, *Giangaleazzo Visconti*, 122; Kohl, *Padua*, 266.

27. Kohl, *Padua*, 267.

28. ASF, Signori-Carteggi, Missive I Cancelleria, 22, fol. 71v.

29. BML, Ashburnham MS 1830, III-68 (27 June 1390); *Corpus chronicorum Bononiensium*, 416.

30. *Cronaca senese*, 735.

31. *Cronica Volgare*, 105.

32. Fumi, *Regesti*, 294.

33. *Corpus chronicorum Bononiensium*, 418.

34. BML, Ashburnham MS 1830, III-68.

35. Ibid., III-73.

36. Gatari, *Cronaca Carrarese*, 423–425.

37. BML, Ashburnham MS 1830, III-75.

38. The Florentines hired Stephen with two thousand lances back in April. Rambaldi, "Stefano III," 28.

39. Romano, "Giangaleazzo Visconti," 311.

40. ASF, Dieci di balia, Deliberazioni, condotte e stanziamenti, 4, fol. 190r.

41. *Cronica Volgare*, 106–107; Cognasso, "L'unificazione," 555.

42. ASF, CP, 28; *Cronica Volgare*, 106–107.

43. *Cronica Volgare*, 107.

44. Gatari, *Cronaca Carrarese*, 433; *Chronicon Estense*, col. 520.

45. Pastorello, *Nuove ricerche*, 72; Gatari, *Cronaca Carrarese*, 433; *Corpus chronicorum Bononiensium*, 425–426; Ganguzza Billanovich, "Francesco da Carrara," 657.

46. *Cronica Volgare*, 110.

47. Discussions in the Florentine Signoria relating to Armagnac are in ASF, CP, 28, fols. 85v, 86r, 88v, 96r.

48. Jarry, *La vie politique*, 28–35; Mirot, *La politique Française;* Cognasso, "L'unificazione," 558.

49. Cognasso, "L'unificazione," 557. The correspondence between Armagnac and Florence is published in Durrieu, *Les Gascons en Italie.* For the agreement with Florence of 16 October, see 51–52.

50. Temple-Leader and Marcotti, *Sir John Hawkwood*, 246.

51. BML, Ashburnham MS 1830, II-161.

52. Vergerio, *Epistolario*, 48.

53. BML, Ashburnham MS 1830, III-106 (15 December 1390); *Corpus chronicorum Bononiensium*, 427.

54. ASF, Dieci di balia, Deliberazioni, condotta e stanziamenti, 5, fol. 22v.

55. *Cronica Volgare*, 114.

56. *Corpus chronicorum Bononiensium*, 427; *Chronicon Estense*, col. 520; Kohl, *Padua*, 273.

57. The legislation was enacted on 16 November 1390. ASF, Provvisioni, registri, 79, fol. 267r; Prestanze, 1252, fol. 54r.

58. BML, Ashburnham MS 1830, III-104.

59. Ibid., III-106.

60. Ibid. The Florentines had been admonishing the Bolognese since at least 6 October. Ibid., II-161.

61. The preparations are noted by Pier Paolo Vergerio in his letter of 22 January to Giovanni da Bologna. Vergerio, *Epistolario*, 46–53 (XXVII). See also Ganguzza Billanovich, "Francesco da Carrara," 655–657.

62. Francesco Novello wrote to Donato Acciaiuoli about the matter on 12 January. BML, Ashburnham MS 1830, II-187. The inventory of the collection incorrectly identifies "Conte Corrado" as Konrad Landau. *Il carteggio Acciaioli*, 266.

63. Gatari, *Cronaca Carrarese*, 434; Rondini, "La dominazione viscontea," 133.

64. *Cronica Volgare*, 115.

65. BML, Ashburnham MS 1830, II-188.

66. *Cronica Volgare*, 116.

67. Vergerio, *Epistolario*, 67–68.

68. BML, Ashburnham MS 1830, I-9.

69. Cognasso, "L'unificazione," 555; Durrieu, *Les Gascons en Italie*, 58.

70. Durrieu, *Les Gascons en Italie*, 58–59.

71. Quoted from Cognasso, "L'unificazione," 558.

72. ASF, Dieci di balia, Deliberazioni, condotte e stanziamenti, 5, fol. 23r.

73. BML, Ashburnham MS 1830, III-44.

74. Ibid., III-45.

75. *Cronica Volgare*, 116.

76. BML, Ashburnham MS 1830, III-252.

77. *Cronica Volgare*, 122.

78. ASF, Capitoli, registri, 1, #79, fols. 160v–163v.

79. ASMi, Registri Panigarola, n. 1, fols. 150r–150v; Ferorelli, *I registri dell'ufficio degli statuti di Milano*, 10 n. 191; Archivio di Stato di Verona, Fondo Zalieri–dal Verme, no. 20. See also Rondini, "La dominazione viscontea," 90.

80. ASF, Camera del comune, Provveditori, poi massai, specchi, 7, fol. 385r; Dieci di balia, Deliberazioni, condotte e stanziamenti, 5, fol. 197r.

81. ASF, Camera del comune, Provveditori, poi massai, specchi, 7, fol. 50r.

82. ASBo, Condotta degli Stipendiari, le bollette, 56, fols. 117r.

83. Ibid., fols. 118r–123v.

84. Ibid., fol. 120r.

85. Ibid., fols. 3r, 63r, 117r.

86. Vergerio, *Epistolario*, 70.

87. ASF, Dieci di balia, Deliberazioni, condotte e stanziamenti, 5, fols. 52v–53r.

88. Ibid., fol. 56v.

89. "curramento dello stato." BML, Asburnham MS 1830, III-252.

90. Durrieu, *Les Gascons en Italie*, 78–79.

91. Cognasso, "L'unificazione," 562; Bigazzi, *Firenze e Milano*, 16–19, documents 8, 10.

92. ASF, Camera del comune, Provveditori, poi massai, specchi, 7, fol. 52v.

93. Bueno de Mesquita, *Giangaleazzo Visconti*, 127–128.

94. Ibid., 126–127; *Chronicon Estense*, 522–523.

95. Minerbetti and Gatari have the date as 10 May; Vergerio has it as 11 May. *Cronica Volgare*, 124; Gatari, *Cronaca Carrarese*, 435; Vergerio, *Epistolario*, 70.

96. *Cronica Volgare*, 125.

97. Vergerio, *Epistolario*, 70.

98. Ibid., 71.

99. *Cronica Volgare*, 125; Ammirato, *Istorie fiorentine*, 443–444.

100. Vergerio, *Epistolario*, 71–72.

101. Ibid., 72.

102. Ibid., 73; *Cronica Volgare*, 130–131.

103. Bueno de Mesquita, *Giangaleazzo Visconti*, 130.

104. Ibid., 127, 130.

105. Dati, *L'istoria di Firenze*, 37.

106. *Cronica Volgare*, 126–127; Cognasso, "L'unificazione," 559.

107. The death of Bernard is recorded in a letter written by Giovanni Bilotti to Donato Accaiauoli on 10 June 1391. "On 29 May," Biliotti wrote, "two corporals at the petition of the Count of Armagnac killed Messer Bernard della Salle, two miles outside of Avignon." BML, Ashburnham MS 1830, III-35. *Cronica Volgare*, 126–127; Cognasso, "L'unificazione," 559.

108. Froissart, *Chronicles*, 490.

109. Gatari, *Cronaca Carrarese*, 435.

110. *Cronica Volgare*, 131.

111. Ibid.

112. The anecdote appears in modern histories but not in contemporary sources. The closest is the reference in the Bolognese chronicle. The author includes a letter from a member of Hawkwood's retreating force: "they thought to have us in their lap ["grembo"] and they said during the skirmishes that the fox was closed in his den." *Corpus chronicorum Bononiensium*, 433. The chronicler of Gubbio mentions "the Fox in the cage," but he wrote nearly a century after the event, and after the Florentine humanist Poggio Bracciolini, who also included the story. *Cronaca di ser Guerriero da Gubbio*, 28.

113. *Cronica Volgare*, 131–132; *Chronicon Estense*, col. 523.

114. *Cronica Volgare*, 132.

115. Sienese ambassadors gave reports on the battle. ASS, Conc., 1829, #38, 39. Jacopo dal Verme's description of his victory, in a letter dated 25 July, is reproduced in French. Durrieu, *Les Gascons en Italie*, 92–93.

116. *Cronica Volgare*, 134.

117. Ibid., 132.

118. Manni, *Commentario*, 641.

119. Bruni, *Istoria fiorentina*, 539.

120. Vergerio, *Epistolario*, 74.

121. ASS, Conc., 1829, #34 (16 July 1391).

122. Gatari, *Cronaca Carrarese*, 435.

123. *Chronicon Estense*, 523.

124. Bruni, *Istoria fiorentina*, 535–537; Wilcox, *Development*, 2–3.

125. Wilcox, *Development*, 5–6.

126. Bracciolini, *Storia Fiorentina*, libro terzo (pages unnumbered, but I count it as the 16th side from beginning of start of chapter 3).

127. Ricotti, *Storia delle compagnie*, 2:191–193.

128. Ammirato, *Istorie fiorentine*, 445–455.

129. Corio, *Storia di Milano*, 1:916.

130. *Cronica Volgare*, 137.

131. ASMa, AG, busta 757, #29–69.

132. ASBo, Governo, Signorie, Provvisioni in Capreto, 302, fol. 30r.

133. *I Capitoli del Comune di Firenze*, 50–51.

134. ASF, Dieci di balia, Deliberazioni, condotte e stanziamenti, 5, fol. 78r–78v.

135. *Cronica Volgare*, 138.

136. ASF, Provvisioni, registri, 80, fols. 78v–80r, 239r–243r, 245r–249r. See Brucker, *Civic World*, 86 n. 137.

137. *Corpus chronicorum Bononiensium*, 405.

138. *Cronica Volgare*, 146.

139. Cognasso, "L'unificazione," 563.

140. *Cronica Volgare*, 153.

*Fourteen • Two Weddings, a Funeral, and a Disputed Legacy, 1392–1394–1412*

*Epigraphs:* Winstanley, *Honour of the Taylors*, 53. Medin, "La morte di Giovanni Aguto," 173.

1. The act stipulated that the minimum marriageable age was fourteen years old, at which point Hawkwood would receive the money. ASF, Capitoli, registri, 1, #79, fols. 160v–163v.

2. ASF, Notarile Antecosmiani, 12063, fols. 257r, 259v–260r.

3. Bradler, *Die Landschaften Allgäu und Oberschwaben*, 173–181.

4. ASB, Condotta degli Stipendiary, le bollette, #56.

5. *Cronica Volgare*, 149.

6. *Corpus chronicorum Bononiensium*, 436.

7. *Cronica Volgare*, 149, 158–159.

8. ASF, Notarile Antecosmiani, 12063, fol. 257v.

9. BML, Ashburnham MS 1830, II-142. Temple-Leader and Marcotti erroneously put the date of this letter at 9 January. Temple-Leader and Marcotti, *Sir John Hawkwood*, 272.

10. Hawkwood was also, as of April 1393, receiving a salary as the head of an honorary brigade of twenty-five lances. Temple-Leader and Marcotti, *Sir John Hawkwood*, 273–274.

11. ASF, Notarile Antecosmiani, 12063, fol. 258r.

12. Selzer, *Deutsche Söldner*, 244.

13. Della Torre served as captain of the people in Florence in 1420 and eleven years later as podestà. Manni, *Commentario*, 646.

14. CLRO, HR, 124/6; *Calendar of Select Pleas*, 308; *London Topographical Record*, 9–15.

15. ASF, Provvisioni, registri, 75, fol. 209v. The second was in 1389. ASF, Mercanzia, 1201, fol. 149r–149v; Notarile Antecosmiano, 10656, fols. 35r–37v. I thank Paula Clarke for alerting me to this document.

16. Dini, "La Rocchetta," 29–30. Dini was unsure whether Hawkwood's property was sold before or after his death. He suggested that the sale probably occurred sometime after 1393 and before 1399. Ibid., 27.

17. ASF, Capitoli, registri, 1, 81, fols. 164v–167r.

18. ASF, Provvisioni, registri, 82, fols. 211r–212v; see now Poggi and Haines, *Il duomo di Firenze*, 2:122–123.

19. ASF, Capitoli, registri, 1, 81, fol. 165v.

20. *Cronica Volgare*, 183.

21. In addition to Minerbetti, the published primary accounts include Naddo da Monte-catini, *Memorie storiche*, and Rinuccini, *Ricordi storici*. An unpublished primary account exists among the papers of the Ricci family. ASF, Carte Bardi, 3a serie, 59. The standard secondary account, with documents, is Medin, "La morte di Giovanni Aguto," 161–171.

22. *Cronica Volgare*, 183.

23. Naddo da Montecatini, *Memorie storiche*, 141; Medin, "La morte di Giovanni Aguto," 173.

24. Medin, "La morte di Giovanni Aguto," 173.

25. Strocchia, *Death and Ritual*, 110.

26. Ibid., 55.

27. Ibid., 79–82.

28. Mueller, "Veronesi e Capitali Veronesi," 371; Borsook, *Mural Painters*, 75–76; Mallett, *Mercenaries and Their Masters*, 129; Valentiner, "Equestrian Statue of Paolo Savelli"; Scalini, "L'armatura fiorentina" and "Note sulla formazione dell' armatura di Piastra," 15–26.

29. Mueller, "Veronesi e Capitali Veronesi," 371.

30. *Cronaca senese*, 735–736.

31. Caferro, *Mercenary Companies*, 25.

32. *Cronaca senese*, 735–736.

33. ASS, Reg 4, fol. 295r.

34. Caferro, *Mercenary Companies*, 156–171.

35. *Cronaca senese*, 747–748.

36. *Cronaca senese*, 748.

37. Jacopo de' Cavalli is remembered by a more elaborate monument in Venice, portraying him on horseback. Konrad Aichelberg lies beneath a simple stone slab in a Pisan church, depicting him with his sword and shield in full armor. The tomb is sometimes mistaken for that of Konrad von Landau. Schäfer, "Kirchen und Grabmäler," 279–283; Selzer, *Deutsche Söldner*, 173–175; Valentiner, "Equestrian Statue of Paolo Savelli."

38. H. W. Janson states that there were five equestrian monuments in Tuscany before 1400: Guidoriccio da Fogliano, Piero Farnese, Hawkwood, Gian "tedesco," and Giovanni degli Ubaldini. The Pietramala memorial was destroyed in 1506. Janson, *Sculpture of Donatello*, 157–158.

39. Parronchi, *Paolo Uccello*; Borsook, *Mural Painters*, 75–76.

40. Borsook, *Mural Painters*, 76.

41. Boskovits, *Pittura fiorentina*, 117–124, 295–304.

42. Cole, *Agnolo Gaddi*, 39, 43–44, 66, 70.

43. Poggi and Haines, *Il duomo di Firenze*, 1:93.

44. The last point has been persuasively argued by Eve Borsook, who specifically pointed out Uccello's ability to re-create the effect of marble in the subsequent painting of Hawkwood. Borsook, "Power of Illusion." I thank Professor Borsook for sharing her article with me prior to its publication.

45. Poggi and Haines, *Il duomo di Firenze*, 2:124–125.

46. Wegener, "That the Practice of Arms," 132.

47. Forni, *Manuale del pittore restauratore*, 23; Hennessy, *Paolo Uccello*, 141.

48. Borsook, *Mural Painters*, 75.

49. Temple-Leader and Marcotti, *Sir John Hawkwood*, 294; Borsook, *Mural Painters*, 75.

50. Poggi and Haines, *Il duomo di Firenze*, 1:lxxx, 94–95.

51. Wegener, "That the Practice of Arms," 142–158. Mallett has also stressed the propaganda value of the fresco. He saw it as a piece of Medici-inspired propaganda, intended to promote "the praiseworthiness of condottieri to a populace with mixed feelings." Mallett, *Mercenaries and Their Masters*, 129.

52. Vasari, *Le vite de' piu eccellenti pittori*, 211–212; Boccia, "Le armadure di Paolo Uccello," 86. See also Scalini, "Il monumento a Giovanni Acuto."

53. Melli, "Nuove indagine sui disegni di Paolo Uccello," 6. I thank the author for giving me a copy of her offprint.

54. The document is quoted in Temple-Leader and Marcotti, *Sir John Hawkwood*, 295.

55. Gioseffi cited problems of perspective (excessive foreshortening), as did Degenhart and Schmitt. Parronchi thought the problem one of colors. Gioseffi, "Complementi di prospettiva," 131; Degenhart and Schmitt, *Corpus der Italienischen Zeichnungen*, 382; Parronchi, *Paolo Uccello*, 31.

56. Cavalcanti, *Trattato Politico-Morale*, 124, 214.

57. Bracciolini, *Storia fiorentina*, 20, 22.

58. The entire document is reproduced in Medin, "La morte di Giovanni Aguto," 166–167.

59. Ibid., 168.

60. ASF, Capitoli, registri, 1, fol. 50r.

61. Ibid.; Medin, "La morte di Giovanni Aguto," 168.

62. The document is reproduced in the appendix of Temple-Leader and Marcotti, *Sir John Hawkwood*, 359–360 (document 69).

63. *Calendar of Close Rolls, Richard II, 1377–1381*, 367–368; *Calendar of Close Rolls, Richard II, 1381–1385*, 137–138; Morant, *History and Antiquities of Essex*, 379–380.

64. Davies, *Guide to the Church*, 2.

65. The document is reproduced in Manni, *Commentario*, 644.

66. Saul, *Richard II*, 461; Jones, *Royal Policy of Richard II*.

67. CLRO, HR, 124/6; *London Topographical Record*, 11–12.

68. Guildhall Library, MS 9171/1.

69. PRO, C 66/348 (9m, reverse side). See also *Calendar of the Patent Rolls, Richard II, 1396–1399*, 312.

70. There are numerous documents relating to William's life in the Public Record Office in London and the Essex Record Office in Chelmsford. PRO, DL 41/428; C 4/12/5, C 1/5/97; ERO, D/DL/T 1/248, D/DXa/5. See also *Calendar of the Patent Rolls, Richard II, 1381–1385*, 84–84, 139, 400, 437, 591; *Calendar of the Patent Rolls, Richard II, 1385–1389*, 176, 260; *Calendar*

*of the Patent Rolls, Richard II, 1388–1391,* 53, 321, 462, 517, 518; *Calendar of the Patent Rolls, Richard II, 1391–96,* 91, 234, 236; *Calendar of the Patent Rolls, Richard II, 1396–1399,* 212, 559; *Calendar of Inquisitions Post Mortem, 1–7 Richard II,* 118. Additional information is in Ward, *Essex Gentry* and "Sir John Coggeshale." See also Roskell, *Commons of the Parliament of 1422,* 169–170, and Roskell, Clark, and Rawcliffe, *History of Parliament.*

71. PRO, C 270/29, #17.

72. Santoro, *La politica finanziaria,* 2:5–6.

73. Archivio dell' Opera di Santa Maria del Fiore, Florence, Italy, II, 1, fol. 50. I thank Lorenzo Fabbri for opening the archive to allow me to see the document. See also Baldinucci, *Notizie de' professori del disegno,* 58, and Wegener, "That the Practice of Arms," 132.

74. The first to describe the tomb was John Weever in his book on English funeral monuments written in 1631. Weever, *Ancient Funeral Monuments,* 623.

75. A description of the monument is in a letter dated 23 February 1713/14. ERO, D/Y 1/1/70. See also Sperling, "Sir John Hawkwood," 72–74, and Gough, *Memoirs of Sir John Hawkwood,* 30.

76. Monumental brasses were popular in Essex. The figure was usually affixed to the wall with pitch. Soldiers were common subjects. Norris, *Monumental Brasses;* Stephenson, *List of Monumental Brasses;* Crossley, *English Church Monuments.*

77. *Westminster Chronicle,* 521.

78. Walsingham, *Historia Anglicana,* 215.

79. Rymer, *Foedera,* vol. 4, pt. 1, 104 (3 November 1406).

80. *Calendar of Close Rolls, Henry IV, 1405–1409,* 522.

81. Sperling, "Hawkwood Family," 174–175.

82. In 1409, John junior sold land to a John Barton. ERO, D/DCw/T 37/37.

83. The antiquarian Morant asserts that he eventually married and had a daughter Anne. Temple-Leader gives the name of John's wife as Margaret and claims that the two survived into old age, until 1464. Morant, *History and Antiquities of Essex,* 329, 379. Temple-Leader and Marcotti, *Sir John Hawkwood,* 310.

84. John Doreward senior served as Speaker of the House of Commons in 1399 and 1413. *Essex Sessions of Peace,* 18–20. A Doreward is mentioned alongside Coggeshale in the document of 1409 granting John Hawkwood junior rights to the properties of Scotneys and others in Toppesfield. We do not know whether this refers to Doreward senior or junior. Morant says that Doreward died in 1420 and was subsequently remembered by a chantry. Morant, *History and Antiquities of Essex,* 107.

85. Roskell, *Commons of the Parliament of 1422,* 170; Chancellor, *Ancient Sepulchral Monuments,* 162–164.

86. Rymer, *Foedera,* vol. 4, pt. 2, 18, 120; PRO, C 67 (8 January 1382).

87. The chantry was also dedicated to "the souls of John Oliver, esquire, and Thomas Newington, esquire," described by Temple-Leader and others as "military companions" of Hawkwood. The identities of these men remain a mystery. I have found no overt mention of them in Hawkwood's armies in Italy. There is, however, evidence of a John Oliver, who was the father-in-law of John Doreward, husband of Hawkwood's daughter Blanche from his first marriage. This John Oliver (if indeed it is the same) appears in the sources as a prominent Essex man: member of Parliament in 1368 and sheriff of both Essex and Herts from 1366 to 1368. There is also documentary reference to John Oliver owning manors in Gosfield and estates in

Stisted and Great Yeldham. ERO, D/DAy/m1, D/DAy/T1/15; Morant, *History and Antiquities of Essex*, 275, 279, 291, 307, 380.

88. On chantries of the period, see Kemp, "English Church Monuments during the Period of the Hundred Years War," 208–209, and *English Church Monuments*, 35–38. See also Starr, *Guide to Essex Churches*.

89. PRO, C 143/443/24a (Chancery: Inquisitions ad quod damnum, Henry III to Richard II). See also *Calendar of the Patent Rolls, Henry IV, 1408–1413*, 452–453.

90. *London Topographical Record*, 14.

91. PRO, C 143/443/11; Clark, "College of Halstead," 311–337.

92. ASF, Dieci di balia, Deliberazioni, condotte e stanziamenti, 1, fol. 153r, Dieci di balia, Deliberazioni, condotte e stanziamenti, 3, fol. 26v; Dieci di balia, Deliberazioni, condotte e stanziamenti, 4, fols. 45v, 131r; Dieci di balia, 5, fol. 185r, Camera del comune, uscita, 300, fol. 15r.

93. ERO, D/P/19/25/13.

94. An anonymous manuscript in the Essex Record Office describes the chantry at Castle Hedingham. ERO, D/DMh/F35 7.

95. Davies, *Guide to the Church*, 12.

## Conclusion

*Epigraph:* Charny, *Book of Chivalry*, 92.

1. An excellent discussion of the parameters of medieval chivalry is in Kaeuper, *Chivalry and Violence*, 8, 161, 176–185.

2. The view was shared by the most influential writer on chivalry in the Middle Ages, Ramon Lull. Lull, *Book of Knighthood and Chivalry*, 25.

3. Jones, *Chaucer's Knight*.

4. Keen, "Chaucer's Knight," 54.

5. Wedgwood, "John of Gaunt," 624; Walker, *Lancastrian Affinity*, 267, 273.

6. Hale, *War and Society in Renaissance Europe*, 8.

7. Trundle has stressed this point with regard to ancient mercenaries. Trundle, "Identity and Community," 28–38.

8. For Stisted, see ASF, Dieci di balia, Deliberazioni, condotte e stanziamenti, 1, fol. 153r, Dieci di balia, Deliberazioni, condotte e stanziamenti, 3, fol. 26v; Dieci di balia, Deliberazioni, condotte e stanziamenti, 4, fols. 45v, 131r; Dieci di balia, Deliberazioni, condotte e stanziamenti, 5, fol. 185r, Camera del comune, uscita, 300, fol. 15r.

John Northwood, whom Hawkwood sent to King Richard in 1381, is named with respect to rental property in Priory of Earl's Colne at Finchingfeld in 1380. ERO D/DPr/5.

John Oliver's name appears in documents relating to estates near Gosfield, Stisted, and Great Yeldham. ERO, D/DAy/m1, D/DAy/T1/15; Morant, *History and Antiquities of Essex*, 275, 279, 291, 307, 380.

For Giffard, see ERO, D/DBm /m164.

9. Klapisch-Zuber, "Parenti," 953–982.

10. Mockler, *New Mercenaries*, 9; Arnold, *Mercenaries*, ix.

11. For the general notion of patriotism in late Middle Ages, see Kantorowicz, "Pro Patria

Mori," 472–92; Post, "Two Notes on Nationalism," 81–320; and Housley, "Pro Deo et Patria Mori," 221–248. See also Tyerman, *England and the Crusades.*

12. Allmand, *Hundred Years War,* 53, 138–139.

13. ASMa, AG, 2338, #242.

14. ASF, Signori-Carteggi, Missive I Cancelleria, 18, fol. 8r.

15. Petrarch, *Sonnets and Songs,* 202–206.

16. ASF, Capitoli, registri, 12.

17. Hay and Law, *Italy in the Age of the Renaissance,* 64–71.

18. Nussbaum, *Ten Thousand.*

19. ASF, Dieci di balia, Deliberazioni, condotte e stanziamenti, 6, fol. 36v.

20. Meek, *Lucca, 1369–1400,* 48.

21. ASS, Regolatori 3, fol. 215r.

22. Hunt, *Medieval Super-companies,* 25.

23. Dyer, *Standards of Living,* 29.

24. Lane, "Economic Consequences of Organized Violence," 413.

25. The situation is such as to warrant D. C. Coleman's assessment, applied to European history in general, that the subject of war and economy is a "border country . . . remarkably neglected by economic historians." Coleman, *What Has Happened to Economic History?* 29.

26. ASPe, Consigli e riformanze, 29, fol. 189r–189v.

27. Professione, *Siena e le compagnie,* 92.

28. Caferro, *Mercenary Companies,* 174–177.

29. The subject is treated in detail in ibid., 42, 113–155.

30. Kohl, *Padua under the Carrara,* 288–289; Schäfer, *Vatikanische Quellen zur Geschichte,* 427, 434, 646, 647.

31. Caferro, *Mercenary Companies,* 107–109, 111, 114–115, 176–177.

32. Mueller, *Venetian Money Market,* 359–360.

33. Barducci, "Politica e speculazione finanziaria," 202.

34. Molho, *Florentine Public Finances,* 141–150.

35. Mueller, *Venetian Money Market,* 577.

36. Caferro, *Mercenary Companies,* 175.

37. McFarlane, "The Investment of Sir John Fastolf's Profits," 91–116, and "War, the Economy and Social Change," 3–13; Postan, "The Costs of the Hundred Years' War," 34–35.

38. *Calendar of Close Rolls, Richard II, 1389–1392,* 265.

39. *Calendar of Inquisitions Post Mortem, 1–6 Henry IV (1399–1405),* 21–22; *Calendar of the Patent Rolls, Edward III, 1370–1374,* 104; *Calendar of the Patent Rolls, Richard II, 1381–1385,* 75.

40. Thornbury's investments, from 1384 to 1395, are outlined in documents in the Public Record Office. PRO, C 143/403/38; E 210/5550; E 211/310/b; E 211/310/e, e, f, g. See also Roskell, Clarke, and Rawcliffe, *History of Parliament,* 4:589–593.

41. CLRO, HR, 122/53; *Calendar of Select Pleas,* 253–255.

42. Wycliff, *Sermones,* 341.

43. *Rotuli Parliamentorum,* 332.

44. Selzer, *Deutsche Söldner,* 174–175, 384–385.

45. Gessler, "Huglin von Shönegg," 75–126; Selzer, *Deutsche Söldner,* 176–177.

46. Von Stromer, *Oberdeutsche Hochfinanz,* 64–65.

47. Selzer, *Deutsche Söldner*, 110.

48. ASPe, Conservatore della Moneta, 13, fol. 9v.

49. Waley, "Army of the Florentine Republic," 99.

50. Mattingly, *Renaissance Diplomacy*, 58.

51. Selzer, *Deutsche Söldner*, 308–311.

52. Burckhardt, *Civilization of the Renaissance in Italy*, 17.

53. Greenblatt, *Renaissance Self-Fashioning*, 227–228. See also Biagioli, *Galileo, Courtier.*

54. Lerner, *Passing of Traditional Society*, 224–225.

55. Foucault, *Power/Knowledge*, 78–108.

*Archival Sources*

ENGLAND

*Chelmsford*

Essex Record Office

| | |
|---|---|
| D/DAy/m1 | D/DMh/Z4 |
| D/DAy/T1/9 | D/DPr/5 9 |
| D/DAy/T1/15 | D/DQ 61/194 |
| D/DBm/m 164 | D/DU 40/50 |
| D/DCw/T 33/2–3 | D/DXa/5 |
| D/DCw/T 37/13, 31, 37 | D/P 19/25/13 |
| D/DCw/T 46/3 | D/Y 1/1/66–72 |
| D/DL/T 1/248 | T/A 293/2 |
| D/DMh/F32 | T/A 316/334–333 |
| D/DMh/F35 | T/Z 20/19 |

*London*

British Library

| | |
|---|---|
| Additional Charter 6719 | Additional MS 6395 |
| Additional Charter 70744 | Additional MS 8540 |
| Additional MS 33, 526 | Harleian MS 1110 |
| Additional MS 41 | Harleian MS 6148 |
| Additional MS 5702 | Harley MS 6989 |

Corporation of London Record Office

Hustings Roll, 114/14, 20; 122/53; 124/6; 144/42, 152/68; 186/14

Guildhall Library

MS 9171/1

Public Record Office

C 1/5/97; C 47/2/34; C 47/2/39; C 47/2/46; C 47/13/6; C 47/14/4; C 47/28/6; C 49/12/5; C 66/348; C 81/1348/18; C 81/1352; C 81/1355; C 143/396/7; C 143/239/6; C 143/297/2; C 143/443/11; C 143/403/38; C 143/443/23–24a,b; C 270/29 DL 15/1999; DL 25/518; DL 25/731; DL 25/1724; DL 25/1731; DL 25/1734; DL 25/1736; DL 25/1737; DL 25/1897; DL 25/1999; DL 41/428

E 36/20; E 36/203–204; E 101/393/11; E 101/400/8; E 153/2783; E 326/2571; E 326/
2574; E 358/1; E 358/1 (rot. 4); E 358/2 (rot. 4d, 8, 24); E 358/5 (rot. 2d); E 364/12; E
364/13–14; E 364/21, 28; E 403/336; E 403/465; E 403/468; E 403/490; E 403/517–
519; E 403/521; E 403/548.
SC 8/143/7130B

ITALY
*Bologna*

Archivio Albornoziano
    Busta 361 (46)
Archivio di Stato di Bologna
    Archivio della famiglia Pepoli, serie I/A: Istrumenti e scritture, 3
    Carteggio, lettere al comune, 413
    Carteggio, lettere patenti, 412
    Comune, Capitano del popolo, Giudici del capitano, 805
    Comune, Curia del Podestà, giudici a dischi in materia civile, 20
    Comune, Curia del Podestà, giudici ad maleficia, sentenze, 20, 22
    Comune, Feudi, nobiltà e cittadinanza straniere, 428
    Comune, Soprastanti alle prigioni
    Comune, Ufficio delle bollette e presentazione dei forestieri, ufficio della condotta degli
    Feudi, nobiltà e cittadinanza straniere, 428
    Stipendiari, le bollette, 56
    Governo, Signorie, Provvisioni in Capreto, 299–302
    Notarile, Miscellanea, Busta 1, Matteus Jacobini Angellini, 1366–1383
    Notarile, Miscellanea, Busta 1, 2
    Tesoreria e controllatore di tesoreria, 14, 15, 16
Biblioteca Comunale dell'Archiginnasio
    B. 1145 (Lettere di Signori e del Comune di Firenze ed oltre missive responsive)

*Florence*

Archivio dell'Opera di Santa Maria del Fiore di Firenze
    II-1-50
Archivio di Stato di Firenze
    Balie, 13, 16, 18
    Camera del comune, Camarlinghi, uscita 176–178, 220, 226, 238–300, entrata, 93, 166
    Camera del comune, Provveditori, poi massai, specchi, poi campioni di entrata e uscita, 3–9
    Camera del comune, scrivano di camera uscita, 20–22, 77
    Capitoli, registri, 1, 12, 22, 32
    Carte Bardi, 3a serie, 59
    Consulte e Pratiche, 4, 10–28
    Dieci di balia, Deliberazioni, condotte e stanziamenti, 2–9
    Dieci di balia, Legazioni e commissarie, 1
    Mercanzia 1177, 1201, 7126
    Miscellanea repubblicana, buste 2, 120

Monte Comune, part II, 694

Notarile Antecosmiani, 12063, 11053, 10656

Prestanze, 957, 1252

Provvisioni, registri, 50–85

Signori-Carteggi, Missive I Cancelleria, 13–23

Signori, responsive originali, 6

Stipendiati del comune, 3

Biblioteca Medicea Laurenziana di Firenze

Ashburnham MS 1830

Biblioteca Riccardiana di Firenze

MS 786

*Lucca*

Archivio di Stato di Lucca

Anziani al Tempo della Libertà, 2–4, minute di riformagioni (1371–1400)

Anziani al Tempo della Libertà, 131–133, deliberazioni

Anziani al Tempo della Libertà, 439, lettere originali

Anziani al Tempo della Libertà, 529–530, carteggio

Anziani al Tempo della Libertà, 571–572, ambascerie e carte originali, Capitoli 25, 32

Consiglio Generale, 5–9, Riformagioni Pubbliche, 1369–1400

*Mantua*

Archivio di Stato di Mantova, Archivio Gonzaga

| | |
|---|---|
| Buste 48–51 | 1339 (Mirandola) |
| 740 (Monferrato) | 1367 (Parma and Piacenza) |
| 757 (Genova) | 1397 (Guastella) |
| 805 (Napoli/Sicilia) | 1418 (Venice) |
| 839 (Rome) | 1430 (Venice) |
| 1140 (Bologna) | 1591 (Padua) |
| 1066 (Urbino and Pesaro) | 1595 (Verona) |
| 1085 (Florence) | 1599 (Brescia) |
| 1099 (Florence) | 1602 (Milan) |
| 1180 (Ferrara and Modena) | 1606 (Milan) |
| 1224 (Ferrara) | 1619 (Milan) |
| 1225 (Ferrara) | 1791 (Cremona) |
| 1227 (Ferrara) | 2093 (Internal letters) |
| 1288 (Reggio and Modena) | 2184 (Minute) |
| 1306 (Carpi) | 2373 (Internal letters) |
| 1310 (Carpi) | 2374 (Cingulo) |
| 1313 (Correggio) | 2383 (Revere) |
| 1321 (Correggio) | 2388 (Internal letters, from Revere) |
| 1329 (Mirandola) | 2389 (Internal letters) |

*Milan*

Archivio della Fabbrica del Duomo di Milano
    Eredità e Legati, cartelle, 62, 74–77, 81, 86
    Libri registri, nos. 1, 1 bis
    Testamenti e donazioni, cartelle 53, 55
Archivio di Stato di Milano
    Fondo notai, n. 20
    Fondo notarile, nos. 2, 20
    Notai appendice, 35
    Notai esteri, 35
    Notai incerti, n. 1
    Registri Ducali, 1 (Paci e feudi del tempo di Bernabò Visconi), 57, 59
    Registri Panigarola, nos. 1, 2

*Modena*

Archivio di Stato di Modena, Archivio d'Este
    Archivi per materie: capitani di ventura, Busta 1
    Cancelleria Marchionale, leggi e decreti
    Carteggio principi esteri, busta 1286, 1291/5, 1292/6
    Casa e Stato, busta 486
    Casa e Stato, cassette 20, 11

*Padua*

Archivio di Stato di Padova
    Archivio Notarile, 31, 33

*Perugia*

Archivio di Stato di Perugia
    Conservatore della Moneta, 13–32
    Consigli e riformanze, 24–39
    Diplomatico, cassetta 36

*Pisa*

Archivio di Stato di Pisa
    Com A 62–63, 79, 136–139, 141, 207–208

*Siena*

Archivio di Stato di Siena
    Biccherna, 237
    Capitoli, 70, 71, 72, 78, 86, 89
    Concistoro, 77, 1774–1829, 2304 (lettere senza dati)
    Consiglio Generale, 171, 176
    Particolari, Famiglie forestiere, Buste 1–10

*Turin*

Archivio di Stato di Torino

    Archivio camerale, conti della tesoria generale di Savoia, camerale Piemonte, castellania,
        Lanzo, mazzo 5–6, #27, 28

    Corti stranieri (esteri), Inghilterra, mazzo 1

    Ducato di Monferrato, mazzo 4, docs. 15, 18

    Principi del sangue, mazzo 7, docs. 6, 16

    Trattati diversi, mazzo 1, docs. 26, 27, 30, 32; mazzo 2, docs. 1, 4

*Vatican City*

Archivio Segreto Vaticano

    Camera Apostolica, introitus et exitus, 268, 270, 336–359, 365–366

    Registri Vaticani, 228, 239–290, 310, 311

*Venice*

Archivio di Stato di Venezia

    Cancelleria Inferiore, notai, 6, 169, 193, 194, 227

    Collegio secreti e lettere secreti, registri, 1–2

    Commemoriali, 8

    Senato, secreti, reg. unico per 1376

*Verona*

Archivio di Stato di Verona

    Fondo Zalieri–dal Verme, cit cassetto, vi, n. 20

## Printed Sources

Ammirato, Scipione. *Istorie fiorentine.* Edited by F. Ranalli. Florence, 1848.

Angelucci, Angelo, ed. *Documenti inediti per la storia delle armi da fuoco italiane.* Vol 1. Turin, 1869.

*Annales Forolivienses ab origine urbis usque ad annum MCCCCXXII.* Edited by G. Mazzatini. Rerum Italicarum Scriptores, vol. 22. Città di Castello, 1903–1909.

*Annales Mediolanenses.* Edited by L. A. Muratori. Rerum Italicarum Scriptores, vol. 16. Milan, 1730.

*The Anonimalle Chronicle.* Edited by V. H. Galbraith. Manchester, England, 1970.

Azario, Pietro (Azarii, Petrii). *Liber Gestorum in Lombardia.* Edited by Francesco Cognasso. Rerum Italicarum Scriptores, vol. 16, pt. 4. Bologna, 1925–1939.

Azzi-Vitelleschi, G. degli. *Le relazioni tra la Repubblica di Firenze e l'Umbria nel sec XIV.* Vol. 1. Perugia, 1904.

Baker, Geoffrey le. *Chronicon.* Edited by E. M. Thompson. Oxford, 1889.

Bartolomeo di Ser Gorello. *Cronica dei fatti d'Arezzo.* Edited by Arturo Bini and Giovanni Grazzini. Rerum Italicarum Scriptores, vol. 15, pt. 4. Bologna, 1917.

Benton, G. Montagu, ed. "Essex Wills at Canterbury." In *Transactions of the Essex Archaeological Society*, vol. 21, pt. 2. Colchester, England, 1934.

Benvenuto de' Rambaldi di Imola. *Commentum super Dantis Aldigheri Comoediam*. Vol. 2. Edited by Giovanni Tamburini. Reprint, Florence, 1887.

*Biblioteca comunale dell'Archiginnasio, Bologna*. Edited by Pierangelo Belletini. Florence, 2001.

Bracciolini, Poggio. *Storia fiorentina*. Edited by Eugenio Garin. Arezzo, 1984.

Bruni, Leonardo. *Istoria fiorentina*. Translated by Donato Accaiaouli. Florence, 1861.

*Calendar of Close Rolls, Edward III, 1327–1330*. Vol. 1. London, 1896.

*Calendar of Close Rolls, Edward III, 1343–1346*. Vol. 7. London, 1901.

*Calendar of Close Rolls, Edward III, 1349–1354*. Vol. 9. London, 1906.

*Calendar of Close Rolls, Edward III, 1354–1360*. Vol. 10. London, 1908.

*Calendar of Close Rolls, Edward III, 1360–1364*. Vol. 11. London, 1909.

*Calendar of Close Rolls, Edward III, 1364–1369*. Vol. 12. London, 1910.

*Calendar of Close Rolls, Edward III, 1369–1374*. Vol. 13. London, 1911.

*Calendar of Close Rolls, Edward III, 1374–1377*. Vol. 14. London, 1913.

*Calendar of Close Rolls, Richard II, 1377–1381*. Vol. 1. London, 1914.

*Calendar of Close Rolls, Richard II, 1381–1385*. Vol. 2. London, 1920.

*Calendar of Close Rolls, Richard II, 1385–1389*. Vol. 3. London, 1921.

*Calendar of Close Rolls, Richard II, 1389–1392*. Vol. 4. London, 1922.

*Calendar of Close Rolls, Richard II, 1392–1396*. Vol. 5. London, 1925.

*Calendar of Close Rolls, Henry IV, 1405–1409*. Vol. 3. London, 1931.

*Calendar of Entries in the Papal Registers Relating to Great Britain and Ireland, 1362–1404: Papal Letters*. Vol 4. Edited by W. H. Bliss and J. A. Twemlow. London, 1902.

*Calendar of Fine Rolls, Edward II, 1307–1319*. Vol. 2. London, 1912.

*Calendar of Fine Rolls, Edward II, 1319–1327*. Vol. 3. London, 1912.

*Calendar of Fine Rolls, Edward III, 1337–1347*. Vol. 5. London, 1915.

*Calendar of Fine Rolls, Edward III, 1347–1357*. Vol. 6. London, 1921.

*Calendar of Fine Rolls, Edward III, 1356–1368*. Vol. 7. London, 1923.

*Calendar of Fine Rolls, Edward III, 1368–1377*. Vol. 8. London, 1924.

*Calendar of Fine Rolls, Richard II, 1377–1383*. Vol. 9. London, 1926.

*Calendar of Fine Rolls, Richard II, 1383–1391*. Vol. 10. London, 1929.

*Calendar of Fine Rolls, Richard II, 1391–1399*. Vol. 11. London, 1929.

*Calendar of Inquisitions, Miscellaneous (Chancery), 1377–1388*. Vol. 4. London, 1957.

*Calendar of Inquisitions, Miscellaneous (Chancery), 1387–1393*. Vol. 5. London, 1962.

*Calendar of Inquisitions Post Mortem, Edward III*. Vol. 10. London, 1921.

*Calendar of Inquisitions Post Mortem, 1370–1373*. Vol. 13. London, 1954.

*Calendar of Inquisitions Post Mortem, 1–7 Richard II*. Vol. 15. London, 1970.

*Calendar of Inquisitions Post Mortem, 15–23 Richard II*. Vol. 17. London, 1988.

*Calendar of Inquisitions Post Mortem, 1–6 Henry IV (1399–1405)*. Vol. 18. Edited by J. L. Kirby. London, 1987.

*Calendar of Inquisitions Post Mortem, 7–14 Henry IV (1405–1413)*. Vol. 19. Edited by J. L. Kirby. London, 1992.

*Calendar of Papal Registers, Petitions to the Pope, 1342–1419*. Vol. 1. Edited by W. H. Bliss. London, 1896.

*Calendar of Select Pleas and Memoranda of the City of London.* Edited by A. H. Thomas. Cambridge, 1932.

*Calendar of State Papers and Manuscripts, Existing in Archives and Collections of Venice.* Vols. 4, 5. Edited by Rawdon Brown. Reprint, Nendeln, Liechtenstein, 1970.

*Calendar of State Papers and MSS., Milan.* Vol. 1. Edited by Allen B. Hinds. London, 1912.

*Calendar of the Patent Rolls, Edward III, 1348–1350.* Vol. 8. London, 1908.

*Calendar of the Patent Rolls, Edward III, 1361–1364.* Vol. 12. London, 1912.

*Calendar of the Patent Rolls, Edward III, 1364–1367.* Vol. 13. London, 1912.

*Calendar of the Patent Rolls, Edward III, 1367–1370.* Vol. 14. London, 1913.

*Calendar of the Patent Rolls, Edward III, 1370–1374.* Vol.15. London, 1914.

*Calendar of the Patent Rolls, Edward III, 1374–1377.* Vol. 16. London, 1916.

*Calendar of the Patent Rolls, Richard II, 1377–1381.* Vol. 1. London, 1895.

*Calendar of the Patent Rolls, Richard II, 1381–1385.* Vol. 2. London, 1897.

*Calendar of the Patent Rolls, Richard II, 1385–1389.* Vol. 3. London 1900.

*Calendar of the Patent Rolls, Richard II, 1388–1391.* Vol. 4. London, 1902.

*Calendar of the Patent Rolls, Richard II, 1391–1396.* Vol. 5. London, 1905.

*Calendar of the Patent Rolls, Richard II, 1396–1399.* Vol. 6. London, 1909.

*Calendar of the Patent Rolls, Henry IV, 1408–1413.* Vol. 4. London, 1909.

Catherine of Siena. *The Letters of St. Catherine of Siena.* Translated and edited by Suzanne Noffke. Binghamton, N.Y., 1988.

Cavalcanti, Giovanni. *The Politico-Morale of Giovanni Cavalcanti (1381–1451).* Edited by Marcella T. Grendler. Geneva, 1973.

Caxton, William. *The Book of the Ordyre of Chivalry.* Edited by A. T. P. Byles. London, 1926.

Charny, Geoffroi. *The Book of Chivalry of Geoffroi de Charny.* Edited by Richard W. Kaeuper and Elspeth Kennedy. Philadelphia, 1996.

*Chaucer's Life Records.* Edited by Martin M. Crow and Clair C. Olson. Oxford, 1966.

Child, Francis James, ed. *The English and Scottish Popular Ballads.* Vols. 1, 2. Boston, 1884, 1885.

Chinazzo, Daniele di. *Cronica de la guerra da Veniciani a Zenovesi.* Edited by Vittorio Lazzarini. Venice, 1958.

*Chronica di Pisa.* Edited by L. A. Muratori. Rerum Italicarum Scriptores, vol. 15. Milan, 1729.

*Chronicon Angliae.* Edited by Edward Maunde Thompson. London, 1874.

*Chronicon Bergomense guelpho-ghibellinum.* Edited by Carlo Capasso. Rerum Italicarum Scriptores, vol. 16, pt. 2. Bologna, 1926.

*Chronicon Estense.* Edited by Giulio Bertoni and Emilio Paolo Vicini. Rerum Italicarum Scriptores, vol. 15, pt. 3. Bologna, 1933.

*Chronicon Regiense.* Edited by Ludovico A. Muratori. Rerum Italicarum Scriptores, vol 18. Milan, 1977.

*Chronicon Siculum incerti authoris ad anno 340 ad annum 1396.* Edited by Joseph de Blasiis. Società Napoletana di Storia Patria, Monumenti Storici. Naples, 1887.

*Chronicon Tarvisum.* Edited by L. A. Muratori. Rerum Italicarum Scriptores, vol. 19. Milan, 1729.

*Chronique de Jean le Bel.* Vol. 2. Edited by Jules Viad and Eugene Deprez. Paris, 1905.

*Chronique Normande du XIVe siècle.* Edited by A. Molinier and E. Molinier. Paris, 1882.

*Codex Diplomaticus, Dominii Temporalis S. Sedi.* Vol 2. Edited by Augustin Theiner. Rome, 1862.

*Codex Italiae diplomaticus.* 4 vols. Edited by J. C. Lünig. Frankfurt, 1725–1735.

Conforto da Costoza. *Frammenti di storia vicentina.* Edited by C. Steiner. Rerum Italicarum Scriptores, vol. 13. Città di Castello, 1915.

Coopland, G. W., ed. and trans. *The Tree of Battles.* Liverpool, 1949.

Corio, Bernardino. *Storia di Milano.* Vols. 1, 2. Edited by Anna Morisi Guerra. Turin, 1978.

*Corpus chronicorum Bononiensium.* Edited by Albano Sorbelli. Rerum Italicarum Scriptores, vol. 18, pt. 1. Città di Castello, 1935.

*Cronaca di ser Guerriero da Gubbio.* Edited by Giuseppe Mazzatinti. Rerum Italicarum Scriptores, vol. 21, pt. 4. Città di Castello, 1902.

"Cronaca del Laurenzi." In *Storia di Città di Castello,* ed G. Magherini. Città di Castello, 1912.

*Cronaca d'Orvieto.* Edited by L. A. Muratori. Rerum Italicarum Scriptores, vol. 15. Milan, 1729.

*Cronache malatestiane.* Edited by Aldo Francesco Masséra. Rerum Italicarum Scriptores, vol. 15, pt. 2. Bologna, 1922–1924.

*Cronache senesi.* Edited by Alessandro Lisini and Fabio Iacometti. Rerum Italicarum Scriptores, n.s., vol. 15, pt. 4. Bologna, 1931–1937.

*Cronica Volgare di Anonimo Fiorentino* (Piero di Giovanni Minerbetti). Edited by Elina Bellondi. Rerum Italicarum Scriptores, vol. 17, pt. 2. Bologna, 1937.

Dati, Gregorio. *L'istoria di Firenze di Gregorio Dati.* Edited by Luigi Pratesi. Norcia, 1902.

Del Graziani. "Cronaca della Città di Perugia (Diario Del Graziani)." Edited by F. Bonaini and F. Polidori. *Archivio Storico Italiano* 16 (1850): 71–750.

"Diario d'anonimo fiorentino dall'anno 1358 al 1389." Edited by A. Gherardi. In *Cronache dei secoli XIII e XIV.* Florence, 1876.

Doyle, Arthur Conan. *The White Company.* New York, 1988.

*Ephemerides Urbevetanae.* Edited by Luigi Fumi. Rerum Italicarum Scriptores, vol. 15, pt. 5. Città di Castello, 1903.

*Essex Sessions of the Peace, 1351, 1377–1379.* Edited by Mary Chapin Furber. Colchester, England, 1953.

*Feet of Fines for Essex, 1272–1422.* Vols. 2, 3. Colchester, England, 1928–1949.

Fenwick, Carolyn C., ed. *The Poll Taxes of 1377, 1379, 1381, Bedfordshire-Leicestershire.* Oxford, 1998.

Ferorelli, Nicola, ed. *I registri dell'ufficio degli statuti di Milano.* Milan, 1971.

"Frammenti della Cronaca di Messer Luca di Totto Panzano." Edited by Vincenzio Borghini. Giornale Storico degli Archivi Toscani, vol. 5. Florence, 1861.

Franceschini, Gino, ed. *Documenti e registri per servire alla storia dello stato di Urbino e di conti di Montefeltro, 1202–1376, 1376–1406.* Vols. 1, 2. Urbino, 1982.

Froissart, Jean. *Chronicles of England, France and Spain.* Vol. 1. Edited by J. Johnes. London, 1868.

———. *Chroniques.* 26 vols. Edited by Kervyn de Lettenhove. Brussels, 1867–1877.

Frontinus. *The Stratagems and the Aqueducts of Rome.* Translated by Charles Bennett. London, 1925.

Fuller, Thomas. *The Worthies of England.* Edited by John Freeman. London, 1952.

Fumi, L., ed. *Regesti del R. Archivi di Stato: Carteggio degli Anziani, 1368–1400.* Vol. 2, pt. 2. Lucca, 1903.

Gatari, Galeazzo, with Bartolomeo and Andrea. *Cronaca Carrarese.* Edited by Antonio Medin and Guido Tolomei. Rerum Italicarum Scriptores, vol. 17, pt. 1. Città di Castello, 1909.

Gherardi, A., ed. "La guerra dei fiorentini con papa Gregorio XI detta la Guerra degli Otto Sancti." *Archivio Storico Italiano,* 3d ser., 5 (1867): 34–131; 6, pt. 1:209–221; 6, pt. 2:229–251; 7 (1868), pt. 1:210–232; 8, pt. 1:235–296.

Ghirardacci, Cherubino. *Historia di Bologna.* Vol 2. Bologna, 1657.

Giovanni da Legnano. *Tractatus de bello, de represaliis et de duello.* Edited by Thomas Erskine Holland. Oxford, 1917.

Giovio, Paolo. *Elogia veris clarorum virorum bellica virtute illustrium.* Edited by Renzo Meregazzi. Rome, 1972.

Glasscock, Robin E., ed. *The Lay Subsidy of 1334.* London, 1975.

Gower, John. *The French Works.* Vol. 1 of *The Complete Works of John Gower.* Edited by G. C. Macaulay. Oxford, 1899.

Gregory XI. *Lettres secrètes et curiales interéssant les pays autres que la France.* Edited by G. Mollat. Paris, 1962–1965.

Gregory XI. *Lettres secrètes et curiales relatives à la France (1370–1378).* Edited by G. Mirot et al. Paris, 1935–1957.

Guasti, Cesare, ed. *Lettere di un notaio a un mercante del secolo XIV.* Vol. 1. Florence, 1880.

Guicciardini, Francesco. *Opere inedite.* Vol 3. Florence, 1857–1867.

Higden, Ranulph. *Polychronicon Ranulphi Higden.* Vol. 8. Edited by Joseph Rawson Lumby. London, 1882.

*I Capitoli del Comune di Firenze.* Vol 1. Florence, 1865.

*Il carteggio Acciaioli della biblioteca medicea laurenziana di Firenze.* Edited by Ida Giovanna Rao. Rome, 1996.

Jensovsky, Frederic, ed. *Monumenta Vaticana. Res Gestas Bohemicas Illustrantia.* Vol. 3. Prague, 1944.

John of Gaunt. *John of Gaunt's Register, 1379–1383.* Edited by Robert Somerville. London, 1937.

*Knighton's Chronicle, 1337–1396.* Edited by G. H. Martin. Oxford, 1995.

Knowles, C., ed. and trans. *Les enseignements de Théodore Paléologue.* London, 1983.

*L'archivio Gonzaga di Mantova.* Edited by Alessandro Luzio and Pietro Torelli. Ostiglia, 1920–1922.

Lattes, E., ed. *Repertorio Diplomatico Visconteo.* Vol. 2. Milan, 1918.

*Les chroniques de la ville de Metz.* Edited by J. F. Huguenin. Metz, France, 1838.

"Lettere alla signoria relative alla venuta in Toscana di Giovanni Acuto." In *Miscellanea Fiorentina di erudizione e storia,* vol. 1, ed. Iodoco del Badia. Reprint, Rome, 1978.

*Life of Cola di Rienzo.* Edited and translated by John Wright. Toronto, 1975.

*London Topographical Record.* Vol. 13. Issued by the Office of the London Topographical Society. London, 1923.

Lunt, William E., ed. *Accounts Rendered by the Papal Collectors in England, 1317–1378.* Philadelphia, 1968.

Machiavelli, Niccolò. *The Discourses.* Edited by Bernard Crick and translated by Leslie J. Walker. New York, 1989.

———. *Florentine Histories.* Translated by Laura Banfield and Harvey C. Mansfield. Princeton, N.J., 1988.

———. *The Prince.* Edited and translated by David Wootton. Indianapolis, 1995.

*Magnum bullarium Romanum, vol III or Bullarum Privilegiorum ac Diplomatum Romanorum Pontificium, Tomus III.* Reprint, Graz, Austria, 1964.

Manni, D. M. *Commentario della vita del famoso capitano Giovanni Aguto Inglese, General condottiere d'armi fiorentini.* Edited by L. A. Muratori. Rerum Italicarum Scriptores, supplementum II. Florence, 1777.

*Marcha di Marco Battagli da Rimini.* Edited by Aldo Francesco Messèra. Rerum Italicarum Scriptores, vol. 16, pt. 3. Città di Castello, 1913.

Monaldi, Guido. *Istorie pistolesi (Diario del Monaldi).* Florence, 1733.

Monteleone, Duca di. *I Diurnali del Duca di Monteleone.* Edited by Michele Manfredi. Rerum Italicarum Scriptores, n.s., vol. 21, pt. 5. Bologna, 1958.

Morelli, Giovanni di Pagolo. *Ricordi.* Florence, 1969.

Mugnier, François. "Lettres des Visconti de Milan et de divers autres personnages aux comtes de Savoie, Amadée VI, VII, VIII (1360–1415)." *Mémoires et Documents Publiés par la Société Savoisienne d'Histoire et Archéologie* 35 (1896).

Muntaner, Ramon. *The Chronicle of Muntaner.* Translated by Lady Goodenough. London, 1920.

Murimuth, Adam. *Adae Murimuth Continuatio Chronicarum.* Edited by E. M. Thompson. London, 1889.

Mussis, Johannis de. *Chronicon Placentinum.* Edited by L. A. Muratori. Rerum Italicarum Scriptores, vol. 16. Reprint, Milan, 1977.

Naddo da Montecatini. *Memorie storiche dal anno 1374 al anno 1398.* Edited by Ildefonso di San Luigi. Delizie degli Eruditi Toscani, vol. 18. Florence, 1784.

Nicolas, Nicholas Harris, ed. *Testamenta Vetusta.* London, 1826.

Osio, Luigi. *Documenti diplomatici tratti degli archivi Milanesi.* Vol. 1. Milan, 1864.

Petrarch, Francesco. *Letters on Familiar Matters (Rerum Familiarium Libri XVII–XXIV).* Translated by Aldo S. Bernardo. Baltimore, 1985.

———. *Sonnets and Songs.* Translated by Anna Maria Armi. New York, 1946.

Pucci, Antonio. *Delle poesie di Antonio Pucci.* Edited by Ildefonso di San Luigi. Delizie degli Eruditi Toscani, vol. 6. Florence, 1775.

*Register of Edward, the Black Prince, Preserved in the Public Record Office.* 4 vols. Edited by Alfred Stamp, M. C. B. Dawes, and Michael Charles Burdett. London, 1933.

*Regest Imperii; Die Regeste des Kaiserreichs unter Kaiser Karl IV, 1346–1378.* Vol. 8. Edited by J. H. Böhmer. Reprint, Hildesheim, Germany, 1968.

*Ricordo della compra di Arezzo fatta dai Fiorentini, tratto del libro segreto di Guccio Benvenuti, del popolo di Santa Maria sopra Porta di Firenze (Nov 1383).* Edited by Giovanni Grazzini. Rerum Italicarum Scriptores, vol. 24, pt. 1. Città di Castello, 1909.

Rinuccini, Filippo di Cino. *Ricordi storici di Filippo di Cino Rinuccini dal 1282 al 1460 colla continuazione di Alemanno e neri suoi figli fino al 1506.* Edited by G. Aiazzi. Florence, 1840.

Roncioni, Raffaello. *Istorie pisane.* Vol. 1, pt. 2. Edited by Francesco Bonaini. Florence, 1844.

*Rotuli Parliamentorum ut et petitiones et placita in Parliamento: Tempore Edward I [-Hen. VII].* Vol 2. London, 1783.

Ruskin, John. *The Works of John Ruskin.* Vol. 27. Edited by E. T. Cook and Alexander Wedderburn. London, 1907.

Rymer, Thomas, ed. *Foedera, Conventiones, Litterae et cuiuscunque generis Acta Publica inter Reges Angliae et alios quovis Imperatores, Reges, Pontifices, Principes, vel Communitates.* 4 vols. in 7 pts. London, 1816–1819. Original ed., 20 vols., London, 1704–1735.

Sacchetti, Franco. *Il trecentonovelle.* Edited by Vincenzo Pernicone. Florence, 1946.

Salutati, Coluccio. *Epistolario.* Edited by Francesco Novati. Fonti per la Storia d'Italia, vols.15–18. Rome, 1891–1911.

Sardo, Ranieri. *Cronaca di Pisa.* Edited by O. Banti. Fonti per la Storia d'Italia. Rome, 1963.

Schäfer, K. H. *Die Ausgaben der apostolichen Kammer unter den Päpsten Urban V und Gregor XI (1362–1378).* Paderborn, Germany, 1937.

Scott, Walter. *Quentin Durward.* New York, 1967.

Sercambi, Giovanni. *Le croniche Lucchesi.* Edited by Salvatore Bonsi. Fonti per la Storia d'Italia, vol. 1. Rome, 1963.

Servion, Jehan. *Gestez et Croniques de la Mayson de Savoye.* Edited by F.-E. Bollati di Saint Pierre. Vol. 2. Turin, 1879.

Sozomen of Pistoia. *Specimen Historiae Sozomeni Pistoiensi.* Edited by L. A. Muratori. Rerum Italicarum Scriptores, vol. 15. Milan, 1729.

Stefani, Marchionne di Coppo. *Cronaca fiorentina di Marchionne di Coppo Stefani.* Edited by Niccolò Ridolico. Rerum Italicarum Scriptores, n.s., vol. 30, pt. 1. Città di Castello, 1903.

Stella, Giorgio. *Annales Genuenses.* Edited by Giovanna Petti Balbi. Rerum Italicarum Scriptores, n.s., vol. 17. Bologna, 1975.

Stow, John. *The Annales or General Chronicle of England.* London, 1631.

Thalamus parvus. *Le petit Thalamus de Montpellier.* Pt. 4. Montpellier, France, 1840.

*Thesaurus Novus Anecdotorum.* Vol. 2. Edited by Edmund Martene and Ursinus Durant. New York, 1717.

Thompson, David, ed. *Petrarch: A Humanist among Princes.* New York, 1971.

Urban V. *Lettres communes analysées d'après les registres dits d'Avignon et du Vatican.* Edited by M. Hayez and A.-M. Hayez, 3d ser. Rome, 1974.

———. *Lettres secrètes et curiales se rapportant à la France du Pope Urbain V (1362–1370).* Edited by P. Lecacheaux and G. Mollat. Paris, 1902.

Vasari, Giorgio. *Le vite de' piu eccellenti pittori, scultori ed architettori.* Edited by Gaetano Milanesi. London, 1906.

Vegetius. *Epitome of Military Science.* Translated by N. P. Milner. Liverpool, 1996.

Velluti, Donato. *La Cronica Domestica di Messer Donato Velluti.* Edited by Isidoro del Lungo and Guglielmo Volpi. Florence, 1914.

Venette, Jean de. *The Chronicle of Jean de Venette.* Edited by R. A. Newhall and translated by by J. Birdsall. New York, 1953.

Vergerio, Pier Paolo. *Epistolario.* Edited by Leonard Smith. Fonti per la Storia d'Italia. Vol. 1. Rome, 1935.

Villani, Giovanni. *Cronica di Giovanni Villani.* Vol. 5. Florence, 1823.

Villani, Matteo, and Filippo Villani. *Cronica di Matteo e Filippo Villani con le vite d'uomini illustri fiorentini di Filippo e la cronica di Dino Compagni.* Vols. 3–5. Florence, 1826.

Walsingham, Thomas. *Historia Anglicana.* Vol. 1. Edited by Henry Thomas Riley. London, 1863.

Ward, Jennifer C., ed. *The Medieval Essex Community: The Lay Subsidy of 1327.* Chelmsford, England, 1983.

Weever, John. *Ancient Funeral Monuments.* Reprint, Amsterdam, 1979.

*Westminster Chronicle, 1381–1394.* Edited and translated by L. C. Hector and Barbara F. Harvey. Oxford, 1982.

Wrottesley, George. *Crécy and Calais from Public Records.* London, 1898.

Wycliff, John. *Select English Works.* Vol. 1. Edited by Thomas Arnold. Oxford, 1869.

———. *Sermones.* Vol. 2. Edited by Johann Loserth. London, 1887.

Xenophon. *The Persian Expedition.* Translated by Rex Warner. New York, 1979.

## Secondary Sources

Allmand, Christopher. *The Hundred Years War.* Cambridge, 1989.

———, ed. *Society at War.* New York, 1973.

———, ed. *War, Literature and Politics in the Late Middle Ages.* Liverpool, 1976.

Ancona, Clemente. "Milizie e condottieri." In *Storia d'Italia,* vol. 5, ed. Giulio Einaudi, 646–665. Turin, 1973.

Anderson, Verily. *The De Veres of Castle Hedingham.* Suffolk, England, 1993.

Ansidei, Vincenzo. "La tregua del 21 Marzo 1380." *Bolletino della Deputazione di Storia Patria per l'Umbria* 22 (1916).

Ansidei, Vincenzo, and Francesco Briganti. "Barolomeus de Gabrillibus de Regno Francie e Ugo de Belciampo de Ingilterra, conestabili al servizio del comune di Perugia nel 1321." *Bolletino della Deputazione di Storia Patria per l'Umbria* 21 (1915): 221–250.

Argiolas, Tommaso. *Armi ed eserciti del Rinascimento italiano.* Rome, 1991.

Arnold, Guy. *Mercenaries: The Scourge of the Third World.* London, 1999.

Ayton, Andrew. "Arms, Armour and Horses." In *Medieval Warfare: A History,* ed. Maurice Keen. Oxford, 1999

———. "English Armies in the Fourteenth Century." In *Arms, Armies, and Fortifications in the Hundred Years War,* ed. Anne Curry and Michael Hughes. Woodbridge, England, 1994.

———. "The English Army and the Normandy Campaign of 1346." In *England and Normandy in the Middle Ages,* ed. David Bates and Anne Curry. London, 1994.

———. *Knights and Warhorses: Military Service and the English Aristocracy under Edward III.* Woodbridge, England, 1994.

———. "Sir Thomas Ughtred and the Edwardian Military Revolution." In *The Age of Edward III,* ed. J. Bothwell. Woodbridge, England, 2001.

Bacci, Don Antonio. *Strade romane e medioevali nel territorio aretino.* Cortona, 1986.

Balduinucci, Filippo. *Notizie de' professori del disegno da Cimabue in qua secolo III e IV dal 1400–1540.* Florence, 1728.

Balduzzi, Luigi. "Bagnacavallo e Giovanni Acuto." *Atti e Memorie della R Deputazione di Storia Patria per le Provincie di Romagna,* 3d ser., 2 (1885): 72–74.

Balestracci, D. *Le armi, i cavalli e l'oro: Giovanni Acuto e i condottieri nell'Italia del Trecento.* Bari, 2003.

Banti, O. "Jacopo d'Appiano e le Origini della sua signoria." *Bolletino Storico Pisano,* 3d ser., 20–21 (1951–1952).

Barber, Richard. *Edward, Price of Wales and Aquitaine.* London, 1978.

Barducci, Roberto. "Politica e speculazione finanziaria a Firenze dopo la crisi del primo trecento, 1343–1358." *Archivio Storico Italiano* 137 (1979): 177–219.

Barlozzetti, Ugo, and Marco Giuliani. "La prassi guerresca in Toscana." In *Guerre e assoldati inToscana, 1260–1364.* Katalog Museo Stibbert. Florence, 1982.

Barni, G. "La formazione interna dello stato Visconteo." *Archivio Storico Lombardo* 6 (1941): 132–157.

Barnie, John. *War in Medieval Society.* London, 1974.

Baron, Hans. *The Crisis of the Early Italian Renaissance.* Princeton, N.J., 1966.

Bayley, C. C. *War and Society in Renaissance Florence.* Toronto, 1961.

Beck, William. *Hawkwood the Brave: A Tale of Medieval Italy.* London, 1911.

Becker, Marvin. *Florence in Transition.* 2 vols. Baltimore, 1968.

Bedell, John. "Memory and Proof of Age in England, 1272–1327." *Past and Present* 162 (1999): 3–27.

Bellucci, Alessandro. "Riccardo da Pavia e altri conestabili agli stipendi di Rieti nel 1396–1398: Documenti illustrati e capitolati in volgare." *Bolletino della Deputazione di Storia Patria per l'Umbria* 7 (1901): 585–602.

Biagioli, Mario. *Galileo, Courtier: The Practice of Science in the Culture of Absolutism.* Chicago, 1993.

Bianchi, Silvana Anna. "Gli eserciti delle signorie venete del Trecento fra continuità e trasformazione." In *Il Veneto nel medioevo: Le signorie trecenesche*, ed. Andrea Castagnetti and Gian Maria Varanini. Verona, 1995.

Bigazzi, Pietro. *Firenze e Milano: Saggio di lettere diplomatiche del secolo XIV e XV.* Florence, 1869.

Bignami, Luigi. *Sotto l'insegna del Biscione: Condottieri Viscontei e Sforzeschi.* Milan, 1934.

Bigwood, Georges. "Le régime juridique et économique du commerce de l'argent dans la Belgique du moyen âge." *Académie Royale de Belgique, Mémoires, Classe des Lettres.* 2d ser., 14. Brussels, 1921–1922.

Billot, Claudine. "Les mercenaires étrangers pendant la guerre de Cent Ans comme migrants." In *Le combattant au moyen âge*, ed. Société des Historiens Médiévistes de l'Enseignement Supérieur Public. Paris, 1991.

Biscaro, Girolamo. "Le relazioni dei Visconti con la chiesa." *Archivio Storico Lombardo*, 2d ser., 15 (1937): 119–193.

———. "Le relazioni dei Visconti di Milano con la chiesa." *Archivio Storico Lombardo* 46 (1919): 84–229.

Blastenbrei, Peter. *Die Sforza und ihr Heer: Studien zur Struktur-, Wirtschafts- und Sozialgeschichte des Söldnerwesens in der italienischen Frührenaissance.* Heidelberg, Germany, 1987.

Block, Willibald. *Die Condottieri: Studien über die sogenannten "unblutigen Schlachten."* Berlin, 1913.

Boccia, Lionello G. *Armi e armature Lombarde.* Milan, 1980.

———. "'Hic iacet miles': Immagini guerriere da sepolcri toscani del Due e Trecento." In *Guerre e assoldati in Toscana, 1260–1364.* Katalog Museo Stibbert. Florence, 1982.

———. "Le armadure di Paolo Uccello." *L'arte* 11–12 (1970).

Bonoli, Girolamo. *Della storia di Cottignola.* Reprint, Bologna, 1976.

Borlandi, A. "Moneta e congiuntura a Bologna (1360–1364)." *Bulletino Istituto Storia per il Medio Evo* 82 (1970).

Borosy, András. "The Militia Portalis in Hungary before 1526." In *From Hunyadi to Rákóczi*, ed. Janos Bak and Béla Király. New York, 1982.

Borsook, Eve. "L' Hawkwood d'Uccello et le vie de Fabius Maximus de Plutarque." *Revue Art* 55 (1982).

———. *The Mural Painters of Tuscany.* 2d ed. Oxford, 1980.

———. "The Power of Illusion: Fictive Tombs in Santa Maria del Fiore." In *Santa Maria del Fiore: The Cathedral and Its Sculpture*, ed. Margaret Haines. Florence, 2001.

Boskovits, M. *Pittura fiorentina alla vigilia del Rinascimento.* Florence, 1975.

Boüard, Michel de. *Les origines des guerres l'italie: La France et l'Italie au temps du grand scisme d'occident.* Paris, 1936.

Boutruche, R. "La dévastation des campagnes pendant la Guerre de Cent Ans et la reconstruction agricole de la France." In *Publications de la Faculté des Lettres de l'Université de Strasbourg,* vol 3. Paris, 1947.

Bradbury, Jim. *The Medieval Archer.* New York, 1985.

Bradler, Günther. *Die Landschaften Allgäu und Oberschwaben in geographischer und historicher Sicht.* Göppingen, Germany, 1973.

Braudel, Fernand. *The Mediterranean and the Mediterranean World in the Age of Philip II.* Vol. 2. Translated by Sian Reynolds. New York, 1966.

Bresc, Henri. "Albornoz et le royaume de Naples de 1363 a 1365." In *El Cardenal Albornoz y el Colegio de España,* vol. 1, ed. Evelio Verdera y Tuells. Bologna, 1972.

——. *La correspondence de Pierre Ameihl, archevêque de Naples, puis d'Embrun, 1363–1369.* Paris, 1972.

Bridge, Joseph C. "Two Cheshire Soldiers of Fortune of the XIV Century: Sir Hugh Calveley and Sir Robert Knolles." *Journal of Architectural, Archaeological and Historic Society,* n.s., 14 (1908).

Britnell, R. H. *Growth and Decline in Colchester, 1300–1525.* Cambridge, 1986.

Brucker, Gene A. *The Civic World of Early Renaissance Florence.* Princeton, N.J., 1977.

——. *Florentine Politics and Society, 1343–1378.* Princeton, N.J., 1962.

——. *Renaissance Florence.* New York, 1969.

Brun, Robert. "Notes sur le commerce des armes a Avignon au XIV siècle." *Bibliothèque de l'École des Chartres* 109 (1951): 209–231.

Brunetti, Mario. "Nuovi documenti Viscontei tratti dall'Archivio di Stato di Venezia: Figli e nipoti di Bernabò Visconti." *Archivio Storico Lombardo,* 2d ser., 36 (1909): 5–90.

Brunner, Cristoph H. *Zur Geschichte der Grafen von Hapsburg-Laufenburg. Aspekte einer süddeutschen Dynastie im späten Mittelalter.* Samedan, Switzerland, 1969.

Bueno de Mesquita, D. M. *Giangaleazzo Visconti, Duke of Milan (1351–1402).* Cambridge, Mass., 1941.

——. "The Place of Despotism in Italian Politics." In *Europe in the Late Middle Ages,* ed. John Hale, Roger Highfield, and Beryl Smalley. London, 1965.

——. "Some Condottieri of the Trecento." *Proceedings of the British Academy* 32 (1946): 301–331.

Buongiorno, Mario. *Il bilancio di uno stato medievale: Genova, 1340–1529.* Genoa, 1973.

——. "Organizzazione e difesa dei castelli della Repubblica di Genova nella seconda metà del XIV secolo." *Studi Genuensi* 9 (1972): 35–72.

Burckhardt, Jacob. *The Civilization of the Renaissance in Italy.* Translated by S. G. C. Middlemore. Reprint, New York, 1954.

Burns, R. I. "The Catalan Company and the European Powers." *Speculum* 29 (1954): 751–771.

Caferro, William. " 'The Fox and the Lion': The Hundred Years War in Italy." In *The Hundred Years War: A Wider Focus,* ed. L. J. Andrew Villalon and Donald J. Kagay. Leiden, 2005.

——. "Giovanni Acuto." In *Dizionario Biografico degli Italiani.* Vol. 61. Rome, 2003.

——. "Italy and the Companies of Adventure in Fourteenth Century Italy." *Historian* 32 (Summer 1996): 795–810.

————. "Mercenaries and Military Expenditure: The Costs of Undeclared Warfare in Fourteenth Century Siena." *Journal of European Economic History* 23 (1994): 219–247.

————. *Mercenary Companies and the Decline of Siena.* Baltimore, 1998.

————. "Slaying the Hydra-Headed Beast: Italy and the Companies of Adventure in the Fourteenth Century." In *Crusaders, Condotierri, and Cannon: Medieval Warfare in Societies around the Mediterranean,* ed. L. J. Andrew Villalon and Donald J Kagay. Leiden, the Netherlands, 2002.

Canestrini, Giuseppe. "Documenti per servire della milizia italiana del secolo XIII al XVI." *Archivio Storico Italiano,* 1st ser., 15 (1851).

Capasso, C. "I provissionati di Bernabo Visconti." *Archivio Storico Lombardo,* 4th ser., 15 (1911): 285–304.

Cardini, Franco. *Guerre di primavera.* Florence, 1991.

————. *L'acciar de' cavalieri.* Florence, 1997.

————. *Quell'antica festa crudele: Guerra e cultura della guerra dall'età feudale alla grande rivoluzione.* Florence 1982.

Cardini, Franco, and Marco Tangheroni, eds. *Guerra e guerrieri nella Toscana del Rinascimento.* Florence, 1990.

Carus-Wilson, E. M. *Medieval Merchant Venturers.* London, 1954.

Castagnetti, Andrea, and Gian Maria Varanini, eds. *Il Veneto nel medioevo: Le signorie trecenesche.* Verona, 1995.

Caturegli, Natale. *La signoria di Giovanni dell'Agnello.* Pisa, 1920.

Cecchini, Giovanni. "Boldrino da Panicale." *Bolletino della Deputazione di Storia Patria per l'Umbria* 59 (1962): 43–95.

Cessi, Roberto. "Prigionieri illustri durante la guerra fra Scaligeri e Carraresi (1386)." In *Padova mediovale, studi e documenti,* ed. Donato Galli. Padua, 1985.

Chamberlain, E. R. *The Count of Virtue.* New York, 1965.

————. "The English Mercenary Companies in Italy." *History Today* 6 (May 1956): 334–343.

Chancellor, Frederick. *Ancient Sepulchral Monuments of Essex.* London, 1890.

Chérest, Aimé. *L'Archiprêtre, épisodes de la guerre de cent ans au xivᵉ siècle.* Paris, 1879.

Cibrario, Luigi. *Storia della Monarchia di Savoia.* 3 vols. Turin, 1844.

Clark, Duncan W. "The College of Halstead or the Bourchier Chantry." *Transactions of the Essex Archaeological Society* 14 (1918): 311–337.

Clark, George N. *War and Society in the Seventeenth Century.* Cambridge, 1958.

Clode, Cecil M. *The Early History of the Guild of Merchant Taylors.* Vols. 1, 2. London, 1888.

Cognasso, Francesco. *I Visconti.* Milan, 1966.

————. *La formazione dello stato visconteo.* Turin, 1953.

————. "L'unificazione della Lombardia sotto Milano." In *Storia di Milano,* vol. 5. UTET. Milan, 1955.

————. "Note e documenti sulla formazione dello stato visconteo." *Bolletino della Societa Pavese di Storia Patria* 23 (1923): 23–169.

————. "Per un giudizio del Conte Verde sulle compagnie di ventura." *Bolletino della Società Pavese di Storia Patria* 28 (1928): 5–11.

Cole, Bruce. *Agnolo Gaddi.* Oxford, 1977.

Cole, Hubert. *Hawkwood.* London, 1967.

————. *Hawkwood and the Towers of Pisa.* London, 1973.

————. *Hawkwood in Paris.* London, 1969.

Coleman, D. C. *What Has Happened to Economic History?* Cambridge, 1972.

Collino, Giovanni. "La guerra veneto-visconteo contro i Carraresi nelle relazioni di Firenze e di Bologna col conte di Virtù (1388)." *Archivio Storico Lombardo* 36 (1909): 5–58, 315–386.

————. "La guerra Viscontea contro gli Scalgeri nelle relazioni diplomatiche fiorentine- bolognesi col conte di Virtù (1386–1387)." *Archivio Storico Lombardo* 34 (1907): 105–159.

————. "La politica fiorentino-bolognese dall'avvento al principato del Conte di Virtù alle sue prime guerre di conquista." *Memorie delle Reale Accademia di Scienze Lettere ed Arti di Torino* 2, no. 54 (1904): 109–184.

————. "La preparazione della guerra veneto-visconteo contro i Carraresi nelle relazioni diplomatiche fiorentino-bolognesi col Conte di Virtù (1388)." *Archivio Storico Lombardo* 34 (1907): 209–289.

Colombo, G. "Le milizie di ventura e la formazione delle signorie prima di Enrico VII." *Bolletino Storico Bibliografico Subalpino* 8 (1903).

Connell, William J. "Il Commissario e lo stato territoriale fiorentino." *Ricerche Storiche* 3 (September–December 1988): 591–617.

Contamine, Philippe, ed. *War and Competition between States.* Oxford, 2000.

————. *War in the Middle Ages.* New York, 1984.

Cook, A. S. "The Last Months of Chaucer's Earliest Patron." *Transactions of the Connecticut Academy of Arts and Sciences* 21 (1916).

Copinger, W. A. *History and Records of the Smith-Carrington Family.* London, 1907.

Covini, Nadia. "Condottieri ed eserciti permanenti negli stati italiani nel XV secolo in alcuni studi recenti." *Nuova Rivista Storica* 49 (1985): 329–352.

————. *L'esercito del duca: Organizzazione militare e istituzioni al tempo degli Sforza.* Rome, 1998.

————. "Political and Military Bonds in the Italian State System." In *War and Competition between States,* ed. Philippe Contamine. Oxford, 2000.

Cox, Eugene. *The Green Count of Savoy.* Princeton, N.J., 1967.

Cozzi, Gaetano, and Michael Knapton. *La Repubblica di Venezia nell' età moderna.* Turin, 1986.

Crosland, Jessie. *Sir John Fastolfe.* London, 1970.

Crossley, F. H. *English Church Monuments, AD 1150–1550.* London, 1921.

Curry, Anne. *The Hundred Years War.* New York, 1993.

Curry, Anne, and Michael Hughes, eds. *Arms, Armies, and Fortifications in the Hundred Years War.* Woodbridge, England,1994.

Cutolo, Alessandro. *Re Ladislao d'Angio Durazzo.* Naples, 1969.

Cuvelier, J. *Chronique de Betrand du Guesclin.* Edited by E. Charriere. 2 vols. Paris, 1883.

Da Mosto, Andrea. "Ordinamenti militari delle soldatesche dello stato romano dal 1430 al 1470." *Quellen und Forschungen aus italienischen Archiven und Bibliotheken* 5 (1903): 19–34.

Davidsohn, Robert. *Forschungen zur Geschichte von Florenz.* Vol. 4. Berlin, 1908.

————. "Tre orazioni di Lapo di Castiglion ambasciadore fiorentino a Papa Urbano V alla curia in Avignon." *Archivio Storico Italiano,* 5th ser., 20 (1897): 225–245.

Davies, G. Howard. *Guide to the Church of St. Peter Sible Hedingham.* Chelmsford, England, 1969.

Degenhart, B., and A. Schmitt. *Corpus der Italienische Zeichnungen, 1300–1450.* Vol. 2. Berlin, 1960.

Deiss, Joseph Jay. *Captains of Fortune*. New York, 1967.

Delachenal, R. *Histoire de Charles V (1358–1364)*. Paris, 1909.

De la Roncière, Charles M. *Florence, centre économique régional au xiv$^e$ siècle*. Vol 2. Aix-en-Provence, France, 1976.

Del Migliore, F. L. *Firenze città nobilissima*. Florence, 1689.

Del Treppo, Mario, ed. *Condottieri e uomini d'arme nell'Italia del Rinascimento*. Naples, 2001.

———. "Gli Aspetti organazzativi economic e sociali di una compagnia di ventura Italiana." *Rivista Storica Italiana* 85 (1973): 253–275.

Denifle, H. *La désolation des églises, monastères et hôpitaux en France pendant la guerre decent ans*. 2 vols. Paris, 1899.

De Regibus, A. "Il declino degli Angioni d'Ungeria sotto Carlo III di Durazzo." *Rivista Storica Italiana* 52 (1935): 369–410.

De Roover, Raymond. *The Medici Bank*. New York, 1966.

———. *Money, Banking and Credit in Medieval Bruges*. Cambridge, 1948.

Descroix, Bernard. *Seguin de Badefol "ce fils d'iniquité."* Lyon, 1986.

Devlin, M. "An English Knight of the Garter in the Spanish Chapel at Florence." *Speculum* 4 (1929).

DeVries, Kelly. "The Impact of Gunpowder Weaponry on Siege Warfare in the Hundred Years War." In *The Medieval City under Seige*, ed. Ivy A. Corfis and Michael Wolfe. Woodbridge, England, 1995.

Diehl, Adolf. "Graf Konrad von Landau als Reiterführer." *Württembergische Vierteljahrshefte für Landesgeschichte* 42 (1936): 263–269.

Dini, Francesco. "La Rocchetta di Poggibonsi e Gio. Acuto." *Miscellanea Storica della Valdelsa* 5 (1893): 13–31.

Ditchburn, David. *Scotland and Europe*. East Linton, Scotland, 2000.

Donati, Patrizia. *Bagnacavallo (VII–XIX)*. Faenza, 1996.

Dupré Theseider, E. "La rivolta di Perugia nel 1375 contro l'abate di Monmaggiore e i suoi precedenti politici." *Bolletino della Deputazione di Storia Patria per l'Umbria* 35 (1938): 69–85.

Durrieu, Paul. "La prise d'Arezzo par Enguerrand VII, sire de Coucy en 1384." *Bibliothèque del'École des Chartres* 41 (1880): 161–194.

———. *Les Gascons en Italie*. Auch, France, 1885.

Dyer, Christopher. *Standards of Living in the Later Middle Ages*. Cambridge, 1989.

Edge, David, and John Miles Paddock. *Arms and Armor of the Medieval Knight*. New York,1988.

Elders, E. A. "A Medieval English Mercenary." *Country Life* 139, 550.

Erben, Dietrich. *Bartolomeo Colleoni: Die künstlerische Repräsentation eines Condottiere im Quattrocento*. Centro Tedesco di Studi Veneziani, Studi 15. Sigmaringen, Germany, 1996.

Esch, Arnold. "Brandolino Brandolino." In *Dizionario Biografico degli Italiani*. Vol. 14. Turin, 1987.

Even, Y. "Paolo Uccello John Hawkwood: Reflections of a Collaboration between Agnolo Gaddi and Giuliano Pesello." *Source* 4 (1985): 6–8.

Fabretti, Ariodante. *Biografie dei Capitanei Venturieri dell'Umbria*. Montepulciano, 1842–1844.

Fantuzzi, M. *Monumenti ravennati de secoli di mezzo*. Vol. 5. Venice, 1801–1804.

Favale, Sarah. "Siena nel quadro della politica viscontea nell'Italia Centrale." *Bolletino Senese di Storia Patria*, n.s., 7 (1936): 315–382.

Favier, Jean. *Les finances pontificales a l'époque du Grand Schisme d'Occident 1378–1409.* Paris, 1966.

Feliciangeli, Bernardino. "Sul passagio di Luigi I d'Angiò e di Amedeo VI di Savoia attraverso la Marca e l'Umbria: Note di corografia storica." *Atti e Memorie della Deputazione di Storia Patria per le Provincie delle Marche,* n.s., 4 (1907): 369–462.

Ferrer i Mallol, M. "Cavalieri catalani e aragonesi al servizio dei Guelfi in Italia, Medioevo." *Saggi e Rassegne* 20 (1995): 161–185.

Filippini, Francesco. *Il Cardinale Egidio Albornoz.* Bologna, 1933.

Fleckenstein, Josef. "Vom Stadtadel im spätmittelalterlichen Deutschland." *Zeitschrift für Siebenbürgische Landeskunde,* 3 (1980): 1–13.

Fleming, Peter. *Family and Household in Medieval England.* Hampshire, England, 2001.

Fontenay, Michel. "Corsaires de la foi ou rentiers du sol? Les chevaliers de Malte et le corso méditerranéen au XVIIe siècle." *Revue d'Histoire Moderne et Contemporaine* 35 (1988): 361–384.

Fop, Maria Pecugi. "Il comune di Perugia e la chiesa durante il periodo Avignonese." *Bolletino della Deputazione di Storia Patria per l'Umbria* 65 (1968).

———. "Lineamenti di una storia dei rapporti tra il cardinal Egidio Albornoz ed il Comune di Perugia, attraverso i documenti perugini." In *El Cardenal Albornoz y el Colegio de España,* vol. 1, ed. Evelio Verdera y Tuelles. Bologna, 1972.

Forni, Ulisse. *Manuale del pittore restauratore.* Florence, 1866.

Foucault, Michel. *Power/Knowledge: Selected Interviews and Other Writings, 1972–1977.* Edited by Colin Gordon and translated by Colin Gordon, Leo Marshall, John Mepham, and Kate Soper. New York, 1980.

Fowler, Kenneth. *The Age of Plantagenet and Valois.* New York, 1969.

———. *Medieval Mercenaries.* Oxford, 2001.

———. "Sir John Hawkwood and the English Condottieri in Trecento Italy." *Renaissance Studies* 11 (1998): 131–148.

Franceschi, Franco. *Oltre il "tumulto": Lavoratori fiorentini dell' Arte della Lana fra Tre e Quattrocento.* Florence, 1993.

Franceschini, Gino. "Boldrino da Panicale: Contributo alla storia delle milizie mercenarie italiane." *Bolletino della Deputazione di Storia Patria per l'Umbria* 46 (1949): 118–139.

———. *I Malatesta.* Sansepolcro, 1973.

———. "La prima compagnia di ventura italiana." *Bolletino Senese di Storia Patria* 48 (1941): 140–146, 231–246, 265–279.

———. "Soldati inglesi nell'alta valle del Tevere seicent'anni fa." *Bolletino della Deputazione di Storia Patria per l'Umbria* 42 (1945): 178–208.

Frangioni, Luciana. "Bacinetti e altre difese della testa nella documentazione di un' azienda mercantile 1366–1410." *Archeologia Medievale* 11 (1984): 507–522.

———. "Matino da Milano fa i bacinetti in Avignone (1379)." *Ricerche Storiche* 14 (1984): 69–115.

Frati, Ludovico. "La guerra di Gian Galeazzo Visconti contro Mantova." *Archivio Storico Lombardo* 14 (1887): 241–277.

———. "La lega dei Bolognesi e dai Fiorentini." *Archivio Storico Lombardo,* 2d ser., 6 (1889).

———. "Una raccolta di lettere politiche del secolo XIV nella Biblioteca Municipale di Bologna." *Archivio Storico Italiano* 8 (1842): 129–144.

Freville, E. de. "Des Grandes Compagnies au Quatorzième siècle." *Bibliothèque de l'École des Chartres* 3 (1841–1842): 258–281.

Fryde, E. B. "The Deposits of Hugh Despenser the Younger with Italian Bankers." *Economic History Review* 3 (1951): 344–362.

Fubini, Riccardo. "Diplomacy and Government in the Italian City-States of the Fifteenth Century." In *Politics and Diplomacy in Early Modern Italy*, ed. Daniela Frigo and trans. Adrian Belton. Cambridge, 2000.

Gabotto, Ferdinando. "La guerra del Conte Verde contro i Marchesi di Saluzzo e di Montferrato nel 1363." *Piccolo Archivio Storico dell'Archivio Machesato di Saluzzo* 1 (1901): 6–47.

———. "L'età del Conte Verde in Piemonte." *Miscellanea di Storia Italia* 23 (1895).

Gaier, Claude. "Art et organisation militaire dans la Principauté de Liège et dans le Comté de Looz au Moyen Âge." *Académie Royale del Belgique, Classe des Lettres, Mémoires 59.3.* Brussels, 1968.

Galli, Ettore. *Facino Cane e le Guerre guelfo-Ghibellino nell'Italia settentrionale.* Milan, 1897.

Ganguzza Billanovich, Maria Chiara. "Francesco da Carrara." In *Dizionario Biografico degli Italiani.* Vol. 20. Turin, 1977.

Gaupp, Friedrich. "The Condottiere John Hawkwood." *History* 23 (March 1939): 305–321.

———. *Pioniere der Neuzeit in der Frührenaissance.* Bern, Switzerland, 1945.

Geraud, H. "Les Routiers au Douzième siècle." *Bibliothèque de l'École des Chartres* 3 (1841–1842): 125–147.

Gessler, Eduard A. "Huglin von Shönegg. Ein Basler Reiterführer des 14. Jahrhunderts in Italien. Ein Beitrag zur damaligen Bewaffnung." *Basler Zeitschrift für Geschichte und Altertumskunde* 21 (1923): 75–126.

Gilbert, Creighton. "When Did a Man Grow Old in the Renaissance?" *Studies in the Renaissance* 14 (1967): 7–32.

Gioseffi, D. "Complementi di prospettiva." *Critica d'Arte* 5 (1958).

Given-Wilson, C. *The Royal Household and the King's Affinity: Service, Politics and Finance in England, 1360–1413.* New Haven, 1986.

Glénisson, Jean. "La politique de Louis de Gonzague, seigneur de Mantoue pendant la guerra Entre Gregoire XI et Bernabo Visconti (1371–1375)." *Bibliothèque de l'École des Chartres* 109 (1951): 232–276.

———. "Les origines de la révolte de l'état pontifical en 1375: Les subsides extraordinaires dans les provinces italiennes de l'Église au temps de Grégoire XI." *Rivista di Storia della Chiesa in Italia* 5 (1951): 145–168.

———. "Quelques lettres de défi du XIV siècle." *Bibliothèque de l'École de Chartres* 107 (1947–1948): 235–254.

Glénisson, Jean, and Guillaume Mollat, eds. *Gil Albornoz et Androin De La Roche (1353–1367).* Paris, 1964.

Goldthwaite, Richard. *The Building of Renaissance Florence.* Baltimore, 1980.

Goodman, A. *John of Gaunt: The Exercise of Princely Power in Fourteenth-Century Europe.* London, 1992.

———. "The Military Subcontracts of Sir Hugh Hastings." *English Historical Review* 95 (1980): 114–120.

Gordon, Victor. *The Duel in European History: Honour and the Reign of Aristocracy.* Oxford, 1988.

Gori, G. "L'eccidio di Cesena." *Archivio Storico Italiano* 8 (1852): 3–37.

Gough, Richard. *The Memoirs of Sir John Hawkwood.* London, 1776.

Granger, James. *A Biographical History of England from Egbert the Great to the Revolution.* Vol. 1. 4th ed. London, 1804.

Green, Louis. *Castruccio Castracani: A Study on the Origins of a Fourteenth-Century Italian Despotism.* Oxford, 1986.

Greenblatt, Stephen. *Renaissance Self-Fashioning.* Chicago, 1980.

Gregorovius, Ferdinand. *Geschichte der Stadt Rom im Mittelalter.* Vol. 2. Munich, 1988.

Grimaldi, N. *La signoria di Bernabò Visconti e di Regina della Scala in Reggio (1371–1385).* Reggio, 1921.

Gualdo, G. "I libri delle Spese di Guerra del Cardinal Albornoz in Italia conservati nell'Archivio Vaticano." In *El Cardenal Albornoz y el Colegio de España,* vol. 2, ed. Evelio Verdera y Tuells. Bologna, 1972.

Guigue, Georges. *Les Tard-Venus en Lyonnais, Forez et Beaujolais 1356–1369: Récits de la guerre de cent ans.* Lyon, 1886.

Guldescu, S. *History of Medieval Croatia.* The Hague, 1964.

Hale, J. R. *Renaissance Venice.* London, 1973.

———. *Renaissance War Studies.* London, 1983.

———. *War and Society in Renaissance Europe, 1450–1620.* Baltimore, 1985.

Hall, Bert S. *Weapons and Warfare in Renaissance Europe.* Baltimore, 1997.

Hallam, Henry. *The History of Europe during the Middle Ages.* New York, 1899.

Hanawalt, Barbara A. *The Ties That Bound.* New York, 1986.

Hanlon, Gregory. *The Twilight of a Military Tradition: Italian Aristocrats and European Conflicts, 1560–1800.* London, 1988.

Harvey, Margaret. *The English in Rome, 1362–1420.* Cambridge, 1999.

Hay, Denys, and John Law. *Italy in the Age of the Renaissance, 1380–1530.* London, 1989.

Hayez, Anna-marie. "Travaux à l'Enceinte d'Avignon sous les Pontificats d'Urbain V et de Grégoire XI." In *La guerre et la paix: Frontières et violences au Moyen Age.* Paris, 1978.

Held, Joseph. "Military Reform in Early Fifteenth Century Hungary." *East European Quarterly* 11 (1977): 129–139.

Henneman, John B. *Royal Taxation in Fourteenth Century France.* Philadelphia, 1976.

Hennessy, John Pope. *Paolo Uccello.* London, 1969.

Herde, Peter. "Politische Verhaltenweisen der Florentiner Oligarchie 1382–1402." In *Geschichte und Verfassungsgefüge: Frankfurter Festgabe für Walter Schlesinger.* Wiesbaden, Germany, 1973.

Hewitt, H. J. *The Black Prince's Expedition of 1355–1357.* Manchester, England, 1958.

———. *The Organization of War under Edward III, 1338–1362.* Manchester, England, 1966.

Hinze, Otto. "Der Commisarius und seine Bedeutung in der allgemeinen Verfassungsgeschichte in Staat und Verfassung." In *Gesammelte Abhandlungen zur allgemeinen Verfassungsgeschichte,* vol 2, ed. G. Oestreich. Göttingen, Germany, 1962.

Hlaváček, Ivan. *Das Urkunden- und Kanzleiwesen des böhmischen und römischen Königs Wenzel (1376–1419). Ein Beitrag zur spätmittelalterlichen Diplomatik.* Stuttgart, Germany, 1970.

Holmes, George A. "Florentine Merchants in England, 1346–1436." *English Historical Review* 13 (1960).

———. *The Good Parliament.* Oxford, 1975.

Hóman, Bálint. *Gli Angioni di Napoli in Ungheria.* Rome, 1938.

Housley, Norman. *The Avignon Papacy and the Crusades, 1305–1378.* Oxford, 1981.

———. "King Louis the Great of Hungary and the Crusades (1342–1382)." *Slavonic and East European Review* 62 (1984): 192–207.

———. "The Mercenary Companies, the Papacy, and the Crusades, 1356–1378." *Traditio* 38 (1982): 253–280.

———. "Pro Deo et Patria Mori: Sanctified Patriotism in Europe, 1400–1600." In *War and the Competition between States,* ed. Philippe Contamine. Oxford, 2000.

Howard, Michael. *War in European History.* Cambridge, 1974.

Hunt, Edwin S. *The Medieval Super-companies.* Cambridge, 1994.

Hyde, J. K. *Society and Politics in Medieval Italy.* New York, 1973.

Ilardi, Vincent. *Studies in Italian Renaissance Diplomatic History.* London, 1986.

Ilardi, Vincent, and Paul Kendall. *Dispatches with Related Documents of Milanese Ambassadors in France and Burgundy, 1450–1483.* 3 vols. Athens, Ohio, 1970–1981.

Ingrao, Charles. *The Hessian Mercenary State: Ideas, Institutions, and Reform under Frederick II, 1760–1785.* Cambridge, 1987.

Jamison, D. F. *Life and Times of Betrand du Guesclin: A History of the Fourteenth Century.* Charleston, S.C., 1864.

Janson, H. W. *The Sculpture of Donatello.* Vol. 2. Princeton, N.J., 1957.

Jarry, Eugène. *La vie politique de Louis de France, Duc d'Orleans, 1372–1407.* Orlèans, France, 1899.

Jones, George F. *Oswald von Wolkenstein.* New York, 1973.

Jones, Michael. "The Fortunes of War: The Military Career of John, Second Lord Bourchier." *Essex Archaeology and History* 26 (1995).

Jones, P. J. *The Malatesta of Rimini and the Papal State.* Cambridge, 1974.

Jones, Richard H. *The Royal Policy of Richard II: Absolutism in the Later Middle Ages.* Oxford, 1968.

Jones, Terry. *Chaucer's Knight: The Portrait of a Medieval Mercenary.* Baton Rouge, La., 1980.

Jorga, N. *Philippe de Mézières, 1327–1405 et la croisade au XIVe siecle.* Paris, 1896.

———. *Thomas III, Marquis de Saluces.* Paris, 1893.

Kaeuper, Richard W. *Bankers to the Crown: The Riccardi of Lucca and Edward I.* Princeton, N.J., 1973.

———. *Chivalry and Violence in Medieval Europe.* Oxford, 1999.

———. *Violence in Medieval Society.* Rochester, N.Y., 2000.

Kantorowicz, Ernst H. "Pro Patria Mori in Medieval Political Thought." *American Historical Review* 56 (1951): 472–492.

Keen, Maurice Hugh. "Chaucer's Knight." In *English Court Culture in the Later Middle Ages,* ed. V. J. Scattergood and J. W. Sherborne. New York, 1983.

———. *Chivalry.* New Haven, 1984.

———. "Chivalry, Nobility and the Man-at-Arms." In *War, Literature and Politics in the Late Middle Ages,* ed. C. T. Allmand, Liverpool, 1976.

———. *The Laws of War in the Middle Ages.* London, 1965.

Kemp, Brian. *English Church Monuments.* London, 1980.

—— "English Church Monuments during the Period of the Hundred Years War." In *Arms, Armies, and Fortifications in the Hundred Years War*, ed. Anne Curry and Michael Hughes. Woodbridge, England, 1994.

Ketter, Elke. *Hugo von Montfort (1357–1423): Eine Biographie*. Salzburg, Austria, 1987.

Kiernan, Victor Gordon. *The Duel in European History: Honour and the Reign of Aristocracy*. Oxford, 1988.

Kilgour, Raymond L. *The Decline of Chivalry as Shown in the French Literature of the Late Middle Ages*. Cambridge, Mass., 1937.

Klapisch-Zuber, Christiane. "Parenti, amici, vicini." *Quaderni Storici* 33 (1976): 953–982.

Klein, Herbert. "Das salzburgische Söldnerheer im 14. Jahrhundert." *Mitteilungen der Gesellschaft für Salzburger Landeskunde* 66 (1926): 99–158.

Kohl, Benjamin. *Padua under the Carrara, 1318–1405*. Baltimore, 1998.

Körner, Hans. *Grabmonumente des Mittelalters*. Darmstadt, Germany, 1997.

Kowaleski, Maryanne. *Local Markets and Regional Trade in Medieval Exeter*. Cambridge, 1995.

Kruger, S. "Das Rittertum in den Schriften des Konrad von Megenberg." In *Herrschaft und Stand: Untersuchungen zur Sozialgeschichte im 13. Jh*, ed. J. Fleckenstein. Göttingen, Germany, 1977.

Kuhl, E. T. "Why Was Chaucer Sent to Milan in 1378?" *Modern Language Notes* 62 (1947): 15–18.

Labande, Edmond René. *Rinaldo Orsini Comte de Tagliacozzo*. Monaco, 1939.

Labande, L. H. "L'occupation du Pont-Saint-Esprit par les grandes compaignes (1360–1361)." *Revue Historique de Provence* 1 (1905): 79–95, 146–164.

Labarge, Margaret Wade. *Gascony, England's First Colony, 1204–1453*. London, 1980.

Labroue, Émile. *Le livre de vie Les Seigneurs et les Capitaines de Perigord Blanc au XIVe siecle*. Paris, 1891.

Lacaille, H. "Enguerran de Coucy au service de Grègoire XI." *L'Annuaire-Bulletin de la Société de 'Histoire de France* (1895).

Landogna, Francesco. "Le relazioni tra Bernabo e Pisa nella seconda metà del sec. xiv." *Archivio Storico Lombardo*, 5th ser., 50 (1923): 53–72.

Lane, Frederic C. "Economic Consequences of Organized Violence in Venice and History." In *Venice and History*. Baltimore, 1966.

—— *Venice: A Maritime Republic*. Baltimore, 1981.

Larner, John. "Crossing the Romagnol Appenines in the Renaissance." In *City and Countryside in Late Medieval and Renaissance Italy*, ed. Trevor Dean and Chris Wickham. London, 1988.

——. *The Lords of Romagna*. Ithaca, N.Y., 1965.

Law, John E. "La caduta degli Scaligeri." In *Istituzioni, societa e potere nella Marca Trivigiana e Veronese, secoli XIII–XIV*, ed. G. Ortalli and M. Knapton. Rome, 1988.

——. "Venice, Verona and the della Scala." *Atti e Memoria della Academia di Verona*, 6th ser, 29 (1977–1978).

Lazzarini, Isabella. *Fra un principe e altri stati: Relazioni di potere e forme di servizio a Mantova nell'eta di Ludovico Gonzaga*. Rome, 1996.

Leoni, L. "La peste e la Compania del Capelletto a Todi nel 1363." *Archivio Storico Italiano* 2 (1878): 1–11.

Lerner, Daniel. *The Passing of Traditional Society: Modernizing the Middle East*. Glencoe, Ill., 1958.

Lewin, Alison W. *Negotiating Survival: Florence and the Great Schism, 1378–1417.* Teaneck, N.J., 2003.

Liddell, W. H., and R. G. Wood. *Essex and the Great Revolt of 1381.* Essex Record Office Publication, #84. Chelmsford, England, 1982.

Lloyd, M. E. H. "John Wyclif and the Prebend of Lincoln." *English History Review* 61 (1946): 388–393.

Luce, S. *Histoire de Betrand Du Guesclin et de son époque.* Paris, 1876.

Lull, Ramon. *The Book of Knighthood and Chivalry.* New York, 2001.

Luttrell, Anthony. "English Levantine Crusaders, 1363–1367." *Renaissance Studies* 2 (1988): 143–153.

———. "Juan Fernandez de Heredia at Avignon." In *El Cardenal Albornoz y el Colegio de España*, vol. 1, ed. Evelio Verdera y Tuells. Bologna, 1972.

Macquarrie, Alan. *Scotland and the Crusades, 1095–1560.* Edinburgh, 1985.

Maddicott, J. R. "Sir Henry Beaumont." In *The Dictionary of National Biography: Missing Persons*, ed. C. S. Nichols. Oxford, 1994.

Magherini, G., ed. *Storia di Città di Castello.* Vol 3. Città di Castello, 1912.

Magna, L. "Gli Ubaldini del Mugello: Una Signoria feudale nel contado fiorentino (secc. XII–XIV)." In *I ceti dirigenti del età comunale nei secoli XII e XIII.* Pisa, 1982.

Mainoni, Patrizia. "Capitali e imprese: Problemi di indentita del ceto mercantile a Milano nel XIV secolo." In *Strutture di potere ed elites economiche nelle citta dei secoli, XII–XVI.* Naples, 1996.

———. *Economia e politica nella Lombardia medievale: Da Bergamo a Milano fra XIII e XV secolo.* Cavallermaggiore, 1994.

———. "Gli atti di Giovnnolo Oraboni, notaio di Milano (1375–1382)." In *Studi di storia padana (in onore di prof. Giuseppe Martini).* Milan, 1978.

———. *Le radici della discordia: Ricerche sulla fiscalità a Bergamo tra XIII e XV secolo.* Milan, 1997.

———. *Mutui alle compagnie al servizio dei Visconti.* Milan, 1980.

Mallett, Michael. *Mercenaries and Their Masters: Warfare in Renaissance Italy.* Totowa, N.J., 1974.

———. "The Theory and Practice of Warfare in Machiavelli's Republic." In *Machiavelli and Republicanism*, ed. Gisela Bock, Quentin Skinner, and Maurizio Viroli. Cambridge, 1990.

———. "Venice and Its Condottieri, 1404–1454." In *Renaissance Venice*, ed. J. R. Hale. London, 1973.

Mallett, Michael, and J. R. Hale. *The Military Organization of a Renaissance State.* Cambridge, 1984.

Malpeli, Michel-Luigi. *Dissertazioni sulla storia antica di Bagnacavallo.* Faenza, 1806.

Mancarella, Andrea. "Firenze, la chiesa e l'avvento di Ladislao di Durazzo al trono di Napoli." *Archivio Storico per le Provincie Napoletane* 44 (1919): 93–158; 45 (1920): 28–60; 46 (1921): 206–220.

Masi, Gino. "Un capitulo di storia del diritto internazionale: Alcuni usi di guerra in Italia all'epoca dei comuni." *Revista di Storia del Diritto Italiano* 29 (1955): 19–37.

Mattingly, Garrett. *Renaissance Diplomacy.* New York, 1955.

Mazzatinti, Giuseppe. "Il Cardinale Albornoz nell'Umbria e nelle Marche." *Archivio Storico per le Marche e per l'Umbria* 4 (1889): 466–493.

McFarlane, K. B. "The Investment of Sir John Fastolf's Profits of War. *Transactions of the Royal Historical Society*, 5th ser., 7 (1957): 91–116.

———. "War, the Economy and Social Change: England and the Hundred Years War." *Past and Present* 22 (1962): 3–13.

McKisack, May. *The Fourteenth Century, 1307–1399*. Oxford, 1959.

Medin, A. "La morte di Giovanni Aguto." *Archivio Storico Italiano* 17–18 (1886): 161–171.

Meek, Christine E. *The Commune of Lucca under Pisan Rule*. Cambridge, Mass., 1980.

———. *Lucca, 1369–1400*. Oxford, 1979.

Melli, Lorenza. "Nuove indagine sui disegni di Paolo Uccello agli Uffizi: Disegno sottostante, tecnica, funzione." *Mitteilungen des Kunsthistorischen Institutes in Florenz* 42 (1998).

Minois, Georges. *Du Guesclin*. Paris, 1993.

Mirot, Léon. "Dom Bévy et les comptes des trésoriers des guerres: Essai de restitution d'un fonds disparu de la chambre des comptes." *Bibliothèque de l'École des Chartres* 86 (1925): 245–379.

———. *La politique Française en Italie de 1380 a 1422: Les préliminaires de l'alliance florentine.* Vol. 1. Paris, 1934.

———. "Sylvestre Budes et Les Bretons en Italie." *Bibliothèque de l'École des Chartres* 58 (1897): 579–614; 59 (1898): 262–324.

Mirot, Léon, and E. Déprez. "Les Ambassades Anglaises pendant la guerre de Cent Ans (1327–1450)." *Bibliothèque de l'École des Chartres* 50 (1899): 177–214.

Mockler, Anthony. *The Mercenaries*. New York, 1969.

———. *The New Mercenaries*. London, 1985.

Molho, Anthony. *Florentine Public Finances in the Early Renaissance, 1400–1433*. Cambridge, Mass., 1971.

Mollat, Guillaume. *Les papes d'Avignon (1305–1378)*. 10th ed. Paris, 1965.

———. "Pourparlers de paix entre le cardinal Albornoz et Bernabò Visconti en 1361." *Mélanges d'Archéologie et d'Histoire* 78 (1966): 191–206.

———. "Préliminaires de la guerre entre Grégoire XI et les Visconti (1371–1373)." *Journal de Savants* (1962): 237–244.

Monicat, Jacques. *Les Grandes Compagnies en Velay 1358–1392*. Paris, 1928.

Montanelli, Indro. *L'Italia dei secoli d'oro: Il medio evo dal 1250 al 1492*. Milan, 1968.

Morant, P. *The History and Antiquities of Essex*. Vol 2. London, 1768.

———. *The History and Antiquities of the Most Ancient Town and Borough of Colchester.* London, 1748.

Morgan, Philip. *War and Society in Medieval Cheshire, 1277–1403*. London, 1987.

Mosely, Charles. *Burke's Peerage and Baronetage*. Vol 1. London, 1999.

Motta, Emilio. "Notai milanesi del Trecento." *Archivio Storico Lombardo* 22 (1895): 331–376.

Mueller, Reinhold C. *The Venetian Money Market: Banks, Panics, and the Public Debt, 1200–1500*. Baltimore, 1997.

———. "Veronesi e Capitali Veronesi a Venezia in Epoca Scaligeri." In *Gli Scaliger, 1277–1387*, ed. Gian Maria Varanini. Verona, 1988.

Najemy, John M. *Corporatism and Consensus in Florentine Electoral Politics, 1280–1400*. Chapel Hill, N.C., 1982.

Naldini, L. "La 'tallia militum societatis tallie Tuscie' nella seconda metà del sec. XIII." *Archivio Storico Italiano* 78 (1920): 75–113.

Neillands, Robin. *The Hundred Years War.* London, 1990.

Neveux, H. *Vie et déclin d'une structure économique: Les grains du Cambrésis, fin du xiv<sup>e</sup> début du xvii<sup>e</sup> siècle.* Paris, 1980.

Nicholson, R. *Edward III and the Scots.* Oxford, 1965.

Nicolas, N. *The Controversy between Sir Richard Scrope and Sir Robert Grosvenor in the Court of Chivalry.* Vol. 1. London, 1832.

Norris, Malcolm. *Monumental Brasses, the Craft.* London, 1978.

Novati, Francesco. "Trattive di Giangaleazzo Visconti con condottieri di ventura durante la guerra contro Antonio della Scala (1387)." *Archivio Storico Lombardo* 39 (1912): 572–577.

———. "Un venturiero toscano del Trecento: Filippo Guazzalotti." *Archivio Storico Italiano,* 5 ser., 11 (1893): 86–103.

Nussbaum, G. B. *The Ten Thousand: A Study in Social Organization and Action in Xenophon's Anabasis.* Leiden, the Netherlands, 1967.

Oman, Charles. *A History of War in the Sixteenth Century.* London, 1989.

Ormerod, George. *The History of the County Palatine and the City of Chester.* Vol 2. London, 1882.

Ormrod, W. M. *The Reign of Edward III.* New Haven, 1990.

O'Rourke, Andrew P. *Hawkwood.* New York, 1989.

Packe, Michael. *King Edward III.* Edited and finished by L. C. B. Seaman. London, 1983.

Page, William, and J. Horace Round, eds. *The Victoria History of the County of Essex.* Vol. 2. London, 1907.

Page-Phillips, J. *Macklin's Monumental Brasses.* London, 1969.

Palmer, J. J. N. *England, France and Christendom, 1377–1399.* London, 1972.

———. "England, France, and the Flemish Succession." *Journal of Medieval History* 2 (1976): 339–364.

Palmieri, Arturo. "La congiura per sottomettere Bologna al Conte di Vertù." *Atti e Memorie della R Deputazione di Storia Patria per le Provincie di Romagna* 6 (1916).

Paret, Peter. *Understanding War.* Princeton, N.J., 1996.

Parronchi, Alessandro. *Paolo Uccello.* Bologna, 1974.

Partner, Peter. "Florence and the Papacy, 1300–1370." In *Europe in the Late Middle Ages,* ed. John Hale, Roger Highfield, and Beryl Smalley. London, 1965.

———. "Gil Albornoz, Androin de la Roche, Florence and the Great Company, July 1357–July 1359." In *El Cardenal Albornoz y el Colegio de España,* vol. 4, ed. Evelio Verdera y Tuells. Bologna, 1979.

———. *The Lands of St. Peter.* Berkeley and Los Angeles, 1972.

Pasquali-Lasagni, A., and E. Stefanelli. "Note di storia dell'artigliera nei secoli xiv e xv." *Archivio della Reale Deputazione Romana di Storia Patria* 60 (1937): 149–189.

Pastorello, Ester. *Nuove ricerche sulla storia di Padova e dei prinicpi da Carrara al tempo di Gian Galeazzo Visconti.* Padua, 1908.

Patzelt, Edwin. "Ulrich von Treuchtlingen, der Goldene Ritter, und sein Geschlecht." *Treuchtlinger Heimatblätter* 6 (1977).

Pauler, Roland. *La Signoria dell'Imperatore: Pisa e l'Impero al tempo di Carlo IV, 1354–1369.* Pisa, 1995.

Pellegrini, F. C. *Sulla repubblica fiorentina al tempo di Cosimo il Vecchio.* Pisa, 1889.

Perroy, Édouard, ed. *The Anglo-French Negotiations at Bruges, 1374–1377.* London, 1952.

———, ed. *The Diplomatic Correspondence of Richard II.* London, 1933.

———. "Gras profits et rançons pendant la Guerre de Cent Ans. L'affaire du Comte de Denia." *Mélanges d'Histoire du Moyen Âge dédiés à la mémoire de Louis Halphen.* Paris, 1958.

———. *The Hundred Years War.* New York, 1946.

———. *L'Angleterre et le grand schisme d'occident.* Paris, 1933.

Peterson, David S. "State-Building, Church Reform and Politics." In *Florentine Tuscany,* ed. William J. Connell and Andrea Zorzi. Cambridge, 2000.

Pieri, Piero. *Il Rinascimento e la crisi militare italiana.* Turin, 1952.

———. "Le compagnie di ventura e l'avviamento degli eserciti mercenari permanenti." In *La crisi degli ordinamenti comunali e le origini dello stato del Rinascimento,* ed. Giorgio Chittolini. Bologna, 1979.

———. "Milizie e capitani di ventura in Italia nel Medio Evo." *Atti della Reale Accademia Peloritana di Messina* 40 (1937–1938).

Pini, Antonio Ivan. *Città medievale e demografia storica: Bologna, Romagna, Italia (secc xiii– xiv).* Bologna, 1996.

Pinto, Giuliano. *Toscana medievale.* Florence, 1993.

Pirchan, Gustave. *Italien und Kaiser Karl IV in der Zeit der Zweiten Romfahrt.* 2 vols. Prague, 1930.

Pizzagalli, Daniela. *Bernabò Visconti.* Milan, 1994.

Poggi, Giovanni, ed. *Il duomo di Firenze.* Vol. 1. Berlin, 1909.

Poggi, Giovanni, and Margaret Haines, eds. *Il duomo di Firenze.* Vol. 2. Florence, 1988.

Poos, R. L. *A Rural Society after the Black Death, 1350–1525.* New York, 1991.

Post, Gaines. "Two Notes on Nationalism in the Middle Ages." *Traditio* 9 (1953): 281–320.

Postan, Michael M. "The Costs of the Hundred Years' War." *Past and Present* 27 (1964): 34–53.

Powel, W. R., ed. *A History of the County of Essex.* Oxford, 1987.

Pratt, R. A. "Geoffrey Chaucer Esq. and Sir John Hawkwood." *Journal of English Literary History* 16 (1949): 188–193.

Prescott, A. J. "Essex Rebel Bands in London." In *Essex and the Great Revolt of 1381,* ed. W. H. Liddell and R. G. E. Wood. Chelmsford, England, 1982.

———. "London in the Peasants' Revolt: A Portrait Gallery." *London Journal* 7 (1981): 125–143.

Prestwich, Michael. *Armies and Warfare in the Middle Ages.* New Haven, 1996.

———. "'Miles in Armis Strenuus': The Knight at War." *Transactions of the Royal Historical Society,* 6th ser., 5 (1995): 201–220.

———. "Money and Mercenaries in English Medieval Armies." In *England and Germany in the High Middle Ages,* ed. Alfred Haverkamp and Hannah Vollrath. Oxford, 1996.

Prince, A. E. "The Army and Navy." In *The English Government at Work, 1327–1336,* ed. J. F. Willard and W. A. Morris. Cambridge, Mass., 1940.

———. "The Strength of English Armies in the Reign of Edward III." *Economic History Review* 46 (1931): 353–371.

Professione, Alfonso. *Siena e le compagnie di ventura.* Civitanova, 1898.

Puddu, Raffaele. "Istituzioni militari e stato tra Medioevo e Rinascimento." *Rivista Storica Italiana* 87 (1975): 449–469.

Pullan, Brian. *A History of Early Renaissance Italy.* New York, 1973.

Quaglioni, Diego, ed. *La crisi del Trecento e il Papato Avignonese 1274–1378: Storia della chiesa.* Milan, 1994.

Rambaldi, Pier L. "Stefano III Duca di Baviera al servizio della lega contro Gian Galeazzo Visconti (luglio-agosto 1390)." *Archivio Storico Lombardo* 28 (1901): 286–326.

Raulich, I. *La casata dei Carraresi.* Padua, 1890.

Reaney, P. H. *Essex.* London, 1928.

———. *The Origin of English Surnames.* New York, 1967.

Redlich, Fritz. *De Praeda Militari: Looting and Booty, 1500–1815.* Wiesbaden, Germany, 1956.

———. *The German Military Enterpriser and His Work Force.* Vols. 1, 2. Wiesbaden, Germany, 1964–1965.

"Regestro e documenti." *Archivio Storico Italiano,* 1st ser., 16 (1851): 547–553.

Rendina, Claudio. *I capitani di ventura.* Rome, 1985.

Renouard, Yves. *The Avignon Papacy, 1305–1403.* Translated by Denis Bethell. London, 1970.

———. *Les hommes d'affaires italiens du Moyen Age.* Paris, 1968.

Repetti, Emanuele. *Dizionario geografico fisico storico della Toscana.* Vols. 1–6, apps. Florence, 1829–1841.

Reynolds, S. *An Introduction to the History of English Medieval Towns.* Oxford, 1977.

Richards, John. *Altichiero.* Cambridge, 2000.

Ricotti, Ercole. *Storia delle compagnie di ventura in Italia.* 2 vols. Turin, 1845–1847.

Rigg, J. M. "Sir John Hawkwood." In *Dictionary of National Biography,* vol. 9, ed. Leslie Stephen and Sidney Lee. London, 1917.

Robertson, Jan. "Cesena: Governo e Società dal Sacco dei Brettoni al Dominio di Cesare Borgia." In *Storia di Cesena,* vol. 2, ed. Augusto Vasina. Rimini, 1985.

Rogers, Clifford J. "The Vegetian Science of Warfare in the Middle Ages." *Journal of Medieval Military History* 1 (2002).

———. *War, Cruel and Sharp: English Strategy under Edward III.* Woodbridge, England, 2000.

Romano, Giacinto. "Giangaleazzo Visconti e gli eredi di Bernabò." *Archivio Storico Lombardo* 18 (1891): 5–59, 291–341.

———. "La guerra tra i Visconti e la chiesa (1360–1376)." *Bolletino della Societa Pavese di Storia Patria* 3 (1903): 412–437.

———. "Niccolò Spinelli da Giovenazzo" *Archivio Storico per le Province Napoletane* 24 (1899).

Rondini, Gigliola Soldi. "La dominazione viscontea a Verona (1387–1404)." In *Verona e il suo territorio,* vol 4. Verona, 1981.

Rosenberger, Hans. *John Hawkwood, ein englischer Soldführer in Italien.* Chur, Switzerland, 1914.

Roskell, J. S. *The Commons and Their Speakers in English Parliaments, 1376–1523.* Manchester, England, 1965.

———. *The Commons of the Parliament of 1422.* Manchester, England, 1954.

———. "John Doreward of Bocking, Speaker in 1399 and 1413." *Transactions of the Essex Archaeological Society* 8 (1976): 209–223.

Roskell, J. S., Linda Clarke, and Carole Rawcliffe, eds. *The History of Parliament: The House of Commons, 1386–1421.* Vols. 1–4. Stroud, England, 1992.

Round, J. H. "John Doreward's Chantry, Bocking." *Transactions of the Essex Archaelogical Society,* n.s., 13 (1913–1914): 73–78.

Russell, M. P. E. *The English Intervention in Spain and Portugal in the Time of Edward III and Richard II.* Oxford, 1955.

Ryder, Alan. *The Kingdom of Naples under Alfonso the Magnanimous.* Oxford, 1976.

Sablonier, R. *Krieg und Kriegertum in der Cronica des Ramon Muntaner.* Bern, Switzerland, 1971.

Salvemini, Stefano. *I balestrieri nel comune di Firenze.* Bologna, 1905.

Salvestrini, Francesco. "San Miniato al Tedesco: The Evolution of a Political Class." In *Florentine Tuscany,* ed. William J. Connell and Andrea Zorzi. Cambridge, 2000.

Sambin, Paolo. "La guerra del 1372–1373 tra Venezia e Padova." *Archivio Veneto,* 5th ser., 38–41 (1946–1947).

Santini, P. "Gli Acciaiouli e la poesia napoletana." *Rivista Critica della Letteratura Italiana* 3 (1886): 122–125.

Santoro, Caterina, ed. *La politica finanziaria dei Visconti.* Vols. 1, 2. Verona, 1976–1979.

Sapori, Armando. *Il libro di commercio dei Peruzzi.* Milan, 1934.

———.*La crisi delle compagnie mercantili dei Bardi e dei Peruzzi.* Florence, 1926.

Saul, Nigel. *Knights and Esquires: The Gloucestershire Gentry in the Fourteenth Century.* Oxford, 1981.

———. *Richard II.* London, 1997.

Saunders, Frances Stonor. *Hawkwood: Diabolical Englishman.* London, 2004.

Sautier, Albert. *Papst Urban V und die Söldnerkompagnien in Italien in den Jahren 1362–1367.* Zürich, 1911.

Scalini, M. "Il monumento a Giovanni Acuto ed i modi operativi di Paolo Uccello." In *Echi e memorie di un condottiero: Giovanni Acuto, Atti del convegno (Castiglion Fiorentino).* Tavernelle, 1995.

———. "L'armatura fiorentina del quattrocento e la produzione d'armi in Toscana." In *Guerra e guerrieri nella Toscana del Rinascimento,* ed. Franco Cardini and Marco Tangheroni. Florence, 1990.

———. "Note sulla formazione dell' armatura di Piastra, 1380–1420." *Zeitschrift für Historische Waffen und Kostümkunde* 1 (1980): 15–26.

Schäfer, Karl-Heinrich. *Castruccio Castracane e i cavalieri Teutonici.* Florence, 1933.

———. *Deutsche Ritter und Edelknechte in Italien während des XIV. Jahrhunderts.* Vols.1–4. Paderborn, Germany, 1911–1940.

———. "Kirchen und Grabmäler deutscher Ritter in Pisa und Lucca." *Der deutsche Herold* 44–— (1913): 279–283.

———. *Vatikanische Quellen zur Geschichte.* Paderborn, Germany, 1937.

Schevill, Ferdinand. *Siena.* New York: 1909.

Segre, Arturo. "I dispacci di Cristoforo di Piacenza, procuratore mantovano alla corte (1371–1383)." *Archivio Storico Italiano,* 5th ser., 43 (1909).

Selzer, Stephan. *Deutsche Söldner im Italien des Trecento.* Tübingen, Germany, 2001.

Seregni, G. "Un disegno federale di Bernabo Visconti 1380–1381." *Archivio Storico Lombardo,* 4th ser., 38 (1911–1912): 162–182.

Settia, Aldo A. *Comuni in guerra: Armi ed eserciti nell'Italia delle citta.* Bologna, 1994.

———. "Gli 'Insegnamenti' di Teodoro di Monferrato e la prassi bellica in Italia all'inizio del Trecento." In *Condottieri e uomini d'arme nell'Italia del Rinascimento,* ed. Mario del Treppo. Naples, 2001.

———. "Il fiume in guerra: L'Adda come ostacolo militare." *Studi Storici* 40 (1999): 487–512.

———. "I Milanese in guerra: Organizzazione militare e tecniche di combattimento." In *Atti del II Congresso Internazionale di Studi dull' Alto Medioevo,* vol. 1. Spoleto, 1989.

———. *Rapine, assedi, battaglie. Guerra nel Medioevo*. Bari, 2003.

Sherbourne, James. "The Defence of the Realm and the Impeachment of Michael de la Pole in 1386." In *Politics and Crisis in Fourteenth-Century England*, ed. John Taylor and Wendy Childs. Gloucester, England, 1990.

———. " 'Sont inobediens et refusent servir': Il principe e l'esercito nel Monferrato dell'età avignonese." In *Piemonte medievale: Forme del potere e della società. Studi per Giovanni Tabacco*. Turin, 1985.

Shubring, K. *Die Herzoge von Urslingen: Studien zu ihren Besitz-, Sozial-, und* Familienge-schichten. Stuttgart, Germany, 1974.

Silva, Pietro. *Il governo di Pietro Gambacorta*. Pisa, 1910.

———. "Il governo di Pietro Gambacorta in Pisa." *Annali della R. Scuola Normale di Pisa* 23 (1912): 1–352.

Simeoni, L. "La crisi decisivi della signoria scaligera." *Archivio Veneto-Tridentino* 9 (1926).

Solieri, G. *L'antica casa degli Attendoli Sforza in Cotignola e gli uomini illustri Cotignolesi*. Ravenna, 1899.

Sperling, C. F. D. "Hawkwood Family." *Transactions of the Essex Archaeological Society*, n.s., 6 (1898): 174–175.

———. "Sir John Hawkwood." *Essex Review* 39 (1930): 72–74.

Spufford, Peter. *Money and Its Use in Medieval Europe*. Cambridge, 1988.

Staçul, Paolo. *Il cardinale Pileo da Prata*. Rome, 1957.

Stanley, Arthur. "Sir John Hawkwood." *Blackwood's* (March 1929).

Starr, Christopher, ed. *A Guide to Essex Churches*. Essex, England, 1980.

Stephenson, M. *A List of Monumental Brasses in the British Isles*. Ashford, England, 1964.

Strickland, Matthew. *War and Chivalry*. Cambridge, 1996.

Strocchia, Sharon. *Death and Ritual in Renaisance Florence*. Baltimore, 1992.

Sumption, Jonathan. *The Hundred Years War*. Vl 2. London, 1999.

Tabanelli, Marco. *Giovanni Acuto, Capitano di Ventura*. Faenza, 1975.

Tagliabue, C. "La politica finanziaria nel governo di Gian Galeazzo Visconti." In *Bolletino di Società Pavese di Storia Patria* 15 (1915): 19–75.

Taylor, F. L. *The Art of War in Italy, 1494–1529*. Westport, Conn., 1921.

Taylor, J. "The Good Parliament and Its Sources." In *Politics and Crisis in Fourteenth-Century England*, ed. J. Taylor and W. Childs. Gloucester, England, 1990.

Temple-Leader, John, and Giuseppe Marcotti. *Sir John Hawkwood*. Translated by Leader Scott (Lucy B. Baxter). London, 1889.

Thorndyke, Lynn. *A History of Magic and Experimental Science*. Vol. 2. New York, 1923.

Thrupp, Sylvia L. *The Merchant Class of Medieval London, 1300–1500*. Ann Arbor, Mich., 1976.

Thurn und Zurlauben, Baron von. "Histoire d'Arnaut de Cervole, dit l'Archiprêtre." In *Histoire de l'Académie Royale des Inscriptions et Belles Lettres*. Vol. 25. Paris, 1759.

Tilly, Charles. *The Politics of Collective Violence*. New York, 2003.

Trautz, Fritz. *Die Könige von England und das Reich, 1272–1377*. Heidelberg, Germany, 1961.

Trease, Geoffrey. *The Condottieri*. London, 1970.

Trexler, Richard C. " 'Correre la Terra': Collective Insults in the Late Middle Ages." *Mélanges de l'École Français de Rome. Moyen âge-Temps modernes* 96 (1984).

———. *Economic, Political and Religious Effects of the Papal Interdict, 1376–1378*. Frankfurt am Main, 1964.

————. "Follow the Flag: The Ciompi Revolt Seen from the Streets." *Bibliothèque d'Humanisme et Renaissance* 46 (1984): 357–392.

————. *The Spiritual Power: Republican Florence under Interdict.* Leiden, the Netherlands, 1974.

Trundle, Matthew. "Identity and Community among Greek Mercenaries in the Classical World: 700–323 BCE." *Ancient History Bulletin* 13 (1999): 28–38.

Tuchman, Barbara. *A Distant Mirror.* New York, 1978.

Tuck, Anthony. "Richard II and the House of Luxemburg." In *Richard II: The Art of Kingship,* ed. Anthony Goodman and James Gillespie. Oxford, 1999.

Tyerman, C. J. *England and the Crusades, 1095–1588.* Chicago, 1988.

Unwin, George, ed. *Finance and Trade under Edward III.* Manchester, England, 1918.

Valente, A. "Margherita di Durazzo vicaria di Carlo III e tutrice di re Ladislao." *Archivio Storico Italiano* 19 (1918).

Valentiner, W. "The Equestrian Statue of Paolo Savelli in the Frari." *Art Quarterly* 16 (1953).

Valeri, Nino. *L'Italia nell'età dei principati.* Vol. 1. Verona, 1949.

Valois, Noël. *La France et le grand schisme d'Occident.* Vol. 2. Paris, 1898.

Vancini, Oreste. *La rivolta dei Bolognesi al governo dei vicari della chiesa, 1376–1377.* Bologna, 1901.

Varanini, Gian Maria, ed. *Gli Scaligeri 1277–1387.* Verona, 1988.

————. "Mercenari tedeschi in Italia nel Trecento: problemi e linee di ricerca." In *Comunicazione e mobilita nel Medioevo,* ed. Siegfried de Rachewiltz and Josef Riedmann. Bologna, 1998.

Verbruggen, J. F. *The Art of Warfare in Western Europe during the Middle Ages.* New York, 1977.

Verci, Giambatista. *Storia della Marca Trivigiana e Veronese.* Vol 15. Venice, 1790.

Verdera y Tuells, Evelio, ed. *El Cardenal Albornoz y el Colegio de España,* vol. 1. Bologna, 1972.

Vittani, Giovanni. "Quattro lettere di Bernabò Visconti sui fatti di Pisa nel 1364,"*Archivio Storico Lombardo* 56 (1940): 157–160.

Von Stromer, Wolfgang. *Oberdeutsche Hochfinanz, 1350–1450.* Wiesbaden, Germany, 1970.

Waley, Daniel P. "The Army of the Florentine Republic from the Twelfth to the Fourteenth Century." In *Florentine Studies,* ed. Nicolai Rubinstein. Evanston, Ill., 1968.

————. "Condotte and Condottieri in the Thirteenth Century." *Proceedings of the British Academy* 61 (1975): 337–371.

————. "I mercenari e la guerra nell'età di Braccio da Montone." In *Braccio da Montone: Le compagnie di ventura nell'Italia del XV secolo,* Atti del Convegno Internazionale di Studi (Montone 23–25 Marzo 1990), vol. 9. Narni, 1993.

Walker, Simon. *The Lancastrian Affinity, 1361–1399.* Oxford, 1990.

————. "Profit and Loss in the Hundred Years War: The Subcontracts of John Strother, 1374." *British Institute for Historical Research* 58 (1985): 100–106.

Ward, Jennifer C. *The Essex Gentry and the County Community in the Fourteenth Century.* Essex, England, 1991.

————. "Sir John Coggeshale, an Essex Knight of the Fourteenth Century." *Essex Archaeology and History* 22 (1991).

Wedgwood, J. C. "John of Gaunt and the Packing of Parliament." *English Historical Review* 45 (1930).

Wegener, W. J. "Mortuary Chapels of Renaissance Condottieri." Ph.D. diss., Princeton University, 1989.

————. "That the Practice of Arms Is Most Excellent Declare the Statues of Valiant Men: The Luccan War and the Florentine Political Ideology in Paintings by Uccello and Castagno." *Renaissance Studies* 7 (1993).

Werunsky, Emil. *Kaiser Karl IV und seine Zeit*. Vol. 3. Innsbruck, Austria, 1892.

Wilcox, Donald J. *The Development of Florentine Humanist Historiography in the Fifteenth Century*. Cambridge, Mass., 1969.

Williams, Alan. *The Knight and the Blast Furnace: A History of Metallurgy of Armour in the Middle Ages and the Early Modern Period*. Boston, 2003.

Winstanley, William. *The Honour of the Taylors or the Famous and Renowned History of Sir John Hawkwood, Knight, containing his many rare and singular adventures, witty exploits, heroick achievements and noble performances relating to love and and arms in many lands*. London, 1687.

Wright, N. A. R. "'Pillagers' and 'Brigands' in the Hundred Years War." *Journal of Medieval History* 9 (March 1983): 15–24.

Zdekauer, Ludovico. "Tre lettere di M. Alberto Guidalotti, lettore dello studio di Perugia a M. Bartolomeo di Biagio, lettore dello studio di Siena." *Bulletino Senese di Storia Patria* 5 (1898).

Zerbi, Tommaso. *La banca nell'ordinamento finanziario visconteo*. Como, 1935.

Zorzi, Andrea. "Piero Farnese." *Dizionario Biografico degli Italiani*. Vol. 45. Rome, 1995.

Abbey del Pino, 247, 249, 313

Abbey of Sant' Alberto, 17, 255

Acciaiuoli, Andreina, 57

Acciaiuoli, Donato, 275, 290, 293, 295, 298, 311, 408, 409

Agnello, Giovanni dell', 5, 114, 116–17, 125, 130–31, 138, 140, 193, 314; fall of, 135, 137; and Hawkwood, 116–17

Aichelberg, Konrad von, 24, 69, 279, 284–86, 290, 297, 299, 301, 304, 306, 311, 315, 334, 345, 411; rivalry with Hawkwood, 14

Albarno, Montreal d', 18, 23, 65–66, 83, 145. See also Great Companies; mercenaries

Alberghettino, Giovanni, 217, 222, 224

Alberti, Spinello, 103, 164–65, 168, 176–78, 197, 207–8, 224–25, 230, 384

Albornoz, Egidio, 130, 376

Albornoz, Gil, 118, 128

Albornoz, Gomes, 131

Alessandria, battle of, 304–5

Alexander the Great, 4

Alidosi, Bertrando di, 187, 192

Amadeus VI, Count of Savoy, 23, 62, 78, 149, 205, 234, 236–38, 261, 291, 349; opposition to the White Company, 51–55, 57; war with the Visconti, 150–56, 158–60

Ammirato, Scipione, 108, 111–12, 306

Anjou, French house of, 63, 232

Anne of Bohemia, 203, 223

Antelminelli, Alderigo degli, 138, 147, 164, 198–99, 240, 258; debts owed to Hawkwood and Thornbury, 243–46

Armagnac, Jean III, Count of, 11, 294–95, 306, 407, 409; defeat at Alessandria, 304–5; recruitment by Florentines of, 298–303

armies: billeting of, 80–81; composition and size of 74, 80, 88–99; social aspects of, 7, 334–37; wages for, 74–77. See also Companies of Adventure; guastatori; mercenaries; warfare

Arnold, Guy, 335

Arrighi, Giuliano, 317. See also Pesello

Arrighi, Jacopo, 287

Arrighi, Matteo, 286

artillery, 84–86. See also warfare

Asciano, Guido d', 273

Asti, siege of, 149–50

Astolfo da Pavia, 213

Astor, Robert, 101

astrology, use in war of, 86, 300

Attendoli, Micchelotto, 67, 87

Attendoli, Muzio (Sforza), 8, 9, 211–12

Attendoli clan, 211–12

Avignon, 44–46, 51, 54, 57, 62, 79, 107, 118, 187, 303, 361

Ayton, Andrew, 354, 360

Azario, Pietro (Milanese chronicler), 46–50, 56, 59–60, 146, 160, 365

Bagnacavallo, 181–82, 185, 208, 210–25, 395; sale of, 223–24; size and condition of, 223–24

Baldinotti, Baldinotto di Antonio, 313

Baldovinetti, Pera, 282

Balduzzi, Luigi, 190, 214, 395

balie, 86. See also warfare

Ball, John, 26, 331

Ball, Thomas, 272

Balzan, John, 281, 296, 300

Barbiano, Alberigo da, 65, 145, 190, 211, 219, 228–30, 237, 239, 295, 336

Barbiano, Giovanni da, 76, 290–91, 294–95, 297, 306

*barbuta* unit, 73, 76, 103. *See also* armies; mercenaries; warfare

Bardi, Doffo dei, 118–19, 123–25, 130, 164

Barducci, Roberto, 341

Baron, Hans, 6

Bartolomeo of Piacenza, 241

Bascot of Mauleon, 58

Bastari, Filippo di Cionetti, 164, 176, 187, 189

Baumgarten, Hannekin, 69, 73, 103–7, 125, 127, 145, 156, 343–44, 374. *See also* Great Companies; mercenaries

Bayley, C. C., 374

Baynard (Bernard) family, 33, 348, 350

Beccanugi, Leonardo, 298

Beck, William, 3

Belisarius, 211

Belmont, Andrew, 47, 100–101, 106–8, 129–30, 144, 183, 335, 349, 361, 371–72; appearance of, 8, 45

Belmont, Thomas, 183

Beltoft, John, 72, 220, 229, 276, 277–79, 290, 308, 343, 404

Bentivoglio, Saluccio, 186

Benvenuti, Guccio, 248

Benvenuto of Imola, 209

Berensen, Bernard, 106

Berkeley, Edward de, 191, 203

Berton, Thomas, 101

Berwick (Barwick), John, 73, 219, 222, 229

Best, William, 163

Beston, Thomas, 163

Biancardi, Ugolotto, 262–63, 290, 297

Biliotti, Bilotti, 288

Black Company, 48

Black Death, 5

Black Prince, 116. *See also* Edward, Prince of Wales

Bloyes, 215

Boccaccio, Giovanni, 121, 317

Boccia, Lionel, 320

Bohun, Humphrey, 23, 132

Bohun, William (Earl of Northampton), 132, 145; and Hawkwood, 40–42

*bombarde. See* gunpowder weapons

Bonauiti, Andrea, 47, 145

Bonintende, Domenico, 179

Bonoli, Girolamo, 214

Bornago, 194, 255, 326

Borsook, Eve, 412

Boson, William, 45, 101, 126, 146, 153, 230, 349; as captain of Society of Genoa, 134, 136

Botarch, Hannekin, 202

Bourchier, John, 23, 40

Bourchier, Robert, 33, 39, 40, 351

Bourchier, Thomas, 39

Bourchier family, 33, 40, 331, 351, 358; chantry dedicated to, 360

Bouvet, Honore, 91

Bracciolini, Poggio, 2, 113, 409; assessment of Hawkwood by, 305–6, 321

Brandolino, Brandolino, 211, 285

Brandolino, Tibertino, 24, 201, 211, 315

Braudel, Fernand, 6

Brentelles, battle of, 259–60

Brètigny, treaty of, 43

Bretons, 187–90, 195–97. *See also* mercenaries; warfare

Brice (Birch), John, 146, 153, 159, 161, 163, 178, 183–86, 199, 374; capture of son Lawrence, 184, 186

Brignais, battle of, 364; Hawkwood's supposed role in, 57–58. *See also* Hawkwood, John; mercenaries

Brinton, Thomas, 335, 357

Brucker, Gene, 171, 273, 384

Bruni, Leonardo, 2, 113, 223, 271, 370; assessment of Hawkwood by, 305, 321

Brunswick, Otto von, 23, 153, 234, 281–82, 284, 350

Buch, Captal de, 43, 267

Budes, Silvestre, 187

Burckhardt, Jacob, 2, 7, 85, 117, 345–46

Burgoforte, siege of, 132, 135

Butler, Johnny, 281

Buzzacarini, Francesco, 265

Byzantium, 64, 65

Caesar, 4

Caimmi, Giovanni, 59

Calisten, Ugo, 224

Calth, John, 347, 351

Calveley, Hugh, 23, 43, 357

Camerino, Rodolfo da, 9, 115, 139

Campaldino, battle of, 71, 89

Cancellieri, Bartolomeo de, 148

Cane, Facino, 145, 220, 290, 304

Cane, Ruggiero, 149, 187–88, 193, 198, 203, 216, 248, 385; friendship with Hawkwood, 176–77

Canestrini, Giuseppe, 3

cannon. *See* artillery

Canturino, battle of, 55, 60–61, 90, 101, 147, 160

Carlino, Niccolò di, 237, 241, 249, 397

Carmagnola, Francesco, 9

Carrara, Conte da, 297, 301–2

Carrara, Francesco (Novello), 260. *See also* Novello, Francesco

Carrara, Francesco (il Vecchio), 259–60, 269

Carrington, John, 5

Carugate, 194, 255

Cascina: first battle of (1364), 109–13, 115; second battle of (1369), 137–39, 147

Castagnaro, battle of, 19, 41, 88, 253–70

Castel, Robin, 101

Castelbaldo, 259–61, 265, 297, 304–5

Castellani, Lotto, 278

Castello, Azzo da, 309

Castiglionchio, Lapo da, 321

Castle Hedingham, 39, 324

Castracane, Castruccio, 338

Catalans, 64–65

Catherine of Siena, 2, 23, 147, 165–66

Cavalcante, Giovanni, 176–77, 321

Cavalcante, Guido, 282–83

Cavalli, Cavallino da, 149

Cavalli, Jacopo, 187, 200, 315–16, 411

Cavendish, John, 215, 227, 351–52

Caxton, William, 27

Cervole, Arnaud de, 23

Cesena, 22, 24, 178, 191, 195, 216, 388; massacre at, 188–90

chantry, 331, 414. *See also* Hawkwood, John; Saint Peter's Church, Sible Hedingham

Charles of Durazzo, 26, 169, 205, 219, 228–29, 232, 234, 236, 274, 396, 398–99; advent in Italy (1380) of, 220–22; disagreement with Urban VI, 257; payments to Hawkwood by, 246–49; reaction in Florence to, 220–21; war against French Angevins, 237–42

Charles IV (Holy Roman Emperor), 63, 118, 131–33, 135–37, 203

Charles IV (King of France), 38

Charles V (King of France), 94

Charles VI (King of France), 295, 299

Charny, Geoffroi de, 332–33

Chaucer, Geoffrey, 2, 134, 191, 197, 200–201, 333, 376–77, 391; to Milan with Hawkwood, 203

Chieri, Broglia da, 262, 285, 309

Chinazzo, Daniele di, 19, 219

chivalry, 9, 69, 332–33. *See also* mercenaries; warfare

Ciompi, 207

Clark, G. N., 7

Clement VII (Robert of Geneva, anti-pope), 24, 189–90, 199, 203, 221, 232, 234–36, 239, 257, 274–75, 295; role in massacre at Cesena of, 189–90

Clifford, John, 73, 163, 170, 191 163

Clifton, Nicholas, 210

Clifton, Robert, 333

Clode, Cecil, 359

Codelupo, Bartolino, 192

Coe, John, 26, 272, 331, 335

Coggeshale, John, 33, 39–40, 351

Coggeshale, Thomas, 27, 33, 36, 146, 312; coat of arms of, 39–40; and Hawkwood's last will and testament, 324–26

Coggeshale, William, 23, 325, 330–31, 335, 352, 412–13; daughters of (Blanche and Alice), 330–31; inheritance in England of, 210; Italian service of, 26, 146, 206, 221; marriage to Antochia Hawkwood, 13, 33, 146, 193, 206, 210, 221

Coiser, Albert, 300

Colchester, 31

Cole, Hubert, 3, 13, 36, 43, 97

Coleman, John, 163

Colepepper, John, 281, 333

Coln River, 31

commissaries (*collaterali*), 81, 367

Companies of Adventure (Free Companies), 22, 91–94; composition of, 65–68; economic and business aspects of, 67–71; employment of exiles in, 242; extortion of bribes by, 92–93; formation of, 63–64; manipulation of, 116–117; nationalities in, 65–66, 80; political and social pressure exerted by, 207–8, 219, 221, 228–29, 242, 291; relation to feudalism, 68–70; role of women in, 66, 80; tactics of, 92–93

Companies of Saint George, 69; (1365–66), 122–28, 147, 207, 219–21; (1380), 224, 228–30

Company of the Flower, 65

Company of the Hat, 65, 94, 107, 125

Company of the Hook, 65

Company of the Rose, 65, 250–59

Company of the Star, 65, 69, 92, 107, 122, 216, 336

*condotte* (contracts for service), 71–79, 93; bonuses (*paggia doppia*) and gifts, 76, 78; compared to English indenture contract, 71; compensation for horses (*mendum*), 77; fines, 77, 369; inspections (*mostre*), 77, 367; payment in cloth, 75–76; pay rates in, 73–76

Contarini, Giovanni, 267

Corbizzi, Giovanni, 236, 397

Corbrigg, Robin, 231

Corio, Bernardino, 133, 170, 254, 291, 306, 377, 386–87, 389, 391

Corona, Piero della, 282–83

Corrugate, 326

Cortegiano, Gino, 285–86

Cortona, 127

Costoza, Conforto da, 236, 266

Cotignola, 181–82, 185, 211–15, 223–24

Coucy, Enguerrand, 23, 26, 151–53, 156, 235, 257, 271, 380; sale of Arezzo by, 248–50

Cox, Eugene, 156, 159

Crécy, 41–42, 60, 110, 111, 156

Crusades, 23, 115, 333. *See also* mercenaries

Cunio, 211–12

Dagworth, Nicholas, 223, 257

Dante, 2, 317, 318

Dati, Gregorio, 253, 290, 302

Datini, Francesco (merchant of Prato), 24, 169, 339

Dei, Benedetto, 314

Deiss Joseph Day, 8, 112

Del Graziani (Perugian chronicler), 47–48, 84, 85, 101, 207

Del Mayno bank, 344

Denifle, Henri, 361

Dent, John, 163

Desio, Filippo da, 142–43

Despenser, Edward le, 5, 134, 144, 335, 378

Despenser, Henry, 234

Despenser, Hugh, 134, 139

De Vere, Aubrey, 227

De Vere, John, 35, 42, 267, 351, 362; retinue of, 39–41, 360

De Vere, Robert, 323–24

De Vere, Thomas, 35, 352

De Vere (Veer) family, 31, 35, 39, 323–24

diplomacy, 4, 6–7, 25–26, 59, 118, 186–88, 198–200, 203–4, 223, 257–58, 344–45; Florentine-Sienese policy compared, 125–26; strategy of Florence toward Hawkwood, 118–20, 141–43, 217–20

Dombellinghi, Francesco, 291, 406

Dombellinghi, Niccolò, 228

Donati, Manno, 111

Donato di Neri (Sienese chronicler), 112–13, 126, 219, 370

Donfol, Allan, 201

Doreward, John, senior and junior, 330, 413

Dovadola, Francesco di, 222–23

Doyle, Arthur Conan, 3, 31, 48

Drake, Sir Francis, 3

Durward, Quentin, 31

Dyer, Christopher, 339

Eberhardsweiler, Johann von, 75, 144, 253, 278–79

Edward II (King of England), 17, 101

Edward III (King of England), 2, 33, 37, 38, 118, 144, 194; relations with English mercenaries, 26, 131–32

Edward, Prince of Wales, 41–42, 153, 361. *See also* Black Prince

Edwardian military revolution, 38–39

Edwardston, Thomas, 198–99

Engestorp, Robotus von, 344

espionage, importance of in war, 82–83, 290; use of by Hawkwood, 20–22

Essex Record Office, 36, 42, 414

Este, Alberto d', 258, 294

Este, Francesco, 156–57

Este, Isabel, 310

Este, Niccolò d', 132, 141, 147–48, 153, 184–85, 192, 213, 223, 344, 380, 395

Este family, 18, 214–15

exiles, 82, 154, 228–29, 242, 291, 337–38, 345; Hawkwood and, 20–21; use of in war, 207–8, 219. *See also* Companies of Adventure; warfare

Fabius Maximus, 20, 321

Faenza, 22, 24, 178, 186, 188–90, 192, 195, 216, 222, 224, 387; sack of, 182–86

Falcan (Falcon), David, 300, 405

Farnese, Piero, 60, 98, 99, 115, 313, 317, 411

Farnese, Ranuccio, 115

Favella, Giovanni, 184

Filibach, Wilhelm, 229, 396

Finchingfield, 33, 358

Flor, Roger de, captain of Great Company (1302), 64–65, 68

Florentine-Milanese war (1390–92), 289–309; diplomatic tension and military buildup, 273–80, 284–88; Sienese front, 271–80, 250–90

Folifet, William, 362

Fontana, Donadazio Malvicini, 154

Fontenay, Michael, 5

Fop, Maria Pecugi, 129

Foresta, Guido della, 100

Forteguerra, Bartolomeo, 283

fortifications (*bastite*), 83–84, 88. *See also* warfare

Fortini, Benedetto di ser Landi, 207

Foucault, Michel, 414

Fowler, Kenneth, 3, 354, 361, 364

Foy, John, 163, 166

Francigena, via, 18, 51, 92, 177, 232

Froissart, Jean, 2, 11, 68, 134, 152, 156, 294, 303, 361, 364; description of Brignais, 58–59

Frontinus, 19, 304

Fuller, Thomas, 31, 38

Gaddi, Agnolo, 317–18, 320

Gaggio, Bartolomeo da, 163, 180

Gaier, Claude, 81

Galuzzi, Alberto, 165, 168, 182, 184–88, 384

Gambacorta, Piero, 135, 140, 286, 288

Gatari, Bartolomeo, 259–70, 305

Gatari, Galeazzo, 259–70, 305

Gaupp, Fritz, 7, 25

Gazzuolo, 18, 193–95, 210, 212; possession and management by Hawkwood of, 213; relations with Mantua, 213–14

Gibbon, Edward, 2

Giffard (Giffart), John, 189, 335

Giovio, Paolo, 2, 8, 36

Glénisson, Jean, 160

Gold, Beltram, 219

Gold (Cocco), William, 14, 22, 101, 105, 146, 153, 163, 165, 166, 180, 184–85, 198, 200–202, 208–9, 222, 335, 343, 356; love affair with Janet, 203–4; possessions at death of, 390; service for Venice, 218–19

Gonzaga, Ludovico, 156, 159–60, 165, 170, 193, 200, 204, 213–14, 294, 381; negotiations with Hawkwood, 141–43

Gorello, Bartolomeo di Ser, 136, 377, 385

Gosfield, 33–35, 37, 215, 227, 329–31, 347, 351, 393

Gough, Richard, 2–3, 8, 11, 25, 37, 355

Gower, John, 144

Grandson, William de, 54

Granger, James, 1

Graveshale, John, 34–35, 38, 347, 351

Great Companies, 64–68, 92, 100, 107; in France, 43–44, 54, 58, 361; in Italy, 46, 54, 57–60, 66, 145, 345. *See also* Avignon; Flor, Roger de; mercenaries; White Company

Great Schism, 63

Great Yeldham, 33–34

Greenblatt, Stephen, 345–46

Gregorovius, Ferdinand, 1

Gregory XI (pope), 162, 177, 181, 187–88, 198–99, 345, 380, 383; recruitment of Hawkwood by, 149–53; wars with Milan, 151–61. *See also* Hawkwood, John; War of Eight Saints

Grimoard, Anglic (cardinal), 209, 211

Guapp, Fritz, 7, 25, 377

*guastatori*, 89, 103. *See also* armies; warfare

Guazzalotti, Filippo, 223, 292, 344–45

Gucci, Guccio, 218

Guccio, Giovanni, 44

Guicciardini, Francesco, 392

Guinigi, Francesco, 240

Guinigi, Michele, 283

Guinigi bank, 25, 215–16, 393; relationship with English mercenaries of, 344

gunpowder weapons (*bombarde*), 85–86

Hale, John, 6, 7

Hales, Robert, 226

Halstead, 33, 358, 360

Hanawalt, Barbara, 36, 358

Hannibal, 4, 20, 102, 247, 290

Hapsburg, Johann von, 69, 102, 112, 126, 127

Hapsburg, Rudolf von, 8, 69, 97, 102–3, 111, 114, 118

Harvey, Margaret, 357

Hawkwood, Agnes, 34–35, 38, 348

Hawkwood, Alice, 34–35, 348

Hawkwood, Anna, 14, 312, 321–22

Hawkwood (Coggeshale), Antiochia, 13, 33, 210, 227, 325, 330–31

Hawkwood, Catherine, 14, 210, 258, 272; children of, 312; marriage to Konrad Prassberg of, 310–12

Hawkwood, Gilbert, 33–35, 37, 39, 215, 358, 359; last will and testament of, 37, 347–49; transactions of, 34–35

Hawkwood, Janet, 14, 210, 272; marriage to Brezaglia di Porciglia of, 310–11

Hawkwood, Johanna, 34–35, 348

Hawkwood, John (Acuto, Aguto, Aucgunctur, Auchevud, Augudth, de Hakeude, Hankelvode, Haucod, Haughd, Haukevvod, Haukwode, Hauvod), 62, 348–50; birth and childhood of, 31, 35, 37; brothers and sisters of, 33–35; capture of, 136–37; career in France, 40–46; career as a tailor, 37–38, 359; children with Donnina Visconti, 14, 210, 258, 272, 310–12, 321–22; comparisons: —to a fox, 37; —to an Italian state, 338–41; —to Lutz von Landau, 345; death and funeral of, 313–17; diplomatic activities of, 25, 59, 186–88, 196–200, 217–19, 257–58; domestic life of, 13, 159, 210–15, 387, 393; education and learning of, 11–12; English investments of, 215–16, 393; English language letters of, 12–13; English loyalties of, 12–13, 25–27; establishment of hospice in Rome by, 357; feud with Astorre Manfredi, 216–19, 221–22, 225; first campaign as captain general, 100–108; Florentine service, 25, 192–93, 195–96, 219–23, 225, 227–30, 234–35, 270–80, 284–309; great raid on Tuscany (1375), 162–71; honesty and fidelity of, 4, 13–18, 106–9; Italian properties and pensions of, 17–18, 146–47, 159, 209–25, 230–32, 255, 299, 341; last will and testament, 324–327; marriage to Donnina Visconti, 13–14, 193–95; meeting with Geoffrey Chaucer, 202–3; memorials: —in England, 13, 327–31; —in Florence, 317–21, 412; Milanese service, 116–17, 132–43, 192–95, 205; military qualities of, 15–23, 128, 136–37, 143–47, 155–59, 110–13, 146–47, 335; mistresses and illegitimate children of, 14, 146, 159, 184, 186, 331; modern biographies of, 2–4; Neapolitan service, 232, 235–41, 280–84; negotiations with Venetians, 101, 186–88, 218–19; Paduan service, 259–70; papal service, 153–61, 177–90; pardon granted to, 191–92; personal qualities of as

chivalrous knight, 9, 332; physical characteristics of, 8–9, 97–98; Pisan service, 97, 100–117, 130–32; relationship with Giangaleazzo Visconti, 254–58; religious nature of, 23–24; Romagnol patrimony, 209–25; salaries and finances of, 16–17, 175, 339–41; service to King Richard II, 4, 7, 25–27, 202–3, 223, 226, 234, 257–58; settlement of Florentine holdings, 312–14; Tuscan patrimony, 230–32; variations on name, 9–11, 98, 358

Hawkwood, John the Elder (senior), 35–36, 215, 330, 348–49, 359; son named John, 35; transactions involving, 351–52

Hawkwood, John, Jr. (bastard son of John Hawkwood, mercenary captain), 14, 331; church office in England granted to, 159

Hawkwood, John, Jr. (legitimate son and heir of John Hawkwood, mercenary captain), 14, 253, 312–13, 322, 327; legacy in England of, 328–30

Hawkwood, Margaret, 34–35, 348

Hedingham, John, 26, 231, 255

Henry IV (King of England), 328, 333

Henry VII (Holy Roman Emperor), 63

Heton, Hugh, 119, 128, 362

Higdon, Ranulf, 38, 379. See also *Polychronicon*

Hinckford Hundred, 31–32, 38

Hoding, Thomas, 38, 351

Hoding (Hodinge) family, 33, 38, 351

Hood, Robin, 3

Horváti, John (Giovanni Bano, John Ban), 65, 69, 205–6, 224, 237–39

Howard, Michael, 355

Hundred Years War, 1, 20, 38–46, 332–33, 342

Hungarians, 63–66, 205. See also Companies of Adventure; mercenaries

Hyde, J. K., 62

Ingrao, Charles, 5

Innocent VI (pope), 44–46, 58

James I (King of England), 2

Jansen, H. W., 411

Jewish moneylenders, 118, 341. See also armies; mercenaries

Johanna, Queen of Naples, 151–52, 168–69, 196, 220, 232, 380, 396

John of Gaunt, 202, 333

Kaeuper, Richard, 355, 357, 414
Keen, Maurice, 9, 69–70, 200
Kirkeby, John, 36, 333
Kirkeby, William, 349
Klapisch-Zuber, Christiane, 335
Knighton, John, 44–46
Knights Templars, 64
Knowles, Robin, 23, 27, 43, 45, 226–27, 357, 362
Krabice, Benesch, 136

Ladenhall, 27, 324, 331, 342
Ladislaus of Naples, 274–75
lance unit, 74–75, 88. *See also* armies; warfare
Landau, Eberhard von, 16, 105, 144–45, 205–8, 219, 224, 246, 273, 276
Landau, Konrad von, 24, 57, 59, 60, 62, 65, 74, 90, 100, 104, 145, 160, 290, 349
Landau, Lutz von, 24, 139, 144, 145, 193, 195, 197, 200, 205–8, 223, 259, 336, 345, 389
Lane, Frederic, 339
Larner, John, 392
La Rocchetta, 232, 283, 312, 405
leagues (*taglie*) 93–94, 127, 336–37, 365, 369
Le Baker, Geoffrey, 42
Le Bel, John, 41, 43
Legnano, Giovanni da, 145
Leopold of Austria, 186
Lerner, Daniel, 346
Leslie (Lesley), Walter, 23, 44, 46, 107, 118, 361–62
Lindsey, Robert, 191, 215–16, 227
Lionel, Duke of Clarence, 5, 132, 147–49, 198, 203, 376–77; wedding to Violante Visconti, 134–35
Liston, John, 38, 39–41, 351
Liston, Thomas, 39, 40
Liston (Lystones) family, 33, 38, 227, 324, 329, 351, 393
Liverpool, Johnny, 281
long bow, 38–39, 60. *See also* armies; warfare; White Company
Longwood, John, 39
Longwood family, 34, 39, 351
Louis of Anjou, 232, 234–39, 241, 248, 396–97, 399
Lucignano, 271–72, 308
Ludwig of Bavaria, 63
Lull, Ramon, 414
Lunt, William, 382
Lupi, Raimondino, 157–58

Lupo, Bonifazio di, 115
Lye, John, 281
Lyons, Richard, 227, 230, 352

Machiavelli, Lorenzo, 286, 288
Machiavelli, Niccolò, 2, 19, 71, 93, 98, 116, 120
Majendie family, 36
Malastroit, Jean, 187–88
Malatacca, Giovanni, 138–39
Malatesta, Galeotto, 23, 109, 110–13, 115, 137, 153, 180–81, 188, 217, 222, 236, 338, 371
Malatesta, Pandolfo, 104–5, 115
Malavolti, Jacopo, Naddo, and Bertoccio, 72
Malavolti, Niccolò, 402
Mallett, Michael, 6, 49, 88, 412
Malpeli, Luigi, 392
Manfredi, Astorre, 195, 221–22, 224–25, 248, 291, 295, 297–98, 338; feud with Hawkwood, 216–17
Manfredi, Francesco, 217, 290
Mangiadori, Giovanni, 138
Manni, Domenico Maria, 3, 24–25, 305, 327
Margherita of Naples (Queen Margherita), 274–75, 280–82, 294
Marshal, Thomas, 121, 128
Marsigli, Luighi de', 317–18
Martinelli, Niccolo, 168
Mattingly, Garrett, 6, 345, 355
Mauleon, Bascot de, 68
Maurice, John Lord, 2
Mazzei, Lapo, 24
McFarlane, K. B., 342
Medici, Coppo dei, 115
Medici bank, 169
Megenberg, Konrad of, 70
Melchingen, Hugo von, 75, 103
*mendum*. See *condotte*
mercenaries: citizenships and honors granted to, 344–45; as crusaders, 23, 118, 333; diplomatic service by, 6–7; and employers, 79–81; English against Germans, 116–21; fighting ability of, 70–71; investments of, 342–44; and Jewish moneylenders, 118, 341; papal condemnations of, 116, 127; patriotism and national identity of, 4, 335–37; personal qualities of, 5, 357; recruitment of, 70–71; religious sentiment of, 23–24; rivalries among, 117–20; social status of, 334–35; wages of, 73–77, 79–80

Méziéres, Philippe de, 82

Michelotti, Biordo, 262, 309

Migliari, 247, 249, 313

Minerbetti, Piero di Giovanni, 261, 263, 265–
66, 273, 277, 280, 285, 289, 292, 295, 298,
301, 303–5, 307, 313, 404, 409, 411

Mino di Simone, 272

Mockler, Anthony, 335

Molho, Anthony, 341

Monaldi, Dinolus Bindi, 136

Monch, Berthold, 153

Montanelli, Indro, 8

Montanini, Mino di Carlo, 139

Montauri, Tommaso, 237, 271, 316–17

Montecatini, Naddo da, 314, 411

Montecchio, 1, 247, 249, 272, 276, 284, 313,
399

Montefeltro, Antonio da, 181, 217, 222, 281

Montefeltro, Federigo da, 11

Montefeltro, Niccolò da, 128–29, 147

Monteleone, 237

Montematre, Ugolino de, 128, 130

Montepulciano, 271–72, 308, 404

Montferrat, John II Paleologus, Marquis of, 9,
45–46, 51, 55, 57, 62, 72, 148–49, 291, 349–
351; contract with Great Company, 45, 54–
55, 467

Montfort-Tettnang, Heinrich von, 102, 105, 111

Montichiari, battle of, 156–59, 161, 381–82

Montone, Braccio da, 4, 8, 76

Morant, Philip, 9

Morelli, Giovanni di Pagolo, 111–12, 114, 372

Morgan, Philip, 38, 357

Mortimer, Roger, 101

Mountjoy, Lord, 282

Mugello, 102–3

Munne family, 34, 348, 351

Musard, Robert (Black Squire), 44, 54, 57, 134,
361; member of the Order of the Collar, 54

Narni, Erasmo da (Gattamelata), 10

Neville, Hugh, 39

Newington (Newton), Thomas, 413–14

Nicolai, Alessio (astrologer), 300–301

Nicolaus of Frisia, 163

Noellett, Guillaume, 184

Northwood, John, 26, 203, 223, 335, 414

Nostradamus, 2

Nottingham, Roger, 300

Novello, Francesco (Carrara), 9, 260–70, 286,
290, 292–98, 301, 305, 308, 408

Nussbaum, G. B., 338

Oliver (Olyver), John, 38, 335, 352, 413–14

Olney, William, 209

Oman, Sir Charles, 262, 401

Ongharrro, Lando, 199

Ordelaffi, Francesco, 217

Ordelaffi, Giovanni, 253, 261–63, 268

Ordelaffi, Sinibaldo, 181, 183

Order of the Collar, 54

Order of the Garter, 69

Order of the Star, 69

Orlandini, Bartolomeo di Fortini, 318, 321

Orlandini, Benedetto di Lando Fortini, 310, 318,
322

Orlandini, Giovanni di Jacopo, 281, 322

O'Rourke, Andrew P., 3

Orsini, Rinaldo, 83, 239, 241–42, 291, 398

Ostag, John, 38

Ostag (Ostage) family, 33, 324, 329, 331, 347,
351

Pace, Andrea del, 21

Paer, Heinrich, 16, 72

Paleologus, Teodoro, 19, 50, 82, 85

Panaro river, Hawkwood's victory at, 155

Panicale, Boldrino da, 242, 247, 253

Panzano, Luca di Totto, 100, 108

Papal-Milanese wars, 50, 55–62, 117, 122–28,
130–37, 141–44, 147–61

Paret, Peter, 6

Partner, Peter, 232

Payton, Nicholas, 272

Peasants' Revolt, 31, 395; profit from by Hawkwood, 226–27

Pepoli, Giovanni, 72, 153

Peruzzi, Simone di Ranieri, 12, 164, 165, 170,
235, 336

Peruzzi bank, 339

Pesello, 317–18, 320. *See also* Arrighi, Giuliano

Pessano, 194, 255, 326

Petit Thalamus of Montpellier, 364

Petrarch, Francis, 2, 49, 71, 79, 133–34, 187, 317,
336

Phoebus, Gaston, Count of Foix, 298

Picard, Nicholas, 41

Piccinino, Niccolò, 320

Pico, Giovanni, 142, 150–52, 168, 170, 187

Pieri, Piero, 6

Pietramala, Giovanni "Tedesco," 259, 262–65, 411; funeral of, 316–17

Pietrasanta, Jacopo da, 21, 147, 194, 208, 230, 238–41, 254, 274, 280, 338

Pin, Robin du, 36, 46, 349

Pinto, Giuliano, 75

Pip, Johnny, 300

Pirchan, Gustave, 377

Pisan-Florentine war (1362–64), 97–115

*pittura infamante*, 290

Pizan, Christine de, 27, 94

Poitiers, 19, 41–42, 60, 153, 158, 262, 266–67

Pole, William de la, 373

Polenta, Guido da, 181, 217

Polenta, Ostasio da, 262–63, 265

*Polychronicon*, 38, 42, 359

Pommiers, Amanieu de, 23, 153–54

Porro, Stefano, 149

Porta, Giovanni della, 288

Postan, M. M., 343

Prassberg, Konrad, 69, 286–87, 290, 297, 299–300, 306, 311, 334

Prayers family, 358

Pucci Antonio, 2, 61

Puer, Philip, 163, 184, 186, 189

Pusterla, Giovanni, 139

Puy, Gerard du, 179–81


Rat, Diego de, 73, 345

Raymond, Viscount of Turenne, 153

Rayner, John, 223

Redlich, Fritz, 5, 354

Renouard, Yves, 70

retinue, 38–41

Richard II (King of England), x, 4, 6, 25–26, 197, 203, 206, 215, 221, 223, 226–27, 231, 234–35, 257, 275, 322–24, 327, 338

Ricotti, Ercole, 3, 24, 81, 269, 306, 355, 363–64

Rieschach, Johann Flach von, 136, 138, 144, 147

Rietheim, Johann von, 136, 138, 140, 144, 147, 343–44

Robbis, Matttino di Giacomo, 21

Robert of Geneva. *See* Clement VII

Roche, David, 163

Rodisten, Konrad, 300

Romsey, Isabel (wife of Richard), 231, 249, 334

Romsey, Richard, 15–16, 101, 139, 146, 153, 163, 166, 208, 220, 222, 229, 231, 239, 241–42, 245, 248–50, 334, 335, 398

Roncioni, Raffaele, 112, 371–72

Rossi, Lapo Fornaino dei, 107, 232

Roughy, Thomas, 35, 38

*routiers*, 68

Rubiera, battle of, 141, 143–44, 147, 153, 267

Ruskin, John, 2–3, 47

Rykedon, Robert, 215–16, 328, 331, 395; properties attacked during Peasants' Revolt, 227


Sabraham, Nicholas, 200–201, 333, 390

Sacchetti, Franco, 1, 193, 321, 345, 354, 393. See also *Trecentonovelle*

Saint Peter's Church, Sible Hedingham, 13, 23, 37, 215, 323, 327–28, 331, 347

Saint Thomas hospice, Rome, 23

Sala, Bonio da, 184–85

Sale, Adam, 212–14

Sale, John, 281

Saliceto, Roberto da, 184

Salle, Bernard de La, 44, 180, 199, 273, 274, 278, 284–85, 303, 409

Salutati, Coluccio, 16, 96, 130, 165, 169, 170, 256, 275, 315, 336, 338, 403

Salvemini, Stefano, 89

Sampson, John, 26, 312–13, 324, 326

San Donato a Torre, Polverosa, 18, 232, 246, 269, 283, 310, 312

San Miniato al Tedesco, 83, 137–39

San Severino, Tommaso da, 239

Santa Maria alle Malgora, 194, 255, 326

Sardo, Ranieri (Pisan chronicler), 109, 111–12, 130, 139, 166, 168, 372

Sargeant, John, 191, 215–16, 227, 352

Savelli, Paolo, 285, 287, 290, 315

Savignano, Ugolino da, 129–30, 153

Scala, Antonio della, 86, 259, 277, 297

Scala, Cansignorio della, 131, 197

Scala, Mastino, 197

Scala, Regina, 197

Scali, Giorgio, 177, 224

Scatizza (Jacopo di Bartolomeo Amati), 227

Schevill, Ferdinand, 93–94

Schöneck, Huglin von, 73, 343–44

Scott, Adam, 362

Scott, Walter, 31

Seaver, Robert, 166

Sercambi, Giovanni, 100, 112–13, 135, 171, 355, 372–73

Servion, Jehan, 45–46, 51, 155, 261, 363

Shardelowe, Thomas, 41

Sibille, Walter, 325

Sible Hedingham, 13, 19, 23, 27, 33–34, 38, 41, 215, 323–24, 327, 329, 331, 347, 348, 351, 358

Simonetti, Simone, 118–19

Skirlaw, Walter, 223

Soderini, Niccolò, 161

Sozomen of Pistoia, 97, 100, 170, 401

Spinelli, Niccolò, 302

Stefani, Marchionne di Coppo, 15, 98, 170, 183–84, 187–88, 199, 206–7, 216, 218, 235, 237, 248, 380, 394

Stephen, Duke of Bavaria, 288, 293–96, 407

Stella, Giorgio, 126

Sterz, Albert, 44, 45, 49, 50, 55, 59, 67, 69, 72, 99–100, 106–9, 119–20, 126, 129, 145, 344, 349–50, 374; death of, 129

Stisted, John, 26, 272, 335, 414

Stow, John, 42, 354, 357, 359

Strada, Dioniso della, 21, 398

Strada, Donato, 282

Strada, Massolus della, 153

Sulz, Philip von, 10

Svim, Johnny, 281

*taglie. See* leagues

Tansild, Nicholas, 163

Tard-Venus, 361

Taylor, F. L., 89

Temple-Leader, John, 3, 4, 25, 37, 39, 112, 159, 210, 359–60, 364, 377, 389, 410, 412–13

Terrell, John, 330–31

Thod, Nicholas, 101, 147

Thomas, Marquis of Saluzzo, 2

Thornbury (Wenlock), John, 12, 27, 79, 145–46, 153, 161, 163, 165–67, 170, 177–78, 182, 184–86, 199–202, 208, 333–34, 343, 358, 380, 383, 415

Thornbury, Naverina, 334

Thornbury, Philip, 182, 184, 343

Thornton, William, 101

Thorpe, Walter, 197, 203

Threlkeld, John, 245, 369

Thrupp, Sylvia, 38

Tilly, Charles, 4

Tilly, William, 163, 166

Tiptoft, John, 331

Tolentino, Niccolò, 318

Tolomei, Raimondo, 21, 232

Toppesfield, 33, 215, 330–31

Torelli, Primerano, 72

Torre, Ambroglio di Piero della, 312, 410

Torre, William de la, 73

Tortona, 56–58

Trease, Geoffrey, 14, 16

trebuchet (mangonel). *See* artillery

*Trecentonovelle*, 1, 354. *See also* Sachetti, Franco

Trotto, Andrelino, 270

Ubaldini, Ghisello, 99

Ubaldini, Giovanni d'Azzo degli, 21, 74, 83, 123, 165, 241–47, 245, 248, 250, 253, 259, 260–64, 268, 273–74, 285, 292–93, 312, 402, 411; funeral of, 316–17

Uccello, Paolo, 1, 8–9, 20, 207, 327, 346; painting of Hawkwood, 318–21, 412; political context of painting, 24–25, 320–21

Ufford, Thomas, 118

Urban V (pope), 26, 108–9, 117, 119, 127, 130–33, 136–37, 217

Urban VI (pope), 199, 206–7, 211, 220, 223, 227, 234–36, 237, 240–41, 246, 257, 271, 276–77, 336

Urslingen, Werner of, 5, 64–66, 343. *See also* Great Companies

Valera, 194, 255, 326

Varano, Rodolfo da, 145, 192–93, 195, 197, 345, 389

Vasari, Giorgio, 320

Vegetius, 19, 21, 38, 80, 304

Velluti, Donato, 106, 112, 115, 137–40, 370

Venette, Jean de, 44

Vergerio, Pier Paolo, 11, 24, 295, 298, 301, 305, 409

Vergiolesi, Giovanni, 226

Veringen, Wolfard von, 102

Verme, Jacopo dal, 23, 145, 149, 254, 262, 290, 291, 297, 299, 302–12, 333, 345, 409

Verme, Luchino dal, 58, 59, 137

Verme, Taddeo, 262, 290, 301, 307

Verme, Ugolino, 262–63

Verney, John, 44

Vettori, Andrea, 14, 284

Vicecamerato, Guidone da, 142

Villa Demidoff, 18, 232

Villa I Tatti, 105

Villani, Filippo, 10–11, 19, 36–37, 39, 43, 48–50, 60–61, 97–100, 102, 104–6, 109–14, 117, 146, 363; description of Hawkwood, 97–98

Villani, Matteo, 43, 45–46, 48–50, 66, 85, 99, 209, 363, 364

Villanozzo of Brumfort, 228, 230, 237–39

Vinciguerra, Francesco, 216, 393

Visconti, Ambrogio, 130–31, 141–43, 147, 149–51, 154–55, 157–58, 160, 376, 379, 381; captain of Company of Saint George, 122–28

Visconti, Bernabò, 9, 13, 15, 26, 45, 58, 83–84, 108, 116–17, 121–22, 126–27, 131–36, 148–59, 170, 176, 189, 192–94, 197–98, 201, 203–6, 216, 219, 225, 234–36, 248, 255, 259, 269, 293, 345, 374, 380; and Agnello of Pisa, 116–17, 130–31, 140–41; capture and deposition by Giangaleazzo of, 254–57; dismissal of Hawkwood and Landau, 205–8; and Hawkwood, 149–53; intrigues in Emilia Romagna (1370–72), 141–43; in Tuscany (1368–69), 137–40; war against Verona, 200–204

Visconti, Carlo, 254–55, 259, 277, 279, 280–81, 286–87, 291, 294, 296, 300, 302, 403

Visconti (Hawkwood), Donnina, 9, 11, 13–15, 27, 158, 193, 210, 213, 231, 253–54, 255, 269, 299, 311, 314, 331; journey to Bagnacavallo, 210–11; personal characteristics of, 13–14; settlement of accounts, 313, 321–27

Visconti, Galeazzo, 45, 51, 56, 57, 58–61, 134, 137, 148–49, 152, 160

Visconti, Giangaleazzo (Count of Virtu), 6, 15, 149–50, 156–58, 230–31, 256, 261, 269–70, 273, 276, 278–80, 283–84, 405; capture of Bernabò, 254–55; relations and war with Florence, 284–309

Visconti, Lodrisio, 122

Visconti, Lucchino, 300

Visconti, Mastino, 302

Visconti family, 25–26, 51, 59, 62, 82, 162

Vitelli, Paolo, 85

Viviano, Francesco, 67

Volterra, Andrea da, 15, 21, 241, 283; negotiations with Hawkwood, 243–46

Waley, Daniel, 87, 354

Wallace, William, 1

Walsingham, Thomas, 144, 328, 363, 379

War of Chioggia, 63, 74, 201, 218, 259

War of Eight Saints, 74, 84, 175–92, 195–98, 200–202, 207–8, 210, 217–18, 221, 234, 240, 246, 386–87; peace negotiations and treaty ending, 199–200; recruitment of Hawkwood by Florence and Milan, 161–71, 192–93

warfare: casualties resulting from, 87; cultural aspects of, 334, 344; economic aspects of, 81, 341–44; kidnap and ransom, 78, 91; poisoning, 83, 368; psychological aspects of, 84; reconnaissance, 82–83; recourse to sieges, 84–85; social and political aspects of, 7, 82; strategy and tactics, 15–19, 86–87, 337–38; techniques of, 81–87, 333–35; use of gestures and insults, 84, 99, 113. *See also* armies; artillery; astrology; fortifications; Hawkwood, John; mercenaries

Wauton, John, 39, 41

Wauton, William, 39, 41

Weever, John, 413

Wegener, Wendy, 320

Weitingen, Konrad von, 72, 139, 144, 343

Wencelaus (Holy Roman Emperor), 26, 208, 223, 234, 345

Wenlock, John (son of Thornbury) 281, 296. *See also* Thornbury (Wenlock), John

*Westminster Chronicle*, 2, 26, 38, 257, 328, 359

Wethersfield, 215, 227

White Company (Great Company), 1, 19, 47–50, 61–62, 64–67, 72, 86, 97–103, 108, 119, 121, 144, 146–47, 152, 163, 231–32, 335, 341, 373, 377; activities in Piedmont, 50–55; contract with Marquis of Montferrat, 349–50; defeat by Germans at San Mariano, 120; fighting methods of, 47–50; origin of name, 46–48, 362–63; Pisan service, 60–61, 97–101; size and composition, 46, 362; victory at Lanzo, 54–55. *See also* Great Companies; mercenaries

Winden, Hermann von, 75, 103

Winstanley, William, 2, 13, 310, 359

Witham, 215, 227

Wolkenstein, Osvald von, 5, 191

Wycliff, John, 182, 226, 343

Xenophon, 68

Xerxes, 236

Zouche, Hugh Mortimer de la, 67, 101, 106, 144, 227, 335, 343